KU-161-462

CONTENTS

STUDY GUIDE FOR

Stiglitz and Walsh's *Economics*

THIRD EDITION

LIVERPOOL JMU LIBRARY

3 1111 01046 9144

LIVERPOOL JOHN MOORES UNIVERSITY
Aldham Robarts L.R.C.
TEL. 051 231 3701/3634

STUDY GUIDE FOR

Stiglitz and Walsh's
Economics

THIRD EDITION

Lawrence W. Martin

MICHIGAN STATE UNIVERSITY

W · W · NORTON & COMPANY · NEW YORK · LONDON

Copyright © 2002, 1997, 1993 by W. W. Norton & Company, Inc.

All rights reserved

Printed in the United States of America

ISBN 0-393-97782-X (pbk.)

W. W. Norton & Company, Inc., 500 Fifth Avenue, New York, N.Y. 10110
www.wwnorton.com
W. W. Norton & Company, Ltd., Castle House, 75/76 Wells Street, London W1T 3QT

1 2 3 4 5 6 7 8 9 0

PREFACE

This Study Guide is designed to aid in your understanding, assimilation, and the use of the material in Joseph Stiglitz and Carl Walsh's *Economics, Third Edition*. The chapters in this volume correspond those in the main text, and each one is divided into three parts. The first part contains a Chapter Review, an Essential Concepts section, and a Behind the Essential Concepts section. The Chapter Review begins with a brief paragraph explaining how each chapter in Stiglitz and Walsh fits into the overall structure of the text, the Essential Concepts section is a summary of the chapter, bringing out the main points covered. Behind the Essential Concepts offers suggestions about how to avoid common mistakes and provides some intuitive explanations for difficult concepts. This section also brings out the similarities among related ideas and the common structure of many economic theories and concepts.

The second part of each chapter provides a Self-Test with true-or-false, multiple-choice, and completion questions. After reading the chapter in the text and going over the first part of the Study Guide chapter, you should take the self-test. It will help you determine those areas that need further study.

The final part of each chapter is called "Doing Economics: Tools and Practice Problems." This part is designed to teach you the basic skills of economics. The only way to do this is to sharpen up your pencil and try some exercises. If you're willing (or your teacher has assigned this material), I think you'll find the program useful. For each type of problem, there is a Tool Kit box that gives step-by-step instructions about how to use the appropriate tool, a worked problem with a step-by-step solution that follows the procedure outlined in the Tool Kit box, and several practice problems for you to do. Answers are provided at the end of each chapter.

Best of success with your course!

PART ONE | Introduction

CHAPTER 1 | Economics and the New Economy

Chapter Review

The story of computers and the internet is a rich one, introducing as it does the principal ideas of economics. The dominant idea is that economics is about the choices made by the three major groups of participants: individuals or households, firms, and the government. These choices control the allocation of resources, another central concern of economics. This story also highlights the three markets on which this book focuses: product, labor, and capital. The chapter closes with a discussion of how economists use models and theories to describe the economy and why they sometimes disagree. This chapter sets the stage for the introduction of the basic economic model in Chapter 2.

ESSENTIAL CONCEPTS

1 The brief history of computers and the Internet given here illustrates the broad and varied subject matter of economics and many of the important themes of this book. We see vigorous competition among firms as the industry moves from the main frame period, where a single firm, IBM, dominated market share, to the time of the personal computer and Microsoft's rise, and finally to the era of the Internet. We see the importance of investors and entrepeneurs and the risks they face and the central roles of research, technological advance, and patents. A large government presence in funding basic research and promoting competition mixes with private goals of profit seeking and wealth creation.

2 Economics studies how **choices** are made by individuals, firms, governments, and other organizations and how those choices determine the allocation of resources. **Scarcity,** the fact that there are not enough resources to satisfy all wants, requires that choices must be made by individuals and by the economy as a whole. The fundamental questions that an economy must answer are the following:
   a What is produced, and in what quantities?
   b How are these goods produced?
   c For whom are these goods produced?
   d Who makes economic decisions, and by what process?

3 There are two broad branches in economics. **Microeconomics** studies the product, labor, and capital markets, focusing on the behaviour of individuals, households, firms, and other organizations that make up the economy. **Macroeconomics** looks at the performance of the economy as a whole and at such aggregate measures as unemployment, inflation, growth, and the balance of trade.

4 The U.S. economy is a mixed one that relies primarily on private decisions to answer the basic economic questions. **Markets,** which exist wherever and whenever exchanges occur, influence the choices of individuals and firms, but government also plays a prominent role. For starters, the government sets the legal structure within which market forces operate. It also regulates private activity, collects taxes, produces some goods and services, and provides support for the elderly, poor, and others.

5 Trade takes place between individuals and firms in three major markets: the **product market,** the **labor market,** and the **capital market.** Figure 1.1 sketches the interactions. Notice that in general, individuals buy goods and services from firms; they also supply labor and funds for investment to firms.

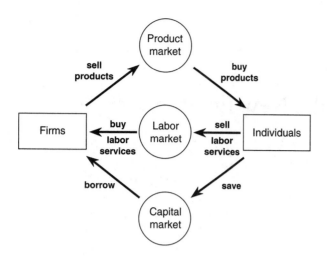

Figure 1.1

6 Economics uses models and **theories**, which are sets of assumptions and conclusions, to understand and predict the behaviour of the economy. Economists want to discover and interpret relationships among economic variables and especially to distinguish where there is causation and where there is only correlation.

7 Economists are frequently asked to give advice regarding public policy, and often they disagree, for two major reasons: they disagree about what is the appropriate theoretical model of the economy and about the effects a policy will have.

BEHIND THE ESSENTIAL CONCEPTS

1 In this book you will learn many economic theories and models. Models and theories are simplified representations of the vast and complex economic world. The way that a model is made simple and workable is through assumptions. We assume that only certain factors are relevant to the problem at hand. Then we derive conclusions from the assumptions and test the model by comparing its predictions with what we know of the world.

You need to do two different things with the models that you will come across in your study of economics. First, you must understand how the model works—specifically, what is assumed and how the conclusions follow. The second task is to evaluate how well the model explains what it is supposed to explain. As you read the many arguments and pieces of evidence, keep in mind how they fit with the model's basic assumptions and conclusions.

2 Economic **variables** are measurable, and they change. The price of potatoes is an economic variable; so is the

rate of unemployment. We look for two types of relationships among these variables. First, we are interested in whether certain economic variables move together. For example, during the 1980s, the U.S. government ran up unprecedented peacetime budget deficits and also very high trade deficits. These two deficit variables were **correlated.** But we are also interested in whether a change in one variable **causes** a change in another variable. Specifically, did the high government budget deficits of the 1980s cause the large trade deficits? Before economists make conclusions, they require a sound model that shows how a change in an economic variable was caused and also some evidence that the model's assumptions are appropriate and that its predictions have actually occurred.

3 **Positive economics** focuses on questions about how the economy works. What does it do, and why does it do it? For example, how were the budget and trade deficits of the 1980s related? **Normative economics,** on the other hand, typically asks what should be done. Should we reduce the federal budget deficit? Keep in mind, however, that normative economics cannot prescribe which value to hold; it describes the appropriate policy given the value.

4 Microeconomics and macroeconomics are two ways of looking at the economy. Microeconomics looks from the bottom up; it starts with the behavior of individuals and firms and builds up to an understanding of markets and the economy as a whole. Macroeconomics, on the other hand, is a top-down look, beginning with a description of the performance of aggregate economic variables and then constructing explanations. Micro- and macroeconomics must fit together. The models that explain how individuals, firms, and markets work must be consistent with the models that we use to describe the economy as a whole. An important theme of this book is that the microeconomics in Parts One, Two, Three and Four provides a firm foundation for the macroeconomics to follow in Parts Five, Six, Seven and Eight.

SELF-TEST

True or False

1 In the 1950s the computer industry produced and marketed mainframe computers.
2 One firm, IBM, has dominated the personal computer market from its inception to the present.
3 Government played little role in the development of the Internet.
4 With the development of hypertext, the World Wide Web opened new opportunities for using the internet.

5 The U. S. government failed in its suit accusing Microsoft of abusing its dominance in the market for personal computer operating systems.

6 Economics studies how individuals, firms, governments, and other organizations make choices and how those choices determine the allocation of the economy's resources.

7 The four basic questions concerning how economies function are what is produced and in what quantities, how are the goods produced, for whom are they produced, and who makes the decisions?

8 Most resource allocation decisions are made by governments in the U.S. economy.

9 In centrally planned economies, most decisions are made by the government.

10 Microeconomics focuses on the behavior of the economy as a whole.

11 Macroeconomics studies the behavior of firms, households, and individuals.

12 The three major markets are the product, labor, and insurance markets.

13 Two economic variables are correlated if there is a systematic relationship between them.

14 When two variables are correlated, it is because changes in one cause changes in the other.

15 Normative economics deals with questions concerning how the economy actually works.

Multiple Choice

1 The market for mainframe computers was dominated by
  a IBM.
  b Microsoft.
  c Xerox.
  d Apple.
  e The World Wide Web.

2 As software programs became more complex, hundreds of programmers might be needed to develop a new program. This
  a enhanced competition in the software market.
  b led to the demise of IBM.
  c limited the impact of the World Wide Web.
  d led to government intervention in the computer market.
  e created a barrier that limited the entry of new firms in the software market.

3 The government's role in the computer industry included
  a funding basic research.
  b regulating competition.
  c playing the watchdog to ensure fair competition.
  d all of the above.
  e none of the above.

4 Because resources are scarce,
  a questions must be answered.
  b choices must be made.
  c all except the rich must make choices.
  d governments must allocate resources.
  e some individuals must be poor.

5 Which of the following is *not* a fundamental question concerning how economies funtion?
  a What is produced, and in what quantities?
  b How are the goods produced?
  c For whom are they produced?
  d Who makes the decisions?
  e All of the above are fundamental questions.

6 In market economies, the four basic questions are answered
  a by elected representatives.
  b in such a way as to ensure that everyone has enough to live well.
  c by private individuals and firms, interacting in markets.
  d according to the traditional way of doing things.
  e by popular vote.

7 In market economies, goods are consumed by those who
  a are most deserving.
  b work the hardest.
  c are politically well connected.
  d are willing and able to pay the most.
  e produce them.

8 The detailed study of firms, households, individuals, and the markets where they transact is called
  a macroeconomics.
  b microeconomics.
  c normative economics.
  d positive economics.
  e aggregate economics.

9 The study of the behavior of the economy as a whole, especially such factors as unemployment and inflation, is called
  a macroeconomics.
  b microeconomics.
  c normative economics.
  d positive economics.
  e market economics.

10 Which of the following is not one of the three major markets?
  a Goods market
  b Labor market
  c Capital market
  d Common Market
  e All of the above

11 An economic theory or model is a
  a mathematical equation.
  b prediction about the future of the economy.

c recommended reform in government policy that pays attention to the laws of economics.

d set of assumptions and conclusions derived from those assumptions.

e small-scale economic community set up to test the effectiveness of a proposed government program.

12 Which of the following is an example of causation?

a Taxes are too high.

b The trade deficits of the 1980s were the direct result of the decade's budget deficits.

c During the 1980s the United States experienced high trade and budget deficits.

d In mixed economies there is a role for government and a role for markets.

e Interest rates in the United States fell during the early 1990s.

13 Which of the following is an example of correlation?

a The high budget deficits of the 1980s caused the trade deficits.

b Taxes are too high.

c During recessions, output falls and unemployment increases.

d In mixed economies, there is a role for markets and a role for government.

e Economics studies choices and how choices determine the allocation of resources.

14 Which of the following is an example of normative economics?

a The high budget deficits of the 1980s caused the trade deficits.

b During recessions, output falls and unemployment increases.

c Lower interest rates would encourage investment.

d Interest rates should be reduced to encourage investment.

e Expansionary monetary policy will reduce interest rates.

15 Which of the following is an example of positive economics?

a Taxes are too high.

b Savings rates in the United States are too low.

c Lower interest rates would encourage investment.

d Interest rates should be reduced to encourage investment.

e There is too much economic inequality in the United States.

16 In the United States, the question of what is produced and in what quantities is answered

a primarily by private decisions influenced by prices.

b by producing what was produced the previous year.

c primarily by government planning.

d randomly.

e according to majority vote.

17 In which of the following does the government determine what is produced, how, and for whom?

a Market economies

b Mixed economies

c Centrally planned economies

d Tradition-bound economies

e All of the above

18 Choices must be made because

a resources are scarce.

b human beings are choice-making animals.

c government regulations require choices to be made.

d economic variables are correlated.

e without choices, there would be no economics as we know it.

19 Anything that can be measured and that changes is

a a correlation.

b a causation.

c a variable.

d a value.

e an experiment.

20 In the labor market,

a households purchase products from firms.

b firms purchase the labor services of individuals.

c firms raise money to finance new investment.

d households purchase labor services from firms.

e borrowing and lending are coordinated.

Completion

1 Exchanges take place in _____.

2 In a _____ economy, some decisions are made chiefly by government and others by markets.

3 All the institutions involved in borrowing and lending money make up the _____ market.

4 The behavior of the economy as a whole, and especially of certain aggregate measures such as unemployment and inflation, is called _____.

5 The branch of economics that focuses on firms, households, and individuals and studies product, labor, and capital markets is called _____.

6 The statement that crime rates are higher in low-income areas is an example of _____.

7 The statement that poverty leads to crime is an example of _____.

8 Economists use _____, which are sets of assumptions, conclusions, and data, to study the economy and evaluate the consequences of various policies.

9 _____ economics rests on value judgments; _____ economics describes how the economy behaves.

10 The four basic questions that economists ask about the economy are (1) what is produced and in what quantities, (2) _____, (3) for whom

are they produced, and (4) who makes the decisions?

Answers to Self-Test

True or False

1	t	6	t	11	f
2	f	7	t	12	f
3	f	8	f	13	t
4	t	9	t	14	f
5	f	10	f	15	f

Multiple Choice

1	*a*	6	*c*	11	*d*	16	*a*
2	*e*	7	*d*	12	*b*	17	*c*
3	*d*	8	*b*	13	*c*	18	*a*
4	*b*	9	*a*	14	*d*	19	*c*
5	*e*	10	*d*	15	*c*	20	*b*

Completion

1 markets
2 mixed
3 capital
4 macroeconomics
5 microeconomics
6 correlation
7 causation
8 theories or models
9 Normative, positive
10 how are these goods produced

CHAPTER 2 | Thinking Like an Economist

Chapter Review

The concept of scarcity discussed in Chapter 1 implies that choices must be made. This chapter begins to explain how economists think about choice, and how choices are influenced and coordinated by markets. A basic economic assumption is that of **rational choice**, which simply says that people select the alternative they prefer most from among all those that are available. The alternatives available to any particular firm or individual, of course, depend upon the choices made by other firms and individuals. All of these rational choices must somehow fit together, and markets serve the function of coordinating them. How they do so is the subject of Chapters 3 through 5.

ESSENTIAL CONCEPTS

1 The **basic competitive model** includes three elements: individuals, firms, and markets. Economic decisions such as what and how much of each type of good to produce, how to produce them, what kind of career to pursue, and how to spend one's earnings are made by **rational, self-interested individuals** and **rational, profit-maximizing firms. Markets** serve the economic role of coordinating these decisions.

2 The basic economic model assumes that markets are **perfectly competitive.** In perfectly competitive markets, there are many consumers and firms, and each is small relative to the size of the overall market. One key feature of perfect competition is that any firm charging more than the going price will lose all its customers. Without any ability to influence the market price, the firm is a **price taker.** (Later in this book, we will encounter monopolists and others known as **price**

makers, who have the power to charge higher prices without losing all their customers.)

3 Private **property rights** play an important role in the basic model. They include the right to use resources in certain ways and the right to sell them in markets. These two aspects of property rights provide incentives to use resources efficiently and to transfer resources to their most valuable use. Inefficiencies can arise when property rights are ill-defined or restricted.

4 When compensation is tied to performance, people have strong incentives to work hard and be productive, but those who are more fortunate and successful also will earn higher incomes. On the other hand, distributing the output more equally undermines incentives. This **incentive-equality trade-off** is one of the basic questions facing societies: how should the tax and welfare system be constructed to balance the competing ends of providing strong incentives and promoting equality?

5 **Scarcity** implies that not everyone who desires a good or resource can have it: there is an allocation problem. In market economies, goods are allocated to the highest bidder. Another solution to the allocation problem is to **ration.** Rationing schemes include queues, first-come-first-served, lotteries, and coupons. Unless supplemented by markets, rationing schemes will likely lead to inefficiencies.

6 The basic economic model assumes that decisions are made rationally, which simply means that individuals and firms balance the benefits and costs of their decisions. Economists see rational decision making as a two-step process. First, find what alternatives are available. This step is the construction of the **opportunity set.** Next, select the best alternative from those within the opportunity set.

7 The chapter presents three types of opportunity sets. The **budget constraint** shows what combinations of goods can be consumed with a limtied amount of money. The **time constraint** indicates to what uses limited time can be put. Finally, the **production possibilities curve** depicts the combinations of goods that a firm or an entire economy can produce given its limited resources and the quality of the available technology.

8 The best alternatives in an opportunity set will lie along the outer edge. This is because people prefer more goods to less. Operating on the outer edge also implies that there will be a **trade-off:** more of one option means less of another. For example, on the budget constraint, consuming more of one good means that less money is available to spend on another good. On the time constraint, if an individual devotes more time to one activity, there is less time available for other endeavors. A society that chooses to produce more of one good must settle for less production of other goods.

9 The **opportunity cost** of a good or activity is the option forgone. The opportunity cost of consuming more of one good is consuming less of some alternative good. The opportunity cost of an activity is the other endeavor that would have been, but now cannot be, undertaken. The opportunity cost of producing one good is the necessarily lower production of another.

10 The opportunity cost, not the price, is the proper measure of the economic cost of any choice. For example, in addition to the ultimate purchase price, the opportunity cost of buying an automobile includes the time and expense devoted to investigating alternatives, searching for the best deal, and negotiating the terms.

11 Opportunity costs are measured in total and at the margin. When a firm is deciding where to locate its plant, it compares the **total costs** at each location. When a firm is considering how large a plant to build, it looks at the costs of increasing or decreasing the size. These arc the **marginal costs,** the costs of a little bit more or a little bit less.

12 The value of a dollar today is greater than the value of a dollar to be received in the future. In other words, money has a time value. Any decision that involves present and future dollars must account for the time value of money. Economists calculate the present discounted value; they convert future dollars to their present equivalent. The formula for the present discounted value of $1 next year is $1/(1 + \text{interest rate})$.

BEHIND THE ESSENTIAL CONCEPTS

1 The basic competitive model introduced in this chapter is critical to your understanding of economics. It will be

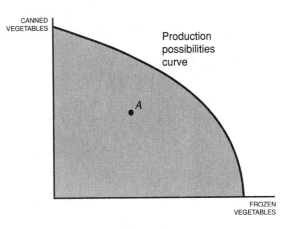

Figure 2.1

expanded and applied in all the chapters that follow, but you should master the concepts given in this chapter: rational individuals choose the best combinations of goods along their budget constraints, firms maximize profits, and trading takes place in competitive markets, where each individual and firm is a price taker.

2 The opportunity set itself shows all of the alternatives that are available. Because more is generally preferred to less, however, economists focus on the outer boundary of the opportunity set. For example, Figure 2.1 shows an opportunity set for a firm that must divide its resources between the production of canned and frozen vegetables. The entire shaded area shows all of the combinations that are possible. The economist's attention is drawn to the outer edge, the production possibilities curve, because to choose a combination inside (such as point *A*) would be inefficient.

3 The terms *opportunity set, budget constraint, trade-off,* and *opportunity cost* are related, but they are distinct, and you should take care to understand each one. Figure 2.2 shows the opportunity set for a student who consumes hamburgers and pizzas. The **opportunity set** shows all of the combinations of hamburgers and pizzas that are affordable. Points *A* and *B* are affordable; they lie within the opportunity set, but have the critical characteristic of lying along its outer edge, which is the budget constraint. The trade-off is that more hamburgers mean fewer pizzas. If Joe chooses *B* rather than *A,* he eats another pizza and exactly two fewer hamburgers. The trade-off between any two points measures the opportunity cost. In this case, the opportunity cost of this extra pizza is the two forgone burgers. When the outer edge of the opportunity set is a straight line, the trade-offs will be the same all along the line; when it is a curve, the trade-offs will change.

4 Opportunity costs are forgone alternatives—not money, not time, and not resources. For example, if you spend

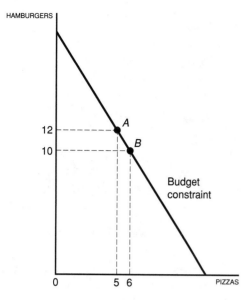

Figure 2.2

one hour in class tomorrow, the opportunity cost of attending that class is not the hour itself. That hour will pass whether you go to the class or not. The opportunity cost is what you would have done with that hour. It is the activity you give up. Strictly speaking, the opportunity cost of buying a book for $20 is not the money, but what would have been purchased with the $20 if it had not been spent on the book.

5 **Sunk costs,** outlays that cannot be recovered, are not opportunity costs. Because these expenditures are not affected by the choice of any alternative, they do not represent the opportunity cost of any alternative. For example, suppose that you sign a one-year lease on an apartment and are forbidden to sublet it. When you consider whether to stay in town for the summer or travel abroad, the rent owed your landlord is irrelevant. You cannot do anything about it. Regardless of which alternative you choose, you must pay the rent. The rent is a sunk cost, not an opportunity cost.

6 Be clear about the difference between total costs and marginal costs. Marginal costs are the costs of a little more or a little less of some activity. Before considering going into business, you evaluate that total opportunity costs of the enterprise—all of the costs of setting up the plant, designing and producing the product, and locating the market. When you are considering whether to produce another unit of output, however, it is the marginl opportunity cost that is important. The marginal cost of producing a little bit more is just the added cost incurred when producing more with the plant already set up, the product designed, and the market found. These latter costs are not marginal.

7 **Diminishing returns** can be confusing at first. What the term means is that as more inputs are used in a

production process, output increases at a diminishing rate. For example, suppose more migrant workers are hired to pick apples. Each additional worker results in more apples being picked in total, but the marginal contribution of the newest worker, how many extra apples are picked when he is hired, is not as great as that of the previously hired new workers. We can also say that the opportunity cost of increasing output—the marginal cost—is higher as output increases.

8 Another way to approach diminishing returns is to think about why the output of the marginal input is declining. The extra inputs are just as good at producing; however, as more are used, the production process becomes crowded. For example, when more workers are hired to pick apples, there are fewer apple trees per workers, and it is more difficult to pick apples.

9 The distinction between real and nominal interest rates is very important, especially in macroeconomics. When you deposit money in your bank account, the bank pays you the nominal interest rate. Say it is 5 percent. Your money grows at 5 percent each year, but your purchasing power may not, because each year prices may also be changing. Suppose that the inflation rate (the rate of increase in the general price level) is 4 percent. This means that each year goods become 4 percent more expensive, and you can buy only 5 percent − 4 percent 1 = percent more goods. The 1 percent is the real interest rate, and also the rate of increase in your purchasing power.

SELF-TEST

True or False

1 The basic model of economics seeks to explain why people want what they want.

2 According to the basic competitive model, firms maximize profits (or stock market value).

3 Generally, inequality will be greater when society is organized to provide stronger incentives to perform efficiently.

4 A firm selling in a perfectly competitive market is a price taker because it cannot raise its price without losing all of its customers.

5 Both the right to use a resource in certain ways and the right to transfer that resource are important aspects of private property rights.

6 Commonly owned property is the reason for diminishing returns.

7 A legal entitlement—that is, the right to use a resource in certain ways but not to sell or trade it—probably prevents the resource from going to its highest valued use.

8 Lotteries are an inefficient means of allocating resources because they do not allocate goods to the highest bidder.

9 Rationing by queues wastes the time spent waiting in line.

10 The opportunity set includes only the best available alternative.

11 The production possibilities curve shows the boundary of the opportunity set.

12 The principle of diminishing returns says that as more units of any input are added to a production process, total output eventually falls.

13 If an economy is not using its resources in the most productive way, economists say that there is inefficiency.

14 Sunk expenditures do not represent opportunity costs.

Multiple Choice

1 Which of the following is *not* a building block of the basic economic model?
   a Assumptions about how firms behave
   b Assumptions about how consumers behave
   c Assumptions about markets
   d Assumptions about the behavior of government
   e All of the above are building blocks of the basic economic model.

2 Individuals and firms in the economy must make choices because of
   a diminishing returns.
   b rationality.
   c scarcity.
   d all of the above.
   e none of the above.

3 The concept of rationality refers to the
   a fact of scarcity.
   b principle of diminishing returns.
   c assumption that individuals have sensible goals.
   d assumption that individuals and firms weigh the costs and benefits of their choices.
   e assumption that individuals and firms are certain of the consequences of their choices.

4 A firm that cannot influence the price it sells its product for is called a
   a price maker.
   b price taker.
   c rational decision maker.
   d none of the above.
   e all of the above.

5 In a pure market economy, incentives to work hard and produce efficiently are provided by
   a the profit motive.
   b government regulations.
   c private property rights.

   d both the profit motive and private property rights.
   e all of the above.

6 When property is commonly owned, users
   a do not maximize profits.
   b violate the principle of rationality.
   c ignore the principle of diminishing returns.
   d have little incentive to maintain and preserve the value of the property.
   e none of the above.

7 If owners are not allowed to sell their resources, then
   a the resources will not go to the highest value users.
   b the owners will not act rationally.
   c their choices will not be limited to their opportunity sets.
   d the market will be perfectly competitive.
   e none of the above.

8 Allocating goods by lotteries, queues, and coupons are examples of
   a rationing.
   b not selling to the highest bidder.
   c efficient ways of allocating resources.
   d the profit motive.
   e a and b.

9 Rationing by queues
   a leads to an efficient allocation of resources.
   b allocates goods to those willing to pay the most money.
   c wastes the time spent waiting in line.
   d is an efficient way of allocating scarce goods.
   e a and c.

10 When goods are rationed by coupons and the coupons are not tradable,
   a the goods do not go to the individuals who value them most.
   b a black market may be established.
   c individuals will not act rationally.
   d a and b.
   e none of the above.

11 Choices of individuals and firms are limited by
   a time constraints.
   b production possibilities.
   c budget constraints.
   d all of the above.
   e none of the above.

12 Fred has $10 to spend on baseball cards and hamburgers. The price of baseball cards is $.50 per pack. Hamburgers sell at a price of $1 each. Which of the following possibilities is not in Fred's opportunity set?
   a 10 hamburgers and zero packs of baseball cards
   b 5 hamburgers and 10 packs of baseball cards
   c 2 hamburgers and 16 packs of baseball cards
   d 1 hamburger and 18 packs of baseball cards
   e All of the above are in Fred's opportunity set.

13 The production possibilities curve
   a shows the amounts of goods a firm or society might produce.
   b is not a straight line because of the principle of diminishing returns.
   c illustrates the trade-offs between goods.
   d all of the above.
   e none of the above.
14 Henry spends an hour shopping and buys one sweater for $30. The opportunity cost of the sweater is
   a one hour.
   b $30.
   c one hour plus $30.
   d the next-best alternative uses of the hour and the $30.
   e none of the above.
15 Renting an apartment, Jorge signs a lease promising to pay $400 each month for one year. He always keeps his word, and therefore he will pay the $400 each month whether he lives in the apartment or not. The $400 each month represents
   a an opportunity cost.
   b a sunk cost.
   c a trade-off.
   d a budget constraint.
   e diminishing returns.
16 One box of Nature's Crunch Cereal sells for $2.55. Each box comes with a coupon worth $.50 off the purchase price of another box of Nature's Crunch Cereal. The marginal cost of the second box of this product is
   a $2.55.
   b $3.05.
   c $2.05.
   d $1.55.
   e none of the above.
17 Making a rational choice involves
   a identifying the opportunity set.
   b defining the trade-off.
   c calculating the opportunity costs.
   d all of the above.
   e none of the above.
18 Fred is considering renting an apartment. A one-bedroom apartment rents for $400, and a nice two-bedroom apartment can be had for $500. The $100 difference is
   a the opportunity cost of the two-bedroom apartment.
   b the marginal cost of the second bedroom.
   c a sunk cost.
   d the marginal cost of an apartment.
   e none of the above.

Completion

1 Economists assume that people make choices _____, taking into consideration the costs and benefits of their alternatives.
2 A market with large numbers of buyers and sellers, each of whom cannot influence the price, is an example of _____.
3 The right of an owner of a resource to use it in certain ways and to sell it is called a _____.
4 Allocating goods and services by some means other than selling to the highest bidder is called _____.
5 The collection of all available opportunities is called the _____.
6 _____ limit choices.
7 The amount of goods that a business firm is able to produce is called its _____.
8 The idea that as more inputs are used in a production process each successive input eventually adds less to output is an example of the principle of _____.
9 The fact that more time spent studying means less time available for other activities illustrates a _____.
10 An expenditure that cannot be recovered is a _____ cost.

Answers to Self-Test

True or False

1	f	6	f	11	t
2	t	7	t	12	f
3	t	8	t	13	t
4	t	9	t	14	t
5	t	10	f		

Multiple Choice

1	d	6	d	11	d	16	c
2	c	7	a	12	e	17	d
3	d	8	e	13	d	18	b
4	b	9	c	14	d		
5	d	10	d	15	b		

Completion

1 rationally
2 perfect competition
3 property right
4 rationing
5 opportunity set
6 Constraints
7 production possibilities
8 diminishing returns
9 trade-off
10 sunk

Doing Economics: Tools and Practice Problems

For the problem sets in this section, we reach into the economist's tool box for five important techniques, each of which will reappear throughout the remainder of the book. Three relate to the opportunity set: budget and time constraints, for which the outer edge of the opportunity set is a straight line; multiple constraints involving, for example, limits on both time and money; and production possibilities curves, which can be straight lines but more often exhibit diminishing returns and are curved. The next two techniques relate to costs: the distinction between sunk and opportunity costs, and the use of marginal analysis to balance costs and benefits. Finally, we turn to the time value of money.

STRAIGHT-LINE OPPORTUNITY SETS

The simplest type of opportunity set has an outer boundary that is a straight line. Examples include budget constraints, time constraints, and production possibilities, when there are constant returns. The budget constraint indicates what combinations of goods can be purchased with a limited amount of money. The time constraint indicates what combinations of time-consuming activities can be undertaken with a limited amount of time. The production possibilities curve (in this case it is a straight line) indicates what combinations of goods can be produced. Tool Kit 2.1 shows how to construct these opportunity sets.

Tool Kit 2.1 Plotting the Straight-Line Opportunity Set

Budget constraints, time constraints, and production possibilities are examples of straight-line opportunity sets. To draw the budget constraint you must know the size of the budget and the prices of the goods. The time constraint can be drawn given the total time available and the time requirements for each activity. To plot the production possibilities curve you need to know the resources and the technology. Follow this procedure to plot these straight-line opportunity sets.

Step one: Draw a set of coordinate axes. Label the horizontal axis as the quantity of one good or activity and the vertical axis as the quantity of the other good or activity.

Step two: Calculate the maximum quantity of the good or activity measured on the horizontal axis. Plot this quantity along the horizontal axis.

Step three: Calculate the maximum quantity of the good or activity measured on the vertical axis. Plot this quantity along the vertical axis.

Step four: Draw a line segment connecting the two points. This line segment is the relevant part of the opportunity set.

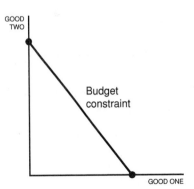

Step five: The slope is the opportunity cost of the good or activity measured on the horizontal axis. In the case of the budget constraint, it is called the relative price, the ratio of the price of the good measured on the horizontal axis divided by the price of the good measured on the vertical axis.

1 (Worked problem: budget constraint) Diana has an entertainment budget of $200 each month. She enjoys lunches with friends and going to the movies. The price of a typical lunch is $10. Movie tickets are $5 each. Construct her opportunity set.

Step-by-step solution

Step one: Draw coordinate axes and label the horizontal one "Lunches" and the vertical one "Movies." (There is no rule as to which good goes where. It would be fine if lunches were measured on the vertical axis and movies on the horizontal.)

Step two: Calculate the maximum quantity of lunches. This number is $200/$10 = 20 lunches. Plot this quantity along the horizontal axis.

Step three: Calculate the maximum quantity of movies. This number is $200/$5 = 40 movie tickets. Plot this quantity along the vertical axis.

Step four: Draw a line segment connecting these two points. This line segment is the budget constraint.

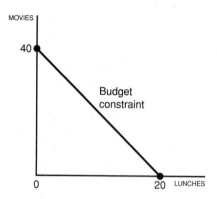

Step five: The slope of the budget constraint is 40/20 = 2. The price ratio is $10/$5 = 2. (Strictly speaking, these slopes are negative, but we follow the practice of dropping the negative sign as long as there is no confusion.)

2 (Practice problem: budget constraint) Velma Thomas must pay for both prescription medicine and nursing care for her elderly father. Each bottle of pills costs her $40, and the price of nursing care is $100 per day. She has been able to scrape together $1,000 each month for these expenses. Construct her opportunity set, going through all five steps.

3 (Practice problem: budget constraint) Construct the following opportunity sets.
  a Clothing budget per year = $900; price of suits = $300; price of shoes = $90.
  b Food budget = $200 per week; price of restaurant meals = $20; price of in-home meals = $5.
  c School expense budget = $1,200 per semester; price of books = $50; price of courses = $200.
  d Annual state transportation department budget = $100,000; cost of fixing potholes = $200; cost of replacing road signs = $500.

4 (Worked problem: time constraint) Ahmed likes to visit his invalid father across town. Each visit, including transportation and time with Dad, takes 3 hours. Another of Ahmed's favorite activities is his tango lessons. These are given downstairs in his apartment building and take only an hour each. With work and night school, Ahmed has only 15 hours each week to divide between visiting his father and tango lessons. Construct his opportunity set.

Step-by-step solution

Step one: The time constraint works very much like the budget constraint. Plot coordinate axes and label the horizontal one "Visits" and the vertical one "Lessons."

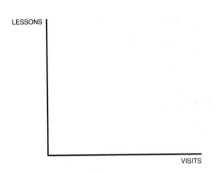

Step two: Calculate the maximum number of visits to his father. This number is 15/3 = 5 visits. Plot this quantity along the horizontal axis.

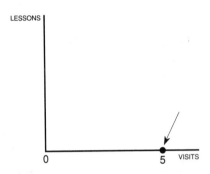

Step three: Calculate the maximum number of tango lessons. This number is 15/1 = 15 lessons. Plot this quantity along the vertical axis.

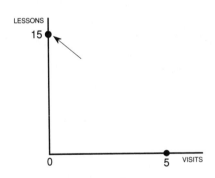

Step four: Draw a line segment connecting these two points. This line segment is the time constraint.

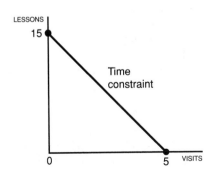

Step five: The slope of the time constraint is 15/5 = 3. The time-requirement ratio is 3/1 = 3.

5 (Practice problem: time constraint) Michael Terranova has 2 hours to make his house as clean as possible. The place needs vacuuming and dusting. He can dust one piece of furniture in 10 minutes. Each room takes 20 minutes to vacuum. Plot his time constraint.

6 (Practice problem: time constraint) Construct the following opportunity sets.

   a Total time available = 6 hours; time required to iron each shirt = 15 minutes; time required to iron each dress = 30 minutes.

   b Total time available = 20 days; time required to study each chapter = 1/2 day; time required to write book reports = 2 days.

   c Total time available = 40 hours; time required to counsel each disturbed teenager = 2 hours; time required to attend each meeting = 1 hour.

   d Total time available = 8 hours; time required to visit each client = 4 hours; time required to telephone each client = 10 minutes.

7 (Worked problem: production possibilities curve) First, assume that there is one resource, which can be used in the production of either of two goods, and that there are no diminishing returns. In this case, the production possibilities curve is a straight line, and we treat it just as we did the budget and time constraints.

There are 25 migrant farm workers employed at San Pueblo vegetable farm. Each worker can pick 4 bushels of cucumbers an hour. Alternatively, each worker can pick 1 bushel of peppers each hour. Each worker can work 8 hours a day. Plot the daily production possibilities curve.

Step-by-step solution

Step one: Plot coordinate axes and label the horizontal one "Cucumbers" (measured in bushels) and the vertical one "Peppers."

Step two: Calculate the maximum number of cucumbers that can be picked each day. This number is 25 (workers) × 8 (hours) × 4 (bushels an hour) = 800 bushels of cucumbers. Plot this number along the horizontal axis.

Step three: Calculate the maximum number of peppers that can be picked each day. This number is 25 (workers) × 8 (hours) × 1 (bushel an hour) = 200 bushels of peppers. Plot this number along the vertical axis.

Step four: Draw a line segment connecting these two points. This line segment is the production possibilities curve.

Step five: The slope is 200/800 = 1/4, which means that the opportunity cost of 1 bushel of cucumbers is 1/4 bushel of peppers.

8 (Practice problem: production possibilities curve) Coach Hun has four assistant coaches. They make recruiting visits and also run clinics for local youth. Each can make 32 recruiting visits a week. Alternatively, each can run 8 clinics in a week. Plot the production possibilities curve.

9 (Practice problem: production possibilities curve) Construct the following opportunity sets.

 a Total amount of land available = 10 acres of land; output of corn per acre = 2,000 bushels; output of wheat per acre = 1,000 bushels.

 b Total amount of labor available = 40 hours; output of donuts per hour = 150; output of sweet rolls per hour = 50.

 c Total amount of floor space available = 1,000 square feet; sales of women's sportswear per square foot = $500; sales of housewares per square foot = $200.

 d Total amount of fuel available = 5,000 gallons; miles per gallon for tank travel = 3; miles per gallon for armored personnel carriers = 9.

MULTIPLE CONSTRAINTS

Individuals often face more than one constraint. For example, many activities cost money and take up time. This means that the opporunity set includes only those alternatives that do not exceed both the budget and time con-

straints. Tool Kit 2.2 shows how to combine multiple constraints into a single opportunity set. Notice how the resulting opportunity set is convex.

Tool Kit 2.2 Plotting Multiple Constraints

When activities take both time and money, opportunities will be limited by two constraints. This is one example of the problem of multiple constraints. To plot the opportunity set when more than one constraint applies, follow this three-step procedure.

Step one: Plot the first constraint. (For example, this might be the budget constraint.)

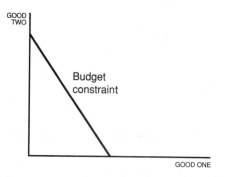

Step two: Plot the second constraint. (For example, this might be the time constraint.)

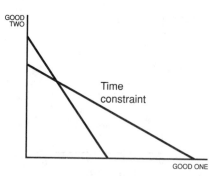

Step three: Darken the section of each constraint that lies under the other constraint. This is the outer edge of the opportunity set.

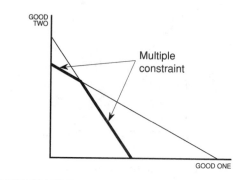

10 (Worked problem: multiple constraints) Out of work for six months, Donna feels that it is time to start looking for a job. Her father (gently) suggests that she apply in person to several of the retail stores on the west side of town. Each store application would require $5 in out-of-pocket expenses for transportation and dry cleaning. (She realizes that only those who wear clean clothes stand any chance of receiving an offer.) Each trip would require 5 hours.

Donna's mother (not so gently) says that she should mail letters of application to a wide variety of potential employers. Each letter of application would require only $1 in mailing and copying costs and 1/2 hour of time.

Donna can devote 30 hours and $50 dollars each week to her job search campaign. Plot her opportunity set.

Step-by-step solution

Step one: Follow the procedure for plotting her budget constraint. Label the horizontal axis "Personal applications" and the vertical one "Mail applications." Your answer should look like this.

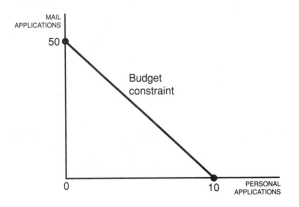

Step two: Follow the procedure for plotting her time constraint. Your answer should look like this.

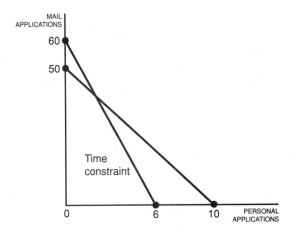

Step three: Darken the section of each constraint that lies under the other constraint. Notice that between points *A* and

B on the diagram, it is the budget constraint that is binding, but between *B* and *C,* the time constraint is the limiting one.

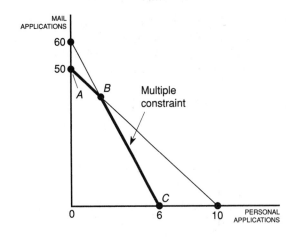

11 (Practice problem: multiple constraints) Harold's leaf-raking business is taking off. He has so many jobs to do that he is thinking of renting a leaf blower. This would cost him $20 per day. With a leaf blower, he could clean 10 lawns each day. He can only do 4 each day with his trusty rake, which costs nothing. Harold works 7 days each week, but has only $100 to spend. Plot his opportunity set for the week. (Hint: The axes should be labeled "Lawns cleaned with a leaf blower" and "Lawns raked by hand.")

12 (Practice problem: multiple constraints) The maintenance department at Alberti Van and Storage has 8 mechanic-hours to tune truck engines and replace the mufflers. It takes 1 hour to tune an engine and 1/2 hour to replace the muffler. In addition, the parts budget is only $100, the parts required to tune an engine cost $10, and each muffler costs $20. Construct the department's opportunity set.

13 (Practice problem: multiple constraints) Lamont tests swimming pools and cleans locker rooms for local country clubs. He has 20 hours available, and it takes him 1 hour to test each pool and 1/2 hour to clean each locker room. He has a budget of $50 to spend. It costs him $10 to test each pool and $1 to clean each locker room. Construct his opportunity set.

PRODUCTION POSSIBILITIES WITH DIMINISHING RETURNS

Usually, production is subject to diminishing returns. This means that as more of a resource is used in production, the extra (or marginal) output is less. In other words, although output increases, it does so at a diminishing rate. With diminishing returns the production possibilities curve acquires a convex shape. Tool Kit 2.3 shows how to plot the production possibilities curves when there are diminishing returns.

Tool Kit 2.3 Plotting the Production Possibilities Curve with Diminishing Returns

Diminishing returns mean that as more of some resource is used in production, the extra (or marginal) output declines. Follow this five-step procedure to plot the production possibilities curve with diminishing returns.

Step one: Draw and label a set of coordinate axes.

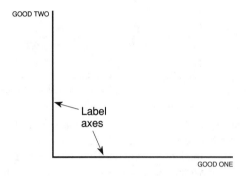

Step two: Calculate the total amount of the good measured on the horizontal axis that can be produced if all the resource is used. Plot this quantity along the horizontal axis.

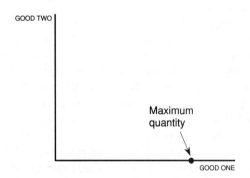

Step three: Calculate the total amount of the good measured on the vertical axis that can be produced if all the resource is used. Plot this quantity along the vertical axis.

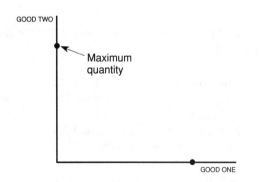

Step four: Calculate and plot several other feasible combinations.

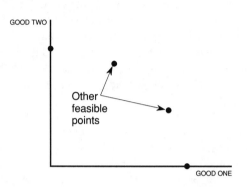

Step five: Draw a smooth curve connecting these points. This curve is the production possibilities curve.

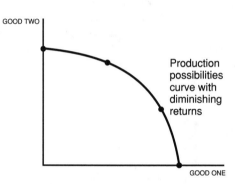

Step six: Verify that the slope is increasing along the curve. Since the slope is the marginal opportunity cost of the horizontal axis good, this reflects diminishing returns.

14 (Worked problem: production possibilities curve with diminishing returns) Iatrogenesis, a medical laboratory, employs 4 lab technicians. Each is equally adept at analyzing throat cultures and distilling vaccines. The table below shows output per day for various numbers of lab technicians.

Technicians doing cultures	Throat cultures	Technicians doing vaccines	Vaccines
1	50	1	20
2	90	2	35
3	120	3	45
4	140	4	50

Plot the production possibilities curve for Iatrogenesis.

Step-by-step solution

Step one: Draw coordinate axes. Label the horizontal one "Throat cultures" and the vertical one "Vaccines."

Step two: Calculate the maximum number of throat cultures. If all 4 technicians do throat cultures, the number is 140. Plot this number.

Step three: Calculate the maximum number of vaccines. If all 4 technicians do vaccines, the number is 50. Plot this number.

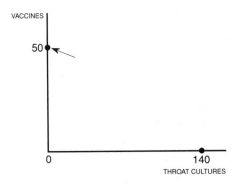

Step four: Calculate several other feasible points. For example, if 1 technician does throat cultures, then 3 can do vaccines. Reading off the table, we see that the combination produced is 50 throat cultures and 45 vaccines. Similarly, if 2 do throat cultures and 2 do vaccines, the outputs are 90

throat cultures and 35 vaccines. Another feasible combination is 120 cultures and 20 vaccines. Plot these points.

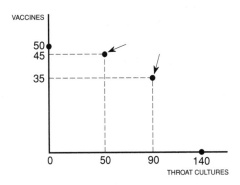

Step five: Draw the production possibilities curve through the points that have been plotted.

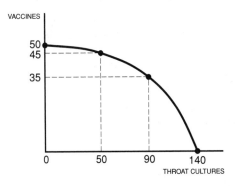

Step six: Observe that, as expected, the slope gets steeper as the number of throat cultures is increased. This indicates diminishing returns.

15 (Practice problem: production possibilities curve with diminishing returns) Enormous State University has a crime problem. Members of the criminal element have stolen many bicycles and a great deal of stereo equipment. To address this crime wave, the campus police has hired 5 new officers. The following table gives the expected number of thefts for various assignments for these new officers.

New police officers assigned to bicycle duty	Reduction in bicycle thefts	New police officers assigned to dorm patrol	Reduction in thefts of stereo equipment
1	25	1	10
2	45	2	18
3	60	3	25
4	70	4	31
5	75	5	36

Plot the production possibilities curve.

16 (Practice problem: production possibilities curve with diminishing returns) Movaway Company has employed 4 maintenance inspectors for their fleet of trucks and forklifts. The following table shows how assigning inspectors leads to fewer breakdowns.

Reduced Inspectors assigned to check trucks	Inspectors number of truck breakdowns	Reduced assigned to check forklifts	number of forklift breakdowns
1	5	1	3
2	9	2	5
3	12	3	6
4	14	4	6

Plot Movaway's production possibilities curve, and verify that it shows diminishing returns.

17 (Practice problem: production possibilities curve with diminishing returns) The Dukakis vegetable farm (located on erstwhile corn-growing land in Iowa) has 800 tons of fertilizer. The following table shows how output of endive and bib lettuce is expected to respond to different amounts of fertilizer.

Fertilizer used on endive crop (tons)	Output of endive (bushels)	Fertilizer used on lettuce crop (tons)	Output of bib lettuce (bushels)
0	1,400	0	2,000
200	2,400	200	3,400
400	3,200	400	4,200
600	3,600	600	4,700
800	4,000	800	5,000

Plot the farm's production possibilities curve, and verify that it exhibits diminishing returns.

SUNK COSTS

Rational individuals make choices by carefully weighing the benefits and costs of their alternatives. Doing this requires a clear understanding of exactly what an opportunity cost is. Expenditures that cannot be recovered are not true opportunity costs. They are sunk costs and should be ignored when making decisions. Opportunity costs are foregone alternatives, and they are the only costs to consider. Tool Kit 2.4 shows how to distinguish true opportunity costs from sunk costs.

Tool Kit 2.4 Distinguishing Opportunity Costs and Sunk Costs

When an expenditure must be made regardless of what action is chosen, that expenditure is not an opportunity cost, it is a sunk cost. To find the opportu-

nity cost of an action, it is necessary to see what is changed by undertaking that action rather than its alternative. Follow this four-step procedure.

Step one: To find the opportunity cost of an action, first specify the next-best alternative. This is what would be done if the action in question were not chosen.

Step two: Calculate the total cost for the action and its alternative.

Step three: Calculate the opportunity cost. Subtract the cost for the alternative from the cost for the action. This difference is the opportunity cost of the action.

Step four: Calculate the sunk costs. Any costs that are the same for both the chosen action and its alternative are sunk costs.

18 (Worked problem: opportunity costs and sunk costs) Upper Peninsula Airlines is studying the question of when to cancel flights for its Marquette to Detroit route. Flying nearly empty planes seems like bad business. The company wants to know the opportunity cost of going ahead with a scheduled round-trip flight. There are two scheduled flights each day. Here are some relevant cost data.

Salaries of crew	$ 1,000 per day
Fuel	$ 400 per round trip
Mortgage on plane	$ 100 per day
Landing fees	$ 50 in Marquette
	$ 100 in Detroit
Other in-flight costs	$ 100 per round trip

Calculate the opportunity cost of each round trip.

Step-by-step solution

Step one: The next-best alternative to going ahead with the scheduled round-trip flight is not flying.

Step two: Calculate the total cost for going ahead with the flight and canceling it. If the flight is made, the expenditures are all of those listed above. If the flight is canceled, the company saves on fuel, landing fees, and other in-flight costs. The salaries of the crew and the mortage must be paid whether the flight happens or not.

Expenditures if flight is not canceled
= $1,000 + $400 + $100 + $150 + $100 = $1,750.

Expenditures if flight is canceled
= $1,000 + $100 = $1,100.

Step three: Calculate the opportunity costs: $1,750 − $1,100 = $650. This is the opportunity cost of the flight.

Step four: Calculate the sunk costs. The remaining $1,100 for salaries and mortgage are sunk costs. Whether or not the flight is canceled, these cannot be recovered.

19 (Practice problem: opportunity costs and sunk costs) Often during the summer term, courses are scheduled but canceled at Enormous State University's downtown education building. In order to see whether this is a good policy, the administration needs to know the opportunity cost of going ahead with a scheduled course offering. Here are some cost data.

Compensation for instructor	$4,000
Air conditioning and lighting	$1,000
Custodial services	$2,000
Property taxes	$2,500

Each course requires one room. Any rooms not used for summer courses can be rented to local groups for $1,200 for the summer term.

a Find the opportunity cost of offering a course.
b How much are sunk costs?

20 (Practice problem: opportunity cost and sunk costs) The Commerce Department is downsizing under Governor Scissorhands. It is considering offering early retirement to 8 bureaucrats in its strategic investment division. Each is 2 years from regular retirement age. (For simplicity, you may ignore discounting the second year's dollars in this problem.)

Salaries	$50,000 each (per year)
Fringe benefits	$20,000 each (per year)
Office space for all 8	$10,000 annually (lease signed for 1 more year)
Pension benefit	$20,000 each if retired (per year)

a If the 8 do receive early retirement, what is the opportunity cost?
b How much are sunk costs?

MARGINAL BENEFITS AND MARGINAL COSTS

The rational individual always considers the benefits and costs of any action. Once you decide to do something, however, there is the question of how much of it to do. Answering this question involves looking at the benefits and costs of a little more or a little less, the marginal benefits and marginal costs. Tool Kit 2.5 shows how to calculate and balance the marginal benefits and marginal costs of economic decisions.

Tool Kit 2.5 Using Marginal Benefits and Marginal Costs

The marginal benefit of an activity is the extra brought about by increasing that activity a little. The marginal cost is the corresponding cost. Rational individuals make efficient decisions by carefully balancing benefits and costs "at the margin." Follow this four-step procedure.

Step one: Identify the objective of the activity and the benefits and costs of various levels of the activity.

Step two: Calculate marginal benefits. These are the extra gains from a little bit more of the activity.

Step three: Calculate the marginal costs. These are the extra costs from a little bit more of the activity.

Step four: Choose the level of the activity for which the marginal benefits equal the marginal costs.

---

21 (Worked problem: marginal costs and marginal benefits) A new inoculation against Honduran flu has just been discovered. Presently, 55 people die from the disease each year. The new inoculation will save lives, but unfortunately, it is not completely safe. Some of the recipients of the shots will die from adverse reactions. The projected effects of the inoculation are given in Table 2.1.

Table 2.1

Percent of population inoculated	Deaths due to the disease	Deaths due to the inoculations
0	55	0
10	45	0
20	36	1
30	28	2
40	21	3
50	15	5
60	10	8
70	6	12
80	3	17
90	1	23
100	0	30

How much of the population should be inoculated?

Step-by-step solution

Step one: Identify the objective, benefits, and costs. The objective is to minimize total deaths from the disease and the inoculations, and the problem is to choose the percentage of the population to inoculate. The benefits are reduced deaths caused by the disease, and the costs are the deaths caused by the shots.

Step two: Calculate the marginal benefits. The first 10 percent of the population inoculated reduces deaths caused by the disease from 55 to 45. The marginal benefit of the first 10 percent is 10. From the second 10 percent (increasing the percentage from 10 to 20), the marginal benefit is $45 - 36 = 9$. The schedule of the marginal benefit is given in Table 2.2.

Table 2.2

Percent of population	Marginal benefits
10	10
20	9
30	8
40	7
50	6
60	5
70	4
80	3
90	2
100	1

Step three: Calculate the marginal costs. Inoculating the first 10 percent causes no deaths. The second 10 percent (increasing the percent of the population getting the shots from 10 to 20 percent) causes 1 death. The schedule for the marginal costs is shown in Table 2.3.

Table 2.3

Percent of population	Marginal costs
0	0
10	1
20	1
30	1
40	1
50	2
60	3
70	4
80	5
90	6
100	7

Step four: Choose the level of inoculation percentage for which marginal benefits equal marginal costs. The percentage of the population to inoculate is 70. To see why this is correct, notice that inoculating 10 percent of the population saves 10 lives (marginal benefits = 10) and causes no deaths (marginal costs = 0). The net savings in lives is 10. Increasing the percentage to 20 percent saves 9 lives at a cost of 1 death. The net savings is 9 lives. Continuing as long as deaths do not rise gives 70 percent. Notice that increasing the percentage to 80 percent saves fewer people (marginal benefits = 2) than it kills (marginal costs = 4). This is a bad idea. We should stop at 70 percent.

22 (Practice problem: marginal costs and marginal benefits) The transportation department has 10 workers fixing potholes. It is considering allocating some of these workers to reprogram traffic lights. Each activity saves travel time for commuters, and this is the objective of the transportation department. Table 2.4 gives time savings of each activity as the number of workers assigned to it varies. Remember that if a worker is assigned to reprogram lights, he cannot fix potholes.

Table 2.4

Workers assigned to reprogramming	Total time saved	Workers assigned to fix potholes	Total time saved
1	100	1	125
2	190	2	225
3	270	3	305
4	340	4	365
5	400	5	415
6	450	6	455
7	490	7	485
8	520	8	510
9	540	9	530
10	550	10	540

How should the workers be assigned? (Hint: Let the number of workers assigned to reprogramming be the activity. What are the costs of assigning these workers?)

23 (Practice problem: marginal costs and marginal benefits) Bugout pesticide kills insects that eat lettuce leaves. Currently 11 leaves per head are eaten by the insects. In the right concentrations, Bugout can be effective. On the other hand, there are side effects. When the concentration is too great, leaves fall off the lettuce head. Table 2.5 shows the relationship between concentrations of Bugout, leaves eaten, and leaves fallen. What concentration should the manufacturer recommend?

Table 2.5

Concentration (parts per million)	Leaves eaten per head	Leaves fallen per head
1	7	0
2	4	1
3	2	3
4	1	6
5	0	10
6	0	15

Answers to Problems

8

11

9

12

13

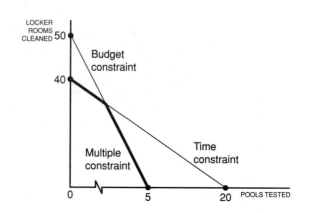

15

Reduction in bicycle thefts	Reduction in thefts of stereo equipment
0	36
25	31
45	25
60	18
70	10
75	0

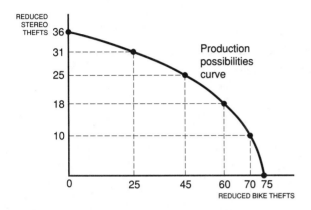

16

Reduced number of truck breakdowns	Reduced number of forklift breakdowns
0	6
5	6
9	5
12	3
14	0

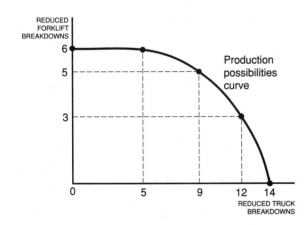

17

Endive (bushels)	Lettuce (bushels)
1,400	5,000
2,400	4,700
3,200	4,200
3,600	3,400
4,000	2,000

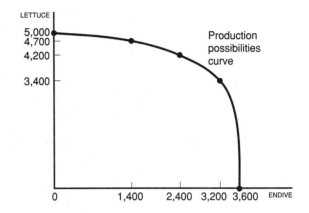

19

	Costs of holding class	Costs of canceling class
Compensation for instructor	$4,000	0
Air conditioning and lighting	$1,000	$1,000
Custodial services	$2,000	#2,000
Property taxes	$2,500	$2,500
Rent	0	−$1,200
Total	**$9,500**	**$4,300**

a Opportunity cost = $9,500 − $4,300 = $5,200.
b Sunk cost = $4,300.

20

	Cost of early retirements	Cost of retaining bureaucrats
Salaries	0	$50,000 × 8 × 2
Fringe benefits	0	$20,000 × 8 × 2
Office space for all 8	$10,000	$20,000
Pension benefit	$20,000 × 8 × 2	0
Total	$330,000	$1,140,000

a Opportunity cost = $1,140,000 − $330,000 = $810,000.
b Sunk cost = $330,000.

22 The marginal benefit of assigning a worker to reprogram the lights is the time saved; the marginal cost is the time lost because the worker was not assigned to fix potholes.

Workers assigned to reprogramming	Marginal benefits	Marginal costs
1	100	10
2	90	20
3	80	25
4	70	30
5	60	40
6	50	50
7	40	60
8	30	80
9	20	100
10	10	125

Assign 6 to reprogramming and 4 to fixing potholes.

23 The benefit of recommending higher concentrations of pesticides are the fewer leaves eaten; the costs are the leaves that fall off.

Concentration of pesticide	Marginal benefits	Marginal costs
1	4	0
2	3	1
3	2	2
4	1	3
5	1	4
6	0	5

The manufacturer should recommend a concentration of 3 ppm.

CHAPTER 3 | Trade

Chapter Review

Chapter 3 takes up the key feature of markets: exchange. The fundamental aspect of market-based economies is voluntary trade. By definition, voluntary trade is mutually beneficial; it creates a **surplus** for both buyer and seller. If this were not true, the trade would not take place! An important insight of trade theory is the principle of comparative advantage, which shows how individuals and countries can specialize in production and thereby increase the gains they receive from trade. Economists emphasize these **gains from trade** and see little sense in protectionist arguments that trade between countries should be limited. The next two chapters will show how markets help realize some of the potential gains from trade.

ESSENTIAL CONCEPTS

1. Voluntary trade between rational individuals is **mutually beneficial;** it is good for both buyer and seller. Naturally, the buyer would like a lower price, and the seller prefers a higher price. Both might also benefit from better information. Nevertheless, the fact that the exchange takes place implies that given the information each has at the time of the transaction, both judge that they are better off trading than not trading.

2. Trade between individuals within a country and trade between individuals in different countries take place in markets. The three broad classes of markets are the product, labor, and capital markets. These three markets are all integrated internationally; this has led to a high degree of economic interdependence among nations.

3. **Trade** is many sided, or **multilateral**. A typical person sells labor to an employer and uses the wages she earns both to purchase goods and services from many other firms and to save for future consumption. Similarly, a country may import more from some trading partners and export very little to those countries. With other trading partners, the country may export more than it imports. A country may also buy more goods and services than it sells abroad, and make up the difference by borrowing in capital markets or sending its workers to foreign labor markets.

4. The principle of **comparative advantage** says that individuals and countries will specialize in those goods that they are relatively more efficient in producing. To be relatively efficient means to have a lower opportunity cost. Countries will have a comparative advantage in different goods. Each can import certain goods from abroad for a lower opportunity cost than it would incur producing them at home. Similarly, each can export to foreign countries those goods for which it has a comparative advantage.

5. Comparative advantage leads to **specialization** in trade, but specialization itself increases productivity and further lowers opportunity costs. First, individuals and countries grow more efficient at their specialties through practice. Second, producing for others allows a larger scale of operations, more **division of labor** into separate tasks, and more specialization. Finally, specialization creates conditions in which invention and innovation flourish.

6. Different countries and individuals have comparative advantages in different activities. Reasons for a comparative advantage can include natural endowments such as climate (for a country) or manual dexterity (for a tailor), human or physical capital, knowledge, and experience. These factors may be gifts of nature, or they may be the result of investment, experience, education, training, or other past actions.

7 **Protectionism** is the idea that the economy needs safeguarding against the perceived harmful effects of trade. Proponents of protectionism use many arguments; chief among them are the loss of domestic jobs, the vulnerability to foreign influences, the unfair trade practices of foreign governments, trade imbalances, and the potential damage to weak economies. To economists, none of these arguments is convincing.

BEHIND THE ESSENTIAL CONCEPTS

1 An exchange creates and divides a surplus. The surplus is the difference between the value to the seller of what is traded and its value to the buyer. If there is no surplus, the exchange does not take place; the seller simply refuses to trade if he thinks the good is worth more than the buyer is willing to pay. The division of the surplus is another matter. Both the buyer and seller will receive some of the surplus. This is what economists mean when they say that trade is mutually beneficial: each party receives some of the surplus. The buyer pays somewhat less than the maximum she is willing to pay, and the seller receives somewhat more than the minimum he is willing to accept. Of course, whatever the division of the surplus, each would prefer to receive more.

2 When individuals trade, both buyer and seller gain. Each is better off with the trade than he or she would be if the trade did not take place. Likewise, countries also gain from trade. Trade allows specialization on the basis of comparative advantage, and countries benefit from more goods and services. But although each country as a whole gains from trade, not every individual in each country is better off. Some businesses lose out to foreign competition, and some workers lose jobs. Other businesses gain new markets, and new jobs are created. Thus, international trade creates both gains and losses, but overall, the gains outweigh the losses.

3 The problem with protectionism is that it looks only at the losers from international trade. Tariffs, quotas, and other protectionist policies can, at least temporarily, protect the losers, but only by limiting the trade. Limiting the trade means limiting the gains as well as the losses. Because the gains from trade exceed the losses, protectionism can only make matters worse for the economy as a whole.

4 To better understand comparative advantage, it helps to distinguish it from **absolute advantage.** A country has an absolute advantage in the production of a good or service if it requires fewer inputs to produce the good than another country. Comparative advantage, on the other hand, pertains to opportunity costs. As we have seen, the opportunity cost is not the inputs used in production; rather, it is the alternative use of those inputs. Thus, a country (or individual) has the comparative advantage in the production of a good or service if it has the lower opportunity cost.

For instance, assume that only labor is required to produce tomatoes or bookcases. Workers in country A can produce a carload of tomatoes in 40 hours, while workers in country B require 80 hours. Country A has an absolute advantage in producing tomatoes. To determine comparative advantage, however, we must look at how productive those workers are elsewhere in the economy. If the 40 hours of labor in country A produce 2 bookcases, but 80 hours in country B produce only 1, then country B has a comparative advantage in tomatoes. Why? Because a carload of tomatoes has an opportunity cost of 1 fewer bookcase in country B.

SELF-TEST

True or False

1 Unless the gain from trade is divided equally between buyer and seller, an exchange cannot be mutually beneficial.

2 While United States imports as a percentage of gross domestic product (GDP) have grown over the past three decades, the percentage of GDP devoted to exports has fallen.

3 Because of problems of information, problems of estimating risks, and difficulties in forming expectations about the future, many exchanges are not mutually beneficial.

4 With multilateral trade, imports from a particular country may not equal exports to that country.

5 The country that can produce a good with the least amount of labor is said to have a comparative advantage in the production of that good.

6 Trade on the basis of comparative advantage leads to complete specialization.

7 The extent of the division of labor is limited by the size of the market.

8 Comparative advantage is determined by the endowment of natural resources, human and physical capital, knowledge, and the experience that comes from specialization.

9 The marginal rate of transformation measures the trade-off between two commodities, indicating how much more of one commodity can be produced at the sacrifice of a given amount of another commodity.

10 Opposition to trade between nations is called protectionism.

11 A country that exports more than it imports will run a trade deficit.

12 Although trade benefits the country as a whole, many individuals may lose from trade in a particular product.

13 A country that runs a trade deficit must borrow from abroad.

14 The United States has comparative advantage in high-technology manufactured products, such as airplanes and computers, but must import wheat.

15 The North American Free Trade Agreement will eliminate all trade barriers between the United States, Canada, and Mexico within fifteen years.

Multiple Choice

1 Voluntary trade between two rational individuals benefits
   a the buyer only.
   b the seller only.
   c the buyer or the seller but not both.
   d both the buyer and the seller.
   e none of the above.

2 The gain from trade, that is, the difference between the value of a good to the buyer and its value to the seller,
   a accrues entirely to the seller.
   b accrues entirely to the buyer.
   c is always divided equally.
   d accrues to the government.
   e none of the above.

3 When economists argue that both parties benefit from voluntary trade, they are assuming
   a that both parties are well informed.
   b that both parties place the same value on the traded good.
   c that both parties desire the same price.
   d that the surplus is divided evenly between buyer and seller.
   e none of the above.

4 Goods produced in the United States and sold in foreign countries are called
   a imports.
   b exports.
   c either imports or exports.
   d capital flows.
   e none of the above.

5 For decades, Japan has imported raw materials from Australia, while Australia has purchased heavy equipment from the United States. Furthermore, Japan has exported consumer goods to the United States. This is an example of
   a multilateral trade.
   b bilateral trade.
   c absolute advantage.
   d protectionism.
   e trade deficit.

6 If the United States has a comparative advantage in the production of a good, then
   a fewer resources are required to produce the good in the United States.
   b the United States also has an absolute advantage in the production of the good.
   c the relative cost of producing the good is lower in the United States.
   d the United States will import the good.
   e all of the above.

7 If the United States has absolute advantage in the production of a good,
   a production of the good in the United States is more efficient and requires fewer resources.
   b the United States also has comparative advantage in the production of the good.
   c the relative cost of producing the good is lower in the United States.
   d the United States will import the good.
   e the United States will export the good.

8 The trade-off between two commodities is called the
   a comparative advantage.
   b specialization.
   c absolute advantage.
   d marginal rate of transformation.
   e none of the above.

9 Suppose that in the United States increasing wheat output by 1,000 tons would require a reduction in steel output of 500 tons, but in Canada increasing wheat output by 1,000 tons would require reducing steel output by 1,000 tons. Then we can infer that
   a Canada has an absolute advantage in wheat.
   b the United States has an absolute advantage in wheat.
   c the United States will export steel.
   d the United States has a comparative advantage in steel.
   e the United States has a comparative advantage in wheat.

10 The slope of the production possibilities curve is called the
   a marginal rate of transformation.
   b comparative advantage.
   c trade deficit.
   d marginal benefit.
   e marginal rate of production.

11 The principle of comparative advantage
   a applies only to international trade.
   b always leads to complete specialization.
   c forms the basis for the division of labor.
   d is relevant only in the absence of protection.
   e all of the above.

12 Which of the following is *not* a reason why specialization increases productivity?

a Workers and countries grow more efficient by repeating the same tasks.

b Specialization saves time needed to switch from one task to another.

c Specialization allows larger-scale production with greater efficiency.

d Specialization allows the assignment of tasks to those who have a comparative advantage.

e All of the above, are reasons.

13 Important sources of comparative advantage include

a natural endowments.

b human and physical capital.

c superior knowledge.

d experience.

e all of the above.

14 If two countries have identical relative opportunity costs,

a there will never be any basis for trade.

b they might specialize in the production of certain goods and acquire a comparative advantage in those goods over time.

c each will gain from protectionist policies.

d the country with an absolute advantage will reap all of the gains from trade.

e none of the above.

15 When two countries trade,

a each individual and firm in both countries benefits.

b any individual benefits from the trades that she engages in.

c particular groups in each country may be hurt by trade in some goods.

d *b* and *c*.

e none of the above.

16 Increased immigration of unskilled workers into the United States will likely

a lower consumer goods prices.

b make U.S. firms more competitive in international markets.

c lower wages of unskilled workers already in the United States.

d all of the above.

e *a* and *b*.

17 If a country runs a trade deficit for several years,

a it is importing more goods and services than it exports.

b it is exporting more goods and services than it imports.

c it must borrow from abroad.

d *b* and *c*.

e *a* and *c*.

18 Which of the following is *not* a basis of comparative advantage?

a Natural endowments

b Acquired endowments

c Superior knowledge

d Protectionism

e Specialization

19 With voluntary trade between countries,

a all individuals are made better off.

b all individuals in the larger country are made better off.

c some individuals are made worse off, but the gainers could more than compensate the losers.

d businesses gain but consumers lose.

e workers lose but consumers gain.

20 The North American Free Trade Agreement will lower trade barriers between which of the following countries?

a All countries in North America

b All countries in North America and the Caribbean

c All countries in North and South America

d The United States, Canada, and Mexico

e The United States and Canada

Completion

1 The difference between what a person is willing to pay for an item and what she has to pay is a gain from trade, or _____.

2 If a country is relatively more efficient at producing a good than its trading partners, then that country is said to have the _____ in the production of that good.

3 _____ refers to having superior production skills or lower resource costs.

4 Because of trade possibilities, individuals and countries can produce more of what each has a comparative advantage in. This specialization or division of labor is limited by the _____ of the market.

5 _____, such as location, natural resources, and climate, are bases of comparative advantage.

6 Acquired endowments, such as physical and human _____, represent other sources of comparative advantage.

7 The doctrine that the economy of a country is injured by trade is called _____.

8 The marginal rate of transformation is the _____ of the production possibilities frontier.

9 The trade-off in producing two commodities is called the _____.

10 The _____ will reduce trade barriers among the United States, Canada, and Mexico over the next fifteen years.

Answers to Self-Test

True or False

1	f	6	f	11	f
2	f	7	t	12	t
3	f	8	t	13	t
4	t	9	t	14	f
5	f	10	t	15	t

Multiple Choice

1	*d*	6	*c*	11	*c*	16	*d*
2	*e*	7	*a*	12	*e*	17	*e*
3	*e*	8	*d*	13	*e*	18	*d*
4	*b*	9	*e*	14	*b*	19	*c*
5	*a*	10	*a*	15	*d*	20	*d*

Completion

1 surplus
2 comparative advantage
3 Absolute advantage
4 size
5 Natural endowments
6 capital
7 protectionism
8 slope
9 marginal rate of transformation
10 North American Free Trade Agreement

Doing Economics: Tools and Practice Problems

This chapter introduces comparative advantage, a very important concept. The principle of comparative advantage illustrates how individuals, firms, and countries can benefit by specializing in performing tasks or producing goods and trading with each other. This problem set will help you to identify comparative advantage and to see why comparative advantage determines the division of labor and the pattern of trade. You will also study the gains from trade when they proceed according to comparative advantage. Finally, you will use the idea of comparative advantage to construct the production possibilities curve for the case in which resources differ.

COMPARATIVE ADVANTAGE

The most important concept in exchange and production is comparative advantage. Countries have comparative advantage when their opportunity cost is lower. They will export the goods in which they have comparative advantage. Tool Kit 3.1 shows how to use production possibilities curve to identify comparative advantage and determine the pattern or production and trade.

Tool Kit 3.1 Identifying Comparative Advantage

When a country or individual has a comparative advantage in performing some task or producing some good, that country or individual is relatively more efficient, which means that the country or individual has the lower opportunity cost. The following procedure shows how to identify comparative advantage and predict the pattern of trade. It is written for the case of two-country trade.

Step one: Plot the production possibilities curves for each country. Be sure to be consistent and measure units of the same good along the horizontal axis in each case.

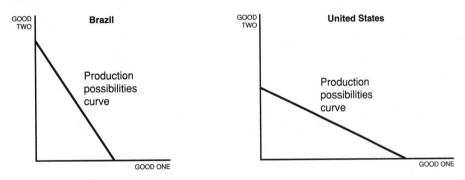

Step two: The slope of the production possibilities curve is the opportunity cost of the good on the horizontal axis, and it indicates the trade-off. The flatter slope implies comparative advantage for producing the good on the horizontal axis.

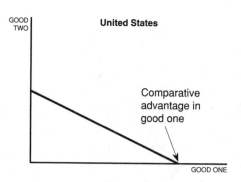

Step three: The steeper slope indicates comparative advantage for the good on the vertical axis.

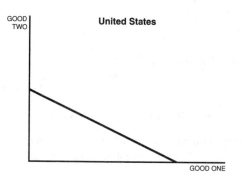

Step four: In a system of free trade, each country will produce more of the good in which it has a comparative advantage, and the relative price will lie somewhere between the opportunity costs of the two countries.

1 (Worked problem: comparative advantage) Workers in the United States and Brazil can produce shoes and computers. The annual productivity of a worker in each country is given in the table below.

Country	Computers	Shoes
United States	5,000	10,000
Brazil	200	5,000

a Which country has a comparative advantage in computers? in shoes?
b Predict the pattern of trade.
c Indicate the range of possible relative prices that would bring about this pattern of trade.

Step-by-step solution

Step one (a): Plot the production possibilities curves. In this problem, the production possibilities curve for one worker in each country will suffice. Measure computers on the horizontal axis.

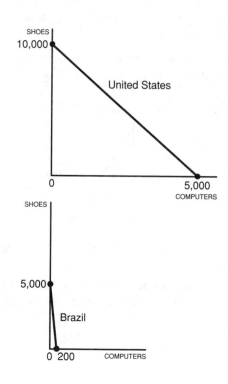

Step two: The production possibilities curve for the United States has the flatter slope; therefore, the U.S. worker has a comparative advantage in the production of computers.

Step three: The production possibilities curve for Brazil is steeper, and the Brazilian worker has a comparative advantage in shoes.

Step four (*b* and *c*): Brazil will trade shoes for U.S. computers. The relative price must lie between 2 shoes per computer (the U.S. opportunity cost) and 25 shoes per computer (the Brazilian opportunity cost).

2 (Practice problem: comparative advantage) Workers in Nigeria and neighboring Niger produce textiles and sorghum. The productivities of each are given in the table below.

Country	Textiles (bales)	Sorghum (bushels)
Nigeria	100	500
Niger	50	400

   a Which country has a comparative advantage in textiles? in sorghum?
   b Predict the pattern of trade.
   c Indicate the range of possible relative prices that would bring about this pattern of trade.

3 (Practice problem: comparative advantage) For each of the following, determine which country has a comparative advantage in each good, predict the pattern of trade, and indicate the range of possible relative prices consistent with this pattern of trade.

a

Country	Fish	Wheat (bushels)
Greece	60	80
Poland	35	70

b

Country	Heart bypass operations	Auto parts (containers)
United States	5,000	10,000
Canada	3,000	9,000

c

Country	Scrap steel (tons)	Finished steel (tons)
Thailand	20	20
Laos	10	2

d

Country	Wine (barrels)	Wool (bales)
Portugal	2	2
Great Britain	4	8

GAINS FROM TRADE

When countries trade there is mutual gain, in the sense that their opportunity sets expand beyond their production possibilities curves. To exploit the potential of trade, production and trade must be organized according to comparative advantage. Tool Kit 3.2 shows how both trading partners can gain from trade.

Tool Kit 3.2 Showing the Gains form Trade

When the pattern of trade is based upon comparative advantage, both countries can gain. Specifically, they each can consume a bundle of goods that lies beyond their own production possibilities curve. Follow these five steps.

Step one: Draw the production possibilities curve for each country, identify the country with a comparative advantage in each good, and identify the trade-offs for each country.

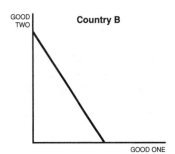

Step two: Choose a relative price between the trade-offs.

Step three: For the country with the comparative advantage in the horizontal intercept *A* and draw a line segment from *A* with a slope equal (−) the relative price. This line segment shows the bundles of goods that the country can consume by trading at the given relative price.

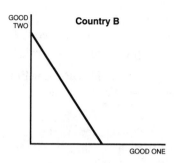

Step four: For the country with the comparative advantage in the vertical-axis good, label the vertical intercept *A* and draw a line segment from *A* with a slope equal to (−) the relative price. This line segment shows the bundles of goods that the country can consume by trading at the given relative price.

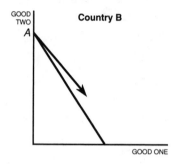

Step five: Pick a pair of consistent points, where A's exports equal B's imports, one on each line segment, and show how each country can benefit from trade.

4 (Worked problem: gains from trade) This problem builds on problem 1. Show that a worker in Brazil and a worker in the United States can benefit by trading on the basis of comparative advantage.

Step-by-step solution

Step one: Identify the country with a comparative advantage in each good and the trade-offs for each country. The U.S. worker has the comparative advantage in computers, and the trade-off is 2 shoes per computer. The Brazilian worker has the comparative advantage in shoes, and the trade-off is 25 shoes per computer.

Step two: Choose a relative price between the trade-offs. Let's choose 20 shoes per computer.

Step three: For the country with the comparative advantage in computers, which is the United States, label the horizontal intercept *A* and draw a line segment from *A* with a slope equal to −20. This line segment shows the bundles of goods that the United States can consume by trading at the given relative price.

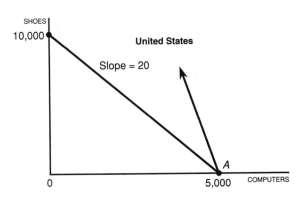

Step four: For the country with the comparative advantage in shoes, label the vertical intercept *A* and draw a line segment from *A* with a slope equal to −20. This line segment shows the bundles of goods that Brazil can consume by trading at the given relative price.

Step five: Pick a pair of consistent points, one on each line segment, and show how each country can benefit from trade.

Let the U.S. worker produce 4,800 computers for domestic consumption. This leaves 200 for trade. At a relative price of 20 shoes, the 200 computers trade for 4,000 shoes. Plot the point (4,000, 4,800) and label it *B*.

The Brazilian worker must then produce 4,000 shoes for trade. This leaves 1,000 shoes for domestic consumption. The 4,000 shoes for trade 200 computers. Plot the point (200, 1,000) and label it *B*. At this point, the United States exports 200 computers and imports 4,000 shoes, while Brazil imports 200 computers and exports 4,000 shoes. Trade is balanced, and each country consumes beyond its production possibilities curve.

5   (Practice problem: gains from trade) This problem builds upon problem #2. Show that workers in Nigeria and Niger can benefit by trading according to comparative advantage.

TRADE WITH THE WORLD

Another view of comparative advantage and the gains from trade sees one country trading with the world at given world prices. We show that comparative advantage results from comparing domestic trade-offs with world relative prices and that trade leads to a budget constraint higher than the production possibilities. In other words, by exploiting its comparative advantage, a country can consume more than it could produce.

Tool Kit 3.3 Trade at World Prices

When a country can trade at fixed world prices, its comparative advantage yields the most revenue and its budget constraint lies above its production possibilities curve. Follow these steps.

Step one: Plot the production possibilities curve.

Step two: Compute the revenue from selling the maximum amount of each good on the world market.

Revenue from good one = price of good one × maximum output of good one.

Revenue from good two = price of good two × maximum output of good two.

Step three: Identify comparative advantage. This is the good with the most revenue compute in step two.

Step four: Compute the maximum consumption of the good in which the country does *not* have comparative advantage by dividing the revenue from selling the maximum amount of the comparative advantage good (computed in step three) by the price of the other good.

Maximum consumption = revenue from comparative advantage good/price of other good

Step five: Draw the budget constraint. Connect the intercept of the comparative advantage good with the maximum quantity of the other good (computed in step 4). This shows that the country can consume more goods than it can produce.

6 (Worked problem: trade with the world) In a season a worker in New Zealand can produce as much as 2,000 pounds of kiwis or 100 barrels of ale. World prices are $1 per pound of kiwis and $10 per barrel of ale.
  a In which good does New Zealand have comparative advantage?
  b Show the potential gains from trade.

Step-by-step solution

Step one: Plot the production possibilities curve.

Step two: Compute the revenue from selling the maximum amount of each good on the world market.

Revenue from kiwis = $1 × 2,000 = $2,000.

Revenue from ale = $10 × 100 = $1,000.

Step three: Identify the comparative advantage. Comparative advantage lies in growing kiwis.

Step four: Compute the maximum consumption of the good in which the country does *not* have comparative advantage.

Maximum consumption = $2,000/$10 = 200 barrels of ale.

Step five: Draw the budget constraint.

7 (Practice problem: trade with the world) A worker in Hungary can produce one case of wine per week or twenty bushels of rye. The world prices are $100 and $3, respectively.
  a In which good does Hungary have comparative advantage?
  b Show the potential gains from trade.

8 (Practice problem: trade with the world) A worker in South Africa can produce 1 ounce of gold per day or 1/2 ton of coal. The world prices are $25 per ounce of gold and $20 per ton of coal.
  a In which good does South Africa have a comparative advantage?
  b Show the potential gains from trade.

Production Possibilities with Different Resources

Free trade assigns to each country the task of producing those goods in which it has a comparative advantage. The same is true for trade between individuals. To see why this is efficient we consider the joint production possibilities curve in the case where there are two or more different types of resources that can be used in the production of two goods. To do this efficiently it is necessary to assign resources to produce the good in which they have comparative advantage. Tool Kit 3.4 shows how. Compare its shape with Chapter 2's opportunity sets for multiple constraints and diminishing returns.

Tool Kit 3.4 Plotting the Production Possibilities Curve When Resources Are Different

When resources differ in their productivity, plotting the production possibilities curve requires that they be assigned to produce goods according to the principle of comparative advantage. Follow these six steps.

Step one: Draw a set of coordinate axes. Label the horizontal axis as the quantity of one good and the vertical axis as the quantity of the other good.

Step two: Calculate the maximum quantities of each good that can be produced. Plot the quantity along the vertical axis and label the point *B*. Plot the quantity along the horizontal axis and label this point *A*.

Step three: Identify the resource with the comparative advantage for each good.

Step four: Choose the resource with the comparative advantage in the horizontal-axis good and assign it to produce this good, while keeping the other resource producing the vertical-axis good. Calculate the total quantities produced, and plot this point. Label it *C*.

Step five: Connect the points *BCA* with line segments. This is the production possibilities curve.

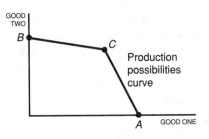

Step six: Verify that the slope is increasing. Because the slope measures the opportunity cost of the horizontal-axis good, this means that the opportunity cost is increasing, which is an implication of the principle of diminishing returns.

9 (Worked problem: production possibilities curve) Harrigan and her daughter have formed a two-person firm to handle business incorporations and real estate transactions. The hours required for each type of task are given below. Each works 48 hours every week.

Lawyer	Hours required to perform each incorporation	Hours required to complete each transaction
Harrigan	4	8
Daughter	8	24

Plot their weekly production possibilities curve.

Step-by-step solution

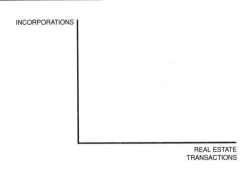

Step one: Draw and label a set of coordinate axes. Put real estate transactions on the horizontal axis and incorporations on the vertical.

Step two: Calculate the maximum number of incorporations they can do in a week. For Harrigan, this number is 48/4 = 12; for her daughter, it is 48/8 = 6. The pair can complete 18 incorporations. Plot this point along the vertical axis, and label it *A*. Concerning real estate transactions, Harrigan can do 48/8 = 6; her daughter, 48/24 = 2. The pair can do 8. Plot this point along the horizontal axis, and label it *B*.

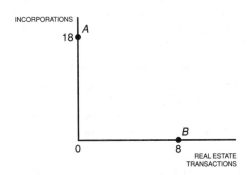

Step three: Identify the resource with the comparative advantage for each good. Since it takes Harrigan 8 hours to complete each real estate transaction but only 4 to do an incorporation, each real estate transaction requires enough time to do 2 incorporations. The opportunity cost of a real estate transaction for Harrigan is, then, 2 incorporations. By the same argument, the opportunity cost for her daughter is 24/8 = 3 incorporations; thus, Harrigan has the comparative advantage in real estate transactions, while her daughter has the comparative advantage in incorporations.

Step four: We assign to Harrigan the task of real estate transactions, leaving her daughter to do the incorporations. With this assignment, they can do 6 incorporations and 6 real estate transactions (see step two). Plot this point, and label it *C*.

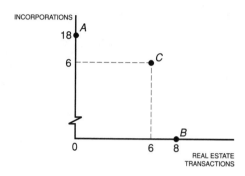

Step five: Draw line segments connecting the points. This is the production possibilities curve.

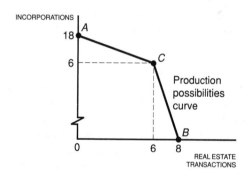

Step six: Note that between *A* and *C* the slope is 2, but between *C* and *B* the slope increases to 3. The shape of the production possibilities curve thus indicates diminishing returns.

10 (Practice problem: production possibilities curve) A farmer has 3 acres of land. Owing to various characteristics of the land, his ability to produce his two cash crops (corn and soybeans) differs on each acre. The technology of production is given in the table below.

Maximum outputs of each crop per acre (bushels)

	Acre 1	Acre 2	Acre 3
Corn	200	200	100
Soybeans	400	200	50

These figures represent the maximum output of each crop, assuming that only one crop is grown on the acre. That is, acre #1 can produce either 200 bushels of corn or 400 bushels of soybeans. Of course, the farmer can also divide the acre into one part corn and one part soybeans. For example, he can grow 100 bushels of

corn and 200 bushels of soybeans on acre #1. Plot the production possibilities curve.

11 (Practice problem: production possibilities curve) Plot the following production possibilities curves.
   a Maximum harvest of each type of fish per trawler (tons)

	Trawler 1	Trawler 2	Trawler 3
Salmon	2	3	4
Tuna	2	6	6

   b Maximum amounts of pollutants removed (tons)

Smokestack scrubbers	Coal treatment	
Sulphur	100	50
Particulates	500	100

Answers to Problems

2 *a* Nigeria has a comparative advantage in textiles. Niger has a comparative advantage in sorghum.
   b Nigeria will trade its textiles for sorghum from Niger.
   c The relative price will lie between 8 bushels of sorghum per bale of textiles and 5 bushels of sorghum per bale of textiles.
3 *a* Greece has a comparative advantage in fish. Poland has a comparative advantage in wheat. Greece will trade its fish for Polish wheat. The relative price will lie between 4/3 bushels of wheat per fish and 2 bushels of wheat per fish.
   b The United States has a comparative advantage in heart bypass operations, and Canada in auto parts. The United States will trade heart bypass operations for Canadian auto parts. The relative price will lie between 2 containers of auto parts per operation and 3 containers of auto parts per operation.
   c Thailand has a comparative advantage in finished steel, Laos in scrap steel. Thailand will trade its finished steel for Laotian scrap steel. The relative price will lie between 5 tons of scrap steel per ton of finished steel and 1 ton of scrap steel per ton of finished steel.
   d Portugal has a comparative advantage in wine, Great Britain in wool. British wool will be traded for Portuguese wine. The relative price will lie between 1 and 2 bales per barrel of wine.
5 Choose, for example, 6 bushels of sorghum per bale of textiles as the relative price. Nigeria can produce 100 bales of textiles and trade 20 to Niger for 120 bushels of sorghum. The point (80, 120) lies outside its production possibilities curve. Niger can produce 400 bushels of sorghum and trade 120 bushels to Nigeria for 20 bales of textiles. The point (20, 280) lies outside its production possibilities curve.

7 *a.* wine

8 *a.* gold

b.

10

11

PART TWO | Perfect Markets

CHAPTER 4 | Demand, Supply, and Price

Chapter Review

Trade, the markets in which it occurs, and the gains it provides for both buyers and sellers are all important ideas from Chapter 3. Chapter 4 builds the basic model of markets, which is the supply and demand model. The focus is on prices and quantities—how they are determined and how they change when other factors change. Chapter 5 then applies the supply and demand model to major areas of concern to economists: what happens to the quantity demanded or supplied when prices change and what happens when prices do not adjust, as when the government sets price floors or ceilings.

ESSENTIAL CONCEPTS

1 Consumers **demand** goods and services. They are willing and able to pay, and given a price, they will buy a certain quantity. Several factors influence demand, but the most important is **price.** As the price falls, people buy more of the good or service; as the price rises, they purchase less. The entire relationship between the price and the quantity that a person buys is called the individual **demand curve.**

2 Adding all the individual demand curves gives the **market demand curve.** For every price, ask how much each individual will buy. Add these quantities. The result is the market demand curve, which shows the total amount of the good that will be purchased by all individuals at each price.

3 Firms **supply** goods and services. They are willing and able to produce and sell the good, and at a given price, they will sell a certain quantity. Several factors influence the supply, but the most important is price. As the price rises, producers will supply more; as the price falls, producers will supply less. The entire relationship between the price and the quantity that the producer will sell is called the individual **supply curve.**

4 Adding up all of the individual supply curves gives the **market supply curve.** For every price, ask how much each producer will sell. Add these quantities. The result is the market supply curve, which shows how much of the good will be sold by all producers at each price.

5 The price at which consumers want to buy exactly the quantity that firms want to sell is the **equilibrium price.** This quantity, which is the same for demand and supply, is the **equilibrium quantity.** It is an **equilibrium** because there are no forces that would cause it to change.

6 If the price were higher than the equilibrium price, firms would want to sell more than consumers would buy. Unable to sell all of their goods, many firms would compete, by lowering prices, to attract the relatively few consumers. Because this higher price would change, it is not an equilibrium. Similarly, if the price were lower than the equilibrium price, consumers would want to buy more than firms would sell. Seeing the glut of consumers, firms would raise their prices. In sum, if the price is above equilibrium, it falls; if it is below equilibrium, it rises. When price equals the equilibrium price, it does not change.

7 Many factors affect the demand and supply. For demand, these factors include changes in income, prices of **substitutes** and **complements,** the composition of the population, and people's tastes. This is only a partial list. When one of these factors—or anything else that affects the willingness to pay for the good—changes, the entire demand curve **shifts,** and a new equilibrium must be found.

Supply is affected by changes in technology and input price—more generally, anything that causes costs to change. Again, changes in these factors **shift** the supply curve and lead to a new equilibrium.

BEHIND THE ESSENTIAL CONCEPTS

1 The demand curve is the entire range, or schedule, that indicates how many goods will be purchased at each price. At a given price, this number is called the quantity demanded. In diagrams of demand curves, the quantity demanded is measured along the horizontal axis. To find the quantity demanded, simply read it off the demand curve at the current price. Economists, students, and sometimes professors are sloppy and say "change in demand" without being clear whether they mean a shift in the demand curve or a change in the quantity demanded. The latter is brought about by a change in price, and it involves only a movement along the same demand curve. To guard against confusion in stressful situations (like tests!), say "demand curve" when you refer to the entire schedule of prices and quantities and "quantity demanded" when you want to indicate the number of goods purchased.

2 It is very important to understand why the market demand curve is drawn as it is. When the price rises, the market quantity demanded falls for two reasons. First, each individual buys less. The principle of substitution says that other available goods and services can serve as alternatives, and at higher prices, people switch to consume these substitutes. Second, some individuals find the price to be too high altogether, and they leave the market completely. When the price falls, the opposite happens. People substitute away from other goods and buy more of the one with the lower price. Furthermore, the lower price attracts new consumers to the market.

3 The market supply curve slopes upward. This means that as the price rises, more is offered for sale. Again, there are two reasons. First, firms are willing to sell more at higher prices. Second, higher prices attract new products to the market.

4 Other factors that shift the demand curve include consumer income, tastes, prices of substitutes and complements, and the composition of the population. The supply curve shifts with changes in technology or input prices. While these factors are the most common causes of shifts, they do not comprise a complete list. Anything that affects the willingness and ability to pay for goods shifts the demand curve, and anything that affects costs shifts the supply curve. For example, if it rains in April, the supply of crops may increase, and the demand for umbrellas may also increase.

5 Successful supply and demand analysis proceeds in four steps:
  a Start with an equilibrium.
  b Figure out which curve shifts.
  c Shift the curve and find the new equilibrium.
  d Compare the price and quantity at the original and new equilibria.

Be careful to avoid a common pitfall. Suppose you are asked to show the effect of a change in tastes that shifts demand to the right. The failing student's analysis goes like this: "Demand shifts to the right, which increases quantity and price, but the increase in price leads producers to want to supply more, so the supply also shifts to the right." What is wrong with this answer? Stop before the "but." True, the demand shift does raise price and quantity, but that is the end of the story. The increase in price does lead producers to want to supply more. As they supply more, there is a movement along the supply curve, but not a shift. Changes in the price of a good *never shift* the demand curve for that good or the supply curve for that good; rather, changes in the price of a good cause a *movement* along the demand curve or supply curve. There is more discussion on this point and lots of practice problems in the Doing Economics section of this chapter.

SELF-TEST

True or False

1 Prices provide incentives to help the economy use resources efficiently.
2 As the price falls, the quantity demanded decreases.
3 The market demand curve is the sum of the quantities and prices of each individual demand.
4 The individual demand curve is an example of an equilibrium relationship.
5 One reason why the supply curve slopes upward is that at higher prices, more producers enter the market.
6 In equilibrium, there is neither excess demand nor excess supply.
7 If the price is above the equilibrium price, consumers can buy as much as they are willing.
8 If the price is below the equilibrium price, sellers cannot sell as much as they are willing.
9 The law of supply and demand says that the equilibrium price will be that price at which the quantity demanded equals the quantity supplied.
10 The individual supply curve is an example of an identity.
11 The price of diamonds is higher than the price of water because diamonds have a higher value in use.
12 A change in a consumer's income will shift her demand curve.

13 A change in the price of a good will shift its market demand curve to the right.

14 An increase in the price of a substitute will shift the demand curve for the good in question to the right.

15 A decrease in the price of a complement will shift the demand curve for the good in question to the left.

Multiple Choice

1 Market prices
   a measure scarcity.
   b communicate information.
   c provide incentives.
   d all of the above.
   e a and b.

2 The individual demand curve for a good or service
   a gives the quantity of the good or service the individual would purchase at each price.
   b gives the equilibrium price in the market.
   c shows which other goods or services will be substituted according to the principle of substitution.
   d all of the above.
   e a and c.

3 The idea that there are other goods or services that can serve as reasonably good alternatives to a particular good or service is called the
   a law of demand.
   b principle of substitution.
   c market demand curve.
   d principle of scarcity.
   e none of the above.

4 If you knew the individual demand curves of each consumer, you could find the market demand curve by
   a taking the average quantity demanded at each price.
   b adding all of the prices.
   c adding up, at each price, the quantities purchased by each individual.
   d taking the average of all prices.
   e none of the above.

5 As the price rises, the quantity demanded decreases along an individual demand curve because
   a individuals substitute other goods and services.
   b some individuals exit the market.
   c some individuals enter the market.
   d the quantity supplied increases.
   e a and b.

6 As the price rises, the quantity demanded decreases along the market demand curve because
   a individuals substitute other goods and services.
   b some individuals exit the market.
   c some individuals enter the market.
   d the quantity supplied increases.
   e a and b.

7 As the price rises, the quantity supplied increases along an individual supply curve because
   a higher prices give firms incentives to sell more.
   b the principle of substitution leads firms to substitute other goods and services.
   c the market supply curve is the sum of all the quantities produced by individual firms at each price.
   d b and c.
   e none of the above.

8 As the price rises, the quantity supplied increases along the market supply curve because
   a at higher prices, more firms are willing to enter the market to produce the good.
   b each firm in the market is willing to produce more.
   c the market supply curve is the sum of all the quantities produced by individual firms at each price.
   d at higher prices, more firms substitute other goods and services.
   e a and b.

9 If the market price is below equilibrium, then
   a there is excess demand.
   b there is excess supply.
   c consumers will want to raise the price.
   d firms will want to lower the price.
   e all of the above.

10 If the market price is at equilibrium, then
   a the quantity that consumers are willing to buy equals the quantity that producers are willing to sell.
   b there is excess demand.
   c there is excess supply.
   d there are no forces that will change the price.
   e a and d.

11 If the market price is above equilibrium, then
   a there is excess supply.
   b there is excess demand.
   c firms will not be able to sell all that they would like.
   d consumers will not be able to buy all that they would like.
   e a and c.

12 The law of supply and demand is an example of
   a an identity.
   b an equilibrium relationship.
   c a behavioral relationship.
   d none of the above.
   e all of the above.

13 The statement that market supply is equal to the sum of individual firms' supplies is an example of
   a an identity.
   b an equilibrium relationship.
   c a behavioral relationship.
   d all of the above.
   e none of the above.

14 A diamond sells for a higher price than a gallon of water because
  a luxuries always have higher prices than necessities.
  b only a few people demand diamonds, but everyone needs water.
  c the total use value of diamonds exceeds the total value of water.
  d the total cost of diamond production exceeds the total cost of water production.
  e none of the above.

15 Stationary exercise bicycles and stair-stepper machines are substitutes, according to the aerobically correct. An increase in the price of exercise bicycles will
  a shift the demand for stair-stepper machines to the right.
  b increase the price of stair-stepper machines.
  c increase the quantity of stair-stepper machine sales.
  d all of the above.
  e none of the above.

16 As people have grown more concerned about saturated fat in their diets, the demand for beef has shifted to the left. The quantity of beef sold has also fallen. This change is a
  a movement along the demand curve for beef.
  b shift in the supply curve for beef.
  c movement along the supply curve for beef.
  d *a* and *b*.
  e none of the above.

17 Which of the following is *not* a source of shifts in market demand?
  a An increase in consumer income
  b A change in tastes
  c An increase in the population
  d A technological advance
  e All are sources of shifts.

18 If the price of an input falls,
  a supply shifts to the left.
  b demand shifts to the right.
  c demand shifts to the left.
  d supply shifts to the right.
  e none of the above.

19 If ski-lift tickets and skiing lessons are complements, then an increase in the price of lift tickets shifts
  a demand for skiing lessons to the left.
  b demand for skiing lessons to the right.
  c supply of skiing lessons to the left.
  d supply of skiing lessons to the right.
  e *a* and *d*.

20 A recent regulation requires tuna fishing companies to use nets that allow dolphins to escape. These nets also allow some tuna to escape. This regulation causes
  a the supply of tuna to shift to the left.
  b the demand for tunas to shift to the right.
  c the demand for tunas to shift to the left.
  d the supply of tunas to shift to the right.
  e none of the above.

Completion

1 _____ is defined as what is given in exchange for a good or service.
2 If the price of a good or service falls, the quantity demanded _____.
3 The quantity of the good or service purchased at each price is given by the _____.
4 The quantity of the good or service offered for sale at each price is given by the _____.
5 In an economic equilibrium, there are no forces for _____.
6 The law of supply and demand says that at the equilibrium price, the _____ equals the _____.
7 The statement that market supply equals market demand is an example of an _____.
8 The statement that market supply is the total of all individual supplies is an example of an _____.
9 An increase in the price of a good leads to a _____ its demand curve.
10 A change in technology leads to a _____ the supply curve.

Answers to Self-Test

True or False

1	t	6	t	11	f
2	f	7	t	12	t
3	f	8	f	13	f
4	f	9	t	14	t
5	t	10	f	15	f

Multiple Choice

1	d	6	e	11	e	16	c
2	a	7	a	12	b	17	d
3	b	8	e	13	a	18	d
4	c	9	a	14	e	19	a
5	a	10	e	15	d	20	a

Completion

1 Price
2 increases
3 demand curve
4 supply curve
5 change
6 quantity demanded, quantity supplied
7 equilibrium relationship
8 identity
9 movement along
10 shift in

Doing Economics: Tools and Practice Problems

Three techniques receive attention in this section. The first technique shows how to add individual demand and individual supply curves to get market demand and market supply curves. The next technique involves finding the equilibrium price and quantity, where the market clears. Finally, some general instructions about supply and demand analysis are given and developed in several problems. Each of these techniques is fundamental and will appear repeatedly throughout this book.

MARKET DEMAND AND MARKET SUPPLY

When the price falls, individual demanders want to buy more, and individual suppliers want to sell less. These individual demand and supply curves are behavioral relationships. The market demand and market supply curves are found by adding up all of these individual demands and supplies. Tool Kit 4.1 shows how to do this.

Tool Kit 4.1 Calculating Market Demand and Supply

The market demand is the sum of the individual demands. The market supply is the sum of the individual supplies. This tool kit shows how to add the individual demands and supplies.

Step one: Make two columns. Label the left-hand column "Price" and the right-hand column "Quantity."

Price	Quantity

Step two: Choose the highest price at which goods are demanded. Enter this in the first row of the price column.

Price	Quantity
p_1	

Step three: Find how many goods each individual will purchase. Add these quantities. Enter the total in the first row of the quantity column.

Price	Quantity
p_1	$Q_1 = Q_a + Q_b + Q_c + \cdots$

Step four: Choose the second highest price, and continue the process.

---

1 (Worked problem: market demand) The individual demands of Jason and Kyle for economics tutoring are given in Table 4.1. Calculate the market demand. (Jason and Kyle are the only two individuals in this market.)

Table 4.1

Jason		Kyle	
Price	Quantity	Price	Quantity
$10	6	$10	4
$ 8	8	$ 8	5
$ 6	10	$ 6	6
$ 4	12	$ 4	7

Step-by-step solution

Step one: Make and label two columns.

Price	Quantity

Step two: Choose the highest price. This is $10. Enter this in the first row under price.

Price	Quantity
$10	

Step three: Find the market quantity. Jason would buy 6; Kyle would buy 4. The total is 6 1 4 5 10. Enter 10 in the corresponding quantity column.

Price	Quantity
$10	10

Step four: Repeat the process. The next lower price is $8. Jason would buy 8; Kyle would buy 5. The total is 8 1 5 5 13. Enter $8 and 13 in the appropriate columns.

Price	Quantity
$10	10
$ 8	13

Continue. The entire market demand is given below.

Price	Quantity
$10	10
$ 8	13
$ 6	16
$ 4	19

2 (Practice problem: market demand) Gorman's tomatoes are purchased by pizza sauce makers, by submarine sandwich shops, and by vegetable canners. The demands for each are given in Table 4.2. Find the market demand.

Table 4.2

Pizza sauce		Submarine shops		Vegetable canners	
Price	Quantity (bushels)	Price	Quantity (bushels)	Price	Quantity (bushels)
$5	25	$5	5	$5	55
$4	35	$4	6	$4	75
$3	40	$3	7	$3	100
$2	50	$2	7	$2	150
$1	80	$1	7	$1	250

3 (Practice problem: market supply) The technique for finding the market supply curve is the same as for the market demand. Simply sum the quantities supplied at each price. There are three law firms that will draw up partnership contracts in the town of Pullman. Their individual supply curves are given in Table 4.3. Find the market supply curve.

Table 4.3

	Jones		Jones and Jones		Jones, Jones, and Jones
Price	Quantity	Price	Quantity	Price	Quantity
$200	0	$200	6	$200	4
$220	0	$220	8	$220	8
$240	0	$240	12	$240	10
$260	8	$260	24	$260	11

EQUILIBRIUM

In equilibrium, markets clear. The market price will settle where the quantity that demanders would like to purchase exactly equals the quantity that suppliers choose to sell. Tool Kit 4.2 shows how to find the equilibrium.

Tool Kit 4.2 Finding the Equilibrium Price and Quantity

The equilibrium price in the demand and supply model is the price at which the buyers want to buy exactly the quantity that sellers want to sell. In other words, the quantity demanded equals the quantity supplied. The equilibrium quantity in the market is just this quantity. Here is how to find the equilibrium in a market.

Step one: Choose a price. Find the quantity demanded at that price and the quantity supplied.

Step two: If the quantity demanded equals the quantity supplied, the price is the equilibrium. Stop.

Step three: If the quantity demanded exceeds the quantity supplied, there is a shortage. Choose a higher price and repeat step one. If the quantity demanded is less than the quantity supplied, there is a surplus. Choose a lower price and repeat step one.

Step four: Continue until the equilibrium price is found.

---

4 (Worked problem: equilibrium price and quantity) The supply curve and demand curve for cinder blocks are given in Table 4.4. The quantity column indicates the number of blocks sold in one year.

Table 4.4

Demand		Supply	
Price	Quantity	Price	Quantity
$2.00	50,000	$2.00	200,000
$1.50	70,000	$1.50	160,000
$1.00	100,000	$1.00	100,000
$0.75	150,000	$0.75	50,000
$0.50	250,000	$0.50	0

a Find the equilibrium price and quantity.

b If the price is $1.50, is the market in equilibrium? Will there be a surplus or a shortage? If so, what is the size of the surplus or shortage? What will happen to the price? Why?

c If the price is $0.75, is the market in equilibrium? Will there be a surplus or a shortage? If so, what is the size of the surplus or shortage? What will happen to the price? Why?

Step-by-step solution

Step one (a): Choose a price. At a price of, say, $2.00, the quantity demanded is 50,000 and the quantity supplied is 200,000.

Step two: The quantities are not equal.

Step three: There is a surplus. The equilibrium price will be lower.

Step four: Continue. Try other prices until the quantity supplied equals the quantity demanded. The equilibrium price is $1.00, where the quantity equals 100,000. We can now see the answers to parts b and c.

Step five (b): If the price is $1.50, the quantity demanded is 70,000, and it is less than the quantity supplied, which is 160,000. There is a surplus of 90,000 (160,000 − 70,000). The price will fall because producers will be unable to sell all that they want.

Step six (c): If the price is $0.75, the quantity demanded is 150,000, and it is greater than the quantity supplied, which is 50,000. There is a shortage of 100,000 (150,000 − 50,000). The price will rise because producers will see that buyers are unable to buy all that they want.

5 (Practice problem: equilibrium price and quantity) The demand curve and supply curve in the market for billboard space space along Interstate 6 are given in Table 4.5. The price is the monthly rental price. The quantity column shows numbers of billboards.

Table 4.5

Demand		Supply	
Price	Quantity	Price	Quantity
$100	5	$100	25
$ 80	8	$ 80	21
$ 60	11	$ 60	16
$ 40	14	$ 40	14
$ 20	22	$ 20	3

   a Find the equilibrium price and quantity.

   b If the price is $20, is the market in equilibrium? Will there be a surplus or a shortage? If so, what is the size of the surplus or shortage? What will happen to the price? Why?

   c If the price is $80, is the market in equilibrium? Will there be a surplus or a shortage? If so, what is the size of the surplus or shortage? What will happen to the price? Why?

6 (Practice problem: equilibrium price and quantity) Find the equilibrium price and quantity in each of the following markets.

   a The supply and demand curves for new soles (shoe repair) are given in Table 4.6.

Table 4.6

Demand		Supply	
Price	Quantity	Price	Quantity
$35	17	$35	53
$30	21	$30	37
$25	25	$25	25
$20	30	$20	15
$15	35	$15	0

   b The supply and demand curves for seat cushions are given in Table 4.7.

Table 4.7

Demand		Supply	
$8	4	$8	32
$7	8	$7	28
$6	12	$6	22
$5	16	$5	19
$4	17	$4	17

SUPPLY AND DEMAND

Supply and demand is probably the most useful technique in microeconomics. Economists use it to study how markets are affected by changes, such as tastes, technology, government programs, and many others. Supply and demand offers

---

Tool Kit 4.3 Using Supply and Demand

Supply and demand analysis provides excellent answers to questions of the following form: "What is the effect of a change in _____ on the market for _____?" You are well on your way to success as a student of economics if you stick closely to this procedure in answering such questions.

Step one: Begin with an equilibrium in the relevant market. Label the horizontal axis as the quantity of the good or service and the vertical axis as the price. Draw a demand and a supply curve and label them *D* and *S,* respectively.

Step two: Figure out whether the change shifts the supply curve, the demand curve, or neither.

Step three: Shift the appropriate curve.

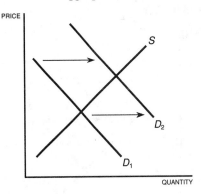

Step four: Find the new equilibrium, and compare it with the original one.

LIVERPOOL JOHN MOORES UNIVERSITY
LEARNING SERVICES

a wealth of insights into the workings of the economy. It is very important to master the procedure spelled out in Tool Kit 4.3.

7 (Worked problem: using supply and demand) In response to concern about the fumes emitted by dry cleaning establishments, the Environmental Protection Agency has issued regulations requiring expensive filtering systems. How will this regulation affect the dry cleaning market?

Step-by-step solution

Step one: Start with an equilibrium.

Step two: Figure out which curve shifts. The mandated filtering systems increase the dry cleaning firm's costs, shifting supply to the left.

Step three: Shift the curve.

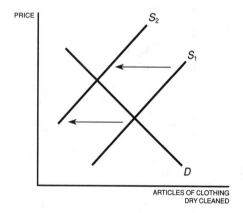

Step four: Find the new equilibrium and compare. The effect of the regulation is to raise the price and lower the quantity of clothes dry cleaned.

8 (Practice problem: using supply and demand) As the oil market comes to the realization that Kuwait's production will not return to prewar levels, the price of oil has increased by $4 per barrel. Explain the effect of this oil price increase on the market for natural gas.

9 (Practice problem: using supply and demand) For each of the following, show the effects on price and quantity. Draw the diagrams and follow the procedure.
  a An increase in income in the market for a normal good
  b A decrease in income in the market for a normal good
  c An increase in the price of a substitute
  d A decrease in the price of a substitute
  e An increase in the price of a complement
  f A decrease in the price of an complement
  g An increase in the price of an input
  h A decrease in the price of an input
  i An improvement in technology

Answers to Problems

2 | Price | Quantity (bushels) |
   |---|---|
   | $5 | 85 |
   | $4 | 116 |
   | $3 | 147 |
   | $2 | 207 |
   | $1 | 337 |

3 | Price | Quantity |
   |---|---|
   | $200 | 10 |
   | $220 | 16 |
   | $240 | 22 |
   | $260 | 43 |

5 a Equilibrium price = $40; quantity = 14.
   b If the price is $20, there is a shortage of 22 − 3 = 19. The price will be driven up.
   c If the price is $80, there is a surplus of 21 − 8 = 13. The price will be driven down.

6 *a* Price = \$25; quantity = 25.
   b Price = \$4; quantity = 17.

8 Oil and natural gas are substitutes, and therefore the demand curve shifts to the right, the price increases, and the quantity increases.

9 *a* Demand shifts to the right, driving the price up and increasing the quantity.

   b Demand shifts to the left, driving the price down and decreasing the quantity.

c Demand shifts to the right, driving the price up and increasing the quantity.

d Demand shifts to the left, driving the price down and decreasing the quantity.

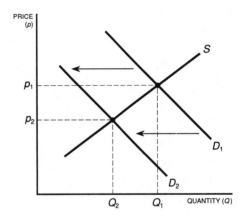

e Demand shifts to the left, driving the price down and decreasing the quantity.

f Demand shifts to the right, driving the price up and increasing the quantity.

g Supply shifts up (vertically), increasing the price but decreasing the quantity.

h Supply shifts down (vertically), decreasing the price but increasing the quantity.

i Supply shifts down (vertically), decreasing the price but increasing the quantity.

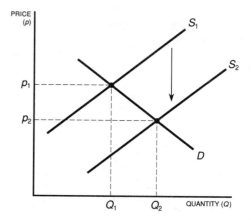

CHAPTER 5 | Using Demand and Supply

Chapter Review

The model of demand and supply introduced in Chapter 4 is one of the most useful in all of the social sciences. The ideas of demand and supply form the basis of all economic study, and will be used throughout this text. This chapter develops the model in more detail and introduces the concept of elasticity. Elasticity is best thought of as "sensitivity." The price elasticity of demand, for instance, measures how sensitive the quantity demanded is to a change in price. The chapter then applies the model to the study of the effects of taxes and price controls. Chapter 6 extends the supply and demand framework to markets in which future goods and risk are exchanged.

ESSENTIAL CONCEPTS

1 When price falls, quantity demanded increases. If the demand curve is steep, the increase in quantity is smaller than it would be if the curve were flat. Although it might seem natural to measure how the quantity responds to price changes by the slope of the demand curve, economists employ the concept of **elasticity.** They do so because elasticity will produce the same measure no matter what units are used. The **price elasticity of demand** is the percentage change in the quantity demanded brought about by a 1 percent change in price.

2 The **price elasticity of supply** is the percentage change in the quantity supplied brought about by a 1 percent change in price. It is the basic measure of how sensitive the quantity supplied is to changes in price.

3 The price elasticity of demand is greater when there are good, close substitutes available. Usually it is greater when the price is higher, because at higher prices, only those who consider the good essential remain in the market. Both the price elasticity of demand and the price elasticity of supply are greater in the long run because individuals and firms have more time to find substitutes and make adjustments.

4 When demand shifts, both the equilibrium price and quantity change. The price elasticity of supply determines which change is larger. If supply is more elastic, quantity changes by a greater percentage than price; if supply is less elastic, price changes more. Similarly, it is the price elasticity of demand that determines the relative changes in price and quantity when supply shifts. The more elastic the demand, the more quantity changes and the smaller is the change in price.

5 The economic effects of a tax are seen by focusing on the market affected by the tax. For example, a tax on the sale of gasoline shifts the supply curve up (vertically) by the amount of the tax, raises consumer prices, and reduces the quantity of gasoline sold. Except in a case where supply or demand is perfectly inelastic or perfectly elastic, the increase in consumer price is less than the amount of the tax. This means that producers are able to pass on only part of the tax to their customers and must bear some of the burden themselves.

6 **Price ceilings,** when set below the market-clearing price, lead to **shortages,** which means that the quantity demanded exceeds the quantity supplied. **Price floors,** when set above the market-clearing price, result in **surpluses**; in this case, the quantity demanded is less than the quantity supplied. In each case, the quantity actually exchanged is less than it is at the market-clearing price.

BEHIND THE ESSENTIAL CONCEPTS

1 The concept of elasticity appears many times throughout the text and is worth mastering. Suppose that price falls by 1 percent. We know that quantity will increase as consumers substitute toward the lower price, but by how much? The price elasticity provides the answer. It is the percent change in quantity brought on by a 1 percent change in price.

2 The relationship between elasticity and total revenue is very important. Total revenue is just price multiplied by quantity. If the price of a bicycle is $200 and there are 20 sold, then total revenue is $200 × 2 = $4,000. When price falls, total revenue is pushed down because each unit sells for less money; however, total revenue is pushed up because more units are sold. Whether on balance total revenue rises or falls depends on the elasticity. Table 5.1 helps to keep the relationship between elasticity and total revenue straight.

Table 5.1

If price rises,
   total revenue *falls* if the price elasticity of demand is greater than 1 (elastic).
   total revenue *rises* if the price elasticity of demand is less than 1 (inelastic).
   total revenue *does not change* if the price elasticity of demand equals 1 (unitary elasticity).

If price falls,
   total revenue *rises* if the price elasticity of demand is greater than 1 (elastic).
   total revenue *falls* if the price elasticity of demand is less than 1 (inelastic).
   total revenue *does not change* if the price elasticity of demand equals 1 (**unitary elasticity**).

3 What makes the demand for some goods (like motor boats) elastic, while the demand for others (like milk) is inelastic? The most important factor is the availability of substitutes. The **principle of substitution** says that consumers will look for substitutes when the price rises. If there are good, close substitutes available, then finding substitutes will be easy and consumers will switch. If good, close substitutes are not available, the consumers are more likely to swallow the price increase and continue purchasing the good.

4 Suppose that the government levies a tax on the supply of hotel rooms. Who pays the tax? While it is natural to think that the hotel pays the tax because it actually writes the check to the government, when you look at the issue through the lens of supply and demand, you see the value of economics. The tax increases the hotel's costs, and therefore it shifts the supply curve up and raises the price. Because they must pay higher prices for hotel rooms, consumers pay some of the tax.

5 The key to tax analysis is to find the market or markets in which the burden of the tax falls. Sometimes this is easy. A hotel room tax falls on the market for hotel rooms. In other cases, its not so clear. For example, an income tax affects the labor market, because workers must give up some of the earnings. It also affects the capital market because some of the interest earnings must be paid to the government. Once you find the relevant market, simply apply the basic method of supply and demand: start with an equilibrium, figure out which curve shifts (which side of the market is taxed), shift the curve, find the new equilibrium, and compare.

6 Price ceilings only make a difference if they are set below the market-clearing price (where the supply and demand curves intersect). A price ceiling set above the market-clearing price has no effect. Similarly, a price floor set below the market-clearing price does not do anything.

7 Price floors and ceilings also affect the quantity traded in the market. If there is a price ceiling, then the quantity demanded exceeds the quantity supplied. The supply is the short side of the market, and although consumers would like to buy more of the good, the quantity traded is what producers are willing to sell. This is shown in Figure 5.1A. With price floors, the opposite is true. The demand is the short side of the market, and the quantity traded equals the amount that consumers are willing to buy, as shown in panel B. In each case, we say that the short side of the market determines the actual quantity traded, and the actual quantity trade is less than the market-clearing quantity.

Figure 5.1

SELF-TEST

True or False

1 The price elasticity of demand is greater for goods and services that have better close substitutes.
2 The price elasticity of demand is always constant along the demand curve.
3 Total revenue increases as price falls when the demand is elastic.
4 A horizontal demand curve is perfectly elastic.
5 A vertical supply curve is perfectly inelastic.
6 If the supply curve is unitary elastic, then total revenue is constant as price changes.
7 If the supply curve is upward sloping, a rightward shift in the demand curve increases the equilibrium price and the equilibrium quantity.
8 If the demand curve is downward sloping, a rightward shift in the supply curve increases the equilibrium price and the equilibrium quantity.
9 When the demand curve is very elastic, relatively more of a tax on the production of some good or service will be borne by producers.
10 A tax on the sale of beer shifts the supply curve vertically by the amount of the tax.
11 When prices are sticky, shortages and surpluses can result in the short run.
12 A price ceiling set above the equilibrium price will have no effect on the market.
13 A price ceiling set below the equilibrium price will have no effect on the market.
14 A price floor set above the equilibrium price in the milk market will lead to a surplus of milk.
15 When demand and supply are more elastic, minimum wages set above the equilibrium wage lead to relatively more unemployment.

Multiple Choice

1 The quantity demanded is more sensitive to price changes when
  a supply is relatively inelastic.
  b close substitutes are available.
  c consumers are rational.
  d consumers are relatively more informed about quality for some goods.
  e all of the above.
2 Suppose that price falls by 10 percent and the quantity demanded rises by 20 percent. The price elasticity of demand is
  a 2.
  b 1.
  c 0.
  d 1/2.
  e none of the above.

3 Suppose that the price elasticity of demand is 1/3. If price rises by 30 percent, how does the quantity demanded change?
  a Quantity demanded rises by 10 percent.
  b Quantity demanded falls by 10 percent.
  c Quantity demanded rises by 90 percent.
  d Quantity demanded falls by 90 percent.
  e Quantity demanded does not change.
4 Suppose that the price elasticity of demand is 1.5. If price falls, total revenue will
  a remain the same.
  b fall.
  c rise.
  d double.
  e c and d.
5 Suppose that the price elasticity of demand is 0.7. The demand for this good is
  a perfectly inelastic.
  b inelastic.
  c unitary elastic.
  d elastic.
  e perfectly elastic.
6 Which of the following are true statements concerning the price elasticity of demand?
  a The price elasticity is constant for any demand curve.
  b Demand is more price elastic in the short run than in the long run.
  c If total revenue falls as price increases, the demand is relatively inelastic.
  d a and c.
  e None of the above.
7 If the supply curve is vertical, then the price elasticity of supply is
  a 0.
  b inelastic.
  c 1.
  d elastic.
  e infinite.
8 The long-run elasticity of supply is greater than the short-run elasticity of supply because
  a in the long run, the stock of machines and buildings can adjust.
  b in the long run, new firms can enter and existing firms can exit the industry.
  c in the long run, customers can discover substitutes.
  d all of the above.
  e a and b.
9 Suppose that supply is perfectly elastic. If the demand curve shifts to the right, then
  a price and quantity will increase.
  b quantity will increase, but price will remain constant.
  c price will increase, but quantity will remain constant.
  d neither price nor quantity will increase.
  e price will increase, but quantity will decrease.

10 Suppose that demand is perfectly inelastic, and the supply curve shifts to the left. Then
   a price and quantity will increase.
   b quantity will increase, but price will remain constant.
   c price will increase, but quantity will remain constant.
   d neither price nor quantity will increase.
   e price will increase, but quantity will decrease.

11 The price elasticity of demand for tires is 1.3, and the supply curve is upward sloping. If a $1-per-tire tax is placed on the production of tires, then the equilibrium price will
   a not change because the tax is on production and not on consumption.
   b increase by $1.
   c increase by less than $1.
   d fall by less than $1.
   e fall by $1.

12 In general, consumers bear more of a tax when the demand is
   a relatively inelastic.
   b unitary elastic.
   c relatively elastic.
   d such that consumers always bear the entire burden.
   e none of the above.

13 Suppose that the supply of a good is perfectly elastic. A tax of $1 on that good will raise the price by
   a less than $1.
   b $1.
   c more than $1.
   d $.50.
   e none of the above.

14 A price ceiling set below the equilibrium price will
   a create a shortage.
   b increase the price.
   c create a surplus.
   d a and b.
   e have no effect.

15 A price ceiling set above the equilibrium price will
   a create a shortage.
   b increase the price.
   c create a surplus.
   d a and b.
   e have no effect.

16 A price ceiling set below the equilibrium price will
   a increase the quantity demanded.
   b increase the quantity supplied.
   c decrease the quantity supplied.
   d a and c.
   e have no effect.

17 Rent control
   a creates a shortage of rental housing.
   b leads to a larger shortage in the long run.
   c lowers rents for renters who have apartments.

   d all of the above.
   e none of the above.

18 A price ceiling on insurance rates will shift
   a demand to the left.
   b demand to the right.
   c supply to the left.
   d supply to the right.
   e none of the above.

19 Which of the following is *not* a cause of surpluses or shortages?
   a Price ceilings
   b Price floors
   c Taxes
   d Sticky prices
   e All of the above cause surpluses or shortages.

20 Recently, the demand for housing has fallen in the northeast United States. Housing prices are sticky, and therefore
   a temporary shortages of housing have appeared.
   b temporary surpluses of housing have appeared.
   c the housing market has cleared.
   d supply has also shifted to the left.
   e none of the above.

Completion

1 The percentage change in the quantity demanded as a result of a 1 percent price change is called the _____.
2 Price changes have no effect on revenue if the price elasticity of demand is _____.
3 If the price elasticity of demand lies between 0 and 1, then we say that demand is relatively _____.
4 A horizontal demand curve indicates that demand is _____.
5 If the supply curve is vertical, then the price elasticity of supply equals _____.
6 A $.50-per-gallon tax on the production of gasoline can be expected to shift the supply curve by _____.
7 If demand is relatively inelastic, most of the tax is borne by _____.
8 A price ceiling set below the equilibrium price will create a _____.
9 A price floor set above the equilibrium price will create a _____.
10 The minimum wage is an example of a _____.

Answers to Self-Test

True or False

1	t	6	f	11	t
2	f	7	t	12	t
3	t	8	f	13	f
4	t	9	t	14	t
5	t	10	t	15	t

Multiple Choice

1	b	6	e	11	c	16	d
2	a	7	a	12	a	17	d
3	b	8	e	13	b	18	e
4	c	9	b	14	a	19	c
5	b	10	c	15	e	20	b

Completion

1 price elasticity of demand
2 1
3 inelastic
4 perfectly elastic
5 zero
6 vertically; $.50
7 consumers
8 shortage
9 surplus
10 price floor

Doing Economics: Tools and Practice Problems

Three techniques receive attention in this section. You'll first learn how to calculate elasticity, then how to measure the effects of taxes, and finally how to analyze the effects of price controls.

ELASTICITY

When price changes, how much does quantity change? Economists answer this question with the concept of elasticity. The price elasticity of demand measures how responsive quantity demand is to changes in the price. Similarly, the elasticity of supply measures the responsiveness of quantity supplied to price changes. Tool Kit 5.1 shows how to calculate elasticity. The problems focus on elasticity of demand

---

Tool Kit 5.1 Calculating Elasticity

Elasticity measures how sensitive the quantity is to changes in price. Follow these steps to calculate elasticity.

Step one: To find the elasticity between two points on the demand or supply curve, let p_1 and Q_1 be the price and quantity at the first point and p_2 and Q_2 be the price and quantity at the second point.

Step two: Substitute the prices and quantities into the formula

$$\text{elasticity} = (Q_1 - Q_2)(p_1 + p_2)/(Q_1 + Q_2)(p_1 - p_2).$$

---

and illustrate the relationship between elasticity and total revenue.

1 (Worked problem: calculating elasticity) The demand curve for bulletin boards is given below.

Price	Quantity
$35	800
$30	1,000
$25	1,200
$20	1,300

a Calculate total revenue for each price.
b Calculate the price elasticity of demand between $35 and $30, between $30 and $25, and between $25 and $20. Does elasticity change along this demand?
c Verify the relationship between elasticity and total revenue.

Step-by-step solution

Step one (a): Total revenue at $35 is 800 × $35 = $28,000. Total revenue at $30 is 1,000 × $30 = $30,000. Continue, and enter the numbers in the table.

Price	Quantity	Total revenue
$35	800	$28,000
$30	1,000	$30,000
$25	1,200	$30,000
$20	1,300	$26,000

Step two (b): Let $35 = p_1, 800 = Q_1, $30 = p_2, and 1,000 = Q_2. Substituting into the formula gives

$$\text{elasticity} = (35 + 30)(1,000 - 800)/(800 + 1,000)(35 - 30)$$
$$= 1.44, \quad \text{which is elastic.}$$

Step three: Between $30 and $25,

$$\text{elasticity} = (30 + 25)(1,200 - 1,000)/(1,000 + 1,200)(30 - 25)$$
$$= 1, \quad \text{which is unitary elastic.}$$

Step four: Between $25 and $20,

$$\text{elasticity} = (25 + 20)(1,300 - 1,200)/(1,200 + 1,300)(25 - 20)$$
$$= 0.36, \quad \text{which is inelastic.}$$

Clearly, the elasticity is not constant. The demand curve is less elastic at lower prices.

Step five (c): Between $35 and $30, where the demand is elastic, total revenue rises from $28,000 to $30,000 as price falls. Between $30 and $25, where the demand is unitary elastic, total revenue is constant at $30,000 as the price falls. Between $25 and $20, where the demand is inelastic, total revenue falls from $30,000 to $26,000 as the price falls.

Check Table 5.1 to verify that these numbers are consistent with the general relationship between price elasticity of demand and total revenue.

2 (Practice problem: calculating elasticity) The demand curve for bookends is given below.

Price	Quantity
$10	70
$8	90
$6	120
$4	130

a Calculate total revenue for each price.
b Calculate the price elasticity of demand between each of the adjacent prices. Does elasticity change along this demand?
c Verify the relationship between elasticity and total revenue.

3 (Practice problem: calculating elasticity) For each of the following, calculate the total revenue for each price and the price elasticity for each price change, and verify the relationship between elasticity and total revenue.

a
Price	Quantity
$12	6
$10	8
$8	10
$6	12

b
Price	Quantity
$100	80
$80	85
$60	90
$40	95

c
Price	Quantity
$9	10
$8	8
$7	6
$6	4

TAX INCIDENCE

The economic effects of taxes can be analyzed using the method of supply and demand introduced in Chapter 4. The key idea is that the burden of a tax—its incidence–does not necessarily fall on the person or firm that must deliver the money to the government. Taxes affect exchanges, and their impact must be analyzed by looking at the markets where the affected exchanges occur. The basic conclusions of this analysis are that, except when demand or supply is perfectly elastic or perfectly inelastic, consumers and producers share the burden of the tax, taxes reduce the level of economic activity, and, perhaps surprisingly, the effects of the tax are the same whether the supplier or the demander pays. Tool Kit 5.2 shows how to use supply and demand to do tax incidence.

Tool Kit 5.2 Using Supply and Demand for Tax Incidence

Supply and demand analysis shows how markets are affected by taxes and how the burden of taxes is allocated between suppliers and demanders. Follow this five-step procedure.

Step one: Start with an equilibrium in the relevant market.

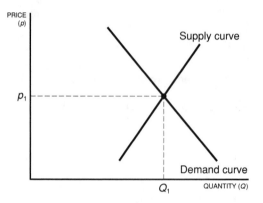

Step two: Identify whether the demander or supplier must pay the tax.

Step three: If the supplier must pay the tax, shift the supply curve up (vertically) by exactly the amount of the tax. If the demander must pay the tax, shift the demand curve down by exactly the amount of the tax.

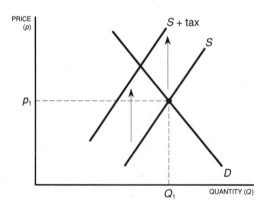

Step four: Find the new equilibrium.

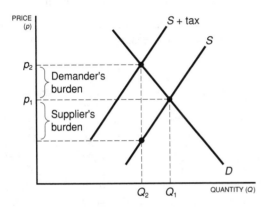

Step five: Determine the economic incidence of the tax. If the supplier must pay the tax, then use the following formulas to calculate economic incidence.

Demander's burden
= new equilibrium price − original equilibrium price.

Supplier's burden
= original equilibrium price − new equilibrium price
+ tax.

If the demander must pay the tax, use the following formulas to calculate tax incidence.

Demander's burden
= new equilibrium price + tax − original equilibrium price.

Supplier's burden
= original equilibrium price − new equilibrium price.

4 (Worked problem: tax incidence) The demand curve and supply curve for two-bedroom apartments in Takoma Park are given in Table 5.2.

Table 5.2

Demand		Supply	
Price	Quantity	Price	Quantity
$800	100	$800	500
$750	200	$750	500
$700	300	$700	450
$650	400	$650	400
$600	500	$600	300

a Find the equilibrium price and quantity.
b Suppose that landlords are required to pay $100 per apartment in a renter's tax to the city government. Use supply and demand analysis to determine the incidence of the tax.
c Now suppose that rather than being paid by the sellers of an apartment, the tax must be paid by the demanders. Use supply and demand analysis to determine the incidence of the tax.
d Does it matter who pays the tax?

Step-by-step solution

Step one (a): Find the no-tax equilibrium. When the price is $650, the market clears with 400 apartments rented. This is the answer to part a.

Step two (b): Identify whether the demander or supplier must pay the tax. For part b, the supplier pays the tax.

Step three: Because the tax is paid by sellers, the supply curve shifts up by $100, the amount of the tax. The new supply curve is found by adding $100 to the price column, as in Table 5.3

Table 5.3

Supply	
Price	Quantity
$900	500
$850	500
$800	450
$750	400
$700	300

Step four: Find the new equilibrium. The market clears at a price of $700 and a quantity of 300.

Step five: Determine the economic incidence of the tax.

Demander's burden
= new equilibrium price − original equilibrium price
= $700 − $650 = $50.

Supplier's burden
= original equilibrium price − new equilibrium price
+ tax
= $650 − $700 + $100 = $50.

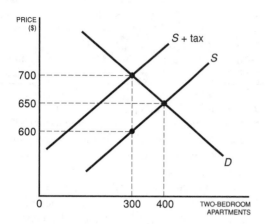

Step six (*c*): To answer part *c*, we repeat the procedure for the case where the demander must pay the tax.

Step seven (*one*): The original no-tax equilibrium is the same with the price equal to $650 and 400 apartments rented.

Step eight (*two*): In this case, the demanders pay the tax.

Step nine (*three*): We shift the demand curve down by $100. The new demand curve is given in Table 5.4.

Table 5.4

Demand	
Price	Quantity
$700	100
$650	200
$600	300
$550	400
$500	500

Step ten (*four*): The market clears at a price of $600 and a quantity of 300.

Step eleven (*five*): We determine the incidence as follows.

Demander's burden
= new equilibrium price + tax − original equilibrium price
= $600 + $100 − $650 = $50.

Supplier's burden
= original equilibrium price − new equilibrium price
= $650 − $600 = $50.

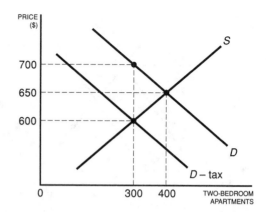

Step twelve (*d*): It does not matter who pays the tax! In either situation, the total amount that demanders pay is $700, the net amount that sellers receive is $600, and the equilibrium quantity is 300. The diagrams illustrate the solution.

5   (Practice problem: tax incidence) The demand curve and supply curve for unskilled labor are given in Table 5.5.

Table 5.5

Demand		Supply	
Wage	Quantity	Wage	Quantity
$6.50	1,000	$6.50	1,900
$6.00	1,200	$6.00	1,800
$5.50	1,400	$5.50	1,700
$5.00	1,600	$5.00	1,600
$4.50	1,800	$4.50	1,500
$4.00	2,000	$4.00	1,400

a   Find the equilibrium wage and quantity hired.
b   Consider the effect of the unemployment insurance tax. Suppose that it equals $1.50 per hour and is paid by the employers (they are the demanders in this market). Use supply and demand analysis to determine the incidence of this tax.
c   Now suppose that rather than being paid by the employers, the tax must be paid by the workers. Use supply and demand analysis to determine the incidence of this tax.
d   Does it matter who pays the tax?

PRICE CONTROLS

When the government interferes with the law of supply and demand and sets price controls, the effects can be analyzed with the basic method of supply and demand. To see the effects, start with an equilibrium.

The price control (if it is effective) will change the price without changing either the demand curve or the supply curve. The new equilibrium occurs at the price set by the government, but the quantity demanded is read off the demand curve, and the quantity supplied is read off the supply curve. The actual quantity transacted is always the short side of the market (the smaller of the quantity demanded and the quantity supplied).

The basic results of this analysis are that price ceilings, when set below the market-clearing price, lower the price, cause shortages, and reduce the quantity transacted. Price floors, when set above the market-clearing price, raise the price, cause surpluses, and reduce the quantity transacted. Tool Kit 5.3 shows how to use supply and demand to analyze price controls.

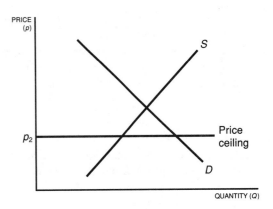

Step four: Determine the shortage or surplus. For a price floor set above the market-clearing price, there is a surplus:

shortage = quantity supplied − quantity demanded.

For a price ceiling set below the market-clearing price, there is a shortage:

surplus = quantity demanded − quantity supplied.

Tool Kit 5.3 Using Supply and Demand for Price Controls

The impact of price controls is made clear through the use of supply and demand. This four-step procedure shows how to analyze price controls.

Step one: Start with a market-clearing equilibrium.

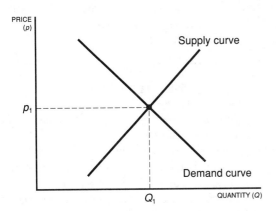

Step two: Identify the controlled price, and decide whether it is a floor or a ceiling.

Step three: Find the new equilibrium price. If it is a price floor set below the market-clearing price or a price ceiling set above the market-clearing price, then the equilibrium is the market-clearing one found in step one. If it is a price floor set above the market-clearing price or a price ceiling set below market clearing, then the controlled price is the equilibrium price.

6 (Worked problem: price controls) Dental bills in Yellowville rose again last year. The City Council is considering a bill to place a ceiling on fees that dentists can charge for teeth cleaning. The supply curve and demand curve for teeth cleanings are given in Table 5.6.

Table 5.6

Demand		Supply	
Price	Quantity	Price	Quantity
$65	100	$65	190
$60	120	$60	180
$55	140	$55	170
$50	160	$50	160
$45	180	$45	150
$40	200	$40	140

a Find the equilibrium price and quantity for teeth cleanings in Yellowville.

b The City Council passes a price ceiling ordinance, setting the maximum price at $40 per cleaning. Use supply and demand analysis to determine the effects of the price control.

Step-by-step solution

Step one (*a*): Find the equilibrium price and quantity. The market clears at a price of $50 and quantity equal to 160.

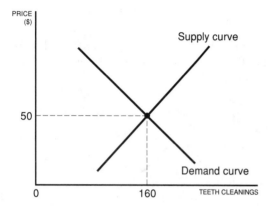

Step two (*b*): Identify the controlled price and whether it is a floor or a ceiling. The price control is a price ceiling set at $40.

Step three: Determine the new equilibrium price. The ceiling is below the market-clearing price; therefore, the new price is equal to the ceiling price of $40.

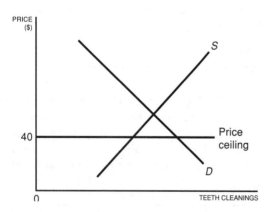

Step four: Determine the shortage or surplus. When the price is $40, the quantity demanded is 200 and the quantity supplied is 140. Although consumers would like more, there are only 140 cleanings actually performed. This results in a shortage of 200 − 140 = 60 teeth cleanings. The diagram illustrates the solution.

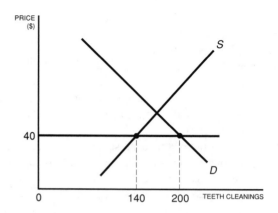

7 (Practice problem: price controls) Many states are considering price ceilings on automobile insurance premiums. In West Dakota, the supply curve and demand curve for automobile insurance policies ($250 deductible on liability, no collision) are given in Table 5.7.

Table 5.7

Demand		Supply	
Price	Quantity	Price	Quantity
$800	1,000	$800	1,800
$750	1,100	$750	1,500
$700	1,200	$700	1,200
$650	1,400	$650	900
$600	1,600	$600	600

a Find the equilibrium price and quantity.
b Suppose that a price ceiling of $650 is imposed. Use supply and demand analysis to determine the effects of the price control.
8 (Practice problem: price controls) Fearful of a restless urban population, Corporal Thug, the new supreme ruler of Costa Guano, attempts to mollify the masses with a wage increase. He mandates that employers must pay at least $8 per day. The supply and demand curves for urban labor are given in Table 5.8.

Table 5.8

Demand		Supply	
Wage	Quantity	Wage	Quantity
$8.50	400	$8.50	4,000
$8.00	600	$8.00	3,200
$7.50	700	$7.50	2,600
$7.00	800	$7.00	2,200
$6.50	900	$6.50	1,800
$6.00	1,000	$6.00	1,000

a Find the quantity demanded, the quantity supplied, and the size of the surplus or shortage, if any.

b Democracy comes to Costa Guano! Corporal Thug is overthrown and the minimum wage repealed. Use supply and demand analysis to determine the effects of the price control.

Answers to Problems

2 *a*

Price	Quantity	Revenue
$10	70	$700
$8	90	$720
$6	120	$720
$4	130	$520

b Between $10 and $8,
elasticity = (10 + 8)(90 − 70)/(10 − 8)(90 + 70)
= 1.125.
Between $8 and $6,
elasticity = (8 + 6)(120 − 90)/(8 − 6)(120 + 90)
= 1.
Between $6 and $4,
elasticity = (6 + 4)(130 − 120)/(6 − 4)(130 + 120)
= 0.2.

c When elasticity is 1.125, the demand curve is elastic, and total revenue rises from $700 to $720 as price falls. When elasticity is 1, the demand curve is unitary elastic, and total revenue remains constant at $720 as price falls. Finally, when elasticity is 0.2, the demand curve is inelastic, and total revenue falls from $720 to $520 as price falls.

3 In the following tables, the number in the elasticity column corresponding to each price refers to the elasticity over the interval between that price and the next highest price.

a

Price	Quantity	Total revenue	Elasticity
$12	6	$72	
$10	8	$80	1.57
$8	10	$80	1.00
$6	12	$72	0.64

b

Price	Quantity	Total revenue	Elasticity
$100	80	$8,000	
$80	85	$6,800	0.26
$60	90	$5,400	0.20
$40	95	$3,800	0.14

c

Price	Quantity	Total revenue	Elasticity
$9	10	$90	
$8	14	$112	2.430
$7	18	$126	1.875
$6	22	$132	1.300

5 *a* Wage = $5.00; quantity = 1,600.
b The new supply is given in Table 5.9.

Table 5.9

Supply	
Wage	*Quantity*
$8.00	1,900
$7.50	1,800
$7.00	1,700
$6.50	1,600
$6.00	1,500
$5.50	1,400

The new equilibrium wage = $5.50; quantity = 1,400. Demander's burden = $5.50 − $5.00 = $.50; supplier's burden = $5.00 + $1.50 − $5.50 = $1.00.

c The new demand curve is given in Table 5.10.

Table 5.10

Demand	
Wage	*Quantity*
$5.00	1,000
$4.50	1,200
$4.00	1,400
$3.50	1,600
$3.00	1,800
$2.50	2,000

The new equilibrium wage = $4.00; quantity = 1,400. Demander's burden = $4.00 + $1.50 − $5.00 = $0.50; supplier's burden = $5.00 − $4.00 = $1.00.

d No. The demander's burden, supplier's burden, and equilibrium quantity are the same in each case.

7 *a* Price = $700; quantity = 1,200.
b Price = $650; quantity demanded = 1,400; quantity supplied = 900; shortage = 1,400 − 900 = 500.

8 *a* Wage = $8.00; quantity demanded = 600; quantity supplied = 3,200; surplus = 3,200 − 600 = 2,600.
b Price = $600; quantity = 1,000.

CHAPTER 6 | The Consumption Decision

Chapter Review

The detailed study of microeconomics, the branch that focuses on the behavior of individuals and firms and builds up to an understanding of markets, begins in this chapter and continues throughout Parts Two and Three of the text. The basic competitive model of the private economy developed here is one you'll use throughout this course. Chapters 6-10 build on this model; exploring first the decisions individuals make—how much to consume, save, invest, and work—and then the decisions firms take—what and how much to produce and by what method. The entire model is put together in Chapter 10.

ESSENTIAL CONCEPTS

1   The consumer's decisions about how much of each good to purchase—that is, the demand for each—are made in a two-step procedure. First, the consumer finds how much can be consumed given the amount of money available. This step is the construction of the **opportunity set,** the outer edge of which is the **budget constraint.** Second, he chooses the best alternative along the budget constraint. Figure 6.1 depicts a budget constraint.

2   The budget constraint shows how much of each good can be purchased with the money available. The **slope** of the budget constraint is the **relative price** of the good measured on the horizontal axis. This relative price indicates the **trade-off:** how much of one good must be forgone to consume one more unit of the other.

3   The benefit or utility that a consumer derives from a good is measured by how much she is willing to pay. Consumers focus on the margin (the next unit) and

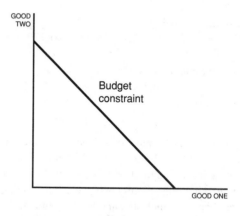

Figure 6.1

continue to purchase more of the good until the *marginal benefit equals the price.*

4   When income increases, the budget constraint shifts out, but its slope does not change. Consumers buy more normal goods. Goods that people buy less of as income increases are called inferior goods, but these are the exceptions. The **income elasticity of demand** measures how much the quantity demanded changes as income changes. It is positive for **normal goods** and negative for **inferior goods.**

5   When price changes, the budget constraint rotates, becoming steeper if the price of the good on the horizontal axis rises and flatter if it falls. Introduced in Chapter 5, the **price elasticity of demand** measures how much the quantity demanded changes as price changes.

6   Price changes cause substitution and income effects. Suppose the price of a good rises. Because the good is relatively more expensive, the principle of substitution says that consumers will shift some of their

consumption to other goods. This change is the **substitution effect.** At the same time, when the price is higher, the consumer is worse off and tends to buy less if the good is normal but more if the good is inferior. This change is the **income effect.**

7 **Utility** is the term economists use for the benefits that individuals receive for consuming goods. As people consume more of a particular good, they get smaller increments of utility. In other words, there is **diminishing marginal utility.** When the consumer has chosen the best bundle of goods, her utility is maximized and the marginal utility of each good equals its price.

8 **Consumer surplus** equals the difference between what the consumer is willing to pay for goods and the price (what he has to pay). Figure 6.2 shows a demand curve for apples, which also represents what the consumer is willing to pay for apples. When the price is $.25, the consumer purchases 8 apples. The consumer surplus, shown as the area between the demand curve and the price, measures the consumer's gain from trade.

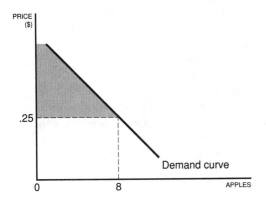

Figure 6.2

BEHIND THE ESSENTIAL CONCEPTS

1 The budget constraint shows what quantities of goods are affordable. If you know the prices of goods and an individual's income, you can draw her budget constraint. As you might expect, people who have the same income and must pay the same prices have the same budget constraint. As price changes, each individual's budget constraint changes in the same way. The budget constraint indicates opportunities; it says nothing about the value that the consumer places on the goods. Individual tastes only come into the picture when the actual choices are made.

2 The slope of the budget line depends only on prices, not on income. Therefore, changes in income cannot change the slope of the budget line. Changes in income bring about a parallel shift in the budget constraint. Price changes, on the other hand, do change the slope.

The budget constraint rotates when price changes.

3 Economists measure the responsiveness of quantity to income or price changes by using elasticities. In this chapter, there are two elasticities: the income elasticity of demand and the price elasticity of demand. Elasticities are relative percentage changes. The income elasticity equals the percentage that the quantity demanded changes when income changes by 1 percent. The price elasticity tells the percentage change in quantity demanded as the result of a 1 percent change in price.

4 The distinction between substitution and income effects is important, and it will reappear in the next chapter and throughout the course. Two points are key here. First, income effects are small in the consumption decision. Suppose that the price of milk rises by 10 percent. If I were spending $10 per month on milk, now I must spend $1 more to buy the same amount of milk. This makes me worse off by approximately $1, not a very important change in my well-being. The income effect captures how much extra milk can be bought with $1 of extra income. The second point is that the relatively more important substitution effect governs many important issues concerning the response to price changes, such as how elastic are demand curves, whether goods are substitutes or complements, and why taxes lead to inefficiencies.

5 The basic economic model says that individuals balance the benefits and costs of their decisions. It emphasizes choice at the margin, for the next unit of a good or service. Individuals continue buying until the marginal benefit equals the marginal cost. For the consumer, the marginal benefit (called the marginal utility) is just how much she is willing to pay for another unit. The marginal cost is the price. When marginal utility equals price, the consumer has realized all the possible gains from the purchase of the good.

6 There are two important diagrams in this chapter: the budget constraint and the demand curve. Although each is downward sloping, they should not be confused. The budget constraint drawn in Figure 6.1 shows the combinations of goods that a person can afford. Quantities of goods are measured on each axis. The demand curve drawn in Figure 6.2 shows how much of *one* good will be purchased at each price. The quantity of the good is measured on the horizontal axis, and the price is measured on the vertical.

SELF-TEST

True or False

1 The budget constraint indicates that the amount spent on goods cannot exceed after tax income.

2 The slope of the budget constraint shows the trade-off between two goods.

3 Income determines the slope of the budget constraint.
4 The amount that an individual is willing to pay for coffee is called the marginal utility of coffee.
5 The amount that an individual is willing to pay for an extra cup of coffee is called the marginal utility of coffee.
6 A rational individual will increase her consumption of a good until the marginal utility equals the price.
7 When income increases, the budget constraint rotates, becoming flatter.
8 When income increases, the consumer demands more of inferior goods.
9 If an individual demands more of a good when income falls, the good is a complement.
10 If the income elasticity is less than zero, then the good is an inferior good.
11 The long-run income elasticity of demand is greater than the short-run income elasticity of demand.
12 If when the price of one good rises the demand for another also rises, the goods are substitutes.
13 If when the price of one good falls the demand for another also falls, the goods are complements.
14 When the price of a good falls, the substitution effect encourages more consumption of that good.
15 When the price of a normal good falls, the income effect encourages more consumption of that good.

Multiple Choice

1 Assuming that there is no saving or borrowing and a consumer's income is fixed, his budget constraint
   a defines his opportunity set.
   b indicates that total expenditures cannot be greater than total income.
   c shows that marginal utility is decreasing.
   d all of the above.
   e *a* and *b*.
2 Suppose that the price of a movie ticket is $5 and the price of a pizza is $10. The trade-off between the two goods is
   a one pizza for one movie ticket.
   b two movie tickets for one pizza.
   c two pizzas for one movie ticket.
   d $2 per movie ticket.
   e none of the above.
3 The marginal utility of a good indicates
   a that the usefulness of the good is limited.
   b the willingness to pay for an extra unit.
   c that the good is scarce.
   d that the slope of the budget constraint is the relative price.
   e none of the above.
4 Diminishing marginal utility means that
   a the usefulness of the good is limited.
   b the willingness to pay for an extra unit decreases as more of that good is consumed.

   c the good is less scarce.
   d the slope of the budget constraint is flatter as more of that good is consumed.
   e none of the above.
5 If Fred is willing to pay $100 for one espresso maker and $120 for two, then the marginal utility of the second espresso maker is
   a $20.
   b $120.
   c $100.
   d $60.
   e $50.
6 When the income of a consumer increases, her budget constraint
   a shifts outward parallel to the original budget constraint.
   b rotates and becomes steeper.
   c rotates and becomes flatter.
   d shifts inward parallel to the original budget constraint.
   e none of the above.
7 The percentage change in quantity demanded brought about by a 1 percent increase in income is
   a 1.
   b greater than 0.
   c the income elasticity of demand.
   d the price elasticity of demand.
   e none of the above.
8 If the share of income that an individual spends on a good decreases as her income increases, then the income elasticity of demand is
   a greater than 1.
   b between 0 and 1.
   c 0.
   d less than 1.
   e less than 0.
9 In the long run,
   a the price elasticity of demand is greater than in the short run.
   b the income elasticity of demand is greater than in the short run.
   c the price elasticity of demand is less than in the short run.
   d the income elasticity of demand is less than in the short run.
   e *a* and *b*.
10 When the price of a good (measured along the horizontal axis) falls, the budget constraint
   a rotates and becomes flatter.
   b rotates and becomes steeper.
   c shifts out parallel to the original budget constraint.
   d shifts in parallel to the original budget constraint.
   e none of the above.
11 If demand for a good falls as income rises, then
   a the good is a normal good.
   b the good is an inferior good.

c the income elasticity is less than 0.

d the income elasticity is between 0 and 1.

e *b* and *c*.

12 When the price of a good falls, the substitution effect

a encourages the individual to consume more of the good.

b encourages the individual to consume less of the good.

c leads to more consumption if the good is an inferior good but less if the good is a normal good.

d leads to less consumption if the good is an inferior good but more if the good is a normal good.

e *a* and *c*.

13 When the price of a good falls, the income effect

a encourages the individual to consume more of the good.

b encourages the individual to consume less of the good.

c leads to more consumption if the good is an inferior good but less if the good is a normal good.

d leads to less consumption if the good is an inferior good but more if the good is a normal good.

e *a* and *c*.

14 The rational consumer chooses her purchases for each good so that the

a utility equals total expenditure.

b marginal utility equals price.

c consumer surplus equals 0.

d marginal utility is diminishing.

e income elasticity equals 1.

15 The difference between what the consumer is willing to pay for an item and what she has to pay is called the

a marginal utility.

b substitution effect.

c consumer surplus.

d income effect.

e price elasticity of demand.

16 In general, the price elasticity of demand is greater when

a the good is an inferior good.

b there are good, close substitutes available.

c there are good, close complements available.

d the income elasticity of demand is less.

e none of the above.

17 For normal goods, when income rises,

a the budget constraint shifts out, parallel.

b the demand curve shifts to the right.

c quantity demanded increases.

d more money is spent on the good.

e all of the above.

18 For normal goods, as price rises,

a the substitution effect encourages less consumption.

b the income effect encourages less consumption.

c the quantity demanded falls.

d the demand for substitute goods increases.

e all of the above.

19 For inferior goods, as price rises,

a the substitution effect encourages less consumption.

b the income effect encourages less consumption.

c the income effect encourages more consumption.

d the quantity demanded rises.

e *a* and *c*.

20 The slope of the budget constraint depends on

a the relative price of the goods.

b the income of the consumer.

c the availability of substitute goods.

d whether the good is normal or inferior.

e *a* and *b*.

Completion

1 The opportunity set for the consumer is defined by the _____, which says that expenditures cannot exceed income.

2 The slope of the budget line equals the _____ of the two goods.

3 The benefits of consumption are called _____.

4 The willingness to pay for an extra unit of some good is its _____.

5 When income increases, the budget constraint shifts outward in a _____ way.

6 The _____ of demand measures how consumption of a good changes in response to a change in income.

7 When the price of a good changes, the budget constraint _____.

8 The _____ of demand measures how consumption of a good changes in response to a change in price.

9 When the price of a good falls, the _____ effect always encourages more consumption of the good.

10 The difference between what the consumer is willing to pay for an item and what she has to pay is called _____.

Answers to Self-Test

True or False

1	t	6	t	11	t
2	t	7	f	12	t
3	f	8	f	13	f
4	f	9	f	14	t
5	t	10	t	15	t

Multiple Choice

1	*e*	6	*a*	11	*e*	16	*b*
2	*b*	7	*c*	12	*a*	17	*e*
3	*b*	8	*d*	13	*d*	18	*e*
4	*b*	9	*e*	14	*b*	19	*e*
5	*a*	10	*a*	15	*c*	20	*a*

Completion

1 budget constraint

2 relative price

3 utility
4 marginal utility
5 parallel
6 income elasticity
7 rotates
8 price elasticity
9 substitution
10 consumer surplus

Doing Economics: Tools and Practice Problems

The most important model in this chapter is the opportunity set for the consumer: the budget constraint. This section will first review how to construct the budget constraint and then explain how the budget constraint changes when price and income change. A somewhat more advanced topic follows, as we explore how to illustrate the substitution and income effects of price changes. Next, there are some applications: in-kind transfers and tax-subsidy schemes. Finally, we turn to marginal utility and consumer surplus.

THE BUDGET CONSTRAINT

Because we have limited income, we must limit our purchases. The budget constraint shows what combinations of goods are affordable. Tool Kit 6.1 shows how to plot the budget constraint. After some practice problems, we study the effects of income and price changes. The basic technique is to first draw the budget constraint using the original income and price, then draw a new budget constraint using the new income and prices. Finally, we compare the old and new budget constraints.

Tool Kit 6.1 Plotting the Budget Constraint

The budget constraint shows what combinations of goods can be purchased with a limited amount of money. Constructing the budget constraint is one of the essential techniques needed in Part Two. Follow these four steps.

Step one: Draw a set of coordinate axes. Label the horizontal axis as the quantity of one good consumed and the vertical axis as the quantity of a second good consumed.

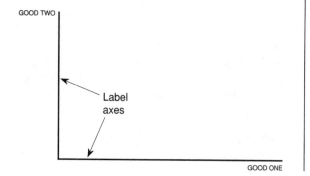

Step two: Calculate the quantity of the good measured on the horizontal axis that can be purchased if all the consumer's money is spent on it. Plot this quantity along the horizontal axis.

Step three: Calculate the quantity of the good measured on the vertical axis that can be purchased if all the consumer's money is spent on it. Plot this quantity along the vertical axis.

Step four: Draw a line segment connecting the two points. This line segment is the budget constraint.

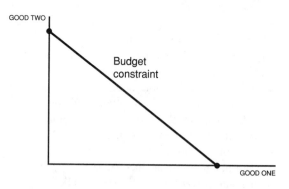

Step five: Verify that the slope of the budget constraint is (minus) the price of the good measured on the horizontal axis divided by the price of the good measured on the vertical axis.

---

1 (Worked problem: budget constraint) Dick has a budget of $500 to paint and paper the rooms in his new condominium. The price of enough paint for 1 room is $25; the price of wallpaper is $50 per room. Draw Dick's budget constraint.

Step-by-step solution

Step one: Draw a set of coordinate axes, and label the horizontal one "Rooms painted" and the vertical one "Rooms papered." (There is no rule as to which good goes on which axis. It is fine either way.)

Step two: Calculate how many rooms can be painted with the entire $500. This number is $500/$25 = 20 rooms. Plot this quantity along the horizontal axis.

Step three: Calculate how many rooms can be papered with the entire $500. This number is $500/$50 = 10 rooms. Plot this quantity along the vertical axis.

Step four: Draw a line segment connecting these two points. This line segment is the budget constraint.

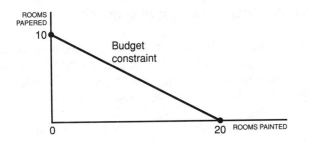

Step five: Verify the slope. The slope of the budget constraint is 10/20 = 1/2. The price ratio is $25/$50 = 1/2.

2 (Practice problem: budget constraint) Dean Lewis would like to have some of the practice pianos tuned in the charming but decaying music building. She could use some of the $1,000 in the supplies and services budget, but that money must pay for repairing broken lockers. The piano tuner charges $50 per piano, and the carpenter charges $40 per locker. Plot her budget constraint and verify that the slope is the relative price.

3 (Practice problem: budget constraint). Draw the following budget constraints.
   a Budget for hiring groundskeepers = $100,000; price of a full-time employee = $20,000; price of a part-time employee = $8,000.
   b Budget for food = $250; price of microwave snacks = $2.00. (Plot expenditures on all other food on the vertical axis.)
   c Budget for landscaping = $2,000; price of lilac bushes = $50; price of cherry trees = $80.
   d Budget for library acquisitions = $50,000; price of books = $40; price of journal subscriptions = $100.

4 (Worked problem: budget constraint with income and price changes) Bill Kutt, a somewhat diminutive and lazy student, has decided to take a course on the nineteenth-century American novel. Many books are assigned, and all are available in the abridged "Fred's Notes" versions at $8 each. The unabridged versions are $3 each. Bill has $72 to spend.
   a Plot his budget constraint.
   b Show how it changes when Bill finds that he has another $24 (for a total of $96).

Step-by-step solution

Step one (*a*): Plot Bills budget constraint using the procedure outlined above. He can afford $72/$8 = 9 abridged and $72/$3 = 24 unabridged notes. Note that the slope is 9/24 = $3/$8, which is the ratio of the prices.

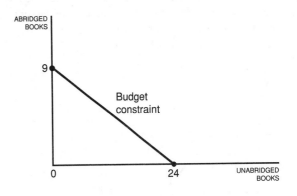

Step two (*b*): Plot Bills budget constraint with $96 to spend. He can now afford $96/$8 = 12 abridged and $96/$3 = 32 unabridged notes.

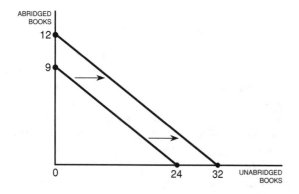

Step three: Verify that the shift in the budget constraint is parallel. The slope is 12/32 = $3/$8, which is the ratio of the prices. Because the prices have not changed, the slope has not changed. The income increase causes a parallel shift.

5 (Practice problem: budget constraint with income and price changes) Helen is nervous about graduate school. She is considering hiring a tutor for her economics course at $10 per hour. Another possibility is to attend sessions on how to improve the score of her GMAT test. These cost $30 each. She has $90.

    a Plot her budget constraint.
    b Oops! Unexpectedly stuck with the tab at Ernie's Ice House, Helen now has only $60 to spend. Plot her new budget constraint.

6 (Worked problem: budget constraint with income and price changes) Dissatisfied with his social life, Horatio has budgeted $400 for self-improvement. He is considering elocution lessons at $25 per hour and ballroom dancing classes at $10 each.
    a Plot Horatio's budget constraint.
    b Good news! A new elocution studio offers lessons at the introductory price of $20. Plot the new budget constraint.

Step-by-step solution

Step one (a): Plot the budget constraint at the $25 price. Horatio can afford $400/$25 = 16 elocution lessons or $400/$10 = 40 classes. Note that the slope is 40/16 = $25/$10, which is the ratio of the prices.

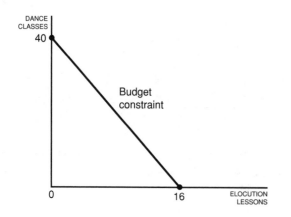

Step two (b): Plot the budget constraint at the $20 price. Horatio can now afford $400/$20 = 20 elocution lessons, which is 4 more, but he still can only buy 40 dance lessons.

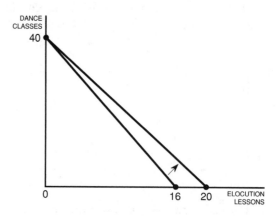

Step three: Verify that the budget constraint rotates. The slope is now 40/20 = $20/$10, which is the ratio of the new prices and is flatter. The price decrease rotated the budget constraint. The point at 0 elocution lessons and 40 dance classes does not change, because when no elocution lessons are purchased, the price change makes no difference.

7 (Practice problem: budget constraint with income and price changes) With some of her extra cash ($100 each month), Sho-Yen buys meals and blankets and donates them to the nearby shelter for the homeless. The meals cost $2 each, and she buys the blankets for $5 each.

    a Plot her budget constraint.
    b The supplier of meals cuts the price to $1. Plot the new budget constraint.

8 (Practice problem: budget constraint with income and price changes) For each of these problems, draw the budget constraints before and after the change. Plot "Expenditures on other goods" on the vertical axis.
    a Income = $400; price of potatoes = $1 per sack; price of potatoes rises to $2 per sack.
    b Income = $5,000; price of therapy sessions = $100 per hour; income rises to $6,000.
    c Income = $450; price of housecleaning = $45; income falls to $225.
    d Income = $100; price of pizzas = $5; price increases to $10.

SUBSTITUTION AND INCOME EFFECTS

Price changes rotate the budget constraint and bring about two effects, substitution and income. The substitution effect indicates that consumers buy more when the price falls and less when it rises. The income effect, on the other hand, is not necessarily in the opposite direction of the price change. Tool Kit 6.2 uses the budget constraint to distinguish substitution and income effects.

Tool Kit 6.2 Distinguishing Between Substitution and Income Effects

When the price of a good changes, there are two effects: substitution and income. These can be illustrated using the budget constraint. This technique clarifies the point that while the substitution effect is always in the opposite direction to the price change, the income effect may go either way. Follow these steps.

Step one: Draw the budget line with the original price.

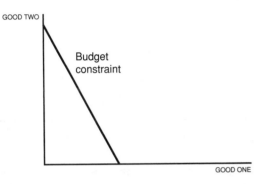

Step two: Find the chosen quantities along the budget line. Label this point *A*.

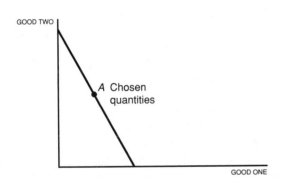

Step three: Draw the budget line with the new price.

Step four: Draw a dashed line through point *A* and parallel to the *new* budget line.

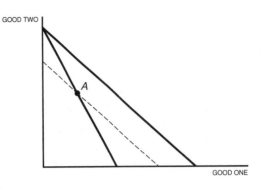

Step five: Darken the portion of the dotted-line segment that lies above the original budget line. The points along this darkened segment represent the quantities made possible by the substitution effect of the price change. The income effect shifts this line parallel out to the new budget line drawn in step three.

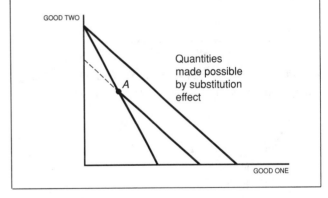

9 (Worked problem: substitution and income effects) Always diligent in keeping up with out-of-town friends and acquaintances, Lurleen budgets $30 per month for postage and phone calls. A long-distance call costs her $2 on average, and the price of a stamped envelope is $.30. She makes 6 calls and mails 60 letters each month.

a Plot her budget constraint, and label the point that she has chosen.

b Headline news! The price of a stamped envelope falls to $.20. Illustrate the substitution and income effects of the price change.

Step-by-step solution

Step one (*a*): Draw the original budget constraint. The maximum quantity of calls is $30/$2 = 15, and the maximum quantity of letters is $30/$.30 = 100.

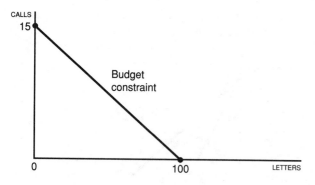

Step two: Plot and label the chosen point (6 calls, 60 letters). Note that this is on the budget constraint because (6 × $2) + (60 × $.30) = $30. Label this point *A*.

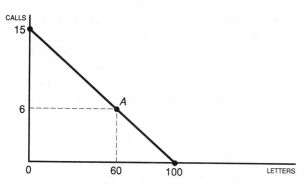

Step three (*b*): Draw the new budget constraint. The maximum quantities are 15 calls and 30/$.20 = 150 letters.

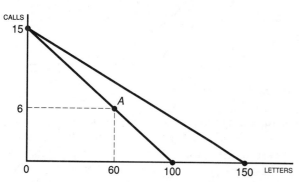

Step four: Draw a dashed line segment through *A* parallel to the new budget constraint.

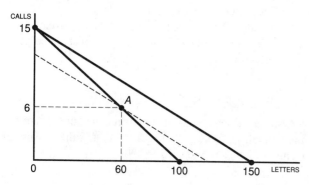

Step five: Darken the portion of the dashed line segment that lies above the original budget constraint. Notice that the sub-

stitution effect would lead Lurleen to choose a point like *B* along this segment, where the quantity of letters is greater. We say that the substitution effect of a price decrease is always to increase the quantity demanded. The income effect moves this darkened segment out to the new budget constraint. Lurleen would write more letters if letters were a normal good, but she would write fewer if letters were inferior. The income effect can go either way in principle, although most goods are normal.

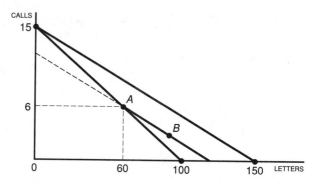

10 (Practice problem: substitution and income effects) Yves loves to wear whites for tennis. He sends his outfits to the cleaners at a price of $3.60 each. Playing tennis also requires new balls, which cost $2. Yves' tennis budget is $36 per week, which allows him his current consumption levels of 8 cans of balls and 5 clean outfits.
   a Plot his budget constraint, and show his current consumption choice.
   b The price of tennis balls has risen to $4.50. Illustrate the substitution and income effects of this price increase.

11 (Practice problem: substitution and income effects) For each of the following, illustrate the substitution and income effects of the price change. Plot "Expenditures on other goods" on the vertical axis, and pick any point on the original budget line as the quantities consumed before the price change.
   a Income = $100; price of bricks = $.10 each; price changes to $.20.
   b Income = $1,000; price of haircuts = $20; price changes to $25.
   c Income = $500; price of pies = $5; price changes to $4.
   d Income = $10; price of baseball cards = $.50; price changes to $.25

APPLICATIONS

Now that you have mastered plotting the budget constraint and analyzing how it changes when price or income changes, you are ready for some applications. The following problems look at how the budget constraint is affected by in-kind transfers, such as food stamps and tax changes. These latter problems illustrate the relationship between the substitution effect and tax distortions.

12 (Worked problem: applications) Many government programs deliver benefits in kind to people. For example, food stamps can only be used to buy food. Economists often argue that cash transfers are better. The typical food stamp recipient has $200 per week in income in addition to $80 per week in food stamps.
a Draw the budget constraint.
b One proposal is to substitute $80 in cash for the stamps. Draw the budget constraint that results from this proposal.
c Which would the recipient prefer? Why?

Step-by-step solution

Step one (*a*): Draw the budget constraint with the food stamps. Label the axes "Food consumption in dollars" and "Expenditures on other goods." The slope is 1 because $1 less spent on other goods means $1 spent on food. Note that no more than $200 may be spent on other goods.

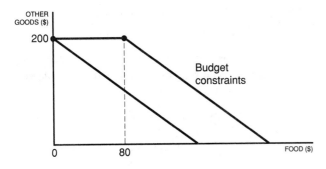

Step two (*b*): Draw the budget constraint with the cash grants replacing the food stamps.

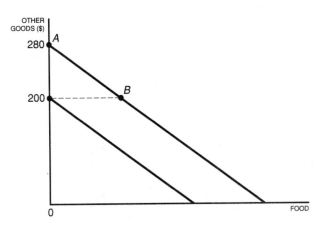

Step three (*c*): Compare. The difference is that the cash grant allows the recipient to choose the points between *A* and *B*. Many recipients would not choose these low levels of food consumption anyway; so there would be no difference. Some might, however, and these people would prefer the cash.

13 (Practice problem: applications) The city of Lansing, Michigan, recently planted 2 trees (worth $20 each) in every yard. The typical Lansing resident has $4,000 in disposable income this summer.
a Plot the budget constraint with the in-kind transfer of 2 trees.
b Plot the budget constraint with the $40 refunded through the tax system.
c Which opportunity set is preferred? How could the tree planting be justified?

14 (Worked problem: applications) When less consumption of some good or service is needed, economists often recommend putting a tax on the good or service. One objection is that the taxes lead to higher prices, which make people worse off. If the tax revenue is refunded, however, people can be approximately as well off, yet still face higher prices for the good or service. In essence, it is possible to put the substitution effect to work and reduce consumption of the good or service without reducing the well-being of consumers very much. The city of Pleasantville is running out of room at the dump. The typical resident purchases 6 bags weekly at $.10 each.
a Plot the budget constraint for the typical resident, and show the current consumption choice.
b In an effort to encourage recycling and discourage disposal, the city institutes a user fee of $1.90 per trash bag. (Trash bags now cost $2.) Keeping to their "No new taxes" pledge, the city council members vote to combine the user fee with a tax refund. Each citizen receives a tax refund of $1.90 × 6 = $11.40. Plot the new budget constraint.
c Discuss the user fee–tax refund plan.

Step-by-step solution

Step one (*a*): Plot the budget constraint with neither a user fee nor a tax refund. Label the resident's chosen point *A*.

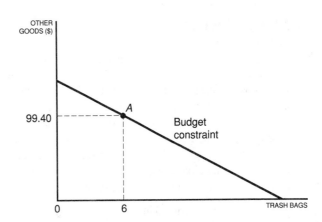

Step two (*b*): Plot the budget constraint with the user fee and tax refund.

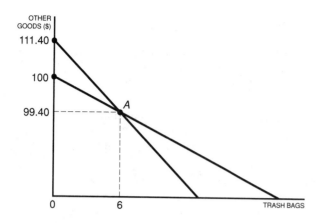

Step three (c): We see that the net effect of the entire user fee–tax refund scheme is only the substitution of the increase in the price of bags to $2. The resident is no worse off (because he can still consume as he did before the user fee), but he will be motivated to use fewer bags. (One minor flaw in the program is that as people substitute away from trash bags, they will pay less in user fees than is needed to finance the tax relief.)

15 (Practice problem: applications) Since the Gulf War, gasoline consumption has been on the mind of Senator Adam Smith. He proposes a $1-per-gallon tax on gasoline, which currently sells for $1. Assume that this tax will increase the price of gas to $2. The senator also proposes refunding the gas-tax revenues through an income tax cut large anough to allow consumers to buy the same amount of gas as before the tax.
  a Plot the budget constraint with no added gas tax.
  b Plot the budget constraint with the gas tax and the refund.
  c Columnist Kirk Jimpatrick writes, "This plan will have no effect. The government takes money away with one hand and gives it back with the other." Is he right? Why or why not?

UTILITY AND PREFERENCES

The first step in the consumption decision is to determine what is affordable—to plot the budget constraint. The second step is to choose the best bundle of goods from all those that lie along the budget constraint. Economists say that the best bundle gives the greatest utility. When the consumer has chosen the best bundle, the marginal utility (what she would be willing to pay for another unit) equals the price. Tool Kit 6.3 shows how to use marginal utility to interpret the consumption decision and also calculate consumer surplus.

16 (Worked problem: marginal utility) Table 6.1 gives Ching-Fan's willingness to pay (utility) for various hours of on-line access per week. On-line time is priced at $12 per hour.

Tool Kit 6.3 Using Marginal Utility to Choose the Best Bundle of Goods

The rational consumer demands the quantity of a good for which marginal equals price. The difference between what she is willing to pay and her expenditure is consumer surplus. Follow these steps to see how it works.

Step one: Identify the product price and utility (willingness to pay) for each quantity of the good.

Step two: Compute marginal utility for each quantity of the good.

Marginal utility = change in utility
          = utility of one fewer unit − utility.

Step three: Choose the quantity for which marginal utility equals price.

Step four: Compute her expenditure.

Expenditure = price × quantity.

Step five: Calculate consumer surplus.

Consumer surplus = utility − expenditure.

Step six: Confirm that consumer surplus equals the difference between marginal utility and price, added up over each unit purchased.

Consumer surplus = marginal utility of the first unit
          − price
          + marginal utility of the second unit − price
          + ...
          + marginal utility of the last unit − price.

Table 6.1

Number of on-line hours	Utility (willingness to pay)
0	0
1	$ 20
2	$ 38
3	$ 54
4	$ 68
5	$ 80
6	$ 90
7	$ 98
8	$104

a Compute marginal utility for each hour.
b How many hours will Ching-Fan purchase?
c Compute his consumer surplus for this good.

Step-by-step solution

Step one: Identify utility for each quantity and the price. The price is $12 and utility is given in Table 6.1.

Step two: Compute marginal utility. The first unit raises utility from $0 to $20. The marginal utility is then $20 − $0 = $20. Similarly, marginal utility for the second unity equals $38 − $20 = $18. Continuing, we have Table 6.2. Notice that marginal utility diminishes as quantity increases.

Table 6.2

Number of on-line hours	Utility (willingness to pay)	Marginal utility
0	0	
1	$ 20	$20
2	$38	$18
3	$ 54	$16
4	$ 68	$14
5	$ 80	$12
6	$ 90	$10
7	$ 98	$ 8
8	$104	$ 6

Step three: Choose the quantity for which marginal utility equals price. The price ($12) equals marginal utility when 5 hours are purchased.

Step four: Calculate expenditure. Expenditure is $12 × 5 = $60.

Step five: Calculate consumer surplus. His utility is $80 when he buys 5 hours. Consumer surplus is $80 − $60 = $20.

Step six: Calculate consumer surplus using marginal utilities. The marginal utility of the first unit is $20 less the price of $12 gives consumer surplus of $20 − $12 = $8 on the first unity. Proceeding similarly, we have

consumer surplus = ($20 − $12) + ($18 − $12) + ($16 − $12) + ($14 − $12) + ($12 − $12)
= $8 + $6 + $4 + $2 + $0 = $20,

which equals the total computed in step five.

17 (Practice problem: marginal utility) Table 6.3 gives Marneta's willingness to pay for concert tickets. The price of concerts is $20 each.
   a Compute marginal utility for ticket.
   b How many hours will Marneta purchase?
   c Compute her consumer surplus.

Table 6.3

Number of tickets	Utility (willingness to pay)
0	$0
1	$35
2	$65
3	$90
4	$110
5	$125
6	$135
7	$140

18 (Practice problem: marginal utility) Table 6.4 gives Charlie's consumer surplus for tennis balls, which sell for $2 each.
   a Compute marginal utility for each can.
   b How many hours will Charlie purchase?
   c Compute his consumer surplus for this good.

Table 6.4

Number of cans of tennis balls	Utility (willingness to pay)
0	$0
1	$10
2	$16
3	$20
4	$22
5	$23
6	$23.50
7	$23.75

Answers to Problems

2

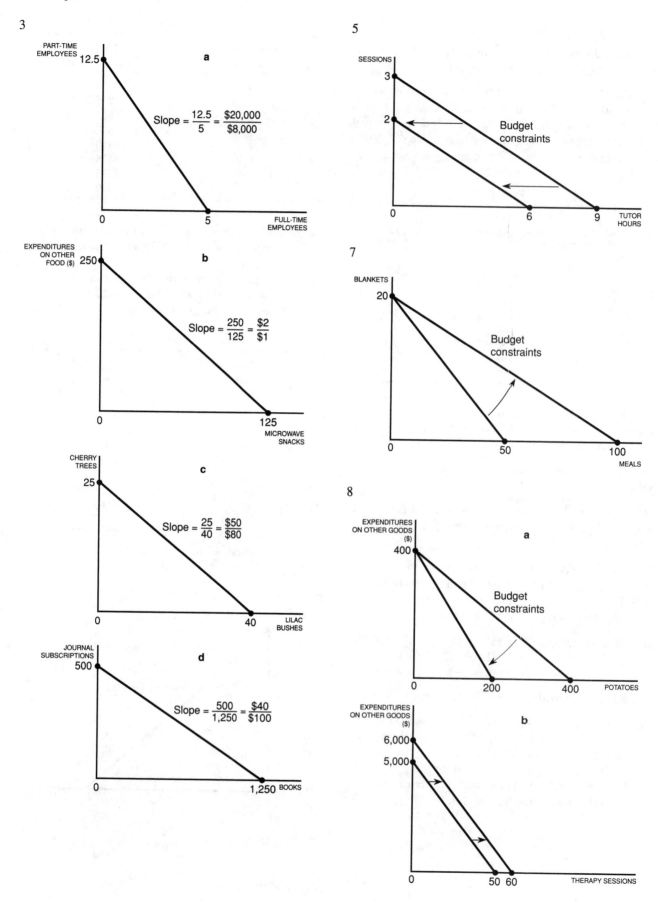

3

a

PART-TIME EMPLOYEES

12.5

Slope = $\frac{12.5}{5}$ = $\frac{\$20,000}{\$8,000}$

0   5   FULL-TIME EMPLOYEES

b

EXPENDITURES ON OTHER FOOD ($)

250

Slope = $\frac{250}{125}$ = $\frac{\$2}{\$1}$

0   125   MICROWAVE SNACKS

c

CHERRY TREES

25

Slope = $\frac{25}{40}$ = $\frac{\$50}{\$80}$

0   40   LILAC BUSHES

d

JOURNAL SUBSCRIPTIONS

500

Slope = $\frac{500}{1,250}$ = $\frac{\$40}{\$100}$

0   1,250   BOOKS

5

SESSIONS

3

2

Budget constraints

0   6   9   TUTOR HOURS

7

BLANKETS

20

Budget constraints

0   50   100   MEALS

8

a

EXPENDITURES ON OTHER GOODS ($)

400

Budget constraints

0   200   400   POTATOES

b

EXPENDITURES ON OTHER GOODS ($)

6,000

5,000

0   50 60   THERAPY SESSIONS

c

b

d

c

d

10

11

a

13

a

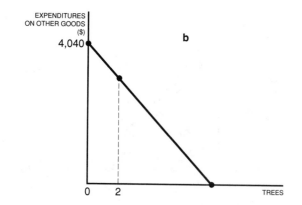

c The budget constraint with the tax refund, which is shown in part *b,* is preferred because it allows more choices. If desired, the resident can spend as much as $4,040 on other goods, and with the in-kind transfer of trees, she can spend a maximum of $4,000 on other goods.

15

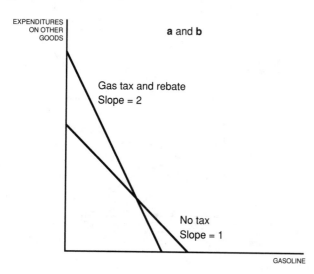

c He is wrong. The gas tax and rebate program results in a budget constraint with more alternatives that involve less gasoline consumption. It motivates individuals to substitute other goods for gasoline.

17 *a*

Table 6.5

Number of tickets	Utility (willingness to pay)	Marginal Utility
0	0	
1	$35	$35
2	$65	$30
3	$90	$25
4	$110	$20
5	$125	$15
6	$135	$10
7	$140	$5

b 4.
c $110 − ($20 × 4) = $30.
d ($35 − $20) + ($30 − $20) + ($25 − $20) + ($20 − $20) = $30

18 *a*

Table 6.6

Number of cans of tennis balls	Utility (willingness to pay)	Marginal Utility
0	$0	
1	$10	$10
2	$16	$6
3	$20	$4
4	$22	$2
5	$23	$1
6	$23.50	$0.50
7	$23.75	$0.25

b 4.
c $22 − ($2 × 4) = $14.
d ($10 − $2) + ($6 − $2) + ($4 − $2) + ($2 − $2) = $14.

| The Firm's Costs

Chapter Review

One side of the competitive model, the household's, is complete. Business enterprises—firms—occupy the other side. This chapter begins the discussion of the role of firms in a market-based economy. We learn about the production function, which summarizes the relationship between the inputs that the firm demands (especially in the labor market) and the outputs that it supplies in the product market. Payments to purchase inputs make up most of the firm's costs, and this chapter treats these costs in depth. How the costs are balanced against revenues is the subject of Chapter 8.

ESSENTIAL CONCEPTS

1 In the basic competitive model, the firm's objective is to maximize its market value. Because the value of the firm depends on its profit-making potential, another way to put this is to say the firm's objective is to maximize its (long-term) profits. **Profits** equal revenues minus costs, and **revenues** are simply price times quantity.

2 The **production function** shows the relationship between inputs and outputs. The increase in output resulting from a small increase in the use of an input is called the **marginal product.** The **principle of diminishing returns** states that as more of one input is used, holding other inputs fixed, the marginal product declines. While diminishing returns represent the usual case, some production functions exhibit **increasing returns,** where the marginal product increases as more of an input is used. If doubling the input doubles the output, then there are **constant returns.** Inputs that do not change as output changes are called **fixed inputs;**

inputs that do change with output are called **variable inputs**.

3 There are costs associated with each type of input: either **fixed costs,** which do not change when output changes, or **variable costs,** which do. The important concept to grasp is how the various measures of costs change as output changes. The **average cost** curve is typically U-shaped; the **marginal cost** curve lies below it when average cost falls, equals average cost at the minimum, and lies above it when average cost increases.

4 In the long run, firms can increase in the same proportion, there are **constant returns to scale** if output increases in the same proportion. If output increases by less, there are **diminishing returns to scale. Increasing returns to scale** imply that output increases by a greater proportion than do inputs. **Economies of scope** refer to the cost savings from producing several goods together rather than separately.

5 The **principle of substitution** says that as the price of an input increases, firms substitute other inputs. The firm always chooses the least-cost production technique. In the long run, all inputs are variable; the firm has more choices. The **long-run average cost curve** is the lower boundary of all possible short-run average cost curves.

BEHIND THE ESSENTIAL CONCEPTS

1 Of the many diagrams in this chapter, there are four that you should master. Each is explained below. Notice how the economic idea (such as diminishing returns or increasing returns to scale) determines the shape of the curves.

a The first diagram to master is the production
function (Figure 7.1, which is similar to Figure 7.4
in the text). The production function indicates how
output (measured on the vertical axis) changes as the
quantity of the variable input (measured on the
horizontal axis) changes. There are two important
facts to know. The first is that the shape indicates
whether the production function has diminishing,
constant, or increasing returns. Figure 7.1 shows
diminishing returns. Also, the slope of the
production function is equal to the marginal product.

Figure 7.1

b The second diagram is the total cost curves, shown
in Figure 7.2 (which summarizes Figure 7.5 A, B,
and C of the text). Output is measured along the
horizontal axis, and cost along the vertical one.
Again, there are two important features to observe.
First, **total cost** is the sum of fixed and variable
costs. Because by definition fixed costs don't
change, the difference between the parallel variable
and total cost curves equals fixed cost. The second
feature is that the total cost curve inherits its shape
from the production function. This will be explored
in the analysis part of this chapter.

Figure 7.2

c Third, there is the average cost-marginal cost
diagram, shown in Figure 7.3 (which duplicates
Figure 7.6 in the text). The important concept here is
the relationship between the marginal and average
cost curves. The average cost curve is typically U-
shaped. When marginal cost is below average cost,
average cost is downward sloping. Marginal cost
equals average cost at the minimum of average cost,
and marginal cost is above average cost when
average cost is upward sloping. Average cost falls as
fixed costs are spread over more units. Average cost
rises because diminishing returns drive the marginal
cost curve above the average cost curve.

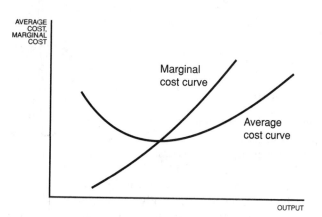

Figure 7.3

d Finally, there is the long-run average cost curve. For
every production process, there are fixed inputs and
an associated average cost curve. The long-run
average cost curve is the lower boundary, as shown
in Figure 7.4 (which duplicates Figure 7.14 in the
text). The curve is drawn flat, which represents
constant returns of scale.

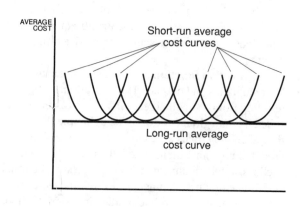

Figure 7.4

2 In reviewing these four diagrams, keep in mind three
pointers.

a Remember to note what is measured along each axis. It's easy to make the mistake of memorizing the shapes of the curves while forgetting how to label the axes.

b Note the relationships among the curves, especially the marginal cost and average cost relationship.

c The shape of the curves illustrate the economic properties. It's important to be able to recognize economic properties like diminishing returns and economies of scale in the diagrams of production functions and cost curves.

3 Diminishing returns refer to production processes in which some, but not all, inputs are variable. Diminishing returns imply that the marginal product decreases as more inputs are used. Economists add the words "to scale" when describing a production process in which all inputs are variable. Thus, decreasing returns to scale mean that as all inputs are increased in a certain proportion, output increases by less.

4 The marginal product is the additional output produced by one more worker (or other variable factor). The marginal cost is the additional cost of one more unit of output. These are two distinct ideas, but they are related. Suppose that you have a business digitizing legal documents. If you pay your workers $10 per hour and they digitize 50 documents per hour, then the marginal product of an hour of labor is 50 documents. The marginal cost of digitizing a document is $10/50 = p. 20. If your workers become more productive and their marginal product rises to, say, 100 documents per hour, then your marginal cost falls to $10/100 = p. 10. In general, a higher marginal product means a lower marginal cost; so if the marginal product curve is downward sloping, then the marginal cost curve is upward sloping.

SELF-TEST

True or False

1 According to the basic competitive model, firms maximize profits.

2 Firms in competitive markets are price takers.

3 The marginal product is the last unit of output.

4 The principle of diminishing returns says that as more of one input is added, while other inputs remain unchanged, the marginal product of the added input diminishes.

5 With constant returns, if all inputs are increased by one-third, then output increases by one-third.

6 Costs associated with inputs that change as output changes are called variable costs.

7 Total costs are the sum of average and marginal costs.

8 If labor is the only variable input, then marginal cost equals the wage divided by the marginal product.

9 The average variable cost curve lies below the average total cost curve.

10 The marginal cost curve intersects the average cost curve at the minimum of the marginal cost curve.

11 Short-run average cost curves are typically U-shaped.

12 If there are economies of scale, the long-run average cost curve slopes downwards.

13 The long-run average cost curve is the lower boundary of all short-run average cost curves.

14 Economies of scope imply that producing a set of goods is cheaper than producing each of them singly.

15 If the price of an input rises, the firm will substitute other inputs to some extent, but its cost curves will still shift up.

Multiple Choice

1 In the basic competitive model, a firm that charges more than the going price
a will lose some of its customers slowly over time.
b will lose all its customers.
c may keep its customers if its goods are of higher quality than those of its competitors.
d will lose no customers if its price equals its marginal cost.
e none of the above.

2 The statement that firm in competitive markets are price takers means that
a firms accept the price set by the market.
b firms maximize profits.
c production has constant returns.
d marginal cost is upward sloping.
e average cost equals marginal cost at the minimum of average cost.

3 Profits equal
a fixed costs minus average costs.
b revenues minus fixed costs.
c revenues minus variable costs.
d price minus average cost.
e revenues minus total cost.

4 The marginal product of an input is
a the cost of producing one more unit of output.
b the extra output that results from hiring one more unit of the input.
c the cost required to hire one more unit of the input.
d output divided by the number of inputs used in the production process.
e a and c.

5 According to the principle of diminishing returns,
a as more of one input is added, the marginal product of the added input diminishes.

b as more of one input is added, holding other inputs unchanged, the marginal product of the added input diminishes.

c as more of the output is produced, the cost of production diminishes.

d as more of the output is produced, the marginal cost of production diminishes.

e none of the above.

6 If the production function exhibits increasing returns,

a the marginal product of input increases with the amount produced.

b the marginal cost increases with output.

c productivity is higher.

d the production function is downward sloping.

e *a* and *d*.

7 If, when the total quantity of all inputs is doubled, output exactly doubles, the production function exhibits

a constant returns.

b diminishing returns.

c increasing returns.

d economies of scale.

e none of the above.

8 Fixed inputs are inputs that

a cannot be moved.

b can be purchased in only one fixed configuration.

c can be purchased at a fixed price.

d do not depend on the level of output.

e none of the above.

9 Fixed costs

a are the costs associated with fixed inputs.

b do not change with the level of output.

c include payment to some variable factors.

d all of the above.

e *a* and *b*.

10 The relationship between the marginal product of labor and the marginal cost of output is:

a Marginal cost is the inverse of marginal product.

b Marginal cost equals the wage divided by the marginal product.

c Marginal cost is downward sloping when marginal product is downward sloping.

d Marginal cost is constant, but marginal product is subject to diminishing returns.

e *b* and *d*.

11 The principle of diminishing returns implies that

a marginal product diminishes as more of the input is hired.

b marginal cost increases with the level of output.

c productivity is higher in large firms.

d all of the above.

e *a* and *b*.

12 Total cost equals

a the sum of fixed and variable costs.

b the product of fixed and variable costs.

c the ratio of fixed and variable costs.

d the sum of average costs and average variable costs.

e none of the above.

13 When the marginal cost curve is above the average cost curve, the

a average cost curve is at its minimum.

b marginal cost curve is at its maximum.

c marginal cost curve is downward sloping.

d average cost curve is downward sloping.

e average cost curve is upward sloping.

14 The difference between the long and the short runs is

a that in the short run, there are constant returns but in the long run there are not.

b that in the long run, all inputs can be varied.

c three months.

d that in the short run, the average cost is decreasing but, in the long run, it is increasing.

e *a* and *b*.

15 In the short run, the typical average cost curve is

a upward sloping.

b downward sloping.

c U shaped.

d horizontal.

e none of the above.

16 The long-run average cost curve is

a the sum of the short-run average cost curves.

b the lower boundary of the short-run average cost curves.

c the upper boundary of the short-run average cost curves.

d horizontal.

e none of the above.

17 The long-run average cost curve

a may slope down because of overhead costs.

b may eventually slope up because of managerial problems.

c always exhibits increasing returns to scale.

d *a* and *c*.

e *a* and *b*.

18 The concept of increasing returns to scale means that

a it is more expensive to produce a variety of goods together than to produce them separately.

b it is more expensive to produce a large quantity than a small quantity.

c the average cost of production is lower when a larger quantity is produced.

d the marginal cost curve is downward sloping.

e *a* and *b*.

19 The concept of economies of scope means that

a it is less expensive to produce a variety of goods together than to produce them separately.

b it is more expensive to produce a large quantity than a small quantity.

c the average cost of production is lower when a larger quantity is produced.

d the marginal cost curve is downward sloping.

e *a* and *b*.

20 According to the principle of substitution,

   a marginal cost equals average cost at the minimum of average costs.

   b an increase in the price of an input will lead the firm to substitute other inputs.

   c a decrease in the price of an input will lead the firm to substitute other inputs.

   d if the firm does not know its marginal cost curve, it can substitute its average cost curve.

   e none of the above.

Completion

1 The relationship between the inputs used in production and the level of output is called the _____.

2 The increase in output that results from using one more unit of an input is the _____.

3 The principle of _____ says that as more and more of one input is added, while other inputs remain unchanged, the marginal product of the added input diminishes.

4 Costs that do not depend upon output are called _____ or overhead costs.

5 The _____ is the extra cost of producing one more unit of output.

6 The marginal cost curve intersects the average cost curve at the _____ of the _____ cost curve.

7 If marginal costs are above average costs, then producing an additional unit will _____ the average.

8 If the average cost is lower when the firm produces a larger quantity, then there are economies of _____.

9 If it is less expensive to produce a variety of goods together than to produce each good separately, then there are economies of _____.

10 An increase in the price of one input will lead a firm to substitute other inputs. This is a statement of the _____.

Answers to Self-Test

True or False

1	t	6	t	1	t
2	t	7	f	12	t
3	f	8	t	13	t
4	t	9	t	14	t
5	t	10	f	15	t

Multiple Choice

1	*b*	6	*a*	11	*e*	16	*b*		
2	*e*	7	*a*	12	*a*	17	*e*		
3	*e*	8	*d*	13	*e*	18	*c*		
4	*b*	9	*e*	14	*b*	19	*a*		
5	*b*	10	*b*	15	*c*	20	*b*		

Completion

1 production function
2 marginal product
3 diminishing returns
4 fixed
5 marginal cost
6 minimum, average
7 raise
8 scale
9 scope
10 principle of substitution

Doing Economics: Tools and Practice Problems

There is quite a bit of technical detail in this chapter, including production functions and a host of cost curves. First, we will explore the production function, calculating the marginal and average product and plotting the curves. It is important to understand how the shape of the production function exhibits diminishing, constant, or increasing returns. Next, we turn our attention to the cost curves; we calculate the various cost concepts and plot the curves. Again, it is important to understand the relationships between the curves and the economic meaning of the shapes of the curves.

THE PRODUCTION FUNCTION

The relationship between inputs and outputs is given by the production function. It shows how much output will result from the efficient use of each possible quantity of the inputs. Economists are interested also in the marginal product, the extra returns brought about by using one more input, and the average product, output per input. In order to understand the decisions of firms, you must understand the production function and its relationship to marginal and average product. Table 7.1 lists the key facts and Tool Kit 7.1 shows how to calculate and graph the key concepts.

Table 7.1 Production Function

The marginal product is the slope of the production function:
marginal product = change in number of inputs
change in output.
If returns are diminishing,
  the marginal product is decreasing and
  the slope of the production function is becoming flatter.
If returns are constant,
  the marginal product is constant and
  the slope of the production function is constant.
If returns are increasing,
  the marginal product is increasing and
  the slope of the production function is becoming steeper.

Tool Kit 7.1 Calculating and Graphing Marginal and Average Products

The production function summarizes the relationship between inputs and outputs. It is important to understand its relationship with the marginal and average product, which can be calculated from the information in the production function and also can be derived from the graph of the production function. Here is how it is done.

Step one: Identify and graph the production function.

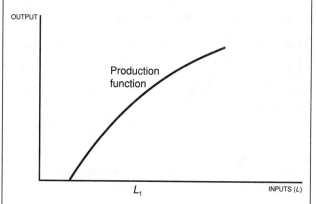

Step two: Calculate the average product, which is output per unit of the input:

average product = output/number of inputs.

Step three: Calculate the marginal product, which is the extra output resulting from the use of one more unit of the input.

marginal product = change in output/change in input.

The marginal product equals the slope of the production function.

1 (Worked problem: marginal and average products) Table 7.2 gives the production function for keyboards at Tek-Tek computer products.

a Compute the average and marginal product, and fill in the table.

b Plot the production function. For each point, verify that the slope of the line from the origin to the production function equals the average product.

Table 7.2

Number of workers	Output	Average product	Marginal product
1	80		
2	150		
3	210		
4	260		
5	300		

c Between each two adjacent points on the production function, verify that the slope equals the marginal product.

d Does the production function exhibit diminishing, constant, or increasing returns?

Step-by-step solution

Step one (*a*): Identify and graph the production function. This is given in Table 7.2.

Step two: Calculate. The average product is output divided by the number of workers. If output is 80, the average product is $80/1 = 80$. Enter this number. If output is 150, the average product is $150/2 = 75$. Complete the average product column. The result is given in Table 7.3.

Table 7.3

Number of workers	Output	Average product	Marginal product
1	80	80	80
2	150	75	70
3	210	70	60
4	260	65	50
5	300	60	40

Step three: Calculate the marginal product. The marginal product is the extra output resulting from using one more input. The marginal product of the first worker is 80. Enter this number. When the second worker is used, output rises to 150. The marginal product of this worker is $150 - 80 = 70$. Enter this number. Complete the marginal product column. Table 7.3 gives the result.

Step four (*b*): Plot the production function.

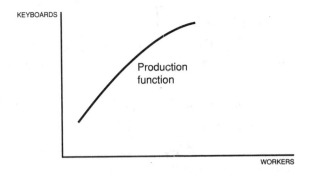

Step five (*c*): Verify that the slope of the production function is the marginal product. The slope of the production function between *A* and *B*, where output is 300 and the number of workers is 5, is (300 − 260)/(5 − 4) = 40, which is the marginal product of the fourth worker.

Step six (*d*): The marginal product is decreasing; this indicates diminishing returns.

2 (Practice problem: marginal and average products) Table 7.4 gives the production function for the insect spray Nobeetle at Bugout Pesticide Company.

Table 7.4

Number of workers	Output	Average product	Marginal product
1	1,200		
2	2,200		
3	3,000		
4	3,600		
5	4,000		

a Compute the average and marginal products, and fill in the table.
b Plot the production function.
c Between each two adjacent points on the production function, verify that the slope equals the marginal product.
d Does the production function exhibit diminishing, constant, or increasing returns?

3 (Practice problem: marginal and average products) For the following production functions, answer parts *a* through *d* in problem 2.
a Bedford Waterbeds

Number of workers	Output	Average product	Marginal product
1	24		
2	42		
3	57		
4	68		
5	75		

b Worry-Free Insurance

Number of sellers	Policies	Average product	Marginal product
10	200		
20	500		
30	700		
40	800		
50	850		

COST

A firm's costs are its payments to inputs. Some of these inputs are fixed and some are variable. We are interested in the total cost curves and also in average and marginal costs. Thus we have many cost curves. Table 7.5 summarizes the important information about cost curves and Tool Kit 7.2 shows how to calculate and graph the key concepts.

Table 7.5 Cost Curves

Variable cost is parallel to the total cost curve, and below it by the amount of fixed cost:

variable cost = total cost − fixed cost.

Marginal cost is the slope of the total cost curve:

marginal cost = change in total cost/
                change in output
If returns are diminishing,
    the marginal cost is increasing and
    the slope of the total cost curve is becoming steeper.
If returns are constant,
    the marginal cost is constant and
    the slope of the total cost curve is constant.
If returns are increasing,
    the marginal cost is decreasing and
    the slope of the total cost curve is becoming flatter.
If marginal cost is below average cost,
    the average cost curve is decreasing.
If marginal cost equals average cost,
    the average cost curve is at its minimum.
If marginal cost is above average cost,
    the average cost curve is increasing.

Tool Kit 7.2 Calculating and Graphing Cost Measures

There are two sets of cost curves: the total curves (total cost, fixed cost, and variable cost) and the average-marginal curves (average cost, marginal cost). It is important to be able to calculate each of the cost concepts and also to recognize their relationships on the graphs. Follow along.

Step one: Identify and graph the total cost curve.

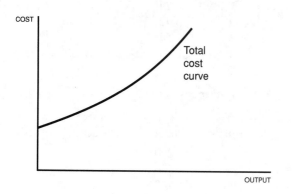

Step two: Calculate and graph the variable cost curve:

variable cost = total cost − fixed cost.

The variable cost curve is parallel to the total cost curve, lying below it by the amount of fixed costs.

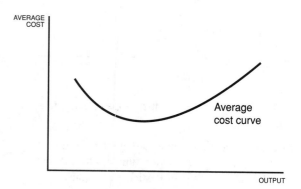

Step three: Calculate and graph the average cost curve: average cost = total cost/output.

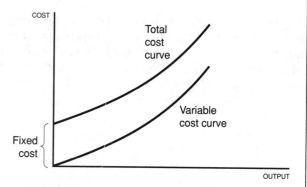

Step four: Calculate and graph the marginal cost curve: marginal cost = change in cost/change in output.

Marginal cost is the slope of the total cost curve.

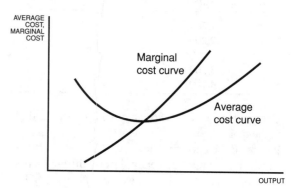

Table 7.5 summarizes the key information about cost curves.

4 (Worked problem: cost curves) The total fixed costs at Stay-Brite Cleaning Company are $100,000. Table 7.6 gives their total costs for different levels of output measured in truckloads of Stay-Brite Cleaning Solution.

  a Compute variable, average, and marginal cost, and enter in the table.

  b Plot the total cost and variable cost curves on one diagram, and verify the relationships given in Table 7.5.

Table 7.6

Output	Total cost	Variable cost	Average cost	Marginal cost
1,000	$180,000			
2,000	$280,000			
3,000	$420,000			
4,000	$600,000			
5,000	$800,000			

  c Plot the average cost and marginal cost curves, and verify the marginal-average relationship.

  d Do the cost curves exhibit increasing, constant, or diminishing returns?

Step-by-step solution

Step one (*a*): Identify and graph the total cost curve.

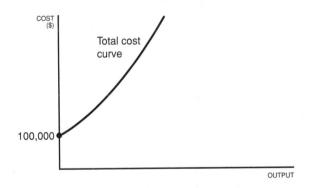

Step two: Calculate and graph the variable cost curve. Variable cost is just the difference between total cost and total fixed cost. The variable cost of 1,000 units is $180,000 − $100,000 = $80,000. Enter this number. Complete the variable cost column.

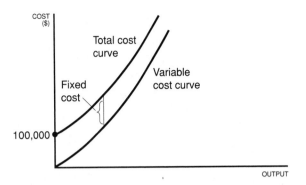

Step three: Calculate and graph the average cost curve. Average cost is total cost divided by output. The average cost of 1,000 units is $180,000/1,000 = $180. Enter this number. Complete the average cost column.

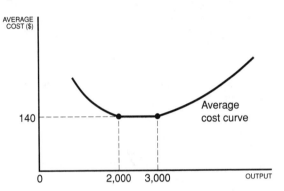

Step four: Calculate and graph the marginal cost curve. Marginal cost is the extra cost of producing one more unit. The marginal cost per unit for the first 1,000 units is $80,000/1,000 = $80. Enter this number, and continue to fill in the column. The complete information appears in Table 7.7.

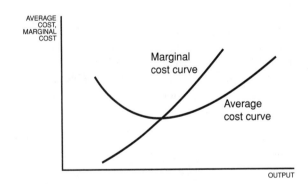

Table 7.7

Output	Total cost	Variable cost	Average cost	Marginal cost
1,000	$180,000	$ 80,000	$180	$ 80
2,000	$280,000	$180,000	$140	$100
3,000	$420,000	$320,000	$140	$140
4,000	$600,000	$500,000	$150	$180
5,000	$800,000	$700,000	$160	$200

Step five (b): Choose a point on the total cost curve, and verify the relationships.

Variable cost is parallel to total cost. For example, between *A* and *B*, the slope of the total cost curve is ($600,000 − $420,000)/(4,000 − 3,000) = 180. The slope of the variable cost curve for the same levels of output is ($500,000 − $320,000)/(4,000 − 3,000) = 180.

The variable cost curve lies below the total cost curve by the amount of fixed cost. The difference all along the curves is $100,000, which is fixed cost.

The slope of the total cost curve equals marginal cost. Between *A* and *B*, the slope is 180, which is the marginal cost at 4,000 workers.

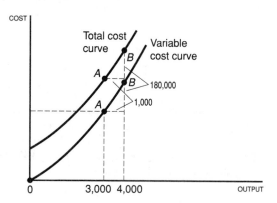

Step six (c): Plot the average and marginal cost curves, and verify the average-marginal relationship. As you can see, marginal cost is above average cost at *A*, where average cost is rising; they are equal at *B*, which is the minimum of average cost; and marginal cost is above average cost at *C*, where average cost is rising.

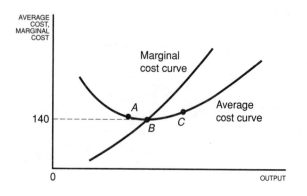

Step seven: The cost curves exhibit diminishing returns. Marginal cost is increasing, and total cost is becoming steeper.

5 (Practice problem: cost curves). The fixed costs at Pestle Mortar Company are $50,000. Table 7.8 gives their costs for different levels of output measured in mortars.

Table 7.8

Output	Total cost	Variable cost	Average cost	Marginal cost
1,000	$ 250,000			
2,000	$ 500,000			
3,000	$ 800,000			
4,000	$1,200,000			
5,000	$1,800,000			

a Compute variable, average, and marginal costs, and enter in the table.
b Plot the total cost and variable cost curves on one diagram, and verify the relationships given in Table 7.5.
c Plot the average cost and marginal cost curves, and verify the marginal-average relationship.
d Do the cost curves exhibit increasing, constant, or diminishing returns?

6 (Practice problem: cost curves) For the following cost data, answer parts *a* through *d* in question 5.
a Fixed costs are $1,000.

Output	Total cost	Variable cost	Average cost	Marginal cost
10	$1,500			
20	$2,200			
30	$3,000			
40	$4,000			
50	$6,000			

b Fixed costs are $0.

Output	Total cost	Variable cost	Average cost	Marginal cost
100	$1,000			
200	$1,800			
300	$2,400			
400	$2,800			
500	$3,200			
600	$3,600			

c Fixed costs are $80,000.

Output	Total cost	Variable cost	Average cost	Marginal cost
1	$140,000			
2	$180,000			
3	$220,000			
4	$260,000			
5	$300,000			
6	$340,000			

Answers to Problems

2   *a*   The marginal and average products are given in Table 7.9.

Table 7.9

Number of workers	Output	Average product	Marginal product
1	1,200	1,200	1,200
2	2,200	1,100	1,000
3	3,000	1,000	800
4	3,600	900	600
5	4,000	800	400

b   The production function is drawn in the figure.
c   The marginal product of the 4th worker, is 600, shown as the slope between points *B* and *C,*

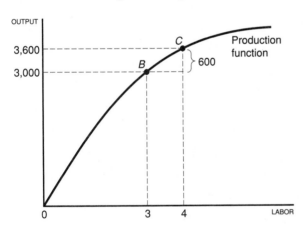

d   The production function exhibits diminishing returns.

3   *a*   Bedford Waterbeds—diminishing returns

Number of workers	Output	Average product	Marginal product
1	24	24	24
2	42	21	18
3	57	19	15
4	68	17	11
5	75	15	7

b   Worry-Free Insurance—diminishing returns

Number of sellers	Policies	Average product	Marginal product
10	200	20.0	20
20	500	25.0	30
30	700	23.3	20
40	800	20.0	10
50	850	17.0	5

5   *a*   The completed table is given in Table 7.10.

Table 7.10

Output	Total cost	Variable cost	Average cost	Marginal cost
1,000	$ 250,000	$ 200,000	$250	$200
2,000	$ 500,000	$ 450,000	$250	$250
3,000	$ 800,000	$ 750,000	$267	$300
4,000	$1,200,000	$1,150,000	$300	$400
5,000	$1,800,000	$1,750,000	$360	$600

b   The diagram shows the total cost and variable cost curves. The variable cost curve is parallel and lies below the total cost curve by $50,000, which is the amount of fixed cost.

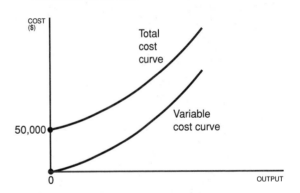

c   The diagram shows the average and marginal cost curves. Average and marginal costs are equal at $250, which is the minimum of the average cost curve. Average cost rises after this point, while marginal cost hovers above.

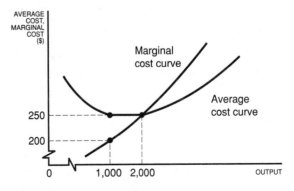

d   The cost curves exhibit diminishing returns.

6 The completed cost tables appear below.

   a These cost curves show diminishing returns.

Output	Total cost	Variable cost	Average cost	Marginal cost
10	$1,500	$ 500	$150	$50
20	$2,200	$1,200	$110	$70
30	$3,000	$2,000	$100	$80
40	$4,000	$3,000	$100	$100
50	$6,000	$5,000	$120	$200

   b These cost curves show increasing returns.

Output	Total cost	Variable cost	Average cost	Marginal cost
100	$1,000	$1,000	$10.00	$10
200	$1,800	$1,800	$ 9.00	$ 8
300	$2,400	$2,400	$ 8.00	$ 6
400	$2,800	$2,800	$ 7.00	$ 4
500	$3,200	$3,200	$ 6.50	$ 4
600	$3,600	$3,600	$ 6.00	$ 4

c These cost curves show increasing returns until output equals 2, and constant returns thereafter.

Output	Total cost	Variable cost	Average cost	Marginal cost
1	$140,000	$ 60,000	$140,000	$60,000
2	$180,000	$100,000	$ 90,000	$40,000
3	$220,000	$140,000	$ 73,333	$40,000
4	$260,000	$180,000	$ 65,000	$40,000
5	$300,000	$220,000	$ 60,000	$40,000
6	$340,000	$260,000	$ 56,667	$40,000

CHAPTER 8 | The Competitive Firm

Chapter Review

This chapter moves the discussion from the firm's costs to decisions firms must make regarding production. In the process, it shows the role of the firm in the competitive model as a supplier in product markets. The chapter also explains why and when new firms will enter an industry and why and when existing firms will shut down. Each of these issues requires carefully distinguishing opportunity costs from sunk costs, and profits from rents. This close examination of the firm's production decision completes the discussion of the product markets.

ESSENTIAL CONCEPTS

1 Firms choose output to **maximize profits.** Profit is the difference between total revenue and total costs. The output decision can be illustrated in two ways. One way, shown in Figure 8.1A, is to draw the total revenue and total cost curves and find the quantity where the total **revenue curve** is above the total cost curve by the greatest amount. At this point, the curves are parallel and their slopes are equal. The second way, shown in panel B, uses the marginal revenue curve. The slope of the total revenue curve is **marginal revenue**, which for the competitive firm equals the price of its product. The slope of the total cost curve is marginal cost. Therefore, at this point, marginal revenue (price) equals marginal cost, and profit maximization can be shown by the intersection of these two curves.

2 If the market price for a good or service exceeds the minimum average cost, then it pays new firms to enter the market. In deciding whether to *exit* the market, however, a firm must pay attention to those costs it cannot recover.

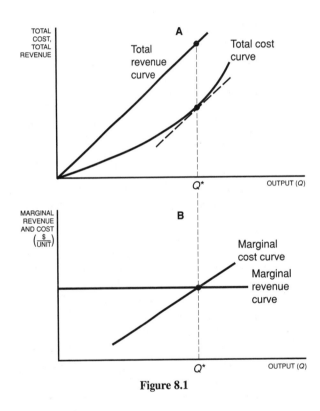

Figure 8.1

Costs that the firm must pay whether or not it leaves the market are called **sunk costs.** The firm should stay in the market whenever it can earn revenues greater than all the costs not sunk. If all the fixed costs are nonrecoverable sunk costs, then the firm will exit when price falls below the minimum of the average variable cost curve.

3 The *supply curve of the firm* is the marginal cost curve above the minimum price needed to keep the firm from exiting. The *market supply curve* is the sum of the quantities supplied of all firms in the market, and it takes

into account both the adjustments made by existing firms and the new entrants attracted to the market as the price rises. This curve is more elastic in the long run than in the short run, because existing firms have time to adjust to the lowest-cost production techniques and new firms have time to enter the market and produce.

4 When the going price in a competitive industry exceeds the minimum of the average cost, new firms will enter. The reason is that they will be able to earn higher profits in this industry than elsewhere in the economy. (Recall that the normal rate of return to capital is included in average cost.) Competition thus forces all firms to produce at minimum cost and drives any inefficient firms out of the market. In a similar vein, the theory of **contestable markets** argues that the threat of entry alone will compel a firm to earn zero profits even if it is the only one in the industry.

5 Firms exit an industry when they can no longer earn enough revenues to cover their costs, but the focus is on recoverable costs. Sunk costs are ignored in making the exit decision. The existence of significant sunk costs breaks down the theory of contestible market. The threat of entry is not so strong if the entrant risks losing its investment.

BEHIND THE ESSENTIAL CONCEPTS

1 It is important that cost include all opportunity costs of production borne by the firm. Not only are such explicit costs as wages, energy, raw materials, and interest included, but also more subtle *opportunity costs* are taken into account, such as the value of the entrepreneur's time or the alternative earnings on the equity invested by the owners of the firm. These are considered opportunity costs because if the firm did not produce, the entrepreneur would devote time to some other activity, and the owners would take their investment capital elsewhere.

When a firm is making zero *economic* profits, its revenues are sufficient to cover all costs, including normal returns on the invested financial capital. An economist would say that the firm is only making enough to compensate the owners for the opportunity cost of putting their money into the firm. An accountant would view the situation differently, saying that a firm earning normal returns was actually making positive accounting profits.

2 Another difference between the way economists and accountants view profits concerns rent. **Economic rent** is the return to anything that is supplied inelastically. For example, suppose a firm's superior location enables it to earn 50 percent more than its competitors. An accountant would say that this firm's profits are 50

percent higher. An economist would call this extra return a rent, because the firm's earnings are higher than the minimum necessary to induce it to stay in its location. Although land is a good example, the concept of rent applies to any payment to a factor of production above the minimum necessary to bring the factor on to the market.

3 Sunk costs and fixed costs are distinct ideas. *Sunk costs* cannot be recovered no matter what the firm does. The firm can shut down production, sell off all its assets, and even go out of business, but it cannot recover its sunk costs. *Fixed costs* do not change as output changes, but they may be recoverable if the firm exits the industry. For example, the firm may own a plant, and the alternative earnings (the opportunity cost) of its plant do not depend on whether the firm produces a little or a great deal of output. If the firm can sell the factory when it exits the industry, then the costs of the plant are fixed but not sunk.

4 The competitive firm has four basic decisions to make: when to enter, when to exit, how much to produce, and how many inputs to hire. Table 8.1 summarizes the first three. The latter appears the next chapter.

Table 8.1

Entry	Enter when price > minimum average cost.
Exit	Exit when revenues < nonrecoverable costs.
Supply	Produce the quantity of output for which price equals marginal cost.

SELF-TEST

True or False

1 The firm is choosing the profit-maximizing level of output when price equals marginal cost.
2 The relationship between revenue and output is shown by the production function.
3 The slope of the revenue curve equals marginal revenue.
4 In the competitive model, marginal revenue is less than price because increasing output leads to a fall in price.
5 All fixed costs are sunk, but not all sunk costs are fixed.
6 Accounting profits are always less than economic profits.
7 In the long run in a competitive industry, economic profits are zero for any potential entrant.
8 Firms exit the industry when price falls below the minimum of the average cost.
9 A firm will enter an industry if the price is above the minimum of the average variable cost curve.
10 Economic rent is any payment to an input in excess of that needed to keep the input in its current use.

11 Land is the only input that can earn economic rent.
12 The long-run supply is more elastic than the short-run supply for the industry but not for the individual firm.
13 The long-run supply curve is the sum of the supply curves of individual firms, including those that enter at high prices.
14 Even if a firm's supply curve is upward sloping in the short run, it may be perfectly elastic in the long run.
15 Correctly measured, total cost should include all opportunity costs of operating.

Multiple Choice

1 Marginal revenue
   a is less than price for the competitive firm because as it sells more output, it must lower the price.
   b equals price for the competitive firm.
   c is the revenue that the firm receives for selling another unit of output.
   d is the extra profit that the firm receives from selling another unit of output, after accounting for all opportunity costs.
   e b and c.

2 The firm supplies the profit-maximizing level of output when
   a marginal revenue equals price.
   b marginal revenue equals marginal cost.
   c economic profits are zero.
   d accounting profits are zero.
   e sunk costs equal fixed costs.

3 The extra cost of producing an additional unit of output is called
   a marginal cost.
   b fixed cost.
   c overhead cost.
   d sunk cost.
   e marginal revenue.

4 It pays a firm to enter a market whenever
   a the market price is greater than the minimum average cost at which the firm can produce.
   b the firm can earn revenues greater than any nonrecoverable costs.
   c price is greater than the minimum of the average variable cost curve.
   d price equals marginal cost.
   e marginal revenue equals marginal cost.

5 The firm should exit the market whenever
   a it cannot earn revenues equal to at least its recoverable costs.
   b price is less than marginal cost.
   c price is less than the minimum of the average cost curve.
   d price is less than the minimum of the average variable cost curve.
   e all of the above.

6 Sunk costs are
   a costs that do not change when output changes.
   b the costs of starting the business.
   c nonrecoverable costs.
   d variable costs.
   e opportunity costs.

7 Which of the following is true?
   a Accounting costs are always greater than economic costs.
   b Economic costs are always greater than accounting costs.
   c Accounting profits are always greater than economic profits.
   d Economic profits are always greater than accounting profits.
   e None of the above.

8 The firm's economic costs include
   a the opportunity cost of the time of the entrepreneur.
   b the revenue that could be earned in alternative uses by the assets that the firm owns.
   c the return on the equity invested in the firm by the owners.
   d depreciation on company-owned buildings and machinery.
   e all of the above

9 The long-run supply curve for the industry is
   a perfectly elastic.
   b more elastic than the short-run supply curve.
   c less elastic than the short-run supply curve.
   d the lower boundary of the short-run supply curves.
   e the sum of the short-run supply curves.

10 Economic rent refers to
   a economic profit minus sunk cost.
   b any payment to an input above the minimum needed to keep the input in its present use.
   c payments from tenants to landlords.
   d the wages of especially skilled labor.
   e revenues received by efficient firms.

11 In the basic competitive model, profits are driven to zero. This means that
   a revenues are just enough to cover all nonrecoverable costs.
   b revenues are just enough to cover all costs, including the opportunity cost of invested financial capital.
   c price equals the minimum of the average variable cost curve.
   d accounting profits are equal to zero.
   e b and d.

12 When price is greater than the minimum of the average variable cost curve, the firm
   a enters the market.
   b exits the market.
   c may continue or exit depending on the magnitude of sunk costs.

d shuts down production but does not exit.

e enters the market only if overhead costs are zero.

13 The market supply curve is

   a the sum of the quantities of the supply curves of all of the firms.

   b less elastic than the supply curves of all of the firms.

   c the marginal cost curve of the last firm to enter the market.

   d always horizontal.

   e none of the above.

14 The relationship between revenue and output is shown by the

   a average cost curve.

   b average revenue curve.

   c marginal revenue curve.

   d revenue curve.

   e cost curve.

15 Which of the following statements is *not* true?

   a In the very short run, firms may not be able to adjust output.

   b In the short run, firms may be able to adjust variable inputs such as labor.

   c In the long run, firms may adjust the size of their plant and equipment.

   d In the long run, new firms may enter.

   e All of the above are true.

16 If a firm reports a 10 percent return on its capital and could earn 4 percent by investing its capital elsewhere, then its economic rate of return is

   a 10 percent.

   b 4 percent.

   c 14 percent.

   d 6 percent.

   e 16 percent.

17 If all of a firm's fixed costs are sunk, then it shuts down when

   a price is less than marginal cost.

   b price is less than the minimum of the average cost curve.

   c price is less than the minimum of the average variable cost curve.

   d accounting profits fall below zero.

   e economic profits fall below zero.

18 If none of a firm's fixed costs are sunk, then it shuts down when

   a price is less than marginal cost.

   b price is less than the minimum of the average cost curve.

   c price is less than the minimum of the average variable cost curve.

   d economic profits fall below zero.

   e *b* and *d*.

19 If a firm with a U-shaped short-run average cost curve doubles its output by doubling the number of plants and keeps its average cost the same, then the long-run supply is

   a perfectly elastic.

   b perfectly inelastic.

   c upward sloping.

   d downward sloping.

   e none of the above.

20 A firm paid $20 million to build its plant, but it could sell the plant for only $5 million. Its sunk costs equal

   a $20 million.

   b $5 million.

   c $25 million.

   d $15 million.

   e $0.

Completion

1 The extra revenue that a firm receives for selling another unit of output is the _____.

2 In the basic competitive model, the marginal revenue equals the _____.

3 The extra cost that the firm bears for producing another unit of output is the _____.

4 The level of output that maximizes profits is found by setting _____ equal to _____.

5 The supply curve of the competitive firm is the same as the _____ curve when price is high enough to keep the firm in the market.

6 Costs that are not recoverable are called _____ costs.

7 Economic profits equal revenues received in excess of all _____ costs of operating the firm.

8 The demand for inputs is the _____ of the _____.

9 New firms enter the industry whenever price is greater than the minimum of the _____ curve.

10 The difference between the price actually paid and the price needed to induce a firm to produce a good is called _____.

Answers to Self-Test

True or False

1	t	6	f	11	f
2	f	7	t	12	f
3	t	8	f	13	t
4	f	9	f	14	t
5	f	10	t	15	t

Multiple Choice

1	e	6	c	11	b	16	d
2	b	7	e	12	c	17	c
3	a	8	e	13	a	18	e
4	a	9	b	14	d	19	a
5	a	10	b	15	e	20	d

Completion

1 marginal revenue
2 price
3 marginal cost
4 price, marginal cost
5 marginal cost
6 sunk
7 opportunity
8 value, marginal product
9 average cost
10 economic rent

Doing Economics: Tools and Practice Problems

The firm's decision of how much output to supply requires marginal benefit and marginal cost reasoning. In this section, we will do problems involving the profit-maximizing quantity of output. Next, we will investigate the entry and exit decisions, reviewing opportunity and sunk costs. A good understanding of costs allows us to derive the entire supply curve of output.

SUPPLY OF OUTPUT

Firms must decide how much output to offer for sale. This supply decision involves balancing marginal revenue and marginal cost. Competitive firms are price takers, so marginal revenue equals price. All this implies that price must equal marginal cost, and this is the rule for profit maximization in the supply of output. Tool Kit 8.1 shows how to solve the problem of how much output to supply.

Tool Kit 8.1 Finding the Quantity of Output to Supply

The quantity of output that maximizes the firm's profits is found by setting marginal revenue equal to marginal cost. When the firm is a price taker, the marginal revenue equals the product price. The rule is then to find the quantity for which price equals marginal cost.

Step one: Calculate the marginal cost for each unit of output.

Step two: Identify the market price.

Step three: Find the greatest level of output for which price equals marginal cost. This is the quantity supplied.

---

1 (Worked problem: quantity supplied) Barbara's Carpet Cleaners has fixed costs of $100 per month and a total cost curve as given in Table 8.2. Output is the number of carpets cleaned.

Table 8.2

Output	Total cost
10	$ 200
20	$ 320
30	$ 460
40	$ 620
50	$ 800
60	$1,000

a The current price for cleaning a carpet is $18. How many carpets must be cleaned to maximize profits? What will the profit be?

b Suppose that the price falls to $14. Calculate the profit-maximizing output and the total profits.

Step-by-step solution

Step one (*a*): Marginal cost is the extra cost of cleaning another carpet. When output is increased from 0 to 10, total costs increase by $200 − $100 = $100; therefore, the marginal cost is $100/10 = $10. Derive the marginal cost curve shown in Table 8.3.

Table 8.3

Output	Total cost	Marginal cost
10	$ 200	10
20	$ 320	12
30	$ 460	14
40	$ 620	16
50	$ 800	18
60	$1,000	20

Step two: Identify the market price. It is $18.

Step three: Find the greatest level of output for which price equals marginal cost. The $18 price equals marginal cost when output is 50.

Step four: Calculate profits. Profits equal revenues minus costs. Revenues equal $900 (50 × $18); profits equal $900 − $800 = $100. So the firm makes profits equal to $100.

Step five (*b*): If the price falls to $14, then price equals marginal cost at 30 units. Profits = (30 × $14) − $460 = −$40, and the firm loses $40.

2 (Practice problem: quantity supplied) The fixed cost for Martin Block, Inc., is $10,000. The company's cost curve is given in Table 8.4.

Table 8.4

Output	Total cost	Marginal cost
10,000	$21,000	
20,000	$32,100	
30,000	$43,300	
40,000	$54,600	
50,000	$66,000	
60,000	$77,500	

a The current price for blocks is $1.12. Find the profit-maximizing quantity of blocks to produce. What will the profit be?

b Suppose that the price rises to $1.15. Calculate the profit-maximizing output and the total profits.

3 (Practice problem: quantity supplied) For each of the following, find the profit-maximizing output level, and calculate total profits.

a Fixed costs = $40,000; price = $600.

Output	Total cost	Marginal cost
100	$ 80,000	
200	$120,000	
300	$170,000	
400	$230,000	
500	$300,000	
600	$380,000	
700	$470,000	

b Fixed costs = $900; price = $3.00.

Output	Total cost	Marginal cost
1,000	$ 1,900	
2,000	$ 2,900	
3,000	$ 4,600	
4,000	$ 6,600	
5,000	$ 9,400	
6,000	$12,400	
7,000	$16,000	
8,000	$20,000	

c Fixed costs = $0; price = $80.

Output	Total cost	Marginal cost
1	$ 40	
2	$ 90	
3	**$150**	
4	$210	
5	$280	
6	$360	
7	$450	
8	$550	

ENTRY AND EXIT

A firm should seize the opportunity and enter an industry whenever it can make positive (or at least zero) economic profits. This occurs when price is greater than the minimum of the average cost curve. A firm should give up and exit an industry whenever it can no longer earn revenues in excess of its nonrecoverable costs. If all fixed costs are recoverable, then the firm exits whenever price falls below the minimum of the average cost curve. If none of the fixed costs are recoverable, then the firm exits when price falls below the minimum of the average *variable* cost curve. If some costs are recoverable, the exit price lies somewhere in between. Tool Kit 8.2 explores this idea.

Tool Kit 8.2 Determining Entry and Exit Prices

Firms enter the market when the price rises above the minimum average cost. They exit when the price falls below the minimum average recoverable cost. Follow this procedure to find these prices.

Step one: Calculate the average cost for each level of output.

Step two: Find the minimum average cost; this is the entry price. When the price is greater than or equal to the minimum average cost, then the firm should enter the market.

Step three: Identify all costs that are not sunk (nonrecoverable).

Step four: Calculate the average of the costs that are not sunk.

Step five: Find the minimum average nonsunk cost; this is the exit price. When the price falls below this level, the firm should exit the market.

---

4 (Worked problem: entry and exit prices) Let's return to Barbara's Carpet Cleaners in problem 1. The total cost curve is given in Table 8.5.

Table 8.5

Output	Total cost
10	$ 200
20	$ 320
30	$ 460
40	$ 620
50	$ 800
60	$1,000

a Find the entry price, which is the minimum price that will induce the firm to enter the market.

b Assume that all the fixed costs are sunk. Find the exit price, which is the maximum price that will induce the firm to exit the market.

c Now assume that $50 of the fixed cost is recoverable. Find the exit price.

Step-by-step solution

Step one (a): Calculate the average cost for each level of output, and enter in the table. The average cost at 10 carpets is $200/10 = $20. Continue to fill in the column as in Table 8.6.

Table 8.6

Output	Total cost	Average cost
10	$ 200	$20.00
20	$ 320	$16.00
30	$ 460	$15.33
40	$ 620	$15.50
50	$ 800	$16.00
60	$1,000	$16.66

Step two: The minimum of the average cost curve is $15.33, and this is the entry price. This is the answer to part a.

Step three (b): Identify the costs that are not sunk. If all fixed costs are sunk, then only the variable costs can be recovered. In this case, the exit price is the minimum of the average variable cost curve. First, compute variable cost by subtracting fixed costs from total cost. The variable cost for 10 units of output is $200 − $100 = $100. Continue to fill in this column as in Table 8.7.

Table 8.7

Output	Total cost	Variable cost
10	$ 200	$100
20	$ 320	$220
30	$ 460	$360
40	$ 620	$520
50	$ 800	$700
60	$1,000	$900

Step four: Compute average variable cost. For 10 carpets, the average variable cost is $100/10 = $10. Enter the results as given in Table 8.8.

Table 8.8

Output	Total cost	Variable cost	Average variable cost
10	$ 200	$100	$10
20	$ 320	$220	$11
30	$ 460	$360	$12
40	$ 620	$520	$13
50	$ 800	$700	$14
60	$1,000	$900	$15

Step five: The minimum of the average variable cost curve is $10; therefore, the firm should exit when the price falls below $10. This is the answer to part b.

Step six (c): Only $50 is sunk; thus, the firm exits when revenues fall below variable costs plus $50. To find the recoverable costs, simply add $50 to the variable cost. Next, find the average of these numbers, and the minimum of these averages is the exit price. The results appear in Table 8.9.

Table 8.9

Output	Variable cost	Recoverable cost	Average recoverable cost
10	$100	$150	$15.00
20	$220	$270	$13.50
30	$360	$410	$13.66
40	$520	$570	$14.25
50	$700	$750	$15.00
60	$900	$950	$15.83

The minimum of the average recoverable cost column is $13.50, which is the exit price. When the price is $13.50, the firm loses $50, which means that revenues cover all but the nonrecoverable costs.

5 (Practice problem: entry and exit prices) Now let's return to Martin Block in problem 2. The total cost curve is reprinted in Table 8.10. Fixed costs equal $10,000.

Table 8.10

Output	Total cost
10,000	$21,000
20,000	$32,100
30,000	$43,300
40,000	$54,600
50,000	$66,000
60,000	$77,500

a Find the entry price, which is the minimum price that will induce the firm to enter the market.

b Assume that all of the fixed costs are sunk. Find the exit price, which is the maximum price that will induce the firm to exit the market.

6 (Practice problem: entry and exit prices) Find the entry price and the exit price for the firms in problem 3. Assume that all the fixed costs are sunk.

Answers to Problems

2 a The marginal cost is given in Table 8.11. When the price is $1.12, output is 30,000, and profits equal ($1.12 × 30,000) − $43,300 = −$9,400.

Table 8.11

Output	Total cost	Marginal cost
10,000	$21,000	—
20,000	$32,100	$1.11
30,000	$43,300	$1.12
40,000	$54,600	$1.13
50,000	$66,000	$1.14
60,000	$77,500	$1.15

b When the price is $1.15, output is 60,000, and profits equal ($1.15 × 60,000) − $77,500 = −$8,500.

3 *a* The marginal cost is given in Table 8.12.

Table 8.12

Output	Total cost	Marginal cost
100	$ 80,000	$400
200	$120,000	$400
300	$170,000	$500
400	$230,000	$600
500	$300,000	$700
600	$380,000	$800
700	$470,000	$900

Output = 400; profits = ($600 × 400) − $230,000 = $10,000.

b The marginal cost is given in Table 8.13.

Table 8.13

Output	Total cost	Marginal cost
1,000	$ 1,900	$1.00
2,000	$ 2,900	$1.00
3,000	$ 4,600	$1.70
4,000	$ 6,600	$2.00
5,000	$ 9,400	$2.80
6,000	$12,400	$3.00
7,000	$16,000	$3.60
8,000	$20,000	$4.00

Output = 6,000; profits = ($3.00 × 6,000) − $12,400 = $5,600.

c The marginal cost is given in Table 8.14.

Table 8.14

Output	Total cost	Marginal cost
1	$ 40	$ 40
2	$ 90	$ 50
3	$150	$ 60
4	$210	$ 60
5	$280	$ 70
6	$360	$ 80
7	$450	$ 90
8	$550	$100

Output = 6; profits = (6 × $80) − $360 = $120.

5 The cost measures are given in Table 8.15.

Table 8.15

Output	Total cost	Average cost	Variable cost	Average variable cost
10,000	$21,000	$2.10	$11,000	$1.10
20,000	$32,100	$1.61	$22,100	$1.11
30,000	$43,300	$1.43	$33,300	$1.11
40,000	$54,600	$1.37	$44,600	$1.12
50,000	$66,000	$1.32	$56,000	$1.12
60,000	$77,500	$1.29	$67,500	$1.13

a Entry price = $1.29.

b Exit price = $1.10.

6 *a* The cost measures appear in Table 8.16.

Table 8.16

Output	Total cost	Average cost	Variable cost	Average variable cost
100	$ 80,000	$800	$ 40,000	$400
200	$120,000	$600	$ 80,000	$400
300	$170,000	$567	$130,000	$433
400	$230,000	$575	$190,000	$475
500	$300,000	$600	$260,000	$520
600	$380,000	$633	$340,000	$567
700	$470,000	$671	$430,000	$614

Entry price = $567; exit price = $400.

b The cost measures appear in Table 8.17.

Table 8.17

Output	Total cost	Average cost	Variable cost	Average variable cost
1,000	$ 1,900	$1.90	$ 1,000	$1.00
2,000	$ 2,900	$1.45	$ 2,000	$1.00
3,000	$ 4,600	$1.53	$ 3,700	$1.23
4,000	$ 6,600	$1.65	$ 5,700	$1.43
5,000	$ 9,400	$1.88	$ 8,500	$1.70
6,000	$12,400	$2.07	$11,500	$1.92
7,000	$16,000	$2.29	$15,100	$2.16
8,000	$20,000	$2.50	$19,100	$2.39

Entry price = $1.45; exit price = $1.00.

c The cost measures appear in Table 8.18.

Table 8.18

Output	Total cost	Average cost	Variable cost	Average variable cost
1	$ 40	$40.00	$ 40	$40.00
2	$ 90	$45.00	$ 90	$45.00
3	$150	$50.00	$150	$50.00
4	$210	$52.50	$210	$52.50
5	$280	$56.00	$280	$56.00
6	$360	$60.00	$360	$60.00
7	$450	$64.29	$450	$64.29
8	$550	$68.75	$550	$68.75

Entry price = $40; exit price = $40.

CHAPTER 9

Labor and Capital Markets

Chapter Review

Chapter 6 explored the individual's decision to spend her income. This chapter returns to the discussion of household decision making. First, it examines the labor supply decision, the choice between leisure and the income needed for consumption. As with the consumption decision in Chapter 6, the individual chooses the best alternative along the budget constraint. This chapter examines how much labor time to offer, what level of education to pursue, and when to retire. The discussion turns next to the demand side of the market, where firms choose the profit-maximizing quantity of labor. Putting together demand and supply gives a complete model of the labor market. The capital market is the topic of the last part of the chapter, where the household's choice of the supply of savings reflects the trade-off of present and future consumption. Bringing in the firms's demand for capital to finance investment completes the model of the capital market.

ESSENTIAL CONCEPTS

1   The decision to supply labor is primarily a time-allocation problem. Individuals have only so much time available, and they must divide their time between working and other activities. Any time not devoted to working and earning money, whether it is spent in recreation, sleep, chores, or errands, is called leisure. The income earned while working is available for consumption; therefore, the *trade-off* is between **leisure** and **consumption,** between consuming time and consuming goods.

2   The chapter focuses on the budget constraint between leisure and consumption, shown here in Figure 9.1. The

slope is the wage rate, and changes in the wage rate rotate the budget constraint, causing income and substitution effects. When an individual's wage increases, leisure becomes more expensive; thus, the *substitution effect* encourages less leisure and more work. On the other hand, the *income effect* leads the individual to want to consume more leisure, which results in less work. Because the income and substitution effects work in opposite directions, the supply curve for labor may slope upward or even bend backward.

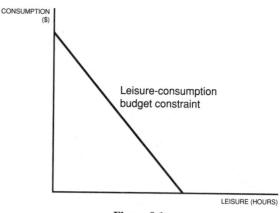

Figure 9.1

3   There are more dimensions to labor supply than hours worked. Individuals choose whether or not to participate in the workforce. They must also decide how much education and training to acquire and when to retire. Each of these decisions can be understood as the choice of the best alternative within an appropriately specified budget constraint.

4   According to **human capital** theory, individuals invest

in education and training to acquire human capital, or skills that increase their productivity and wages. Another view is that education signals to employers which potential workers are innately more productive. This signal leads to credentials competition, the process by which people gather degrees not for any learning that takes place but rather to show that they will be productive if hired.

5 The firm's demand for inputs follows from its decision about how much to produce. More formally, the demand for an input is the **value of its marginal product,** which equals its marginal product (how much extra output the marginal input produces) times the product price (how much revenue the firm receives in selling the output). Again, the market demand is just the sum of the quantities demanded by all firms in the market. Because labor is by far the most important input in production, it is used as the main example of an input in the text. Nevertheless, the demand for any input is the value of its marginal product.

6 The **savings decision** is basically a decision about *when* to consume; households choose whether to spend all of their income now or to save it for future consumption. The **two-period budget constraint** employs the techniques we learned in Chapter 6 to show which combinations of consumption in the present and consumption in the future are affordable, given present and future incomes and the interest rate. As in Chapter 6, the slope of the budget constraint indicates the *trade-off,* and it equals the relative price. Since current consumption is measured on the horizontal axis, the slope is the **relative price of current consumption,** which is **1 plus the interest rate.**

7 When the interest rate changes, the budget constraint rotates, becoming steeper if the interest rate increases and flatter if it decreases. In exactly the same manner as Chapter 6's analysis of the consumption decision, the change in the budget constraint causes income and substitution effects. Higher interest rates make savers better off, and because current consumption is a normal good, the *income effect* makes them want to consume more today, thus reducing savings. On the other hand, higher interest rates lower the relative price of future consumption. The resulting *substitution effect* increases savings. In the decision to save, the substitution and income effects work in opposite directions.

8 There are several motives for saving. People save during their working lives to provide for retirement. This is called **life-cycle savings.** People set aside **precautionary savings** to guard against the chance of accident or illness. The **bequest motive** leads people to save for their heirs. People save to meet a particular goal, such as buying a house or starting a business. We call this motive **target savings.** Furthermore,

government policies affect savings; some encourage saving, others do not. For example, Social Security benefits tend to reduce life-cycle savings because people do not feel as compelled to save for retirement. Taxes on interest lower the after-tax rate of interest and thus provide less incentive to save.

9 Firms make up the demand side of the **capital market,** also called the **market for loanable funds.** They borrow funds for investment. The interest rate, which is the price in this market, reflects the cost of capital. As it rises, the cost of capital increases and firms reduce their borrowing and their investment.

BEHIND THE ESSENTIAL CONCEPTS

1 The basic diagram for the first part of the chapter is the budget constraint for leisure and consumption. It is important to understand that this diagram is very much like the consumer's budget constraint in Chapter 6. Each shows which combinations are affordable. The slopes are the relative prices; in this case, the relative price of leisure is the wage rate. If the individual wants to consume another hour of leisure, the opportunity cost is the money that could be earned in that hour. Changes in nonwage income, such as investment returns, bring about a parallel shift in the budget constraint, but changes in the wage rate rotate it. Again, this is very similar to the Chapter 6 budget constraint.

2 Changes in the wage rate rotate the budget constraint and cause substitution and income effects. The income effect leads to more leisure (less work) when the wage rate increases. The substitution effect, on the other hand, causes less leisure (more work) when the wage rate increases. As with the savings decision, the substitution and income effects of wage changes work in opposite directions. For consumption, however, they work in the same direction. Thus, while the demand curves for goods and services are downward sloping the supply curves for savings and labor may be upward sloping or bend backward.

3 Table 9.1 may help you keep straight the substitution and income effects.

Table 9.1

If the wage rate rises,
  the *substitution* effect leads to more work because leisure is more expensive and
  the *income* effect leads to less work because the worker is better off and demands more leisure.
If the wage rate falls,
  the *substitution* effect leads to less work because leisure is less expensive and
  the *income* effect leads to more work because the worker is worse off and demands less leisure.

4 Be sure not to confuse the budget constraint with the labor supply curve. The budget constraint shows the combinations of leisure and consumption the individual can afford given the wage rate and any nonwage income. The labor supply curve shows the quantity of labor she supplies at each wage rate. As usual, it is important to pay attention to what is measured along each axis.

5 The basic diagram in the second part of this chapter is the two-period budget constraint shown in Figure 9.2. It is important to see how similar this diagram is to the consumer's budget constraint of Chapter 6. There, the trade-off was between consuming different goods. Here, the trade-off involves consuming at different time periods. In each case, the slope is the relative price. When the relative price changes, there are substitution and income effects. Price changes rotate the budget constraint, but income changes bring about a parallel shift. This basic approach will also be used later for the labor supply decision and for other issues throughout the course.

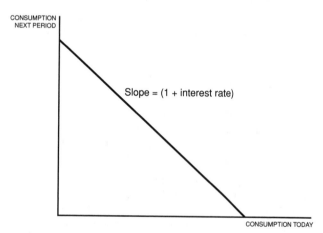

Figure 9.2

6 Think about the slope of the two-period budget constraint. If an individual desires to consume more in the future, he can save today. One dollar saved today results in (1 plus the interest rate) dollars of consumption in the future. That is, he can buy $(1 + r)$ dollars of future consumption at an opportunity cost of only 1 dollar today. Conversely, when he buys 1 more dollar of current consumption, he must give up $(1 + r)$ dollars of future consumption. The relative price of current consumption is, then, 1 plus the interest rate.

7 One plus the interest rate is also the slope of the budget constraint; therefore, only changes in the interest rate can change the slope. If the interest rate rises, the budget constraint becomes steeper. If the interest rate falls, the budget constraint becomes flatter. Income changes, either now or in the future, only shift the

budget constraint in a parallel way.

8 Table 9.2 may help you keep the substitution and income effects straight.

Table 9.2

If the interest rate rises,
   the *substitution* effect leads to more savings because current consumption is relatively more expensive and
   the *income* effect leads to less savings because the saver is better off and desires to consume more today.
If the interest rate falls,
   the *substitution* effect leads to less savings because current consumption is relatively less expensive and
   the *income* effect leads to more savings because the saver is worse off and desires to consume less today.

SELF-TEST

True or False

1 The percentage change in hours worked resulting from a 1 percent change in the real wage is the elasticity of supply of labor.

2 The income effect of a decrease in wages is to increase the quantity of labor supplied.

3 The substitution effect of a decrease in wages is to increase the quantity of labor supplied.

4 Investment in education is an example of human capital.

5 An increase in nonwage income rotates the budget constraint.

6 The firm chooses the profit-maximizing demand for an input when the value of the marginal product equals the input price.

7 The labor force participation of women has increased since World War II.

8 According to human capital theory, education increases the productivity of students, enabling them to earn more in the labor market.

9 The slope of the budget constraint equals the rate of interest.

10 As the interest rate increases, the income effect leads individuals with savings to save less.

11 As the interest rate increases, the substitution effect leads people to save less.

12 As the interest rate increases, the budget constraint shifts out in a parallel way.

13 In the market for loanable funds, the demander borrows money to invest.

14 When the interest rate changes, the income and substitution effects work in the same direction.

15 A cut in interest taxes matters because people are concerned with the after-tax rate of interest.

16 The present discounted value of a future dollar is what one would pay today for that future dollar.

Multiple Choice

1 If a person can earn $10 per hour, then the slope of the leisure-consumption budget constraint is
   a .10.
   b 10.
   c .01.
   d 1.0.
   e none of the above.

2 If nonwage income increases, then the budget constraint
   a rotates, becoming steeper.
   b rotates, becoming flatter.
   c shifts out parallel.
   d shifts in parallel.
   e none of the above.

3 If the wage increases, then the budget constraint
   a rotates, becoming steeper.
   b rotates, becoming flatter.
   c shifts out parallel.
   d shifts in parallel.
   e none of the above.

4 An increase in nonwage income will usually lead to
   a a decrease in the quantity of labor supplied through the substitution effect.
   b a decrease in the quantity of labor supplied through the income effect.
   c an increase in the quantity of labor supplied through the substitution effect.
   d an increase in the quantity of labor supplied through the income effect.
   e none of the above.

5 The substitution effect of a wage increase leads to
   a a decrease in the quantity of labor supply.
   b an increase in the quantity of labor supply.
   c a decrease in leisure.
   d a parallel shift in the budget constraint.
   e *b* and *c*.

6 The value to the firm of hiring one more worker is equal to the marginal
   a cost.
   b revenue.
   c product of labor.
   d product of labor multiplied by the product price.
   e product of labor multiplied by the wage.

7 The value of the marginal product is
   a the revenue that the firm receives for the last unit of output.
   b the revenue that the firm entering the market.
   c the marginal product multiplied by the wage.
   d the marginal product multiplied by the product price.
   e none of the above.

8 The market demand for labor equals
   a the market supply of output.
   b the sum of the demands for labor of all the firms.

c the wage.
   d the marginal product of labor.
   e none of the above.

9 Increased lifetime wealth leads to
   a earlier retirement through the income effect.
   b later retirement through the substitution effect.
   c earlier retirement through the substitution effect.
   d later retirement through the income effect.
   e *a* and *c*.

10 Which of the following is *not* an example of investment in human capital?
   a Formal schooling
   b On-the-job learning
   c Technical training
   d Plant and equipment
   e All of the above are examples.

11 The opportunity costs of attending college do not include
   a tuition expenses.
   b costs of materials and books.
   c room and board.
   d forgone earnings while attending class and studying.
   e All of the above are opportunity costs of attending college.

12 Most capital in the United States is
   a human capital.
   b credentials.
   c capital goods.
   d compensating differentials.
   e About 50 percent of the capital are goods and 50 percent human.

13 Using the budget constraint to analyze the savings decision underscores the fact that the individual is really deciding
   a when to consume.
   b what the slope of the budget constraint should be.
   c without knowing what the future will bring.
   d what the interest rate should be.
   e none of the above.

14 The slope of the intertemporal budget constraint
   a equals 1 plus the interest rate.
   b shows the trade-off between consuming now and waiting to consume.
   c indicates the relative price of current and future consumption.
   d all of the above.
   e *a* and *b*.

15 If the interest rate falls, the budget constraint
   a shifts to the left in a parallel way.
   b shifts to the right in a parallel way.
   c rotates, becoming steeper.
   d rotates, becoming flatter.
   e none of the above.

16 If the interest rate falls, the substitution effect
   a encourages people to consume more in the future, because the relative price of future consumption is less.

b increases savings.

c decreases savings.

d encourages people to consume less in the future, because the relative price of current consumption is lower.

e *c* and *d*.

17 If the interest rate rises, the income effect for people who are saving

a encourages people to consume more in the future, because the relative price of future consumption is less.

b leads people to want to consume more both now and in the future.

c increases savings.

d decreases savings.

e *b* and *d*.

18 If the interest rate rises, the substitution effect increases life-cycle savings because

a the relative price of future consumption is higher.

b people are better off and want to consume more today.

c the budget constraint rotates, becoming flatter.

d people are worse off and want to consume more today.

e none of the above.

19 When the interest rate rises, the cost of capital

a increases, causing the quantity of capital goods demanded to decrease.

b decreases, causing the quantity of capital goods demanded to increase.

c decreases, causing the quantity of capital goods demanded to decrease.

d increases, causing the quantity of capital goods demanded to increase.

e none of the above.

20 New technology

a increases the marginal product of capital, shifting demand to the right.

b decreases the marginal product of capital, shifting demand to the right.

c increases the marginal product of capital, shifting demand to the left.

d decreases the marginal product of capital, shifting demand to the left.

e none of the above.

21 If you are to receive $1,000 from a client one year from today, and the interest rate is 10 percent, what is the present discounted value of that future receipt?

a $1,100

b $1,000

c $1,200

d $979

e None of the above

22 Suppose that the interest rate offered for certificates of deposit is 8 percent. The inflation rate is expected to be 5 percent. What is the real rate of interest?

a 8 percent

b 5 percent

c 13 percent

d 3 percent

e None of the above

Completion

1 The decision concerning how much labor to supply is a choice between _____ and _____.

2 The slope of the budget line is equal to (minus) the _____.

3 When the nonwage income of an individual decreases, his labor supply _____.

4 The _____ effect of a wage decrease leads individuals to decrease their labor supply.

5 If an individuals labor supply is backward bending, then the _____ effect is stronger.

6 The labor supply of women is usually _____ elastic than the labor supply of men.

7 The relative price of consumption today and consumption tomorrow is 1 plus the _____.

8 If the interest rate increases, the budget constraint for the savings decision becomes _____.

9 The income effect of higher interest rates _____ savings.

10 The firm demands the profit-maximizing quantity of labor when the wage equals the _____.

True or False

1	t	6	t	11	f	16	t
2	t	7	t	12	f		
3	f	8	t	13	t		
4	t	9	f	14	f		
5	f	10	t	15	t		

Multiple Choice

1	b	6	d	11	c	16	e	21	b
2	c	7	d	12	a	17	e	22	d
3	a	8	b	13	a	18	e		
4	b	9	a	14	d	19	a		
5	e	10	d	15	d	20	a		

Completion

1 leisure, consumption

2 wage

3 increases

4 substitution

5 income

6 more

7 interest rate

8 steeper

9 reduces

10 value of the marginal product

Doing Economics: Tools and Practice Problems

LABOR SUPPLY

The most important model in the first part of this chapter is the opportunity set for the labor supply decision: the leisure-consumption budget constraint. In this section, we first review how to construct the budget constraint. We then see how the budget constraint changes when the wage rate or nonwage income changes. As in Chapter 6, the substitution and income effects of wage changes can be illustrated using the budget constraint. Finally, there are some applications.

THE LEISURE-CONSUMPTION BUDGET CONSTRAINT

We work in order to earn money for consumption, but we give up time that could be used for leisure. Economists see the labor supply decision as involving a trade-off between leisure and consumption. The basic tool for analyzing labor supply is the budget constraint. Tool Kit 9.1 shows how to construct the leisure-consumption budget constraint.

Tool Kit 9.1 Plotting the Leisure-Consumption Budget Constraint

The budget constraint shows what combinations of leisure and consumption can be afforded given the wage rate and the amount of nonwage income. To plot the budget constraint, follow this five-step procedure.

Step one: Draw a set of coordinate axes. Label the horizontal axis as the quantity of leisure consumed and the vertical axis as the consumption level.

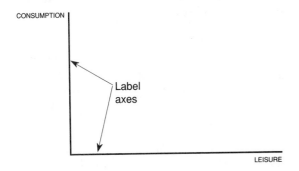

Step two: If an individual chooses to do no work, leisure equals the total time available, and consumption is equal to the nonwage income. Plot this point.

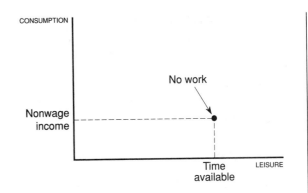

Step three: Calculate the maximum earnings if the individual consumes no leisure. Add this amount to the nonwage income, and plot this quantity along the vertical axis.

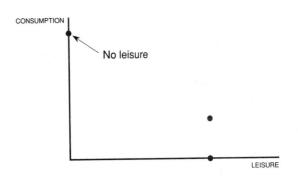

Step four: Draw a line segment connecting the two points. This line segment is the leisure-consumption budget constraint.

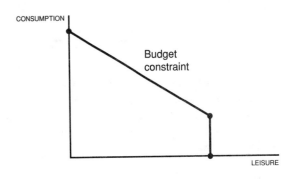

Step five: Verify that the slope of the budget constraint is (minus) the wage rate.

---

1 (Worked problem: leisure-consumption budget constraint) In his spare time, Mike, a student at Enormous State University, referees intramural basketball games. Each game pays $7, and if he could stand the abuse, Mike could referee as many as 60 each month. On average, each game takes 1 hour. This is not Mike's only source of income; each month his parents send him $200 for expenses.

a Construct Mike's budget constraint.

b Suppose that Mike chooses to referee 20 games. Label his chosen alternative, and indicate his total income, income from refereeing, hours worked, and leisure.

Step-by-step solution

Step one (*a*): Draw the two axes, and label the vertical one "Consumption" and the horizontal one "Leisure."

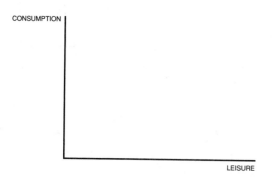

Step two: Plot the no-work consumption point. If Mike referees no games, he consumes all 60 hours as leisure. This leaves him $200 (from his parents) for consumption. Plot this point.

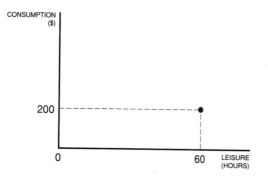

Step three: Calculate total income if Mike works all the time available. If he referees the maximum number of games, 60, he earns $420 from refereeing and retains the $200 from his parents. This leaves him with $620 for consumption but no time for leisure. Plot this point.

Step four: Draw a line segment between the two plotted points. This is the budget constraint.

Step five: The slope of the budget constraint is $(620 - 200)/60 = 7$, which is the wage.

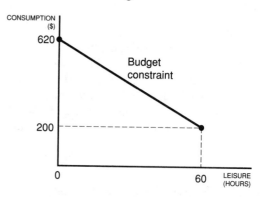

Step six (*b*): If Mike referees 20 games, then he is left with 40 hours of leisure, and he earns $140 in wage income for a total of $340. Plot the point, and label appropriately.

2   (Practice problem: leisure-consumption budget constraint) College professors can earn extra cash by reviewing papers for journals. Editors pay around $50 per paper for an academic opinion about whether it should be accepted for publication. Reviewing a paper takes 1 hour. Professor Cavendish has 15 hours available each month for outside work such as reviewing. He draws $3,000 monthly from McCavendish College, and that is his only other source of income.

a   Plot Cavendish's budget constraint.

b   Suppose that the professor reviews 6 papers in March. Plot and label his chosen alternative.

3   (Practice problem: leisure-consumption budget constraint) For each of the following, draw a budget constraint. Also, choose a point along the budget constraint, and show the corresponding amount of leisure, work, nonwage income, and wage income.

Wage	Total time	Nonwage income
a $25/hour	80 hours	$ 1,000
b $200/day	30 days	$0
c $1,000/week	50 weeks	$15,000
d $5/hour	100 hours	$0

4   (Worked problem: leisure-consumption budget constraint) When either nonwage income or the wage rate changes, the budget constraint moves. The basic technique here is to draw the budget constraint using the original nonwage income and wage rate, following the procedure shown above. Then draw a new budget constraint using the new nonwage income and wage rate. Compare the two budget constraints, and verify that the shift is parallel when nonwage income changes, but the budget constraint rotates when the wage rate changes. Art supplements his pension by repairing automatic teller machines. Each service call takes an hour, and he receives $50 per call. His

pension and other nonwage income is $200 per week. Art has 30 hours available and can work as much as he likes.

a Plot Arts budget constraint.

b His pension fund has done well with its investments and increases Arts nonwage income to $300. Plot his new budget constraint.

c How will Art change his work effort?

Step-by-step solution

Step one(*a*): Plot his budget constraint in the usual way. If he consumes all 30 hours as leisure, Art can consume $200. If he works all 30 hours, he can consume $200 + ($50 × 30) = $1,700. Note that the slope is (1,700 − 200)/30 = 50, which is the wage.

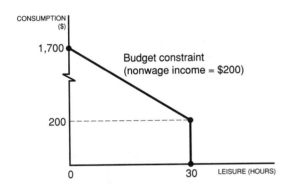

Step two (*b*): Plot his budget constraint with nonwage income equal to $300. His no-work consumption is now $300 + (30 × $50) = $1,800, if he works all of the available time. Note that the nonwage income increase brings about a parallel shift.

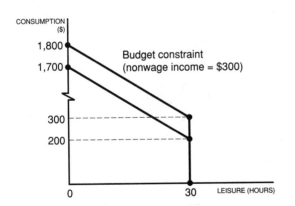

Step three (*c*): The change in the budget constraint is an income effect. The income effect reduces work effort when income rises. Art will work less.

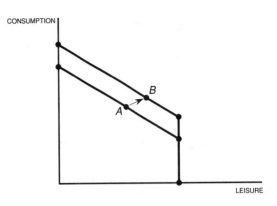

5 (Practice problem: leisure-consumption budget constraint) Liza's job as a broker requires making unsolicited, or "cold," calls to potential clients in an attempt to persuade them to put their portfolio in her hands. On average, cold calls earn Liza $10 each. She can make 4 per hour, and she can work as much as 80 hours per week. Her base salary (nonwage income) is $100 per week.

a Plot her budget constraint.

b Suppose that the firm offers her an increase in the base salary to $150 per week. Plot her new budget constraint.

c Will Liza make more or fewer cold calls? Why?

6 (Practice problem: leisure-consumption budget constraint) Sara is offered a position as tour guide for a local museum. She can conduct 2 tours per hour and earn $10 each. She has no nonwage income, but she must pay 25 percent of her salary in taxes. The museum will allow her to work as much as 20 hours each week.

a Plot her budget constraint.

b Taxes are reduced to 20 percent. Plot her budget constraint.

7 (Practice problem: leisure-consumption budget constraint) Theodore tutors some of his fellow students in economics for $10 per hour. He also receives $2,000 in expense money per semester from his scholarship. He can work as much as 100 hours per semester.

a Plot his budget constraint.

b Students realize that there is a plethora of semi-intelligent grad students who will take less pay. Theodore now only receives $8 per hour. Plot his new budget constraint.

8 (Practice problem: leisure-consumption budget constraint) For each of the following, plot the budget constraint before and after the change.

a Nonwage income = $100; wage = $20 hour; total time available = 40 hours; nonwage income changes to $0.

b Nonwage income = $0; wage = $500/week; total time available = 52 weeks; wage changes to $300/week.

c Nonwage income = $10,000; wage = $40/hour; total time available = 50 hours; available time increases to 60 hours.

d Nonwage income = $500; wage = $200/week; total time available = 52 weeks; wage changes to $400/week.

SUBSTITUTION AND INCOME EFFECTS

As in the case of Chapter 6's budget constraint, price changes cause two kinds of effects: substitution and income. When the wage increases, the substitution effects motivate household to supply more labor, but the income effects indicate that they supply less labor. These concepts show how the labor supply curve can bend backward. Tool Kit 9.2 uses the budget constraint to distinguish between substitution and income effects.

Tool Kit 9.2 Distinguishing between Substitution and Income Effects of Wage Changes

When the wage rate changes, there are two effects: substitution and income. These can be illustrated using the leisure-consumption budget constraint. This technique clarifies the fact that, as in the case of savings, the substitution and income effects work in opposite directions.

Step one: Draw the budget line with the original wage.

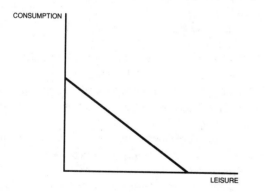

Step two: Find the chosen point along this budget line. Label this point *A*.

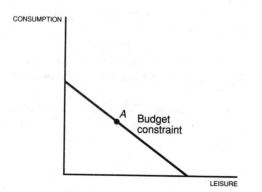

Step three: Draw the budget line with the new wage.

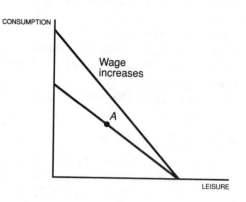

Step four: Draw a dotted line segment through point *A* and parallel to the *new* budget line.

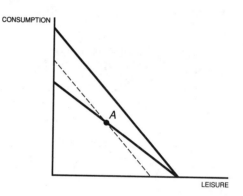

Step five: Darken the portion of the dotted line segment that lies above the original budget line. The points along this darkened segment represent the new alternatives made possible by the substitution effect of the wage change. The income effect shifts this line parallel out to the new budget line drawn in step three.

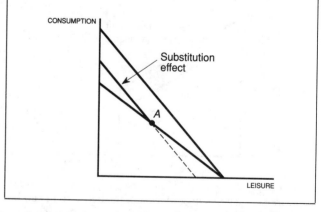

---

9 (Worked problem: wage changes/applications) John currently works 45 hours per week tuning pianos at a wage of $20 per hour. This is his only income. He is offered a raise to $30 per hour. He has 80 hours available for work each week.

a Draw the budget constraint at $20 per hour. Label his chosen alternative along this budget line.

b Draw the budget constraint at $30 per hour.

c Show the substitution effect of the wage increase. Why must the substitution effect lead John to work no less at the new, higher wage?

Step-by-step solution

Step one (a): Draw the budget constraint at the original wage. We label the horizontal axis "Leisure" and the vertical one "Consumption." If John does not work, he has 80 hours of leisure and no consumption. If he works all 80 hours (leisure = 0), he consumes $1,600. Draw John's budget constraint connecting the two points.

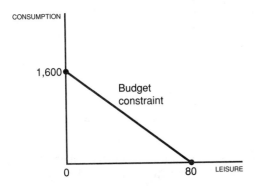

Step two: Find the chosen point along this budget line. John chooses 80 − 45 = 35 hours of leisure, which give him 45 × $20 = $900. Label this point *A,* and note that it does lie along the budget constraint.

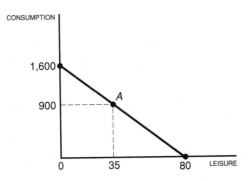

Step three (b): Draw the budget constraint when the wage is $30. The no-work alternative still offers consumption equal to $0, but now if John works the 80 hours available, he consumes $30 × 80 = $2,400. Plot and connect the two endpoints.

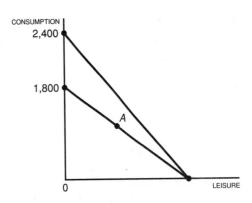

Step four (c): Draw a dotted line parallel to the $30 budget constraint through point *A.*

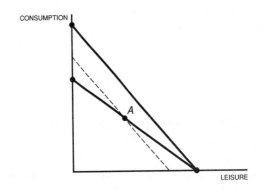

Step five: Darken the portion that lies above the budget constraint drawn in step one. These are the alternatives made possible by the substitution effect of the wage increase. All of these points involve more work than at point *A,* the alternative chosen when the wage is $20.

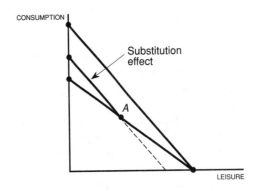

10 (Practice problem: applications) Arna loves her job as a design consultant. She can earn $60 per hour and has

been able to work as much as she likes up to 50 hours per week. She has no nonwage income. She is currently working 15 hours per week.

  a   Plot her budget constraint. Find her chosen alternative, and label the point *A*.

  b   A new city income tax of 10 percent is passed. Arna now takes home only $54 per hour. Plot her new budget constraint.

  c   Show the substitution effect of the wage decrease.

11 (Practice problem: substitution and income effects) For each of the following, draw the budget constraint with the wage in the first column and a new budget line with the wage in the second column. Pick an alternative along the first budget constraint, and show the substitution effect. There is no nonwage income.

	Old wage	New wage	Total time
a	$25/hour	$50/hour	80 hours
b	$200/day	$100/day	30 days
c	$1,000/week	$1,500/week	50 weeks
d	$5/hour	$4/hour	100 hours

APPLICATIONS OF THE LEISURE-CONSUMPTION BUDGET CONSTRAINT

The following applications use the leisure-consumption budget constraint. We analyze welfare programs, overtime pay, and even divorce arrangements. The basic technique is to draw the budget constraint without the policy in question, draw another budget constraint with the policy in place, and compare the two using substitution and income effects.

12 (Worked problem: application) In Smithsville, the welfare system pays $100 per week. Anyone in Smithsville can earn the minimum wage of $4 per hour at the local pickle plant, but welfare recipients cannot receive more than $100 per week. This means that any earnings are subtracted from welfare benefits. There are 80 hours available for work.

  a   Draw the budget constraint for a Smithsville welfare recipient.

  b   A new proposal would substitute a job subsidy for the welfare system. Under the job subsidy proposal, the town pays nothing to those who do not work and $.50 for every dollar earned, up to a total payment of $100. Draw the new budget constraint, and compare it with the one under the welfare system.

  c   Do you think job subsidies are a better program than unconditional welfare? What other factors are involved?

Step-by-step solution

Step one (*a*): Draw a set of axes labeled "Leisure" and "Consumption." If the recipient does no work, she consumes $100. Plot this point, and label it *A*.

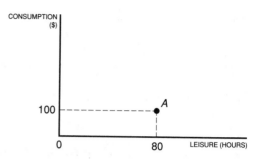

Step two: If the recipient earns $100, she loses all of her benefits and still consumes $100. At $4 per hour, $100 is earned in $100/$4 = 25 hours, which leaves 80 − 25 = 55 hours of leisure. Plot the point (100, 55). Label this point *B*.

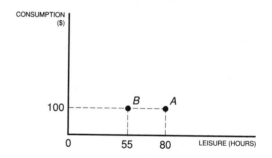

Step three: If the recipient works all 80 hours, she consumes $4 × 80 = $320. Plot this point, and label it *C*.

Step four: Draw line segments connecting points *A* and *B* and points *B* and *C*. This is the budget constraint under the welfare system.

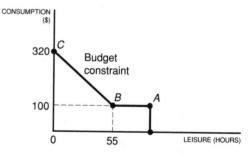

Step five (*b*): Under the job subsidy program, if the person works no hours, he consumes nothing. Plot the point (0.80). Label it *D*.

Step six: If the person earns $200, he receives the maximum subsidy, which is $100. The total consumption is then $300.

To earn $200 (and consume $300) takes $200/$4 = 50 hours of work, leaving 80 − 50 = 30 hours of leisure. Plot the point (300, 30), and label it *E*.

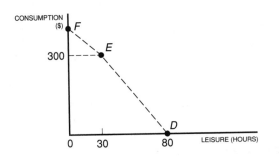

Step seven: If the person works all 80 hours, he consumes $100 + (80 × $4) = $420. Plot the point (420, 0); label it *F*.

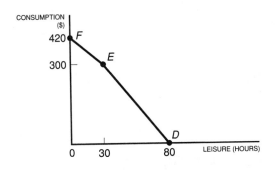

Step eight: Draw line segments connecting *DEF.* This is the budget constraint for job subsidies.

13 (Practice problem: applications) The management at Acme Manufacturing is disturbed that although the typical factory worker is required to work 250 days each year, most only work 230. It proposes a $100 bonus for any employee who works more than 240 days each year. The wage of the typical factory worker is $120 per day.

   a Draw the budget constraint without the attendance bonus.

   b Draw the budget constraint with the attendance bonus. How is attendance likely to change for the typical factory worker?

   c Suppose that the company simply gives each worker $100. How is the opportunity set different from the one with the attendance bonus?

   d Under which scheme will the typical worker work more? Why?

14 (Practice problem: applications) The Quantity Bakery Company has paid its workers $6 per hour to make donuts, cakes, and pies. There are always sweets to make, and the workers can work as many hours as they choose, up to 80 hours per week. Recently, the company union won a new contract that, although it keeps the wage at the same level, now allows for

overtime pay of "time and a half" for any hours worked in excess of 40 per week.

   a Draw the budget constraint under the old contract with no provision for overtime pay.

   b Draw the budget constraint with the overtime pay.

   c What is likely to happen to the number of hours that Quantity Bakery workers work under the new contract? Explain.

15 (Practice problem: applications) Under the U.S. tax code, earnings below $20,000 or so are taxed at 15 percent. Any earnings above $20,000 incur a 28 percent tax rate. Lucinda Gamez, a private investigator, earns $800 per week, and she has 50 weeks per year available for work.

   a Draw her budget constraint if she pays no taxes.

   b Draw her budget constraint under the schedule described above. How do progressive income taxes shape the budget constraint.

16 (Practice problem: applications) Harry Gold makes $5,000 by working 20 days each month as a plumber. His wage is $250 per day, and he can work as many as 30 days each month (except February, of course). The income tax rate for Harry is 20 percent. Also, he pays $1,000 monthly in property taxes on a very nice condo down by the river. His nonwage income is $4,000 per month. (Hint: Review the solutions to problems 14 and 15 of Chapter 6.)

   a What is Harry's net wage after taxes?

   b Draw his budget constraint.

   c The new governor proposes eliminating the income tax and increasing property taxes. Harry figures that his property tax bill will rise to $2,000. Draw his budget constraint under the governor's proposed tax changes.

   d Will Harry work more or less under the new tax plan? Why?

   e Is Harry better off under the new tax plan? Why or why not?

17 (Practice problem: applications) After 10 miserable years, Al and Norma Bennet are getting a divorce. They have agreed that Norma will retain custody of their two children. Al makes $50 per hour from his job as a marriage counselor, and this is his only income. Although he could work as much as 40 hours, Al is only working 20 hours currently. The court has ruled that Al must pay $250 per week in child support regardless of his earnings. (Hint: Review the solutions to problems 14 and 15 of Chapter 6.)

   a Draw Al's (postdivorce) leisure-consumption budget constraint.

   b Many states (for example, Wisconsin and Michigan) have established fixed guidelines for child support payments. Suppose the guideline requires that noncustodial parents pay 25 percent of their income per child. Draw Al's budget line for this child care payment.

c Under which plan will Al work more? Why?

DEMAND FOR INPUTS

Profits are always maximized by setting marginal revenue equal to marginal cost. When the firm is a price taker in both product and input markets, the marginal revenue from hiring another input is the value of the marginal product, which is the marginal product of that input multiplied by the product price. The marginal cost of hiring another input is the input price. In the case of labor, the input price is the wage. Tool Kit 9.3 shows how to solve for the input demand.

Tool Kit 9.3 Finding the Quantity of an Input to Demand

The demand for an input is its value of the marginal product. This is found by multiplying the marginal product by the product price. Follow this five step procedure to determine the profit maximizing quantity of an input.

Step one: Calculate the marginal product for each level of the input.

Step two: Identify the product price.

Step three: Compute the value of the marginal product by multiplying the marginal product by the product price for each level of the input:

value of the marginal product =

marginal product × product price.

Step four: Identify the input price. (In the case of labor, this is the wage.)

Step five: Find the level of the input for which the value of the marginal product equals the input price. This is the quantity demanded.

---

18 (Worked problem: quantity demanded) The new company The Hair Cuttery is ready to start hiring. The price of haircuts is $8, and the production function is given in Table 9.3.

Table 9.3

Stylists	Haircuts per day	Marginal product	Value of the marginal product
1	8		
2	16		
3	23		
4	29		
5	34		
6	38		

a The wage paid to hair stylists is $40 per day. Find the profit-maximizing number of hair stylists to hire.

b Suppose that the wage rises to $64 per day. Find the number of hair stylists that maximizes profits.

Step-by-step solution

Step one (*a*): The marginal product is the extra output that results from hiring one more input. When the first hair stylist is hired, output rises from 0 to 8. The marginal product is 8. Enter this number. When the second hair stylist is hired, output rises from 8 to 16. The marginal product is $16 - 8 = 8$; enter this number and continue. The marginal product column is given in Table 9.4.

Table 9.4

Stylists	Haircuts per day	Marginal product	Value of the marginal product
1	8	8	
2	16	8	
3	23	7	
4	29	6	
5	34	5	
6	38	4	

Step two: The product price is $8.

Step three: The value of the marginal product equals the product price multiplied by the marginal product. The value of the marginal product of the first worker is 8 × $8 = $64. Continue to enter the results in the appropriate column. The completed information is given in Table 9.5.

Table 9.5

Stylists	Haircuts per day	Marginal product	Value of the marginal product
1	8	8	$64
2	16	8	$64
3	23	7	$56
4	29	6	$48
5	34	5	$40
6	38	4	$32

Step four: The wage is $40 per day.

Step five: Profits are maximized when the wage is set equal to the value of the marginal product. The wage is $40, which equals the value of the marginal product when 5 hair stylists are hired.

Step six (*b*): When the wage is $64, it equals the value of the marginal product if 2 stylists are hired.

19 (Practice problem: quantity demanded) Moe's Lawn Service mows lawns for $20 each. Moe's production

function is given in Table 9.6. Output is measured as the number of lawns mowed.

Table 9.6

Workers	Output per day	Marginal product	Value of the marginal product
1	5.0		
2	9.0		
3	13.0		
4	16.5		
5	19.5		
6	22.0		
7	24.0		

Moe pays his lawn mowers $40 per day.
a Find the profit-maximizing number of mowers to hire.
b Suppose that the wage rises to $70 per day. Find the profit-maximizing number of mowers to hire.

20 (Practice problem: quantity demanded) For each of the following, complete the table and find the profit-maximizing number of inputs.
a Product price = $10; wage = $100 per day.

Workers	Output per day	Marginal product	Value of the marginal product
10	200		
20	360		
30	500		
40	620		
50	720		
60	800		

b Product price = $10,000; wage = $10,000 per month.

Workers	Output per day	Marginal product	Value of the marginal product
10	20		
20	40		
30	55		
40	65		
50	70		
60	70		

c Product price = $5; input price = $40.

Workers	Output per day	Marginal product	Value of the marginal product
1,000	10,000		
2,000	18,000		
3,000	25,500		
4,000	31,500		
5,000	36,000		
6,000	40,000		

SAVINGS

Now we turn to the saver's opportunity set: the two-period budget constraint. Given the wealth or income of the household and the interest rate, we can construct the two-period budget constraint. We see how the budget constraint is altered when income (either present or future) and interest rates change. We show the substitution and income effects by using the rotation and shift technique introduced in the last chapter. Finally, we learn some applications: different borrowing and lending interest rates, individual retirement, college and housing accounts, and how Social Security benefits affect savings.

The Two-Period Budget Constraint

When we save money, we forgo current consumption in order to increase consumption at some later date. The trade-off involves current and future consumption. Tool Kit 9.4 shows how to plot the two-period budget constraint, which is the economist's basic tool for analyzing savings.

Tool Kit 9.4 Plotting the Two-Period Budget Constraint

The two-period budget constraint shows what combinations of consumption in each period are possible, given the income and interest rate. Follow the steps.

Step one: Draw a set of coordinate axes. Label the horizontal axis consumption in period one and the vertical axis consumption in period two.

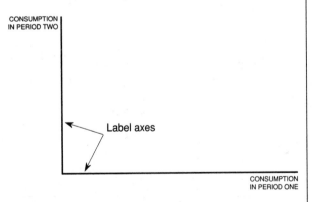

Step two: Calculate the maximum possible consumption in period one. (This quantity is the present discounted value of income.) Plot this quantity along the horizontal axis.

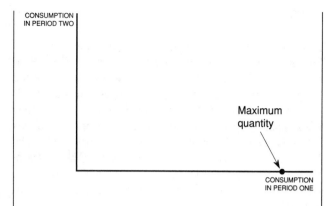

Step three: Calculate the maximum possible consumption in period two. (This quantity is the future value of income.) Plot this quantity along the vertical axis.

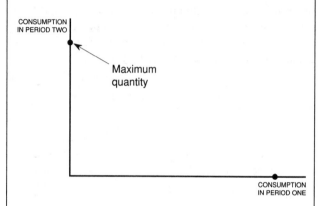

Step four: Draw a line segment connecting the two points. This line segment is the two-period budget constraint.

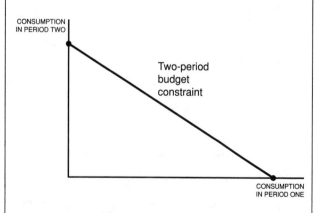

Step five: Verify that the slope of the budget constraint is (minus) $1 + r$, where r is the interest rate.

21 (Worked problem: two-period budget constraint) Nancy won the lottery! It is only $5,000, but that looks pretty good to someone making $18,000 per year. Her interest rate is 6 percent, and the capital market is perfect. Plot her two-period budget constraint.

Step-by-step solution

Step one: Draw coordinate axes, labeling the horizontal axis "Consumption now" and the vertical axis "Consumption next year."

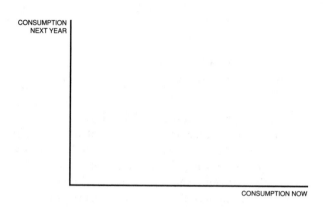

Step two: The maximum consumption today is the present discounted value of all income. Make the following table, and compute and plot the amount along the horizontal axis.

Year	Income	Discount factor	Present discounted value
Now	$23,000	1	$23,000
Next year	$18,000	1/(1.06)	$16,980

Present discounted value = $39,980.

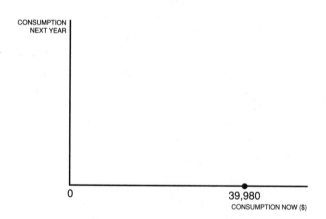

Step three: The maximum consumption next year is

$$\$23,000 \ (1 + .06) + \$18,000 = \$42,380.$$

Plot this point.

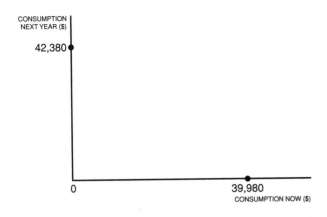

parallel when either current or future income changes, but the budget constraint rotates when the interest rate changes. Michael is earning $25,000 as a secretary and expects to earn the same in the future. His interest rate is 5 percent.

a   Plot his two-period budget constraint.

b   He receives word that his aunt is sick and has one year to live. She plans to leave him $50,000. Plot his two-period budget constraint.

Step-by-step solution

Step one (*a*): Follow the procedure to plot the two-period budget constraint. The slope is $1 + r = 1.05$, and it passes through the point $25,000 now and $25,000 next year.

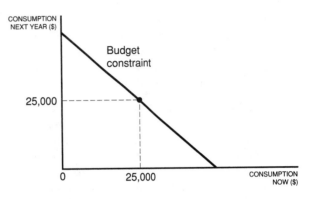

Step four: Draw a line segment connecting the two points.

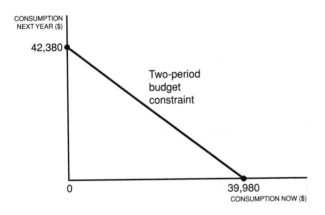

Step five: Verify that the slope equals 1 plus the interest rate. It is 42,380/39,980 = 1.06 = 1 + r.

22   (Practice problem: two-period budget constraint) Current income is $40,000. Retirement income is $15,000. The interest rate for the period between now and retirement is 150 percent. Plot the two-period budget constraint.

23   (Practice problem: two-period budget constraint) Plot the two-period budget constraints for the following.

	Interest rate	Present income	Future income
a	100%	$100,000	$ 25,000
b	50%	$ 40,000	$ 10,000
c	250%	$ 20,000	$0
d	80%	$0	$150,000

24   (Worked problem: two-period budget constraint) When the interest rate, current income, or future income changes, the two-period budget constraint moves. The basic technique here is to draw the two-period budget constraint using the original income and interest rate, and then draw a new two-period budget constraint using the new incomes and interest rate. Compare the two budget constraints and verify that the shift is

Step two (*b*): Plot the new budget constraint. Because the interest rate is the same, the slope does not change. The new budget constraint passes through the point $25,000 now and $75,000 next year.

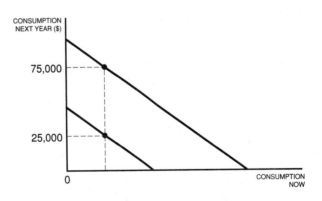

25   (Practice problem: two-period budget constraint) Boris currently takes home $45,000 as a skilled lathe operator. His union contract guarantees him the same salary next year. The credit union at the plant pays 8 percent interest.

a   Plot his two-period budget constraint.

b   Boris's employer is experiencing low profits this year. He proposes that Boris accept $35,000 this year and $55,000 next year. Plot his two-period budget constraint. Does the offer shift the budget constraint? How?

26 (Practice problem: two-period budget constraint) Monica plans to retire in 20 years. She now takes home $40,000 and expects $20,000 in retirement income. The interest rate for the 20 years is 180 percent.
  a Plot her budget constraint.
  b A new broker promises her a 20-year return of 250 percent. She believes him. Plot her new budget constraint.

27 (Practice problem: two-period budget constraint) The Coddingtons now take home $375,000 per year, but they have no retirement income planned. Their portfolio will earn them 100 percent over the 12 years left until retirement.
  a Plot their budget constraint.
  b Tax increases reduce their after-tax return to 60 percent. Plot their new budget constraint.

28 (Practice problem: two-period budget constraint) Plot the budget constraints before and after the change.

	Current income	Future income	Interest rate	Change
a	$100,000	$0	40%	Interest rate = 60%
b	$100,000	$0	40%	Future income = $100,000
c	$0	$50,000	10%	Current income = $25,000
d	$ 60,000	$80,000	50%	Interest rate = 20%

SUBSTITUTION AND INCOME EFFECTS

As in the case of the other budget constraints that you have studied, price changes cause two kinds of effects: substitution and income. When the interest rate increases, the substitution effects motivate household to save more, but the income effects indicate that they save less. These concepts show why the supply curve of savings may bend backward. Tool Kit 9.4 uses the budget constraint to distinguish between substitution and income effects of changes in interest rates.

Tool Kit 9.5 Distinguishing between Substitution and Income Effects of Changes in Interest Rates

When the interest rate changes, there are two effects: substitution and income. These effects can be illustrated by using the two-period budget constraint. Follow this procedure.

Step one: Draw the two-period budget line with the original interest rate.

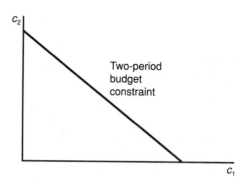

Step two: Find the chosen current and future consumption level along this budget line. Label this point *A*.

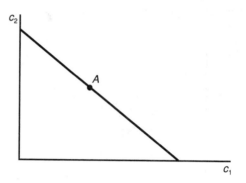

Step three: Draw the two-period budget line with the new interest rate.

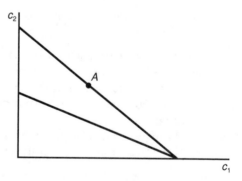

Step four: Draw a dotted line segment through point *A* and parallel to the *new* budget line.

Step five: Darken the portion of the dotted line segment that lies above the original budget line. The points along this darkened segment represent the quantities made possible by the substitution effect of the interest rate change. The income effect shifts this line out in a parallel way to the new budget line drawn in step three.

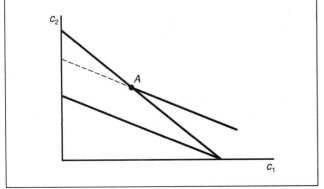

29 (Worked problem: substitution and income effects) Show the substitution and income effects of the change in the rate of return for Monica's portfolio in problem 26. She is currently saving $5,000 per year.

Step-by-step solution

Step one: Draw the two-period budget constraint with the interest rate equal to 180 percent. It must pass through the point ($40,000, $20,000).

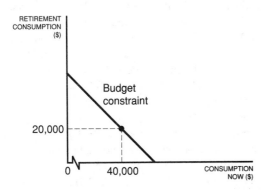

Step two: Label Monica's current consumption ($40,000 $5,000 = $35,000) point A.

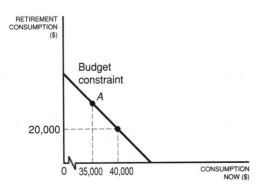

Step three: Draw the two-period budget constraint with the interest rate equal to 250 percent. It also must pass through the point ($40,000, $20,000).

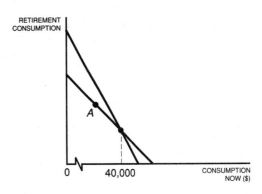

Step four: Draw a dotted line with a slope of 1 + 2.50 = 3.50 through A.

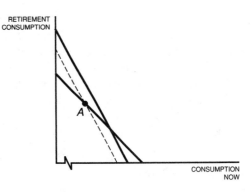

Step five: Darken the portion of the dotted line that lies above the original budget constraint drawn in step one. These are the alternatives made possible by the substitution effect of the interest rate change. All of these involve more savings; thus, the substitution effect of an increase in the interest rate is an increase in savings. The income effect shifts this darkened line segment out parallel to the budget constraint drawn in step two and reduces savings.

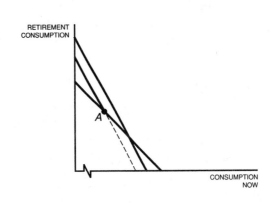

30 (Practice problem: substitution and income effects) Show the substitution and income effects for the change in the Coddingtons after-tax interest rate in problem 24. Currently they have no savings.

31 (Practice problem: substitution and income effects) Show the substitution and income effects for parts a through d in problem 25. In each case, savings equal $10,000 before the interest rate changes.

APPLICATION OF THE TWO-PERIOD BUDGET CONSTRAINT

The following applications show how the two-period budget constraint can be used to analyze imperfect capital markets, Social Security, and government programs that affect savings incentives. Again, the procedure is to draw budget constraints with and without the feature of interest and compare using substitution and income effects.

32 (Worked problem: applications) If the capital market were perfect, then the interest rates for borrowing and lending would be the same. The rates for borrowing, however, are higher. Haywood and Myrna take home $40,000 each year. They can earn 4 percent on any savings, but they must borrow at 14 percent. Plot their two-period budget constraint.

Step-by-step solution

This is an application of the opportunity set with multiple constraints introduced in Chapter 2.

Step one: Plot the budget constraint with the 4 percent interest rate. The slope is 1.04, and it passes through the point $40,000 now and $40,000 next year.

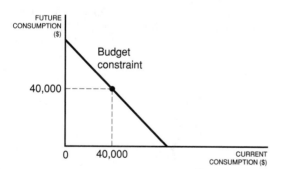

Step two: Plot the budget constraint with the 14 percent interest rate. The slope is 1.04, and it passes through the point $40,000 now and $40,000 next year.

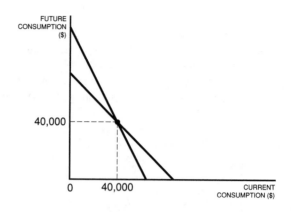

Step three: Darken the portion of each budget constraint that lies under the other constraint.

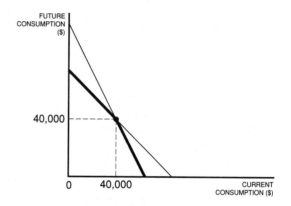

33 (Practice problem: applications) Bob takes home $20,000 this year, but he anticipates taking home $30,000 next year. He can earn 8 percent on savings, but he has a poor credit rating and must pay 19 percent to borrow. Plot his two-period budget constraint.

34 (Worked problem: applications) Concern about low U.S. savings rates, among other motivations, has prompted a number of proposals for tax-exempt savings accounts. They range from the Bush administrations family savings accounts to special tax-exempt accounts for college expenses or down payments on a first home. The Davidsons take home $100,000 per year after taxes. If he gets his grades up, David, their son, will enter college in 3 years. The Davidsons can earn a 25 percent real rate of return before taxes over the three-year period.

a Draw their two-period budget constraint.

b The Davidsons face a 40 percent marginal tax rate. Draw their budget constraint with the tax on interest. (Hint: What is their after-tax real rate of return on savings?)

c A new college savings plan is proposed that offers parents an opportunity to deposit up to $3,000 in a special tax-exempt account. Any money withdrawn and not used for college tuition payments is subject to penalty. Draw their two-period budget constraint if the plan becomes law.

d   Before the plan, the Davidsons were saving $3,500 each year. Use the concepts of substitution and income effects to explain how their savings will be affected by the college savings plan.

Step-by-step solution

Step one (*a*): Plot the two-period budget constraint. The slope is $1 + 0.25 = 1.25$, and the budget constraint must pass through the point where current and future income are each $100,000.

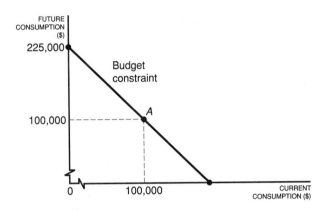

Step two (*b*): Plot the two-period budget constraint with the tax on interest. Taxes take 40 percent of the interest, so their after-tax interest rate for the three years is 15 percent. The slope is now 1.15. Interest taxes make the budget constraint flatter.

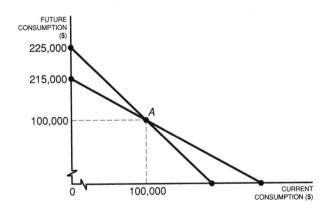

Step three (*c*): The college savings plan allows the Davidsons to save along the tax-free budget constraint, where the slope is 1.25 until their savings reach $3,000. At that point (*B*), there is a kink, and the slope of the budget constraint returns to the flatter after-tax slope of 1.15.

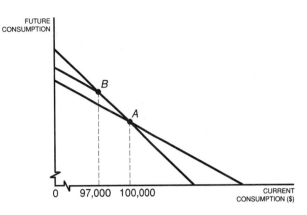

Step four (*d*): Since the Davidsons save more than $3,000, the program will have only an income effect. The program will not change their after-tax marginal rate of return, because only the first $3,000 of savings is tax exempt.

35   (Practice problem: applications) The Shades do not know where they will find the money to send their four bright but impecunious children to college in 5 years. They make $26,000 per year and have been unable to save a nickel. Their marginal tax rate is 20 percent, and they could earn 40 percent interest on savings over the five-year period.
   a   Plot the Shades' two-period budget constraint ignoring the tax on interest.
   b   Plot their two-period budget constraint including the tax on interest.
   c   Plot their two-period budget constraint under the college savings plan spelled out in problem 31.
   d   Use the concepts of substitution and income effects to explain how their savings will be affected by the college savings plan.

36   (Worked problem: applications) Social Security reduces the incentives that individuals have to save for retirement, and because it is financed on a pay-as-you-go basis, it reduces national savings. Melissa is already fantasizing about retirement, even though it is 40 years away. She estimates that a dollar deposited today will return $3.50 in interest when she retires. She currently takes home $25,000 after paying taxes, including $3,250 annually in Social Security taxes, and expects to draw $14,625 in Social Security benefits. Although she is thinking about retirement, Melissa has no savings.
   a   Calculate the present discounted value of Melissa's Social Security benefits.
   b   Draw her two-period budget constraint, and label her levels of consumption now and in the future.
   c   Suppose that the entire Social Security system (taxes and benefits) is eliminated. Draw her two-period budget constraint.
   d   How much does Melissa save?

Step-by-step solution

Step one (a): The present discounted value of her benefit payment is $\$14,625/(1 + r) = \$3,250$, which is exactly her taxes.

Step two (b): Draw Melissa's two-period budget constraint. Label the axes "Current consumption" and "Consumption 40 years in the future." The slope is $1 + r$, and the interest rate for the 40-year period is 350 percent. Also, the budget constraint must pass through her current choice: $25,000 now and $14,625 in 40 years.

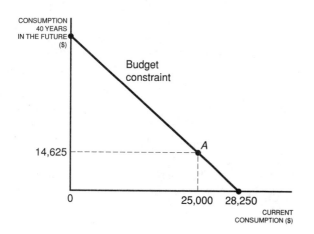

Step three (c): Eliminating Social Security reduces her future income to $0, but because she no longer pays Social Security taxes, her current after-tax income rises to $28,250. Because the present discounted value of her two-period income does not change, the budget constraint does not change. (In general, the Social Security system shifts out the budget constraint for low-income people and shifts it in for high-income people.)

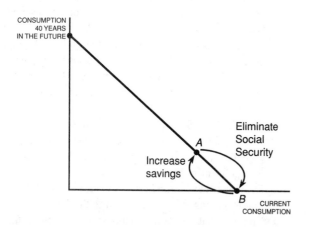

Step four (d): Because Melissa has the same budget constraint, she chooses the same point. This means that she must save $3,250 (which returns $14,625 in 40 years), which is exactly the amount she now pays in taxes. Eliminating Social Security would (for Melissa) lead to the same consumption, but greater national savings.

37 (Practice problem: applications) Melissa's uncle is only 10 years from retirement. He can expect to receive $1 in interest for every $1 saved for retirement. He takes home $50,000 annually, saves $10,000, and expects Social Security benefits of $20,000 when he retires.
   a Plot his two-period budget constraint.
   b Suppose that the American Association of Retired Persons has a banner year lobbying Congress and wins a 50 percent increase in benefits. Taxes also rise, so that the budget constraint of Melissa's uncle does not change. How will his earnings change? How will his consumption now and during retirement change?

THE TIME VALUE OF MONEY

Payments to be received in the future are not worth as much as payments received today. This statement reflects the time value of money. Decisions involving present and future costs and returns require a consistent standard for comparison. This standard is present discounted value, and it is illustrated in Tool Kit 9.6.

Tool Kit 9.6 Calculating the Present Discounted Value

To compare the worth of present and future payments, it is necessary to compute the present discounted value, which is the current dollar equivalent of an amount to be rendered in the future. Follow the steps.

Step one: Make a table with four columns, and label them as shown.

Year	Amount	Discount factor	Present discounted value

Step two: For every payment or receipt, enter the year and the amount. Let Y_1 be the amount in the first year, Y_2 the amount the second year, and so on.

Year	Amount	Discount factor	Present discounted value
1	Y_1		
2	Y_2		

Step three: Calculate the discount factor for each year. The formula is $1/(1 + r)^n$, where r is the interest rate and n is the number of years until the payment or receipt. Enter these discount factors in the table.

Year	Amount	Discount factor	Present discounted value
1	Y_1	$1/(1 + r)$	
2	Y_2	$1/(1 + r)^2$	

Step four: Multiply the number in the amount column by the corresponding discount factor. Enter the product in the present discounted value column.

Year	Amount	Discount factor	Present discounted value
1	Y_1	$1/(1 + r)$	$Y_1 \times 1/(1 + r)$
2	Y_2	$1/(1 + r)^2$	$Y_2 \times 1/(1 + r)^2$

Step five: Add the numbers in the right-hand column. The sum is the present discounted value.

Year	Amount	Discount factor	Present discounted value
1	Y_1	$1/(1 + r)$	$Y_1 \times 1/(1 + r)$
2	Y_2	$1/(1 + r)^2$	$Y_2 \times 1/(1 + r)^2$

Present discounted value
$$= Y_1 \times 1/(1 + r) + Y_2 \times 1/(1 + r)^2.$$

38 (Worked problem: present discounted value) Ethel has two years before retirement from a career of teaching unruly high school delinquents. Her salary is $40,000, paid at the end of each year. The school board has offered her $70,000 now to retire early. The relevant interest rate is 7 percent. In monetary terms alone, is working worth more than retiring?

Step-by-step solution

First, calculate the present discounted value of continuing to work.

Step one: Make a table with four columns, and label them as shown.

Year	Amount	Discount factor	Present discounted value

Step two: For every payment or receipt, enter the year and the amount. Ethel receives $40,000 each year for two years.

Year	Amount	Discount factor	Present discounted value
1	$40,000		
2	$40,000		

Step three: Calculate the discount factor for each year. For the first year, the discount factor is $1/(1 + .07) = 0.93$, and for the second year it is $1/(1 + .07)^2 = 0.86$. Enter these discount factors in the table.

Year	Amount	Discount factor	Present discounted value
1	$40,000	0.93	
2	$40,000	0.86	

Step four: Multiply the number in the amount column by the corresponding discount factor. Enter the product in the present discounted value column.

Year	Amount	Discount factor	Present discounted value
1	$40,000	0.93	$37,380
2	$40,000	0.86	$34,400

Step five: Add the numbers in the right-hand column. The sum is the present discounted value.

Year	Amount	Discount factor	Present discounted value
1	$40,000	0.93	$37,380
2	$40,000	0.86	$34,400

Present discounted value = $71,780.

Next, compare the lump-sum payment with the present discounted value of continuing to work. Ethel can postpone retirement and increase the present discounted value of her earnings by only $1,780. The reason that the gain is so little is that earnings come in the future and must be discounted, while the retirement bonus is paid now.

39 (Practice problem: present discounted value) The Transportation Department is considering the bids of two paving companies for repaving South Street. The Do-It-Rite firm will do the job for $200,000, and they will guarantee that their new process will make the road free of potholes for 3 years. The Let-It-Go company only charges $100,000, but estimated pothole repair costs are $40,000 each year. The interest rate is 8 percent.
   a Calculate the present discounted value of the entire cost with the Let-It-Go firm.
   b Which is the least expensive bid?

40 (Practice problem: present discounted value) Calculate the present discounted value of each of the following.

   a Interest rate equals 10 percent.

Year	Amount	Discount factor	Present discounted value
1	$10,000		
2	$15,000		

   b Interest rate equals 5 percent.

Year	Amount	Discount factor	Present discounted value
1	$0		
2	$20,000		

   c Interest rate equals 15 percent.

Year	Amount	Discount factor	Present discounted value
1	$5,000		
2	$5,000		
3	$5,000		

d Interest rate equals 5 percent.

Year	Amount	Discount factor	Present discounted value
1	$5,000		
2	$0		
3	$25,000		

Answers to Problems

2

3

5

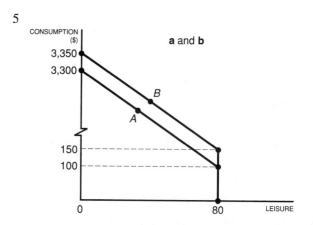

c Liza will make fewer cold calls, she will consume more leisure when her income increases, as shown by the movement from point *A* to point *B*.

6

7

8

10

11

13

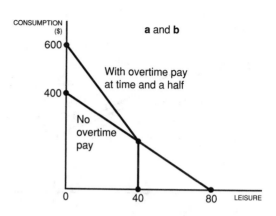

c All the new alternatives made possible by the overtime provision involve working more than 40 hours. Work time probably will increase.

15

16

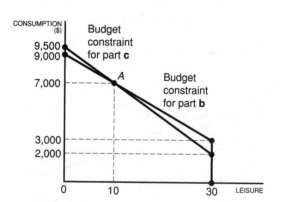

d An unconditional bonus of $100 simply shifts the budget constraint up in a parallel way, causing an income effect. The typical worker consumes more leisure at point *C*. The attendance bonus does not offer the points along the dashed budget constraint. Point *B* or another point involving even more work will be chosen. Clearly, there is a greater incentive to work with the attendance bonus.

a $200/day.

d He will work more because the tax change offers him new alternative with more work. In effect it leaves him with the substitution effect of a wage increase, with the income effect being canceled by the property tax increase.

e He is better off because he can continue to choose point *A*, but he also has some new alternatives.

17

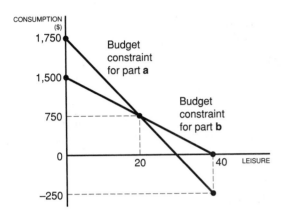

c Al will likely work more under the lump-sum child care requirement. The other system leaves him with the substitution effect of a wage decrease.

19 The value of the marginal product is given in Table 9.7

Table 9.7

Workers	Output per day	Marginal product	Value of the marginal product
1	5.0	5.0	$100
2	9.0	4.0	$ 80
3	13.0	4.0	$ 80
4	16.5	3.5	$ 70
5	19.5	3.0	$ 60
6	22.0	2.5	$ 50
7	24.0	2.0	$ 40

a When the wage is $40, it equals the vmp if 7 are hired.

b When the wage is $70, it equals the vmp if 4 are hired.

20 a The value of the marginal product is given in Table 9.8. The quantity demanded is 50 workers.

Table 9.8

Workers	Output per day	Marginal product	Value of the marginal product
10	200	20	$200
20	360	16	$160
30	500	14	$140
40	620	12	$120
50	720	10	$100
60	800	8	$ 80

b The value of the marginal product is given in Table 9.9. The quantity demanded is 40 workers.

Table 9.9

Workers	Output per day	Marginal product	Value of the marginal product
10	20	2.0	$20,000
20	40	2.0	$20,000
30	55	1.5	$15,000
40	65	1.0	$10,000
50	70	0.5	$ 5,000
60	70	0	$0

c The value of the marginal product is given in Table 9.10. The quantity demanded is 2,000 workers.

Table 9.10

Workers	Output per day	Marginal product	Value of the marginal product
1,000	10,000	10.0	$50.00
2,000	18,000	8.0	$40.00
3,000	25,500	7.5	$37.50
4,000	31,500	6.0	$30.00
5,000	36,000	4.5	$22.50
6,000	40,000	4.0	$20.00

22

23

25

26

27

28

30

31

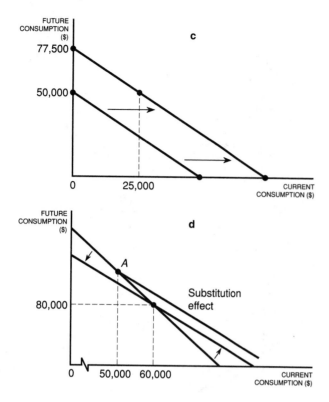

c

d

Substitution effect

33

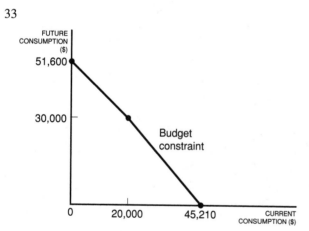

Budget constraint

35

d If the Shades save less than $3,000, the program has both substitution and income effects.

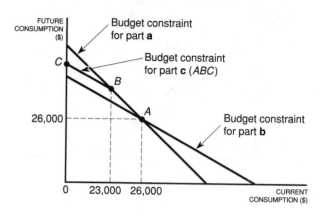

Budget constraint for part **a**

Budget constraint for part **c** (*ABC*)

Budget constraint for part **b**

37

a

Budget constraint

Savings

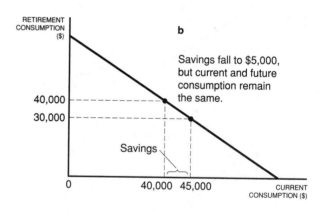

b

Savings fall to $5,000, but current and future consumption remain the same.

Savings

39 *a*   Firm   Cost

Do-It-Rite $200,000

Let-It-Go $\displaystyle + \$100,000 + \frac{\$40,000}{1.08}$

$\displaystyle + \frac{\$40,000}{(1.08)^2} + \frac{\$40,000}{(1.08)^3}$

$203,083.

40 *b* The Do-It-Rite bid.
    a $21,488.
    b $18,141.
    c $12,447.
    d $26,358.

CHAPTER 10 | The Efficiency of Competitive Markets

Chapter Review

The elements of the basic competitive model have been presented over the last six chapters of the text. In Chapter 13, these elements—from individuals and their decisions regarding consumption, savings, investment, and work, to firms and their choices regarding production and costs—are brought together in the general equilibrium model. The focus of the model is on the interdependencies of the product, labor, and capital markets. Another major topic is a normative one: how well does the competitive economy perform? The notion of Pareto efficiency provides a tool with which economists can evaluate how well the market economy answers the basic economic questions. This chapter completes the presentation of the competitive model and closes Part Two. In Part Three, attention shifts to imperfect markets.

ESSENTIAL CONCEPTS

1   The basic competitive three-market model is a relatively simple general equilibrium model, and is very good for analyzing the interactions among markets. The three markets are the labor, capital, and product markets. They are interdependent in that as the price changes in one market, demand and supply curves shift in the others. In **general equilibrium**, the three prices (wage, interest rate, and product price) are set so that each market clears.
    a   Demand equals supply in the labor market.
    b   Demand equals supply in the capital market.
    c   Demand equals supply in the goods market.
2   To evaluate how well the competitive market economy allocates resources, economists use the concept of **total surplus:** the sum of consumer and **producer surplus**. Consumers gain the difference between what they are willing to pay and the price. Producers gain the difference between price and marginal cost. The sum of the gains is the total surplus. If the conditions of the basic competitive model are satisfied, the market will maximize total surplus. In this sense the allocation of resources is efficient.
3   The concept of efficiency used by economists is called **Pareto efficiency.** An allocation of resources is Pareto efficient if there is no way to reallocate resources to make anyone better off without hurting someone else. The equilibrium of the competitive economy is Pareto efficient. There is **exchange efficiency** because the goods and services produced by the economy are distributed efficiently among individuals, **production efficiency** because the economy is on its production possibilities curve, and **product-mix efficiency** because the mix of goods matches consumers' tastes.
4   **Partial equilibrium analysis** looks at one market in isolation. This kind of analysis can be inappropriate if changes in the market under consideration cause disturbances in the rest of the economy, which then feed back in an important way to the original market. **General equilibrium analysis** takes into account the relationships among different markets and keeps track of the interactions.
5   While the competitive economy allocates resources efficiently, it does not necessarily distribute then fairly. An unequal outcome results in some households with enormous wealth, some in deep poverty, and many in between. According to the competitive model, however, more equitable divisions of the economy's goods can be achieved by redistributing initial wealth. Once this is done, the market can make all of the remaining

resource allocation decisions efficiently. Public education can be seen as an example of this idea, providing everyone with a more equal measure of human capital.

BEHIND THE ESSENTIAL CONCEPTS

1 If a firm produces several goods and there exists a way to rearrange its production and increase the output of one good without reducing the output of any other, an economist would say that this firm is inefficient. The firm is wasting inputs, because it is not getting the maximum output from the inputs. The output of the economy is the satisfaction (the utility) of its members. Therefore, if the economy is doing things one way, and there exists another way to do things that increases the utility of one individual (makes her better off) without reducing the utility of anyone else, then, just like the firm above, the economy is inefficient. Pareto efficiency is a natural definition of efficiency for the economy, the important output of which is ultimately not goods and services but human satisfaction.

2 Economists often speak of the trade-off of efficiency and equity. The competitive market brings about an efficient allocation of resources, but its results are by no means fair. The unfortunate fact, as we have seen, is that attempts to redistribute resources often have undesirable consequences for efficiency. For example, rent control can redistribute wealth from landlords to renters. This may promote equality, but it leads to shortages and other porblems that undermine the efficiency of housing markets. In principle we could redistribute initial wealth and then leave the rest to the market. This policy would achieve both efficiency and fairness, but it is unlikely in the real world.

3 The interdependencies of markets demonstrate another facet of the principle of substitution. When the price of one good rises, the demand for its substitutes rises, while the demand for its complement falls. When the price of one input rises, firms substitute other inputs. A change in the capital market affects the wealth of consumers and the costs of firms. The economy is a spider's web, and a movement in any one part reverberates throughout the whole.

4 Even though there are connections among all markets, in many cases the effects beyond a single market may be small. When this is true, it is sufficient to concentrate on the one market, that is, to employ partial equilibrium analysis, and ignore any general equilibrium repercussions. The art of economic analysis is to bring to light the important general equilibrium considerations and leave aside the portion of the economy that remains relatively unaffected.

SELF-TEST

True or False

1 For the most part, in the capital market, firms are demanders and households are suppliers.
2 In the product market, firms are demanders and households are suppliers.
3 In the labor market, firms are demanders and households are suppliers.
4 The economy is in equilibrium when most of its markets clear.
5 The allocation of resources is Pareto efficient in competitive equilibrium.
6 The allocation of resources is equal in competitive equilibrium.
7 Pareto efficiency means that everyone can be made better off by some reallocation of resources.
8 All points along the production possibilities curve are Pareto efficient.
9 Pareto efficiency requires exchange efficiency, production efficiency, and product-mix efficiency.
10 A general equilibrium analysis takes into account all the important interactions among markets.
11 A partial equilibrium analysis focuses on one market only.
12 General equilibrium and partial equilibrium analyses always differ quite dramatically.
13 The burden of the corporate income tax falls on investors in the corporate and noncorporate sectors.
14 Partial equilibrium analysis is appropriate for taxes on individual markets, such as cigarettes.
15 Even when the conditions of the competitive model are satisfied, there is a substantial role for government in correcting market failures.

Multiple Choice

1 In a general equilibrium model, the supply of labor depends on
   a product prices.
   b the wage.
   c interest rates.
   d all of the above.
   e *a* and *b*.
2 In a partial equilibrium model, the supply of products depends on the wage and interest rates because
   a these input prices affect costs.
   b household income is affected by changes in the wage and interest rates.
   c households can substitute leisure or future consumption for current products.
   d the demand for capital depends upon the wage rate.
   e all of the above.

3 Which of the following is *not* necessarily true when the economy is in full, general equilibrium?

  a The supply of labor equals the demand.

  b The supply of products equals the demand.

  c The supply of capital equals the demand.

  d The distribution of income is fair.

  e All of the above are true when the economy is in equilibrium.

4 In the product market,

  a firms are demanders and households are suppliers.

  b firms and households are demanders and the government is the supplier.

  c the government is the demander and households are suppliers.

  d households are demanders and firms are suppliers.

  e the government is the supplier and firms are demanders.

5 In the labor market,

  a firms are demanders and households are suppliers.

  b firms and households are demanders and the government is the supplier.

  c the government is the demander and households are suppliers.

  d household are demanders and firms are suppliers.

  e the government is the supplier and firms are demanders.

6 In the capital market, in general,

  a firms borrow and households save.

  b firms save and households borrow.

  c households pay interest to firms.

  d firms pay wages to households.

  e all of the above.

7 Consumer surplus refers to

  a the gain that consumers receive by paying less than the maximum that they are willing to pay.

  b the gain that sellers receive by selling at a price above marginal cost.

  c accounting profits.

  d economic profits.

  e the total gain from trade in the market.

8 Producer surplus refers to

  a the gain that consumers receive by paying less than the maximum that they are willing to pay.

  b the gain that sellers receive by selling at a price above marginal cost.

  c accounting profits.

  d economic profits.

  e the total gain from trade in the market.

9 In competitive equilibrium,

  a consumer surplus is maximized.

  b producer surplus is maximized.

  c the sum of consumer and producer surplus is maximized.

  d all of the above.

  e none of the above.

10 Exchange efficiency means that

  a the distribution of the goods and services that the economy produces is efficient.

  b the distribution of the goods and services that the economy produces is equitable.

  c the economy is operating along its production possibilities curve.

  d all of the above.

  e *a* and *b*.

11 Production efficiency means that

  a the mix of goods and services that the economy produces reflects the preferences of consumers.

  b the economy is operating along its production possibilities curve.

  c the distribution of what the economy produces is efficient.

  d the distribution of what the economy produces is equitable.

  e all of the above.

12 Which of the following is *not* implied by Pareto efficiency?

  a Exchange efficiency

  b Production efficiency

  c Efficiency of the product mix

  d All individuals share equally in the decisions that the economy makes.

  e All of the above are implied by Pareto efficiency.

13 If the competitive model is an accurate depiction of the economy, then

  a the allocation of resources is Pareto efficient.

  b the distribution of income may be quite unequal.

  c the economy is operating on the production possibilities curve.

  d the economy is operating on the utility possibilities curve.

  e all of the above.

14 In general equilibrium, a tax on business profits will be paid by individuals through

  a increases in product prices.

  b decreases in wages.

  c decreases in dividends.

  d capital losses on stock ownership.

  e all of the above.

15 An increase in the tax rate on commercial property will

  a have no effect on the returns to other forms of capital investment.

  b cause financial capital to flow from commercial property to other forms of capital investment, reducing the average return to capital.

  c have no effect on the allocation of financial capital.

  d have no effect on the returns to capital because all investments must be equally profitable in equilibrium.

  e *a* and *c*.

16 If the allocation of resources is Pareto efficient,
  a the distribution of income is fair.
  b there is a way to reallocate resources and make everyone better off.
  c there is a way to reallocate resources and make some people better off without hurting others.
  d there is no way to reallocate resources and make anyone better off without hurting some other person.
  e none of the above.

17 When an analysis focuses on the interactions between markets, it is called
  a partial equilibrium.
  b interactive equilibrium.
  c disequilibrium.
  d general equilibrium.
  e none of the above.

18 When an analysis looks only at the changes in one market, it is called
  a partial equilibrium.
  b interactive equilibrium.
  c disequilibrium.
  d general equilibrium.
  e none of the above.

19 Which of the following probably does *not* require a general equilibrium analysis?
  a A corporate income tax
  b A ban on foreign investment
  c A national sales tax
  d Elimination of trade restrictions
  e All of the above require general equilibrium analysis.

20 Which of the following probably requires *only* a partial equilibrium analysis?
  a An increase in the supply of green beans
  b Stricter antipollution regulations
  c A reduction in the size of the military by one-half
  d An end to agricultural price supports
  e All of the above

Completion

1 When demand equals supply in all markets, the economy is in _____.
2 The area between the demand curve and the price measures _____.
3 The area between the supply curve and the price measures _____.
4 In competitive equilibrium, _____ is maximized.
5 According to Adam Smith, individual actions are led to produce good social outcomes by the _____.
6 When there is no way to make anyone better off without hurting someone else, the allocation of resources is _____.
7 _____ requires that the economy's output of goods and services be distributed efficiently among its consumers.
8 When the economy is productively efficient, it is operating on its _____ curve.
9 Focusing on a single market while ignoring any spillover effects on other markets is called _____ analysis.
10 _____ analysis takes into account all the interactions and interdependencies between various parts of the economy.

Answers to Self-Test

True or False

1	t	6	f	11	t
2	f	7	f	12	f
3	t	8	f	13	t
4	f	9	t	14	t
5	t	10	t	15	f

Multiple Choice

1	d	6	a	11	b	16	d
2	a	7	a	12	d	17	d
3	d	8	b	13	e	18	a
4	d	9	c	14	e	19	e
5	a	10	a	15	b	20	a

Completion

1 equilibrium
2 consumer surplus
3 producer surplus
4 total surplus
5 invisible hand
6 Pareto efficient
7 Exchange efficiency
8 production possibilities
9 partial equilibrium
10 General equilibrium

Doing Economics: Tools and Practice Problems

The competitive economy is efficient in the sense that it maximizes the sum of consumer and producer surpluses. We begin this section with some problems verifying this idea. Then we turn to general equilibrium analysis. The skill in general equilibrium analysis lies in choosing which interdependencies are important and which can be left aside. In this problem set, we first use the three-market model to analyze the effects of major changes in the economy: the introduction of a national sales tax, an important technological advance, and an increase in savings. Finally, there are a few problems that focus on the connections between two markets. We consider corporate taxation, compensating differentials, and natural resource prices.

Tool Kit 10.1 Maximizing Total Surplus and the Competitive Equilibrium

Consumer surplus measures the gain to the demander in a market. Producer surplus measures the corresponding gain to the supply side of the market. The competitive equilibrium maximizes the sum of consumer and producer surpluses. Follow these steps.

Step one: Identify the demand and supply curves.

Step two: Compute the sum of consumer and producer surplus for first unit. Use the following formula:
Consumer surplus + producer surplus
= (demand price − market price) + (market price − supply price)
= demand price − supply price.

Step three: Find the total surplus for the second unit. This is the sum of the difference between the demand and supply prices for the first and second unit.

Demand		Supply		
Price	Quantity	Price	Quantity	Total surplus
$10	1	$2	1	$10 − $2 = $8
$ 9	2	$3	2	$8 + ($9 − $3) = $14
Etc.				

Step four: Find the quantity that maximizes total surplus.

Step five: Verify that this is the market clearing equilibrium.

1 (Worked problem: maximizing total surplus) The market demand and supply of roses are given below.
  a Find the total surplus for each quantity.
  b Find the quantity that maximizes total surplus.
  c Find the competitive equilibrium and verify that it is the quantity that maximizes total surplus.

Demand		Supply	
Price	Quantity (thousands)	Price	Quantity (thousands)
$20	1	$ 4	1
$18	2	$ 6	2
$16	3	$ 8	3
$14	4	$10	4
$12	5	$12	5
$10	6	$14	6
$ 8	7	$16	7

Step-by-step solution

Step one: Identify the demand and supply curves. They are given above.

Step two: Compute the sum of consumer and producer surplus for the first unit. For the first thousand roses the total surplus is $20 − $4 = $16.

Step three: Find total surplus for the second unit. This is $16 + $18 − $6 = $28. Continuing and entering in the table we have.

Demand		Supply		Total Surplus
Price	Quantity (thousands)	Price	Quantity (thousands)	($thousands)
$20	1	$ 4	1	$20 − $4 = 16
$18	2	$ 6	2	$16 + $18 − $6 = $28
$16	3	$ 8	3	$28 + $16 − $8 = $36
$14	4	$10	4	$36 + $14 − $10 = $40
$12	5	$12	5	$40 + $12 − $12 = $40
$10	6	$14	6	$40 + $10 − $14 = $36
$ 8	7	$16	7	$36 + $8 − $16 = $28

Step four: Find the quantity that maximize total surplus. Total surplus is maximized at 5 thousand roses. (Note that total surplus is also $40 thousand when the quantity is 4 thousand.)

Step five: Verify that this is the market-clearing equilibrium. The market-clearing equilibrium is 5.

2 (Practice problem: maximizing total surplus) The market demand and supply of plaster repairs are given below.
  a Find the total surplus for each quantity.
  b Find the quantity that maximizes total surplus.
  c Find the equilibrium and verify that it is the quantity that maximizes total surplus.

Demand		Supply	
Price	Quantity	Price	Quantity
$100	1	$10	1
$ 80	2	$20	2
$ 60	3	$30	3
$ 40	4	$40	4
$ 20	5	$50	5

3 (Practice problem: maximizing total surplus) The market demand and supply of catered dinners are given below.
  a Find the total surplus for each quantity.
  b Find the quantity that maximizes total surplus.
  c Find the competitive equilibrium and verify that it is the quantity that maximizes total surplus.

Demand		Supply	
Price	Quantity	Price	Quantity
$800	1	$ 200	1
$700	2	$ 400	2
$600	3	$ 600	3
$500	4	$ 800	4
$600	5	$1,000	5

Tool Kit 10.2 Using General Equilibrium Analysis

When doing general equilibrium analysis, keep the following procedure in mind.

Step one: Identify the relevant markets.

Step two: Start with an equilibrium in each market, as in the figure.

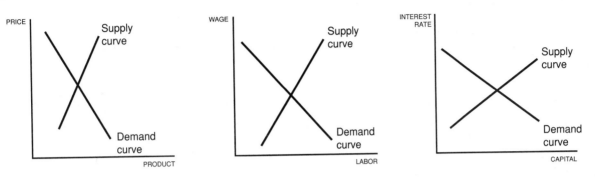

Step three: Identify a change, and determine which curves shift as a direct result of the change. In the second row of the figure, the demand for labor shifts outwards.

Step four: Shift the curves, and find the new equilibrium. In the general equilibrium model, this is only a temporary equilibrium because there are second-round effects to be accounted for. Observe which prices have changed. In the diagram, wages increase.

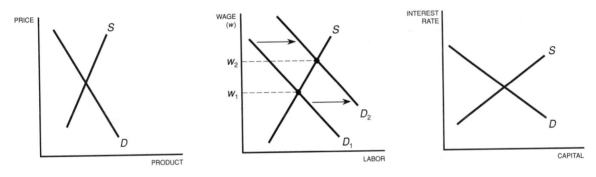

Step five: Determine which curves shift as a result of the price changes observed in step four.

Step six: Shift the curves, as shown here by lower supply in the product market and higher demand in the capital market, and find the new equilbrium.

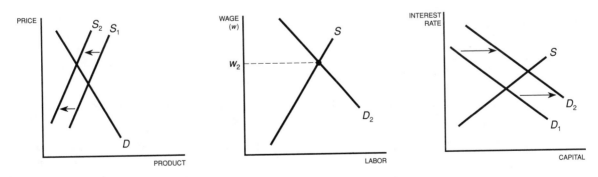

Step seven: Stop. Usually a second round is enough. Compare the new equilbrium with that in step two.

LIVERPOOL JOHN MOORES UNIVERSITY
LEARNING SERVICES

4 (Worked problem: general equilibrium analysis) There are three major markets: labor; capital, and product. They are interrelated in that the prices in other markets cause the demand curves and supply curves tto shift. Because of this interdependance, there will be important second-round effects in the three-market model. Most European countries have value-added taxes, a type of national sales tax.

a Use the three market model to evaluate the effects of a value-added tax.

b Who pays the value-added tax?

Step-by-step solution

Step one (*a*): Identify the relevant markets. We will use the labor, capital, and product markets.

Step two: Start with an equilibrium in each market.

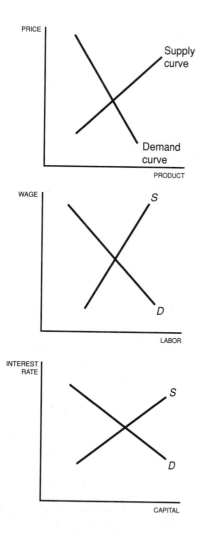

Step three: The value-added tax shifts the product market supply curve up by the amount of the tax. (This step is exactly like the analysis of the effects of taxes in Chapter 5.)

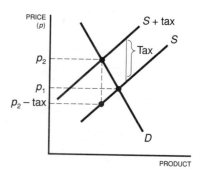

Step four: Find the new (temporary) equilibrium. Note that some of the tax is paid by consumers in the form of higher product prices. On the other hand, firms also receive less after the tax. This completes the first round.

Step five: Determine which curves shift as a result of the price changes observed in step four. The lower net of tax product prices observed in step four implies that the value of the marginal product of inputs is lower. This means that the demand curve for labor and the demand curve for capital must shift to the left.

Step six: Shift the curves, and find the new equilibrium.

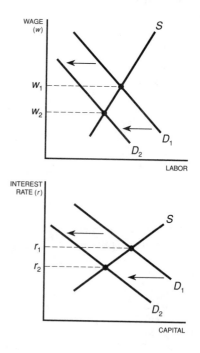

Step seven: Compare the new equilibrium with that in step two. We see that the wage and the interest rate are lower.

Step eight (*b*): The value-added tax is paid for in three ways. First, it is shifted forward to consumers in the form of higher product prices. Second, it is shifted backward to workers through lower wages. Third, it is shifted backward to savers in terms of lower interest rates. A vital lesson of the general equilibrium approach is that all taxes are ultimately paid by individuals. A partial equilibrium treatment in the product market alone would imply that firms pay some of the tax. The full general equilibrium analysis reveals that the producers' share of the tax is passed backward to workers and savers.

5 (Practice problem: general equilibrium analysis) A substantial share in the growth of developed countries is accounted for by technological advance, by improvements in how goods and services are produced, and by the introduction of new and better products. The hope for continued economic progress rests on technological advance in production. Use the three-market model to analyze the effects of a major technological advance.

   a Start with an equilibrium in the three markets.

   b Better technology increases the marginal products of labor and capital. Which curves are shifted? (Hint: Remember the formula for the value of the marginal product and the relationship between marginal product and marginal cost.)

   c In the second round, how does the equilibrium change?

6 (Practice problem: general equilibrium analysis) Many people are concerned about relatively low savings rate. One cause for optimism is that the aging of the relatively large baby boom generation will lead to more savings. Suppose that households decrease their consumption and increase their savings. Trace through the effects using the three-market model.

7 (Worked problem: general equilibrium analysis) Often when a change occurs in one market, there is another market closely linked to the first. In these cases, both markets must be included in the analysis. Investors seeking the highest possible returns can choose to buy stock in corporations or to invest their money in other noncorporate businesses. If the returns were higher in the corporate sector of the economy, then no one would invest in the noncorporate sector. If the returns were higher in the noncorporate sector, all money would flow out of the corporate sector. In equilibrium, then, the rate of return must be equal in the two sectors.

   a Illustrate an equilibrium in the markets for corporate and noncorporate investment.

   b In the United States, corporations must pay taxes on their income. The corporate income tax is in addition to the taxes paid by investors on their dividend income. Show how a tax on corporate income affects the market for corporate investment.

   c Show how the noncorporate investment market will adjust to restore both markets to equilibrium.

   d Who pays the corporate income tax?

Step-by-step solution

Step one (*a*): Start with an equilibrium. In this case, not only must supply and demand be equal in each market, but also each market must pay the same returns.

Step two (*b*): Determine which curve shifts. The corporate tax is paid by the demanders (corporations); therefore, the demand curve in the market for corporate investment shifts down.

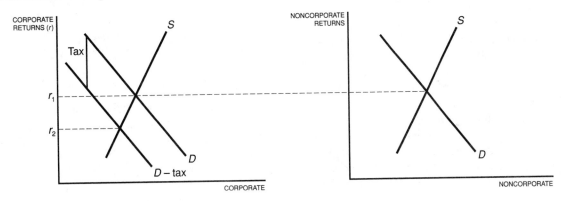

Step three: The (temporary) equilibrium in the market for corporate investment has a lower rate of return than in the market for noncorporate investment.

Step four (c): Determine the effects in the noncorporate investment market. Because they can earn higher after-tax returns in the noncorporate sector, corporate investors will move their money. The supply of corporate investment will shift left, and the supply of noncorporate investment will shift right, until the returns are equal.

 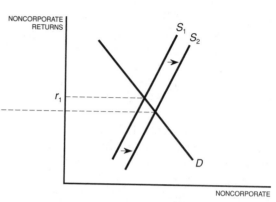

Step five (d): Find the new equilibrium and compare. In the new equilibrium, the returns are equal in each sector, but overall the returns are lower. We conclude that the corporate tax is paid by both noncorporate and corporate investors.

8 (Practice problem: general equilibrium analysis) Differences in wages that reflect differences in the characteristics of jobs are called compensating differentials. Truck drivers who haul freight over long distances are paid more than those who drive local routes. Suppose that the difference is $50 per week in equilibrium.

  a Start with an equilibrium in the markets for local truck drivers and long-haul drivers. Be sure that the difference in wages is $50 per week.

  b A new policy, agreed upon by both union and management, specifies that each driver must earn the same amount. Explain how the markets will adjust.

9 (Practice problem: general equilibrium analysis) Many people are concerned about the possible exhaustion of the limited supplies of natural resources, such as oil. To understand the economics of this issue, consider a two-period problem. Known reserves of oil equal 100,000 barrels. The oil can be sold now or be saved and sold in the future period. The discount rate is 50 percent over the time between the periods. The demand is the same now and in the future, and it is given in Table 10.1.

  a Calculate the present discounted value of each of the prices for the future demand. This is the current value of waiting to sell at the future price.

  b If the current price is greater than the present discounted value of the future price, all the oil will be sold today. If the reverse is true, the oil will be sold in the future. In equilibrium, current price must equal the present discounted value of the future price, and the total quantity sold in both periods must equal 100,000 barrels. Find the equilibrium

Table 10.1

Price	Quantity	Present discounted value of the future price
$50	20,000	
$45	30,000	
$40	40,000	
$35	55,000	
$30	70,000	
$25	80,000	
$20	90,000	
$10	100,000	

price today, the price in the future, and the quantity sold in each period.

Answers to Problems

2 *a*

Demand		Supply		
Price	Quantity	Price	Quantity	Total surplus
$100	1	$10	1	$100 − $10 = $90
$ 80	2	$20	2	$90 + $80 − $20 = $150
$ 60	3	$30	3	$150 + $60 − $30 = $180
$ 40	4	$40	4	$180 + $40 − $40 = $180
$ 20	5	$50	5	$180 + $20 − $50 = $150

  b Total Surplus is maximized when the quantity is 4.
  c The market-clearing equilibrium is also 4.

3 *a*

Demand		Supply		
Price	Quantity	Price	Quantity	Total surplus
$800	1	$ 200	1	$800 − $200 = $600
$700	2	$ 400	2	$900 + $700 − $400 = $900
$600	3	$ 600	3	$900 + $600 − $600 = $900
$500	4	$ 800	4	$900 + $500 − $800 = $600
$600	5	$1,000	5	$600 + $600 − $1,000 = $200

b Total Surplus is maximized when the quantity is 4.

c The market-clearing equilibrium is also 4.

5 *a* The initial equilibrium price is p_1, the wage is w_1, and the interest rate is r_1.

  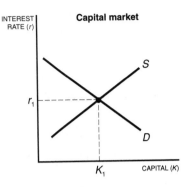

b The technical advance shifts the demands for labor and capital to the right because both factors are made more productive, and it shifts the supply of products to the right because costs are lower. The product price falls to p_2, the wage rises to w_2, and the interest rate rises to r_2.

  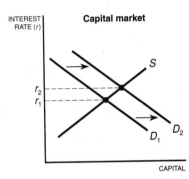

c In the second round, the supply curve for products shifts left (mitigating the effects of the original shift) because wages and interest rates are higher. The demand curves for labor and capital shift back to the left (offsetting somewhat the effects of the original shift) because product prices are lower. (Recall that the demand for a factor of production is the value of the marginal product, which is price multiplied by marginal product.) The ultimate price is p_3, which is higher than p_1 but lower than p_2, because of the general equilibrium repercussions. Similarly, w_3 is greater than w_1 and r_3 is greater than r_1, but the changes are less great than a partial equilibrium analysis would imply.

  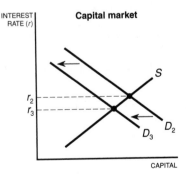

6 *a* The initial equilibrium price is p_1, the wage is w_1, and the interest rate is r_1.

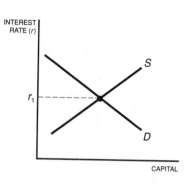

b As people consume less, the demand for output falls. As they save more, the supply shifts to the right in the capital market. Product prices and interest rates fall as a result.

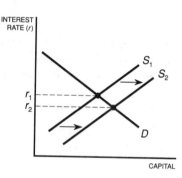

c In the second round, the fall in interest rates shifts the supply of output to the right and further reduces product prices. The fall in product prices, observed in part b, reduces the demand for capital and leads to a further decrease in the interest rate. In the labor market, demand shifts up because of lower interest rates, but shifts down because of lower product prices. The ultimate impact on the wage is not certain.

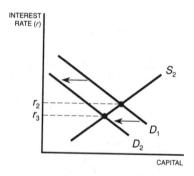

8 a In the initial equilibrium, both markets clear, and the weekly wage is $50 higher in the long-haul market.

b When the same wage is paid in the two markets, there is a shortage of long-haul drivers, and a surplus of drivers in the local market.

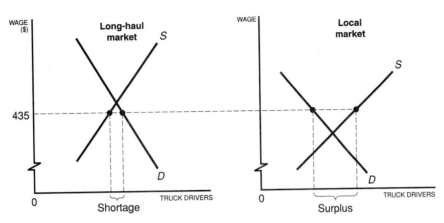

9 *a* The present discounted value of the future price is given in Table 10.2.

Table 10.2

Price	Quantity	Present discounted value of the future price
$50	20,000	$50 / (1 + $.50) = $33.33
$45	30,000	$30.00
$40	40,000	$26.67
$35	55,000	$23.33
$30	70,000	$20.00
$25	80,000	$16.67
$20	90,000	$13.33
$10	100,000	$6.67

b The current price is $30, and 70,000 barrels are sold. The future price is $45, and 30,000 barrels are sold. The total is 70,000 + 30,000 = 100,000. The present discounted value of the future price is $30, which is the current price.

PART THREE

Imperfect Markets

| Introduction to Imperfect Markets

Chapter Review

The focus now shifts away from the efficiency of the basic competitive model to the fascinating world of imperfect competition. The chapter identifies four broad categories of market failures: imperfect market structures, information problems, externalities, and public goods. Subsequent chapters in Part Three study aspects of each of these categories in detail.

ESSENTIAL CONCEPTS

1 While there is only one basic competitive model, markets can be imperfect in a variety of ways. These imperfections lead to **market failures**. Economists see a role for government in correcting market failures.

  a In the basic competitive model, the outputs of each firm are perfect substitutes. This means that if a firm unilaterally raises its price, it loses all of its customers. Therefore, firms are price takers and need not consider the actions of rivals. In imperfect markets, firms set their own prices and must worry about the reactions of rivals.

  b In the basic competitive model, buyers and sellers have all the necessary information. When customers are not informed about product quality or lenders do not know the creditworthiness of borrowers, information problems arise that lead to another type of **imperfect competition**.

  c In the basic competitive model, firms and households bear all of the consequences of their actions. When this is not true, there are **externalities.** For example, polluters may not have

an incentive to consider the damages caused by their effluents. This can lead to market failure.

  d In the basic competitive model, a good is consumed by only one person and should this person not pay for it, he or she is excluded from its benefits. **Public goods** lack these two attributes and this lack causes market failure.

2 There are four important types of **market structure: perfect competition, monopoly, monopolistic competition,** and **oligopoly.** A monopoly has a single seller. Under monopolistic competition there are many firms, each selling a distinct product. Few firms dominate the industry in oligopolies. The essential differences are summarized in Table 11.1.

Table 11.1

Market Structure	Firm's demand curve	Entry	Product differentiation	Examples
Perfect competition	Horizontal	Free entry	Homogenous products	Wheat, corn
Monopoly	Downward sloping	Barriers to entry	Only one	Major league baseball, holders of patents
Monopolistic competition	Downward sloping	Free entry	Differentiated products	Restaurants, designer clothing
Oligopoly	Downward sloping	Barriers to entry	Either homogenous or differentiated products	Aluminum manufacturers, automobiles

3 With imperfect competition, firms see that their **marginal revenue** is less than price and they increase profits by raising price above marginal cost. Government policies to deal with this market failure include antitrust policies and the regulation of natural monopolies.

4 When buyers or sellers lack important information about what is traded, market failures can occur. For example, a buyer who is not confident of the quality of a good may refrain from purchasing the good even though she values it more than its cost. Similar problems arise in labor and capital markets. Markets for information break down because the seller cannot credibly convince the buyer of the information's value. Government policies include consumer protection legislation and financial market regulation.

5 When there are costs of benefits that spill over to others, economists say there are **externalities** and market failures. For example, when the polluting firm ignores the damage that its pollution does to others, the market price reflects only private costs. Government policies include establishing property rights, environmental regulation, taxes, and subsidies.

6 Public goods have two attributes. They are **nonrivalrous.** As more people consume the public good, it remains available for others to consume. They are also **nonexcludable.** Anyone can benefit from the public good without paying. This brings about the **free-rider** problem. Firms that produce public goods cannot make any revenue because customers know that they can benefit without paying.

BEHIND THE ESSENTIAL CONCEPTS

1 One important idea in the theory of imperfect competition is the relationship between marginal revenue and price. Marginal revenue is the extra revenue that the firm takes in when it sells another unit. In perfect competition, this amount is the price. But in imperfect competition, the price falls as more output is sold. Thus, there are two effects on revenue, shown in Figure 11.1. The firm is initially selling 10 units for $10 each. If it chooses to produce and sell 11 units, the price falls to $9.50. The first effect on revenue is that the firm sells more units at $9.50. This is shown as the area with pluses. If the demand curve facing the firm were horizontal, as under perfect competition, this would be the end of the story: the extra revenue would be price times the extra quantity sold. However, the downward-sloping demand curve makes the price drop in order to sell one extra unit. This is the second effect. It means that the firm loses revenue on all its existing sales (because the price is lower for all units). This effect is

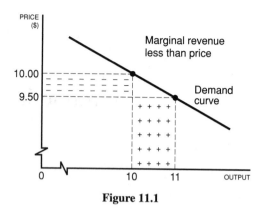

Figure 11.1

shown as the area with minuses, and it makes marginal revenue less than the simple price times quantity calculation.

2 In product markets, buyers may not know all they need to know about the quality of the good. In labor markets, firms may not be confident about the qualifications and effort of their employees. In capital markets, lenders may not be sure about their borrower's creditworthiness. Each of these are examples of the same type of imperfect competition. In each case, the information problems stand in the way of mutually beneficial exchanges.

3 One reason that markets for information do not work well is that information has the two attributes of a public good. It is nonrivalrous. Suppose that I know how to make waffles. You can learn how without affecting me at all. Also, information is nonexcludable. It is difficult for me to prevent you from learning how to make waffles. These two attributes bring about free-riding and market failure.

4 Externalities exist whenever individuals or firms do not face the full costs and benefits of their decisions, and left alone, externalities create incentive problems. Negative externalities are costs borne by others, such as pollution, congestion, and noise. Positive externalities are benefits received by others, such as contributions for medical and other research, innovation, public parks, and endangered species preservation. Because decision makers can ignore the costs that spill over onto others, private firms overproduce negative externalities. Similarly, because they are not compensated, producers of positive externalities do not create enough. Governments can improve the allocation of resources by inducing individuals to produce fewer negative and more positive externalities.

5 Public goods have two important characteristics. Once they are provided, the marginal cost of another consumer's enjoying the good is zero. For example, a second, third, or fourth person can view a public statue without affecting the first person's enjoyment. The

second characteristic is that it is costly to exclude individuals from enjoying the public good. Placing the statue in a private viewing area and charging admission misses the point of a monument. This feature makes it difficult for private individuals to collect enough funds to provide public goods. The fact that people can choose to enjoy public goods without paying for them is called the free-rider problem, and it is one reason economists often recommend that the public sector take a role in providing public goods.

True or False

1   Market structure refers to the organization of the market.
2   A monopoly is the situation where a single firm supplies the entire market quantity.
3   In an oligopoly several firms operate in the market.
4   Firms can ignore the reactions of rivals in monopolistic competition.
5   The fact that college-educated workers are more productive implies, of course, that the college education has increased their productivity.
6   The market system leads to an efficient allocation of resources only if firms know the preferences of consumers.
7   Markets for information are troubled by the facts that the buyer cannot judge the quality of the information before he learns it, and after he learns it, he does not need to buy it.
8   Government policies related to imperfect information include regulations that require the disclosure of information and outlaw deceptive advertising.
9   Government action is distinguished from private sector action in that government always has better information.
10   Externalities are present whenever an individual or a firm can take an action without bearing all the costs and benefits.
11   The marginal cost of an additional consumer is zero for a public good.
12   The marginal cost of production is zero for a public good.
13   It is very costly to exclude those who do not pay from consuming private goods.
14   Markets for new inventions fail if those who benefit from new inventions do not pay the inventor.
15   If the private market provides too little of some good or service, then government can increase the quantity provided by subsidizing the good or service.

Multiple Choice

1   The types of imperfect competition considered in this chapter include
    a   imperfectly competitive market structures.
    b   information problems.
    c   externalities.
    d   public goods.
    e   all of the above.
2   Which of the following assumptions of the basic competitive model is *not* true in the case of monopoly?
    a   Firms are price takers.
    b   Individuals and firms have perfect information about quality.
    c   Actions of individuals affect others only through their effects on prices.
    d   Only the buyer enjoys the benefits of goods.
    e   Output is fairly distributed among all household in the economy.
3   Which of the following assumptions of the basic competitive model is *not* true in the case of imperfect information?
    a   Firms are price takers.
    b   Individuals and firms have perfect information about quality.
    c   Actions of individuals affect others only through their effects on prices.
    d   Only the buyer enjoys the benefits of goods.
    e   Output is fairly distributed among all household in the economy.
4   Which of the following assumptions of the basic competitive model is *not* true in the case of externalities?
    a   Firms are price takers.
    b   Individuals and firms have perfect information about quality.
    c   Actions of individuals affect others only through their effects on prices.
    d   Only the buyer enjoys the benefits of goods.
    e   Output is fairly distributed among all household in the economy.
5   Which of the following assumptions of the basic competitive model is *not* true in the case of public goods?
    a   Firms are price takers.
    b   Individuals and firms have perfect information about quality.
    c   Actions of individuals affect others only through their effects on prices.
    d   Only the buyer enjoys the benefits of goods.
    e   Output is fairly distributed among all household in the economy.
6   In which market structure are resources allocated efficiently?
    a   Monopoly
    b   Oligopoly
    c   Monopolistic competition
    d   Perfect competition
    e   All of the above

7 Firms must consider the reactions of rivals in which market structure?

    a Monopoly

    b Oligopoly

    c Monopolistic competition

    d Perfect competition

    e All of the above

8 Firms are price takers in which market structure?

    a Monopoly

    b Oligopoly

    c Monopolistic competition

    d Perfect competition

    e All of the above

9 Markets for information

    a can never work, and thus we require the government to provide information.

    b are troubled by credibility problems in that buyers cannot judge the quality of information before learning it.

    c work in much the same way as other successful markets.

    d are usually monopolies.

    e usually fail due to excessive government regulation.

10 For competitive markets to allocate resources efficiently,

    a firms must know the preferences of consumers.

    b firms must know the available supplies of all of their inputs.

    c consumers must know the technology of production for products they buy.

    d all of the above.

    e none of the above.

11 Private markets may *not* provide information efficiently because

    a information is scarce.

    b information is costly to produce.

    c certain types of information are public goods.

    d the principle of consumer sovereignty does not apply to information.

    e private markets cannot exercise eminent domain.

12 What important information does the price of potting soil convey to the producer of potting soil?

    a The marginal cost of potting soil

    b The marginal benefit to consumers of potting soil

    c The quantity of potting soil produced by its competitors

    d The productivity of its workers

    e All of the above

13 Government policies to correct information problems include

    a consumer protection legislation.

    b disclosure regulations of the Securities and Exchange Commission.

    c laws against deceptive advertising.

    d truth-in-lending legislation.

    e all of the above.

14 Which of the following is *not* an example of an externality?

    a Environmental pollution

    b Research and development

    c Restoring buildings in decaying areas

    d Contributions to philanthropic organizations

    e All of the above are examples of externalities.

15 Market failure occurs when there are

    a positive externalities.

    b negative externalities.

    c positive or negative externalities.

    d no externalities.

    e none of the above.

16 When there is a negative externality, market output is

    a greater than the efficient level and the market price is too high.

    b less than the efficient level and the market price is too low.

    c greater than the efficient level and the market price is too low.

    d less than the efficient level and the market price is too high.

    e none of the above.

17 Which of the following is/are true of pure public goods?

    a The marginal cost of an additional individual using the good is zero.

    b It is impossible to exclude people from receiving the good.

    c They are efficiently provided through the interaction of supply and demand.

    d *a* and *b*.

    e All of the above.

18 One advantage that government has in the provision of public goods is that it

    a is not subject to scarcity.

    b does not face uncertainty about the demand for public goods.

    c can coerce citizens to pay for them.

    d need not always be rational.

    e none of the above.

19 The free-rider problem refers to

    a the idea that public transportation always runs large deficits.

    b the idea that when people can enjoy a public good without paying for it, they often do not contribute.

    c the idea that markets fail to allocate resources efficiently when there are externalities.

    d the idea that the marginal cost of an additional consumer enjoying a pure public good is zero.

    e none of the above.

20 Which of the following is *not* a reason for market failure?

   a Externalities

   b Public goods

   c Missing markets

   d Lack of competition

   e All of the above are reasons for market failure.

Completion Questions

1 The failure of private markets to produce economic efficiency is called _____.

2 _____ refers to how a market is organized.

3 A single firm supplies the entire market in a _____.

4 If the entire market is supplied by several firms, the market structure is _____.

5 In _____, there is enough competition so that firms can ignore the reactions of rivals, economic profits are driven near zero, and each firm's product is somewhat different.

6 When the market structure is not perfect competition, the marginal revenue is _____ than price.

7 _____ refers to government policies that prevent monopolies from forming, restrain anticompetitive behavior, or break up monopolies that exist.

8 When an individual or firm can take an action without bearing the full costs and benefits, there is said to be an _____.

9 Public goods have two key properties: _____ and _____.

10 Because it is difficult to exclude those who do not pay from benefiting from public goods, the private markets do a poor job of providing public goods. This is the _____ problem.

Answers to Self-Test

True or False

1	t	6	f	11	t
2	t	7	t	12	f
3	t	8	t	13	f
4	t	9	f	14	t
5	f	10	t	15	t

Multiple Choice

1	e	6	d	11	c	16	c
2	a	7	b	12	b	17	d
3	b	8	d	13	e	18	c
4	c	9	b	14	e	19	b
5	d	10	e	15	c	20	e

Completion

1 market failure

2 Market structure

3 monopoly

4 oligopoly

5 monopolistic competition

6 less

7 Antitrust policies

8 externality

9 nonrivalrous; nonexcludable

10 free-rider

Doing Economics: Tools and Practice Problems

When an activity causes positive externalities, or external benefits, the government can often improve matters through subsidies. This section explores two questions. First, how do subsidies encourage more of the subsidized activity? Our analysis will be very much like the treatment of the economic effects of taxation in Chapter 5. The other issue is why decisions are likely to be inefficient when there are externalities. This is an application of the technique of balancing marginal benefits and marginal costs introduced in Chapter 2.

SUBSIDIES

Many goods and services receive subsidies from various levels of government. Sometimes, as in the case of home ownership, the demanders benefit directly. In other cases, as with federal water projects, the subsidies are paid directly to the suppliers. Subsidies have their effects by shifting supply or demand curves, bringing about new equilibrium quantities. Tool Kit 11.1 shows how to analyze the impacts of subsidies.

Tool Kit 11.1 Using Supply and Demand to Determine the Effects of Subsidies

If subsidies are paid directly to demanders, the demand curve shifts. If paid directly to suppliers, subsidies shift the supply curve. The remainder of the analysis parallels the basic method of supply and demand. Follow these steps.

Step one: Start with a no-subsidy equilibrium in the appropriate market.

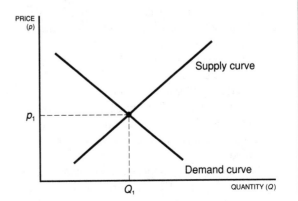

Step two: Identify the magnitude of the subsidy and whether it is paid directly to the demanders or suppliers.

Step three: If the subsidy is paid to demanders, shift the demand curve up (vertically) by exactly the amount of the subsidy. If the subsidy is paid to suppliers, shift the supply curve down by exactly the amount of the subsidy.

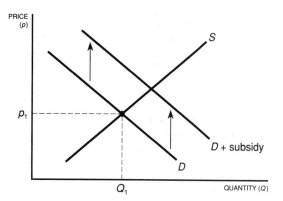

Step four: Find the new equilibrium and compare it with the original equilibrium.

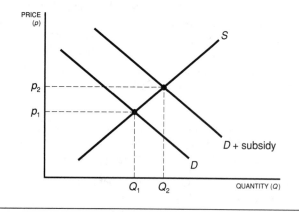

1 (Worked problem: effects of subsidies) Home ownership is treated very favorably by the U.S. tax system. The interest paid on mortgages is tax deductible, and the taxes on capital gains earned by selling at more than the purchase price can be deferred and even avoided altogether. To see how the subsidy affects the housing market, consider the market for three-bedroom bungalows in Little Spoon. The market demand and supply curves without the subsidy are given in Table 11.2.

a Find the equilibrium price and quantity.

b The tax advantages accruing to the home owner amount to $20,000 over the life of the occupancy. Calculate the demand curve with the subsidy included.

c Find the equilibrium price and quantity with the subsidy in place. How does the subsidy change the number of bungalows sold in Little Spoon?

Table 11.2

Demand		Supply	
Price	Quantity	Price	Quantity
$125,000	10	$125,000	50
$100,000	14	$100,000	42
$90,000	25	$90,000	31
$80,000	28	$80,000	28
$70,000	31	$70,000	20

Step-by-step solution

Step one (*a*): Start with a no-subsidy equilibrium in the appropriate market. The price is $80,000; the market clears with 28 houses sold. This is the answer to part *a*.

Step two (*b*): Identify the magnitude of the subsidy and whether it is paid directly to the demanders or suppliers. The subsidy is $20,000, paid to demanders.

Step three: Because it is paid to demanders, the subsidy causes the demand curve to shift vertically by $20,000. To calculate this, add $20,000 to each entry in the price column of the demand curve. The new demand curve is given in Table 11.3, which is the answer to part *b*.

Table 11.3

Demand	
Price	Quantity
$145,000	10
$120,000	14
$110,000	25
$100,000	28
$90,000	31

Step four (*c*): Find the new equilibrium and compare it with the original equilibrium. The new equilibrium price is $90,000, and the market clears at 31 houses sold. The subsidy has increased the number of home owners in Little Spoon from 28 to 31. The price is $10,000 higher, so the $20,000 subsidy makes home owners only $10,000 better off. Producers share in the benefits with a $10,000 higher price. The solution is illustrated in the diagram.

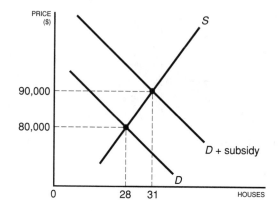

2 (Practice problem: effects of subsidies) Her eyes brightening at the thought of thousands of stressed, child-raising voters, Senator Shill has proposed child care grants of $10,000 per family. The demand and supply curves for child care services (measured in days) are given in Table 11.4.

Table 11.4

Demand		Supply	
Price (thousands)	Quantity (days)	Price (thousands)	Quantity (days)
$50	50,000	$50	100,000
$45	60,000	$45	80,000
$40	70,000	$40	70,000
$35	80,000	$35	60,000
$30	100,000	$30	50,000

a Find the equilibrium price and quantity without the subsidy.
b Calculate the demand with the subsidy.
c Find the equilibrium price and quantity with the subsidy. Compare the equilibria, and explain the effects of the subsidy.

3 (Practice problem: effects of subsidies) To promote conversion to renewable sources of energy, the government has offered various tax deductions and credits for the purchase and installation of solar water heaters. The value to a typical taxpayer of the tax provisions is $3,000. The supply and demand curves for solar water heaters are given in Table 11.5.

Table 11.5

Demand		Supply	
Price	Quantity	Price	Quantity
$8,000	1,000	$8,000	10,000
$7,000	3,000	$7,000	9,000
$6,000	5,000	$6,000	8,000
$5,000	7,000	$5,000	7,000
$4,000	9,000	$4,000	6,000
$3,000	11,000	$3,000	5,000

a Find the equilibrium price and quantity without the subsidy.
b Calculate the demand with the subsidy.
c Find the equilibrium price and quantity with the subsidy. Compare the equilibria, and explain the effects of the subsidy.

POSITIVE EXTERNALITIES

Individuals make decisions by balancing their private benefits and costs at the margin, but efficiency requires that all benefits and costs, not only the private ones, be included in the decision. Thus, when there are externalities, there are costs or benefits ignored by the individual making the decision, and this fact leads to inefficient decisions. This tool kit focuses on positive externalities and the inefficiencies that result.

Tool Kit 11.2 Showing How Positive Externalities Lead to Inefficiencies

Positive externalities occur when decision makers ignore some benefits of their actions. Follow these steps to see how this leads to inefficient decisions.

Step one: Find the private marginal benefits and costs of the relevant activity.

Step two: Find the equilibrium level of the activity, which is the level at which private marginal benefits equal marginal cost.

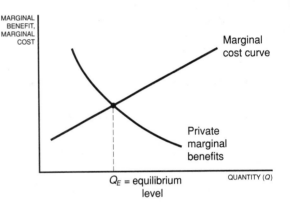

Step three: Calculate the social marginal benefits by adding the external benefit to the private marginal benefit at each level of the activity.

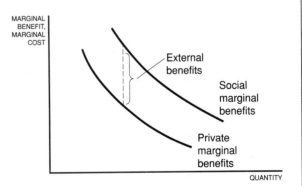

Step four: Find the efficient level of the activity, which is the level at which social marginal benefits equal marginal cost.

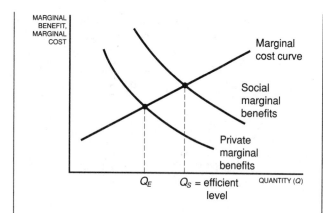

Step five: Compare the equilibrium and efficient levels of the activity.

4 (Worked problem: positive externalities) An important example of an activity that generates positive externalities is worker training. When firms train their employees, the employees not only become more productive in the job, they can also earn higher wages elsewhere. This increase in earning power is a positive externality. The QXV Corporation is considering sending some of its white-collar employees to computer school. The cost is $1,000 per week, and the private marginal benefits to QXV are given in Table 11.6 Also, the value of the external benefit is $500 per week.

Table 11.6

Weeks at school	Private marginal benefits
1	$1,500
2	$1,250
3	$1,000
4	$ 750
5	$ 500
6	$ 250

a How many weeks of computer schooling will the company provide?
b Find the social marginal benefits of computer schooling.
c What is the efficient number of weeks of schooling?

Step-by-step solution

Step one (a): Find the private marginal benefits and costs of the relevant activity. The private marginal benefits are in Table 11.6; the private marginal cost is $1,000 per week.

Step two: Find the equilibrium level of the activity. Private marginal benefits equal $1,000 at 3 weeks.

Step three (b): Calculate the social marginal benefits by adding the external benefit to the private marginal benefit at each level of the activity. The answer is in Table 11.7.

Table 11.7

Weeks at school	Private marginal benefits	Social marginal benefits
1	$1,500	$2,000
2	$1,250	$1,750
3	$1,000	$1,500
4	$ 750	$1,250
5	$ 500	$1,000
6	$ 250	$ 750

Step four (c): Find the efficient level of the activity. Social marginal benefits equal marginal cost at 5 weeks.

Step five: Compare the equilibrium and efficient levels of the activity. The equilibrium number of weeks is 3, which is less than the efficient number, which is 5. The number of weeks provided is too low because the firm ignores the externality.

5 (Practice problem: positive externalities) ZZZX Pharmaceuticals is considering how many scientists to put to work researching a new drug for Angolan flu. Each scientist, complete with equipment and assistance, costs $200,000. The research will bring profits to ZZZX, but it will also bring about advances in viral research that other companies may build on in their own research. The private benefits are given in Table 11.8. The external marginal benefits are $150,000.

Table 11.8

Scientists	Private benefits
1	$400,000
2	$600,000
3	$700,000
4	$750,000
5	$750,000

a How many scientists will the company use? (Hint: First find the private marginal benefits.)
b Find the social marginal benefits of research scientists.
c What is the efficient number of scientists?
6 (Practice problem: positive externalities) Hillside County farmers have been advised to erect earthen dikes for erosion control. Each dike costs $2,000. The private marginal benefits are given in the second column of Table 11.9, but they do not include the external benefit that one farmers erosion control efforts provide to her neighbors. The external benefits appear in the third column of the table.

Table 11.9

Dikes	Private marginal benefits	External marginal benefits
1	$3,000	$8,000
2	$2,000	$7,000
3	$1,500	$6,000
4	$1,000	$5,000
5	$ 500	$4,000
6	$ 0	$3,000
7	$ 0	$2,000

a How many dikes will each farmer erect?
b Find the social marginal benefits of a farmer's dikes.
c What is the efficient number of dikes?

Answers to Problems

2 *a* Price = $40; quantity = 70,000.
b The new demand curve is given in Table 11.10.

Table 11.10

Demand	
Price	Quantity
$60	50,000
$55	60,000
$50	70,000
$45	80,000
$40	100,000

c The new equilibrium price is $45,000, and the quantity is 80,000. The subsidy increases the quantity from 70,000 to 80,000. Consumers are better off by $5,000 ($10,000 subsidy − $5,000 increase in price), and firms are better off by $5,000, which is the increase in price.

3 *a* Price = $5,000; quantity = 7,000.
b The new demand curve is given in Table 11.11.

Table 11.11

Demand	
Price	Quantity
$11,000	1,000
$10,000	3,000
$ 9,000	5,000
$ 8,000	7,000
$ 7,000	9,000
$ 6,000	11,000

c The new equilibrium price is $7,000, and the quantity is 9,000. The subsidy increases the quantity from 7,000 to 9,000. Consumers are better off by $1,000 ($3,000 subsidy − $2,000 increase in price), and firms are better off by $2,000, which is the increase in price.

5 *a* 2 scientists.
b The social marginal benefits are given in Table 11.12.

Table 11.12

Scientists	Private benefits	Private marginal benefits	Social marginal benefits
1	$400,000	$400,000	$550,000
2	$600,000	$200,000	$350,000
3	$700,000	$100,000	$250,000
4	$750,000	$50,000	$200,000
5	$750,000	$ 0	$150,000

c The efficient number is 4 scientists. The company chooses only 2 because it ignores the externality.

6 *a* 2 dikes.
b The social marginal benefits are given in Table 11.13.

Table 11.13

Dikes	Private marginal benefits	External marginal benefits	Social marginal benefits
1	$3,000	$8,000	$11,000
2	$2,000	$7,000	$ 9,000
3	$1,500	$6,000	$ 7,500
4	$1,000	$5,000	$ 6,000
5	$ 500	$4,000	$ 4,500
6	$ 0	$3,000	$ 3,000
7	$ 0	$2,000	$ 2,000

c The efficient number of dikes is 7. Farmers only erect 2 because they ignore the external benefits.

CHAPTER 12 | Monopoly, Monopolistic Competition, and Oligopoly

This chapter takes up the first of the four sources of market failure sketched in Chapter 11. Imperfect market structures include markets dominated by a single firm (monopolies) and two other important cases (monopolistic competition and oligopoly). Understanding why these market structures exist and how they lead to inefficiencies sets the stage for Chapter 13's discussion of how government policy may improve matters.

ESSENTIAL CONCEPTS

1   Like all firms, monopolies maximize profit by setting marginal cost equal to marginal revenue. Unlike for competitive firms, for monopolies marginal revenue is less than price. This fact is shown by the following formula: Marginal revenue = Price (1 − 1/elasticity of demand). Barriers to entry allow monopolists to earn above-normal profits (also called **monopoly rents**). Finally, as price makers, monopolists can sometimes profitably charge different prices to different customers, a practice known as **price discrimination.**

2   When average costs decline throughout the likely range of output, the industry is said to be a **natural monopoly.** By supplying the entire market, the single firm has the lowest possible average cost and can undercut any potential competition. If there are no sunk costs associated with entry, however, the market may be **contestable.** This means that the threat of quick entry of competitors prevents the incumbent firm from raising price above average cost. If there are sunk costs, on the other hand, the incumbent can threaten a price war and deter entry.

3   Monopolistic competition describes the market structure made up of many firms, each ignoring the reactions of the others. The demand curves facing the firms slope down (thus, price is above marginal cost), but new firms enter when there are profit opportunities (thus, in equilibrium, price equals average cost). New entrants produce close substitutes to the products of existing firms. Each entry shifts the demand curves facing existing firms to the left, reducing their profits.

4   In **oligopolies,** a few firms dominate the industry. If any one firm changes its price, produces more, or adopts a new strategy, then the other firms in the oligopoly will notice the change and react to it. It is essential, then, that oligopolists pay careful attention and try to anticipate the reactions of rivals. This strategic interaction is the essential feature of oligopolies, and it makes the study of oligopolies both difficult and fascinating.

5   Because total profits are lower when firms compete, oligopolists have the incentive to form a **cartel** and to collude, fix prices, and share the market. This behavior, however, is difficult to sustain. First, individual firms are tempted to cheat and take advantage of the higher prices charged by others by undercutting their prices. Further, as demand and costs change over time, oligopolies have trouble renegotiating their tacit agreements. Finally, the pure profits earned by successful colluders attract entry and new competition.

6   The conflict between **collusion** and competition is at the heart of oligopoly. The combined profits of firms are highest if they collude. Collectively, their incentives are to fix prices and share the market. But each individual firm is tempted by its own self-interest. If the rivals keep their prices high, a firm can undercut and capture the market. The **Prisoner's Dilemma** summarizes this conflict and shows how collusion might work. If the game is played only once and self-interest quickly takes over, all firms cheat and the

equilibrium is competition. If the game is played repeatedly for an indefinite period of time, firms may be able to threaten cheaters with competitive price wars and motivate one another to continue colluding.

7 Certain **restrictive practices** help sustain collusion. These include assigning exclusive territories to individual firms, requiring exclusive dealing at retail outlets, and insisting upon tie-in arrangements that force a customer who buys one product to buy an additional product. These practices can reduce competition by increasing the costs of capturing the customers of rival firms. Firms also facilitate cooperation through such practices as matching low-price offers of rivals.

8 Factors that prevent entry into markets are called **barriers to entry.** Government policies such as licence requirements and patents create barriers to entry. The cost structure of the industry can also be a barrier, specifically the fraction of market demand accounted for by the output at the minimum of the firm's average cost curve. A monopoly or oligopoly can be sustained if a firm has control over an essential resource or if the firm has information advantages. Finally, strategies of existing firms can create barriers, if they can credibly convince potential competitors that entry would be met with fierce competition.

9 There are three important models of competition in oligopolies.
   a If firms are committed to producing a given amount of output, as is the case in industries where fixed costs are high and changing capacity is very expensive, there is quantity or **Cournot competition.** One such example is the steel industry. Setting up a factory to commence or expand production is very expensive, so the firm gets locked in at certain capacities. It tries to select capacities corresponding to a price where profits will be maximized.
   b If the costs of increasing capacity are low, then price or **Bertrand competition** reigns. An example of this is the catalog marketing industry. Setting up a mail-order firm is inexpensive, and the firm can vary the size of its orders from suppliers. It selects a price corresponding to a quantity where profits will be maximized.
   c The **kinked demand curve** model shows that if firms expect rivals to match a price cut but not price increases, then they are unlikely to change price or quantity.

BEHIND THE ESSENTIAL CONCEPTS

1 All imperfectly competitive firms face a downward-sloping demand curve. Thus, their profit-maximizing price is greater than marginal cost. In monopoly, there are barriers to entry, which allow monopolies to earn pure profits without attracting new competition. Monopoly prices are greater than average costs. In monopolistic competition, however, new entry drives economic profits to zero. When profits are zero, price equals average cost. To sum up,
   a downward-sloping demand implies that price is greater than marginal cost.
   b barriers to entry imply that price is greater than average cost.

2 Monopoly and monopolistic competition are similar in that each firm faces a downward-sloping demand curve and sets marginal revenue equal to marginal cost, which is less than price. The similarities stop here, however, because in a monopoly no new firm may enter even though a firm may earn pure profits. In monopolistically competitive industries, new firms enter, produce close substitutes, and capture customers. This entry shifts demand to the left until price equals average cost. The basic difference in the equilibria is that monopolies earn pure profits.

3 Monopolies are inefficient because price (which equals the marginal benefit of the good to consumers) is greater than marginal cost. Producing another unit would benefit customers more than it would cost. In monopolistic competition, things are not so simple. If all firms produce more goods, there are gains to both consumers and firms because price is greater than marginal cost and also because average cost falls. (Remember that the monopolistically competitive firm produces along the downward-sloping part of average cost.) On the other hand, the overall industry demand is only so and if the firms become bigger, there will be room for fewer firms. Fewer firms mean fewer types of goods, so there is a trade-off between costs and variety.

4 As a group, firms in an oligopoly want to cooperate, charge high prices, and share monopoly profits, but they always run up against the problem of self-interest. Each individual firm would like to cheat while the others abide by the cooperative strategy. It is this noncooperative behavior by individual firms that promotes economic efficiency, because it keeps the oligopolists from cooperating to gouge customers with high prices. It is ironic that if firms were more cooperative, the economy would not work so well.

5 The world of perfect competition is simple and precise. The firm cannot affect the market of any competitor; it simply chooses its quantity to maximize profits. The world of oligopoly is rich and varied. Firms try to limit competition and promote collusion. They have a wealth of strategies to choose from: price and quantity, of course, but also such practices as matching offers of rivals and threatening price wars with new entrants or

existing firms who cheat on tacit agreements to limit price competition. Oligopoly is an area in which economics has made much progress in the last ten or fifteen years.

SELF-TEST

True or False

1 The demand curve facing the firm is downward sloping in perfect competition.
2 The demand curve facing the firm is downward sloping in monopolistic competition.
3 When the demand curve facing the firm is downward sloping, marginal revenue is less than price.
4 Marginal revenue is less than price because price must fall for output to increase.
5 An industry with a single seller is a monopoly.
6 The demand curve facing a monopolist is the same as the industry demand curve.
7 Price is greater than marginal cost in monopoly.
8 If there is a barrier to entry, firms may continue to earn pure profits.
9 In a natural monopoly, one firm can produce at a lower average cost than it could if it shared the market with other firms.
10 An oligopolist considering lowering its price must anticipate the reactions of its rivals.
11 A cartel is a group of firms engaging in price competition.
12 One difficulty that cartels have is that when they succeed in raising price, their members are tempted to undercut the cartel price.
13 Certain restrictive practices such as resale price maintenance and exclusive territories help oligopolies reduce competition and increase profits.
14 In Cournot competition, oligopolists choose their quantity expecting that their rivals will produce the same quantity as they.
15 In Bertrand competition, firms choose their price expecting their rivals to keep price constant.

Multiple Choice

1 In the competitive model,
   a marginal revenue for the firm equals the market price.
   b if the firm raises its price above that charged by its competitors, it will lose all its customers.
   c the demand curve facing the firm is horizontal.
   d the firm is a price taker.
   e all of the above.
2 If a single firm supplies the entire market, the market structure is
   a perfect competition.
   b oligopoly.
   c monopoly.
   d monopolistic competition.
   e none of the above.
3 If the market is dominated by several firms, its market structure is
   a perfect competition.
   b oligopoly.
   c monopoly.
   d monopolistic competition.
   e none of the above.
4 Monopolistic competition is distinguished from oligopoly by the fact that
   a in monopolistic competition, firms do not worry about the reactions of their rivals.
   b there is no competition in oligopoly.
   c oligopoly is a form of imperfect competition.
   d the demand curve facing the firm is downward sloping in monopolistic competition.
   e price is above marginal cost in an oligopoly.
5 When there is imperfect competition, the demand curve facing the firm
   a equals the market demand curve.
   b is horizontal.
   c is downward sloping.
   d is upward sloping.
   e is vertical.
6 When the demand curve facing the firm is downward sloping, marginal revenue is less than price
   a because of the principle of diminishing returns.
   b in the short run, but not in the long run.
   c because as output increases, the price must fall on all units.
   d because taxes must be paid.
   e none of the above.
7 A monopoly increases price above marginal cost by a greater amount when the demand is
   a more elastic.
   b more inelastic.
   c unitary elastic.
   d perfectly elastic.
   e none of the above.
8 Because they are single sellers, monopolies can earn
   a pure economic profits.
   b pure accounting profits.
   c zero profits.
   d the normal rate of return on invested capital.
   e c and d.
9 The measure of a firm's market power is
   a the number of employees it has.
   b the size of its capital stock.
   c the market price of its stock shares.
   d the extent to which the demand curve it faces is downward sloping.
   e all of the above.

10 How much the demand curve facing the firm slopes downward is determined by
   a   the number of firms in the industry.
   b   the extent to which its product is differentiated from those of its competitors.
   c   the size of its capital stock.
   d   the minimum of its average cost curve.
   e   *a* and *b*.

11 The four-firm concentration ratio measures the
   a   number of firms in the industry.
   b   elasticity of industry demand.
   c   extent to which production is concentrated among a few firms.
   d   extent to which foreign firms dominate the industry.
   e   average elasticity among the four largest firms.

12 When the products sold in one industry are differentiated, if one firm raises its price,
   a   it will lose all of its customers.
   b   it will lose none of its customers.
   c   it will lose some but not all of its customers.
   d   it will go out of business.
   e   its profits will rise.

13 Barriers to entry
   a   are factors that prevent new firms from entering the market.
   b   are illegal.
   c   allow firms in the industry to continue to earn economic profits.
   d   imply that marginal revenue is greater than marginal cost.
   e   *a* and *c*.

14 In the equilibrium of monopolistic competition,
   a   firms make zero economic profits.
   b   price equals average cost.
   c   marginal revenue equals marginal cost.
   d   price is greater than marginal cost.
   e   all of the above.

15 The practice of charging different prices to different customers is called
   a   product differentiation.
   b   price discrimination.
   c   predatory pricing.
   d   limit pricing.
   e   natural monopoly.

16 In the Prisoner's Dilemma,
   a   both prisoners act in their own self-interest; this leads to the best alternative from their combined standpoint.
   b   both prisoners cooperate to bring about the best alternative.
   c   acting in their own self-interest, the prisoners bring about the worst alternative.
   d   it is impossible to say what happens because each prisoner must worry about the reactions of the other.
   e   none of the above.

17 Collusion is difficult in practice because
   a   antitrust laws make explicit price-fixing agreements illegal.
   b   individual firms are tempted to cheat and undercut their rivals.
   c   as demand and cost conditions change, it is difficult to renegotiate tacit agreements.
   d   all of the above.
   e   none of the above.

18 In Cournot competition, the firms
   a   compete by choosing quantity, given some conjecture about the quantity that the rival will produce.
   b   compete by choosing price, given some conjecture about the price that the rival will charge.
   c   match price cuts by rivals but not price increases.
   d   collude to fix prices and earn monopoly profits.
   e   divide the market in an orderly way.

19 In Bertrand competition, the firms
   a   compete by choosing quantity, given some conjecture about the quantity that the rival will produce.
   b   compete by choosing price, given some conjecture about the price that the rival will charge.
   c   match price cuts by rivals but not price increases.
   d   collude to fix prices and earn monopoly profits.
   e   divide the market in an orderly way.

20 Restrictive practices restrict competition. These include
   a   resale price maintenance.
   b   exclusive territories.
   c   vertical restrictions.
   d   horizontal restrictions.
   e   all of the above.

Completion

1 The way in which an industry is organized is called its _____.

2 A few firms dominate an industry in _____.

3 An industry with a single seller is called _____.

4 In industries where the characteristics of products are different, there is said to be _____.

5 Any factor that prevents new firms from coming into an industry is called a _____.

6 If the market demand curve intersects the average cost curve for the firm at a point where it is decreasing, the industry is a _____.

7 A group of companies operating jointly as if they were a monopoly is called a _____.

8 Markets in which the threat of competition impels firms to charge the competitive price are called _____.

9 If a firm believes that its rivals will match its price cuts

but not its price increases, then it will perceive its demand curve to be _____ at the current price.

10 Firms that conjecture that rival's quantity is fixed are engaging in _____.

Answers to Self-Test

True or False

1	f	6	t	11	f
2	t	7	t	12	t
3	t	8	t	13	t
4	t	9	t	14	f
5	t	10	t	15	t

Multiple Choice

1	e	6	c	11	c	16	c
2	c	7	b	12	c	17	d
3	b	8	a	13	e	18	a
4	a	9	d	14	e	19	b
5	c	10	e	15	b	20	e

Completion

1 market structure
2 oligopoly
3 monopoly
4 product differentiation
5 barrier to entry
6 natural monopoly
7 cartel
8 contestable
9 kinked
10 Cournot competition

Doing Economics: Tools and Practice Problems

In this section, we start with two basic topics and several applications. First, we calculate marginal revenue and find the profit-maximizing price and quantity for the monopolist. The second topic is price discrimination, which is the practice of firms in imperfectly competitive markets charging different prices to different consumers in order to raise profits. The applications that follow include the effects of taxes and price controls in monopoly markets and a couple of puzzles. Artists, entertainers, and authors are often paid a percentage of revenues. Also, they generally prefer lower prices than their producers and publishers. Two problems toward the end of this problem set show why this is true. Other problems explore the effects of taxes and price ceilings in monopoly markets and show that the monopolist always produces along the elastic portion of the demand curve.

Next this section looks at three issues pertaining to oligopoly. First, we consider collusion and the difficulty that cartels have in enforcing their tacit agreements. We see not only how two firms can divide a market and share monopoly profits, but also how difficult it is to maintain a cartel. The cartel's success in restricting output and raising prices

tempts each of the cartel members to cheat by producing more than their assigned amounts and undercutting the cartel's price. One way to lessen the incentives to cheat is to assign exclusive territories. We look at collusion and cheating in several problems before turning to some simple game theory problems, using the Prisoner's Dilemma framework to investigate collusion.

MARGINAL REVENUE

The key idea that distinguishes perfect from imperfect competition is that for the latter, marginal revenue is less than price. This is because price must be lowered on all units in order to sell more. Tool Kit 12.1 shows how to calculate marginal revenue from the demand schedule.

Tool Kit 12.1 Calculating Marginal Revenue

The first step in solving the monopolist's problem is to calculate marginal revenue.

Step one: Make a table with four column headings: Price, Quantity, Revenues, and Marginal revenue. Enter the demand curve in the first two columns.

Price   Quantity   Revenues   Marginal revenue

Step two: Calculate revenues for each point on the demand curve, and enter the result in the table. Revenues are price multiplied by quantity:

revenues = price × quantity.

Step three: Calculate marginal revenue for each interval along the demand curve, and enter the result in the table. Marginal revenue is the change in total revenue divided by the change in quantity:

marginal revenue = change in quantity, change in revenues.

After calculating marginal revenue, choose the price and quantity for which marginal revenue equals marginal cost.

---

1 (Worked problem: marginal revenue) As the only cement producer within 200 miles, Sam's Cement faces a downward-sloping demand curve, which is given in Table 12.1.

Table 12.1

Price	Quantity (tons)
$4.00	400
$3.50	800
$3.00	1,400
$2.50	2,800
$2.00	4,000

Sam's marginal cost is $2.00 per ton, and he has fixed costs of $1,000.

a Calculate revenues and marginal revenue, and add these two columns to the table.
b Find the profit-maximizing price and quantity.
c Compute Sam's costs and profits at this price.
d Suppose that Sam's fixed costs fall to $500. What is his profit-maximizing price and quantity, and how much does he earn in profits?
e Illustrate your answer with a diagram.

Step-by-step solution

Step one (*a*): Make a table.

Price   Quantity   Revenues   Marginal revenue

Step two: Calculate revenues for each point on the demand curve. When the price is $4, revenues are $4 × 400 = $1,600. Continuing, we derive Table 12.2.

Table 12.2

Price	Quantity	Revenues	Marginal revenue
$4.00	400	$1,600	
$3.50	800	$2,800	
$3.00	1,400	$4,200	
$2.50	2,800	$7,000	
$2.00	4,000	$8,000	

Step three: Calculate marginal revenue for each interval along the demand curve. For the first 400 units, revenue rises from $0 to $1,600. Thus, marginal revenue is $1,600/400 = $4. As output is increased to 800, total revenue grows from $1,600 to $2,800. Marginal revenue is ($2,800 − $1,600)/(800 − 400) = $3. Complete the marginal revenue column as shown in Table 12.3.

Table 12.3

Price	Quantity	Revenues	Marginal revenue
$4.00	400	$1,600	$4.00
$3.50	800	$2,800	$3.00
$3.00	1,400	$4,200	$2.33
$2.50	2,800	$7,000	$2.00
$2.00	4,000	$8,000	$0.83

Step four (*b*): To find the monopoly output and price, set marginal revenue equal to marginal cost. This occurs when the price is $2.50 and output is 2,800.

Step five (*c*): To find total costs, add fixed costs, which are $1,000, plus total variable costs. Each unit costs $2, and 2,800 units are produced. Total costs equal $1,000 + ($2 ×

2,800) = $6,600. Profits equal revenues minus costs. Revenues are $7,000, so profits equal $7,000 − $6,600 = $400.

Step six (*d*): If fixed costs fall, marginal cost does not change. The profit-maximizing price is still $2.50, but total profits now equal $7,000 − ($500 + $5,600) = $900. Unless the firm decides to shut down, fixed costs do not affect the output and pricing decisions.

Step seven (*e*): The solution is illustrated in the diagram.

2 (Practice problem: marginal revenue) The Mudville Nine is the only professional baseball team within several hundred miles. The marginal cost of admitting another fan is $1. Fixed costs, which include player salaries, are $100,000. The demand curve is given in Table 12.4. The quantity column gives the season's attendance.

Table 12.4

Price	Quantity	Revenues	Marginal revenue
$8	100,000		
$7	150,000		
$6	200,000		
$5	250,000		
$4	300,000		
$3	350,000		
$2	400,000		

a Compute marginal revenue, and complete the column.
b Find the profit-maximizing price and quantity.
c Compute Mudville's costs and profits at this price.
d Suppose that the players win the right to negotiate with any team, and the increase in salaries raises fixed costs to $150,000. What is Mudville's profit-maximizing price and quantity, and how much profit does the team earn?
e Illustrate your answer with a diagram.

3 (Practice problem: marginal revenue) For each of the following firms, find the profit-maximizing price and quantity and total profits earned.

a Fixed costs = $0; marginal cost = $8.

Price	Quantity	Revenues	Marginal revenue
$10	1		
$ 9	2		
$ 8	3		
$ 7	4		
$ 6	5		
$ 5	6		
$ 4	7		

b Fixed costs = $50,000; marginal cost = $.10.

Price	Quantity	Revenues	Marginal revenue
$0.50	500,000		
$0.45	600,000		
$0.40	700,000		
$0.35	800,000		
$0.30	900,000		

c Compute marginal cost from the table.

Price	Quantity	Revenues	Marginal revenue	Total costs	Marginal costs
$20	400			$ 5,000	
$18	800			$ 7,000	
$16	1,200			$ 9,400	
$14	1,600			$12,600	
$12	2,000			$16,200	
$10	2,400			$21,000	

d Compute marginal cost from the table.

Price	Quantity	Revenues	Marginal revenue	Total costs	Marginal costs
$1.00	1,000			$ 200	
$0.90	2,000			$ 300	
$0.80	3,500			$ 450	
$0.70	5,500			$ 650	
$0.60	8,000			$ 900	
$0.50	11,000			$1,230	
$0.40	15,000			$1,730	
$0.30	20,000			$2,355	

PRICE DISCRIMINATION

When it is possible to do so, an imperfectly competitive firm can improve profits by charging different prices to different consumers. This is called price discrimination. The idea is to segment the markets and set marginal revenue equal to marginal cost in each market and charge the corresponding price.

4 (Worked problem: price discrimination) Although the sale of the product is illegal, a drug enterprise operates according to sound business practices. It sells addictive designer drugs to two types of customers: nonaddicted experimenters and addicts (former experimenters). The demands for each type of customer are given in Table 12.5. The drug has no fixed costs and has marginal cost equal to $10 per dose.

Table 12.5

Nonaddicts				Addicts			
Price	Quan-tity	Revenues	Marginal revenue	Price	Quan-tity	Revenues	Marginal revenue
$50	100			$50	500		
$40	300			$40	700		
$30	500			$30	1,050		
$20	1,000			$20	1,650		

a Calculate marginal revenue for each demand curve.
b Find the profit-maximizing price and quantity for each type of consumer.
c Calculate total profits.

Step-by-step solution

Step one (*a*): Follow the procedure outlined above to calculate marginal revenue. The result should look like Table 12.6.

Table 12.6

Nonaddicts				Addicts			
Price	Quan-tity	Revenues	Marginal revenue	Price	Quan-tity	Revenues	Marginal revenue
$50	100	$5,000	$50	$50	500	$25,000	$50.00
$40	300	$12,000	$35	$40	700	$28,000	$15.00
$30	500	$15,000	$15	$30	1,050	$31,500	$10.00
$20	1,000	$20,000	$10	$20	1,650	$33,000	$ 2.50

Step two (*b*): Find the profit-maximizing price in each market. Marginal cost, which is $10, equals marginal revenue for nonaddicts at a price of $20 and a quantity of 1,000. For addicts, marginal revenue equals marginal cost at a price of $30 and a quantity of 1,050.

Step three (*c*): Calculate total profits. Revenues are $20,000 from the nonaddicts and $31,500 from the addicts. Costs are $10 × (1,000 + 1,050) = $20,500; so profits equal $51,500 − $20,500 = $31,000.

5 (Practice problem: price discrimination) A common instance of price discrimination is dumping, which occurs when a firm faces less competition in its home market than abroad. In these cases, it will pay the

company to charge different prices in the two markets. Opus Company sells carpet fibres in the foreign and domestic markets. Its marginal cost is $1 per spool, and it has fixed costs of $5,000. The domestic and foreign demands are given in Table 12.7.

Table 12.7

	Home market				Foreign market		
Price	Quan-tity	Revenues	Marginal revenue	Price	Quan-tity	Revenues	Marginal revenue
$10	2,000			$10	2,000		
$ 9	2,500			$ 9	3,000		
$ 8	3,000			$ 8	4,000		
$ 7	3,500			$ 7	5,000		
$ 6	4,000			$ 6	6,000		
$ 5	4,500			$ 5	7,000		
$ 4	5,000			$ 4	8,000		

 a Calculate marginal revenue for each demand curve.
 b Find the profit-maximizing price and quantity for each type of consumer.
 c Calculate total profits.

6 (Practice problem: price discrimination) Mark's Markets is one of the few chains that has not closed its inner-city stores. Mark's has expanded to the suburbs, but he faces more competition there. An example of a product he sells in both markets is hamburger, which has a marginal cost equal to $1. The space required to sell hamburger costs Mark's Markets about $100, and the demand curves in the suburbs and inner city are given in Table 12.8.

Table 12.8

	Suburbs				Inner city		
Price	Quan-tity	Revenues	Marginal revenue	Price	Quan-tity	Revenues	Marginal revenue
$4.00	200			$4.00	100		
$3.50	400			$3.50	120		
$3.00	600			$3.00	140		
$2.50	800			$2.50	160		
$2.00	1,000			$2.00	180		
$1.50	1,200			$1.50	200		

 a Calculate marginal revenue for each demand curve.
 b Find the profit-maximizing price and quantity for each type of consumer.
 c Calculate total profits.

APPLICATIONS

The following problems apply the idea of marginal revenue and monopoly decision-making to percentage of gross revenue contracts, tax incidence, price controls, and elasticity. Simply follow the procedure outlined in Tool Kit 12.1.

7 (Worked problem: marginal revenue) After the surprising success of her first novel, Imelda has negotiated a deal in which she receives 20 percent of the revenues from the sale of her second novel. The demand curve is given in Table 12.9. The publisher has fixed costs of $20,000, and the marginal cost of printing and distributing each book printed is $20.

Table 12.9

Price	Quantity	Revenues	Marginal revenue	Imelda's revenue
$40	10,000			
$35	20,000			
$30	30,000			
$25	40,000			
$20	50,000			

 a Calculate marginal revenue, and enter in the table.
 b Find the profit-maximizing price and quantity.
 c Compute Imelda's revenue for each price, and enter in the table.
 d What price maximizes Imelda's revenues?
 e Draw a diagram illustrating your answer.

Step-by-step solution

Step one (*a*): Calculate marginal revenue. Follow the usual procedure. The answer is in Table 12.10.

Table 12.10

Price	Quantity	Revenues	Marginal revenue	Imelda's revenue
$40	10,000	$ 400,000	$40	
$35	20,000	$ 700,000	$30	
$30	30,000	$ 900,000	$20	
$25	40,000	$1,000,000	$10	
$20	50,000	$1,000,000	$ 0	

Step two (*b*): Find the profit-maximizing price and quantity. Marginal cost equals marginal revenue for the publisher at a price of $30, where the quantity sold is 30,000.

Step three (*c*): Calculate Imelda's revenue. She receives 20 percent of the total. At a price of $40, she receives .20 × $400,000 = $80,000. Continue to calculate, and enter the results. They are given in Table 12.11.

Table 12.11

Price	Quantity	Revenues	Marginal revenue	Imelda's revenue
$40	10,000	$ 400,000	$40	$ 80,000
$35	20,000	$ 700,000	$30	$140,000
$30	30,000	$ 900,000	$20	$180,000
$25	40,000	$1,000,000	$10	$200,000
$20	50,000	$1,000,000	$ 0	$200,000

Step four (d): Imelda prefers a price of $25 or $20, which earns her $200,000, more than the $180,000 that she earns at the publisher's preferred price.

Step five (e): Draw a diagram. Note that the publisher sets marginal revenue equal to marginal cost. Imelda is only concerned with revenues, so she prefers the point where marginal revenue equals zero.

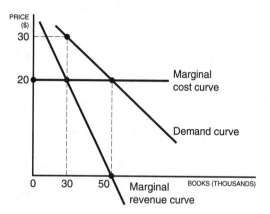

8   (Practice problem: marginal revenue) Magdalena, a budding female recording artist, has just completed her first album. She will receive 25 percent of the revenues. The record company reports that its demand curve is as given in Table 12.12, and its marginal costs are $6 per CD.

Table 12.12

Price	Quantity	Revenues	Marginal revenue	Magdalena's revenue
$20	20,000			
$18	25,000			
$16	30,000			
$14	35,000			
$12	40,000			
$10	48,000			

a   Calculate marginal revenue, and enter in the table.
b   Find the profit-maximizing price and quantity.
c   Compute Magdalena's revenue for each price, and enter in the table.
d   What price maximizes Magdalena's revenues?
e   Draw a diagram illustrating your answer.

9   (Practice problem: marginal revenue) Like most cities, South Potato is a one-newspaper town. The *South Potato Truth* distributes its daily paper for a marginal cost of $.10. The demand curve is given in Table 12.13.

Table 12.13

Price	Quantity	Revenues	Marginal revenue
$1.00	30,000		
$0.95	40,000		
$0.90	50,000		
$0.85	60,000		
$0.80	70,000		
$0.75	80,000		
$0.70	90,000		
$0.65	100,000		
$0.60	110,000		
$0.55	120,000		

a   Calculate marginal revenue, and enter in the table.
b   Find the profit-maximizing price and quantity.
c   Suppose that a tax of $.10 per paper is instituted. The tax will be paid by the newspaper company. Find the new profit-maximizing price and quantity.
d   How much of the tax is paid by consumers?
e   Draw a diagram illustrating your answer.

10   (Practice problem: marginal revenue) In competitive markets, price ceilings lower price and reduce the quantity sold. This is not true in monopoly markets. The demand for cable subscriptions in Motelville is given in Table 12.14. The marginal cost, including payments to cable programming providers, is $15.

Table 12.14

Price	Quantity	Revenues	Marginal revenue
$45	60,000		
$40	80,000		
$35	100,000		
$30	120,000		
$25	140,000		

a   Calculate marginal revenue, and enter in the table.
b   Find the profit-maximizing price and quantity of subscriptions.
c   Now suppose that the town sets a price ceiling equal to $25. How much will the company charge, and how many subscriptions will be sold?
d   Draw a diagram illustrating your answer.

11   (Practice problem: marginal revenue) Because a monopoly is a single seller of a good, it has no competition. Since price elasticity is generally lower when consumers have little opportunity to find substitutes, you might think that the demand for the monopolist's product is always inelastic. Nevertheless, it is true that the monopolist always produces on the elastic portion of its demand curve. To see this,

compute elasticity along the demand curve given in question 3a. Show that at the chosen price and quantity, the price elasticity of demand is greater than 1.

CARTELS, COLLUSION, AND CHEATING

Many firms can secretly organize and agree to cooperate to share monopoly profits. Tool Kit 12.2 shows how they might do this. The following problems use this insight to show how individual firms have incentives to cheat and produce more than they agreed. Tool Kit 12.3 shows that when there is quantity competition (Cournot), the same incentive problem arises. This is developed and extended to price competition in the problems.

Tool Kit 12.2 Organizing a Cartel of Many Price-Taking Firms

To organize a cartel of many firms, one must find the monopoly output and price. Then each firm must be assigned its quota. The following steps show how to proceed.

Step one: Identify and add up the supply curves of the individual firms. The result is the cartel's marginal cost curve.

Step two: Identify the market demand curve, and find its marginal revenue.

Step three: Find the profit-maximizing price and quantity for the cartel by setting marginal revenue equal to marginal cost.

Step four: Determine each firm's output by evenly dividing the cartel's output among its members.

---

12 (Worked problem: collusion and cheating) The Quebec Maple Syrup Board is a cartel of 1,000 maple syrup producers. The demand for maple syrup and the supply curve of one typical producer are given in Table 12.15. The quantity represents gallons.

Table 12.15

Market demand		Firm's supply	
Price	Quantity	Price	Quantity
$10	10,000	$10	60
$ 9	15,000	$ 9	55
$ 8	20,000	$ 8	50
$ 7	25,000	$ 7	45
$ 6	30,000	$ 6	40
$ 5	35,000	$ 5	35
		$ 4	30
		$ 3	25
		$ 2	20

a Find the profit-maximizing price for the cartel as a whole. How many litres will be sold at this price: How many must each firm produce to sustain this price?

b If the cartel charges the price computed in part a, how many units would the individual firm like to produce?

c Now suppose that all firms cheat and the market becomes competitive. Find the equilibrium price and quantity.

Step-by-step solution

Step one (a): Add up the individual supplies. Since there are 1,000 firms, the market supply is simply the quantity supplied by the firm multiplied by 1,000. The market supply is given in Table 12.16.

Table 12.16

Firm's supply		Market supply	
Price	Quantity	Price	Quantity
$10	60	$10	60,000
$ 9	55	$ 9	55,000
$ 8	50	$ 8	50,000
$ 7	45	$ 7	45,000
$ 6	40	$ 6	40,000
$ 5	35	$ 5	35,000
$ 4	30	$ 4	30,000
$ 3	25	$ 3	25,000
$ 2	20	$ 2	20,000

Step two: Derive the marginal revenue curve. First find total revenue, and enter it in the appropriate column. Marginal revenue is the change in total revenue divided by the change in quantity. The answer is given in Table 12.17.

Table 12.17

Market demand		Total revenue	Marginal revenue
Price	Quantity		
$10	10,000	$100,000	
$ 9	15,000	$135,000	$7
$ 8	20,000	$160,000	$5
$ 7	25,000	$175,000	$3
$ 6	30,000	$180,000	$1
$ 5	35,000	$175,000	−$1

Step three: Find the profit-maximizing price for the cartel. The market supply curve is the cartel's marginal cost. Marginal cost equals marginal revenue when the quantity is 25,000. The corresponding price is $7. Each firm produces 25 gallons.

Step four (b): Find how much the firm would like to supply at the cartel price. At a price of $7, the firm would like to produce 45 units (this number is read off the firm's supply curve), which is 20 more than it is assigned.

Step five (c): If all firms cheat, then the market will become a competitive market and will clear at a price of $5, where each firm produces 35 gallons.

13 (Practice problem: collusion and cheating) The 500 mail-order computer equipment suppliers are (discreetly) forming a cartel. The market demand curve and the supply curve of a typical equipment supplier are given in Table 12.18. The quantity represents the number of computers.

Table 12.18

Market demand		Total revenue	Marginal revenue
Price	Quantity		
$1,000	300,000		
$ 900	400,000		
$ 800	500,000		
$ 700	600,000		
$ 600	700,000		
$ 500	800,000		
$ 400	900,000		
$ 300	1,000,000		

Firm's supply		Market supply	
Price	Quantity	Price	Quantity
$1,000	4,000		
$ 900	3,500		
$ 800	3,000		
$ 700	2,400		
$ 600	2,000		
$ 500	1,600		
$ 400	1,000		
$ 300	500		
$ 200	100		

a Derive the marginal revenue for the computer equipment supplier market.

b Add up the 500 individual firm supplies to derive the market supply.

c Find the profit-maximizing price for the cartel as a whole. How many computers will be sold at this price? How many must each firm sell to sustain this price?

d If the cartel charges the price computed in part c, how many units would the individual firm like to sell?

e Now suppose that all firms cheat, and the market becomes competitive. Find the equilibrium price and quantity.

Tool Kit 12.3 Finding the Profit-Maximizing Output in Quantity Competition between Duopolists

In some industries, such as steel or aluminum, the fixed costs of plant and equipment are such a large share of total costs that firms have little discretion in changing output once the machinery is in place. In this case, the competition is over quantity, and the price will be whatever clears the market of the quantities that firms have collectively decided to produce.

Step one: Identify the market demand, marginal cost, and output of the opponent firm.

Step two: Subtract the output of the opponent firm from the market demand. The difference is called the **residual demand curve:**

residual demand = market demand
        − opponent's output.

Step three: Find the marginal revenue for the residual demand curve.

Step four: Choose the output for which marginal revenue equals marginal cost.

---

14 (Worked problem: quantity competition) The New Chairs for Old Company shares the furniture-refinishing market in Southpoint with the Like New Company. Each uses enormous vats of chemicals, which are expensive to set up but cheap to operate. One vat will permit the refinishing of 10 pieces of furniture per day. The marginal cost for each firm is constant and equal to $4. Table 12.19 gives the market demand.

Table 12.19

Price	Quantity
$7.50	0
$7.00	10
$6.50	20
$6.00	30
$5.50	40
$5.00	50
$4.50	60
$4.00	70

a Suppose that the two firms try to operate as a cartel and share the market equally. Find the profit-maximizing quantity for each.

b Now look at the problem from the point of view of the owner of New Chairs for Old. She conjectures that her rival commit to the quantity solved for in part a. Find the profit-maximizing quantity.

Step-by-step solution

Step one (*a*): We follow the usual procedure for the monopolist: find the marginal revenue and set marginal revenue equal to marginal cost. Table 12.20 gives the marginal revenue.

Table 12.20

Price	Quantity	Total revenue	Marginal revenue
$7.50	0	$ 0	—
$7.00	10	$ 70	$7
$6.50	20	$130	$6
$6.00	30	$180	$5
$5.50	40	$220	$4
$5.00	50	$250	$3
$4.50	60	$270	$2
$4.00	70	$280	$1

Marginal revenue equals marginal cost when the total quantity is 40. Each firm then buys two vats and refinishes 20 pieces of furniture.

Step two (*b*): Identify the market demand, marginal cost, and output of the opponent firm. The market demand is given in Table 12.19, the marginal cost is $4, and Like New is expected to produce 20.

Step three: Subtract the output of the opponent firm from the market demand, as shown in Table 12.21.

Table 12.21

Price	Quantity
$7.00	0
$6.50	20 − 20 = 0
$6.00	30 − 20 = 10
$5.50	40 − 20 = 20
$5.00	50 − 20 = 30
$4.50	60 − 20 = 40
$4.00	70 − 20 = 50

Step four: Find the marginal revenue for the residual demand curve, as given in Table 12.22.

Table 12.22

Price	Quantity	Total revenue	Marginal revenue
$7.00	0	0	—
$6.50	0	0	—
$6.00	10	$ 60	$6
$5.50	20	$110	$5
$5.00	30	$150	$4
$4.50	40	$180	$3
$4.00	50	$200	$2

Step five: Choose the output for which marginal revenue equals marginal cost. When output is 30, marginal revenue and marginal cost both equal $4.

15 (Practice problem: quantity competition) The Davis Lead Company competes with its rival Anderson Lead. Because the plant and equipment are so expensive and because marginal production costs are so low (only $5 per ton) until capacity is reached, the two firms compete by choosing quantity. The market demand is given in Table 12.23.

Table 12.23

Price	Quantity (tons)
$22.50	0
$20.00	100
$17.50	200
$15.00	300
$12.50	400
$10.00	500
$ 7.50	600

a Suppose that the two firms try to operate as a cartel and share the market equally. Find the profit-maximizing quantity for each.

b Now look at the problem from the point of view of the owner of Davis. The owner conjectures that the rival firm will commit to the quantity solved for in part a. Find the profit-maximizing quantity.

16 (Worked problem: price competition) There are two dry-cleaning establishments in Mudville: Jay's Cleaners and Fay's Cleaners. Although they hate each other personally, the two owners have decided to form a cartel. This is illegal, of course, but they meet discreetly. Each faces a marginal cost of $1 per item. Consumers always patronize the lower-price establishment; therefore, either Jay or Fay can capture the entire market by pricing below the other. One additional fact is that in Mudville people only carry half dollars, so the price must be a multiple of $0.50. Table 12.24 gives the market demand.

Table 12.24

Price	Quantity
$3.00	1,500
$2.50	3,000
$2.00	4,500
$1.50	6,000
$1.00	7,500

a Derive marginal revenue curve, and enter in the table.

b Find the profit-maximizing price. If they divide the market equally, how many items will each clean?

c Compute the profits for each firm.

d Suppose that Fay decides to undercut Jay and capture the market. What price will Fay charge? How many will Fay sell? Compute Fay's profits.

Step-by-step solution

Step one (*a*): Derive marginal revenue. Follow the usual procedure, as in Table 12.25.

Table 12.25

Price	Quantity	Total revenue	Marginal revenue
$3.00	1,500	$4,500	$3
$2.50	3,000	$7,500	$2
$2.00	4,500	$9,000	$1
$1.50	6,000	$9,000	$0
$1.00	7,500	$7,500	−$1

Step two (*b*): Find the profit-maximizing price. Marginal cost equals marginal revenue at a price of $2.

Step three (*c*): At a price of $2, there are 4,500 items cleaned. If each does one-half, then each cleans 2,250. The profits for each are $2 − $1 = $1 per unit, so each earns $2,250.

Step four (*d*): Fay can capture the market by charging the next-lower price, which is $1.50. Fay will sell 6,000 units. Fay's profit will be $1.50 − $1.00 = $0.50 per unit for a total of $3,000. Fay gains $750 by cheating on their agreement.

17 (Practice problem: price competition) Yuppie Company and its rival Buppie Company sell dark green and gray rag wool sweaters through catalogs. They buy the sweaters from supplier firms for $10 each. The market demand is given in Table 12.26.

Table 12.26

Quantity (sweaters)	Price
0	$27.50
100	$25.00
200	$22.50
300	$20.00
400	$17.50
500	$15.00
600	$12.50

a Derive marginal revenue, and enter in the table.

b Find the profit-maximizing price. If the companies divide the market equally, how many items will each clean?

c Compute the profits for each firm.

d Suppose that Yuppie decides to undercut Buppie and capture the market. What price will it charge? How many will it sell? Compute its profits.

PRISONER'S DILEMMA

The Prisoner's Dilemma is one of the most important models in social science. It shows why groups may have difficulty inducing their members to cooperate and act in the group interest. In this section our interest is in the ability of oligopolists to collude. Tool Kit 12.4 shows how to use this model.

Tool Kit 12.4 Using the Prisoner's Dilemma

The Prisoner's Dilemma highlights the conflict between what is good for the cartel as a whole and what is best for the individual firm. Follows these steps to represent this conflict as a game.

Step one: Draw a box with four cells, and label it as shown.

Step two: Identify the payoffs of each party if both cooperate, and enter in the appropriate cell.

Step three: Identify the payoffs for each party if both compete, and enter in the appropriate cell.

Step four: Identify the payoffs for each party if one competes while the other cooperates, and enter in the corresponding cells.

	Firm A	
	Cooperate	Compete
Cooperate		A's profits = B's profits =
Firm B		
Compete	A's profits = B's profits =	

Step five: In the classic Prisoner's Dilemma, competing is always the best strategy, whatever the opponent chooses. Show that competition is the equilibrium.

18 (Worked problem: Prisoner's Dilemma) Chiaravelli and Fiegenshau are the only two dentists in Plainville. They have been colluding, sharing the market and earning monopoly profits of $100,000 each for several years. Fiegenshau is considering reducing his price. He estimates that if Chiaravelli keeps his price at current levels, Fiegenshau would earn $150,000, although Chiaravelli's earnings would fall to $25,000. There is also the possibility that Chiaravelli would compete against Fiegenshau. The resulting price war would reduce the earnings of each to $40,000.

a Represent this market as a Prisoner's Dilemma game.

b Explain why the equilibrium might be achieved when both dentists compete.

Step-by-step solution

Step one (a): Draw a box with four cells, and label it as shown.

	Chiaravelli	
	Cooperate	Compete
Cooperate		
Fiegenshau		
Compete		

Step two: Identify the payoffs for each party if both cooperate, and enter in the appropriate cell. If both cooperate, they each earn $100,000.

	Chiaravelli	
	Cooperate	Compete
Cooperate	C = $100,000 F = $100,000	
Fiegenshau		
Compete		

Step three: Identify the payoffs for each party if both compete, and enter in the appropriate cell. If both compete, they each earn $40,000.

	Chiaravelli	
	Cooperate	Compete
Cooperate	C = $100,000 F = $100,000	
Fiegenshau		
Compete		C = $40,000 F = $40,000

Step four: Identify the payoffs for each party if one competes while the other cooperates, and enter in the corresponding cell. In this case, the dentist who competes earns $150,000, and the other is left with $25,000.

	Chiaravelli	
	Cooperate	Compete
Cooperate	C = $100,000 F = $100,000	C = $150,000 F = $ 25,000
Fiegenshau		
Compete	C = $ 40,000 F = $150,000	C = $40,000 F = $40,000

Step five (b): Show that competition is the equilibrium. For each party, competition is always the best alternative. If Chiavarelli cooperates, then Fiegenshau can earn more by competing ($150,000 > $100,000). If Chiavarelli competes, again Fiegenshau earns more by competing ($40,000 > $25,000). The same is true for Chiavarelli, and both choose to be competitive.

19 (Practice problem: Prisoner's Dilemma) Upper Peninsula Airlines and Northern Airways share the market from Chicago to the winter resorts in the North. If they cooperate, they can extract enough monopoly profits to earn $400,000 each, but unbridled competition would reduce profits to $50,000 each. If one is foolish enough to cooperate in its pricing policy while the other undercuts it, the cooperating firm would earn $0, and the competing firm would earn $800,000.

a Represent this market as a Prisoner's Dilemma game.

b Explain why the equilibrium might be that both firms choose a competitive strategy.

20 (Practice problem: Prisoner's Dilemma) Rosewood College and Elmwood College are the best private schools in the state. Each also prides itself on its lacrosse team. If neither offers scholarships for promising players, then obviously the cost of scholarships will be zero. For $20,000 in scholarships, either could attract the best players (if the other did not offer scholarships), win the conference championship, and attract at least $50,000 in new donations. In this case, however, donations at the losing school would fall by $30,000. On the other hand, if both offered

scholarships, there would be no advantage, no extra donations, and each would have spent the $20,000 for nothing.

a Represent this market as a Prisoner's Dilemma game.

b Explain why the equilibrium might be achieved when both schools compete.

FACILITATING AND RESTRICTIVE PRACTICES

Oligopolists can use certain practices to facilitate collusion and restrict competition. These practices may enable them to get around the incentive to cheat on collusive arrangements. These problems illustrate how dividing the market into exclusive territories and promising to match competitors' low prices can promote collusion.

21 (Worked problem: facilitating and restrictive practices) This problem builds upon problem 14. Having accumulated several years of experience with the unpleasant results of competition, the owners of Southpoint's two furniture-refinishing firms decide to try a new method of collusion. Henceforth, the New Chairs for Old Company will specialize in refinishing chairs, and the Like New Company will take care of the table share of the market. It so happens in Southpoint that exactly half of the business involves tables and half involves chairs. Their marginal costs remain at $4.

a Compute the profit-maximizing quantity of chairs and tables and the corresponding prices for both companies.

b Compare the answer to the answer to part *a* of problem 14.

Step-by-step solution

Step one (*a*): Divide the market into chair and table markets. The result is given in Table 12.27.

Table 12.27

Price	Quantity of chairs	Quantity of tables
$7.50	0	0
$7.00	5	5
$6.50	10	10
$6.00	15	15
$5.50	20	20
$5.00	25	25
$4.50	30	30
$4.00	35	35

Step two: Compute the marginal revenue for each firm. These are shown in Table 12.28. Note that since the demands are exactly the same, so are the marginal revenue curves. Only one is shown.

Table 12.28

Price	Quantity of chairs	Quantity of tables	Total revenue	Marginal revenue
$7.50	0	0	$ 0	—
$7.00	5	5	$ 35	$7
$6.50	10	10	$ 65	$6
$6.00	15	15	$ 90	$5
$5.50	20	20	$110	$4
$5.00	25	25	$125	$3
$4.50	30	30	$135	$2
$4.00	35	35	$140	$1

Step three (*b*): Marginal revenue equals marginal cost at a quantity of 20 for each. The market price will be $5.50, which is exactly the outcome that was solved for in part *a* of problem 14. Dividing the market promotes collusion.

22 (Practice problem: facilitating and restrictive practices) This problem builds upon problem 15. The Davis and Anderson companies have come up with a scheme to promote collusion. From now on, Davis will advertise and take orders from customers in the West, leaving the eastern half of the market to Anderson. They divide the territories so that exactly half of the customers will go to each firm. The marginal cost remains at $5 per ton, and the market demand is as given in Table 12.24.

a Compute the profit-maximizing quantity and price for each firm.

b Compare with the collusive price and quantity solved for in part *a* of problem 15.

23 (Worked problem: facilitating and restrictive practices) Let's return to Mudville and problem 17, where Fay is considering undercutting Jay.

a Compute profits if she reduces her price by $50 below the collusive price and Jay matches the price cut. Assume that customers divide themselves equally between the firms charging the same price.

b Derive Fay's demand curve under the assumption that Jay will match any price cuts but not price increases. Draw a diagram illustrating your answer.

Step-by-step solution

Step one (*a*): The collusive price is $2.00, and Fay's profits are $2,250. If she cuts price to $1.50 and Jay matches the cut, then the quantity demanded is 6,000, and Fay will serve 3,000 of them.

Step two: Fay earns ($1.50 − $1.00) × 3,000 = $1,500. Because this number is less than collusive profits, the offer to match price cuts by Jay will deter Fay from undercutting him.

Step three (*b*): To find the demand if Jay matches price cuts (below $2) but not price increases, simply divide the market evenly at prices of $2 or below, and give all the customers to Jay for higher prices. Table 12.29 gives the result. Notice the kink at a price of $2.

Table 12.29

Price	Quantity
$3.00	0
$2.50	0
$2.00	2,250
$1.50	3,000
$1.00	3,750

24 (Practice problem: facilitating and restrictive practices) Return to problem 6 and the competition between Yuppie and Buppie. Suppose that each agree to match price offers of the other.

a Compute Yuppie's profits if it cuts price by $2.50 below the collusive price and its cut is matched by Buppie. Assume that customers divide themselves equally between firms charging the same price.

b Derive Yuppie's demand curve assuming that Buppie will match price cuts (below the collusive price) but not price increases.

Answers to Problems

2 *a* Marginal revenue appears in Table 12.30.

Table 12.30

Price	Quantity	Revenues	Marginal revenue
$8	100,000	$ 800,000	—
$7	150,000	$1,050,000	$5
$6	200,000	$1,200,000	$3
$5	250,000	$1,250,000	$1
$4	300,000	$1,200,000	−$1
$3	350,000	$1,050,000	−$3
$2	400,000	$ 800,000	−$5

b Profits are maximized when the price is $5 and the number of fans is 250,000.

c Costs = $100,000 + (250,000 × $1) = $350,000; profits = $1,250,000 − $350,000 = $900,000.

d The price and quantity remain as in part a, but profits fall to $1,250,000 − $400,000 = $850,000.

e The solution is illustrated in the diagram.

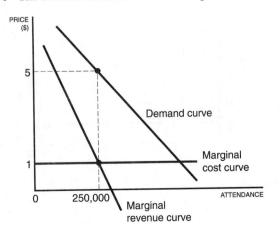

3 *a* Marginal revenue appears in Table 12.31.

Table 12.31

Price	Quantity	Revenues	Marginal revenue
$10	1	$10	—
$ 9	2	$18	$8
$ 8	3	$24	$6
$ 7	4	$28	$4
$ 6	5	$30	$2
$ 5	6	$30	$0
$ 4	7	$28	−$2

Price = $9; quantity = 2; profits = $18 − ($8 × 2) = $2.

b Marginal revenue appears in Table 12.32

Table 12.32

Price	Quantity	Revenues	Marginal revenue
$0.50	500,000	$250,000	—
$0.45	600,000	$270,000	$0.20
$0.40	700,000	$280,000	$0.10
$0.35	800,000	$280,000	$0
$0.30	900,000	$270,000	−$0.10

Price = $0.40; quantity = 700,000; profits = $280,000 − [$50,000 + (700,000 × $0.10)] = $160,000.

c The complete table appears in Table 12.33.

Table 12.33

Price	Quantity	Revenues	Marginal revenue	Total costs	Marginal cost
$20	400	$8,000	—	$ 5,000	—
$18	800	$14,400	$16	$ 7,000	$ 5
$16	1,200	$19,200	$12	$ 9,400	$ 6
$14	1,600	$22,400	$ 8	$12,600	$ 8
$12	2,000	$24,000	$ 4	$16,200	$ 9
$10	2,400	$24,000	$ 0	$21,000	$12

Price = $14; quantity = 1,600; profits = $22,400 − $12,600 = $9,800.

d The completed table appears in Table 12.34.

Table 12.34

Price	Quantity	Revenues	Marginal revenue	Total costs	Marginal cost
$1.00	1,000	$1,000	—	$ 200	—
$0.90	2,000	$1,800	$0.80	$ 300	$0.10
$0.80	3,500	$2,800	$0.67	$ 450	$0.10
$0.70	5,500	$3,850	$0.52	$ 650	$0.10
$0.60	8,000	$4,800	$0.38	$ 900	$0.10
$0.50	11,000	$5,500	$0.23	$1,230	$0.11
$0.40	15,000	$6,000	$0.12	$1,730	$0.12
$0.30	20,000	$6,000	$0	$2,355	$0.14

Price = $0.40; quantity = 15,000; profits = $4,270.

5   *a* The marginal revenue figures appear in Table 12.35.
    b Home market price = $7; quantity = 3,500. Foreign market price = $6; quantity = 6,000.
    c Profits = $24,500 + $36,000 − (3,500 + 6,000) × $1 − $5,000 = $46,000.

Table 12.35

	Home market				Foreign market		
Price	Quan- tity	Revenues	Marginal revenue	Price	Quan- tity	Revenues	Marginal revenue
$10	2,000	$20,000	—	$10	2,000	$20,000	—
$9	2,500	$22,500	$5	$9	3,000	$27,000	$7
$8	3,000	$24,000	$3	$8	4,000	$32,000	$5
$7	3,500	$24,500	$1	$7	5,000	$35,000	$3
$6	4,000	$24,000	−$1	$6	6,000	$36,000	$1
$5	4,500	$22,500	−$3	$5	7,000	$35,000	−$1
$4	5,000	$20,000	−$5	$4	8,000	$32,000	−$3

6   *a* The completed table appears in Table 12.36.

Table 12.36

	Home market				Foreign market		
Price	Quan- tity	Revenues	Marginal revenue	Price	Quan- tity	Revenues	Marginal revenue
$4.00	200	$800	—	$4.00	100	$400	—
$3.50	400	$1,400	$3	$3.50	120	$420	$1
$3.00	600	$1,800	$2	$3.00	140	$420	$0
$2.50	800	$2,000	$1	$2.50	160	$400	−$1
$2.00	1,000	$2,000	$0	$2.00	180	$360	−$2
$1.50	1,200	$1,800	−$1	$1.50	200	$300	−$3

    b Suburbs price = $2.50; quantity = 800. Inner city price = $3.50; quantity = 120.
    c Profits = $2,000 + $420 − (800 + 120) × $1 − $100 = $1,400.

8   *a* and *c* The marginal revenues and Magdalena's revenues are given in Table 12.37.

Table 12.37

Price	Quantity	Revenues	Marginal revenue	Magdalena's revenue
$20	20,000	$400,000	—	$100,000
$18	25,000	$450,000	$10	$112,500
$16	30,000	$480,000	$6	$120,000
$14	35,000	$490,000	$2	$122,500
$12	40,000	$480,000	−$2	$120,000
$10	48,000	$480,000	$0	$120,000

    b and *d* The profit-maximizing price is $16 and the quantity is 30,000, but Magdalena's revenues

are maximized at a price of $14, where 35,000 CDs are sold.
    e The solution is illustrated in the diagram.

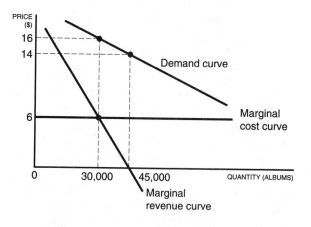

9   *a* Marginal revenue is given in Table 12.38.

Table 12.38

Price	Quantity	Revenues	Marginal revenue
$1.00	30,000	$30,000	—
$0.95	40,000	$38,000	$0.80
$0.90	50,000	$45,000	$0.70
$0.85	60,000	$51,000	$0.60
$0.80	70,000	$56,000	$0.50
$0.75	80,000	$60,000	$0.40
$0.70	90,000	$63,000	$0.30
$0.65	100,000	$65,000	$0.20
$0.60	110,000	$66,000	$0.10
$0.55	120,000	$66,000	$0

    b Price = $0.60; quantity = 110,000.
    c The tax increases marginal cost to $0.20. The price becomes $0.65 and the quantity, 100,000.
    d Consumers pay $.05 of the tax.
    e The solution is illustrated in the diagram.

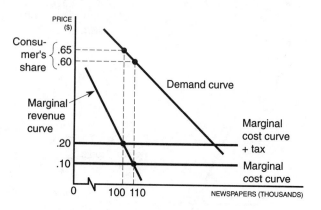

10   *a* Marginal revenue is given in Table 12.39.

Table 12.39

Price	Quantity	Revenues	Marginal revenue
$45	60,000	$2,700,000	—
$40	80,000	$3,200,000	$25
$35	100,000	$3,500,000	$15
$30	120,000	$3,600,000	$ 5
$25	140,000	$3,500,000	–$ 5

b Price = $35; quantity = 100,000.

c Price = $25; quantity = 140,000.

d The solution is illustrated in the diagram.

11 The elasticity for each point on the demand curve is given in Table 12.40.

Table 12.40

Price	Quantity	Revenues	Marginal revenue	Elasticity
$10	1	$10	—	—
$ 9	2	$18	$8	19/3
$ 8	3	$24	$6	17/5
$ 7	4	$28	$4	15/7
$ 6	5	$30	$2	13/9
$ 5	6	$30	$0	11/11
$ 4	7	$28	–$2	9/11

Along the elastic portion of the demand curve, which is where price exceeds $5, marginal revenue is positive. Marginal revenue equals marginal cost at a price of $9, which is on the elastic portion.

13 *a* and *b* The marginal revenue and the market supply appear in Table 12.41.

Table 12.41

Market demand		Total revenue	Marginal revenue
Price	Quantity		
$1,000	300,000	$300,000,000	—
$ 900	400,000	$360,000,000	$600
$ 800	500,000	$400,000,000	$400
$ 700	600,000	$420,000,000	$200
$ 600	700,000	$420,000,000	$ 0
$ 500	800,000	$400,000,000	–$200
$ 400	900,000	$360,000,000	–$400
$ 300	1,000,000	$300,000,000	–$600

Firm's supply		Market supply	
Price	Quantity	Price	Quantity
$1,000	4,000	$1,000	2,000,000
$ 900	3,500	$ 900	1,750,000
$ 800	3,000	$ 800	1,500,000
$ 700	2,400	$ 700	1,200,000
$ 600	2,000	$ 600	1,000,000
$ 500	1,600	$ 500	800,000
$ 400	1,000	$ 400	500,000
$ 300	500	$ 300	250,000
$ 200	100	$ 200	50,000

c Cartel price = $800; market quantity = 500,000; each firm's quantity = 1,000.

d 3,000.

e Price = $500; quantity = 800,000.

15 *a* Marginal revenue for the market demand is given in Table 12.42.

Table 12.42

Price	Quantity (tons)	Revenues	Marginal revenue
$22.50	0	$ 0	
$20.00	100	$2,000	$20
$17.50	200	$3,500	$15
$15.00	300	$4,500	$10
$12.50	400	$5,000	$ 5
$10.00	500	$5,000	$ 0
$ 7.50	600	$4,500	–$ 5

Price = $12.50; market quantity = 400; each firm sells 200 tons.

b The residual demand is found by subtracting 200 from the market demand. This and marginal revenue appear in Table 12.43.

Table 12.43

Price	Quantity (tons)	Revenues	Marginal revenue
$22.50	0	$ 0	—
$20.00	0	$ 0	—
$17.50	0	$ 0	—
$15.00	100	$1,500	$15
$12.50	200	$2,500	$10
$10.00	300	$3,000	$ 5
$ 7.50	400	$3,000	$ 0

Davis will produce 300. The market quantity will be 200 + 300 = 500, and the price will be $10 per ton.

17 *a* Marginal revenue for the market demand is given in Table 12.44.

Table 12.44

Price	Quantity (sweaters)	Revenues	Marginal revenue
$27.50	0	$ 0	—
$25.00	100	$2,500	$25
$22.50	200	$4,500	$20
$20.00	300	$6,000	$15
$17.50	400	$7,000	$10
$15.00	500	$7,500	$5
$12.50	600	$7,500	$0

b Cartel price = $17.50; market quantity = 400; each firm sells 200.

c Profits = (200 × $17.50) − (200 × $10) = $1,500.

d Yuppie's price = $15; quantity = 500; profits = ($15 × 500) − ($10 × 500) = $2,500.

19 *a*

		Upper Peninsula	
		Cooperate	Compete
Northern	Cooperate	UP = $400,000 N = $400,000	UP = $800,000 N = S50
	Compete	UP = $0 N = $800,000	UP = $50,000 N = $50,000

b If Northern competes, UP prefers to compete ($800,000 > $400,000). If Northern cooperates, UP still prefers to compete ($50,000 > $0). If UP competes, Northern prefers to compete ($800,000 > $400,000). If UP cooperates, Northern still prefers to

compete ($50,000 > $0) Since both always prefer competition, the equilibrium is that both compete and profits are $50,000 each.

20 *a*

		Elmwood	
		Cooperate	Compete
Rosewood	Cooperate	E = $0 R = $0	E = $30,000 R = −S30,000
	Compete	E = −$30,000 R = $30,000	C = $20,000 R = −$20,000

b If Rosewood cooperates and does not offer scholarships, Elmwood prefers to compete and offer them ($30,000 > $0). If Rosewood competes and offers scholarships, Elmwood still prefers to offer them (−$20,000 > −$30,000). If Elmwood cooperates and does not offer scholarships, Rosewood prefers to offer them ($30,000 > $0). If Elmwood competes and offers scholarships, Rosewood still prefers to offer them (−$20,000 > −$30,000). Since both always prefer competition, the equilibrium is that both compete, offer scholarships, and lose $20,000 each.

22 The demand for each firm's share of the market and the corresponding marginal revenue appear in Table 12.45.

Table 12.45

Price	Quantity (tons)	Revenues	Marginal revenue
$22.50	0	$ 0	—
$20.00	50	$1,000	$20
$17.50	100	$1,750	$15
$15.00	150	$2,250	$10
$12.50	200	$2,500	$ 5
$10.00	250	$2,500	$ 0
$ 7.50	300	$2,250	−$ 5

a Each firm charges $12.50 and sells 200.

b The price and quantity are the same as under monopoly.

24 *a* If both reduce price by $2.50 to $15.00, the market quantity will equal 500, which implies that each will sell 250. Profits will equal ($15 × 250) − ($10 × 250) = $1,250, which is less than the $1,500 they earn by charging $17.50.

b Yuppie's demand curve if price cuts below $17.50 are matched but price increases are not is given in Table 12.46.

Table 12.46

Price	Quantity (sweaters)
$27.50	0
$25.00	0
$22.50	0
$20.00	0
$17.50	200
$15.00	250
$12.50	300

CHAPTER 13 | Government Policies Toward Competition

Chapter Review

Monopolies and oligopolies, explored in Chapter 12, produce too little output and charge inefficiently high prices. This chapter of the text returns to the role government plays in the economy, this time examining government policies to promote competition. Another important topic is government responses to natural monopolies. Natural monopolies occur in markets like home electric service, where a single firm can produce the good more cheaply than multiple firms can.

ESSENTIAL CONCEPTS

1 Competitive industries allocate resources efficiently. Monopolies and other imperfectly competitive industries, however, often operate inefficiently. Economists study four types of inefficiency.

  a Monopolies restrict output below what it would be if the industry were competitive. The lower output results in higher prices and a transfer of wealth from consumers to the monopoly. There is an additional loss in consumer surplus, because output is below the level at which all gains from trade are realized. This loss is called the deadweight loss of monopoly.

  b Although monopoly profits are higher when their costs are lower, monopolies are not forced to produce at the lowest cost. There is some room for **managerial slack,** which allows monopolies to be inefficient.

  c Although there are examples of monopolies that engage in effective **research and development,** the incentives are less under monopoly.

  d Because monopolies earn rents (profits above the

level necessary to compensate investors), resources are expended to acquire and retain these existing rents. This type of activity is called **rent seeking** and is socially wasteful.

2 In some industries, where there are high fixed and low marginal costs, the lowest cost of production occurs when there is only one firm. Such an industry is called a **natural monopoly.** Figure 13.1 shows that the average cost curve for a natural monopoly is falling and that marginal cost always lies below average cost. Governments sometimes nationalize and operate natural monopolies, but more often governments regulate them. A regulatory agency sets prices designed to limit the firm to a normal rate of return. This policy in turn motivates firms to overinvest. Also, because in both the nationalized and regulated cases the pricing decisions are made politically, products may be sold below cost in some markets and above cost in others. This practice is called **cross subsidization.**

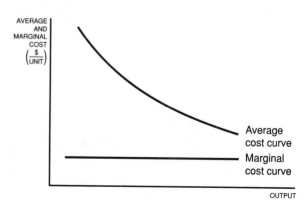

Figure 13.1

3 A final way of dealing with natural monopolies is to increase competition. Examples in the United States include the deregulation of long-distance telephone service and of the trucking and airline industries. Competition provides firms with incentives to innovate and reduce costs, and it eliminates cross subsidization. On the other hand, with more firms in the industry, each firm produces less, that is, chooses a point higher up on the average cost curve.

4 The various ways in which the government attempts to promote competition are called **antitrust policy.** Important pieces of legislation such as the Sherman Act, the Clayton Act, and the establishment of the Federal Trade Commission have outlawed monopolizing, authorized opposition to mergers, and forbidden such types of anticompetitive practices as tying, price discrimination, and exclusive dealing.

BEHIND THE ESSENTIAL CONCEPTS

1 The problem of deadweight loss lies at the heart of economic arguments about making exchange efficient. As an example, look at Figure 13.2, which shows a monopoly output equal to 200. The firm sets the price at $10 and maximizes its profits. Notice, however, that at this point the marginal benefit to consumers of one or more unit (measured, as usual, by the price they're willing to pay) is greater than the marginal cost. This means that producing and selling additional units would create value—there would be gains from trade. The total possible additional gains equal the area of the triangle *ABC*. But these gains are not realized, and therefore they are called the deadweight loss of monopoly.

The idea that exchange creates value and that any reduction in the amount of exchange below the competitive level leads to a deadweight loss (as seen in Figure 13.2) is very important in economics.

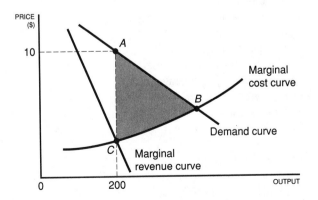

Figure 13.2

2 Firms desiring greater profits seek them in two different ways. First, they offer better products or devise better ways of producing and doing business. These activities do make profits, and they create value and enhance efficiency as well. Firms can also try to convince government to protect them against competition or devise strategies to deter entry. Practices of this type do not create anything, they only redistribute money and reduce economic efficiency. The latter behavior is called rent seeking.

3 In competitive industries, firms are forced to produce at the lowest possible cost. If they do not, new firms will enter the market, undercut the price, and drive existing firms out. In a monopoly, however, whether it is private, nationalized, or regulated, the firm can get away with some slack. It can pay its workers a little more than the going wage, it can postpone adopting the most efficient production techniques, or it can overlook the low-cost suppliers. You can probably see how this could happen in an unregulated monopoly, where there are extra profits, or in a nationalized industry, where the government makes up any losses, but it is also possible in a regulated monopoly because regulators do not always know the lowest cost. The firm has an incentive and the ability to make the regulators believe that it is more costly to do business than it really is. Regulators can prevent fraud, but it is very difficult to find and eliminate waste.

4 In order to determine whether a merger will inhibit competition, the number of firms in an industry and their size relative to the market need to be determined. The geographical size of the market should be considered, as some industries are local, while many have become international. For example, the gold market is a world market. The cement industry, on the other hand, is local. The product is very expensive to transport, and only nearby firms could merge. The similarity of the products also needs to be considered. Is plastic wrap in the same industry as aluminum foil? If so, does a single producer of plastic wrap have a monopoly, or is it simply another firm in the food-wrapping industry? Economists look at the cross-price effect to determine the extent to which firms are competing. How much does a price decrease by one firm reduce another's demand?

5 Antitrust policy is concerned with prohibiting market domination. This brings up the question of what it means to dominate a market. First, there is the issue of the bounds of the market. What products belong in the market? Economists look at the effect of one good's increase in price on the demand for another. If demand rises significantly, then the goods are part of the same market. The second issue is how different are the products. Here, we look at how much business is lost

when price rises. In each case, how prices affect demands is the central idea.

SELF-TEST

True or False

1 Monopolies produce less output than would be produced if the industry were competitive.
2 Monopolies must produce at the lowest cost.
3 Rent seeking refers to anything done in pursuit of monopoly profits.
4 Monopolies have stronger incentives to undertake research and development than do competitive firms.
5 In a natural monopoly, the cost of production is higher because of the lack of competition.
6 Cross subsidization refers to the practice of selling below cost in one market and above cost in another.
7 Regulated natural monopolies are usually forced to charge a price equal to marginal cost.
8 Subjecting a natural monopolist to competition can be an effective strategy if the average cost curve is not too steep.
9 In a horizontal merger, a firm acquires an upstream supplier.
10 Vertical mergers are illegal *per se* in the United States.
11 Enforcement of antitrust laws is the exclusive domain of the U.S. government.
12 One important goal of antitrust policy is to limit the absolute size of firms.
13 Under the rule of reason, a business practice is not illegal if it can be shown to enhance economic efficiency.
14 The Clayton Act outlawed some specific monopoly practices, such as price discrimination.
15 Most current antitrust efforts involve attempting to break up excessively large firms.

Multiple Choice

1 Monopolists set the price
   a equal to marginal cost.
   b equal to average cost.
   c above marginal cost.
   d below marginal cost.
   e below average cost.
2 Monopoly output is
   a the same as the competitive output.
   b less than the competitive output.
   c more than the competitive output.
   d sometimes more and sometimes less than the competitive output.
   e determined by setting marginal revenue equal to price.

3 The deadweight loss caused by monopoly is the
   a difference between consumer surplus under the monopoly and what consumer surplus would have been if the industry were competitive.
   b amount of monopoly profits.
   c increase in cost brought about by managerial slack.
   d total of rent-seeking expenditures.
   e difference between consumer surplus under the monopoly and what consumer surplus would have been if the industry were competitive minus the transfer from consumers to the monopolist.
4 Managerial slack refers to
   a the lack of efficiency in some monopolies.
   b activities designed to protect a monopoly position.
   c the loss in consumer surplus as a result of restricted output.
   d the lessened incentives for research and development under monopoly.
   e the failure of antitrust policies.
5 Among the problems of monopolies are
   a restricted output.
   b managerial slack.
   c reduced incentives for research and development.
   d rent seeking to protect the monopoly position.
   e all of the above.
6 Which of the following is *not* a type of rent seeking?
   a Research aimed at reducing the cost of production
   b Lobbying the legislature for protection against foreign competition
   c Contributions to political campaigns for candidates who support regulations favored by the monopoly
   d Entry-deterring activities
   e Designing the product to be incompatible with competitors' products
7 If the cost of production is lowest when there is only one firm, then the industry is a
   a trust.
   b natural oligopoly.
   c natural monopoly.
   d horizontal merger.
   e vertical merger.
8 In a natural monopoly, marginal cost
   a equals price.
   b equals average cost.
   c is less than average cost.
   d is greater than average cost.
   e is greater than price.
9 Cross subsidization involves selling
   a below cost in some markets and above cost in others.
   b at cost in all markets.
   c above cost in each market.
   d below cost in each market.
   e *a* and *b*.

10 Cross subsidization
  a occurs in nationalized monopolies but not in regulated monopolies.
  b occurs in regulated monopolies but not in nationalized monopolies.
  c occurs in neither regulated nor nationalized monopolies.
  d occurs in both regulated and nationalized monopolies.
  e never occurs.

11 Natural monopoly regulation usually sets price equal to
  a marginal revenue.
  b marginal cost.
  c average revenue.
  d average cost.
  e average variable cost.

12 Regulated natural monopolies often
  a invest too much.
  b invest too little.
  c hire too much labor.
  d hire too few workers.
  e sell too much output.

13 Government policies to promote competition are called
  a antitrust.
  b rent seeking.
  c managerial slack.
  d natural monopoly.
  e horizontal mergers.

14 Which of the following is an example of a horizontal merger?
  a One steel producer buys another steel producer.
  b A meat-packing firm buys a large cattle ranch.
  c A maker of chalk buys a pizza delivery firm.
  d A foreign company buys a U.S. company.
  e A U.S. company buys a foreign company.

15 Which of the following is an example of a vertical merger?
  a One steel producer buys another steel producer.
  b A meat-packing firm buys a large cattle ranch.
  c A maker of chalk buys a pizza delivery firm.
  d A foreign company buys a U.S. company.
  e A U.S. company buys a foreign company.

16 Which of the following is *not* a goal of antitrust policy?
  a Limit anticompetitive practices
  b Prevent market domination
  c Limit the absolute size of firms
  d Make use of private incentive to sue under antitrust law
  e All of the above are goals of antitrust policy.

17 The Federal Trade Commission
  a issues the regulation that made monopolies illegal.
  b investigates unfairly competitive practices.
  c issues orders to cease and desist from unfair practices.

  d determines whether foreign firms engage in unfair trade practices, such as dumping.
  e *b* and *c*.

18 The act that made monopolizing an industry illegal was the
  a Sherman Act.
  b Federal Trade Commission Act.
  c Robinson-Patman Act.
  d Celler-Kefauver Act.
  e Taft-Hartley Act.

19 The hypothesis that regulators eventually serve the interests of the industry that they regulate and not the customers is called
  a the antitrust hypothesis.
  b the rent-seeking hypothesis.
  c the regulatory capture hypothesis.
  d the natural monopoly hypothesis.
  e none of the above.

20 A business practice is anticompetitive under the rule of reason if it
  a is illegal *per se.*
  b is in violation of the Clayton Act.
  c cannot be shown to be a sensible business practice that promotes efficiency.
  d leads to vertical mergers.
  e leads to horizontal mergers.

Completion

1 Monopolies restrict output and cause a loss in consumer surplus, part of which is a transfer to the monopolist, and the remainder is called the _____.

2 The fact that, shielded from competition, monopolists may not produce for the lowest costs is called _____.

3 Political contributions and lobbying expenses for the purpose of winning regulations to restrict competition are examples of _____.

4 Regulated or nationalized firms may sell below cost in some markets and above cost in others, a practice known as _____.

5 In a _____, the cost of production is lowest if there is only one firm in the industry.

6 Government efforts to promote competition by restricting anticompetitive tactics or opposing mergers are called _____.

7 When a firm buys a competitor that was producing a competing product, it is called a _____.

8 The purchase by one firm of an upstream supplier or downstream distributor is called a _____.

9 The monopolization of an industry was made illegal by the _____.

10 The _____ investigates and proscribes unfair trade practices.

Answers to Self-Test

True or False

1	t	6	t	11	f
2	f	7	f	12	f
3	f	8	t	13	t
4	f	9	f	14	t
5	f	10	f	15	f

Multiple Choice

1	c	6	a	11	d	16	c
2	b	7	c	12	a	17	e
3	e	8	c	13	a	18	a
4	a	9	a	14	a	19	c
5	e	10	d	15	b	20	c

Completion

1 deadweight loss
2 managerial slack
3 rent seeking
4 cross subsidization
5 natural monopoly
6 antitrust
7 horizontal merger
8 vertical merger
9 Sherman Act
10 Federal Trade Commission

Doing Economics: Tools and Practice Problems

One of the important costs that monopolies impose on the economy is the deadweight loss, which reflects the losses resulting from the fact that monopolies restrict output. Here, we study how to compute the deadweight loss and then move on to consider the regulation of natural monopolies.

DEADWEIGHT LOSS

When a monopoly controls an industry, it can increase its profits by restricting output below the level where price equals marginal cost. By doing so, the monopoly reduces the number of mutually beneficial trades. Because these trades do not occur, there is a loss in consumer surplus, and this loss is called the deadweight burden. (Consumer surplus falls still further because of the higher price that the monopoly charges, but this loss in consumer surplus is only a transfer from consumers to the monopolist and is not part of the deadweight loss.) Tool Kit 13.1 shows how to compute deadweight loss.

Tool Kit 13.1 Finding the Deadweight Loss of Monopoly

When price is set above marginal cost, the market contracts and there is a deadweight loss. Follow these five steps to compute it.

Step one: Identify the demand and marginal cost curves.

Step two: Calculate marginal revenue.

Step three: Find the monopoly output (Q_m) and price (p_m) by choosing the quantity for which marginal revenue equals marginal cost (MC_m).

Step four: Find the "competitive" quantity (Q_c) by choosing the quantity for which demand equals marginal cost.

Step five: Compute the deadweight loss as the area between the demand and marginal cost curves:

$$\text{deadweight loss} = 1/2(Q_c - Q_m)(p_m - MC_m).$$

(This formula exactly measures the area only when demand is a straight line.)

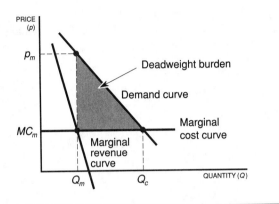

1 (Worked problem: deadweight loss) The West India Tea Company has been granted the sole franchise to sell green tea in Greenville. Its marginal cost is $5 per box. Demand is given in Table 13.1. Solve for its output and price and the deadweight loss.

Table 13.1

Price	Quantity
$10	10,000
$ 9	15,000
$ 8	20,000
$ 7	25,000
$ 6	30,000
$ 5	35,000

Step-by-step solution

Step one: Identify the demand and marginal cost curves. The demand curve is given in Table 13.1; marginal cost is constant and equal to $5.

Step two: Calculate marginal revenue. Follow the usual procedure outlined in Tool Kit 13.1. The marginal revenue for the West India Tea Company is given in Table 13.2.

Table 13.2

Price	Quantity	Total revenue	Marginal revenue
$10	10,000	$100,000	—
$ 9	15,000	$135,000	$7
$ 8	20,000	$160,000	$5
$ 7	25,000	$175,000	$3
$ 6	30,000	$180,000	$1
$ 5	35,000	$175,000	−$1

Step three: Find the monopoly output by choosing the quantity for which marginal revenue equals marginal cost. Marginal revenue equals marginal cost when price is $8 and 20,000 boxes are sold.

Step four: Find the competitive quantity by choosing the quantity for which demand equals marginal cost. The competitive price is $5, and the quantity is 35,000.

Step five: Compute the deadweight loss as the area between the demand and marginal cost curves.

$$\begin{aligned}\text{Deadweight loss} &= 1/2(Q_c - Q_m)(p_m - MC_m) \\ &= 1/2(35,000 - 20,000)(\$8 - \$5) \\ &= \$22,500.\end{aligned}$$

2 (Practice problem: deadweight loss) Although its marginal cost is only $4 for each ride, the Calloway Cab Company has bribed the city council in Venal City to grant it monopoly status at the local airport. The demand for rides is given in Table 13.3.

Table 13.3

Price	Quantity
$7.50	0
$7.00	10
$6.50	20
$6.00	30
$5.50	40
$5.00	50
$4.50	60
$4.00	70

Solve for the company's output and price and the deadweight loss.

3 (Practice problem: deadweight loss) As all baseball fans know, there is only one team in Mudville. The marginal cost of another fan in the park is $1, and the demand is given in Table 13.4.

Table 13.4

Price	Quantity
$3.00	1,500
$2.50	3,000
$2.00	4,500
$1.50	6,000
$1.00	7,500

Solve for the team's output and price and the deadweight loss.

NATURAL MONOPOLY

Natural monopolies are industries with high fixed and low marginal costs. Costs in these industries are lowest when there is only one firm. Many so-called natural monopolies, such as public utilities, cable television companies, and phone companies, are regulated by a public commission that prevents the entry of competitors and sets prices just high enough to allow the firms to earn a normal rate of return. This practice mandates that price equal average cost. Tool Kit 13.2 shows how to set price in a regulated monopoly.

Tool Kit 13.2 Finding the Price for a Regulated Natural Monopoly

Public utility commissions often regulate natural monopolies so that they make a normal rate of return. To this end price must equal average cost. Follow these steps.

Step one: Identify the demand curve, marginal cost, and fixed costs.

Step two: Compute the average cost by dividing total cost by quantity:

average cost = total cost/quantity.

Step three: Find the price for which average cost crosses the demand curve. This is the price for a regulated natural monopoly.

---

4 (Worked problem: natural monopoly) Cutthroat Cable Company is the only provider of cable television services in Kings. Most of its costs are access fees and maintenance expenses, and these fixed costs, which do not vary with the number of customers, total $760,000 monthly. The marginal cost of another subscriber is only $1 per month. The company's demand curve is given in Table 13.5.

Table 13.5

Price (per month)	Number of subscribers
$50	10,000
$40	20,000
$30	30,000
$20	40,000
$10	50,000
$ 1	100,000

The Kings Borough Utility Commission regulates the price of cable service and wants to set the price so that Cutthroat makes a normal rate of return. What price should it mandate?

Step-by-step solution

Step one: Identify the demand curve, marginal cost, and fixed costs. Demand is given in Table 13.5; marginal cost is $1, and fixed costs are $760,000.

Step two: Compute average cost. When price is $50, there are 10,000 subscribers, and total costs are $760,000 + (10,000 × $1) = $770,000. Average cost is $770,000/10,000 = $77. Continuing this procedure, we derive Table 13.6.

Table 13.6

Price	Number of subscribers	Total cost	Average cost
$50	10,000	$770,000	$77.00
$40	20,000	$780,000	$39.00
$30	30,000	$790,000	$26.33
$20	40,000	$800,000	$20.00
$10	50,000	$810,000	$16.20
$ 1	100,000	$860,000	$ 8.60

Step three: Find the price for which average cost crosses the demand curve. This price is $20, and it is the price that the public utility commission will choose.

5 (Practice problem: natural monopoly) The new big-cat exhibit at the Potter Park Zoo is bringing in the public. Demand is given in Table 13.7. The zoo costs the park service only $1 per visitor, but its fixed costs equal $12,000. Governor Scissorhands has declared that no public funds will be used to support zoos, so Potter Park must charge a price just high enough to cover its costs. What price will solve this problem?

Table 13.7

Price	Number of visitors
$8	1,000
$7	2,000
$6	3,000
$5	4,000
$4	5,000
$3	6,000
$2	7,000
$1	8,000

6 (Practice problem: natural monopoly) Country Line Commuter Service runs from rural areas into the city. It has fixed costs of $20,400 and a marginal cost of $10 per commuter. Demand is given in Table 13.8. The Metropolitan Transportation Commission sets the

monthly price for a pass on Country Line, and it wants to allow the firm to earn a normal rate of return. Find the price that allows the service to cover its costs.

Table 13.8

Price (per month)	Number of commuters
$200	100
$180	120
$160	140
$140	160
$120	180
$100	200

Answers to Problems

2   The marginal revenue is given in Table 13.9.

Table 13.9

Price	Quantity	Revenues	Marginal revenue
$7.50	0	$ 0	—
$7.00	10	$ 70	$7
$6.50	20	$130	$6
$6.00	30	$180	$5
$5.50	40	$220	$4
$5.00	50	$250	$3
$4.50	60	$270	$2
$4.00	70	$280	$1

The monopoly output and price are 40 and $5.50, respectively. The competitive output and price would be 70 and $4, respectively. The deadweight loss is

$$\tfrac{1}{2}(70 - 40)(\$5.50 - \$4.00) = \$22.50.$$

The marginal revenue is given in Table 13.10.

Table 13.10

Price	Quantity	Revenues	Marginal revenue
$3.00	1,500	$4,500	$3
$2.50	3,000	$7,500	$2
$2.00	4,500	$9,000	$1
$1.50	6,000	$9,000	$0
$1.00	7,500	$7,500	−$1

The monopoly price and output are $2 and 4,500, respectively. The competitive price and output would be $1 and 7,500, respectively. The deadweight loss is

$$\tfrac{1}{2}(7,500 - 4,500)(\$2 - \$1) = \$1,500.$$

5   Average cost is given in Table 13.11.

Table 13.11

Price	Number of visitors	Total cost	Average cost
$8	1,000	$13,000	$13.00
$7	2,000	$14,000	$ 7.00
$6	3,000	$15,000	$ 5.00
$5	4,000	$16,000	$ 4.00
$4	5,000	$17,000	$ 3.40
$3	6,000	$18,000	$ 3.00
$2	7,000	$19,000	$ 2.70
$1	8,000	$20,000	$ 2.50

The price that allows Potter Park to cover its costs is $3.

6   Average cost is given in Table 13.12.

Table 13.12

Price	Number of commuters	Total cost	Average cost
$200	100	$21,400	$214.00
$180	120	$21,600	$180.00
$160	140	$21,800	$156.00
$140	160	$22,000	$138.00
$120	180	$22,200	$123.00
$100	200	$22,400	$112.00

Average cost equals price when price is $180. The commission should choose this price.

CHAPTER 14 | Imperfect Information in the Product Market

Chapter Review

Chapter 14 begins the exploration of the economics of information with a look at information problems in the product market. Why can't customers always be sure of the quality of a good? Why do customers sometimes pay a higher price for a good than the good is worth? This chapter explains the various ways in which the economy attempts to solve these problems. In doing so, the chapter deviates from the basic competitive model to introduce a fascinating world of signaling, reputation, search, and advertising. Imperfect information causes markets to look a lot like the imperfect competition models discussed in Chapter 12 (on monopoly and oligopoly).

ESSENTIAL CONCEPTS

1 The basic competitive model assumes that information is perfect, that households are well-informed about the prices, quality, and availability of goods and services, and that firms know all input and output prices and the best available technology. Economists now believe that there are important aspects of the economy's performance that are the result of **imperfect information.** For instance, mutually beneficial trades may not occur if customers cannot judge accurately a product's quality.

   If there were such a thing as a market for information, it would not solve the problem. There would be no way for a customer to evaluate information before buying it, and if she already had the information, she would have no need to buy it.

2 **Asymmetric information** exists when one side of the market knows something that the other does not. For

example, the seller of a used car may know more about its reliability than the buyer. Asymmetric information can cause the demand curve to be upward sloping, because buyers reason that only low-quality cars would be sold at low prices and that quality increases with price. This odd situation can lead to more than one possible equilibrium, and can cause markets to be thin or nonexistent in spite of potential gains from trade.

3 One way to send buyers a message in a market with asymmetric information is called **signaling.** For example, a seller of quality used cars can distinguish his product by offering warranties or by building expensive showrooms. Buyers will reason that a seller of lemons could not afford the expenses of honoring the warranty and will conclude that this seller's used cars are reliable. The seller can also charge higher prices, another potentially informative signal. Buyers understand that only lemons would be sold at low prices, and thus they judge the quality according to the price.

4 If buyers can observe the quality of what is sold, then they can provide sellers with good incentives by basing pay on quality. For example, an employer can pay a typist according to the number of errors made. When buyers do not know the quality of goods before purchasing them, markets do not provide built-in incentives for firms to produce high-quality merchandise. Two possible solutions to this incentive problem are **contracts** and **reputations.**

   a Contracts typically include **contingency clauses,** which make payment depend on the quality of the service. For example, a contract might specify that the service must be performed by a certain date unless there is a strike or bad weather. Spelling out contingencies provides incentives and shares the risk, but it makes contracts complicated. When the terms of a contract are violated, one party is said to be in breach, but if the reasons for the breach are ambiguous, contract enforcement becomes an issue. Certainly, contracts help, but they provide only an imperfect solution to the incentive problems accompanying trade in the presence of asymmetric information.

b By repeatedly providing quality goods and service, a firm establishes a reputation, which enables it to earn extra profits. To preserve its valuable reputation, the firm must continue to provide quality. Reputations thus provide firms with incentives to perform well.

5 Because quality is uncertain and also because the same good may be sold at different prices in different locations (**price dispersion**), customers spend time and money in **search.** Rational search balances the benefits (finding better goods at lower prices) against the costs. Customers usually stop searching even though there is more to learn. **Information intermediaries** are firms that gather information to make customer search easier and more effective. Department stores and travel agents are examples of information intermediaries.

6 Firms try to influence customers' purchasing decisions through **informative** and **persuasive advertising.** The goal of advertising is to shift the demand curve to the right, enabling the firm to raise prices and sell more goods. Advertising may also serve as a signal. Customers may reason that only a high-quality product with good sales would justify a large expenditure on advertising.

7 Concern for poorly informed consumers and deceptive advertising has led to **consumer protection legislation,** which attempts to stop false advertising. Such legislation includes truth-in-lending regulations, which require lenders to disclose the true interest rate. Even so, distinguishing between illegal, false advertising and its legal counterparts (confusing and persuasive advertising) is difficult.

BEHIND THE ESSENTIAL CONCEPTS

1 Markets do not necessarily fail when information is imperfect. The market for assets is an example of a very efficient market. Uncertainty in these markets exists, but the uncertainty is symmetric. Neither side knows the ultimate value of the assets they are trading. Efficiency problems arise, however, when information is asymmetric, that is, when one side of the market knows something that the other does not. Many mutually beneficial exchanges do not take place because buyers cannot be sure about quality, and they fear that sellers may exploit their informational advantage and sell lemons.

2 In the basic competitive model, customers ask simple questions such as, "Is the good worth its price?" In the presence of asymmetric information, and, especially signaling, customers must be more sophisticated. The seller of a quality item wants to signal that his goods have value. He could just say, "My goods are great!" but few customers would believe him. If he provides a guarantee and builds an expensive shop, customers may be more confident that he would be there to honor his word should the product fail. The customer infers from the warranty and the shop that the seller's goods are quality goods.

3 The information problems discussed in this chapter lead the market structure away from perfect competition, creating two possible situations: **barriers to entry** and firms with **downward-sloping demand curves.**

a Customers who cannot know the quality of goods buy from businesses with good reputations. Because a reputation is built up over time, firms that would otherwise enter an industry will not be able to justify the investment necessary to establish a good reputation. In this scenario, reputation becomes a barrier to entry and results in less competition.

b Because customers must search to learn about price and quality, it becomes cheaper for them to shop at familiar stores. Although the goods themselves may be identical, the stores are different in the eyes of the customer because he knows about some stores and is ignorant of others. Thus, a firm faces a downward-sloping demand curve, where high demanders are those who have information about the firm and lower demanders do not as yet.

4 Information problems in the product market run parallel to the problems in the insurance market. Again, there are two types of information problems.

a In the insurance market, when the price of insurance is high, only the risky customers buy insurance. The mix of customers is adversely selected when the price rises. Adverse selection also appears in the market for lemons. Customers reason that as the price rises, more quality cars are offered for sale, and the fraction of lemons declines. In other words, there is **adverse selection** in the average quality of used cars when the price falls.

b **Moral hazard** troubles the insurance market because people who have insurance tend to be less cautious. They lose their incentives to be careful when they are protected against loss. Similarly, in this chapter, we see that suppliers must be given incentives to live up to the terms of their contracts. There is a moral hazard that the other party may not fulfill his promise and instead give some excuse that cannot be verified.

5   Although this chapter is about information problems, you should also keep in mind that markets do economize on the need for gathering information. In deciding what to produce and in what quantities and the method of production, firms do not need to know the preferences or incomes of households, the production techniques of other firms, or the overall quantities of inputs available. They only need to know the price. Similarly, households do not need to know others' tastes or anything about firms. Price conveys all relevant information, a great advantage of markets.

SELF-TEST

True or False

1   In the basic competitive model, individuals know their opportunity sets.
2   In the basic competitive model, firms know the opportunity sets of individuals.
3   Markets for information do not work well because once the consumer has enough information to evaluate the worth of the information, she no longer has the incentive to pay for it.
4   In the lemons model, demand may slope upward if average quality increases as price increases.
5   Supply and demand may cross more than once if customers do not know the quality of the goods they are asked to buy.
6   Lemons markets have adverse selection in that as the price falls, the mix of goods offered for sale contains more low-quality goods.
7   Customers may believe that a product that carries a warranty is reliable because if the product were not reliable, the firm would incur costs honoring the warranty.
8   Even if customers judge the quality of goods by their price, the market always clears in equilibrium.
9   In the rental car market, there is an incentive problem because customers have less reason to drive carefully.
10 Contracts attempt to provide incentives through contingency clauses that specify what each party agrees to do in different situations.
11 Problems of specifying and enforcing quality make it difficult to overcome the incentive problems with contracts.
12 The reputation of a firm may persuade customers that its goods are of high quality because if the firm were to lose its reputation, its profits would fall.
13 The reputations of existing firms attract new competitors to the market because these firms earn higher profits.
14 Markets where customers must search to learn price are characterized by perfect competition.

15 Information intermediaries reduce the search costs of firms and customers.

Multiple Choice

1   In the basic competitive model, households are assumed to know
    a their opportunity set.
    b the prices of all goods and services offered for sale.
    c the characteristics of all goods and services.
    d their preferences.
    e all of the above.
2   In the basic competitive model, firms are assumed to know
    a the best available technology.
    b the productivity of each job applicant.
    c all input prices from every possible supplier.
    d the present and future prices for their outputs.
    e all of the above.
3   In the basic competitive model, firms are assumed to know
    a the preferences of individual consumers.
    b the costs of production for their suppliers.
    c the overall quantities of available inputs.
    d all of the above.
    e none of the above.
4   Markets for information do not work well because
    a no firm would be willing to sell information.
    b consumers are not willing to pay for information.
    c consumers cannot know what they are buying before they actually buy the information.
    d markets only work to allocate material goods.
    e all of the above.
5   In the lemons model,
    a customers know the quality of the goods, but sellers do not.
    b sellers know the quality of the goods, but customers do not.
    c neither customers nor sellers know the quality of the goods.
    d both customers and sellers know that the quality of the goods is low.
    e none of the above.
6   In the lemons model, average quality
    a rises as price falls.
    b falls as price falls because sellers know the quality, and owners of lower-quality goods are willing to sell at lower prices.
    c does not change as price falls because consumers know quality and will not buy lower-quality goods.
    d may rise or fall as price falls.
    e none of the above.
7   In the lemons model,
    a demand is downward sloping.
    b supply is upward sloping.

c demand may slope up or down.

d supply may slope up or down.

e *b* and *c*.

8 Which of the following involve(s) adverse selection?

a Consumers sometimes make mistakes and select inferior products.

b Consumers may not be able to find the lowest-price supplier.

c As the price falls, the fraction of used cars that are lemons increases.

d As the automobile insurance premium is increased, those least likely to have an accident drop out of the market.

e *c* and *d*.

9 In markets with imperfect information,

a firms are price takers.

b firms set prices, taking into account the effect that price has as a signal of quality.

c price plays no role because consumers are uncertain about quality.

d markets clear for the usual reasons.

e there is a uniform market price per unit of quality, but the goods of different firms sell for different prices.

10 Which of the following are examples of informative signals?

a The seller claims that her goods are high quality.

b The seller offers a warranty.

c The seller constructs an expensive showroom.

d All of the above.

e *b* and *c*.

11 In markets with imperfect information, the incentive problem arises because firms

a have no incentive to pay lower prices because they do not know the quality.

b have limited incentive to produce good-quality items if they cannot convince consumers.

c can raise price above the consumer's willingness to pay.

d have no incentive to produce quality items unless they can be patented.

e have no incentive to build reputations.

12 Contract provisions that specify what each of the parties must do in certain situations are called

a signals.

b adverse selection.

c contingency clauses.

d reputations.

e none of the above.

13 When a party to contract violates its terms, he

a is in adverse selection.

b writes a contingency clause.

c creates price dispersion.

d is an information intermediary.

e is in breach.

14 In some markets, the reputations of firms help persuade customers that their products are high quality. In these markets,

a price remains above the cost of production.

b firms earn reputation rents.

c the reputations of existing firms act as a barrier to the entry of new competitors.

d all of the above.

e *a* and *b*.

15 A firm with a reputation for high-quality goods might *not* cut its price because

a cutting price would attract more customers.

b customers might infer that at the low price, the firm will not have enough incentive to maintain its reputation.

c lower prices would attract new competitors.

d the firm cannot set its price—it must be a price taker.

e *a* and *b*.

16 When customers do not have perfect information about price, there may be price dispersion, which means

a the same good is sold at different prices.

b the expenses of searching eliminate the gains from trade.

c customers will search for the best value.

d all of the above.

e *a* and *c*.

17 When search is costly for customers,

a the demand curves for a firm's products will be downward sloping.

b firms will be price takers.

c the firm will lose all its customers if it raises its price above the prices of its competitor.

d the firm will gain all its competitors' business if it charges lower prices.

e *c* and *d*.

18 Markets in which customers must search to learn prices and qualities are best described by the

a competitive model.

b pure monopoly model.

c monopolistic competition model.

d *a* or *b*.

e none of the above.

19 An information intermediary

a helps bring together buyers and sellers.

b cannot make money because markets for information do not work well.

c writes contracts for buyers and sellers.

d eliminates the need for advertising.

e *c* and *d*.

20 Advertising

a provides price information to potential customers.

b informs customers about which products are available.

c attempts to persuade customers to buy certain products.

d all of the above.

e *a* and *b*.

Completion

1 In the market for _____, customers do not know the quality of the goods being sold.
2 Actions taken by sellers to convince buyers of the high quality of their goods are called _____.
3 The _____ arises when the individual is not rewarded for what she does or when she does not have to pay the full costs of what she does.
4 Clauses in contracts that make the payment depend on precisely how the service is performed are called _____.
5 Someone who brings buyers and sellers together is called an _____.
6 The reputations of existing firms act as a _____ against new competition.
7 When the same good is sold at different prices, there is _____.
8 When customers must search for price and quality information, competition is _____.
9 Advertising that conveys information about price, product availability, and quality is called _____ advertising.
10 Advertising may _____ to customers that the product is of high quality because if the quality were poor, the firm would soon lose its new customers and would have wasted its advertising expenses.

Answers to Self-Test

True or False

1	t	6	t	11	t
2	f	7	t	12	t
3	t	8	f	13	f
4	t	9	t	14	f
5	t	10	t	15	t

Multiple Choice

1	e	6	b	11	b	16	e
2	e	7	e	12	c	17	a
3	e	8	e	13	e	18	c
4	c	9	b	14	d	19	a
5	b	10	e	15	b	20	d

Completion

1 lemons
2 signals
3 incentive problem
4 contingency clauses
5 information intermediary
6 barrier to entry
7 price dispersion

8 imperfect
9 informative
10 signal

Doing Economics: Tools and Practice Problems

Three topics are discussed in this section. First, we look at the important **lemons model,** where average quality is higher as price increases. In this situation, we may see upward-sloping demand curves, which may cause markets to fail to exist or may create the possibility of more than one equilibrium. Also, when firms are able to set prices in this model, there is the possibility of excess supply. Second, we turn to price dispersion and search. We explore the benefits and costs of searching and see why the consumer will likely stop searching before the lowest price is found. Finally, we study how advertising increases profits.

LEMONS

When consumers do not know the quality of a good until after they make the purchase, there is asymmetric information in the product market. Firms that produce low-quality goods (lemons) can sell their goods in the high-quality market. If information were perfect, there would be two markets; now there is one. In figuring out their own demand, consumers must estimate how average quality changes as the market expands. Tool Kit 14.1 shows how to derive the demand curve under these circumstances and that it may slope upwards, and some problems explore the consequences.

Tool Kit 14.1 Deriving the Demand Curve When Consumers Do Not Know the Quality of the Good

If they cannot observe the quality of a good at the time of purchase, customers must estimate and base their demand on the average quality available on the market. Follow this four-step procedure.

Step one: Add the supplies of low- and high-quality goods to find the market supply curve.

Price	Quantity supplied
p_1	$Q_{low} + Q_{high}$
p_2	$Q_{low} + Q_{high}$
Etc.	

Step two: Find the fractions of high- and low-quality goods at each point on the supply curve.

Fraction of high-quality goods $= Q_{high}/(Q_{low} + Q_{high})$.

Fraction of low-quality goods $= Q_{low}/(Q_{low} + Q_{high})$.

Step three: Find the average value at each point. This number is what consumers are willing to pay; therefore, it is the demand price.

Average value = demand price
= fraction of high quality × value of high quality
+ fraction of low quality × value of low quality.

Step four: Construct the demand curve.

Price = average value	Quantity demanded
p_1	$Q_{low} + Q_{high}$
p_2	$Q_{low} + Q_{high}$
Etc.	

1 (Worked problem: lemons) Many firms sell 50-pound packages of meat at the local farmers' market. Customers place a value of $20 on fatty, low-quality beef, and they place a value of $50 on lean, good-quality beef. The beef is wrapped and frozen, so at the time of purchase, customers cannot distinguish the quality of beef they are buying. The supply curves for low- and high-quality beef appear in Table 14.1.

Table 14.1

Low quality		High quality	
Price	Quantity	Price	Quantity
$15	1,000	$15	0
$20	2,000	$20	0
$25	3,000	$25	1,000
$30	4,000	$30	4,000
$35	5,000	$35	10,000
$40	6,000	$40	12,000
$45	7,000	$45	14,000
$50	8,000	$50	16,000

 a Derive the demand curve for beef.
 b Find the market-clearing price (or prices) and quantity (or quantities).
 c For purposes of comparison, suppose that consumers could tell the difference and that there were separate markets for the two types of beef. Find the equilibrium price and quantity for each type of beef. How does the asymmetric information about quality affect the market for high-quality beef?

Step-by-step solution

Step one (a): Add the supplies to find the market supply. For example, if the price is $325, there will be 5,000 low-quality packages of beef and 10,000 high-quality packages for a total of 15,000. Proceeding in this way gives the market supply as shown in Table 14.2.

Table 14.2

	Market supply
Price	Quantity (high and low quality)
$15	1,000
$20	2,000
$25	4,000
$30	8,000
$35	15,000
$40	18,000
$45	21,000
$50	24,000

Step two: Find the fractions of the total that are high and low quality at each point. For example, if the price is $35, there are 10,000 high-quality packages. The total number of packages is 15,000. The fraction is (10,000/15,000) × 100 = 2/3. Enter the number and continue. The corresponding fraction of low-quality goods is then 1/3. The complete information appears in Table 14.3.

Table 14.3

Price	Low-quality quantity	High-quality quantity	Fraction high	Fraction low
$15	1,000	0	0	1
$20	2,000	0	0	1
$25	3,000	1,000	1/4	3/4
$30	4,000	4,000	1/2	1/2
$35	5,000	10,000	2/3	1/3
$40	6,000	12,000	2/3	1/3
$45	7,000	14,000	2/3	1/3
$50	8,000	16,000	2/3	1/3

Step three: Compute the average value for each price. For example, when the price is $35, there are 5,000 packages valued at $20 and 10,000 valued at $50. The average value is [($20 × 5,000) + ($50 × 10,000)]/15,000 = $40. Continue and complete the table as shown in Table 14.4. Note that average value increases with price. This is because at a higher price, the percentage of packages that are high quality is greater.

Table 14.4

Price	Low-quality quantity	High-quality quantity	Fraction high	Average value
$15	1,000	0	0	$20.00
$20	2,000	0	0	$20.00
$25	3,000	1,000	1/4	$27.50
$30	4,000	4,000	1/2	$35.00
$35	5,000	10,000	2/3	$40.00
$40	6,000	12,000	2/3	$40.00
$45	7,000	14,000	2/3	$40.00
$50	8,000	16,000	2/3	$40.00

Step four: Construct the demand curve. It is given in Table 14.5 and drawn in the diagram. The price column is the average value, and the quantity column is the sum of the low- and high-quality quantities.

Table 14.5

Market demand	
Price	*Quantity*
$20.00	1,000
$20.00	2,000
$27.50	4,000
$35.00	8,000
$40.00	15,000
$40.00	18,000
$40.00	21,000
$40.00	24,000

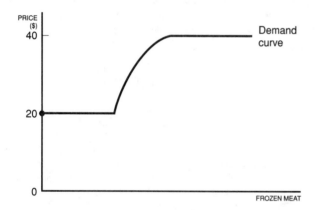

Step five (b): Find the market-clearing prices and quantities. The market clears at a price of $20, where the quantity demanded equals the quantity supplied at 2,000. At this equilibrium, there are no high-quality packages sold. Also, the market clears at a price of $40, where the quantity demanded and the quantity supplied equal 18,000. At this equilibrium, there are 6,000 low-quality and 12,000 high-quality packages. The two equilibria are shown in the diagram.

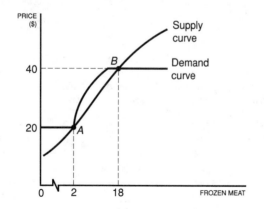

Step six (c): If consumers had perfect information about quality, then there would be a separate low-quality market with 2,000 sold at a price of $20 and a high-quality market with a price of $50 and 16,000 units sold. The asymmetric information destroys the high-quality market in equilibrium *A.* In equilibrium *B,* the high-quality market survives, but the quantity is smaller than it would be with perfect information.

2 (Practice problem: lemons) Trying to appear better educated, many Americans are buying abbreviated guides to culture—lists of novels, operas, and works of art an educated person should know. The guides also include a paragraph or two of witty things to say. The consumers of these books, obviously, cannot judge the quality until they say the wrong thing at the next important social function. The supply curves of low- and high-quality guides are given in Table 14.6. The value of a high-quality guide (complete with video tapes and workbooks) is $300. Low-quality guides are worthless.

Table 14.6

Price	Low-quality guides	High-quality guides
$50	1,000	0
$100	2,000	1,000
$150	4,000	6,000
$200	8,000	16,000
$250	12,000	36,000
$300	16,000	48,000

a Derive the demand curve for guides.
b Find the market-clearing price (or prices) and quantity (or quantities).
c For the purposes of comparison, suppose that consumers could tell the difference and that there were separate markets for the two types of guides. Find the equilibrium price and quantity for each type of guide. How does the asymmetric information about quality affect the market for high-quality guides?

3 (Practice problem: lemons) Several new varieties of tomatoes are coming on to the market. Each promises tasty tomatoes with long shelf lives, and a tomato plant that fulfilled this promise would be worth $4. Consumers cannot observe the quality until the end of the growing season, but they suspect that the new hybrids are no better or worse than existing ones valued at $1 per plant. The supply curves of low- and high-quality tomato plants are given in Table 14.7.
a Derive the demand curve for tomato plants.
b Find the market-clearing price (or prices) and quantity (or quantities).

Table 14.7

Price	Low-quality tomato plants	High-quality tomato plants
$1.00	10,000	0
$1.50	20,000	5,000
$2.00	30,000	20,000
$2.50	40,000	60,000
$3.00	50,000	100,000
$3.50	60,000	300,000
$4.00	70,000	500,000

c For the purposes of comparison, suppose that consumers could tell the difference and that there were separate markets for each of the two types of plants. Find the equilibrium price and quantity for each type of plant. How does the asymmetric information about quality affect the market for high-quality plants?

JUDGING QUALITY BY PRICE

Because it is more expensive to produce high-quality goods than low, consumers may reason that at low prices only the poor-quality items are offered for sale, and that as price increases, so does average quality. If firms understand this sort of reasoning, they will set price so that quality per dollar is as high as possible, even though this price may not be the market-clearing price. It is possible that shortages will occur, and yet no firm will reduce its price because it knows that it will not gain customers, who believe that lower prices imply lower quality. This is a profound result. In normal competitive markets, the role of prices is only to clear the market. In markets where customers do not know quality, however, price acts as a signal of quality. The price that does the best job of signaling quality may not clear the market. Tool Kit 14.2 shows how price is set in this case.

Tool Kit 14.2 Finding the Price That Maximizes Quality per Dollar

If customers judge quality by price, firms will set price to maximize quality per dollar. Follow these steps to find the right price.

Step one: Identify and plot the relationship between quality and price.

Step two: For each price, find the quality-price ratio: quality-price ratio = quality/price.

Step three: Choose the highest quality-price ratio. Label this point *A*.

Step four: Draw a line from the origin to point *A*. It should be tangent to the quality-price curve, and its slope equals the maximum quality-price ratio.

---

4 (Worked problem: quality and price) Consumers of 12-gallon fire extinguishers care deeply about the quality of the item, but they cannot distinguish effective and ineffective goods at the time of purchase. The quality of the fire extinguisher only matters if and when it is used. Consumers may reason that at low prices, firms could not afford the quality-control procedures necessary to ensure effective operation. Suppose consumers believe that the relationship between quality and price is as given in Table 14.8.

Table 14.8

Price	Quality (gallons of fire retardant released)
$5	0
$10	1.0
$15	4.5
$20	7.0
$25	10.0
$30	11.0
$35	12.0
$40	12.0

a Find the price that maximizes quality per dollar.

b Suppose that demand and supply are as given in Table 14.9. Find the equilibrium price. Does it clear the market? Why or why not?

Table 14.9

Price	Demand	Supply
$40	10,000	28,000
$35	12,000	25,000
$30	14,000	21,000
$25	16,000	20,000
$20	17,000	19,000
$15	19,000	17,000
$10	21,000	11,000

Step-by-step solution

Step one (a): Identify and plot the relationship between quality and price. It is given in Table 14.8 and drawn in the diagram.

Step two: For each price, find the quality-price ratio. When the price is $40, the quality-price ratio is 12/$40 = 0.30. Continuing, we derive Table 14.10.

Table 14.10

Price	Quality	Quality-price ratio
$5	0	—
$10	1.0	0.10
$15	4.5	0.30
$20	7.0	0.35
$25	10.0	0.40
$30	11.0	0.37
$35	12.0	0.34
$40	12.0	0.30

Step three: Choose the highest quality-price ratio. It is 0.40, which occurs at a price of $25.

Step four: Draw a line from the origin to point *A*. It should be tangent to the quality-price curve, and its slope should equal the maximum quality-price ratio, as shown in the diagram.

Step five (b): At a price of $25, the quantity demanded is 16,000, and the quantity supplied is 20,000. Even though there is a surplus of 4,000, firms do not reduce the price. They know that customers would interpret the lower price as a signal of lower quality.

5 (Practice problem: quality and price) Tourists come to San Gordo for the shrimp. Dozens of small establishments offer shrimp, but tourists have little ability to judge the quality before eating. They reason, however, that at low prices the firms cannot afford to ensure that the shrimp are tasty. Suppose consumers believe that the relationship between quality and price is as given in Table 14.11.

Table 14.11

Price (dozen shrimp)	Quality (percentage of tasty shrimp)
$1	10
$2	30
$3	60
$4	70
$5	80
$6	85

a Find the price that maximizes quality per dollar.

b Suppose that demand and supply are as given in Table 14.12. Find the equilibrium price. Does it clear the market? Why or why not?

Table 14.12

Price	Demand	Supply
$6	2,000	6,000
$5	2,500	5,500
$4	3,000	5,000
$3	3,500	4,500
$2	4,000	4,000
$1	6,000	3,000

6 (Practice problem: quality and price) The boom in home exercise equipment continues, but there are many purchasers who have given up the quest for the perfect body. These purchasers offer their used equipment for sale. The market also includes those who are selling used lemons, worthless devices that do not perform as advertised. Consumers of used exercise equipment judge that the relationship between price and quality is as given in Table 14.13.

Table 14.13

Price	Quality (calories burned per hour)
$100	100
$200	500
$300	1,100
$400	1,600
$500	1,750

Find the price that maximizes quality per dollar.

SEARCH

In imperfectly competitive markets, different firms may offer the same good for sale at different prices. This situation, called price dispersion, means that consumers must not only decide which goods to purchase, they also must expend time and effort to locate lower price offers and decide which offer to accept. The optimal amount to search is the subject of these problems. As usual, the solution involves carefully balancing benefits and costs. Tool Kit 14.3 shows how.

Tool Kit 14.3 Searching for Lower Prices

When there is price dispersion, customers must search. These steps show how to balance the benefits and costs of searching for lower prices.

Step one: Identify the marginal cost of search and the relationship between search effort and price.

Step two: Calculate the marginal benefits of search:

marginal benefit = change in lowest price/change in search effort.

Step three: Find the amount of search for which the marginal benefits equal the marginal cost.

Step four: Draw a diagram illustrating the solution.

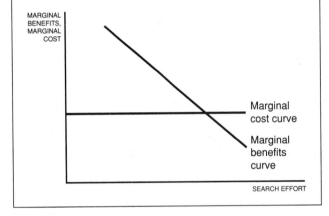

7 (Worked problem: search) Jennifer would like to build a deck behind her new condominium. She has in mind the type she would like and is considering sending away for catalogs offering deck kits. Each catalogue costs $5. The relationship between the lowest appropriate deck kit price and the number of catalogs is given in Table 14.14.

Table 14.14

Number of catalogs ordered	Lowest price found	Marginal benefit
1	$250	
2	$225	
3	$210	
4	$205	
5	$202	
6	$200	

a What is the optimal number of catalogs for Jennifer to order?

b What price does she expect to pay for a deck kit?

c Draw a diagram illustrating your solution.

Step-by-step solution

Step one (a): Identify the marginal cost of search and the relationship between search effort and price. The marginal cost is $5, and the relationship appears in Table 14.14.

Step two: Calculate the marginal benefit of search. The expected price is $250 from the first catalog and $225 from the second. The marginal benefit is thus $25. Continuing, we derive the marginal benefits as shown in Table 14.15.

Table 14.15

Number of catalogs ordered	Lowest price found	Marginal benefit
1	$250	—
2	$225	$25
3	$210	$15
4	$205	$5
5	$202	$3
6	$200	$2

Step three: Find the amount of search for which the marginal benefit equals the marginal cost. This is 4 catalogs, which is the answer to part *a*.

Step four (b): The expected lowest price is $205, when she buys 4 catalogs.

Step five (c): The solution appears in the diagram.

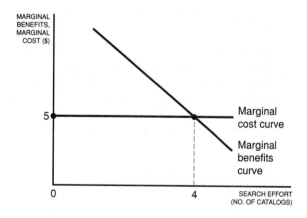

8 (Practice problem: search) Raul wants to refinish his floors. This type of home improvement project is very popular in his neighborhood, and appointments for estimates must be made and paid for weeks in advance. Estimates cost $25, and Raul guesses that the relationship between the number of estimates and the lowest price is as given in Table 14.16.

Table 14.16

Number of estimates	Expected lowest price
1	$800
2	$650
3	$550
4	$500
5	$475
6	$465
7	$460

a What is the optimal number of estimates for Raul to schedule?

b What price does he expect to pay for refinishing his floors?

c Draw a diagram illustrating your solution.

9 (Practice problem: search) The Melling Forging Company needs a new robotic lathe. Several companies offer the lathes, but Melling's management feels there is enough variety that an on-site inspection is needed for each. Time is short, so the company plans to send engineers simultaneously to the plants of some of the firms that sell robotic lathes. The company would like to visit all robotic lathe producers, but a plant visit costs the company $1,000. The relationship between the number of visits and the profits that the new system will earn is given in Table 14.17.

Table 14.17

Number of visits	Expected maximum profitability
1	$18,000
2	$23,000
3	$26,000
4	$27,000
5	$27,500

How many engineers should Melling send?

10 (Practice problem: advertising) Advertising is designed to shift the demand curve to the right. This allows a firm to charge higher prices on the goods that it sells and to adjust the quantity to the profit-maximizing level along the new demand curve. To see how profits change with a successful advertising program, simply follow the procedure outlined in Chapter 12 for deriving marginal revenue and finding the monopoly price and quantity.

Fay's Cleaners has been advertising its new service, which offers customers the opportunity to leave and pick up their dry cleaning at the commuter train station. The demand curves before and after the advertising campaign are given in Table 14.18. Quantity measures suits cleaned and pressed. The marginal cost of each item is $1. Fixed costs equal $1,000.

Table 14.18

Before		After	
Price	Quantity	Price	Quantity
$5.00	100	$5.00	500
$4.50	200	$4.50	1,000
$4.00	300	$4.00	1,500
$3.50	400	$3.50	2,000
$3.00	500	$3.00	2,500
$2.50	600	$2.50	3,000
$2.00	700	$2.00	3,500

a Find the profit-maximizing price and quantity and level of profits before the advertising campaign.

b Find the profit-maximizing price and quantity and level of profits after the advertising campaign.

c How much is the advertising campaign worth to Fay's Cleaners?

11 (Practice problem: advertising) The Gainesville Gekkos, a minor league franchise in the A league, is evaluating its advertising program. The demand curves before and after the advertising campaign are given in Table 14.19. Quantity measures the attendance. The marginal cost of another customer in the park is $0.50. Fixed costs are $50,000.

Table 14.19

Low quality		High quality	
Price	Quantity	Price	Quantity
$10.00	15,000	$10.00	20,000
$9.50	17,500	$9.50	30,000
$9.00	20,000	$9.00	40,000
$8.50	22,500	$8.50	50,000
$8.00	25,000	$8.00	60,000
$7.50	27,500	$7.50	70,000
$7.00	30,000	$7.00	80,000
$6.50	32,500	$6.50	90,000
$6.00	35,000	$6.00	100,000
$5.50	37,500	$5.50	110,000

a Find the profit-maximizing price and quantity and level of profits before the advertising campaign.

b Find the profit-maximizing price and quantity and level of profits after the advertising campaign.

c How much is the advertising campaign worth to the Gainesville Gekkos?

Answers to Problems

2 *a* The market demand and supply curves appear in Table 14.20.

Table 14.20

Price	Low-quality guides	High-quality guides	Total market quantity	Demand price
$50	1,000	0	1,000	$0
$100	2,000	1,000	3,000	$100
$150	4,000	6,000	10,000	$180
$200	8,000	16,000	24,000	$200
$250	12,000	36,000	48,000	$225
$300	16,000	48,000	64,000	$225

b The market clears at a price of $100, with 1,000 high- and 2,000 low-quality guides. Another market-clearing price is $200, where high-quality guides number 16,000 and low-quality, 8,000.

c If there were perfect information, there would be no low-quality guides, 48,000 high-quality guides, and an equilibrium price equal to $300.

3 *a* The market demand and supply curves appear in Table 14.21.

Table 14.21

Price	Low-quality tomato plants	High-quality tomato plants	Total market quantity	Demand price
$1.00	10,000	0	10,000	$1.00
$1.50	20,000	5,000	25,000	$1.60
$2.00	30,000	20,000	50,000	$2.20
$2.50	40,000	60,000	100,000	$2.80
$3.00	50,000	100,000	150,000	$3.00
$3.50	60,000	300,000	360,000	$3.50
$4.00	70,000	500,000	570,000	$3.63

b The market clears at a price of $1 where 10,000 low-quality plants are sold and also at a price of $3 where 50,000 low-quality and 100,000 high-quality plants are sold.

c The equilibrium price of low-quality plants would be $1 with 10,000 sold. In the high-quality market, the price would equal $4, and 500,000 would be sold.

5 *a* The quality-price ratio appears in Table 14.22.

Table 14.22

Price	Quality	Quality-price ratio
$1	10	10.0
$2	30	15.0
$3	60	20.0
$4	70	17.5
$5	80	16.0
$6	85	14.2

Firms choose a price of $3.

b   This results in a surplus of 4,500 − 3,500 = 1,000.

6   The quality-price ratio appears in Table 14.23.

Table 14.23

Price	Quality	Quality-price ratio
$100	100	1.00
$200	500	2.50
$300	1,100	3.67
$400	1,600	4.00
$500	1,750	3.50

8   The marginal benefits of searching appear in Table 14.24.

Table 14.24

Number of estimates	Expected lowest price	Marginal benefits
1	$800	—
2	$650	$150
3	$550	$100
4	$500	$50
5	$475	$25
6	$465	$10
7	$460	$5

a   Raul should get 5 estimates.

b   He expects to pay $475.

c

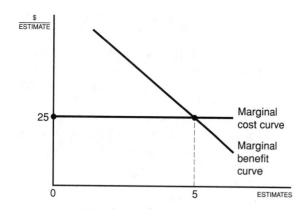

9   The marginal benefits of search appear in Table 14.25.

Table 14.25

Number of visits	Expected maximum profitability	Marginal benefits
1	$18,000	—
2	$23,000	$5,000
3	$26,000	$3,000
4	$27,000	$1,000
5	$27,500	$500

The company should send 4 engineers and expect to earn $27,000.

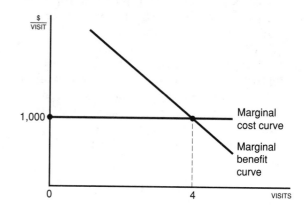

10 a   Price = $3; quantity = 500; profits = ($3 × 500) − ($1 × 500) − $1,000 − $0.

b   Price = $3; quantity = 2,500; profits = ($3 × 2,500) − ($1 × 2,500) − $1,000 = $4,000.

c   The advertising campaign increases profits by $4,000 − $0 = $4,000.

11 a   Price = $6; quantity = 32,500; profits = ($7 × 30,000) − ($0.50 × 30,000) − $50,000 = $145,000.

b   Price = $5.50; quantity = 110,000; profits = ($5.50 × 110,000) − ($0.50 × 110,000) − $50,000 = $500,000.

c   The advertising campaign increases profits by $500,000 − $145,000 = $355,000.

CHAPTER 15 | Imperfections in the Labor Market

Chapter Review

This chapter of the text returns to the labor market and applies the lessons of imperfect competition from Chapter 12 and imperfect information from Chapter 14. The chapter first explores labor unions and compares them to monopolies in the context of the labor they supply to the firm. Next the chapter examines reasons for wage differences. Finally, it takes up the problems of motivating and selecting employees. Particular attention is paid to how different compensation schemes affect incentives.

ESSENTIAL CONCEPTS

1 Employees band together in **unions** to negotiate better working conditions and higher wages. After increasing for decades, the unionized share of the work force has declined since the mid-1950s. Reasons for the decline include an overall improvement in working conditions, relative declines in the sectors of the economy with more unionization, more competitive product markets, and unfavorable government policy, expecially the Taft-Hartley Act.

2 Unions can be thought of as *monopolies* in the supply of labor to the firm. As such, they raise the wage and allow employment to fall. When the employer firm makes monopoly profits in its own product market, however, it is possible for unions to secure higher wages without reduced employment, at least for a while. Overall, higher union wages probably result in somewhat lower wages for nonunion workers and lower union employment in the long run. Unions also promote job security and have advocated job safety regulations, minimum wages, and immigration restrictions through the political process.

3 Because of imperfect information and other factors, labor is somewhat immobile, and wage differentials exist. Wage differentials may be caused by the following factors:

   a **Compensating differentials** are wage differences that reflect characteristics of the job. For example, a police officer may earn more than a firefighter, reflecting the greater danger of police work.

   b **Information-based differentials** reflect a worker's imperfect information. Workers must search for job offers. A worker currently receiving a low wage may not be able to convince another employer to offer a higher wage because the prospective employer will not know the quality of the worker. This is the lemons model from Chapter 18 applied to the labor market. The difficulty that workers have in moving from job to job gives firms some market power and leads to lower wages.

   c **Productivity wage differentials** simply account for differences in abilities to produce output.

4 **Discrimination** reduces the wages of certain groups. This may involve outright prejudice or just **statistical discrimination,** which results from the use of screening devices (such as degrees from well-established schools) that unintentionally sort out certain classes of workers from the hiring pool. **Affirmative action** requires that firms must actively seek out minorities and women and include them in the applicant pool.

5 Employers must **motivate** workers to perform the task for which they were hired. When the marginal product of a worker is observable, a firm can base pay on output. Thus, **piece-rate systems** provide strong incentives to workers but can subject them to substantial risk. Again, there is a risk-incentive trade-

off. When there is concern for the quality, piece-rate systems may fail to give good incentives.

6 Especially when a worker's output is difficult for the employer to observe, the employer may want to **monitor** workers. Also, paying relatively high **efficiency wages** gives workers incentives to work hard and be more productive. Employers can reduce turnover (and training costs) by letting pay and **fringe benefits** increase with seniority.

7 Sometimes the employer may not know whether output is high because the employees are working hard and well or because the demand for the product is high. In this case, one option is to set up **contests** where workers are paid according to how well they do relative to their peers. Also, basing pay on team performance can encourage workers to monitor and help each other.

BEHIND THE ESSENTIAL CONCEPTS

1 The most important idea to keep in mind when thinking about the labor market is that it is a market. Many of the same models that explained aspects of imperfect product markets appear here in the labor market. Consider the following:
   a Just as the firm may be a monopoly in the product market, a union has monopoly power over the labor supply to the firm. In each case, the price (wage) is set above marginal cost (supply curve of labor), and the quantity (employment) is less.
   b Consumers must search for price and quality information, while workers must search for job offers. In the product market, there is price dispersion; in the labor market, there are information-based wage differentials.
   c Firms need incentives to produce quality products just as workers need incentives to be productive. There is always the risk-incentive trade-off. Contracts and reputations create incentives in product markets. Monitoring, efficiency wages, seniority benefits, contests, and team rewards create incentives in labor markets.

2 Not only is information imperfect, but exactly what the employer does not know is important. Based upon what she does not know, the employer must choose a means of selecting and motivating her workers. For example:
   a If the employer does not know the productivity of a job applicant, she may rely on signals. A low wage in the current job may indicate low productivity. A college degree may indicate innate abilities.
   b If the employer can observe the marginal productivity of his workers, then he may offer a piece-rate schedule of wages, but this scheme may expose the employee to substantial risk.

   c If the employer cannot observe the effort of her workers, she can monitor them and pay above-market efficiency wages. High wages make the job valuable and make losing the job something to motivate the worker.
   d If the employer thinks that the worker might have other employment opportunities, the employer may offer higher wages and better working conditions to discourage more senior workers from quitting. This becomes especially important if the employer must pay to train new workers.
   e If the employer does not know whether the output of her workers is due to their productivity or due to market conditions, she may set up contests, paying more to workers who do relatively better.
   f If the employer cannot observe the productivity of his employees but if he thinks that the employees are aware of one another's productivity, he can reward good performance by a team, which serves to induces employees to motivate one another.

SELF-TEST

True or False

1 The Wagner Act set up the National Labor Relations Board, which provided procedures for the certification of unions and the prevention of unfair labor practices.
2 The Taft-Hartley Act allowed states to pass right-to-work laws and authorized the president to temporarily suspend strikes.
3 One reason for the decline in the percent of the work force in the private sector that belongs to unions is that consumers have shifted their demand toward more manufacturing and fewer services.
4 Unions act like monopolies in the supply of labor to the firm.
5 Unions power is limited by threats of replacing striking workers and also by unemployment.
6 Wage differentials resulting from differences in job characteristics are called compensating differentials.
7 Imperfect information will not lead to wage differentials if workers search for job opportunities.
8 Employers may be reluctant to offer jobs to workers who currently earn low wages, if they believe that current wages signal low productivity.
9 Statistical discrimination results from overt prejudice.
10 Affirmative action is designed to eliminate union shops.
11 Under a piece-rate system, workers are insured against any risk related to the overall success of the business.
12 Piece-rate systems do not work well if the firm cannot easily and accurately measure the marginal product of workers.

13 Paying higher efficiency wages may motivate workers to be more productive because they perceive that the high-wage job is worth keeping.

14 Firms that are unsure about a task's difficulty can motivate workers by using contests.

15 When pay depends on team performance, workers have incentives to cooperate, work together, and monitor each other's effort.

Multiple Choice

1 In 1935, Congress passed the Wagner Act, which
   a gave legal status to unions.
   b outlawed right-to-work laws.
   c set up the National Labor Relations Board, which provided procedures for the certification of labor unions and for the prevention of unfair labor practices.
   d all of the above.
   e a and c.

2 The Taft-Hartley Act of 1947
   a allowed individual states to pass right-to-work laws.
   b gave the president the power to declare an 80-day cooling off period during which striking workers must return to work.
   c eliminated the National Labor Relations Board.
   d all of the above.
   e a and b.

3 Reasons for the decline in the percentage of the work force that belongs to unions include the following.
   a An overall improvement in working conditions has reduced the demand of workers for unions.
   b Consumer demand has shifted toward the relatively less unionized sectors, such as services.
   c Increasingly competitive markets have limited the power of unions to negotiate increased wages.
   d All of the above.
   e None of the above.

4 In negotiating wages with firms, unions are most like
   a monopolies.
   b monopsonies.
   c competitive firms.
   d individual consumers.
   e none of the above.

5 Unless the firm is making monopoly profits in its product market, the higher wages negotiated by a union must
   a increase the level of employment at the firm.
   b have no effect on the level of employment at the firm.
   c reduce the level of employment at the firm.
   d lead the firm to substitute labor for capital.
   e a and d.

6 Higher wages for union labor
   a increase the supply of nonunion labor.
   b decrease the supply of nonunion labor.
   c reduce wages received by nonunion labor.
   d a and c.
   e b and c.

7 In a labor-management negotiation, the bargaining surplus refers to
   a the fact that although the firm can hire other workers and workers can find other jobs, both sides can gain by reaching agreement.
   b the costs of negotiation in lawyers' and arbitrators' salaries.
   c the strike funds built up by the firms and unions in anticipation of possible work stoppages.
   d the extra workers that union force management to hire.
   e b and d.

8 Compensating differentials are wage differences resulting from
   a the fact that workers must search to find job offers and learn of alternative wages.
   b the fact that employers are unlikely to make offers to workers who currently earn low wages, inferring that these workers may be less productive.
   c differences in job characteristics.
   d wage differences that compensate for differences in productivity.
   e a and b.

9 Jobs that are similar in all respects
   a must pay the same wage, because no worker would take the lower-paying job when higher-paying ones are available.
   b can have different wages according to the theory of compensating differentials.
   c may pay different wages if it takes time and effort for workers to learn about the alternative job possibilities.
   d may pay different wages because employers can pay whatever they want and workers must accept.
   e none of the above.

10 Wage differences that are due to differences in ability to produce output are called
   a compensating differentials.
   b information-based differentials.
   c statistical discrimination.
   d productivity differentials.
   e affirmative action.

11 When workers are not aware of alternative job possibilities,
   a firms may take advantage of their information-based market power and raise wages.
   b information-based wage differentials may occur.

    c workers can earn compensating differentials.

    d all similar workers must earn the same wage for jobs with the same characteristics.

    e none of the above.

12 Statistical discrimination refers to

    a wage differences based on statistical measures of productivity differentials.

    b requirements that firms keep statistics on the numbers of employees in each ethnic group.

    c requirements that firms actively seek out women and minorities for hiring and promotion.

    d the use of screening devices that unintentionally sort out members of certain groups.

    e paying lower wages to workers who have little statistical information about the labor market and alternative job possibilities.

13 Affirmative action refers to

    a wage differences based on statistical measures of productivity differentials.

    b requirements that firms keep statistics on the numbers of employees in each ethnic group.

    c requirements that firms actively seek out women and minorities for hiring and promotion.

    d the use of screening devices that unintentionally sort out members of certain groups.

    e paying lower wages to workers who have little statistical information about the labor market and alternative job possibilities.

14 The system of payment in which a worker is paid for each item produced is called

    a a compensating differential system.

    b an adverse selection system.

    c a signaling system.

    d monopsony.

    e a piece-rate system.

15 One difficulty with basing workers' pay on their output is that

    a although workers are given appropriate incentives to work hard, they bear considerable risk.

    b although they bear the appropriate amount of risk, workers are given little incentive to work hard.

    c piece-rate schemes are illegal under the Wagner Act.

    d *a* and *c*.

    e none of the above.

16 Most workers are not paid on a piece-rate basis, because

    a piece-rate pay is illegal under the Wagner Act.

    b workers are risk lovers.

    c it is often difficult to measure the quantity and quality of an individual worker's output.

    d all of the above.

    e none of the above.

17 If the employer cannot observe the contribution to output of each worker, she can

    a monitor a worker's effort.

    b pay higher wages to increase the cost to the worker of being fired.

    c set up a piece-work system.

    d all of the above.

    e *a* and *b*.

18 Efficiency wages

    a reduce job turnover.

    b attract more productive job applicants.

    c motivate workers to put forth more effort.

    d increase payments to workers.

    e all of the above.

19 When workers are paid on the basis of relative performance, as in contests,

    a they are given incentives to be productive, even though management does not know their job's difficulty.

    b workers are better off because they bear less risk.

    c workers receive efficiency wages and thus work hard.

    d turnover is reduced.

    e all of the above.

20 When pay is based on team performance,

    a workers are motivated to monitor each other's efforts.

    b worker are motivated to help each other.

    c promotions go the those workers who have been more productive.

    d *a* and *b*.

    e all of the above.

Completion

1 Under _____ legislation, all laborers at unionized establishments must join the union.

2 Unions can raise wages because they have a _____ on the supply of labor to the firm.

3 _____ outlaw union shops.

4 _____ are differences in wages that reflect different job characteristics, such as working conditions or advancement possibilities.

5 _____ results from firms using screening devices that unintentionally sort out members of certain groups from the applicant pool.

6 The system of payment in which a worker is paid for each item produced or each task performed is called a _____ system.

7 The theory that paying higher wages leads to a more productive work force is called _____ theory.

8 Some compensation schemes, such as bonuses for the top sales representatives, base pay on _____ performance.

9 The safety of working conditions is regulated by the _____.

10 The "glass ceiling" that prevents the promotion of women to higher management is an example of _____ discrimination.

Answers to Self-Test

True or False

1	t	6	t	11	f
2	t	7	f	12	t
3	f	8	t	13	t
4	t	9	f	14	t
5	t	10	f	15	t

Multiple Choice

1	e	6	d	11	b	16	c
2	e	7	a	12	d	17	e
3	d	8	c	13	c	18	e
4	a	9	c	14	e	19	a
5	c	10	d	15	a	20	d

Completion

1 union shops
2 monopoly
3 Right to work laws
4 Compensating differentials
5 Statistical discrimination
6 piece-work
7 efficiency wage
8 relative
9 Occupational Safety and Health Administration
10 job

Doing Economics: Tools and Practice Problems

A successful union forms a monopoly in the supply of labor to a firm or industry. We apply the tools of monopoly to study the behavior of unions in several problems in this section. Then we move to compensating differentials, an important source of wage differences among workers. In accepting a job offer, a worker also buys a list of job characteristics, such as safety, advancement potential, training, and the aesthetics of the workplace. We use the budget constraint to show how the labor market offers a choice among job characteristics and establishes an implicit market price for them.

THE WAGE-EMPLOYMENT TRADE-OFF

If a union is able to force the signing of a contract, guaranteeing that only union members will be hired, it is in the po-sition of a monopolist in the supply of labor. Unions may control the supply of labor to an industry, a craft, or an individual firm. The problems here focus on the latter case. Usually unions set wages and let management choose the quantity of labor to hire. In this case, the firm's demand for labor, which is the marginal revenue product, includes all the combinations of wages and employment that the union can achieve. These combinations, in turn, show the trade-off faced by the union. Tool Kit 15.1 shows how to construct the demand for labor and some possible choices that a union might make.

Tool Kit 15.1 Constructing the Union's Trade-off between Wages and Employment

Higher wages usually bring about reduced employment. Follow this procedure to construct the trade-off.

Step-one: Identify the production function and the price of the product, and set up a table as follows.

Workers	Output	Revenues	Marginal revenue product

Step-two: Find the revenue corresponding to each level of labor use by multiplying the output level by price, and enter the results in the table:

revenues = output × price.

Step-three: Compute the marginal revenue product, which is the change in revenue divided by the change in labor, and enter the results in the table:

marginal revenue product
= change in revenues,
change in output.

Step-four: Plot the marginal revenue product. This curve is the schedule of possible wage and employments levels.

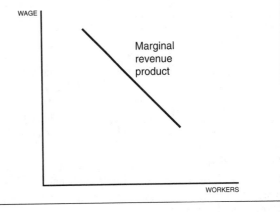

---

1 (Worked problem: unions) The miners of Davis Lead are represented by the Lead Workers Union, which is considering its stance for the upcoming contract negotiations. The union's economist has estimated a production function for lead, as given in Table 15.1. Its current price is $10 per ton.

Table 15.1

Workers	Output (tons per month)
10	20,000
20	40,000
30	60,000
40	75,000
50	85,000
60	90,000
70	90,000

a Calculate the marginal revenue product, plot it, and interpret it as a schedule of wage and employment possibilities.
b What is the maximum wage? How much employment would result at this wage?
c Workers can earn $5,000 elsewhere. What is the maximum level of employment?

Step-by-step solution

Step one (a): Identify the production function and the price of the product. The production function is given in Table 15.1, and the price of lead is $10 per ton.

Step two: Find the revenue corresponding to each level of labor use. We multiply output by $10, which is the price of lead. When there are 10 workers, output is 20,000, and revenue is 20,000 × $10 = $200,000. Continuing, we derive Table 15.2.

Table 15.2

Workers	Output	Revenues
10	20,000	$200,000
20	40,000	$400,000
30	60,000	$600,000
40	75,000	$750,000
50	85,000	$850,000
60	90,000	$900,000
70	90,000	$900,000

Step three: Compute the marginal revenue product, which is the change in revenue divided by the change in labor. The marginal revenue product for the first 10 workers is $200,000/10 = $20,000. Continuing, we derive Table 15.3.

Table 15.3

Workers	Output	Revenues	Marginal revenue product
10	20,000	$200,000	$20,000
20	40,000	$400,000	$20,000
30	60,000	$600,000	$20,000
40	75,000	$750,000	$15,000
50	85,000	$850,000	$10,000
60	90,000	$900,000	$5,000
70	90,000	$900,000	$0

Step four: Plot the marginal revenue product.

Step five (b): The maximum possible wage is $20,000 per month, and 30 workers will have jobs at this wage.

Step six (c): If the company pays $5,000, which is the alternative wage, there will be 60 workers hired.

2 (Practice problem: unions) Rosewood College's faculty has voted to join the United Professorial Workers Union to win high wages from the administration. Its economics department has estimated the production function, which is given in Table 15.4. Tuition nets Rosewood a profit of $1,000 per student after all expenses (except salaries for professors) are deducted.

Table 15.4

Faculty	Students
20	100
30	600
40	1,000
50	1,300
60	1,500
70	1,600
80	1,600

a Calculate and plot the marginal revenue product schedule. Interpret it as a schedule of salary and employment possibilities.

b What is the maximum salary that the union could negotiate? Keep in mind that with its enormous endowment, Rosewood would not shut down even if it lost money.

c The alternative salary for a typical Rosewood professor is $20,000. What is the maximum level of employment?

3 (Practice problem: unions) The cherry pickers at Bingo's Cherry Orchard have won an agreement that the owner will only hire union workers. The production function is given in Table 15.5, and cherries sell for $2 per bushel.

Table 15.5

Pickers	Cherries (bushels per day)
1	24
2	64
3	96
4	120
5	136
6	144
7	148
8	150

a Calculate and plot the marginal revenue product. Interpret it as a schedule of wage and employment possibilities.

b What is the maximum wage? Will the orchard shut down if labor is its only nonsunk cost?

c The workers have an alternative wage of $16 per day. What is the maximum level of employment?

COMPENSATING DIFFERENTIALS

A job offer brings with it a promised wage and a bundle of job characteristics. Workers may not accept the highest-paying job, preferring a lower wage alternative if it offers more attractive nonwage benefits. The additional wage that accompanies a job with some undesirable nonwage aspect is called the compensating differential. The budget constraint allows us to identify and study the trade-off between wages and job characteristics. Tool Kit 15.2 shows the technique.

Tool Kit 15.2 Using Budget Constraints to Analyze Compensating Differentials

When an individual has several job offers, she faces a trade-off between higher wages and other desirable job characteristics. These steps show how to illustrate the trade-off with a budget constraint.

Step one: Draw a set of axes with the wage measured on the vertical axis and the nonwage characteristic on the horizontal.

Step two: Plot a point corresponding to each job offer.

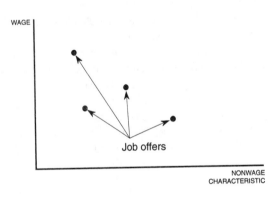

Step three: Cancel the dominated offers. The dominated offers represent jobs with both lower wages and less-attractive job characteristics.

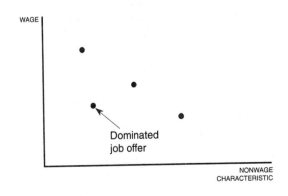

Step four: Draw a smooth curve through the undominated job offers. These are the ones that include higher wages or more attractive job characteristics. This curve is the budget constraint, reflecting the alternative combinations of wages and job characteristics available to the worker.

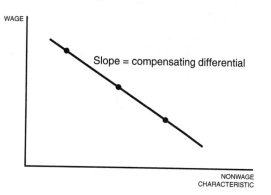

Slope = compensating differential

Step five: Identify the trade-off between several points on the budget constraint. The slope is the compensating differential.

4 (Worked problem: compensating differentials) Many parents in two-earner families worry about day care for infants. Recognizing this concern, some progressive companies offer on-site day care, although the facilities vary greatly in quality. Table 15.6 lists some local firms, the entry-level salaries for management trainees, and the expenditure per child for the day care facility.

a Represent the salaries and day care expenditures as an opportunity set.

b Are there any dominated offers?

c What is the compensating differential for reducing day care expenditures from $5,000 to $4,000? from $1,000 to $0?

Table 15.6

Firm	Salary	Expenditure per child
ALX Corp.	$30,000	$5,000
ABX Corp.	$35,000	$3,000
PBX Corp.	$37,000	$4,000
APX Corp.	$46,000	$0
AXX Corp.	$40,000	$1,000

Step-by-step solution

Step one (a): Draw a set of axes.

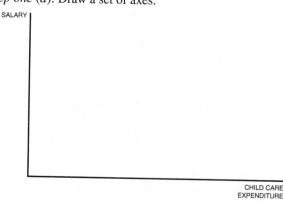

Step two: Plot a point corresponding to each job offer.

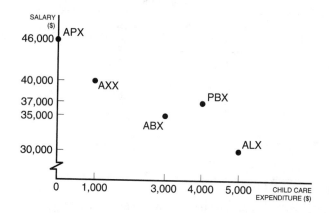

Step three (b): Cancel the dominated offers. The ABX offer, which entails less money and child care expenditure, is dominated by the PBX offer.

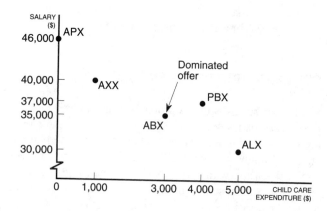

Step four: Draw a smooth curve through the undominated job offers.

Step five (c): Identify the trade-offs between several points on the budget constraint. As the day care expenditure falls from $5,000 to $4,000, salary rises by $37,000 − $30,000 = $7,000. The compensating differential for a decrease from $1,000 to $0 is $46,000 − $40,000 = $6,000.

5 (Practice problem: compensating differentials) Sylvester Stallion is looking for a job. The alternatives, the corresponding annual salaries, and some data on accidental deaths are given in Table 15.7. Sylvester has offers for each type of job, he is qualified for each, and he considers them equally satisfying except for the risk of death.

Table 15.7

Job	Salary	Deaths per 100,000
Night guard	$16,000	2
Shoe seller	$15,000	1 (irate customer)
Clerk in convenience store	$24,000	5
Cab driver	$19,000	6
Armed guard	$22,000	3

a Represent the job offers as an opportunity set.
b Without knowing anything about Stallion's willingness to risk death, can you say if there is a job offer he will definitely refuse? Explain.
c What is the compensating differential for increasing the annual death risk from 1 to 2 deaths per 100,000 workers? What is the compensating differential for increasing the annual death risk from 3 to 5 deaths per 100,000 workers?

6 (Practice problem: compensating differentials) The banking industry in Gotham offers a wide variety of salaries and vacation days. Table 15.8 gives entry salaries and vacation time offered to new hires.

Table 15.8

Bank	Salary	Vacation days
First One	$20,000	5
Bank One	$25,000	8
First Bank	$32,000	5
Premier Bank	$30,000	6
Second Bank	$28,000	7

a Represent the salaries and vacation days as an opportunity set.
b Are there any dominated offers?
c What is the compensating differential for reducing vacation days from 8 to 7? From 6 to 5?

Answers to Problems

2 a The marginal revenue product schedule is given in Table 15.9.

Table 15.9

Faculty	Students	Revenues	Marginal revenue product
20	100	$100,000	—
30	600	$600,000	$50,000
40	1,000	$1,000,000	$40,000
50	1,300	$1,300,000	$30,000
60	1,500	$1,500,000	$20,000
70	1,600	$1,600,000	$10,000
80	1,600	$1,600,000	$0

b The maximum wage is $50,000, at which 30 faculty will be hired.
c The maximum employment occurs at a wage of $20,000, with 60 faculty.
3 a The marginal revenue product schedule is given in Table 15.10.

Table 15.10

Pickers	Cherries	Revenues	Marginal revenue product
1	24	$48	$48
2	64	$128	$80
3	96	$192	$64
4	120	$240	$48
5	136	$272	$32
6	144	$288	$16
7	148	$296	$8
8	150	$300	$4

b The maximum wage is $80, at which there will be 2 pickers.

c The maximum employment is 6, where the wage equals $16.

5 a

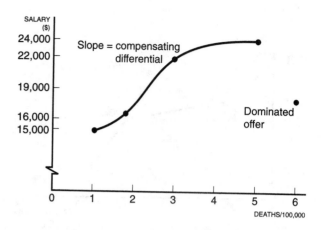

b Stallion will refuse the cab driver offer, which is dominated by the job of clerk in a convenience store.

c $1,000, $2,000.

6 a

b First One.

c $3,000, $2,000.

| # The Public Sector

Chapter Review

Although the private sector accounts for most economic activity, the United States is a mixed economy where a large role is played by the public sector. This chapter studies the role of government in enhancing the performance of the economy. Topics include the tax system, social insurance, and other transfer programs. Reasons why the public sector has difficulties and a discussion of current controversies close the chapter.

ESSENTIAL CONCEPTS

1 Economists see roles for government in correcting market failures. These include stabilizing the economy's fluctuations, enhancing competition, and improving performance when there are externalities, public goods, and information problems. Government is also concerned with the problem of poverty and the redistribution of income. Finally, there are **merit goods** and **bads,** activities that are encouraged or discourages, overriding the principle of **consumer sovereignty.**

2 A good tax system has five important characteristics, the first of which is **fairness.** The second characteristic of a good tax system is **efficiency.** The system should change the economy's resource allocation decisions as little as possible and also impose few extra costs on taxpayers. The U.S. tax system often encourages more consumption and production of some goods with special tax provisions called **tax subsidies.** These reduce taxes for those who engage in the favoured activity and result in lower tax revenues for the government. The lost tax revenue is called **a tax expenditure.** Other characteristics of a good tax system

include **administrative simplicity, flexibility,** and **transparency,** which means that it should be clear who is paying how much of each tax.

3 Transfer programs of the U.S. government include cash assistance to poor families, Medicaid, food stamps, disability payments, and housing subsidies. The welfare programs have been substantially revised to encourage work and responsibility. Housing programs have been refocused away from public housing toward providing subsidies.

4 Many social insurance programs, such as Social Security, unemployment insurance, disability insurance, and Medicare, benefit the middle class. They are financed by payroll taxes, but the ultimate burden is in the form of lower wages. Although they are called insurance programs, the provisions of each cause some income to be redistributed.

5 Although there are many examples of efficient government enterprises and helpful programs, government often allocates resources wastefully. Reasons for **public failures** include improper incentives attributable to the constraints of due process, inability to make long-term commitments, and political pressures. Also budgetary and spending problems such as soft budget constraints, the annual appropriations process, and inflexible cost containment restrictions like competitive bidding requirements undermine efficiency. Finally, there is the general problem of unintended consequences and unforeseen incentives and behavior brought about by the interaction of government policy and the very complex economy.

6 The reform of Social Security and repair of the health care system are two important current controversies.
  a Faced with impending shortfalls in revenues, some have proposed a partial privatization, whereby

private investment accounts would replace part of the current pay-as-you-go system. A related issue is the conversion to a fully funded system.

b The health care system confronts four main problems. Millions have no health insurance. The quality of care is poor for the low-income elderly. Costs must be contained. Finally, there remain issues beyond medical care, such as poor diet, lack of exercise, smoking, drinking, and environmental degradation.

BEHIND THE ESSENTIAL CONCEPTS

1 You can judge the U.S. tax system on how well it meets the five criteria outlined in the text. The following are some arguments:

a Fairness: The **marginal tax rate**, which is the tax paid out of the extra dollar of income, is higher for higher incomes. This aspect and refundable tax credits combine to make U.S. individual **income taxes** mildly **progressive**, although the progressivity is offset somewhat by a variety of special provisions that help higher-income households, such as mortgage interest deductions and capital gains exclusions. **Payroll taxes** and federal and provincial sales taxes are **regressive**, however, and in sum, the total tax system is probably fairly flat, slightly progressive at best.

b Efficiency: Although the 1981 reduction in marginal tax rates and the 1986 tax reform improved the efficiency of the income tax system, many special provisions remain. Further, in 1993 marginal rates rose again.

c Administrative simplicity: By removing many lower-income individuals from the tax rolls and making tax avoidance less profitable (because marginal tax rates are lower), recent tax reforms have made the U.S. income tax system simpler for some. Overall, the goal remains unmet.

d Flexibility: In practice, the U.S. income tax system is not flexible because any proposed tax change seems to open up debate on all aspects of the tax code.

e Transparency: For some taxes, such as the **corporation income tax** and **sales taxes**, it is difficult to determine the actual tax burden.

2 When the private market fails to allocate resources efficiently, there is a potential role for government action. For example, when a public good such as a traffic light is needed, the government is the natural choice to provide it. When negative externalities are present, such as pollution, the government may be able to discourage them. The income distribution produced by private markets may be unacceptable, and the government may be able to redistribute it. Governments are large organizations, however, and policies do not always work as intended.

3 The existence of market failures prompts the call for more government intervention. **Government failures** justify calls for less intervention. Often what is needed is different, better government action, which harnesses market incentives to bring about a better allocation of resources.

4 You can understand certain constraints placed on government decision making as imperfect solutions to larger problems. For example, due process constraints prohibit the arbitrary exercise of government power to seize assets. While this is undoubtedly a good thing, due process unfortunately limits the discretion of bureaucrats to tailor decisions to individual circumstances. Similarly, competitive bidding requirements help to minimize corruption in government procurement, but they mandate cumbersome and costly procedures. The government's ability to make long-term commitments does lead to inefficiencies, but it also limits the ability of current legislature from imposing undue burdens on future generations.

SELF-TEST

True or False

1 The U.S. economic system relies primarily on private markets.

2 Government's role in the economy has remained essentially unchanged since the early 1900s.

3 Redistribution is necessary to promote a more efficient allocation of resources than the market provides.

4 A tax system is progressive if upper-income individuals pay a larger fraction of income in taxes.

5 The U.S. income tax system is quite flexible and able to respond quickly to changes in economic circumstances.

6 The 1986 tax reform reduced administrative complexity somewhat by removing some low-income individuals from the tax rolls and reducing marginal tax rates.

7 The corporate income tax is an example of a transparent tax in that it is easy to see how much each person effectively pays.

8 The earned-income tax credit increases the after-tax income of the working poor.

9 Social Security is an example of a middle-class entitlement program.

10 The United States has a more equal distribution of economic goods than most other developed economies.

11 Even though markets may fail to allocate resources efficiently, government action may make matters worse.

12 Civil service rules and political pressures create incentive problems that may lead to public failures.

13 Due process is designed to protect against arbitrary use of government's coercive powers.

14 The inability to make long-term commitments can undermine the efficiency of public agencies.

15 Soft budget constraints, the annual appropriations process, and rigid procurement rules constrain government budgetary and spending decisions.

Multiple Choice

1 Which of the following is *not* a legitimate role of government?
   a Solving the problem of scarcity
   b Redistributing income
   c Stabilizing the level of economic activity
   d Correcting market failures
   e All of the above are legitimate roles.

2 Which of the following is an example of a market failure?
   a Housing is expensive.
   b The poor often cannot afford adequate health care.
   c The ostentatious displays of wealth by the rich and famous are offensive.
   d Periodic episodes of high unemployment trouble market economies.
   e All of the above.

3 Which of the following is *not* an example of an externality?
   a Environmental pollution
   b Research and development
   c Restoring buildings in decaying areas
   d Contributions to philanthropic organizations
   e All of the above are examples of externalities.

4 Consumer sovereignty means that
   a individuals are the best judges of what is in their own interest.
   b there is no role for government in product-safety regulations.
   c consumers always have good information.
   d consumers are rational decision makers.
   e a and c.

5 Which of the following is *not* a reason for government failure?
   a Imperfect information
   b Government waste
   c Incentives of public administrators
   d Missing markets
   e All of the above are reasons for government failure.

6 Which of the following is *not* a reason for market failure?
   a Externalities
   b Public goods
   c Missing markets
   d Lack of competition
   e All of the above are reasons for market failure.

7 Government can provide incentives to produce more of some good by
   a taxing it.
   b subsidizing it.
   c banning its production.
   d redistributing it.
   e using the "invisible hand."

8 Which of the following is *not* an excise tax?
   a Cigarette tax
   b Tax on alcohol
   c Gasoline tax
   d Tax on air travel
   e Corporate income tax

9 If lower-income individuals pay a larger fraction of their income in tax, the system is
   a progressive.
   b regressive.
   c transparent.
   d efficient.
   e flexible.

10 The marginal tax rate is the
   a extra tax owed on an additional dollar of income.
   b amount of tax expenditure on an additional dollar of income.
   c amount of tax subsidy on an additional dollar of income.
   d ratio of taxes to taxable income.
   e tax rate at which the earned-income credit no longer applies.

11 An efficient tax system
   a distorts economic decisions as little as possible.
   b collects its revenue with as little additional cost to taxpayers as possible.
   c is flexible.
   d all of the above.
   e a and b.

12 Which of the following is *not* an attribute of a good tax system?
   a Efficiency;
   b Vertical equity;
   c Horizontal equity;
   d Transparency.
   e All of the above are attributes of good tax systems.

13 A subsidy that the tax system currently provides to low-wage workers is
   a unemployment insurance.
   b the earned-income tax credit.
   c minimum wage laws.
   d AFDC.
   e b and d.

14 Social insurance programs in the United States
   a have no redistribution effect.
   b are purely redistributive.

c provide insurance and also redistribute from higher-to lower-income households.

d are financed by taxes that have disincentive effects.

e *c* and *d*.

15 The government's role in redistribution is primarily motivated by

a market failure.

b social values concerning those unable to sustain a minimum standard of living.

c imperfect information.

d distrust of consumer sovereignty.

e noncompetitive markets.

16 Procedures developed to protect the public against arbitrary use of government power are called

a due process.

b soft budget constraints.

c the law of unintended consequences.

d rent seeking.

e federalism.

17 The idea that public enterprises can make losses that are funded by taxpayer moneys is called

a due process.

b soft budget constraints.

c the law of unintended consequences.

d rent seeking.

e the principal agent problem.

18 The concept of public failures refers to

a inefficient decisions by government.

b inefficient allocations of resources by market.

c a socially unacceptable distribution of income.

d the voting paradox.

e the free-rider problem.

19 When government subsidies increase demand and raise costs, it is an example of

a soft budget constraints.

b unintended consequences.

c due process.

d externalities.

e market failure.

20 Which of the following are sources of government failure?

a Due process regulations limit flexibility.

b Governments have limited ability to make long-term commitments.

c Expenditures are appropriated on an annual basis.

d Rigid procurement rules impose excessive costs.

e All of the above.

Completion

1 The failure of private markets to produce economic efficiency is called _____.

2 When an individual or firm can take an action without bearing the full costs and benefits, there is said to be a(n) _____.

3 A tax system in which individuals pay a larger fraction of income as income increases is called _____.

4 A good tax system has the characteristics of _____, which means that it is clear what each person is paying in taxes.

5 The tax owned on an additional dollar of income is the _____.

6 Under the _____, low-wage workers receive tax credits.

7 Procedures designed to limit the arbitrary use of government power are called _____.

8 Due to _____, government enterprises can suffer financial losses with the deficit funded out of government revenues.

9 _____ refer to inefficient decisions by governments.

10 Urban renewal led to a decline the housing availability for low-income people. This is an example of a(n) _____.

Answers to Self-test

True or False

1	t	6	t	11	t
2	f	7	f	12	t
3	f	8	t	13	t
4	t	9	t	14	t
5	f	10	f	15	t

Multiple Choice

1	*a*	6	*e*	11	*d*	16	*a*
2	*d*	7	*b*	12	*e*	17	*b*
3	*e*	8	*e*	13	*b*	18	*a*
4	*a*	9	*b*	14	*e*	19	*b*
5	*d*	10	*a*	15	*b*	20	*e*

Completion

1 market failure

2 externality

3 progressive

4 transparency

5 marginal tax rate

6 earned-income tax credit

7 due process

8 soft budget constraints

9 Public failures

10 unintended consequence

Doing Economics: Tools and Practice Problems

When an activity causes positive externalities, or external benefits, the government can often improve matters through subsidies. This section explores two questions. First, how do subsidies encourage more of the subsidized activity? Our analysis will be very much like the treatment of the economic effects of taxation in Chapter 5. The other issue is why decisions are likely to be inefficient when there are externalities. This is an application of the technique of balancing marginal benefits and marginal costs introduced in Chapter 2.

SUBSIDIES

Many goods and services receive subsidies from various levels of government. Sometimes, as in the case of home ownership, the demanders benefit directly. In other cases, as with federal water projects, the subsidies are paid directly to the suppliers. Subsidies have their effects by shifting supply or demand curves, bringing about new equilibrium quantities. Tool Kit 16.1 shows how to analyze the impacts of subsidies.

Tool Kit 16.1 Using Supply and Demand to Determine the Effects of Subsidies

If subsidies are paid directly to demanders, the demand curve shifts. If paid directly to suppliers, subsidies shift the supply curve. The remainder of the analysis parallels the basic method of supply and demand. Follow these steps.

Step one: Start with a no-subsidy equilibrium in the appropriate market.

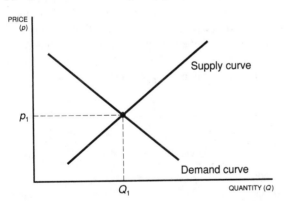

Step two: Identify the magnitude of the subsidy and whether it is paid directly to the demanders or suppliers.

Step three: If the subsidy is paid to demanders, shift the demand curve up (vertically) by exactly the amount of the subsidy. If the subsidy is paid to suppliers, shift the supply curve down by exactly the amount of the subsidy.

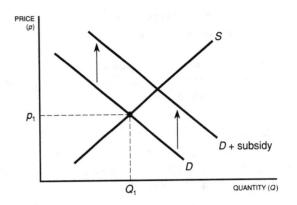

Step four: Find the new equilibrium and compare it with the original equilibrium.

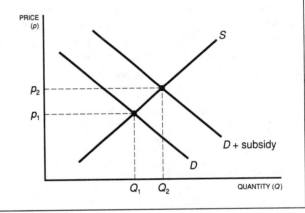

1 (Worked problem: effects of subsidies) Home ownership is treated very favorably by the U.S. tax system. The interest paid on mortagages is tax deductible, and the taxes on capital gains earned by selling at more than the purchase price can be deferred and even avoided altogether. To see how the subsidy affects the housing market, consider the market for three-bedroom bungalows in Little Spoon. The market demand and supply curves without the subsidy are given in Table 16.1.

Table 16.1

Demand		Supply	
Price	*Quantity*	*Price*	*Quantity*
$125,000	10	$125,000	50
$100,000	14	$100,000	42
$90,000	25	$90,000	31
$80,000	28	$80,000	28
$70,000	31	$70,000	20

a Find the equilibrium price and quantity.

b The tax advantages accruing to the home owner

amount to $20,000 over the life of the occupancy. Calculate the demand curve with the subsidy included.

c Find the equilibrium price and quantity with the subsidy in place. How does the subsidy change the number of bungalows sold in Little Spoon?

Step-by-step solution

Step one (a): Start with a no-subsidy equilibrium in the appropriate market. The price is $80,000; the market clears with 28 houses sold. This is the answer to part *a*.

Step two (b): Identify the magnitude of the subsidy and whether it is paid directly to the demanders or suppliers. The subsidy is $20,000, paid to demanders.

Step three: Because it is paid to demanders, the subsidy causes the demand curve to shift vertically by $20,000. To calculate this, add $20,000 to each entry in the price column of the demand curve. The new demand curve is given in Table 16.2, which is the answer to part *b*.

Table 16.2

Demand	
Price	Quantity
$145,000	10
$120,000	14
$110,000	25
$100,000	28
$90,000	31

Step four (c): Find the new equilibrium and compare it with the original equilibrium. The new equilibrium price is $90,000, and the market clears at 31 houses sold. The subsidy has increased the number of home owners in Little Spoon from 28 to 31. The price is $10,000 higher, so the $20,000 subsidy makes home owners only $10,000 better off. Producers share in the benefits with a $10,000 higher price. The solution is illustrated in the diagram.

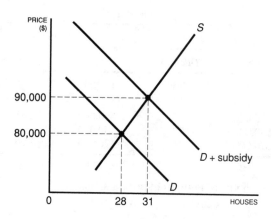

2 (Practice problem: effects of subsidies) Her eyes brightening at the thought of thousands of stressed, child-raising voters, Senator Shill has proposed child care grants of $10,000 per family. The demand and supply curves for child care services (measured in days) are given in Table 16.3.

Table 16.3

Demand		Supply	
Price (thousands)	Quantity (days)	Price (thousands)	Quantity (days)
$50	50,000	$50	100,000
$45	60,000	$45	80,000
$40	70,000	$40	70,000
$35	80,000	$35	60,000
$30	100,000	$30	50,000

a Find the equilibrium price and quantity without the subsidy.
b Calculate the demand with the subsidy.
c Find the equilibrium price and quantity with the subsidy. Compare the equilibria, and explain the effects of the subsidy.

3 (Practice problem: effects of subsidies) To promote conversion to renewable sources of energy, the government has offered various tax deductions and credits for the purchase and installation of solar water heaters. The value to a typical taxpayer of the tax provisions is $3,000. The supply and demand curves for solar water heaters are given in Table 16.4.

Table 16.4

Demand		Supply	
Price	Quantity	Price	Quantity
$8,000	1,000	$8,000	10,000
$7,000	3,000	$7,000	9,000
$6,000	5,000	$6,000	8,000
$5,000	7,000	$5,000	7,000
$4,000	9,000	$4,000	6,000
$3,000	11,000	$3,000	5,000

a Find the equilibrium price and quantity without the subsidy.
b Calculate the demand with the subsidy.
c Find the equilibrium price and quantity with the subsidy. Compare the equilibria, and explain the effects of the subsidy.

POSITIVE EXTERNALITIES

Individuals make decisions by balancing their private benefits and costs at the margin, but efficiency requires that all benefits and costs, not only the private ones, be included in the decision. Thus, when there are externalities, there are costs or benefits ignored by the individual making the decision, and this fact leads to inefficient decisions. Tool kit 16.2 focuses on positive externalities and the inefficiencies that result.

Tool Kit 16.2 Showing How Positive Externalities Lead to Inefficiencies

Positive externalities occur when decision makers ignore some benefits of their actions. Follow these steps to see how this leads to inefficient decisions.

Step one: Find the private marginal benefits and costs of the relevant activity.

Step two: Find the equilibrium level of the activity, which is the level at which private marginal benefits equal marginal cost.

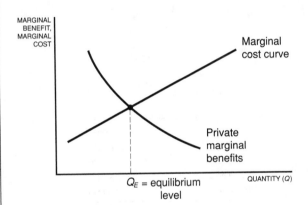

Step three: Calculate the social marginal benefits by adding the external benefit to the private marginal benefit at each level of the activity.

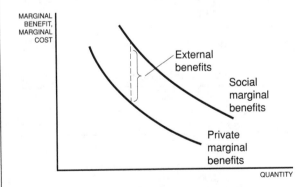

Step four: Find the efficient level of the activity, which is the level at which social marginal benefits equal marginal cost.

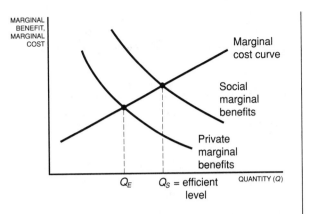

Step five: Compare the equilibrium and efficient levels of the activity.

---

4 (Worked problem: positive externalities) An important example of an activity that generates positive externalities is worker training. When firms train their employees, the employees not only become more productive in the job, they can also earn higher wages elsewhere. This increase in earning power is a positive externality. The QXV Corporation is considering sending some of its white-collar employees to computer school. The cost is $1,000 per week, and the private marginal benefits to QXV are given in Table 16.5. Also, the value of the external benefit is $500 per week.

Table 16.5

Weeks at school	Private marginal benefits
1	$1,500
2	$1,250
3	$1,000
4	$750
5	$500
6	$250

a How many weeks of computer schooling will the company provide?
b Find the social marginal benefits of computer schooling.
c What is the efficient number of weeks of schooling?

Step-by-step solution

Step one (a): Find the private marginal benefits and costs of the relevant activity. The private marginal benefits are in Table 16.5; the private marginal cost is $1,000 per week.

Step two: Find the equilibrium level of the activity. Private marginal benefits equal $1,000 at 3 weeks.

Step three (*b*): Calculate the social marginal benefits by adding the external benefit to the private marginal benefit at each level of the activity. The answer is in Table 16.6.

Table 16.6

Weeks at school	Private marginal benefits	Social marginal benefits
1	$1,500	$2,000
2	$1,250	$1,750
3	$1,000	$1,500
4	$750	$1,250
5	$500	$1,000
6	$250	$750

Step four (*c*): Find the efficient level of the activity. Social marginal benefits equal marginal cost at 5 weeks.

Step five: Compare the equilibrium and efficient levels of the activity. The equilibrium number of weeks is 3, which is less than the efficient number, which is 5. The number of weeks provided is too low because the firm ignores the externality.

5 (Practice problem: positive externalities) ZZZX Pharmaceuticals is considering how many scientists to put to work researching a new drug for Angolan flu. Each scientist, complete with equipment and assistance, costs $200,000. The research will bring profits to ZZZX, but it will also bring about advances in viral research that other companies may build on in their own research. The private benefits are given in Table 16.7. The external marginal benefits are $150,000.

Table 16.7

Scientists	Private benefits
1	$400,000
2	$600,000
3	$700,000
4	$750,000
5	$750,000

a How many scientists will the company use? (Hint: First find the private marginal benefits.)
b Find the social marginal benefits of research scientists.
c What is the efficient number of scientists?

6 (Practice problem: positive externalities) Hillside County farmers have been advised to erect earthen dikes for erosion control. Each dike costs $2,000. The private marginal benefits are given in the second column of Table 16.8, but they do not include the external benefit that one farmer's erosion control efforts provide to her neighbors. The external benefits appear in the third column of the table.

Table 16.8

Dikes	Private marginal benefits	External marginal benefits
1	$3,000	$8,000
2	$2,000	$7,000
3	$1,500	$6,000
4	$1,000	$5,000
5	$500	$4,000
6	$0	$3,000
7	$0	$2,000

a How many dikes will each farmer erect?
b Find the social marginal benefits of a farmer's dikes.
c What is the efficient number of dikes?

Answers to Problems

2 a Price = $40; quantity = 70,000.
   b The new demand curve is given in Table 16.9.

Table 16.9

Demand	
Price	Quantity
$60	50,000
$55	60,000
$50	70,000
$45	80,000
$40	100,000

   c The new equilibrium price is $45,000, and the quantity is 80,000. The subsidy increases the quantity from 70,000 to 80,000. Consumers are better off by $5,000 ($10,000 subsidy − $5,000 increase in price), and firms are better off by $5,000, which is the increase in price.

3 a Price = $5,000; quantity = 7,000.
   b The new demand curve is given in Table 16.10.

Table 16.10

Demand	
Price	Quantity
$11,000	1,000
$10,000	3,000
$9,000	5,000
$8,000	7,000
$7,000	9,000
$6,000	11,000

c The new equilibrium price is $7,000, and the quantity is 9,000. The subsidy increases the quantity from 7,000 to 9,000. Consumers are better off by $1,000 ($3,000 subsidy − $2,000 increase in price), and firms are better off by $2,000, which is the increase in price.

5 a 2 scientists.

   b The social marginal benefits are given in Table 16.11.

Table 16.11

Scientists	Private benefits	Private marginal benefits	Social marginal benefits
1	$400,000	$400,000	$550,000
2	$600,000	$200,000	$350,000
3	$700,000	$100,000	$250,000
4	$750,000	$50,000	$200,000
5	$750,000	$0	$150,000

c The efficient number is 4 scientists. The company chooses only 2 because it ignores the externality.

6 a 2 dikes.

   b The social marginal benefits are given in Table 16.12.

Table 16.12

Dikes	Private marginal benefits	External marginal benefits	Social marginal benefits
1	$3,000	$8,000	$11,000
2	$2,000	$7,000	$9,000
3	$1,500	$6,000	$7,500
4	$1,000	$5,000	$6,000
5	$500	$4,000	$4,500
6	$0	$3,000	$3,000
7	$0	$2,000	$2,000

c The efficient number of dikes is 7. Farmers only erect 2 because they ignore the external benefits.

PART FOUR

Topics in Microeconomics

CHAPTER 17 | A Student's Guide to Investing

Chapter Review

Chapter 16 explored what the household does with its savings. This is the investment decision. Financial markets offer a wide array of investment opportunities, from savings accounts to Treasury bills to corporate stock, all with different characteristics. Why investors value certain characteristics of assets and how returns to assets reflect these characteristics form the central focus of this chapter.

ESSENTIAL CONCEPTS

1 **Financial investments** are purchases of financial assets in the expectation of receiving a return. Among the most important are bank deposits, housing, bonds, shares of stock, and mutual funds.

  a Bank deposits include savings accounts and **certificates of deposit**. Insured by the Federal Deposit Insurance Corporation, they are safe and liquid.

  b Housing is a tax favored investment in that property taxes and interest are deductible, and capital gains taxation usually can be avoided. Housing investment is risky and illiquid, however.

  c Bonds, which are promises to pay a fixed amount in a specified number of years, are a way for businesses and government to borrow. Bondholders bear the risk of default and/or inflation.

  d Shares of stock represent ownership rights in corporations. Investors hold stock in the hopes of receiving **dividends** and **capital gains**.

  e **Mutual funds** combine money from many different investors and purchase a wide variety of assets. This is called **diversification**. Although they are not insured by the federal government, mutual funds are safer than individual stocks or bonds.

2 There are four important properties of financial investments: expected return, risk, tax treatment, and liquidity.

  a Since returns are uncertain, the investor must balance the high returns with the low. The **expected return** is calculated by multiplying the possible returns by the probability each will occur.

  b Assets with a greater chance of very low and very high returns are **risky.** Most individuals are **risk averse;** they prefer safer assets.

  c The returns from some assets, such as housing and municipal bonds, are taxed less than the returns from other assets. The **tax advantages** make these assets more appealing to investors.

  d The ease with which an investment can be converted to cash is called **liquidity.** Bank accounts are very liquid; housing is illiquid. Most investors prefer liquidity.

3 **Assets,** such as land, housing, stocks, and bonds, last a long time and can be bought today and sold in the future. The prices of assets are determined by supply and demand; however, supply and demand are affected by both today's conditions and what people expect future prices to be. Buyers and sellers of assets must form their **expectations** and make forecasts with care; nevertheless, they are likely to make mistakes, disagree, and revise their expectations. Changing expectations explain large changes in asset prices and make asset markets volatile and risky.

4 Many economic activities, from purchasing an asset to making an investment, are oriented toward the future. Households and firms must form expectations about the future. Economists distinguish three ways of forming

expectations. If you think that tomorrow will be like today, then your expectations are **myopic.** You have **adaptive expectations** if you that current trends will continue. Finally, you have **rational expectations** (and are well on your way to becoming an economist) if you use all available information, including what you learn in economics.

5 The **efficient market theory** says that market prices reflect the characteristics of assets, incorporate all currently available information, and change unpredictably. An important implication of this theory is that without inside information, investors cannot continue to earn more than average returns.

6 The chapter closes with some investment advice. Although unlikely to appear on a test, this advice is immensely valuable.

  a Carefully evaluate the characteristics of each asset you own as it relates to your personal situation.

  b Diversify. Give your **portfolio** a broad base.

  c Consider all your risks, not just those in your financial investment portfolio.

  d Think again before you imagine that you can beat the market.

BEHIND THE ESSENTIAL CONCEPTS

1 What do investors want from their financial assets? In addition to high expected returns, individuals value the characteristics of investments with low risk, favorable tax treatment, and liquidity. The demand for investments with these characteristics is higher; therefore, their price is higher. The fact that market prices are higher for assets with desirable characteristics—in other words, that asset prices reflect these characteristics—is one of the central ideas of efficient market theory.

2 Most people are risk averse and would prefer to reduce the uncertainty about future economic conditions. Risky assets are less attractive because they subject their owners to uncertainty about future returns. The lower demand for these assets depresses their price, and economists say that they are "sold at a discount." Another way to look at the same facts shows us that a dollar invested in a risky asset will yield higher expected returns.

3 Efficient market theory says that prices also reflect all available information. For example, when Iraq invaded Kuwait in August 1990, the prices of oil and oil stocks shot up immediately. The new information that oil would be in short supply in the future made firms that owned large oil reserves worth more, and their stock prices immediately reflected this additional worth.

4 Many people are mystified by the notion that in an efficient market, asset prices change randomly. Once you understand the logic, however, you can see why this must be true. Since market prices reflect available information, you can only beat the market if you have information others do not. Anyone who had known in April 1990 that Iraq would invade Kuwait could have bought oil stocks before their prices rose. Once the invasion happened, however, it was too late. Prices had already risen. Since the invasion was a surprise, the sudden changes in the prices of oil stocks were also surprises. This is what is meant by random movements in prices: the changes are unpredictable, though they are not without rational cause.

SELF-TEST

True or False

1 The ease with which an asset can be converted to cash is called its liquidity.

2 To find the expected return, simply take the average of the possible returns.

3 Housing is a tax-favored investment because interest is tax deductible and capital gains taxes may be postponed.

4 If the interest rate rises, bond prices fall.

5 Bondholders bear no risk from inflation.

6 If a company goes bankrupt, bondholders are paid before stockholders.

7 The portion of a company income not paid to stockholders in dividends is called retained earnings.

8 Risky assets pay higher rates of return on average.

9 Illiquid assets pay lower rates of return on average.

10 An increase in the price of a share of stock is called a capital gain.

11 If stock prices vary randomly, then the market cannot be efficient.

12 If the price of an asset rises because people expect that asset to pay higher returns in the future, there is said to be an **asset price bubble**.

13 Because most people prefer safe, tax-favored, liquid assets, those assets yield higher returns.

14 A fund that gathers money from many investors and purchases a range of assets is called a mutual fund.

15 If stock prices reflect all available information, then changes in price must result from unanticipated events and must be random.

Multiple Choice

1 Which of the following are financial investments?

  a Stocks

  b Bonds

  c Money market accounts

   d Certificates of deposit

   e All of the above

2 Which of the following are real investments?

   a Preferred stock

   b Mutual funds

   c Purchases of new factories

   d Bank accounts

   e None of the above

3 Liquidity refers to

   a the correlation of the return on an asset and the market return.

   b the term to maturity of a bond.

   c the ease with which an asset can be converted into cash.

   d the likelihood that an investor will be repaid if a corporation goes bankrupt.

   e *a* and *d*.

4 Which of the following is *not* a risk borne by bondholders?

   a The market interest rate may rise, causing the price of the bond to fall.

   b Inflation may lower the real value of the fixed return.

   c A corporation may go bankrupt and default on the bond.

   d At the end of the term, even if it does not default, a company may not pay a bondholder what she expected to receive.

   e All of the above are risks of holding bonds.

5 Junk bonds are

   a highly risky bonds usually issued by firms with high debt levels.

   b bonds that must be held by the original purchaser and cannot be sold.

   c bonds that have procyclical returns.

   d bonds that are not convertible into stock.

   e bonds issued by firms in the used vehicle industry.

6 The amount of a firm's earnings not paid out to stockholders as dividends is called

   a economic profits.

   b the average return.

   c retained earnings.

   d liquidity.

   e accounting profits.

7 If an investor sells a share of stock for more than he paid for it, he earns a

   a liquidity premium.

   b capital gain.

   c retained earning.

   d risk premium.

   e procyclical return.

8 People who use all available information to form expectations about the future are said to have

   a myopic expectations.

   b adaptive expectations.

   c rational expectations.

   d insider expectations.

   e random walk expectations.

9 Suppose that an antique automobile purchased for $25,000 is to be sold next year. The investor thinks that the sales price may be $20,000 or $40,000, and the probability of each price is one-half. What is its expected return?

   a $5,000

   b $30,000

   c $35,000

   d −$5,000

   e None of the above

10 If there were no differences between assets other than the ways in which they produced returns, then

   a the expected returns to all assets would be the same.

   b the returns to stock ownership would exceed the returns to bond holding.

   c assets that paid returns through capital gains would pay more than assets that paid returns through interest or dividends.

   d no investor would hold bonds.

   e none of the above.

11 Why are stocks risky financial investments?

   a The price of the stock may go up or down.

   b The amount of the dividend payment may go up or down.

   c The firm may go bankrupt.

   d All of the above.

   e *a* and *c*.

12 Most investors are risk averse. This means that they will

   a never purchase risky assets.

   b look only at the risk of an investment, not the expected return.

   c always prefer bonds to stocks.

   d always prefer bank accounts to bonds because bank accounts are insured by the Federal Deposit Insurance Corporation.

   e prefer safe to risky assets of equal expected return.

13 Suppose that an asset has a .5 probability of earning 30 percent and a .5 probability of earning nothing. Its expected return equals

   a 0.

   b 15 percent.

   c 25 percent.

   d 30 percent.

   e 100 percent.

14 When market prices for assets change dramatically, it is usually because of

   a changes in the supply of assets.

   b government price floors.

   c changes in expectations about future prices.

   d changes in tastes.

   e changes in income.

15 State and municipal bonds yield
  a lower returns than corporate bonds chiefly because they are less risky.
  b higher returns than corporate bonds chiefly because they are more liquid.
  c lower returns than corporate bonds of equivalent risks and liquidity because interest on them is tax-exempt.
  d higher returns than corporate bonds of equivalent risk and liquidity because interest on them is tax-exempt.
  e returns equal to those paid by corporate bonds of equivalent risk and liquidity because interest on them is tax-exempt.
16 Housing is a tax-favored investment in that
  a mortgage interest is tax deductible.
  b housing is liquid.
  c it is possible to avoid capital gains taxes on housing.
  d housing is financed by municipal bonds.
  e a and c.
17 Which of the following assets is most liquid?
  a Stocks
  b Bonds
  c Bank accounts
  d Housing
  e Mutual funds
18 The demand for an asset depends on
  a its liquidity.
  b its average returns.
  c its risk.
  d its tax treatment.
  e all of the above.
19 Efficient market theory says that
  a all assets are perfectly liquid.
  b all assets are treated the same by the tax system.
  c asset characteristics are perfectly reflected in their prices.
  d average returns are equal for all assets.
  e a, b, and d.
20 The advice to diversify your portfolio means
  a to own a wide variety of assets with different risks.
  b to stay away from risky assets.
  c to choose only assets with procyclical returns.
  d to follow a random walk strategy.
  e none of the above.

Completion

1 Purchases of new factories and machinery are examples of _____ investment.
2 Purchases of stocks and bonds and deposits in money market accounts are examples of _____ investment.
3 _____ refers to the ease with which an investment can be turned into cash.
4 An unexpected decline in the rate of interest causes the prices of bonds to _____.
5 Because most individuals are _____, risky assets must offer a higher average return than safe assets.
6 When interest rates rise the price of an asset, such as a bond _____.
7 Because municipal bonds are exempt from taxes, their prices are _____ than prices for comparable taxable bonds.
8 The demand for an asset depends on its expected return, _____, tax treatment, and liquidity.
9 To find the expected return on an asset, multiply the possible returns by the corresponding _____.
10 The theory that market prices perfectly reflect the characteristics of assets is called the _____ theory.

Answers to Self-Test

True or False

1	t	6	t	11	f
2	f	7	t	12	f
3	t	8	t	13	f
4	t	9	f	14	t
5	f	10	t	15	t

Multiple Choice

1	e	6	c	11	d	16	e
2	c	7	b	12	e	17	c
3	c	8	c	13	b	18	e
4	d	9	a	14	c	19	c
5	a	10	a	15	c	20	a

Completion

1 real
2 financial
3 Liquidity
4 rise
5 risk averse
6 falls
7 higher
8 risk
9 probabilities
10 efficient market

Doing Economics: Tools and Practice Problems

The concept of expected returns appears in this chapter. We study how to calculate the expected return on an investment and what it means. We go on to consider the opportunity set for the investor and learn how he perceives trade-offs of risk and expected return, and also liquidity and returns. The last issue we take up is the relationship between bond prices and interest rates. A few problems use the concept of present value (introduced in Chapter 4) to show why an increase in interest rates leads to a decrease in bond prices.

EXPECTED RETURNS

When we purchase an asset, we do not know exactly what it will earn in the future. Investors calculate the expected return, which is the average of all the possible returns. The expected return is one of the important desirable properties of financial investments. Tool Kit 17.1 shows how to calculate expected returns.

Tool Kit 17.1 Calculating Expected Returns

Because the returns on financial investments come in the future, at the time the decision is made an investor is uncertain about what the returns will actually be. Good investors think carefully about all the possibilities and calculate the expected returns.

Step one: Make a three-column table showing all the possible returns in the left-hand column and the corresponding probabilities in the middle column.

Returns	Probability	Product
r_1	P_1	
r_2	P_2	

Step two: Multiply each possible return by its probability, and enter the product in the right-hand column.

Returns	Probability	Product
r_1	P_1	$r_1 \times P_1$
r_2	P_2	$r_2 \times P_2$

Step three: Add the numbers in the right-hand column. The sum is the expected return.

Returns	Probability	Product
r_1	P_1	$r_1 \times P_1$
r_2	P_2	$r_2 \times P_2$

Average returns = $(r_1 \times P_1) + (r_2 \times P_2)$.

---

1 (Worked problem: expected returns) Envious of his brother's life-style, Dr. Mendez is considering investing in one of his brother's real estate ventures. His brother promises a return of 100 percent in one year, but Dr. Mendez thinks the probability that this will happen is only 1/4. More likely (probability = 1/2) is a return of 8 percent. Finally, there is another 1/4 probability that

the project will go under and the doctor will lose all his money (return = −100 percent). Calculate the expected return.

Step-by-step solution

Step one: Make a table, and enter the possible returns and the corresponding probabilities.

Returns	Probability	Product
100%	1/4	
8%	1/2	
−100%	1/4	

Step two: Multiply each return by its probability, and enter the result.

Returns	Probability	Product
100%	1/4	25%
8%	1/2	4%
−100%	1/4	−25%

Step three: Add the numbers in the right-hand column.

Returns	Probability	Product
100%	1/4	25%
8%	1/2	4%
−100%	1/4	−25%

Expected returns = 4%.

Thus, in spite of the considerable risk, the investment pays an average of only 4 percent. The good doctor should stick to medicine and put his money in a safe investment.

2 (Practice problem: expected returns) Black Dust, Montana, flush with a consultant's prediction of its future as a high-technology center, is issuing bonds for a new city government building. The bonds pay 20 percent. Most financial analysts think the probability of default is 1/10. In case of default, the bondholders lose their investments (returns = −100 percent). Calculate the expected return on the Black Dust bond.

3 (Practice problem: expected returns) Calculate the expected return on each of the following.

a Returns	Probability	Product
50%	1/4	
12%	5/8	
−100%	1/8	

b Returns	Probability	Product
10%	1/4	
20%	3/4	

c Returns	Probability	Product
200%	1/3	
40%	1/3	
−100%	1/3	

d Returns	Probability	Product
50%	1/3	
12%	2/3	

RISK AND RETURNS

There are four desirable characteristics of financial investments: expected returns, risk, tax treatment, and liquidity. Seeking the best combination of these characteristics, an investor faces trade-offs. Some problems show how this trade-off looks to a potential investor.

4 (Worked problem: risk and returns) The table below gives the returns on six bond issues if there is no default, and also the probabilities of default for each. If there is a default, the investor loses all of her money (returns = −100 percent). Also, note that if the probability of default is .1, then the probability of not experiencing a default must be .9.

    a Compute the expected return for each bond.

    b Measure risk as the probability of default. Construct the opportunity set, and interpret its outer edge as the risk-return trade-off.

    c Are there any bonds a rational investor would never buy? Why or why not?

Company	Returns (if no default)	Probability of default
Do Music Co.	5%	0
Re Music Co.	19%	.1
Mi Music Co.	30%	.2
Fa Music Co.	12%	.05
Sol Music Co.	8%	.02
Fred's Music Co.	15%	.07

Step-by-step solution

Step one (*a*): Calculate the expected returns for each bond. Follow the procedure for calculating expected returns.

Do Music Co.	$(5\% \times 1) - (100\% \times 0) = 5\%$
Re Music Co.	$(19\% \times .9) - (100\% \times .1) = 7.1\%$
Mi Music Co.	$(30\% \times .8) - (100\% \times .2) = 4\%$
Fa Music Co.	$(12\% \times .95) - (100 \times .05) = 6.4\%$
Sol Music Co.	$(8\% \times .98) - (100\% \times .02) = 5.84\%$
Fred's Music Co.	$(15\% \times .93) - (100\% \times .07) = 6.95\%$

Step two (*b*): Plot the expected returns on the vertical axis and risk (measured as the probability of default) on the horizontal. This is the risk-return trade-off.

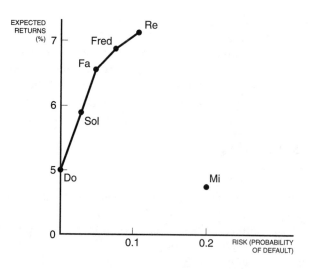

Step three (*c*): Since Mi Music Co.'s bonds do not lie on the outer edge, no one will buy them. All of the other issues offer higher average returns and lower risk, as shown in the figure.

5 (Practice problem: risk and returns) The four hospitals in Greenville are racing to install the latest medical technologies. Each is trying to raise money in the bond market, and their returns and default risks are given below. If there is a default, the return is −100 percent.

    a Calculate the expected returns for each.

    b Plot the risk-return trade-off.

Hospital	Returns (if no default)	Probability of default
Northside	6%	0
Southside	18%	.09
Eastside	22%	.1
Westside	12%	.05

6 (Practice problem: risk and returns) The Kannapans have set aside some money in case of emergency. They are considering where to invest it, but they are concerned about how quickly they will have access to the money when it is needed. The four possible assets, their returns, and the times needed to withdraw the principal (or sell the asset) are given below. Construct the liquidity-return trade-off.

Asset	Returns	Waiting period
Bank account	5%	None
Bond	7%	2 days
Diamonds	4%	1 week
Rental housing	9%	1 month

BOND PRICES AND INTEREST RATES

When interest rates rise, bond prices fall. This fact of financial markets follows from the concept of present discounted value, introduced in Chapter 6. The market price for a bond is the present discounted value of the promised repayments.

7 (Worked problem: present value) Bonds issued by Hitek, Inc., promise to pay $100 at the end of the year for 2 years. In addition, the face value equal to $1,000 is repaid at the end of 3 years. The market interest rate is 8 percent.
   a Calculate the present discounted value of the bond.
   b The interest rate rises to 10 percent. Recalculate the bond value.

Step-by-step solution

Step one (*a*): Make a table, and enter the years and the payments.

Year	Amount	Discount factor	Present discounted value
1	$ 100		
2	$ 100		
3	$1,000		

Step two: Calculate and enter the discount factors for each year. For the first year, the discount factor is $1/(1 + .08) = 0.92$. For the second year, it is $1/(1 + .08)^2 = 0.85$, and for the third, it is $1/(1 + .08)^3 = 0.78$.

Step three: Multiply the amounts by the corresponding discount factor. Enter the product in the right-hand column.

Step four: Add the numbers in the right-hand column.

Year	Amount	Discount factor	Present discounted value
1	$ 100	0.92	$ 92
2	$ 100	0.85	$ 85
3	$1,000	0.78	$780

Present discounted value = $957.

Step five (*b*): Repeat the procedure for a 10 percent interest rate. The table looks like this.

Year	Amount	Discount factor	Present discounted value
1	$ 100	0.90	$ 90
2	$ 100	0.81	$ 81
3	$1,000	0.73	$730

Present discounted value = $901.

The rise in the interest rate from 8 percent to 10 percent causes the bond price to fall by $56 ($957 − $901). It should be clear why ripples in interest rates cause waves in the bond market.

8 (Practice problem: present value) Deuce Hardwear, a franchiser of motorcycle clothing, has issued a bond that promises to pay $800 at the end of each of the next two years and $12,000 at the end of the third year. The interest rate is 7 percent.
   a Calculate the present discounted value of the bond.
   b The interest rate falls to 6 percent. How much does the price of the bond change?

9 (Practice problem: present value) For each of the following, calculate the change in the price of the bond.
   a The interest rate falls from 10 percent to 8 percent.

Year	Amount	Discount factor	Present discounted value
1	$ 88		
2	$ 88		
3	$1,000		

Present discounted value = $

   b The interest rate rises from 10 percent to 13 percent.

Year	Amount	Discount factor	Present discounted value
1	$ 800		
2	$ 700		
3	$13,000		

Present discounted value = $

Answers to Problems

2 Expected return = $(9 \times 20) - (.1 \times 100) = 8\%$.
3 a 7.5%.
   b 17.5%.
   c 46.7%.
   d 24.7%.
5 a The expected returns for each bond are given in the table.

Hospital	Returns (if no default)	Probability of default	Expected returns
Northside	6%	0	6%
Southside	18%	0.09	7.38%
Eastside	22%	0.1	9.8%
Westside	12%	0.05	6.4%

b

6

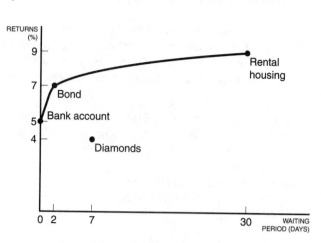

8 *a* Present discounted value = $800/(1.07) +
      $800/(1.07)^2 + $12,000/(1.07)^3= $11,243.

   b Present discounted value = $11,542.

9 *a* Price of the bond rises from $904 to $950.

   b Price of the bond falls from $11,073 to $10,263.

CHAPTER 18 | Trade Policy

Chapter Review

Governments affect the flows of traded goods through tariffs, quotas, other nontariff barriers, and a series of fair trade laws. This chapter discusses how these measures affect markets, who wins, who loses, and their political rationale. There is also discussion of the major international institutions governing trade.

ESSENTIAL CONCEPTS

1 Countries practicing protection use commercial policies to restrict imports. These trade barriers include tariffs, quotas, other nontariff barriers, and fair trade laws. Tariffs, which are taxes on imported goods, raise domestic prices, injuring consumers while providing some benefit to producers. Overall the economy suffers, losing consumer surplus and wasting resources producing goods that could be imported more cheaply.

2 Quotas are limits on the quantity of imports. By restricting supply they force up prices and lead to the same types of deadweight burdens as do tariffs. Rather than collecting tariff revenues, the government confers on certain firms extra profits from importing, called quota rents. Other nontariff barriers, such as voluntary export restraints (VERs), have similar effects. In the case of VERs the quota rent accrues to foreign exporters.

3 While ostensibly designed to promote competition, fair trade laws are protectionist. These include anti-dumping laws that prohibit the sale of imports below the cost of production and subsidies to domestic producers, usually justified to offset the impact of foreign subsidies. Another approach is to impose countervailing duties, taxes on subsidized foreign goods. Finally, there are laws that are designed to offset market surges, sudden increases in imports.

4 The political rationale for trade lies in the fact that certain groups lose from trade. Competition from imports may lead firms to close plants or even cease operations. Their displaced workers suffer large losses. Also, foreign competition may drive down wages in certain sectors or erode market power. Lost profits and laid-off unionized workers create a demand for protectionist relief.

5 Other arguments for protection may have some limited validity. The **infant industry argument** claims that import barriers may allow a young industry time to acquire the experience necessary to be competitive on the world market. Usually, however, direct assistance is a better policy. There is also the strategic trade argument, whereby protected domestic firms exploit economies of scale to undercut their foreign competitors.

6 After World War II the **General Agreement on Tariffs and Trade (GATT)** was founded to reduce trade barriers. Its three basic principles were reciprocity, nondiscrimination, and transparency, and it succeeded in greatly reducing tariffs. In 1995 it was replaced by the **World Trade Organization (WTO)** as attention turned to nontariff barriers and intellectual property. The WTO has procedures for adjudicating trade disputes.

7 Regional trading blocs, such as the **European Union** and the **North American Free Trade Agreement (NAFTA),** remove trading barriers for member countries, and this brings about the benefits of trade creation, expanded trade within the bloc. On the other hand, the discrimination against those outside the bloc

causes trade diversion. Goods that may be less costly from outsiders are produced within the bloc.

BEHIND THE ESSENTIAL CONCEPTS

1   A tariff is just a tax on imports, and we analyze its effects in the same way that we analyze a tax on a domestic good. As you recall from Chapter 3, if the suppliers must pay the tax, it shifts the supply curve up by the amount of the tax and the price rises to the intersection of the demand and the new supply. In the case of a tariff the price is set on the world market. This price simply shifts up by the amount of the tariff, and the new equilibrium is read off the demand and supply curves. There is more on how to do this in Tool Kit 18.1.

2   Tariffs, quotas, and voluntary export restraints are equivalent in one sense. Each raises prices to consumers, reduces the quantity demanded, reduces imports, and increases domestic supply. In another way, however, they are quite different. Tariff revenue is collected by the government. In the case of quotas there is an equivalent amount of money collected by importers. They can earn excess profits because the quota protects them from competition. In the case of voluntary export restraints, the two governments force the foreign suppliers to restrict output. But we know from monopoly theory that this results in higher prices and monopoly profits. In each case there are extra revenues collected: tariff revenue to the government, quota rents to the licensed importer, and VER excess profits to foreign firms.

3   When a country enters a regional trading bloc, it eliminates trade barriers with the other members, while keeping barriers up against nonmembers. This discrimination favors production within the bloc. Trade that otherwise would have occurred with nonmember countries is diverted to member countries. Since this likely goes against the principle of comparative advantage, there is a waste. Balanced against this inefficiency are the benefits of expanded trade among member countries. When trade agreements are global, however, there is no downside. It is all trade creation.

4   Why do we care about dumping? After all, if foreign producers want to sell us goods below cost, then should we not just accept their generosity? One fear is that after driving domestic producers from the market, the foreign firms will take advantage of their monopoly position and raise prices. This practice is called predatory pricing and it is illegal in the United States. In theory, anti-dumping laws make the practice illegal for foreign firms. In practice, however, these laws are used to protect domestic firms from low-cost foreign competition.

5   The infant industry argument claims that temporary protection may allow firms to grow more efficient and ultimately to prosper. The policy is like an investment, sacrificing the current gains from importing cheaper goods for long-run profitability. Of course, it should only be applied if the present value of the future profits exceeds the current costs. But in that case firms in the industry should be able to raise capital to stay in business while they are gaining experience. Governments are in no better position to evaluate the prospects of infant industries than the capital market.

SELF-TEST

True or False

1   Policies that restrict the import of foreign goods are examples of protection.

2   Tariffs are taxes on exports.

3   Tariffs reduce the quantity supplied domestically.

4   Although they also result in higher prices, quotas differ from tariffs in that firms licensed to import earn quota rents.

5   Voluntary export restraints allow foreign firms to collude and raise prices.

6   Anti-dumping laws make it illegal to sell goods abroad below the cost of production.

7   Predatory pricing refers to selling below cost in order to drive rivals from the markets.

8   Strategic trade theory points out the possibility of protecting domestic firms so that they can exploit economies of scale to undercut their foreign rivals.

9   When there is free trade between two countries, the net benefits are positive in each country.

10 When there is free trade between two countries, all individuals gain.

11 Most of the recent decline in wages in the United States is due to international trade.

12 Regional trading blocs can divert trade from nonmember to member countries.

13 Regional trading blocs expand trade both among member and nonmember countries.

14 The GATT successfully reduced tariffs among most of the world's countries.

15 The WTO adjudicates trade disputes among the United States, Canada, and Mexico.

Multiple Choice

1   Which of the following are trade barriers?
   a   Tariffs
   b   Quotas
   c   Voluntary export restraints
   d   Fair trade laws
   e   All of the above

2 Policies that affect imports or exports are called
   a commercial policies.
   b protection.
   c free trade.
   d nontariff barriers.
   e fair trade laws.

3 Tariffs are
   a taxes on exports.
   b subsidies on exports.
   c taxes on imports.
   d subsidies on imports.
   e voluntary export restraints.

4 When a small country imposes a tariff, the domestic price
   a rises by more than the amount of the tariff.
   b rises by an amount equal to the tariff.
   c rises by less than the amount of the tariff.
   d stays the same because only imported goods pay the tariff.
   e falls.

5 Tariffs, quotas, and voluntary exports restraints are similar in that each
   a raises domestic prices.
   b reduces domestic prices.
   c reduces domestic consumption.
   d increases domestic output.
   e a, c, and d.

6 When a tariff is imposed the net loss to the United States includes
   a tariff revenues.
   b lost consumer surplus due to less consumption of the good.
   c higher costs of producing the good domestically.
   d all of the above.
   e b and c.

7 When a quota is imposed, the net loss to the United States includes
   a quota rents.
   b lost consumer surplus due to less consumption of the good.
   c higher costs of producing the good domestically.
   d all of the above.
   e b and c.

8 When a voluntary exports restraint is imposed, the net loss to the United States includes
   a excess profits.
   b lost consumer surplus due to less consumption of the good.
   c higher costs of producing the good domestically.
   d all of the above.
   e b and c.

9 Dumping refers to selling
   a goods abroad for less than the going price.
   b goods abroad without paying tariffs.
   c goods abroad below the cost of production.
   d goods abroad above the cost of production.
   e excess inventories abroad.

10 Predatory pricing refers to
   a pricing above cost to reap excess profits.
   b pricing below cost to drive rivals from the market.
   c bribing politicians to receive licenses to import.
   d not reducing price when the firm is subsidized.
   e using intellectual property without paying for it.

11 Which of the following generally favors free trade?
   a Exporters
   b Unions
   c Firms earning monopoly profits
   d Workers in import industries
   e Low-wage workers

12 Economists estimate that the percentage of the recent fall in wages that is due to trade is
   a 10.
   b 20.
   c 30.
   d 50.
   e 100.

13 Beggar-thy-neighbor policies attempt to
   a increase national consumption by reducing exports.
   b increase national savings by reducing foreign aid.
   c increase national output by reducing imports.
   d decrease national savings by reducing imports.
   e decrease the budget deficit by exporting taxes.

14 During the Great Depression, the Hawley-Smoot tariffs
   a raised tariffs on imported goods.
   b drastically reduced imports.
   c led to foreign retaliation.
   d contributed to the economic downturn.
   e all of the above.

15 During the first years of the Great Depression,
   a U.S. imports fell.
   b U.S. exports fell.
   c U.S. GDP fell.
   d all of the above.
   e none of the above.

16 Which of the following is *not* a result of international trade in the United States?
   a Lower wages for skilled workers
   b Lower wages for unskilled workers
   c Lower profits in industries where competition is limited
   d Lower wages in industries where competition is limited
   e None of the above

17 The infant industry argument advocates
   a temporary protection while firms gain experience needed to compete with foreign rivals.
   b lowering prices to drive foreign rivals out of business.

c protection so that domestic firms can take advantage of economies of scale.

d subsidizing firms that face competition from foreign firms subsidized by their governments.

e quotas rather than tariffs.

18 Strategic trade theory can be used to argue for

a temporary protection while firms gain experience needed to compete with foreign rivals.

b lowering prices to drive foreign rivals out of business.

c protection so that domestic firms can take advantage of economies of scale.

d subsidizing firms that face competition from foreign firms subsidized by their governments.

e quotas rather than tariffs.

19 The organization established after World War II for the purpose of reducing trade barriers is called

a WTO.

b GATT.

c NAFTA.

d European Union.

e OECD.

20 Regional trading blocs can lead to

a the diversion of trade from member to nonmember countries.

b the diversion of trade from nonmember to member countries.

c the creation of trade among member countries.

d the creation of trade between member and nonmember countries.

e *b* and *c*.

Completion

1 _____ involves restricting the import of foreign goods.

2 Policies that affect imports or exports are called _____.

3 Taxes on imports are called _____.

4 When the government imposes quotas, firms licensed to import may earn extra profits, called _____.

5 An agreement whereby foreign firms limit sales of their good in domestic markets is called a _____.

6 Selling products abroad at prices below the cost of production is called _____.

7 The _____ proposes temporary protection while firms gain experience to become competitive.

8 Formed after World War II, the _____ promoted free trade among most of the world's countries.

9 The global trading organization that directed attention toward nontariff barriers, agricultural subsidies, and intellectual property is called _____.

10 Regional trading blocs, such as NAFTA or the European Union, expand trade within the bloc but

the net benefits may not be positive if there is too much _____.

Answers to Self-Test

True or False

1	t	6	t	11	f
2	f	7	t	12	t
3	f	8	t	13	f
4	t	9	t	14	t
5	t	10	f	15	f

Multiple Choice

1	e	6	e	11	a	16	a
2	a	7	e	12	b	17	a
3	c	8	d	13	c	18	c
4	b	9	c	14	e	19	b
5	e	10	b	15	d	20	e

Completion

1 Protection
2 commercial policies
3 tariffs
4 quota rents
5 voluntary export restraint
6 dumping
7 infant industry argument
8 General Agreement on Tariffs and Trade
9 World Trade Organization
10 trade diversion

Doing Economics: Tools and Practice Problems

We use the small open economy model to study the effects of three commercial policies: tariffs, quotas, and voluntary export restraints. This model starts with the idea that price is determined on world markets and that relative to that world market the country's output is too small to affect price. The country, in other words, is a price taker. For each of the policies we will determine the effects upon the market equilibrium and also the deadweight burdens. Tool Kit 18.1 shows how to get started.

Tool Kit 18.1 Finding the Free Trade Equilibrium in a Small Open Economy

In a small open economy the quantity demanded is what consumers demand at the fixed world price, and the quantity supplied is what producers offer for sale at that price. These quantities need not be equal. The difference is the level of imports or exports. Follow these steps.

Step one: Identify the world price, the demand curve, and the supply curve.

Step two: Find the quantity demanded. This is read off the demand curve at the world price.

Step three: Find the quantity supplied. This is read off the supply curve at the world price.

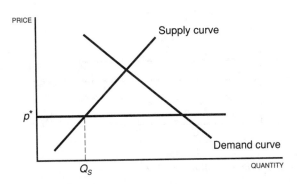

Step four: Find the level of imports or exports. If the quantity demanded exceeds the quantity supplied, then the country imports the goods. Otherwise the good is exported.

Imports = quantity demanded
− quantity supplied (if positive).

Exports = quantity supplied
− quantity demanded (if positive).

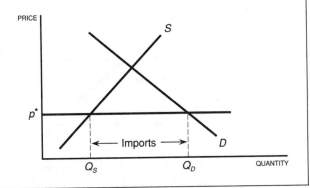

1 (Worked problem: small open economy) The world price of high-grade aluminum is $1,200 per metric ton. The United States demands and supplies are given below in Table 18.1.

Table 18.1

Demand		Supply	
Price	Quantity (metric tons)	Price	Quantity (metric tons)
$2,000	100,000	$2,000	400,000
$1,800	150,000	$1,800	300,000
$1,600	200,000	$1,600	200,000
$1,400	250,000	$1,400	100,000
$1,200	300,000	$1,200	50,000
$1,000	350,000	$1,000	25,000

a Find the quantity demanded and the quantity supplied.
b Is high-grade aluminum exported or imported? What is the amount?

Step-by-step solution

Step one: Identify the world price, the demand curve, and the supply curve. The world price is $1,400 and the demand and supply curves are given in Table 18.1.

Step two: Find the quantity demanded. When the price is $1,200, the quantity demanded is 300,000 metric tons.

Step three: Find the quantity supplied. When the price is $1,400, the quantity supplied is 50,000 metric tons.

Step four: Find the level of imports or exports. The quantity demanded exceeds the quantity supplied, so the country imports the good.

Imports = quantity demanded − quantity supplied
= 300,000 − 50,000 = 250,000.

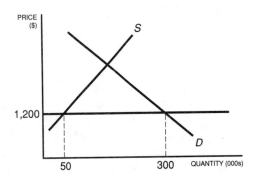

2 (Practice problem: small open economy) The world price of coffee is 4 cents per pound. The United States demands and supplies are given in Table 18.2.

a Find the quantity demanded and the quantity supplied.

b Is coffee exported or imported? What is the amount?

Table 18.2

Demand		Supply	
Price (cents per pound)	Quantity (million pounds)	Price (cents per pound)	Quantity (million pounds)
8	14,000	8	20,000
7	16,000	7	18,000
6	18,000	6	16,000
5	20,000	5	14,000
4	22,000	4	12,000
3	24,000	3	10,000
2	26,000	2	8,000
1	28,000	1	6,000

3 (Practice problem: small open economy) The world price of sugar is 1 cent per pound. The United States demand and supply curves are given in Table 18.3.

a Find the quantity demanded and the quantity supplied.

b Is sugar exported or imported? What is the amount?

Table 18.3

Demand		Supply	
Price (cents per pound)	Quantity (million pounds)	Price (cents per pound)	Quantity (million pounds)
4.0	1,000	4.0	900
3.5	1,100	3.5	850
3.0	1,200	3.0	800
2.5	1,300	2.5	750
2.0	1,400	2.0	700
1.5	1,500	1.5	650
1.0	1,600	1.0	600

Tariffs

Tariffs are taxes on imported goods. Economists analyze their impact by looking at how markets adjust. Like other taxes, they change market outcomes and bring about deadweight burdens. Fewer goods are sold and consumers lose surplus. Also, the economy wastes resources by producing goods that are more cheaply obtained abroad. We follow the usual procedure of starting with an equilibrium, shifting curves, finding the new equilibrium, and comparing. Tool Kit 18.2 shows how to find the deadweight burden of tariffs.

Tool Kit 18.2 Determining the Effects of Tariffs

Tariffs raise domestic prices above world price. This increase reduces consumption and increases production and creates deadweight burdens. These steps show how to analyze tariffs.

Step one: Identify the world price, the demand curve, the supply curve, and the tariff.

Step two: Find the new world price. The new world price increases by exactly the amount of the tariff.

New world price = old world price + tariff.

Step three: Find the new equilibrium quantity demanded, quantity supplied, and level of imports. Follow the steps of Tool Kit 18.1.

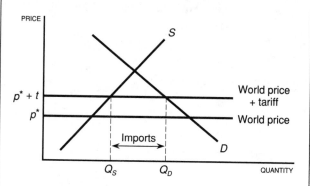

Step four: Calculate tariff revenue.

Tariff revenue = tariff × imports.

Step five: Show the area of the deadweight burden. There are two parts. Triangle *DEF* represents the loss in consumer surplus due to reduced consumption. Triangle *ABC* represents the waste of resources brought about by producing domestically when it is less expensive to import.

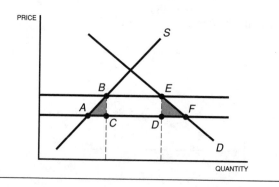

4 (Worked problem: tariffs) This problem continues with the market for high-grade aluminum. The demand and supply data are given in Table 18.1. The world price is $1,400 and the tariff rate is $200 per metric ton.

a Find the new equilibrium.
b Calculate tariff revenue.
c Show the deadweight burden.

Step-by-step solution

Step one: Identify the world price, the demand curve, the supply curve, and the tariff. The world price is $1,200, the demand and supply curves are in Table 18.1, and the tariff rate is $200 per metric ton.

Step two: Find the new world price. The new world price increases by exactly the amount of the tariff.

New world price = old world price + tariff
= $1,200 + $200 = $1,400.

Step three (a): Find the new equilibrium quantity demanded, quantity supplied, and level of imports. When the price is $1,400, the quantity demanded is 250,000, the quantity supplied is 100,000, and the level of imports is 250,000 − 100,000 = 150,000.

Step four (b): Calculate tariff revenue.

Tariff revenue = tariff × imports
= $200 × 150,000
= $30,000,000.

Step five (c): Show the area of the deadweight burden. There are two parts. Triangle *DEF* represents the loss in consumer surplus due to reduced consumption. Triangle *ABC* represents the waste of resources brought about by producing domestically when it is less expensive to import.

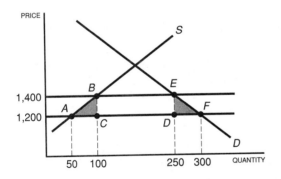

5 (Practice problem: tariffs) This problem continues with the market for coffee. The demand and supply curves are given in Table 18.2. The world price is 6 cents per pound and the tariff rate is 2 cents per pound.
a Find the new equilibrium.
b Calculate tariff revenue.
c Show the deadweight burden.
6 (Practice problem: tariffs) This problem continues with the market for sugar. The demand and supply curves are given in Table 18.3. The world price is 1 cent per pound and the tariff rate is 1/2 cent per pound.

a Find the new equilibrium.
b Calculate tariff revenue.
c Show the deadweight burden.

Quotas and Voluntary Export Restraints

Both quotas and VERs reduce imports. Quotas are imposed by the importing country, and VERs are "voluntarily" agreed to by the exporting country. Both raise prices, reduce consumption, and increase domestic production. Accordingly, both lead to deadweight burdens of exactly the same type as do tariffs. Follow along with Tool Kit 18.3.

Tool Kit 18.3 Quotas

Quotas, whether imposed or voluntary, raise prices, reduce consumption, increase production, and cause deadweight burdens. Follow these steps.

Step one: Identify the world price, the demand curve, the supply curve, and the quota.

Step two: Find the total supply curve. This is just the domestic supply curve added to the quota.

Total supply = domestic supply + quota.

Step three: Find the equilibrium price. Simply equate the total supply with the demand.

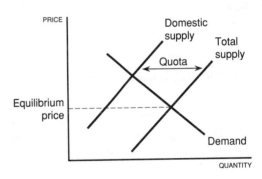

Step four: Find the domestic quantity supplied. This is read off the domestic supply curve.

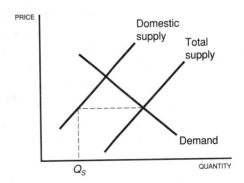

Step five: Calculate the quota rents. This is the extra money earned by licensed importers.

Quota rents = (new price − world price) × imports.

Step six: Show the area of the deadweight burden. There are two parts. Triangle *DEF* represents the loss in consumer surplus due to reduced consumption. Triangle *ABC* represents the waste of resources brought about by producing domestically when it is less expensive to import.

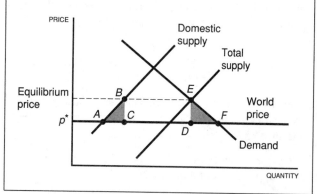

7 (Worked problem: tariffs) This problem continues with the market for high-grade aluminum. The demand and supply curves are given in Table 18.1. The world price is $1,200 and the import quota is 150,000 metric tons.
 a Find the new equilibrium.
 b Calculate quota rents.
 c Show the deadweight burden.

Step-by-step solution

Step one: Identify the world price, the demand curve, the supply curve, and the quota. The world price is $1,200, demand and supply are given in Table 18.1, and the quota is 150,000.

Step two: Find the total supply curve. This is just the domestic supply curve added to the quota.

Total supply = domestic supply + quota.

Supply

Price	Quantity (metric tons)
$2,000	400,000 + 150,000 = 550,000
$1,800	300,000 + 150,000 = 450,000
$1,600	200,000 + 150,000 = 350,000
$1,400	100,000 + 150,000 = 250,000
$1,200	50,000 + 150,000 = 200,000
$1,000	25,000 + 150,000 = 175,000

Step three: Find the equilibrium price. Total supply equals demand when the price is $1,400. The equilibrium quantity is 250,000.

Step four: Find the domestic quantity supplied. When the price is $1,400, domestic supply equals 100,000.

Step five: Calculate the quota rents. This is the extra money earned by licensed importers.

Quota rents = (new price − world price) × imports
= ($1,400 − $1,200) × 150,000.

Step six: Show the area of the deadweight burden. There are two parts. Triangle *DEF* represents the loss in consumer surplus due to reduced consumption. Triangle *ABC* represents the waste of resources brought about by producing domestically when it is less expensive to import.

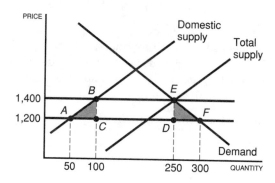

8 (Practice problem: quotas) This problem continues with the market for coffee. The demand and supply curves are given in Table 18.2. The world price is 6 cents and the import quota is 10,000 million pounds.
 a Find the new equilibrium.
 b Calculate quota rents.
 c Show the deadweight burden.
9 (Practice problem: quotas) This problem continues with the market for sugar. The demand and supply curves are given in Table 18.3. The world price is 1 cent and the import quota is 1,000 million pounds.
 a Find the new equilibrium.
 b Calculate quota rents.
 c Show the deadweight burden.

Answers to Problems

2 *a* Quantity demanded = 22,000; quantity supplied = 12,000.
 b Imports = 22,000 − 12,000 = 10,000.
3 *a* Quantity demanded = 1,600; quantity supplied = 600.
 b Imports = 1,600 − 600 = 1,000.
5 *a* Quantity demanded = 18,000; quantity supplied = 16,000; imports = 18,000 − 16,000 = 2,000.
 b Tariff revenue = 2 × 2,000 = 4,000 million cents = $40,000,000.

c

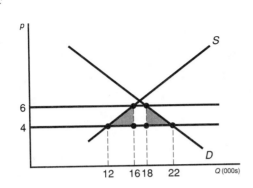

6 *a* Quantity demanded = 1,500; quantity supplied = 650; imports = 1,500 − 650 = 850.

  b Tariff revenue = 0.5 × 850 = 425 million cents = $4,250,000.

c

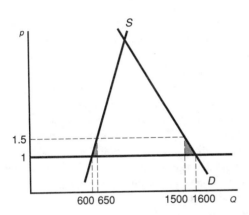

8 *a* New price = 6 cents per pound; quantity demanded = 18,000; quantity supplied = 16,000; imports = 18,000 − 16,000 = 2,000.

b Quota rents = 2 × 2,000 = 4,000 million cents = $40,000,000.

c

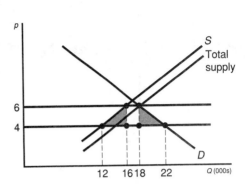

9 *a* New price = 1.5 cents per pound; quantity demanded = 1,500; quantity supplied = 650; imports = 1,500 − 650 = 850.

  b Quota rents = 0.5 × 850 = 425 million cents = $4,250,000.

c

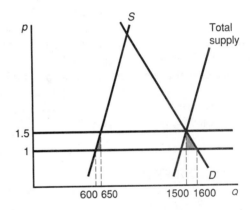

CHAPTER 19 | Strategic Behavior

Chapter Review

When how one's rivals may respond to one's actions is important, it is necessary to think strategically. That is, one must anticipate the rivals' reactions and choose the actions that will result in the best outcome. Game theory studies these sorts of situations. This chapter outlines some of the important insights of game theory with examples from politics, sports, immigration, banking, and many other areas. These ideas give deeper insight into many models of imperfect competition that appeared in Part Three.

ESSENTIAL CONCEPTS

1   **Strategic behavior** occurs when decision makers must take into account the reactions of others in choosing their own best actions. The study of strategic behavior is called game theory.

2   Strategic situations are represented using the game table, which shows the outcomes resulting from the strategy choices of the decision makers, called players. They try to anticipate the strategies of their rivals and choose their own best strategy in order to bring about a good outcome. A game reaches its **Nash equilibrium** when each player's choice is his best strategy given the actions of the other players. Sometimes, however, a strategy is best regardless of what others do. This is called a **dominant strategy**.

3   The Prisoner's Dilemma is a simple game in which players fail to realize potential gains because for each, the dominant strategy is not to cooperate. Thus, partners in crime turn state's evidence, firms compete in price wars, countries engage in arms races, and politicians attack each other with negative advertising. In each case the players pursuit of their own self-interest leads to outcomes that make both parties worse off.

4   In other games, only one player may have a dominant strategy. In these games this player chooses the dominant strategy and the other picks her best response. Still other strategic situations have no players with dominant strategies and may also have two potential Nash equilibria, one more efficient than the other. The case of bank runs is an example of this latter game, where in one equilibrium, all are confident in the bank's solvency. In the other equilibrium, all try to withdraw at once, and the bank fails.

5   When games are played more than once, the players must also consider the future consequences of current strategies. They may threaten retaliation for noncooperative behavior or develop reputations for cooperative behavior. In these **repeated games** the rational decision maker decides what to do by starting from the last period and working backward. This process is called **rollback**, and it may lead players to choose cooperation even when their short-term incentives are to cheat. Also, institutions, such as deposit insurance, may guide the players to cooperative outcomes.

6   In **sequential games**, players take turns moving. These games are represented using a diagram of their **game tree**. This approach is especially useful in evaluating whether threats are credible. Strategies that involve unbelievable threats are said to be time inconsistent. That is, when the time comes to carry out the threat, it is not in the player's best interest to do so. Sometimes, however, players may make commitments that force them to carry out their threats.

BEHIND THE ESSENTIAL CONCEPTS

1 Many problems in economics are made simpler by the absence of strategic behavior. For example, a firm in a competitive market can ignore the reactions of others. It simply observes the price and computes the profit-maximizing level of output and demand for inputs. It need not worry about how its rivals may respond to its actions, because their reactions are too small to affect the market.

2 At the other extreme of possible market structures, a monopolist also may ignore strategic behavior. The market demand shows the output for each price, and the firm simply computes the price that maximizes its profits. There are no other firms in the industry; so the monopolist need never worry about their reactions. Strategic behavior is important for oligopolies, where a few firms dominate the industry. Here an individual firm knows that its rivals will observe its actions and make some response. Thus it is vitally important to have a good idea about what the other firms may do.

3 In the basic competitive model, households and firms are rational and pursue their own self-interest. The outcome, however, is an efficient allocation of resources. In the Prisoner's Dilemma the players again are rational and pursue their self-interest, but the outcome is inefficient. Thus the problem must not be self-interest but rather incentives. Adam Smith's invisible hand is on duty in the competitive market, guiding the self-interested suppliers and demanders to choose efficient actions. In the Prisoner's Dilemma the invisible hand is absent.

4 Players who understand that they are in the Prisoner's Dilemma may want to make promises that they will cooperate. For example, you might say to your roommate, "Please be quiet tonight while I study and I will be quiet in the future when you need to study." In deciding whether to be quiet for you, your roommate must evaluate the credibility of your promise of future cooperation. In thinking about what you will do in the future, he evaluates the time consistency of your proposal and practices rollback. If you cannot convince him, you are in the Prisoner's Dilemma. One solution is an institution, such as a hall monitor, that makes sure that everyone is quiet during study hours. Another solution is for you to develop a reputation for honoring your promises or for punishing people who disturb your study.

SELF-TEST

True or False

1 Strategic behavior involves considering the responses of rivals to one's strategies.

2 In the basic competitive model, firms behave strategically.

3 In oligopolies, firms behave strategically.

4 When the best strategy depends on the strategy chosen by others, the player has a dominant strategy.

5 In the Nash equilibrium, each player chooses the best strategy given that all other players choose their best strategy.

6 In the Prisoner's Dilemma, each player chooses to cooperate.

7 In any game, at least one player has a dominant strategy.

8 There can be only one Nash equilibrium in a game.

9 In repeated games, the players alternate in choosing their strategies.

10 The game table is useful in representing sequential games.

11 The game tree is useful in representing sequential games.

12 Reputations for good behavior are costly to acquire in the short run.

13 When games are repeated, the players start at the end and work backward.

14 The tit-for-tat strategy may help players achieve cooperation in repeated games.

15 There is time inconsistency if when the time comes to carry out a threat, the player may not choose to do so.

Multiple Choice

1 Individuals or firms are engaging in strategic behavior if they
   a maximize profits.
   b choose the best alternative in their opportunity set.
   c act efficiently.
   d consider the responses of rivals to their choices.
   e all of the above.

2 The study of strategic behavior is called
   a strategy theory.
   b reputation theory.
   c equilibrium theory.
   d market theory.
   e game theory.

3 In which of the following market structures do firms behave strategically?
   a Oligopoly
   b Monopoly
   c Monopsony
   d Competition
   e None of the above

4 A diagram showing the players, their strategies, and the payoffs in each outcome for a game played simultaneously is called a
   a sequential game.
   b repeated game.

   c game table.

   d game tree.

   e Prisoner's Dilemma.

5 In the Prisoner's Dilemma game,

   a cooperation is the dominant strategy for each player.

   b cheating (not cooperating) is the dominant strategy for each player.

   c only one player has a dominant strategy.

   d neither player has a dominant strategy.

   e one player's dominant strategy is to cooperate and the other's is to cheat.

6 In the Nash equilibrium of the Prisoner's Dilemma game,

   a the outcome is best for both players.

   b the outcome is worse for both players.

   c one player cooperates.

   d both players cooperate.

   e *a* and *d*.

7 When each player chooses his best strategy given that all other players are choosing their best strategy, the game has reached its

   a Nash equilibrium.

   b dominant strategy.

   c time inconsistency.

   d efficiency equilibrium.

   e rollback.

8 In games where only one of two players has a dominant strategy,

   a there is no equilibrium.

   b there may be two equilibria.

   c one players chooses her dominant strategy and the other chooses his best strategy given the choice of the rival.

   d both players choose the dominant strategy.

   e players choose the tit-for-tat strategy.

9 In the banking panic game,

   a all depositors have a dominant strategy, which is to withdraw their money.

   b one depositor has a dominant strategy, to withdraw her money, and the others follow.

   c no player has a dominant strategy.

   d there is a unique equilibrium outcome.

   e the choices show time inconsistency.

10 When games are repeated, the equilibrium

   a is the same in each period as would occur if the game were played only once.

   b is time inconsistent.

   c may be different than if the game were played only once.

   d is inefficient.

   e *b* and *d*.

11 In repeated Prisoner's Dilemma games,

   a the equilibrium is always inefficient.

   b the players may cooperate.

   c the actions are time inconsistent.

   d the strategy choices are made one following the other.

   e none of the above.

12 When a player starts at the end and works backward, she engages in

   a rollback.

   b her dominant strategy.

   c a Nash equilibrium.

   d time-inconsistent behavior.

   e a tit-for-tat strategy.

13 Which of the following may help players in repeated Prisoner's Dilemma games achieve cooperation?

   a Tit-for-tat strategies

   b Reputations for cooperating

   c Institutions

   d Reputations for punishing noncooperative behavior

   e All of the above

14 If a Prisoner's Dilemma game is played exactly twice, the equilibrium is

   a both players cooperate in each period.

   b one player cooperates in each period.

   c both players cooperate in the first period and neither cooperates in the second.

   d neither player cooperates in the first period and both cooperate in the second.

   e neither player cooperates in either period.

15 If players respond to cooperation by cooperating but punish cheating, they are engaging in

   a time inconsistency.

   b tit-for-tat strategies.

   c dominant strategies.

   d rollback.

   e beggar thy neighbor strategies.

16 If when the time comes to carry out a threat, the player chooses not to do so, the actions are said to be

   a time inconsistent.

   b strategic.

   c cooperative.

   d dominant.

   e inefficient.

17 Economists represent sequential games using the

   a game table.

   b rollback.

   c game tree.

   d tit-for-tat strategy.

   e game room.

18 In a sequential game the second player observes the first player's move before choosing her own strategy. The first player

   a must consider how the second player may respond to his choice.

   b cannot credibly threaten to punish the second player.

   c must choose time inconsistency.

d cannot use rollback.

e must choose time inconsistency unless he has a dominant strategy.

19 An existing firm threatens new entrants with price wars. The new entrants will

a stay out of the market.

b enter and fight.

c evaluate whether the existing firm has the incentive to carry the threat.

d use a tit-for-tat strategy.

e act in a time-inconsistent manner to confuse the existing firm.

20 To make threats credible, players may

a develop a reputation for carrying out threats.

b create a commitment to carry out the threat.

c set up an institution to force the threatened action.

d all of the above.

e none of the above.

Completion

1 When there is a(n) _____, one must consider the reactions of others.

2 A diagram showing the players, their strategies, and the possible outcomes is called a _____.

3 A particular strategy is best regardless of the choices of the rivals is called a(n) _____.

4 In a(n) _____, each player chooses the best strategy given the actual choices by the other players.

5 When games are repeated, players use _____, which is to start at the end and work backward.

6 The _____ strategy promises to cooperate if the other cooperates but to punish cheating.

7 When the game is played more than once, it is called a(n) _____ game.

8 The _____ is used to diagram the sequential game.

9 Players choose their strategies one after another in a(n) _____ game.

10 There is _____ if when the time comes to carry out a threat, it is not in the player's interest to do so.

Answers to Self-Test

True or False

1	t	6	f	11	t
2	f	7	f	12	t
3	t	8	f	13	t
4	f	9	f	14	t
5	t	10	f	15	t

Multiple Choice

1	*d*	6	*b*	11	*b*	16	*a*
2	*e*	7	*a*	12	*a*	17	*c*
3	*a*	8	*c*	13	*e*	18	*a*
4	*d*	9	*c*	14	*e*	19	*c*
5	*b*	10	*c*	15	*b*	20	*d*

Completion

1 strategic situation

2 game tree

3 dominant strategy

4 Nash equilibrium

5 rollback

6 tit-for-tat

7 repeated

8 game tree

9 sequential

10 time inconsistency

Tool Kit 19.1 Playing the Simultaneous Game

To find the Nash equilibrium in the simultaneous game, first set up the game table and then analyze the strategy choices. Follow these steps.

Step one: Identify the players, their strategies, and the payoffs in all of the possible outcomes.

Step two: Set up the game table as shown. Note that there are two players, and each has two strategies. The payoffs lie in the boxes.

		Player B	
		Left	Right
	Top	10 / 8	8 / 6
Player A			
	Bottom	1 / 4	2 / 3

Step three: Find the best responses for player A. First, let player B choose the left column. Then find A's higher payoff and circle it. Let player B choose the right column and circle A's higher payoff. If both circles lie on the same row, then A has a dominant strategy.

		Player B	
		Left	Right
	Top	10 / ⑧	8 / ⑥
Player A			
	Bottom	1 / 4	2 / 3

Step four: Find the best responses for player B. First, let player A choose the top row. Circle B's higher payoff. Then let player A choose the bottom row and circle B's higher payoff.

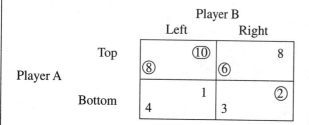

Player B

		Left	Right
Player A	Top	⑧ ⑩	⑥ 8
	Bottom	4 1	3 ②

Step five: Find the equilibrium. Any of the four boxes with two circles is a Nash equilibrium. There may be one or more.

Nash Equilibrium →

Player B

		Left	Right
Player A	Top	⑧ ⑩	⑥ 8
	Bottom	4 1	3 ②

1 (Worked problem: simultaneous games) Two neighboring farmers face the threat of flood damage equal to $25,000 each. They could protect themselves by building a series of dikes for a total cost of $30,000. Thus if they share in the cost, there is no flood damage and each loses only his share of the cost, which is $15,000. If neither does anything, each will lose $25,000 in flood damage. If only one builds the dikes, the builder will lose $30,000 but the other will lose $0. (He will free ride on the flood protection and escape payment.)

a Set up the game table.

b Find the best responses of each player. Does either have a dominant strategy?

c Find the Nash equilibrium.

Step-by-step solution

Step one: Identify the players, their strategies, and the payoffs in all of the possible outcomes. The two farmers are the players and each has two possible strategies: to build or not to build. The payoffs are given in the problem.

Step two: Set up the game table.

Farmer B

	Build a dike	Do not build
Farmer A Build a dike	−$15,000 −$15,000	$0 −$30,000
Do not build	$0 −$30,000	−$25,000 −$25,000

Step three: Find the best responses for player A. Circle the payoffs. If B builds, then A will choose not to build ($0 > −$15,000). If B does not build, then A will also choose not to build (−$25,000 > −$30,000). A has a dominant strategy, which is not to build the dike.

Farmer B

	Build a dike	Do not build
Farmer A Build a dike	−$15,000 −$15,000	$0 −$30,000
Do not build	⓪$0 −$30,000	(−$25,000) −$25,000

Step four: Find the best responses for player B. B also has a dominant strategy, which is also not to build the dike.

Farmer B

	Build a dike	Do not build
Farmer A Build a dike	−$15,000 −$15,000	($0) −$30,000
Do not build	$0 −$30,000	(−$25,000) −$25,000

Step five: Find the equilibrium. The equilibrium is that neither builds the dike.

Farmer B

	Build a dike	Do not build
Farmer A Build a dike	−$15,000 −$15,000	$0 −$30,000
Do not build	$0 −$30,000	(−$25,000) (−$25,000)

2 (Practice problem: simultaneous games) Chiaravelli and Fiegenshau are the only two dentists in Plainville. They have been colluding, sharing the market and earning monopoly profits of $100,000 each for several years. Fiegenshau is considering reducing his price. He estimates that if Chiaravelli keeps his price at current levels, Fiegenshau would earn $150,000, although Chiaravelli's earnings would fall to $25,000. There is also the possibility that Chiaravelli would compete against Fiegenshau. The resulting price war would reduce the earnings of each to $40,000.

a Set up the game table.

b Find the best responses.

c Find the Nash equilibrium.

3 (Practice problem: simultaneous games) Upper Peninsula Airlines and Northern Airways share the market from Chicago to the winter resorts in the North. If they cooperate, they can extract enough monopoly

profits to earn $400,000 each, but unbridled competition would reduce profits to $50,000 each. If one is foolish enough to cooperate in its pricing policy while the other undercuts it, the cooperating firm would earn $0, and the competing firm would earn $800,000.

a Set up the game table.

b Find the best responses of each player. Does either have a dominant strategy?

c Find the Nash equilibrium.

4 (Practice problem: simultaneous games) Rosewood College and Elmwood College are the best private schools in the state. Each also prides itself on its lacrosse team. If neither offers scholarships for promising players, then obviously the cost of scholarships will be zero. For $20,000 in scholarships, either could attract the best players (if the other did not offer scholarships), win the conference championship, and attract at least $50,000 in new donations. In this case, however, donations at the losing school would fall by $30,000. On the other hand, if both offered scholarships, there would be no advantage, no extra donations, and each would have spent the $20,000 for nothing.

a Set up the game table.

b Find the best responses of each player. Does either have a dominant strategy?

c Find the Nash equilibrium.

5 (Practice problem: simultaneous games) There are two suppliers of dilithium in the market. Brobdinagius controls 95 percent of the market towers over its tiny rival Liliputus. Each has the option of a high-price passive or low-price aggressive strategy. Their payoffs are given below.

Strategies		Payoffs	
Borbdinagius	Liliputus	Brobdinagius	Liliputus
Aggressive	Aggressive	$10,000,000	$1,000,000
Passive	Passive	$15,000,000	$1,500,000
Aggressive	Passive	$11,000,000	$1,100,000
Passive	Aggressive	$12,000,000	$3,000,000

a Set up the game table.

b Find the best responses of each player. Does either have a dominant strategy?

c Find the Nash equilibrium.

6 (Practice problem: simultaneous games) Two consulting firms, Blather and Persiflage, plan to join forces for a big project. Unfortunately, they use different statistical software packages. Blather uses Statistica and Persiflage uses Numerology. For the project, they will have to use the same software. The payoffs are given below.

Software		Payoffs	
Blather	Persiflage	Blather	Persiflage
Statistica	Statistica	$4 million	$3 million
Numerology	Numerology	$3 million	$4 million
Statistica	Numerology	$1 million	$1 million
Numerology	Statistica	$0	$0

a Set up the game table.

b Find the best responses of each player. Does either have a dominant strategy?

c Find the Nash equilibrium.

7 (Practice problem: simultaneous games) Computix needs someone trained in the Lynus operating system to maintain its network. Fred Bennet is a qualified person who would love to work at a company like Lynus. Each is considering attending a job fair. Of course, unless both attend, they cannot join. It costs $2,000 for either to attend the fair. If they both go, Computix will meet and hire Fred and each will gain $50,000 − $2,000 = $48,000. If neither goes, their gains will be zero.

a Set up the game table.

b Find the best responses of each player. Does either have a dominant strategy?

c Find the Nash equilibrium.

Tool Kit 19.2 Playing the Sequential Game

To find the equilibrium of the sequential game, first set up the game tree. Begin at the end and roll back to the beginning. Follow these steps.

Step one: Identify the players, their strategies, the timing, and the payoffs.

Step two: Set up the game tree as shown. The payoffs are given in parentheses (payoff for player one, payoff for player two).

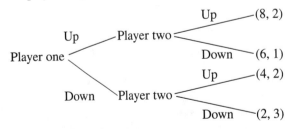

Step three: Determine the choices of player two at the end of the game. Circle the best strategy. If player one chooses Up, then player two will choose Up because 2 > 1. If player one chooses Down, player two will choose Down because 3 > 2.

Step four: Roll back and write player one's payoff under his strategy. (If he chooses Up, then he knows that two will choose Up and he will get a payoff of 8.)

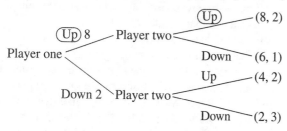

Step five: Determine the choice of player one and circle it.

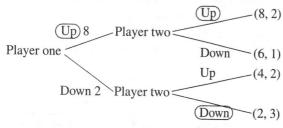

Step six: Follow the circled strategies to the equilibrium payoffs.

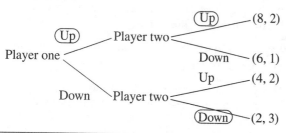

8 (Worked problem: sequential games) Alone in the market for garbage collection, Mr. Tidy earns $100,000 per year. A new firm, Miss Neat 'n Clean, threatens entry. If it enters, Mr. Tidy may passively share the market or fight aggressively. Their net payoffs in each outcome are given below.

Strategies		Payoffs	
Neat 'n Clean	Mr. Tidy	Neat 'n Clean	Mr. Tidy
Stay out		$0	$100,000
Enter	share	$50,000	$50,000
Enter	fight	−$20,000	$10,000

a Set up the game tree.

b Determine Mr. Tidy's best strategy.
c Determine Miss Neat 'n Clean's best strategy.
d Find the equilibrium.

Step-by-step Solution

Step one: Identify the players, their strategies, the timing, and the payoffs. The players are Mr. Tidy, who can fight or share, and Miss Neat 'n Clean, who can enter or stay out. The payoffs appear in the table.

Step two: Set up the game tree. The payoffs are (Miss Neat 'n Clean, Mr. Tidy).

Fight (−$20,000, $10,000)

Mr. Tidy

Enter   Share ($50,000, $50,000)

Miss Neat 'n Clean

Stay out   ($0, $100,000)

Step three: Go to the end and determine the strategies of the second player. If Miss Neat 'n Clean enters, Mr. Tidy will choose to share because $50,000 > $10,000.

Fight (−$20,000, $10,000)

Mr. Tidy

Enter   (Share) ($50,000, $50,000)

Miss Neat 'n Clean

Stay out   ($0, $100,000)

Step four: Roll back and write the first player's payoffs next to its strategies. Miss Neat 'n Clean receives $50,000 because Mr. Tidy will share if it enters.

Fight (−$20,000, $10,000)

Mr. Tidy

Enter   Share ($50,000, $50,000)
($50,000)

Miss Neat 'n Clean

Stay out   ($0, ¢100,000)

Step five: Determine the choice of the first player and circle it. It will choose to enter because $50,000 > $0.

Nash equilibrium

Step six: Follow the circled strategies to the equilibrium. Miss Neat 'n Clean enters and Mr. Tidy shares the market. Each receives $50,000.

9 (Practice problem: sequential games) TicTec is considering spinning off (that is, selling to the market) its successful video game operation and concentrating on its core business of producing special effects for music videos. It worries that the spinoff will compete with TicTec's core business in the future. The payoffs are given below.

Strategies		Payoffs	
TicTec	Spinoff	TicTec	Spinoff
Sell	Compete	$200,000	$200,000
Sell	Do not compete	$300,000	$150,000
Do not sell		$250,000	

a Set up the game tree.
b Determine TicTec's best strategy.
c Determine Spinoff's best strategy.
d Find the equilibrium.

10 (Practice problem: sequential games) Venturo Capital is considering financing a new start-up that promises a new formula for a longer-lasting concrete. The start-up has a great idea, but will it actually make concrete or will the owners use the financing to conduct research for their next business. The payoffs are given below.

Strategies		Payoffs	
Venturo	Start-up	Venturo	Start-up
Finance	make concrete	$2,000,000	$400,000
Finance	no concrete	−$1,000,000	$6,000,000
Do not finance		$0	$0

a Set up the game trees.
b Determine the start-up' best strategy.
c Determine Venturo's best strategy.
d Find the equilibrium.

Answers to Problems

2 a

		Chiaravelli	
		Cooperate	Compete
Fiegenshau	Cooperate	C = $100,000 F = $100,000	C = $150,000 F = $ 25,000
	Compete	C = $ 25,000 F = $150,000	C = $40,000 F = $40,000

b Show that competition is the equilibrium. For each party, competition is always the best alternative. If Chiaravelli cooperates, then Fiegenshau can earn more by competing ($150,000 > $100,000). If Chiaravelli competes, again Fiegenshau earns more by competing ($40,000 > $25,000). The same is true for Chiaravelli.
c The equilibrium is both choosing to compete.

3 a

		Upper Peninsula	
		Cooperate	Compete
Northern	Cooperate	UP = $400,000 N = $400,000	UP = $800,000 N = $50
	Compete	UP = $0 N = $800,000	UP = $50,000 F = $50,000

b If Northern competes, Upper Peninsula prefers to compete ($800,000 > $400,000). If Northern cooperates, Upper Peninsula still prefers to compete ($50,000 > $0). If Upper Peninsula competes, Northern prefers to compete ($800,000 > $400,000). If Upper Peninsula cooperates, Northern still prefers to compete ($50,000 > $0).
c Since both always prefer competition, the equilibrium is that both compete and profits are $50,000 each.

4 a

		Elmwood	
		Cooperate	Compete
Rosewood	Cooperate	E = $0 R = $0	E = $30,000 F = −$30,000
	Compete	E = −$30,000 R = $30,000	C = −$20,000 F = −$20,000

b If Rosewood cooperates and does not offer scholarships, Elmwood prefers to compete and offer them ($30,000 > $0). If Rosewood competes and offers scholarships, Elmwood still prefers to offer them (−$20,000 > −$30,000). If Elmwood cooperates and does not offer scholarships, Rosewood prefers to offer them ($30,000 > $0). If Elmwood competes and offers scholarships, Rosewood still prefers to offer them (−$20,000 > −$30,000).
c Since both always prefer competition, the equilibrium is that both compete, offer scholarships, and lose $20,000 each.

5 a

		Brobdinagius	
		Aggressive	Passive
Liliputius	Aggressive	$10,000,000 $1,000,000	($12,000,000) ($3,000,000)
	Passive	$11,000,000 ($1,100,000)	($15,000,000) $1,500,000

b Brobdinagius has a dominant strategy. It is to be passive. Liliputius is aggressive when Brobdinagius is passive, and passive when Brobdinagius is aggressive.

c   The Nash equilibrium is Brobdinagius passive and Liliputius aggressive.

6   *a*

	Blather	
	Statistica	Numerology
Persiflage Statistica	�)4 ⑤$3$	$0 $0
Numerology	$1 $1	⑥$3$ ⑦$4$

b   If Blather uses Statistic, Persiflage will also. If Blather uses Numerology, Statistic a will use the same. Similarly, Blather's best choice is to match the choice of Numerology.

c   There are two Nash equilibria: one in which both use Statistica and one in which both use Numerology.

7   *a*

	Computix	
	Attend	Do not attend
Fred Attend	⑨$48,000 ⑩$48,000	$0 −$2,000
Do not attend	−$2,000 $0	⑪$0 ⑫$0

b   Fred will attend if he thinks Computix will be there, but will not attend if he thinks it will not be there. The same is true of Computix.

c   There are two Nash equilibria. One has them both attending, the other has neither. The former is better for both players.

9   *a*

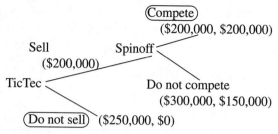

b   If TicTec sells, the spinoff will compete because $200,000 > $150,000. In that case, TicTec will earn only $200,000; therefore, TicTec will not sell because $250,000 > $200,000.

c   The equilibrium is that TicTec will not sell.

10   *a*

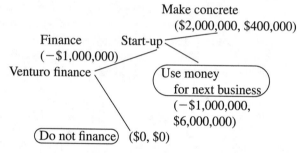

b   The start-up will use the money for its next business because $6,000,000 > $400,000. Venturo will not do the financing because $0 > −$1,000,000.

c   The equilibrium is no financing and no concrete.

CHAPTER 20

Technological Change

Chapter Review

The basic model of perfect competition assumes that the goods produced and the technology used to produce them do not change. In this chapter, the emphasis shifts to firms as they actively compete to discover new products and new ways of producing. Although many firms may be involved, the race for new ideas brings with it many of the aspects of imperfect competition covered in Chapters 12 to 15.

The most important point made in this chapter is that imperfect competition is not all bad. It brings with it the positive benefits of technological advance. Government policy to promote technological change includes granting patents, subsidizing research and development (R & D), and occasionally protecting infant industries.

ESSENTIAL CONCEPTS

1   In the basic competitive model, there is one lowest-cost way of producing, and all firms adopt this technology. The entry of new firms into the market soon drives away any profits, and all firms settle down to produce at the minimum of the average cost curve. The world of **technological change,** however, is vastly different. Firms compete aggressively to develop new products or production processes so that they can earn monopoly profits, at least for a while. For various reasons, the study of technological change must focus on imperfect competition.

2   The development of new ideas fuels the technological change that makes possible new products and new ways of producing. These ideas are **intellectual property**. They differ from basic goods in that they are **nonrivalrous**. That is, the marginal cost of using an

idea is zero. **Patents** give property rights to these ideas. This gives the owner the exclusive right to market the idea, and the marketing profits provide the incentive to produce new ideas.

3   Patent policy involves two types of trade-offs.

   a   The first issue is the **life** of the patent. Longer patents offer greater rewards for winning the race, and at the same time they promote research and development. On the other hand, for the duration of the patent, the firm sells at the monopoly price, which is above marginal cost, and so causes short-run inefficiencies; i.e., deadweight losses.

   b   The second issue is the **breadth** of the patent. Should patents be given for the narrowly defined idea or something more general? More broadly defined patents increase the rewards for R & D; however, access to the idea is restricted, and this restriction inhibits any subsequent innovative activity that might build on the patented idea. Because not all ideas are patentable and because to obtain a patent the firm must disclose details of the idea, firms sometimes forgo applying for one and keep the idea a **trade secret.** In this case, the firm earns monopoly profits until its competitors discover the idea or a better one.

4   **Basic research** on the nature of fundamental ideas generates such widespread external benefits that it has the two characteristics of **public goods:** Basic research produces knowledge, and it is difficult (not to mention undesirable) to exclude others from learning and taking advantage of new knowledge. Also, the marginal cost of giving another user access to new knowledge is certainly zero. Because basic research has the characteristic features of public goods, the government has an important role to play in providing funding for such work.

5 Because R & D creates external benefits not captured through patents, most economists advocate additional government policies to encourage it. Tax credits for increased R & D spending are one form of subsidy used in the United States. Also, the **infant industry argument for protection** says that new industries require protection against foreign competition until they move down the learning curve and acquire sufficient expertise to compete effectively. Further, antitrust laws can be relaxed to allow for joint ventures.

BEHIND THE ESSENTIAL CONCEPTS

1 Most of microeconomics sings the praises of perfect competition, especially to the extent that it allocates resources efficiently given the existing production technology. But does a perfectly competitive economy always find the best way to generate more advanced technologies of production, better products, and new ways of doing things? This chapter suggests that the answer is no. In order to encourage R & D, the government set up the patent system to motivate firms toward innovation by rewarding the winner with a period of freedom from competition. Perhaps paradoxically, government creates monopoly to encourage competition.

2 Technological advance is a vital engine of economic growth. Because it is so important, government promotes it with a wide range of complementary policies. Longer-lived and more broadly defined patents increase the rewards for R & D, while tax subsidies reduce the cost. Government also provides direct funding for basic research.

3 Economists consider the infant industry argument for protection to be valid but dangerous. Sometimes the protected industry gains expertise through experience and becomes a world-class competitor; other times the industry becomes inefficient and requires constant government support to survive. The difficulty is determining which industries will thrive and which will not.

4 You learned the basic logic of externalities in Chapter 11: whenever costs or benefits of some decision are not borne entirely by the decision maker, there is inefficiency. Most important to note in this chapter are the external benefits not captured by the firm that invests in R & D. These **positive externalities** include the fruits of subsequent R & D following an initial discovery, the gains after the expiration of the patent, and the consumer surplus arising from the application of the new idea. The firm ignores these externalities and thus undervalues the true social benefit of the R & D. Government policy can improve matters by promoting additional research efforts.

SELF-TEST

True or False

1 Firms engage in R & D expenditures so that they can participate in competitive markets.
2 A patent confers the exclusive right to produce and market an innovation for a limited period of time.
3 Patents and copyrights are forms of intellectual property.
4 The firm that finishes second in a patent race wins nothing.
5 Holders of patents set the price of their goods equal to marginal cost.
6 Patents promote dynamic efficiency at the expense of short-run inefficiency.
7 The length of patents is set to balance the costs of monopoly pricing by patent holders against the incentives to innovate.
8 Defining a patent more broadly might reduce the rate of innovation by denying access to previous innovations.
9 Any firm eligible for a patent will surely apply for one.
10 The cost of R & D is a variable cost of production.
11. The learning curve shows how fixed costs decline with experience.
12 One advantage that smaller firms have in R & D is their better access to capital markets.
13 Venture capital firms specialize in assessing the prospects of R & D ventures and providing capital to innovating firms.
14 The market is unlikely to provide enough basic research because basic research is a public good.
15 The antitrust laws inhibit firms from engaging in joint ventures.

Multiple Choice

1 Capitalism is a process of
 a steady and smooth growth in the living standards of every individual.
 b stagnation, in which the same goods are produced in the same way and distributed to the same people.
 c creative destruction, in which new products and technologies continually destroy existing jobs, firms, and even entire industries.
 d efficient allocation of resources in the short run, without any incentives for technological advance.
 e b and d.
2 Firms engage in R & D expenditures in order to
 a destroy their rivals.
 b provide beneficial externalities to society.
 c advance knowledge, which is a public good.
 d gain market power and charge prices above costs.
 e promote perfect competition.
3 Research and development refers to expenditures intended to

a discover new ideas and products.

b discover new technologies.

c develop products and bring them to market.

d all of the above.

e *a* and *b*.

4 A patent is

a a property right to an idea.

b the right to produce and sell an invention or innovation for all time.

c the right to produce and sell an invention or innovation for a limited time.

d *a* and *b*.

e *a* and *c*.

5 Patents

a promote short-run efficiency by encouraging firms to set price equal to marginal cost.

b stimulate research and innovation and promote dynamic efficiency.

c are awarded to the firm that has devoted the most resources to researching and developing the idea.

d are given for advances in basic knowledge.

e all of the above.

6 In the United States, the typical patent life is 17 years. The length involves a trade-off between

a short-run inefficiency and incentives to innovate.

b greater incentives to innovate and stimulation of subsequent innovation through greater access to past innovations.

c promoting research and fostering new product development.

d the profits of innovators and those of rivals.

e all of the above.

7 The breadth of patent coverage involves a trade-off between

a short-run inefficiency and incentives to innovate.

b greater incentives to innovate and stimulation of subsequent innovation through greater access to past innovations.

c promoting research and fostering new product development.

d the profits of innovators and those of rivals.

e all of the above.

8 Direct rewards from R & D are given

a in proportion to R & D expenditures.

b in proportion to market share.

c based on how many positive externalities are generated.

d on a winner-take-all basis.

e equally to all who entered the race.

9 A patent might not be awarded for an innovation if

a the innovator chose not to apply for the patent, preferring to hide the advance as a trade secret.

b the idea was too broad to be patentable.

c other firms had tried harder to find this particular innovation.

d too many jobs would be destroyed if the patent were awarded.

e *a* and *b*.

10 When patent holders raise price above marginal cost, there is a sacrifice of

a trade secrets.

b dynamic efficiency.

c infant industries.

d public goods.

e short-run efficiency.

11 R & D expenditures are

a variable costs.

b fixed costs.

c marginal costs.

d U-shaped average costs.

e none of the above.

12 Which of the following is true?

a Large firms have advantages in R & D because they may have better access to capital markets.

b Large firms have advantages in R & D because they can reap the cost savings on sales of more units.

c Small firms have advantages in R & D because of the bureaucratic environment in large corporations.

d All of the above.

e *a* and *b*.

13 Learning by doing refers to

a the fact that education only signals higher productivity; it does not increase productivity.

b the idea that as firms gain experience from production, their costs fall.

c the fact that R & D is wasteful because firms must produce products before they can innovate.

d the fact that R & D is the only way to lower costs.

e none of the above.

14 The learning curve

a shows the trade-off between short-run and dynamic efficiency.

b shows the trade-off between providing incentives to innovate and allowing access to previous innovations.

c shows that patents lead to monopoly profits.

d shows how marginal cost declines as cumulative experience increases.

e disproves the infant industry argument.

15 According to the infant industry argument,

a firms that have higher costs than their foreign rivals should be protected in order to save jobs.

b firms should be protected if foreign labor costs are so low that the domestic firm cannot compete.

c firms that have higher costs than their foreign rivals should be protected until they move down the learning curve.

d free trade is efficient.

e *a*, *b*, and *c*.

LIVERPOOL JOHN MOORES UNIVERSITY
LEARNING SERVICES

16 Which of the following is *not* true?
  a Competition drives firms that do not innovate from the market.
  b Competition inhibits innovation by eliminating profits that could be used to finance R & D.
  c Competition leads firms to imitate innovations, eroding returns.
  d Competition spurs R & D by making it clear that the principal way to earn profits is to innovate and capture market power.
  e All of the above.

17 The market will not supply enough R & D because
  a firms that win patent races do not have to pay for the patents.
  b the benefits of R & D spill over to others not directly involved.
  c firms that lose patent races cannot market the innovation.
  d firms that win patent races set price higher than marginal cost.
  e all of the above.

18 Which of the following is *not* a property of public goods?
  a It is difficult to exclude anyone from the benefits.
  b The marginal cost of an additional user is close to zero.
  c The market is likely to supply too few public goods.
  d All of the above are properties of public goods. *ea* and *b*.

19 Which of the following types of R & D is most likely to be a public good?
  a Basic research
  b Product development
  c Applied research
  d The costs of marketing new goods and services
  e All of the above

20 When firms share research and development efforts, they
  a are in violation of antitrust law.
  b forgo the right to patent their innovations.
  c may restrict access to their discoveries, thereby creating an entry barrier.
  d forgo the right to ask for government subsidies.
  e undermine dynamic efficiency.

Completion

1 As new products and technologies drive older jobs, technologies, and industries from the market, capitalism, in the words of Joseph Schumpeter, is a process of _____.

2 Expenditures designed to discover new ideas, products, and technologies and bring them to market are called _____.

3 The exclusive right to produce and sell an invention or innovation is a _____.

4 The fact that the rewards of research and development are given on a winner-take-all basis makes R & D a _____.

5 Rather than seek a patent, an innovator may try to hide the new knowledge as a _____.

6 _____ refers to the idea that as firms gain experience, their costs fall.

7 The curve showing how marginal costs of production decline as total experience increases is called the _____.

8 The benefits of research and development spill over to others not directly involved and generate positive _____.

9 Basic research produces knowledge from which it is difficult to exclude potential users and which can be used by others at no cost to the producers; therefore, it is an example of a _____.

10 The hope that an industry not currently able to compete with foreign firms may in time acquire the experience to move down the learning curve is called the _____ argument for protection.

Answers to Self-Test

True or False

1	f	6	t	11	f
2	t	7	t	12	f
3	t	8	t	13	t
4	t	9	f	14	t
5	f	10	f	15	t

Multiple Choice

1	c	6	a	11	b	16	e
2	d	7	b	12	d	17	b
3	d	8	d	13	b	18	d
4	e	9	e	14	d	19	a
5	b	10	e	15	c	20	c

Completion

1 creative destruction
2 research and development
3 patent
4 patent race
5 trade secret
6 Learning by doing
7 learning curve
8 externalities
9 public good
10 infant industry

Doing Economics: Tools and Practice Problems

Firms undertake research and development in order to market new products or to find new and less costly ways of producing. They compete to win patents or secure trade secrets that will allow them to enjoy some protection against competition and to earn above-normal profits. In this section we study the rewards that motivate R & D. First, several problems explore the value of new product patents and trade secrets. Next, we study innovations that result in lower production costs and consider whether incumbent monopolies have as much incentive to innovate as do potential entrants.

PATENTS

The incentive to undertake research and development is the expectation of future profits. Patents allow firms to earn these profits by conferring monopoly status for the duration of the patent. Tool Kit 20.1 shows how to compute the value of a patent and thus the reward for successful innovation.

Tool Kit 20.1 Calculating the Value of a Patent

The developer of a new product may be able to win a patent, which grants the exclusive right to market the product for 20 years. The value of the patent is then the present discounted value of monopoly profits for the duration of the patent. Follow these steps to compute the value of a patent.

Step one: Compute monopoly profits resulting from the patent.

Step two: Find the present discounted value of 20 years of profits. This number is the value of the patent:

value of the patent = profits + profits $[1(1 + r)^1]$
+ profits $[1/(1 + r)^2]$ + ...
+ profits $[1/(1 + r)^{19}]$.

(The variable r stands for the real rate of interest. In the problems below, we will set r equal to 3 percent. A shortcut for step two is to multiply profits by 15.23.)

---

1 (Worked problem: patents) Nu Products has come up with another winning idea—a rubberized surface for premium, no-injury waterslide parks. The company wins the patent. Demand for resurfacings is given in Table 20.1, and costs are $20,000 per park. Calculate the value of the patent.

Table 20.1

Price	Parks resurfaced
$60,000	10
$50,000	20
$40,000	30
$30,000	40
$20,000	50

Step-by-step solution

Step one: Compute the monopoly profits resulting from the patent. Table 20.2 gives the marginal revenue for resurfacings.

Table 20.2

Price	Park resurfaced	Revenues	Marginal revenue
$60,000	10	$ 600,000	$60,000
$50,000	20	$1,000,000	$40,000
$40,000	30	$1,200,000	$20,000
$30,000	40	$1,200,000	$ 0
$20,000	50	$1,000,000	−$20,000

Marginal cost equals marginal revenue when price is $40,000 and 30 parks are resurfaced. Profits then equal ($40,000 × 30) − ($20,000 × 30) = $600,000.

Step two: Find the present discounted value of 20 years of profits. This number is the value of the patent.

Value of the patent = $600,000 + $600,000$[1/(1 + r)^1]$
+ $600,000$[1/(1 + r)^2]$ +
+ ... $600,000$[1/(1 + r)^{19}]$
= $600,000 × 13.47 = $8,082,000.

2 (Practice problem: patents) Bugout Pesticide has discovered a new product that kills potato bugs. It wins the patent. The firm's economics department computes that it can expect to earn $100,000 for the length of the patent. Compute the value of the patent.

3 (Practice problem: patents) Nip and Tuck Bodyshapers have developed a new procedure for smoothing those wrinkles that trouble the after-40 generation. They have decided not to apply for a patent, but rather to keep the technique secret. They expect that others will be able to duplicate the procedure in 4 years and that the resulting competition will allow only a normal rate of return thereafter. Their costs are $5,000 per face, and they estimate that the demand curve is as given in Table 20.3. The real interest rate is expected to remain at 5 percent over the period. Find the value of the trade secret.

Table 20.3

Price	Quantity
$30,000	20
$25,000	30
$20,000	40
$15,000	50
$10,000	60
$ 5,000	70

Table 20.4

Price	Offices computerized
$30,000	20
$25,000	30
$20,000	40
$15,000	50
$10,000	60

THE ENTRANT VERSUS THE INCUMBENT

A firm that discovers and patents a new, lower-cost production technique will be able to earn above-normal profits for the duration of the patent. If the firm is already a monopoly, then it merely takes advantage of the lower costs. If the firm is a potential entrant, it can undercut the existing firm, drive it from the market, and take its place as the incumbent monopolist. Here, we compare the incentives that incumbent and entrant firms have to innovate, and demonstrate that monopolists do have lower incentives to innovate, as we learned in Chapter 13. Tool Kit 20.2 shows how to predict the outcome of competition between a new entrant and the incumbent monopolist. The following problems use this idea to compare incentives to innovate.

Tool Kit 20.2 Finding Equilibrium with an Incumbent Monopolist and a Potential Entrant

When a firm discovers how to produce for less, it is in position to take over an industry. It can set price just below the average cost of its rival and capture all sales. Follow these steps.

Step one: Identify the incumbent's costs, the potential entrant's costs, and the demand curve.

Step two: Find the equilibrium. The incumbent sets price equal to the entrant's average cost and captures the entire market. (Actually, the price must be 1 cent less than the average cost of the entrant, but we will round up in the problems below.)

---

4 (Worked problem: monopolist and potential entrant) Dentalcomp has had the monopoly in the market for computerizing dental offices in Roseville. While other firms could set up a computer system for $20,000, Dentalcomp's costs are only $15,000. Demand is given in Table 20.4.

a Find the equilibrium.
b Suppose that a new innovation in programming would lower costs to $10,000. Assume that the incumbent, Dentalcomp, discovers and patents the innovation first. Find the new equilibrium and the incumbent's profits. How much is the innovation worth to Dentalcomp?
c Now assume that a potential entrant discovers and patents the innovation first. Find the new equilibrium and the entrant's profits.
d Who has stronger incentives to innovate?

Step-by-step solution

Step one (a): Identify the incumbent's costs, the potential entrant's costs, and the demand curve. The incumbent, Dentalcomp, has an average cost of $15,000; the entrant has an average cost of $20,000. The demand appears in Table 20.4.

Step two: Find the equilibrium. The incumbent sets price equal to the entrant's average cost, which is $20,000, and captures the entire market of 40 offices. Its profits are ($20,000 × 40) − ($15,000 × 40) = $200,000.

Step three (b): If it discovers the innovation and wins the patent, Dentalcomp is still the low-cost firm. It captures the entire market with the same price of $20,000 and earns profits of ($20,000 × 40) − ($10,000 × 40) = $400,000.

Step four (c): If a potential entrant discovers the patent first, it becomes the low-price firm. It sets price equal to Dentalcomp's average cost, which is $15,000, and captures the entire market of 50 offices. Its profits are ($15,000 × 50) − ($10,000 × 50) = $250,000.

Step five (d): The gain to innovation for Dentalcomp is the difference between its profits before and after the innovation, which equals $400,000 − $200,000 = $200,000. The entrant gains $250,000 by innovating and thus has stronger incentives.

5 (Practice problem: monopolist and potential entrant) Blackdare has patented its unique process for extinguishing oil fires. It can put out a typical well fire for $150,000, but its competitors, without access to the patented process, have average costs equal to $200,000. The demand for extinguishing oil fires is given in Table 20.5.

Table 20.5

Price	Fires
$400,000	10
$350,000	12
$300,000	14
$250,000	16
$200,000	18
$150,000	20
$100,000	22

a Find the equilibrium price and quantity and profits.

b Suppose that a new innovation in firefighting would lower costs to $100,000. Assume that the incumbent, Blackdare, discovers and patents the innovation first. Find the new equilibrium and the incumbent's profits. How much is the innovation worth to Blackdare?

c Now assume that a potential entrant discovers and patents the innovation first. Find the new equilibrium and the entrant's profits.

d Who has the stronger incentives to innovate?

6 (Practice problem: monopolist and potential entrant) PhXXX Pharmaceuticals has a monopoly on the treatment of Rubinksi's Trauma, an obscure ailment of the saliva glands. The average cost of curing a patient is $2,000 for PhXXX. The only other treatment available costs $5,000. Demand for the treatment of Rubinski's Trauma is given in Table 20.6.

Table 20.6

Price	Treatments
$8,000	100
$7,000	200
$6,000	300
$5,000	400
$4,000	500
$3,000	600
$2,000	700
$1,000	800

a Find the equilibrium price and quantity.

b Suppose that a new genetically engineered drug would lower treatment costs to $1,000. Assume that the incumbent, PhXXX, discovers and patents the new drug first. Find the new equilibrium and the incumbent's profits. How much is the innovation worth to PhXXX?

c Now assume that a potential entrant discovers and patents the innovation first. Find the new equilibrium and the entrant's profits.

d Who has the stronger incentives to innovate?

Answers to Problems

2 Value of patent = $100,000 × 13.47 = $1,347,000.

3 Marginal revenue is given in Table 20.7.

Table 20.7

Price	Quantity	Revenues	Marginal revenue
$30,000	20	$600,000	—
$25,000	30	$750,000	$15,000
$20,000	40	$800,000	$ 5,000
$15,000	50	$750,000	−$ 5,000
$10,000	60	$600,000	−$15,000
$ 5,000	70	$350,000	−$25,000

Marginal revenue equals marginal cost at a price of $20,000, where 40 faces are smoothed. Profits = ($20,000 × 40) − ($5,000 × 40) = $600,000. The value of the trade secret is $600,000 + [($600,000) × 1/(1.05)] + [($600,000) × 1/(1.05)^2] + [($600,000) × 1/(1.05)^3] = $2,209,380.

5 *a* Price = $200,000; quantity = 18; profits = $900,000.

b Price = $200,000; quantity = 18; profits = $1,800,000.

c Price = $150,000; quantity = 20; profits = $1,000,000.

d The entrant would gain $1,000,000, while Blackdare would only gain $1,800,000 − $900,000 = $900,000. The entrant has stronger incentives.

6 *a* Price = $5,000; quantity = 400; profits = $1,200,000;

b Price = $5,000; quantity = 400; profits = $1,600,000;

c Price = $2,000; quantity = 700; profits = $700,000.

d The entrant would gain $700,000, while PhXXX would only gain $1,600,000 − $1,200,000 = $400,000. The entrant has stronger incentives.

CHAPTER 21 | Environmental Economics

Chapter Review

Of the three major economic players—individuals, firms, and government—the first two have been center stage so far in the text, while the third has mainly stood silently at the side. Government has been the central focus only of Chapters 13. This is appropriate, because the critical points for you to understand are where markets succeed at answering the main economic questions, where they fail, and how.

Where markets fail, government may have an economic role to play. This chapter wraps up some loose ends with respect to governments role. You have already seen problems of competition, information, and technological change that interfere when private markets are used to answer economic questions. Another major category of market failure is externalities, a concept first introduced in Chapter 7. As you may remember, externalities can be positive or negative. The distinguishing characteristic of externalities is that, positive or negative, they represent benefits or costs that are not captured in the market price. The first example studied in Chapter 21 is pollution. The chapter moves on to natural resources, where the key idea is whether correct incentives exist to conserve.

ESSENTIAL CONCEPTS

1 A market transaction is a voluntary exchange between two parties. Any costs or benefits not captured by market transactions are called **externalities. Positive externalities** are benefits received by others. Markets produce too little activities that generate positive externalities, such as research and development or on-the-job training. Other activities, such as pollution, noise, or congestion, confer costs on others that often do not figure into the market price. Markets create too many of these **negative externalities.**

2 Markets require clearly defined *property rights* in order to allocate resources efficiently. The **Coases theorem** says that any externality problem could be solved if the government would assign property rights for the externalities. For example, direct pollution of a privately owned lake would not occur unless the owner judged that the benefits exceeded the costs. General environmental pollution is a serious problem because the environment is commonly, not privately, owned.

3 Externalities lead to **market failure** because resources are not allocated efficiently. Individuals consider only their private costs and benefits and ignore the larger social costs and benefits. Potential governmental solutions to the problems fall into two categories: **command and control regulations** and marketlike devices such as taxes, subsidies, and **marketable permits.** For example, in the case of pollution, governments can issue regulations requiring pollution-control equipment or banning the use of hazardous materials. Alternatively, they can employ more market-oriented policies, such as taxes on pollution emissions, subsidies for pollution abatement, or even creating a market for pollution permits.

4 Private property and the price system enhance the conservation of natural resources. If all is well, current prices reflect the value of natural resources used today and expected future prices equal their expected value in the future. Seeking the highest value for his property, the natural resource owner sells today if the current price exceeds the present discounted value of the future price. If not, he conserves. Thus, private owners make socially efficient decisions.

5 Two problems with private incentive for natural resource conservation exist. First, property rights may not be secure, especially in resource-rich, less-developed countries. If an owner sees a risk of confiscation, she will likely use her resource at a faster than efficient rate. In the same vein, governments often make poor guardians of commonly owned public lands. Second, if capital markets impose borrowing constraints on resource owners, they may substitute faster extraction for borrowing and thereby foil conservation.

BEHIND THE ESSENTIAL CONCEPTS

1 Individuals and firms make efficient decisions when they bear the full costs and benefits of their choice. When externalities are present, some benefit or cost is ignored, and the decision becomes inefficient. The missing ingredient is property rights. Coases theorem says that if property rights are clearly assigned, decisions will be efficient. The logic can best be understood with an example.

Suppose that your neighbor likes to play the stereo very loudly each evening while you are reading this book. Clearly, there is an externality. You complain to the building manager, and there are two possible reactions. The manager might say that playing the stereo is a right of all tenants, in effect giving the property right (to make noise) to your neighbor. Or the manager may insist on quiet and give the property right (to silence) to you. According to Coases theorem, either way of assigning property rights will do. If your neighbor has the right, then you can buy the right to silence by paying your neighbor to be quiet. If you have the right, she must buy your permission to play the music. Of course, you would prefer the latter; nevertheless, in either case, the externality is eliminated and replaced by a market transaction. (Any reader who lives in a college dorm can judge how realistic it is to apply Coases theorem to externalities.)

2 Pollution is an example of a negative externality. It is a cost ignored by the polluter and borne by others. The inefficiency can be corrected by raising the polluters private marginal **cost** of pollution to the level of the **social marginal cost**. There are three marketlike ways to do this: taxes on pollution, subsidies for pollution abatement, and marketable pollution permits. Here is how they work.

  a Suppose that the firm must pay a *tax* of $10 per unit of pollution. Clearly, any pollution now has a private marginal cost of $10, because the tax must be paid.

  b Suppose that the government pays a *subsidy* of $10 per unit of pollution abatement. Again, the marginal opportunity cost of the pollution is $10, because if the pollution is emitted, it is not abated, and the subsidy is not received.

  c Under the marketable permits scheme, pollution requires a permit, which must be purchased. The purchase price of the permit is the marginal cost of the pollution. All three marketlike policies put a price on pollution and encourage polluters to find economical ways to reduce emissions.

3 Whether we are using our limited natural resources efficiently and whether we are likely to run out of these resources are important economic questions. The key aspects in the answer to these questions are property rights and markets.

  a For those resources, such as oil, minerals, and arable farmland, that are *privately owned,* markets provide good incentives for conservation. Future shortages mean high prices in the future. The profit opportunities from future sales motivate owners to conserve resources for the future.

  b For those resources, such as the ozone layer and endangered species, that are not privately owned, there is no reason for optimism. Since there are *no markets* for these resources, there is no financial incentive to conserve.

SELF-TEST

True or False

1 When there is no government interference, markets will always produce efficient outcomes.

2 The market failures approach assigns to government the task of improving matters when markets allocate resources inefficiently.

3 Markets fail because too many people are motivated by greed.

4 The market will supply too many goods for which there are positive externalities.

5 The social marginal cost is greater than the private marginal cost for a good that generates negative externalities.

6 Coases theorem contends that externality problems require government intervention.

7 Reassigning property rights can sometimes correct a market failure.

8 Because pollution is an example of a negative externality, economists recommend taxing pollution abatement.

9 Goods for which there are negative externalities should be taxed so that the price captures more of the social costs.

10 The regulation requiring catalytic converters on automobiles is an example of the command and control approach.

11 Marketable permits give no incentive to reduce pollution, because firms that want to pollute can simply buy the permits.

12 Because pollution is a negative externality, it should be eliminated on efficiency grounds.

13 We are using up our limited supply of natural resources because they are sold without concern for the needs of potential future users.

14 Both current and future property rights are essential to provide private owners with incentives to conserve natural resources.

15 If natural resource owners face borrowing constraints, they may conserve more natural resources than is socially efficient.

Multiple Choice

1 The market failures approach to the role of government in the economy says that
  a because markets fail, governments must do as much as they can afford.
  b governments have a role to play when markets fail to produce efficient outcomes.
  c government is less likely to fail than markets.
  d Coase's theorem is correct about the role of property rights in producing efficient market outcomes.
  e marketable prices will fail to give incentives for natural resource conservation.

2 Examples of market failures include
  a externalities.
  b a lack of sufficient competition.
  c information problems.
  d insufficient technological innovation.
  e all of the above.

3 The costs of environmental pollution are examples of
  a positive externalities.
  b public goods.
  c negative externalities.
  d private costs.
  e diminishing returns.

4 Social marginal cost includes
  a all marginal costs borne by all individuals in the economy.
  b only those marginal costs not included in private marginal cost.
  c only those marginal costs included in private marginal cost.
  d total revenues minus total private costs.
  e marginal revenue minus marginal cost.

5 Coase's theorem claims that
  a market outcomes are always efficient.
  b when markets fail to produce efficient outcomes, the government should allocate resources.
  c negative externalities should be subsidized.

  d reassigning property rights can solve externality problems.
  e the decisions made by a majority of voters may be inconsistent.

6 Which of the following is *not* an example of a negative externality?
  a Freon gas destroys some of the ozone layer.
  b Carbon dioxide emissions bring about global warming.
  c Industrial smoke emissions increase lung cancer rates.
  d Customers must pay more when the prices of natural resources are increased.
  e Runoff of pesticides pollutes streams and rivers.

7 Which of the following is an example of command and control regulations?
  a Subsidies for the production of goods with positive externalities
  b Taxation of goods with negative externalities
  c Regulations limiting the allowable level of pollution emissions
  d Assigning property rights to victims of environmental pollution
  e Nonrivalrous consumption.

8 To reduce emissions of pollution, the government can
  a tax pollution abatement.
  b subsidize pollution abatement.
  c subsidize the sale of polluting goods, such as steel and chemicals.
  d reassign to polluters the property rights to pollute.
  e take over the production facilities of firms.

9 Under the marketable permits approach to curbing pollution,
  a firms purchase permits from the government.
  b permits allow firms to emit a certain amount of pollution.
  c a market for pollution permits exists for firms to buy and sell the permits.
  d firms have strong incentives to reduce pollution.
  e all of the above.

10 The market system encourages conservation because
  a the price of a natural resource, such as an oil well, equals the present discounted value of potential future uses.
  b wasteful exploitation is punished by fines or imprisonment.
  c markets always allocate resources efficiently.
  d permits from the government are required before natural resources may be sold.
  e there is such an abundance of natural resources.

11 Private owners may undervalue future demand for natural resources if
  a there are negative externalities associated with the current use of the resource.

b there are positive externalities associated with the current use of the resource.

c property rights are not secure.

d owners may face limited borrowing opportunities.

e *b, c,* and *d.*

12 The view that there is a role for government when markets do not produce efficient outcomes is called

a Coases theorem.

b the market failures approach.

c marketable permits.

d the command and control approach.

e none of the above.

13 How does Coases theorem recommend that government solve the problem of overgrazing public lands?

a The government should put a tax on beef.

b The government should sell the grazing land to private owners.

c The government should subsidize beef feedlots.

d The government should issue regulations mandating how many cattle can graze per acre in each season.

e Coases theorem allows no role for government.

14 Which of the following is *not* an example of a problem with command and control regulations of environmental pollution?

a Firms cannot afford to clean up their pollution.

b Regulations do not allow for variations in circumstances among firms.

c The least cost cleanup technology may not be the mandated one.

d There are limited incentives for technological advance in pollution abatement.

e All of the above are problems with command and control regulations.

15 Which of the following methods can reduce environmental pollution?

a Taxes on pollution emissions

b Subsidies for pollution abatement

c Marketable permits

d Command and control regulations

e All of the above

16 When the social marginal cost of an activity exceeds its private marginal cost, it should be

a subsidized.

b taxed.

c outlawed.

d *a* or *b.*

e *a, b,* or *c.*

17 If the government uses the marketable permits policy, firms

a must purchase permits from the government.

b may sell their permits to the government but not to other firms.

c may buy their permits from the government but not from other firms.

d may sell their unused permits, but they may not buy additional permits.

e may buy or sell permits as they choose.

18 The marketable permits system specifies that firms

a purchase permits in order to pollute.

b may buy permits from other firms.

c may sell unused permits to other firms.

d all of the above.

e none of the above.

19 The production of too many goods with negative externalities is an example of

a paternalism.

b consumer sovereignty.

c public failure.

d market failure.

e the voting paradox.

20 In deciding when to extract and sell a mineral deposit, the private owner compares

a the present and expected future prices.

b the present net return and the discounted present value of the future net return.

c the discounted present value of future costs and prices.

d the expected value of future costs and prices.

e present costs and price.

Completion

1 The _____ approach to the role of government calls upon the government when markets fail to produce efficient outcomes.

2 The extra costs and benefits not captured by market transactions are called _____.

3 The _____ cost of pollution is borne entirely by the polluter, while the _____ cost includes all costs borne by individuals in the economy.

4 _____ claims that externality problems can be solved by reassigning property rights.

5 Regulatory measures that set limits on pollution emissions and mandate the use of specific types of pollution-control technologies are examples of the _____ approach.

6 The _____ approach issues to firms permits, which allow them to emit a certain amount of pollution and which can be traded.

7 Government can bring about a reduction in pollution emmissions by subsidizing _____.

8 When social marginal costs exceed private marginal costs there is a _____ externality.

9 High expected future prices motivate private owners to _____ natural resources.

10 When there are negative externalities associated with a good the market will produce too _____.

ANSWERS TO SELF-TEST

True or False

1	f	6	f	11	f
2	t	7	t	12	f
3	f	8	f	13	f
4	f	9	f	14	t
5	t	10	t	15	t

Multiple Choice

1	b	6	d	11	e	16	b
2	e	7	c	12	b	17	e
3	c	8	b	13	b	18	a
4	a	9	e	14	a	19	d
5	d	10	a	15	e	20	b

Completion

1 market failure
2 externalities
3 private, social
4 Coases theorem
5 command and control
6 marketable permits
7 pollution abatement
8 negative
9 conserve
10 much

Doing Economics: Tools and Practice Problems

The first topic of this section is how taxes and subsidies can be used to encourage an activity for which there are positive externalities. We see how firms can be induced to emit less pollution by engaging in pollution abatement. Next, we turn to markets for goods that generate negative externalities such as noise, congestion, and pollution. A few problems show situations in which market equilibrium levels are too high and investigate how taxes can be used to make the market more efficient. The last topic focuses directly on the market for pollution and the way in which the marketable permits system brings about efficient use of the environment.

POLLUTION ABATEMENT

Like other decisions made by firms, the question of the level of pollution abatement involves marginal benefit and cost reasoning. If the government taxes pollution emissions, then abating pollution saves the tax. If the government subsidizes pollution abatement, then abating pollution earns the subsidy. In each case, the marginal benefit of pollution abatement is determined by the governments policy. Tool Kit 21.1 demonstrates this.

Tool Kit 21.1 Determining the Level of Pollution Abatement

Pollution abatement is encouraged by taxing pollution or subsidizing abatements. Each raises the marginal cost of polluting. Follow these steps to find the resulting level of abatement.

Step one: Identify the cost of pollution emission and abatement.

Step two: Calculate the marginal abatement costs:

marginal abatement cost = change in cost change in level of pollution of abatement.

Step three: Determine the marginal benefit of abatement.

Step four: Set the marginal benefit of pollution abatement equal to its marginal cost.

---

1 (Worked problem: pollution abatement) Runoff from the Lower Indiana Quarta Lead Mine has raised lead levels in the Maumee River. The current level of lead effluent is 10 pounds per month. A filtering technology would enable the company to reduce its effluent. The abatement costs are given in Table 21.1.

Table 21.1

Pollution emitted (pounds/month)	Pollution abated (pounds/month)	Total cost	Marginal cost
10	0	$0	—
9	1	$10	
8	2	$25	
7	3	$45	
6	4	$70	
5	5	$100	
4	6	$135	
3	7	$175	
2	8	$225	
1	9	$290	
0	10	$400	

a Suppose that a pollution tax (or fine) of $40 is assessed per kilogram of lead emitted. How much will the company emit? What quantity of pollution will be abated?

b Suppose that rather than a tax, a subsidy of $40 is given per unit of pollution abated. How much will the company emit? What quantity of pollution will be abated?

c The firms profits from the production and sale of lead total $10,000. Compare its profits under the tax and the subsidy plan.

Step-by-step solution

Step one (a): The cost of pollution emission and abatement is given in Table 21.1.

Step two: Calculate the marginal abatement cost. The marginal abatement cost is the extra cost incurred in reducing pollution emissions by 1 more unit. For example, reducing pollution from 10 to 9 units raises costs from $0 to $10; therefore, the marginal abatement cost is $10 for the first unit. The remainder of the schedule is given in Table 21.2.

Table 21.2

Pollution emmited	Pollution emitted	Total cost	Marginal cost
10	0	$0	—
9	1	$10	$10
8	2	$25	$15
7	3	$45	$20
6	4	$70	$25
5	5	$100	$30
4	6	$135	$35
3	7	$175	$40
2	8	$225	$50
1	9	$290	$65
0	10	$400	$110

Step three: Determine the marginal benefit of abatement. Each unit of pollution emitted incurs a tax of $40; thus, the marginal benefit of abatement is $40.

Step four: Set the marginal benefit of pollution abatement equal to its marginal cost. This results in 3 pounds of lead emitted and 7 pounds abated.

Step five (b): When the policy is to subsidize abatement, the marginal benefit is the subsidy, which is $40. Setting $40 equal to the marginal abatement cost again gives 3 pounds of lead emitted and 7 pounds abated. The answer is the same as for part a. Notice that under the subsidy scheme, each unit emitted still costs the firm $40, in the sense that any unit emitted is a unit not abated and a subsidy not received.

Step six (c): Profits under the tax equal $10,000 less the abatement cost and the tax, or

profits = $10,000 − $175 − $40 (3) = $9,705.

Under the subsidy, however,

profits = $10,000 − $175 + $40 (7) = $10,105.

Notice that the difference in profits is $10,105 − $9,705 = $400, which is the magnitude of the tax/subsidy multiplied by the number of units that the firm emits with no regulation. It is the total value of the property right to pollute.

2   (Practice problem: pollution abatement) Avenger of the Sea Tuna kills 20 dolphins during an average harvest. It has various options for reducing the dolphin kill, and the costs are given in Table 21.3.

Table 21.3

Dolphins killed	Dolphins saved	Total cost	Marginal cost
20	0	$0	—
18	2	$100	
16	4	$240	
14	6	$400	
12	8	$600	
10	10	$1,000	
8	12	$1,500	
6	14	$2,200	
4	16	$3,000	
2	18	$5,000	
0	20	$10,000	

a   Suppose that a tax (or fine) of $100 is assessed per dolphin killed. How many dolphins will be killed? What number of dolphins will be saved?

b   Suppose that rather than a tax, a subsidy of $100 per dolphin is granted for reductions in the dolphin kill. How many will the company kill? How many will be saved?

c   With no tax or subsidy, the companys profits are $10,000. Compute its profits with the tax and with the subsidy.

3   (Practice problem: pollution abatement) Flying Turkey Air Transport has its hub in Franklin. Dozens of planes land and take off each night causing considerable noise. By muffling engines or other more advanced techniques, the company can reduce its noise. The costs are given in Table 21.4.

Table 21.4

Average level of noise (decibels)	Total cost	Marginal cost
1,000	$0	—
900	$50	
800	$150	
700	$300	
600	$500	
500	$750	
400	$1,100	

a   Suppose that a pollution tax (or fine) of $2.50 is assessed per decibel of noise created. How much will the company create? What quantity of noise will be abated?

b   Suppose that rather than a tax, a subsidy of $2.50 is granted per unit of noise abated. How much will the company create? What quantity of noise will be abated?

c With no tax or subsidy, the companys profits are $5,000. Compute its profits with the tax and with the subsidy.

MARKETS AND EXTERNALITIES

When there are negative externalities, such as pollution, noise, and congestion, market outcomes will be inefficient. Specifically, there will be more than the socially efficient level. The socially efficient level just balances the social marginal costs with the marginal benefits. But markets ignore the externality and focus only on the private marginal benefits. Tool Kit 21.2 shows how to distinguish private and social benefits and how to compare the market and socially efficient levels.

Tool Kit 21.2 Finding the Efficient Quantity in Markets with Negative Externalities

The production and consumption of many goods causes negative externalities. In these cases, markets brings about too much production and consumption. Follow these steps to compare markets and efficient levels.

Step one: Determine the market equilibrium at the intersection of the supply and demand curves.

Step two: Add the marginal external cost to the supply curve, which is the private marginal cost, to determine the social marginal cost curve.

Step three: Find the efficient quantity at the intersection of the demand curve and the social marginal cost curve.

Step four: Compare the market equilibrium and efficient quantities.

---

4 (Worked problem: negative externalities) Runoff from local feedlots is polluting the Red Cedar River. The negative externality per steer is $100. The demand and supply curves for steer are given in Table 21.5.

Table 21.5

Demand		Supply	
Price	*Quantity*	*Price*	*Quantity*
$200	350	$200	1,100
$180	500	$180	1,000
$160	650	$160	900
$140	800	$140	800
$120	950	$120	700
$100	1,100	$100	600
$80	1,300	$80	500

a Find the market equilibrium quantity and price.
b Calculate the social marginal cost, and determine the efficient quantity of steers.

Step-by-step solution

Step one (*a*): Find the market equilibrium quantity and price. At a price of $140, the market clears with 800 sold.

Step two (*b*): Find the social marginal cost curve. We add the marginal external cost, which is $100, to the supply curve, which is the private marginal cost. Table 21.6 gives the solution.

Table 21.6

Quantity	Social marginal cost
500	$180
600	$200
700	$220
800	$240
900	$260
1,000	$280
1,100	$300

Step three: Find the efficient quantity at the intersection of the demand curve and the social marginal cost curve. This occurs at a quantity of 500 and a price of $180.

Step four: Compare the market equilibrium and efficient quantities. Notice that the efficient quantity is only 500, while the market produces 800. Incorporating the external cost into the supply curve would raise the price and reduce the quantity to the efficient level.

5 (Practice problem: negative externalities) The private flying lessons at Daredevil Airport cause noise that disturbs local residents. The residents are also uneasy about the periodic crashes. One estimate of the magnitude of the negative externalities is $15 per flight. The market supply and demand curves for flight lessons are given in Table 21.7.

Table 21.7

Demand		Supply	
Price	*Quantity*	*Price*	*Quantity*
75	10	$75	100
$70	20	$70	80
$65	30	$65	60
$60	40	$60	40
$55	50	$55	20
$50	60	$50	0

a Find the market equilibrium price and quantity.
b Calculate the social marginal cost, and find the efficient quantity.

6 (Practice problem: negative externalities) New developments of townhouses are springing up in the ex-urban community of Outland. The supply and demand curves for new townhouses are given in Table 21.8.

Table 21.8

Demand		Supply	
Price	Quantity	Price	Quantity
$140,000	100	$140,000	900
$130,000	200	$130,000	800
$120,000	300	$120,000	700
$110,000	400	$110,000	600
$100,000	500	$100,000	500
$90,000	600	$ 90,000	400
$80,000	700	$ 80,000	300

a Find the market equilibrium quantity of townhouses and the corresponding price.

b The new developments impose costs on other current residents for sewage, transportation, and congestion. An estimate of the magnitude of these negative externalities is $20,000 per townhouse. Find the efficient level of townhouse production and the corresponding price.

MARKETABLE PERMITS

The problem of pollution (and other negative externalities) can be attacked more directly by considering the "market" for pollution itself. The polluters are the demanders for pollution, and their demand curve is just the marginal abatement cost curve. If it costs a firm $40 to clean up a ton of sludge from its emissions, then that firm is willing to pay $40 to be given the right to emit the sludge. The efficient level of pollution occurs where the demand curve intersects the social marginal cost curve, which is the marginal damage done by the pollution. These problems explore the issue of the efficient level of pollution and how a marketable permit scheme can bring about this outcome. Use Tool Kit 21.3.

Tool Kit 21.3 Using Marketable Permits to Bring about the Efficient Level of Pollution

The marketable permit policy sells permits to pollute. The market price for these permits gives firms incentives to reduce pollution. The following procedure shows how to find the number of permits to sell the market price.

Step one: Identify the demand for pollution (the sum of all the marginal abatement cost curves) and the social marginal cost curve

Step two: Find the efficient level of pollution, which is the intersection of the demand for pollution and the marginal abatement cost curve.

Step three: Determine how many permits to sell. This quantity is the efficient level of pollution found in step two.

Step four: Find the market price for the permits. Read this price of the demand curve.

---

7 (Worked problem: marketable permits) Discharges from factories, runoff from farmlands, and many other activities pollute the Metatarsal Lakes. The pollution could be reduced, but any reduction would involve expensive abatement procedures. The marginal abatement cost schedule is given in Table 21.9 along with the social marginal cost of the pollution. (BOD means biochemical oxygen demand.)

Table 21.9

Pollution (millions of pounds/BOD)	Marginal abatement cost	Social marginal cost
100	$1,200	$0
200	$1,000	$0
300	$900	$150
400	$800	$300
500	$700	$450
600	$600	$600
700	$500	$800
800	$300	$1,000

Find the efficient level of pollution, and explain how a marketable permits scheme can achieve an efficient outcome.

Step-by-step solution

Step one: Identify the demand for pollution and the social marginal cost curve. The demand is the marginal abatement cost curve given in Table 21.9, which also includes the social marginal cost curve.

Step two: Find the efficient level of pollution. The intersection of the demand for pollution and the marginal abatement cost curve occurs at 600 parts/million.

Step three: Determine how many permits to sell. This number is 600, and each permit entitles the holder to emit 1 part/million of pollution.

Step four: Find the market price for the permits. If 600 permits are offered for sale, their market price will be $600. This price is read off the marginal abatement cost curve at 600 units.

8 (Practice problem: marketable permits) The marginal abatement cost and social marginal cost of pollution in the Northwest Air Shed are given in Table 21.10. Find the efficient level of pollution, and explain how a marketable permits scheme can achieve an efficient outcome. Pollution is measured as metric tons of sulphur oxide.

Table 21.10

Pollution	Marginal abatement cost	Social marginal cost
10	$100	$0
20	$80	$0
30	$60	$5
40	$50	$10
50	$40	$20
60	$30	$30
70	$15	$50

9 (Practice problem: marketable permits) Pesticides, engine oil, chemicals, and other pollutants are finding their way into the groundwater. Abatement is possible but expensive. The marginal abatement cost and social marginal cost of this type of pollution for the Alago Aquifer are given in Table 21.11. Find the efficient level of pollution, and explain how a marketable permits scheme can achieve it.

Table 21.11

Pollution	Marginal abatement cost	Social marginal cost
100	$10,000	$10
150	$8,000	$100
200	$6,000	$1,000
250	$5,000	$5,000
300	$4,000	$10,000
350	$3,000	$20,000

Answers to Problems

1 The marginal abatement cost for reducing the dolphin kill is given in Table 21.12.

Table 21.12

Dolphins killed	Dolphins saved	Total cost	Marginal cost
20	0	$0	—
18	2	$100	$50
16	4	$240	$70
14	6	$400	$80
12	8	$600	$100
10	10	$1,000	$200
8	12	$1,500	$250
6	14	$2,200	$350
4	16	$3,000	$400
2	18	$5,000	$1,000
0	20	$10,000	$2,500

a The firm reduces its dolphin kill by 8 for a total of 12 killed.

b Again, the firm reduces its dolphin kill by 8 for a total of 12 killed.

c Profits under the tax = $10,000 − (12 × $100) = $8,800; profits under the subsidy = $10,000 + (8 × $100) = $10,800.

3 The marginal abatement cost for noise is given in Table 21.13.

Table 21.13

Average level of noise	Total cost	Marginal cost
1,000	$0	—
900	$50	$0.50
800	$150	$1.00
700	$300	$1.50
600	$500	$2.00
500	$750	$2.50
400	$1,100	$3.50

a The firm will emit 500 decibels (abating 500).

b The firm will abate 500 decibels (emiting 500).

c Profits under tax = $5,000 − (500 × $2.50) = $3,750; profits under subsidy = $5,000 + (500 × $2.50) = $6,250.

5 a Market equilibrium quantity = 40; price = $60;

b The social marginal cost is given in Table 21.14.

Table 21.14

Quantity	Social marginal cost
0	$65
20	$70
40	$75
60	$80
80	$85
100	$90

Efficient quantity = 20; price = $70.

6 *a* Market equilibrium quantity = 500; price = $100,000.

b The social marginal cost is given in Table 21.15. Efficient quantity = 400; price = $110,000.

8 Efficient level = 60. If 60 permits are sold, the market price will be $30 each, 60 permits will be purchased, and the level of pollution will be 60.

9 Efficient level = 250. If 250 permits are sold, the market price will be $5,000 each, 250 permits will be purchased, and the level of pollution will be 250.

Table 21.15

Quantity	Social marginal cost
300	$100,000
400	$110,000
500	$120,000
600	$130,000
700	$140,000
800	$150,000
900	$160,000

PART FIVE | Introduction to Macroeconomics

CHAPTER 22 | Macroeconomics and the Macroeconomy

Chapter Review

The focus now shifts to macroeconomics, the study not of particular industries, but of the overall aggregate economy. Macroeconomics began during the Great Depression that followed the stock market crash of 1929 with the publication of John Maynard Keynes's *The General Theory of Employment, Interest, and Prices*. The brief history of macroeconomic performance since this time illustrates the concerns of macroeconomics and forms a backdrop for the ideas developed in this book. The chapter goes on to summarize the basic concepts of modern economics.

ESSENTIAL CONCEPTS

1 The catastrophe of the Great Depression left the economy with a commitment to full employment and growth. Increases in unemployment bring calls for government action to restart growth. Outbreaks of inflation prompt demands for a return to price stability. The Social Security and federal deposit insurance programs, other legacies of the Great Depression, have faced recent difficulties that require policy responses. These remedies will affect savings, growth, and financial stability for decades to come.

2 **Scarcity,** the fact that there are not enough resources to satisfy all wants, requires that **choices** must be made. Economics studies these choices of individuals, firms, and governments and their effects on the use of resources. Because more of one thing necessarily implies having less of something else, the economy confronts **trade-offs.** In facing these trade-offs, decision makers respond to **incentives.** Individuals and

firms participate in voluntary trade in markets. How well markets perform, however, depends importantly on **information** or its absence. While individual decisions and markets often lead to efficient use of the economy's resources, there remain equity concerns about the **distribution** of goods and services.

BEHIND THE ESSENTIAL CONCEPTS

1 There are two broad branches in economics. **Micro economics** studies the product, labor, and capital markets, focusing on the behavior of individuals, households, firms, and other organizations that make up the economy. **Macro economics** looks at the performance of the economy as a whole and at such aggregate measures as unemployment, inflation, growth, and the balance of trade.

2 Microeconomics and macroeconomics are two ways of looking at the economy. Microeconomics looks from the bottom up; it starts with the behavior of individuals and firms and builds up to an understanding of markets and the economy as a whole. Macroeconomics, on the other hand, is a top-down look, beginning with a description of the performance of aggregate economic variables and then constructing explanations. Micro- and macroeconomics must fit together. The models that explain how individuals, firms, and markets work must be consistent with the models that we use to describe the economy as a whole. An important theme of this book is that the microeconomics in Parts One, Two, Three, and Four provides a firm foundation for the macroeconomics to follow in Parts Five, Six, Seven and Eight.

SELF-TEST

True or False

1 The Great Depression followed the stock market crash of October 1929.
2 The birth of macroeconomics as a separate branch of economics dates from the publication of Adam Smith's *The Wealth of Nations*.
3 The Great Depression was largely confined to the United States.
4 After World War II the economy lapsed back into a period of high unemployment.
5 Under President John Kennedy taxes were cut in 1964, but the economy fell into recession.
6 Stagflation indicates a period of high unemployment and high inflation.
7 During the 1980s and early 1990s the United States ran both budget and trade deficits.
8 Deposit insurance may make the banking system less safe.
9 Microeconomics focuses on the behavior of the economy as a whole.
10 Macroeconomics studies the behavior of firms, households, and individuals.

Multiple Choice

1 The author of the first great work of macroeconomics, *The General Theory of Employment, Interest, and Prices* was
  a Adam Smith.
  b John Maynard Keynes.
  c Allan Greenspan.
  d Franklin Delano Roosevelt.
  e Joseph Stiglitz.
2 Which of the following are legacies of the Great Depression?
  a The government's actively pursuing policies that promote full employment
  b Social Security
  c Federal insurance for bank deposits
  d All of the above
  e None of the above
3 The Misery Index is computed as the
  a sum of the inflation rate and the unemployment rate.
  b sum of the growth rate and the inflation rate.
  c growth rate minus the inflation rate.
  d sum of the growth rate and the unemployment rate.
  e unemployment rate minus the inflation rate.
4 The term *stagflation* refers to a period of
  a rising unemployment and rising inflation.
  b falling unemployment and rising inflation.
  c rising unemployment and falling inflation.
  d increasing growth and rising inflation.
  e falling inflation and increasing growth.
5 During the last half of the 1980s the United States experienced
  a budget surpluses and trade deficits.
  b trade surpluses and budget deficits.
  c both trade and budget surpluses.
  d both trade and budget deficits.
  e none of the above.
6 The Social Security system
  a provides income support to the elderly.
  b affects the savings decisions of all households.
  c influences retirement decisions.
  d all of the above.
  e none of the above.
7 Lower unemployment often leads to higher inflation. This is an example of
  a a trade-off.
  b perverse incentives.
  c exchange.
  d information problems.
  e unequal distribution.
8 Deposit insurance can make the banking system
  a less safe because the government can not be trusted to keep its promises.
  b less safe because households will withdraw their money if there is a run on the bank.
  c less safe because it can give banks incentives to invest in risky projects.
  d more safe because it gives banks incentives to invest in safer projects.
  e more safe because the government will reimburse banks for their losses on risky loans.
9 The detailed study of firms, households, individuals, and the markets where they transact is called
  a macroeconomics.
  b microeconomics.
  c normative economics.
  d positive economics.
  e aggregate economics.
10 The study of the behavior of the economy as a whole, especially such factors as unemployment and inflation, is called
  a macroeconomics.
  b microeconomics.
  c normative economics.
  d positive economics.
  e market economics.

Completion

1 The behavior of the economy as a whole, and especially of certain aggregate measures such as unemployment and inflation, is called _____.

2 The branch of economics that focuses on firms, households, and individuals and studies product, labor, and capital markets is called _____.

3 The sum of the inflation rate and the unemployment rate is called the _____.

4 _____ is a period of high inflation and high unemployment.

5 The _____ protects depositors from the risk of losing their money during a bank run.

6 The fact that high inflation results from effort to reduce the unemployment rate is an example of a _____.

7 The fact that deposit insurance may make the banking system less safe is an example of a problem with _____.

8 When a country imports more than it exports it runs a _____.

Answers to Self-test

True or False

1	t	6	t
2	f	7	t
3	f	8	t
4	f	9	f
5	f	10	f

Multiple Choice

1	b	6	d
2	d	7	a
3	a	8	c
4	a	9	b
5	d	10	a

Completion

1 macroeconomics
2 microeconomics
3 misery index
4 Stagflation
5 deposit insurance system
6 trade-off
7 incentives
8 trade deficit

CHAPTER 23 | Macroeconomic Goals and Measurement

Chapter Review

Macroeconomics is concerned with the characteristics of the economy as a whole. This chapter of the text introduces three central macroeconomic variables: the unemployment rate, the inflation rate, and gross domestic product, which is the standard measure of the economy's output. We learn how to measure each variable and discover how each is related to the major goals for the performance of the economy: full employment, price stability, and a high rate of economic growth.

ESSENTIAL CONCEPTS

1 Three major economic goals are rapid economic growth, low unemployment, and low inflation. Economists measure how well the economy approaches these goals with the **Gross Domestic Product (GDP),** the **unemployment rate** and various **price indices.** Although the U.S. economy has recently performed well on all three measures, other countries have experienced difficulties.

2 The **gross domestic product,** or GDP, measures the output of the economy. It is the money value of the goods and services produced within a country in a year. Adjusting the number for inflation gives real GDP. The rate of increase in the real GDP is the primary measure of economic growth.

3 **Potential GDP** measures what the economy could produce if labor and machines were fully employed. The economy fluctuates, producing below potential GDP in the trough of **recession** and sometimes exceeding it during the peaks of **booms.**

4 GDP can be measured in three equivalent ways. The **final goods approach** computes the market value of

goods sold to their ultimate consumers. The **value-added approach** adds up the additional market value created at each step in the process from production to market. The **income approach** adds the total income received by all individuals and profits retained by firms. Another important measure is **net domestic product,** which subtracts depreciation from the GDP.

5 When the economy goes into a downturn, unemployment rises. Beyond the loss of income to jobless workers, unemployment strains family ties, alienates youth, leads to the loss of skills, devastates communities, and exacerbates racial divisions. The lost output due to recessions can be substantial, as much as $1,300 per person for the high unemployment of the early 1980s.

6 The **labor force** includes those individuals who are either employed or actively seeking employment. The fraction of the labor force that is without work is called the **unemployment rate.** The fraction of the population that is employed or looking for work is called the **labor force participation rate.**

7 Economists distinguish among four types of unemployment. **Seasonal unemployment** occurs when the jobs are available for only part of the year. People who are between jobs make up **frictional unemployment. Structural unemployment,** which is more long-term, arises because the skills of the current labor force do not match the skills required by the available jobs. Finally, **cyclical unemployment** is due to a slowdown in the overall level of economic activity. One of the important tasks of macroeconomics is to understand and reduce cyclical unemployment.

8 Okun's Law relates changes in the unemployment rate to changes in output. A 1 percent increase in the unemployment rate corresponds to a 2 to 2.5 percent

decrease in output. The reason for this large change in output is that firms engage in **labor hoarding,** keeping their best workers employed but not fully utilized during downturns. Then as output declines unemployment falls less than proportionately. When it recovers, output increases by more than unemployment falls.

9 The **inflation rate** is the rate of increase in the general level of prices. It is measured using **price indices** such as the consumer price index, or CPI. The annual percentage change in the CPI indicates the increase in the cost of living from one year to the next. Inflation ranged from 3 to 6 percent in the 1980s. Inflation hurts people on fixed incomes because it erodes their purchasing power. When variable, inflation makes borrowing and lending riskier, and it is generally disruptive of the economy.

BEHIND THE ESSENTIAL CONCEPTS

1 If you have a job or are looking for one, then economists count you as a member of labor force. The unemployment rate is the fraction of the labor force that does not have a job. But the unemployment rate may not measure how hard it is to find work, for several reasons. First you would be counted as unemployed even if you were only claiming to look for work in order to be eligible for unemployment insurance, or if you were holding out for an unrealistic offer. On the other hand, if, during a recession, you realistically gave up hope of finding a job and stopped looking, you would not be counted as unemployed, but rather as out of the labor force. A **discouraged worker** would be part of the usual decline in the **labor force participation rate** during recessions.

2 Economists use the price index, which is constructed by comparing the cost of a particular basket of goods in different years, to measure inflation. The consumer price index measures your cost of living only if you consume exactly what is in the market basket. It also gives an inexact measure of quality changes and sometimes underestimates the importance of sale items.

3 Over time, not only does the price level change, but also there are changes in relative prices. When relative prices change, you substitute away from the relatively expensive items and toward those whose relative price has fallen. In other words, you change your market basket. The price index employs a fixed market basket; therefore it becomes increasingly off base as time passes. When adjusting GDP for inflation, the Bureau of Economic Analysis also provides a measure, the **chain-weighted real GDP,** which updates the market basket yearly.

4 Similarly, GDP does not quite measure all the output in the economy. It ignores nonmarketed goods, such as the services of unpaid spouses, and it can only be adjusted imperfectly to capture changes in the quality of goods and the value of services, especially nonmarketed government services. Other measures have recently been developed to incorporate additional aspects of the standard of living, such as literacy and infant mortality rates. There have also been attempts to include environmental measures into a so-called **green GDP.**

SELF-TEST

True or False

1 The three key goals of macroeconomic performance are rapid growth, low unemployment, and low inflation.
2 The gross domestic product measures the money value of goods and services produced within a country during a specific time period.
3 Nominal GDP is real GDP adjusted for inflation.
4 Gross domestic product is the sum of consumption, investment, government expenditures, and net exports.
5 There are three equally valid ways to compute gross domestic product: final goods, value added, and income
6 Value added is computed by subtracting a firm's purchases of inputs from its revenues.
7 The unemployment rate measures the percentage of the working-age population that is unemployed.
8 The labor force includes the entire working-age-population.
9 Structural unemployment includes those unemployed who have skills that do not match the skills required or currently available jobs.
10 When the economy is on an upswing, cyclical unemployment declines.
11 The price index for the base equals 100.
12 The wholesale price index is based upon a market basket of goods sold by wholesalers to retailers.
13 The producer price index is based upon a market basket of goods sold by wholesalers to producers
14 Inflation reduces the purchasing power of people living on fixed incomes.
15 Variable rates of inflation increase the riskiness of borrowing and lending.

Multiple Choice

1 Which of the following is *not* an important macroeconomic goal?
   a Price stability
   b Full employment
   c Perfect competition
   d Rapid growth

e All of the above are important macroeconomic goals.

2 The money value of all goods and services produced within a country in a year is the
a gross national product.
b gross domestic product.
c net domestic product.
d depreciation index.
e producer price index.

3 Inflation-adjusted gross domestic product is called
a gross national product.
b net domestic product.
c nominal gross domestic product.
d real gross domestic product.
e nominal gross national product.

4 If the price level has risen recently, then the real GDP is
a greater than the nominal GDP.
b less than the nominal GDP.
c equal to the nominal GDP.
d greater than the GNP.
e less than the GNP.

5 During recessions, the GDP
a is less than potential GDP.
b is greater than potential GDP.
c is equal to potential GDP.
d bears no predictable relationship to potential GDP.
e rises at a decreasing rate.

6 The final goods approach to GDP
a adds the differences between the revenues and costs of intermediate goods.
b adds all income received by individuals and governments in the economy.
c subtracts the inflation rate from the nominal GDP.
d adds the value of goods, services, and the environment.
e adds the total money value of goods and services purchased by their ultimate users.

7 The value-added approach to GDP
a adds the differences between the revenues and costs of intermediate goods.
b adds all income received by individuals and governments in the economy.
c substracts the inflation rate from the nominal GDP.
d adds the value of goods, services, and the environment.
e adds the total money value of goods and services purchased by their ultimate users.

8 Gross domestic product divided by the number of hours worked equals
a net domestic product.
b real GNP.
c real GDP.
d productivity.
e NDP.

9 The total labor force comprises all
a individuals of working age who are employed.
b individuals of working age who are unemployed.
c individuals of working age.
d heads of households.
e individuals of working age who are either employed or unemployed.

10 The costs of unemployment include
a underutilization of the economy's resources.
b personal difficulties for unemployed individuals.
c financial troubles for communities with high unemployment.
d exacerbated racial and ethnic divisions.
e all of the above.

11 The unemployment rate is the ratio of the number of unemployed to the
a number of employed.
b total labor force.
c inflation rate.
d gross domestic product.
e adult working-age population.

12 Okun's Law says a 1 percent decline in the unemployment rate requires
a a 1 percent decline in output.
b a 2 to 2.5 percent decline in output.
c no change in output.
d a 1 percent increase in output.
e a 2 to 2.5 percent increase in output.

13 Those individuals who are unemployed because they work in seasonal jobs make up
a seasonal unemployment.
b frictional unemployment.
c structural unemployment.
d cyclical unemployment.
e discouraged-worker unemployment.

14 Those individuals who are temporarily between jobs make up
a seasonal unemployment.
b frictional unemployment.
c structural unemployment.
d cyclical unemployment.
e discouraged-worker unemployment.

15 When the skills required by available jobs are *not* the same as the skills of the unemployed, there is
a seasonal unemployment.
b frictional unemployment.
c structural unemployment.
d cyclical unemployment.
e discouraged-worker unemployment.

16 In recessions, the level of economic activity declines and there is an increase in
a seasonal unemployment.
b frictional unemployment.
c structural unemployment.

d cyclical unemployment.

e discouraged-worker unemployment.

17 If prices and wages rise at the same rate, the purchasing power of typical workers

   a increases.

   b decreases.

   c remains the same.

   d doubles.

   e falls to zero.

18 When the inflation rate rises and falls unpredictably,

   a lenders gain at the expense of borrowers.

   b borrowers gain at the expense of lenders.

   c there is no appreciable impact on borrowing and lending.

   d borrowing and lending become riskier.

   e lending increases, but borrowing falls.

19 The producer price index includes in its market basket a representative bundle of goods

   a purchased by consumers.

   b sold by wholesalers to retailers.

   c sold by producers to wholesalers.

   d purchased by government.

   e sold by wholesalers to consumers.

20 The price index used to calculate the real gross domestic product is

   a the consumer price index.

   b the producer price index.

   c the weighted average of the producer and consumer price indices.

   d the GDP deflator.

   e an index of raw material prices.

Completion

1 The money value of all final goods and services produced within the country in a year is called the _____.

2 Dividing nominal GDP by the price level gives _____.

3 The measure of what the economy could produce given normal levels of frictional unemployment and idle productive capacity is called _____.

4 A firm's revenues minus the cost of intermediate goods equal its _____.

5 _____ states that a 1 percent decline in the unemployment rate requires a 2 to 2.5 percent increase in output.

6 The unemployment rate is the ratio of the number of unemployed to the _____.

7 People who are temporarily between jobs comprise part of _____ unemployment.

8 _____ unemployment is due to a mismatch between the skills of those without jobs and the skills needed to perform the available jobs.

9 _____ unemployment rises in recession and falls in booms.

10 The percentage increase in the price level from one year to the next is called the _____.

Answers to Self-Test

True or False

1	t	6	t	11	t
2	t	7	f	12	t
3	f	8	f	13	f
4	t	9	t	14	t
5	t	10	t	15	t

Multiple Choice

1	c	6	e	11	b	16	d
2	b	7	a	12	e	17	c
3	d	8	d	13	a	18	d
4	b	9	e	14	b	19	c
5	a	10	e	15	c	20	d

Completion

1 gross domestic product

2 real GDP

3 potential GDP

4 value added

5 Okun's Law

6 labor force

7 frictional

8 Structural

9 Cyclical

10 inflation rate

Doing Economics: Tools and Practice Problems

In this section, we will explore how economists measure economic performance. After learning how to calculate the rate of inflation, we use this technique to construct the price index and to distinguish real and nominal GDP. Finally, we calculate GDP by the final goods, value-added, and income approaches, verifying that the three techniques give equivalent answers. Although the examples are simplified, you should realize that the government agencies responsible for computing inflation and GDP perform their calculations in the same way.

Inflation

Inflation refers to a general increase in the price level. It is calculated by computing the increase in the cost of purchasing a fixed market basket of goods. The United States government has several inflation measures, including the consumer price index, the producer price index, and the GDP deflator. In these problems we focus on the computation of the consumer price index (CPI). Tool Kit 23.1 shows how it is done.

Tool Kit 23.1 Calculating the Inflation Rate

The inflation rate is the percentage increase in the cost of purchasing a predetermined basket of goods. Follow this procedure to calculate the inflation rate.

Step one: Identify the quantities of each good in the market basket:

Quantity of good 1 =
Quantity of good 2 =
Quantity of good 3 =

Step two: Calculate the cost of purchasing the quantities in the market basket at year 1 prices:

quantity of good 1 × price in year 1
+ quantity of good 2 × price in year 1
+ quantity of good 3 × price in year 1
= cost of living at year 1 prices.

Step three: Calculate the cost of purchasing the quantities in the market basket at year 2 prices:

quantity of good 1 × price in year 2
+ quantity of good 2 × price in year 2
+ quantity of good 3 × price in year 2
= cost of living at year 2 prices.

Step four: Find the percentage change in the two costs of living by using the following formula:

$$\left(\frac{\text{cost of living at year 2 prices}}{\text{cost of living at year 1 prices}} - 1 \right) \times 100 = \text{inflation rate.}$$

1 (Worked problem: inflation rate) There are three goods consumed in Euthanasia: fast cars, parachute jumps, and hang gliders. The prices and quantities for each in 1999 and the prices in 2000 are given below.

Goods	1999 Prices	1999 Quantities	2000 prices
Fast cars	$20,000	20	$30,000
Parachute jumps	$100	2,500	$80
Hang gliders	$500	400	$800

The market basket comprises the 1990 quantities. Calculate the inflation rate.

Step-by-step solution

Step one: Identify the quantities in the market basket. There are 20 fast cars, 2,500 parachute jumps, and 400 hang gliders.

Step two: Calculate the cost of purchasing the market basket at 1999 prices:

($20,000 × 20) + ($100 × 2,500) + ($500 × 400) = $850,000.

Step three: Calculate the cost of purchasing the market basket at 2000 prices:

($30,000 × 20) × ($80 × 2,500) + ($800 × 400) = $1,120,000.

Step four: Find the percentage change:

($1,120,000/$850,000 − 1) × 100 = 32 percent.

The inflation rate is 32 percent.

2 (Practice problem: inflation rate) In order to determine how to adjust stipends for disabled workers, the Paper Profits Company wants to compute the inflation rate. It has identified a market basket for stipend recipients. This is given below, along with the prices in 1990 (the year of the last adjustment) and in 2000.

Good or service	Quantity	1990 prices	2000 prices
Prepared meals	7	$5	$6
Housecleaning	1	$25	$30
Physical therapy	3	$50	$75
Compact discs	4	$10	$10

Compute the inflation rate.

3 (Practice problem: inflation rate) A recent graduate of Enormous State University, Lamont has dozens of job offers. He has narrowed his search to jobs in two cities: Gotham and Smallville. In order to compare the offers, he must compute the relative cost of living in the two cities. His market basket and prices are given below.

Good or service	Quantity	Gotham price	Smallville price
Two-bedroom apartment	1	$1,500	$300
Pickup truck	1	$600	$400
Meals	90	$10	$5

How much more expensive (in percent) is the cost of living in Gotham than in Smallville?

Inflation Adjustment

The distinction between real and nominal values is essential in macroeconomics. Real values are adjusted for inflation; that is, they measure what would have occurred if the dollar maintained its purchasing power. While the technique is appropriate for any dollar value, in these problems we focus on adjusting nominal GDP. Tool Kit 23.2 shows how to adjust for inflation.

4 (Worked problem: adjusting for inflation) The nominal GDP in Monrovia was $2 billion during 1999. The price index for 1998 was 210, and 1999 saw an inflation rate of 30 percent.

a Calculate the price index in 1999.

Tool Kit 23.2 Adjusting for Inflation

The money value of all goods and services purchased during a year is the nominal GDP. To get a better idea of how actual output changes from year to year, it is important to adjust this number for inflation. Real GDP is nominal GDP adjusted for inflation, and it gives the value of output measured in base year dollars. Follow this procedure to calculate real GDP.

Step one: Calculate this year's price index. Multiply last year's price index by 1 plus the inflation rate:

last year's price index × (1 + inflation rate) = current year's price index.

Step two: Calculate this year's real GDP. Divide current nominal GDP by the price index and multiply by 100. The result is current real GDP expressed in base year dollars. (To express real GDP in any other year's dollars, simply multiply by the price index in the desired year and divide by 100.)

(Nominal GDP/price index) × 100 = real GDP.

b Calculate real GDP for 1998. Express it in base year dollars.

c Express real GDP in 1999 dollars.

Step-by-step solution

Step one (*a*): Calculate the price index for the current year (1999). The price index for 1998 was 210. The inflation rate was 30 percent. The price index for 1999 is 210 × 1.30 = 273.

Step two (*b*): Calculate this year's real GDP. The current nominal GDP is $2 billion. The 1999 real GDP is

($2 billion/273) × 100 = $732.6 million.

Step three (*c*): Real GDP in 1998 dollars is

($732.6 × 210)/100 = $1,538 million.

5 (Practice problem: adjusting for inflation) Suppose that the nominal GDP in 2000 is $4 trillion, the 1999 price index is 352, and the 2000 inflation rate is 95 percent.
 a Calculate the price index in 2000.
 b Calculate real GDP for 2000. Express it in base year dollars.
 c Express real GDP in 1999 dollars.

6 (Practice problem: adjusting for inflation) Suppose that sales of new homes total $30 billion in 2000. The 2000 price index is 222. Express the total sales of new homes in base year dollars.

Gross Domestic Product

The market value of all goods and services produced in a year is the gross domestic product. In the macroeconomics section of this book, when we measure the economy's output we will be looking at GDP. It is very important to realize that GDP equals national income; thus it can also be measured by adding all income earned in the economy. Finally, the value added at each step along the production chain gives another equivalent approach to calculating GDP. Tool Kit 23.3 shows how to calculate GDP.

Tool Kit 23.3 Calculating GDP

Gross domestic product is the money value of all goods and services as purchased by their ultimate users. It can be calculated by adding the money value of all final products, by summing the values adde4d by all firms, or by adding the incomes received by all individuals.

Final goods approach

Step one: Determine which goods are purchased by their ultimate users.

Step two: Add the money values (price × quantity) of these goods:

GDP = money value of good 1
+ money value of good 2 + ⋯

Value-added approach

Step one: For each firm, compute the value added by subtracting any payments to other firms from its receipts:

value added = receipts − purchases from other firms.

Step two: Sum the values added of each firm:

GDP = value added at firm 1

+ value added at firm 2 + ⋯

Income approach

Step one: Find the total wages, total dividends, total interest, and any other form of income for all individuals in the economy.

Step two: Add the totals of each kind of income:

GDP = wages + dividends + interest.

7 (Worked problem: calculating GDP) Suppose that the economy produces three goods: wheat, flour, and bread.

All of the wheat is sold to millers. All of the flour is sold to bakers. Consumers buy the bread from the bakers. The income and expenditure accounts for each of the three industries are given in Table 23.1.

Table 23.1

	Expenditures (billions)	Receipts (billions)
Wheat industry		
Wages	$40	$50
Dividends	$0	
Interest	$10	
Flour industry		
Wages	$30	$110
Purchases of wheat	$50	
Dividends	$15	
Interest	$15	
Bread industry		
Wages	$60	$200
Purchases of flour	$110	
Dividends	$30	
Interest	$0	

a   Calculate (nominal) GDP using the final goods approach.
b   Calculate (nominal) GDP using the value-added approach.
c   Calculate (nominal) GDP using the income approach.
d   Compare the three answers.

Step-by-step solution

Step one (a): Determine which goods are purchased by their ultimate users. Only bread is a final output.

Step two: Add the money value of these goods. The value of bread is $200. The GDP thus equals $200.

Step three (b): Find the value added for each firm or industry.

Value added in wheat = $50 − $0 = $50;
value added in flour = $110 − $50 = $60;
value added in bread = $200 − $110 = $90.

Step four: Sum the value-added numbers.

GDP = $50 + $60 + $90 = $200.

Step five (c): Find the total wages, dividends, and interest.

Total wages = $40 + $30 + $60 = $130;
total dividends = $0 + $15 + $30 = $45;
total interest = $10 + $15 + $0 = $25.

Step six: Add the totals of each income type.

GDP = $130 + $45 + $25 = $200.

Step seven (d): Compare. Note that the GDP equals $200 billion according to each method.

8   (Practice problem: calculating GDP) The economy of Literaria cuts down trees in order to make paper and uses all its paper for books. The expenditure and income accounts for each of the three industries are given in Table 23.2.

Table 23.2

	Expenditures (billions)	Receipts (billions)
Tree industry		
Wages	$80	$100
Dividends	$20	
Interest	$0	
Paper industry		
Wages	$100	$250
Purchases of trees	$100	
Dividends	$40	
Interest	$10	
Book industry		
Wages	$150	$500
Purchases of paper	$250	
Dividends	$50	
Interest	$50	

a   Calculate (nominal) GDP using the final goods approach.
b   Calculate (nominal) GDP using the value-added approach.
c   Calculate (nominal) GDP using the income approach.
d   Compare the three answers.

9   (Practice problem: calculating GDP) in Computavia, they produce chips, all of which are used in the production of computer hardware. Half of the hardware is purchased by consumers, and half is sold to the software industry. Consumers purchase all of the software. The expenditure and income accounts for each of the three industries are given in Table 23.

a   Calculate (nominal) GDP using the final goods approach.
b   Calculate (nominal) GDP using the value-added approach.
c   Calculate (nominal) GDP using the income approach.
d   Compare the three answers.

Answers to Problems

2   [(42 + 30 + 225 + 40)/(35 + 25 + 150 + 40) − 1] × 100 = 30 percent.
3   [(1,500 + 600 + 900)/(300 + 400 + 450) − 1] × 100 = 161 percent.

Table 23.3

	Expenditures (billions)	Receipts (billions)
Chip industry		
Wages	$600	$1,000
Dividends	$400	
Interest	$0	
Hardware industry		
Wages	$600	$2,000
Purchases of chips	$1,000	
Dividends	$200	
Interest	$200	
Software industry		
Wages	$600	$2,000
Purchases of hardware	$1,000	
Dividends	$0	
Interest	$400	

5 *a* 2000 price index = 352 × 1.95 = 686.4.
 b 2000 real GDP (base year dollars) = (4/686.4) × 100 = $0.58 trillion.
 c 2000 real GDP (1991 dollars) = (0.58 × 352)/100 = $2.042 trillion.
6 (30/222) × 100 = $14 billion.
8 *a* $500 (books).
 b Value added in tree industry = $100 − 0 = $100.

value added in paper industry = $250 − $100 = $150;
value added in book industry = $500 − $250 = $250;
total value added = $100 + $150 + $250 = $500.
 c Wages = $80 + $100 + $150 = $330;
dividends = $20 + $40 + $50 = $110;
interest = $0 + $10 + $50 = $60;
total income = $330 + $110 + $60 = $500.
 d Each answer is $500, which is the GDP.
9 *a* Hardware purchased by consumers = $2,000/2 = $1,000;
software purchased by consumers = $2,000;
total final goods = $1,000 + $2,000 = $3,000.
 b Value added in chip industry = $1,000 − $0 = $1,000;
value added in hardware industry = $2,000 − $1,000 = $1,000;
value added in software industry = $2,000 − $1,000 = $1,000;
total value added = $1,000 + $1,000 + $1,000 = $3,000.
 c Wages = $600 + $600 + $600 = $1,800;
dividends = $400 + $200 + $0 = $600;
interest = $0 + $200 + $400 = $600;
total income = $1,800 + $600 + $600 = $3,000.
 d Each answer is $3,000, which is the GDP.

PART SIX | Full-Employment Macroeconomics

CHAPTER 24 | The Full-Employment Model

Chapter Review

The full-employment model describes the performance of the economy in the long run, after prices and wages have had time to adjust. Equilibriums in the product, labor, and capital markets combine to bring the economy to full-employment production at the level of its productive capacity or potential GDP. This chapter lays out the essentials of the model, and the points to many of its uses.

ESSENTIAL CONCEPTS

1   This chapter's model is the basic competitive model in which households and firms interact in product, labor, and capital markets. Households supply labor to firms for use in producing goods, and they provide savings that finance firms' investments in plant and equipment. Receiving their wages, interest, and dividends, households purchase the goods in the product market. Wages, interest rates, and product prices adjust to equate supply and demand in each market. The markets are interdependent in the sense that what occurs in any one market affects each of the others.

2   The labor market governs job creation and employment. The demand for labor depends on the productivity of workers, and it slopes downward because as the real wage falls, firms hire labor to substitute for capital and to produce additional output. Households determine their supply of labor, which is assumed to be inelastic. As shown in Figure 24.1, the real wage adjusts to the level at which demand and supply are equal. An increase in labor supply shifts the supply curve to the right, increasing employment and reducing the real wage. An increase in the demand for labor (due to improved technology or additional investment) shifts demand to the right, bidding up wages.

3   The capacity of the economy, also called its **potential gross domestic product** or **full-employment output,** depends on the available technology, its stock of capital, and the supply of labor. With a given capital stock and technology, the **short-run production function** shows how potential output varies with different quantities of labor. Figure 24.2 illustrates the short-run production function and its property of diminishing returns. It is related to the aggregate supply curve shown in Figure 24.3. Notice that aggregate supply does not depend on product price. An increase in labor supply represents a movement along the short-run production function and a rightward shift in aggregate supply. An increase in the capital stock or a technological advance also shifts aggregate supply to the right.

Figure 24.1

Figure 24.2

Figure 24.3

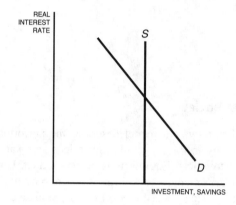

Figure 24.4

4 The savings of households depend upon their disposable income and interest rates. Panel A of Figure 24.4 shows the supply of funds sloping slightly upward; panel B shows it as vertical. The demand for funds, also called the investment function, results from firms' intentions to invest in plant and capital equipment. It depends upon their expectations of future profitability and the real interest rate. In equilibrium savings equals investment. A rightward shift in investment raises the interest rate. It increases investment only if the supply of funds is elastic (panel A).

5 In the economy's general equilibrium all markets clear. There is full employment because the real wage adjusts to bring the demand for labor equal to the supply. Output equals aggregate supply in the product market, and the economy produces its potential GDP. Finally, the real interest rate finds its equilibrium level where savings equal investment.

6 The general equilibrium model provides a coherent way to view the effects of various changes as they work

their way through the three markets. Here are some examples.

a The introduction of personal computers raises the productivity of workers, shifting demand for labor to the right and increasing real wages. In the product market this new technology manifests itself as an increase in aggregate supply. A look at the capital market shows an increase in savings (because households have more income) and an increase in investment.

b An increase in female labor force participation shifts labor supply to the right, driving down the real wage. Output increases. In the loanable funds market, both savings and investment increase. The real interest rate may move up or down.

c When the economy is at full employment, money is neutral. This means that an increase in the supply of money shifts aggregate demand to the right, increasing the price level, but the real wage, real interest rate, real output, and real investment remain unchanged. This separation of money and the real economy is called the classical dichotomy.

7 The **equation of exchange**,

$$MV = PY,$$

shows the relationship between the money supply (*M*),

output (Y), price level (P), and velocity (V), which is how many times a dollar of money is spent in a year. It gives the demand for money $M = PY/V$, which shows that money demand increases with the price level and output. This is because people need more cash to buy more goods at higher prices. Together with the money supply, money demand determines the price level.

BEHIND THE ESSENTIAL CONCEPTS

1 While the basic competitive model employed in this chapter is the same basic competitive model studied in microeconomics, there is a difference in interpretation. In macroeconomics we study the behavior or aggregates: total output, total employment, the price level, and so on. We proceed as if all firms produced a single good and as if there were only one kind of labor. This simplification directs attention away from the complexity of the economy and allows us to see the major forces involved in the movements of broad measures of economic performance.

2 Remember that the real wage refers to the amount of goods that an hour of work will buy. When you decide to take a part time job, you focus on what your earnings will allow you to purchase, not simply on the dollars. Similarly, in the capital market the real interest rate governs savings and investment decisions. Households put aside funds in order to consume additional goods at some future date. It is the real increase in purchasing power that motivates savings. The price level, on the other hand, is the nominal price level. Money affects this price level, but because aggregate supply is vertical, the economy's output is not affected, changes in the money supply affect only the price level, leaving real wages, real interest rates, real investment, and output unchanged. This essential feature of the full-employment economy, is called the **classical dichotomy.**

3 When the interest rate rises, you have an incentive to save more. The reason is, of course, that a given amount of savings results in more goods in the future. This idea is called the **substitution effect:** at higher interest rates people save more, in effect substituting future for current consumption. Why is the supply of funds so insensitive to changes in the interest rate? The reason is the other factor, the **income effect.** As the interest rate increases, savers have more lifetime wealth. As we have seen, when people experience an increase in wealth, they increase their consumption. This extra consumption means that savings must fall. This income effect counteracts the substitution effect, leaving the supply of funds almost inelastic.

4 Study the structure of the full-employment model with care. The basic division of the economy into the three

markets and the channels through which the markets affect each other are constants in macroeconomics. Later in the book, we look at unemployment macroeconomics, where prices are first rigid and then adjust slowly. Although these other models have quite different implications, their basic structures mirror the one studied in this chapter. Furthermore, it is important that you understand them in terms of their difference with the full-employment model. If you think about it, it is "economical" to learn one model well and to use that knowledge as a base for learning the others.

SELF-TEST

True or False

1 In the long run, job creation keeps pace with the growth in the size of the labor force.
2 The real wage equals the nominal wage divided by the price index.
3 As wages fall relative to the cost of machinery, firms substitute workers for machines.
4 If wages and all other prices rise in the same proportion, then the quantity of labor demanded will fall.
5 When new immigrants arrive, the supply of labor shifts to the right and real wages fall.
6 An increase in investment shifts the demand for labor to the left, and wages fall.
7 Along the short-run aggregate production function, an increase in labor increases output at a diminishing rate.
8 When the economy is at full employment, output equals potential GDP.
9 The economy produces its potential GDP only when each firm sells all that it produces.
10 The household supply of savings depends on the nominal rate of interest.
11 In macroeconomics, investment refers to financial investment, such as stocks and bonds.
12 Increases in household savings increase the real rate of interest.
13 As aggregate income rises, household savings must fall.
14 An increase in the price level reduces the demand for money.
15 An increase in the supply of money reduces the price level.

Multiple Choice

1 In the labor market,
  a households supply labor.
  b the real wage adjusts to clear the market.
  c firms use the labor supplied by households to produce output.

d labor supply is assumed to be inelastic.

e all of the above.

2 An increase in the supply of labor causes

    a an increase in both the real wage and employment.

    b a decrease in both the real wage and employment.

    c an increase in the real wage and a decrease in employment.

    d a decrease in the real wage and an increase in employment.

    e no change in the real wage because supply is assumed to be inelastic.

3 An increase in investment most likely will shift

    a the demand for labor to the right.

    b the supply of labor to the right.

    c the demand for labor to the left.

    d the supply of labor to the left.

    e both the supply and demand for labor to the right.

4 The real wage must be

    a greater than the nominal wage.

    b equal to the nominal wage when there is full employment.

    c less than the nominal wage when interest rates are high.

    d less than the nominal wage if there are payroll taxes.

    e none of the above.

5 In this chapter labor supply is assumed to be perfectly inelastic. This means that an increase in the real wage

    a increases the quantity of labor supplied.

    b decreases the quantity of labor supplied.

    c causes no change in the quantity of labor supplied.

    d causes the nominal wage to fall.

    e causes no change in the nominal wage.

6 The relationship between employment and output, holding the technology and capital stock fixed, is called the

    a short-run production function.

    b full-employment gross domestic product.

    c short-run aggregate supply.

    d investment function.

    e labor supply curve, which is assumed to be inelastic.

7 The short-run production function exhibits diminishing returns. This means that as more labor is used in production, output

    a diminishes due to overcrowding.

    b increases at an increasing rate.

    c decreases at an increasing rate.

    d increases at a decreasing rate.

    e decreases at a decreasing rate.

8 All of the following are synonyms *except*

    a full-employment level of output.

    b potential gross domestic product.

    c productive capacity.

    d aggregate supply.

    e aggregate demand.

9 If the labor force grows, in the labor market

    a supply shifts to the right.

    b demand shifts to the right.

    c both supply and demand shift to the right.

    d supply does not shift because it does not depend on price.

    e the real wage rises.

10 According to the circular flow model, in the labor market

    a households are suppliers.

    b firms are demanders.

    c firms are suppliers.

    d households are demanders.

    e *a* and *b*.

11 The income effect of an increase in the real interest rate causes savers to

    a reduce savings because they are better off and want to consume more now.

    b increase savings because consumption in the future is cheaper.

    c reduce savings because they can meet their target level with less savings.

    d increase savings because they are better off and want to consume more in the future.

    e choose no change in the level of savings.

12 The substitution effect of an increase in the real interest rate causes savers to

    a reduce savings because they are better off and want to consume more now.

    b increase savings because consumption in the future is cheaper.

    c reduce savings because they can meet their target level with less savings.

    d increase savings because they are better off and want to consume more in the future.

    e choose no change in the level of savings.

13 Savings depends on

    a the real interest rate.

    b expectations about future profitability.

    c disposable income.

    d *a* and *c*.

    e all of the above.

14 Investment depends on

    a the real interest rate.

    b expectations about future profitability.

    c disposable income.

    d *a* and *b*.

    e all of the above.

15 The relationship between the real interest rate and the level of investment is called the

    a short-run production function.

    b investment function.

    c aggregate supply.

    d potential GDP.

    e aggregate demand.

16 The elasticity of savings is assumed to be
  a perfectly elastic.
  b elastic but not perfectly.
  c 1.
  d inelastic but not perfectly.
  e perfectly inelastic.
17 An increase in the money supply
  a increases the price level.
  b increases the real wage.
  c increases the real interest rate.
  d *a* and *c*.
  e all of the above.
18 The neutrality of money in the full-employment economy refers to the idea that changes in the supply of money do not change
  a investment.
  b output.
  c the real wage.
  d the real interest rate.
  e all of the above.
19 Which of the following is caused by an increase in the supply of money?
  a An increase in output
  b An increase in the price level
  c An increase in the real wage
  d An increase in employment
  e All of the above
20 The demand for money is assumed to depend on
  a the real interest rate.
  b the nominal interest rate.
  c real income.
  d nominal income.
  e the real wage rate.

Completion

1 The nominal wage corrected for inflation is the _____.
2 The real wage equals the nominal wage divided by the _____.
3 The relationship between employment and output with a fixed amount of capital is called the _____.
4 The full-employment level of output is the economy's _____ GDP.
5 In the circular flow model, household savings is a _____ out of the stream of spending.
6 Investment is an _____ into the spending stream.
7 The amount that a household has left after taxes is its _____.
8 The level of real investment at each value of the real rate of interest is given by the _____.
9 When all markets clear, the economy is said to be in _____.
10 The dollar value of transactions supported by each dollar of money holdings is called the _____.

Answers to Self-test

True or False

1	t	6	f	11	f
2	t	7	t	12	f
3	t	8	t	13	f
4	f	9	f	14	f
5	t	10	f	15	f

Multiple Choice

1	*e*	6	*a*	11	*a*	16	*e*
2	*d*	7	*d*	12	*b*	17	*a*
3	*a*	8	*e*	13	*d*	18	*e*
4	*e*	9	*a*	14	*d*	19	*b*
5	*c*	10	*e*	15	*b*	20	*d*

Completion

1 real wage
2 price index
3 short-run aggregate production function
4 potential
5 leakage
6 injection
7 disposable income
8 investment function
9 general equilibrium
10 velocity

Doing Economics: Tools and Practice Problems

The full-employment model occupies a central place in modern economics because in many areas the economy behaves according to its predictions. For example, the long-run performance of the economy corresponds quite closely to the full-employment model. In this chapter we study the full-employment model in four steps. First, we look at the relationship between the short-run production function and the demand for labor. Next, we consider the links between the labor and product markets. Third, we study how the capital and product markets interrelate before we put it all together with some applications. The focus here is on the structure of the full-employment model. Master this subject and unemployment macroeconomics will go smoothly. (The chapter also covers the open economy, but we will defer study of that model until Chapter 25.)

The Short-Run Production Function and the Demand for Labor

The short-run production function shows how much output results from using various amounts of labor, holding the level of capital input and the technology fixed. From this function we can compute the marginal product of labor, which is the extra output resulting from one more unit of the input labor. This curve is the demand for labor. Tool Kit 24.1 shows how to make the derivation.

1 (Worked problem: demand for labor) This problem looks at Costa Guano, whose currency is the guano. The short-run production function is given in Table 24.1.
   a Find the marginal product schedule.
   b Suppose, for example, that the real wage is 300 guanos per year. How much labor is demanded?

Table 24.1

Quantity of labor (million person years)	Output (millions of guanos)
0	0
1	600
2	1,100
3	1,500
4	1,800
5	2,000
6	2,100
7	2,150

Step-by-step solution

Step one: Identify and plot the short-run production function. See Table 24.1.

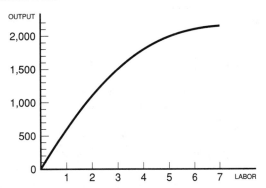

Step two: Compute the marginal product for each level of labor. When the first million workers are used, output rises from 0 to 600 million; therefore the marginal product of this worker is 600. When the second is added, output rises from 600 to 1,100; therefore the second worker's marginal product is $1,100 - 600 = 500$. Continuing in the same manner gives the entire marginal product schedule, given in Table 24.2.

Table 24.2

Quantity of labor (million person years)	Marginal product of labor
1	600
2	500
3	400
4	300
5	200
6	100
7	50

Tool Kit 24.1 Deriving the Demand for Labor from the Short-Run Production Function

Firms hire workers to produce output. The additional output that one more worker produces is called the marginal product of labor. The marginal product schedule is also the demand for labor, in the sense that firms choose the amount of labor to hire by setting the marginal product equal to the real wage. Follow these steps to determine the demand for labor.

Step one: Identify and plot the short-run production function.

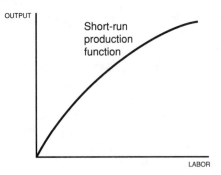

Step two: Compute the marginal product for each level of labor. The marginal product equals the following ratio.

Marginal product = change in output/change in labor.

Step three: Plot the marginal product.

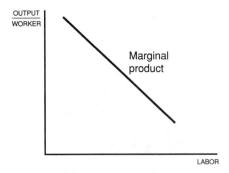

Step four: Identify the real wage. To find the quantity demanded of labor, find the quantity for which the real wage equals the marginal product.

Step three: Plot the marginal product curve.

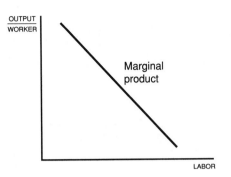

Step four: Find the quantity for which the real wage equals the marginal product. The real wage is 300, which equals marginal product when the quantity of labor is 4.

2 (Practice problem: demand for labor) In El Dorado the short-run production function is given in Table 24.3.
  a Find the marginal product schedule.
  b Suppose that the real wage is 3 thousand dorals. How much labor is demanded?

Table 24.3

Quantity of labor (million person years)	Output (billions of dorals)
0	0
1	25
2	45
3	60
4	70
5	75
6	78
7	80
8	81

3 (Practice problem: demand for labor) In the land of Erehwemos the short-run production function is as given in Table 24.4. The currency is called the wemo.
  a Find the marginal product schedule.
  b Suppose that the real wage is 3,000 wemos per year. How much labor is demanded?

Table 24.4

Quantity of labor (million person years)	Output (billions of wemos)
0	0
1	5
2	9
3	12
4	14
5	15
6	15.5

The Labor Market and the Product Market

The labor market and product market are linked by the short-run production function. The marginal product of labor, derived from the short-run production function, is the demand for labor, which, together with the supply of labor, determines the real wage. We will assume that the supply of labor is perfectly inelastic, an assumption that is not far from the truth. The short-run production function shows how much output will be produced by the supply of labor, and this quantity of output is the aggregate supply in the product market. Note the direction of influence: from the labor market to the product market. The labor market determines the laber supply and, with the production function, it determines the level of output. Changes in the product market have no impact upon the labor market. Tool Kit 24.2 illustrates this linkage.

Tool Kit 24.2 Deriving Aggregate Supply from the Labor Market and Short-Run Production Function

With the supply of labor and the short-run production function, we can find the economy's aggregate supply, which is also called potential GDP, full-employment output, or capacity. The labor market gives the real wage and the production function gives the aggregate supply. Follow these steps.

Step one: Identify the supply of labor and the short-run production function.

Step two: Find the demand for labor. Follow the steps of Tool Kit 24.1.

Step three: Find the equilibrium real wage. This is the real wage that clears the labor market.

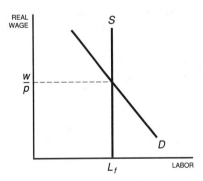

Step four: Find the economy's full employment output. This is the output corresponding to the equilibrium level of labor.

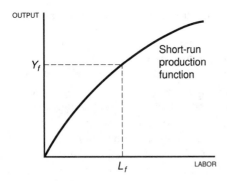

Step five: Plot the aggregate supply curve. This is a vertical line drawn with output equal to its full employment level.

24. *a* Calculate the marginal product schedule.
   b Find the equilibrium real wage. Draw a diagram of the labor market.
   c Find the economy's potential GDP. Draw the aggregate supply curve.

Step-by-step solution

Step one: Identify the supply of labor and the short-run production function. The production function is given in Table 24.1 and the labor supply equals 5 million.

Step two: Find the demand for labor. The demand for labor is as follows. Notice that it is the same as the marginal product schedule.

Quantity of labor (person years)	Real wage
1	600
2	500
3	400
4	300
5	200
6	100
7	50

Step three: Find the equilibrium real wage. Demand equals supply (5 million) when the wage equals 200.

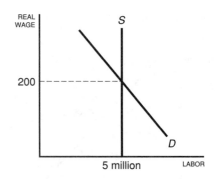

Step four: Find the economy's full-employment output. From the production function, output at 5 million person years equals 2,000 million guanos.

Step five: Plot the aggregate supply curve. Note that output equals 2,000 for each price level.

5 (Practice problem: aggregate supply) We continue with the analysis of El Dorado from problem 2. Suppose that the production function is given in Table 24.2 and that the labor supply is inelastic, equal to 3,000 person years.
   a Find the demand for labor.
   b Find the equilibrium real wage. Draw a diagram of the labor market.
   Find the economy's potential GDP. Draw the aggregate supply curve.

6 (Practice problem: aggregate supply) We continue with the country of Erehwemos, where the production function is given in Table 24.3. Suppose that the labor supply is inelastic, equal to 5 million.
   a Find the demand for labor.
   b Find the equilibrium real wage. Draw a diagram of the labor market.

   Find the economy's potential GDP. Draw the aggregate supply curve.

The Product Market and the Capital Market

The capital market determines the quantity of investment. Recall that the real interest rate adjusts to balance the demand and supply of funds. The product market is affected in that investment is one of the components of aggregate demand. In this case the effects go both ways because the product market affects the capital market through the link between output (which equals income) and savings. For example, an increase in the level of the economy's output will lead households to increase their savings. Tool Kit 24.3 illustrates these linkages.

Tool Kit 24.3 Linking the Product and Capital Markets

The product market determines the economy's output, which equals its income. The capital market is affected because households save a fraction of their income. The capital market then determines the level of investment, which is one of the components of aggregate demand. Keep straight this two-way influence with the following procedure.

Step one: Identify aggregate supply, the investment function, and consumption.

Step two: Find the savings supply (assumed to be inelastic). First, observe that aggregate supply equals output and output equals income. Next, subtract consumption from income. The difference is total savings.

Total savings = income − consumption.

Step three: Find the equilibrium real interest rate and investment level by equating the investment function with total savings.

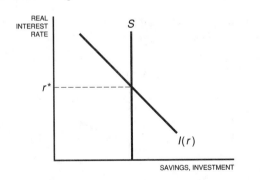

---

7 (Worked problem: product and capital markets) Continuing the analysis of Costa Guano, recall that the short-run production function is given in Table 24.1 and output equals 2,000 million guanos. Costa Guanoans consume 1,800 million. The investment function is given in Table 24.5.

Table 24.5

Investment function	
Investment (millions of guanos)	Real interest rate
50	10
75	9
100	8
125	7
150	6
175	5
200	4
225	3

a Compute total savings.
b Find the equilibrium real interest rate. Draw a diagram of the capital market.
c Now suppose that the demand for investment rises by 50 million guanos at each interest rate. Show on the diagrams.
d Now suppose that savings falls by 25 million. Of course, consumption will also increase by this same amount. Show on the diagrams.

Step-by-step solution

Step one: Identify aggregate supply, the investment function, and consumption. See Table 24.4 for the investment function. Aggregate supply is 2,000 (from problem 4) and consumption equals 1,000 million.

Step two: Find the savings supply (assumed to be inelastic). Total savings = 2,000 − 1,000 = 200 million.

Step three: Find the equilibrium real interest rate and investment level by equating the investment function with total savings. The capital market clears when the real interest rate equals 4 percent. Equilibrium investment is then 200.

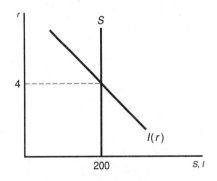

8 (Practice problem: product and capital markets) Continuing the analysis of El Dorado, recall that the short-run production function is given in Table 24.2 and

output equals 60 billion dorals. Households consume 50 billion. The investment function is given in Table 24.6.

a Compute total savings.

b Find the equilibrium real interest rate. Draw a diagram of the capital market.

c Now suppose that the demand for investment rises by 5 billion dorals at each interest rate. Show on the diagrams.

d Now suppose that savings falls by 5 billion. Of course, consumption will also increase by this same amount. Show on the diagrams.

Table 24.6

Investment function	
Investment (billions of dorals)	Real interest rate
3	9
4	8
5	7
6	6
8	5
10	4
15	3
20	2

9 Continue with the analysis of Erehwemos, the production function of which is given in Table 24.4. Households consume 10 billion. The investment function is given in Table 24.7. National income equals 15 billion wemos.

Table 24.7

Investment function	
Investment (billions of wemos)	Real interest rate
1	10
2	9
3	8
4	7
5	6
6	5
7	4
8	3
9	2

a Compute total savings.

b Find the equilibrium real interest rate. Draw a diagram of the capital market.

c Now suppose that the demand for investment rises by 3 billion wemos at each interest rate. Trace through the impact of this change in the economy. Show on the diagrams.

d Now suppose that savings falls by 1 billion. Of course, consumption will also increase by this same amount. Trace through the impact of this change in the economy. Show on the diagrams.

MONEY DEMAND AND SUPPLY

The classical dichotomy implies that money matters are separate from the real economy. Thus changes in the money supply cannot affect such real variables as the real wage or level of output. Money does affect the price level, however, and in this section we see how. The main idea underlying this model goes by the name of the quantity theory of money. Tool Kit 24.4 shows how the price level depends upon money supply and demand.

Tool Kit 24.4 Determining the Price Level

Money demand depends on nominal GDP and the velocity of money. Together with supply, it determines the price level.

Step one: Identify the (real) output (Y), velocity (V), and supply of money (M).

Step two: For each price level, calculate the quantity of money demanded.

Money demand $= (P \times Y)/V$.

Step three: Complete the money demand schedule.

Price level	Money demand
P_1	$(P_1 \times Y)/V$
P_2	$(P_2 \times Y)/V$
Etc.	

Step four: Find the price level for which money demand equals money supply.

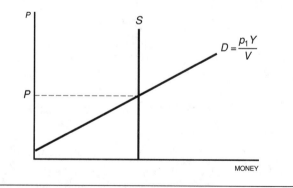

---

10 (Worked problem: money demand and supply) In Costa Guano output equals 2,000 million guanos. The velocity equals 5 and the money supply is 800 million guanos.

a Find the money demand.

b Find the equilibrium price level.

c Suppose the money supply increases to 1,200 million. Find the new price level.

Step-by-step solution

Step one: Identify the (real) output (Y), velocity (V), and supply of money (M). The output is 2,000 million, velocity is 5, and money supply is 800 million.

Step two: For each price level, calculate the quantity of money demanded. Let's pick $P = 1$.

Money demand = $(P \times Y)/V = (1 \times 2,000)/5 = 400$.

Step three: Complete the money demand schedule.

Price level	Money demand
1	400
2	$(2 \times 2,000)/5 = 800$
3	$(3 \times 2,000)/5 = 1,200$
4	$(4 \times 2,000)/5 = 1,600$

Step four: Find the price level for which money demand equals money supply.

This occurs at $P = 2$.

Step five (b): If the money supply increases to 1,200, then the price level rises to 3.

11 In El Dorado output equals 60 billion dorals. The velocity equals 6 and the money supply is 50 billion dorals.

a Find the money demand.

b Find the equilibrium price level.

c Suppose that the money supply falls to 40 billion dorals. Find the new equilibrium price level.

12 In Erewemos output equals 15,000 billion wemos. The velocity equals 2 and the money supply is 5,000 wemos.

a Find the money demand.

b Find the equilibrium price level.

c Suppose that the money supply rises to 8,000 billion wemos. Find the new equilibrium price level.

THE FULL-EMPLOYMENT MODEL

Now we are ready to put the pieces together and use the entire full-employment model to show the effects of various exogenous changes, including shifts in the supply of money, the supply of labor, and the short-run production function (technological progress). There will be a worked problem and a couple of practice problems. As usual, the basic method involves starting with an equilibrium, identifying an

exogenous change, shifting curves, and finding the new equilibrium. This general equilibrium model is complicated because adjustment in one market affects the others, and these effects must be traced through. We will pay special attention to these linkages. For simplicity, however, we will focus on the labor, product, and money markets, leaving the capital market to the next chapter.

13 (Worked problem: full-employment model) Review problems 1, 4, and 10. This problem continues the analysis of Costa Guano.

a Draw a diagram illustrating the general equilibrium in the Costa Guano economy as solved for in the answers to problems 1, 4, and 10. In the following always begin with this equilibrium.

b Suppose that the money supply increases to 1600 million. Trace through the impact of this change in the economy. Show on the diagrams.

c The short-run production function doubles for each level of labor input.

d The supply of labor decreases to 3 million.

Step-by-step solution

Step one (a): Start with equilibrium in the product, labor, and capital markets.

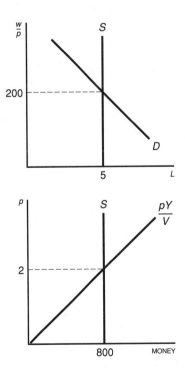

Step two (b): The increase in the shifts the supply to the right, increasing the price level to 4. There are no other changes in the real economy.

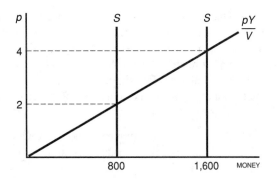

Step three (c): The technological advance shifts the short-run production function up. Usually, this will shift the demand for labor to the right. In this case, we can calculate the new demand for labor by following the steps sketched in Tool Kit 24.1. Also, because the same amount of labor now produces more output, aggregate supply will shift to the right.

Quantity of labor (million person years)	Output (millions of guanos)	Real wage (same as marginal product)
0	0	
1	1,200	1,200
2	2,200	1,000
3	3,000	800
4	3,600	600
5	4,000	400
6	4,200	200
7	4,300	100

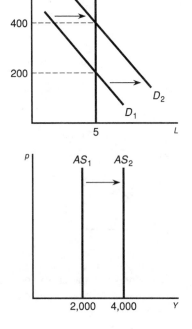

In the money market, demand shifts to the right reducing the price level to $P = 1$.

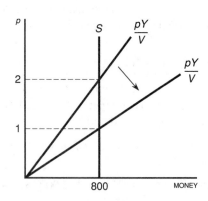

Labor supply, which equals 5 million, equals labor demand at a real wage of 400. Output increases to 4,000.

Step four (a): Labor supply shifts to the left to 3 million, and the real wage increases to 400.

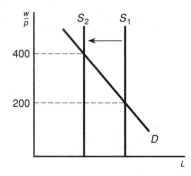

Step five: The reduction in labor reduces output to 1,500 million; thus aggregate supply shifts to the left.

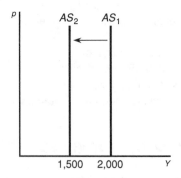

Step six: Find the new general equilibrium and compare.

14 (Practice problem: full-employment model) Review problems 2, 5, and 11. This problem continues the analysis of El Dorado.

    a Draw a diagram illustrating the general equilibrium in the El Dorado economy as solved for in the answer to problems 2, 5, and 11. In the following always begin with this equilibrium.

b Suppose that the money supply increases to 20 percent. Trace through the impact of this change in the economy. Show on the diagrams.

c The short-run production function doubles for each level of labor input.

d The supply of labor increases to 5 million.

15 (Practice problem: full-employment model) Review problems 3, 6, and 12. This problem continues the analysis of Erewhemos.

a Draw a diagram illustrating the general equilibrium in the Erewhemos economy as solved for in the answer to problems 3, 6, and 12. In the following always begin with this equilibrium.

b Suppose that the money supply increases to 23 percent. Trace through the impact of this change in the economy. Show on the diagrams.

c The short-run production function doubles for each level of labor input.

d The supply of labor increases to 5 million.

Answers to Problems

2 *a* The marginal product schedule is as follows:

Quantity of labor (million person years)	Marginal product
1	25
2	20
3	15
4	10
5	5
6	3
7	2
8	1

b The quantity of labor demanded is 6 thousand person years of labor.

3 *a* The marginal product schedule is as follows:

Quantity of labor (million person years)	Marginal product
1	5,000
2	4,000
3	3,000
4	2,000
5	1,000
6	500

b The quantity of labor demanded is 3 million person years.

5 *a* The demand for labor is as follows:

Quantity of labor (million person years)	Real wage (dorals per year)
1	25
2	20
3	15
4	10
5	5
6	3
7	2
8	1

b Real wage = 15; output = 60.

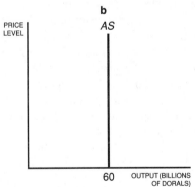

6 *a* The demand for labor is as follows:

Quantity of labor (million person years)	Real wage (wemos per year)
1	5,000
2	4,000
3	3,000
4	2,000
5	1,000
6	500

b Real wage = 1,000 per month; output = 15,000.

8 *a* Total savings = 10 billion dorals.

b Real interest rate = 4 percent. Investment = 10 billion dorals.

c The real interest rate rises to 7 percent. Because the supply of funds is inelastic, the level of investment remains at 10 billion. If the supply of funds sloped upward, investment would increase.

d The real interest rate rises to 7 percent. Investment falls to 5 billion.

9 *a* Total savings = $1/3 \times 15$ = 5 billion.

b Real interest rate = 6 percent. Investment = 5 billion.

c The real interest rate rises to 9 percent. Because the supply of funds is inelastic, the level of investment remains at 5 billion. If the supply of funds sloped upward, investment would increase.

d The real interest rate rises to 7 percent. Investment falls by 1 billion.

11 *a* $M = (60 \times P/6) = 10P$.

P	M_0
1	10
2	20
3	30
4	40
5	50
6	60

b $P = 5$.

c Price level falls to 4.

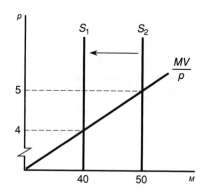

12 *a* $M = (15,000 \times P/2) = 7,500\,P$.

P	M_0
1	7,500
2	15,000
3	22,500
4	30,000
5	37,500
6	45,000

b $P = 2$.

c Price level rises to 4.

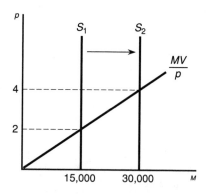

13 *a* General equilibrium is shown below.

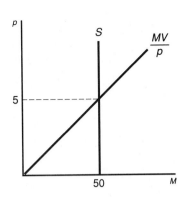

b Money supply shifts right and the new price level equals 6, but there are no other changes. Money is neutral in the full-employment model.

c The real wage doubles to 30. Aggregate supply shifts right to 120 and the price level falls to 2.5.

d The supply of labor shifts to the right, driving the real wage down to 5. Output increases to 75.

14 *a* General equilibrium is shown below.

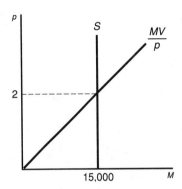

b Money supply shifts right and the new price level equals 3, but there are no other changes. Money is neutral in the full-employment model.

c The real wage doubles to 2,000, and output increases to 30. Aggregate supply shifts right to 30 and the price level falls to 1.

d The supply of labor shifts to the left, driving the real wage down to 2,000. Output increases to 14 billion; therefore aggregate supply shifts to the left.

CHAPTER 25 | Money, Banking, and Credit

Chapter Review

This chapter begins the study of money. The financial system, what money is, and the purposes it serves in the economy are the first topics. The discussion then introduces the concept of the money supply and explains how the banking system creates money. The chapter also discusses the Federal Reserve, the institution of government responsible for regulating the money supply, ensuring the availability of credit, and promoting the stability of the banking system and the Federal funds market where Federal Reserve actions first affect the economy.

ESSENTIAL CONCEPTS

1 The **financial system** includes all the institutions that help savers and borrowers transact. **Financial intermediaries,** such as banks and savings and loan associations, are the firms that stand between savers and borrowers. The **Federal Reserve** is the central bank of the United States. It regulates banks to ensure their financial health and also controls the money supply and availability of credit to promote and stabilize overall economic activity.

2 Economists define **money** by what it does. Money serves three functions. It is a **medium of exchange,** facilitating trades between firms and households. It is a **store of value,** permitting individuals to buy and sell at different times. Finally, it is a **unit of account,** helping people measure the relative value of different goods.

3 Since there are many financial assets that perform money's three functions to some degree, the **money supply** is measured in several ways. The most important measure is **M1,** which includes currency, traveler's checks, and **demand deposits** (checking accounts). Other measures, such as **M2** and **M3,** include progressively less liquid assets. The liquidity of an asset refers to how easy it is to convert into M1. The now rather common practice of buying on credit using credit cards or home equity loans makes specifying the size of the money supply more difficult.

4 While the Federal Reserve (or Fed) controls the money supply, money itself is created by the banking system. Banks operate on the **fractional reserve system,** which means that they keep only a fraction of deposits on hand as reserves. Thus, an intitial deposit (or other increase in reserves) results in additional loans, which ultimately return to the banking system as more deposits. The process of deposit expansion continues until total deposits have grown by a multiple of the initial deposit. The money **multiplier** is the relationship between the initial deposit and the ultimate change in total deposits.

5 Banks borrow and lend reserves on the **federal funds** market, where the "price" of reserves in the **federal funds rate.** The demand for reserves depends chiefly on this interest rate and the level of deposits. The Federal Reserve sets the supply of funds and thereby effectively determines the federal funds rate, the level of reserves, and by extension, the money supply.

6 The Federal Reserve has three instruments for controlling the supply of reserves. Most important, it buys and sells government bonds. This activity is called **open market operations.** The Fed also specifies the level of **required reserves** that banks must keep on hand or on deposit at the Fed. Finally, the Fed sets the **discount rate,** which is the interest rate charged to banks when borrowing from the Fed.

7 The precise way that the Fed implements its monetary

policy is called its **operating procedures.** If it sets a target for the federal funds rate, it is using an interest rate operating procedure. The alternative procedure targets the money supply and is called a money supply operating procedure. Due to recent financial innovations and financial market deregulation, central banks, such as the Fed, have abandoned money supply operating procedures. When a (nominal) interest rate target is used, however, the quantity of money automatically increases as prices rise, further contributing to inflation. Slowing inflation requires a higher interest rate target.

8 Ensuring the stability of the U.S. banking system and reducing the threat of bank runs are important responsibilities of the Federal Reserve and other government agencies. The Fed acts as a lender of last resort, providing liquidity to troubled banks, and it sets reserve requirements. Government-mandated capital requirements add to the incentives that bank owners have to manage risks carefully. The Federal Deposit Insurance Corporation insures depositors against bank failure.

BEHIND THE ESSENTIAL CONCEPTS

1 How do the Fed's instruments affect the money supply? Each works by increasing or decreasing banks' reserves, affecting the money available for loans.
 a When the Fed engages in open market operations, it buys and sells bonds. If it buys a bond, for example, the money that it pays is deposited in a bank. The bank's reserves increase, and it in turn can grant new loans.
 b When the Fed decreases reserve requirements, banks can reduce their reserves and again make new loans.
 c When the Fed increases the discount rate, banks know that borrowing from the Fed will be more expensive. They guard against having to borrow by keeping more reserves and making fewer loans.

2 Figure 25.1 will help you keep straight how open market operations affect the money supply. On the left

is the Fed's vault, where it keeps stacks of bonds and currency. The currency in the vault is not money, because it is not in the economy. On the right is the economy. If the Fed buys bonds, currency flows from the vault into the economy and increases the money supply. If the Fed sells bonds, the money it receives leaves the economy and goes into the vault, where it is no longer money.

3 Both the Federal Reserve and the U.S. Treasury sell government bonds. You can keep the two straight if you remember why the bonds are sold. The Treasury sells bonds to borrow money to finance government spending. When the Treasury sells bonds, the money is spent, and it stays in the economy. The Fed sells bonds to reduce the money supply. When the Fed sells bonds, the money it receives goes into the Fed's vault and leaves the economy.

SELF-TEST

True or False

1 The financial system includes all institutions involved in moving funds from savers to borrowers.
2 Financial intermediaries are firms that provide a link between savers and borrowers.
3 The store of value function of money refers to its use as a measure of the relative value of goods.
4 M1 includes currency, traveler's checks, and demand deposits.
5 A bank's net worth equals its liabilities minus its assets.
6 Banks operate on the fractional reserve system, which means that they hold only a fraction of the amount of deposits in reserve.
7 The money multiplier implies that total deposits increase by a multiple of an initial deposit.
8 The Federal Reserve is the central bank of the United States.
9 The Federal Reserve controls the money supply by mandating maximum interest rates that banks can charge their best customers.
10 Banks borrow and lend reserves overnight in the federal funds market.
11 The discount rate is the interest rate that the Fed charges on loans to banks.
12 Open market operations refer to the buying and selling of government bonds by the Federal Reserve.
13 When the Federal Reserve sells bonds, the total amount of nonborrowed reserves falls and the federal funds rate rises.
14 Among its three major policy instruments, the Federal Reserve uses the discount rate most often.
15 After 1980 the velocity of money became more unstable and difficult to predict.

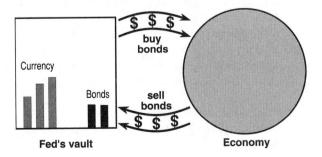

Figure 25.1

Multiple Choice

1 Which of the following are *not* financial intermediaries?
   a Banks
   b Savings and loans
   c Mutual funds
   d Life insurance companies
   e All of the above are financial intermediaries.

2 Which of the following is *not* a task performed by financial intermediaries?
   a Ascertaining the risks of potential borrowers
   b Collecting deposits
   c Monitoring loans
   d Diversification across many investments
   e All of the above

3 Trade without the use of money is called
   a double coincidence of wants.
   b medium of exchange.
   c barter.
   d unit of account.
   e multiple deposit.

4 Double coincidence of wants refers to the
   a fact that in order for two individuals to barter, each must have what the other wants and want what the other has.
   b fact that money must be both a store of value and a medium of exchange.
   c unlikely possibility that two individuals will have exactly the same tastes.
   d fact that dividends are taxed twice.
   e fact that the Federal Reserve engages in open market operations and sets the discount rate.

5 The use of money to facilitate exchange is its
   a medium of exchange function.
   b store of value function.
   c unit of account function.
   d double coincidence of wants function.
   e fractional reserve function.

6 The use of money to measure the relative value of goods and services is its
   a medium of exchange function.
   b store of value function.
   c unit of account function.
   d double coincidence of wants function.
   e fractional reserve function.

7 The use of money as a means of preserving purchasing power for a time period is its
   a medium of exchange function.
   b store of value function.
   c unit of account function.
   d double coincidence of wants function.
   e fractional reserve function.

8 The economic definition of money is
   a currency, traveler's checks, and demand deposits.
   b M1.
   c anything that acts as a medium of exchange, store of value, and unit of account.
   d anything that avoids the double coincidence of wants problem.
   e a and b.

9 Which of the following is *not* included in M1?
   a Currency
   b Demand deposits (checking accounts)
   c Traveler's checks
   d Certificates of deposit
   e All of the above are included.

10 Which of the following is *not* included in M2?
   a M1
   b Certificates of deposit
   c Eurodollar accounts
   d Savings accounts up to $100,000
   e All of the above are included.

11 Which of the following is *not* included in M3?
   a M1
   b M2
   c Savings accounts over $100,000
   d Institutional money-market mutual funds
   e Corporate retained earnings

12 An agreement by a bank to lend up to some specified amount is a
   a money market mutal fund.
   b certificate of deposit.
   c line of credit.
   d unit of account.
   e savings account.

13 The fractional reserve system in banking means that banks
   a lend a fraction of their money to consumers and a fraction to businesses.
   b hold a fraction of the amount on deposit in reserves.
   c hold a fraction of the amount on loan in reserves.
   d lend a fraction of their money to foreign businesses and a fraction to domestic businesses.
   e may or may not belong to the Federal Reserve system.

14 The money multiplier shows that
   a the rich get richer.
   b an increase in aggregate expenditures brings about a larger increase in national income.
   c an increase in reserves leads to a larger increase in total deposits.
   d a multiple of deposits must be held as reserves.
   e deregulation leads to instability in the banking system.

15 The federal funds rate is the
   a interest rate charged by the Fed for loans to member banks.
   b interest rate paid on Treasury bonds.

c interest rate on overnight loans between banks.

d interest rate on tax delinquencies.

e tax rate on interest earned on federal government bonds.

16 In the federal funds market, an increase in deposits

    a shifts demand to the right.

    b shifts demand to the left.

    c shifts supply to the right.

    d shifts supply to the left.

    e creates a surplus of reserves.

17 Open market operations, the most important means by which the Fed controls the money supply, involve

    a changing the discount rate.

    b setting interest rates.

    c changing the reserve requirement.

    d buying and selling government bonds.

    e placing varying restrictions on foreign borrowing and lending.

18 Which of the following is *not* a way in which the Federal Reserve can increase the money supply?

    a Lower the discount rate.

    b Reduce the reserve requirement.

    c Buy government securities.

    d Sell government securities.

    e All of the above are ways to increase the money supply.

19 If the economy's nominal income equals $10 trillion and the money supply is $2 trillion, then velocity equals

    a 20.

    b 5.

    c 40.

    d 18.

    e 22.

20 The modern banking system protects against the threat of bank runs by

    a acting as a lender of last resort.

    b setting reserve requirements.

    c mandating capital requirements.

    d insuring bank depositors.

    e all of the above.

Completion

1 For a trade to take place in a barter economy, each individual must have what the other wants and want what the other has; that is, there must be a _____.

2 Money facilitates exchange; it is performing its _____ function.

3 Money holds on to its purchasing power; it is performing its _____ function.

4 People use money as a measuring rod, taking advantage of the _____ function of money.

5 Currency, traveler's checks, and checking accounts are included in the _____ measure of money.

6 Firms that act as go-betweens for savers and borrowers are called _____.

7 The central bank in United States is called the _____.

8 When the Federal Reserve buys and sells bonds, it is engaging in _____.

9 The minimum level of reserves that banks must keep on hand is its_____.

10 The interest rate charged to banks by the Federal Reserve is called the _____.

Answers to Self-Test

True or False

1	t	6	t	11	t
2	t	7	t	12	t
3	f	8	t	13	t
4	t	9	f	14	f
5	f	10	t	15	t

Multiple Choice

1	*e*	6	*c*	11	*e*	16	*c*
2	*e*	7	*b*	12	*c*	17	*d*
3	*c*	8	*c*	13	*b*	18	*d*
4	*a*	9	*d*	14	*c*	19	*b*
5	*a*	10	*e*	15	*c*	20	*e*

Completion

1 double coincidence of wants

2 medium of exchange

3 store of value

4 unit of account

5 M1

6 financial intermediaries

7 Federal Reserve

8 open market operations

9 required reserves

10 discount rate

Doing Economics: Tools and Practice Problems

In this section, we learn about the balance sheet of banks, where assets, liabilities, and net worth are recorded, and use this tool to see how open market operations lead to changes in deposits, to trace through the deposit expansion process, and to compute the money multiplier. Finally, we study the workings of the Federal Funds market.

THE BALANCE SHEET

Before we can understand how banks create money, we must master the balance sheet. This keeps track of assets and liabilities as they change when money is deposited and loaned. Tool Kit 25.1 shows how to construct the bank's balance sheet and to compute its net worth.

Tool Kit 25.1 Constructing the Balance Sheet

The balance sheet is a "T-account," with assets listed on the left and liabilities and net worth on the right. When anything changes, net worth must adjust to keep the right and left sides in balance. To create a balance sheet, follow this procedure.

Step one: Make a T-account. Label the left column "Assets" and the right column "Liabilities and net worth."

Assets	Liabilities and net worth

Step two: Enter each of the assets (outstanding loans, bond holdings, reserves) in the left column, and sum the assets.

Assets	Liabilities and net worth
Loans	
Bonds	
Deposits	
Total assets	

Step three: Enter each of the liabilities (deposits) in the right column, and sum the liabilities.

Assets	Liabilities and net worth
Loans	Deposits
Bonds	
Deposits	
Total assets	

Step four: Compute net worth by subtracting liabilities from assets:

$$\text{net worth} = \text{assets} - \text{liabilities}.$$

Enter net worth in the right column.

Assets	Liabilities and net worth
Loans	Deposits
Bonds	
Deposits	Net worth
Total assets	

Step five: Sum the right and left columns, and check that the balance sheet is in balance.

Assets	Liabilities and net worth
Loans	Deposits
Bonds	
Deposits	

Total assets = total liabilities + net worth.

---

1 (Worked problem: balance sheet) President Bank has $18 million in outstanding loans, $3 million in government bonds, reserves of $4 million, and deposits equal to $20 million. Compute its net worth, and construct the balance sheet.

Step-by-step solution

Step one: Make a T-account.

President Bank's Balance Sheet

Assets	Liabilities and net worth

Step two: Enter each of the assets (outstanding loans, bond holdings, reserves) in the left column, and sum the assets.

President Bank's Balance Sheet

Assets	Liabilities and net worth
Loans outstanding = $18 million	
Government bonds = $3 million	
Reserves = $4 million	
Total assets = $25 million	

Step three: Enter each of the liabilities (deposits) in the right-hand column, and sum the liabilities.

President Bank's Balance Sheet

Assets	Liabilities and net worth
Loans outstanding = $18 million	Deposits = $20 million
Government bonds = $3 million	
Reserves = $4 million	
Total assets = $25 million	

Step four: Compute net worth:

net worth = 18 + 3 + 4 − 20 = $5 million.

Enter net worth in the right-hand column.

President Bank's Balance Sheet

Assets	Liabilities and net worth
Loans outstanding = $18 million	Deposits = $20 million
Government bonds = $3 million	
Reserves = $4 million	Net worth = $5 million
Total assets = $25 million	

Step five: Sum the right and left columns, and check that the balance sheet is in balance.

President Bank's Balance Sheet

Assets	Liabilities and net worth
Loans outstanding = $18 million	Deposits = $20 million
Government bonds = $3 million	
Reserves = $4 million	Net worth = $5 million
Total assets = $25 million	Total liabilities plus net worth = $25 million

2 (Practice problem: balance sheet) First Bank has $220 million in outstanding loans, $10 million in government bonds, $25 million in reserves, and $240 million in deposits. Compute its net worth, and construct its balance sheet.

3 (Practice problem: balance sheet) Second Bank has $400 million in outstanding loans, $25 million in government bonds, $50 million in reserves, and $450 million in deposits. Compute its net worth, and construct its balance sheet.

MONEY CREATION

Using the fractional reserve system, banks create money. When banks receive a new deposit, they keep only a fraction on hand in reserve and loan out the remainder. But the loans find their way back into the banking system, increasing deposits further and setting off a new round of loans. When the process settles down, total deposits in the banking system have increased by a multiple of the initial deposit.

4 (Worked problem: deposit expansion and money multiplier) The banking system in Costa Guano has $4 billion in outstanding loans, $1 billion in government bonds, $1 billion in reserves, and deposits of $5 billion. Its reserve ratio is 0.20. (Monetary magnitudes are converted to U.S. dollar equivalents.)

   a Construct the combined balance sheet.

   b A new deposit of $1 billion arrives from abroad. Trace through three rounds of the deposit expansion process, and compute the final deposit expansion.

Step-by-step solution

Step one (*a*): Construct a combined balance sheet for the banking system.

Costa Guano's Combined Balance Sheet

Assets	Liabilities and net worth
Loans outstanding = $4 billion Government bonds = $1 billion Reserves = $1 billion Total assets = $6 billion	Deposits = $5 billion Net worth = $1 billion Total liabilities plus net worth = $6 billion

Step two (*b*): Identify the initial deposit, and add it to the banking system's deposits. The deposit is $1 billion.

Step three: Identify the reserve ratio. Calculate the required increase in reserves made necessary by the initial deposit, and add it to the banking system's reserves:

new required reserves = 0.20 × 1 = $0.2 billion.

Step four: Calculate the new loans that the deposit allows, and add the amount to the banking system's loans:

new loans = 1 − 0.2 = $0.8 billion.

Tool Kit 25.2 Understanding Deposit Expansion and the Money Multiplier

Banks create money. Through the fractional reserve system deposits result in additional loans and further deposits. Follow these steps to see how the money creation process works through the banking system.

Step one: Construct a combined balance sheet for the banking system.

Step two: Identify the initial deposit, and add it to the banking system's deposits.

Step three: Identify the reserve ratio. Calculate the required increase in reserves made necessary by the initial deposit, and add it to the banking system's reserves:

new required reserves = reserve ratio × initial deposit.

Step four: Calculate the new loans that the deposit allows, and add the amount to the banking system's loans:

new loans = initial deposit − new required reserves.

This completes round one of the deposit expansion process. (Remember to recompute the total assets and liabilities and net worth.)

Step five: Trace through a few more rounds by repeating steps two through four. the initial deposit for round two is the amount of new loans from round one.

Step six: Compute the final expansion in deposits. This will be the increase in the money supply:

final deposit expansion = initial deposit/reserve ratio.

Because there are no other leakages in this example, the money multiplier equals 1/reserve ratio.

Costa Guano's Combined Balance Sheet (round one)

Assets	Liabilities and net worth
Loans outstanding = $4.8 billion Government bonds = $1 billion Reserves = $1.2 billion Total assets = $7 billion	Deposits = $6 billion Net worth = $1 billion Total liabilities plus net worth = $7 billion

This completes round one of the deposit expansion process. (Note the new totals.)

Step five: Trace through a few more rounds by repeating steps two through four. The initial deposit for round two is the amount of new loans from round one.

Costa Guano's Combined Balance Sheet (round two)

Assets	Liabilities and net worth
Loans outstanding = $5.44 billion	Deposits = $6.8 billion
Government bonds = $1 billion	
Reserves = $1.36 billion	Net worth = $1 billion
Total assets = $7.8 billion	Total liabilities plus net worth = $7.8 billion

Costa Guano's Combined Balance Sheet (round three)

Assets	Liabilities and net worth
Loans outstanding = $5.95 billion	Deposits = $7.44 billion
Government bonds = $1 billion	
Reserves = $1.49 billion	Net worth = $1 billion
Total assets = $8.44 billion	Total liabilities plus net worth = $8.44 billion

Step six: Compute the final expansion in deposits. this will be the increase in the money supply:

final deposit expansion = $1/(0.2)$ = $5 billion.

5 (Practice problem: deposit expansion and money multiplier) In El Dorado, the banking system has outstanding loans of $200 million, government bonds of $10 million, reserves of $30 million, reserves of $30 million, and deposits of $210 million. Its reserve ratio is 1/7. (Monetary magnitudes are converted to dollar equivalents.)
  a Construct the combined balance sheet.
  b A new deposit of $49 million arrives from abroad. Trace through two rounds of the deposit expansion process, and compute the final deposit expansion.
6 (Practice problem: deposit expansion and money multiplier) The Erehwemos banking system has outstanding loans of $45 billion, government bonds of $2 billion, reserves of $5 billion, and deposits of $50 billion. Its reserve ratio is 0.10. (Monetary magnitudes are converted to U.S. dollar equivalents.)
  a Construct the combined balance sheet.
  b A new deposit of $5 billion arrives from abroad. Trace through three rounds of the deposit expansion process, and compute the final deposit expansion.

THE FEDERAL FUNDS MARKET

Banks borrow and lend overnight in the federal funds market. The demand is the demand for reserves and the supply is determined by the Federal Reserve through the use of its policy instruments: the discount rate, reserve requirement,

and open market operations. We trace through the effects of changes in these instruments and in the level of deposits. Again we employ the usual method of starting with equilibrium, shifting curves, and finding the new equilibrium.

Tool Kit 25.3 Supply and Demand in the Federal Funds Market

When deposits increase or when the Fed alters one of its policy instruments, equilibrium in the federal funds market changes. We follow the effects with this procedure.

Step one: Start with an equilibrium.

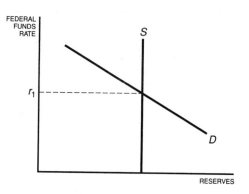

Step two: Observe the exogenous change and determine which curve shifts. Refer to the following table.

Exogenous change	Shift
Deposits increase.	Demand shifts to the right.
The Discount rate increases.	Supply shifts to the left.
The reserve requirement increases.	Supply shifts to the left.
The Fed buys bonds.	Supply shifts to the right.
The Fed sells bonds.	Supply shifts to the left.

Step three: Shift the curve.

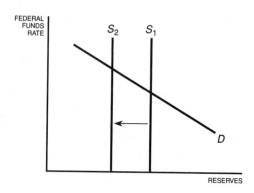

Step four: Find the new equilibrium and compare.

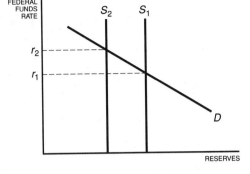

7 (Worked problem: federal funds) The Federal Reserve implements a major bond purchase. Analyze the impact on the federal funds market.

Step-by-step solution

Step one: Start with an equilibrium.

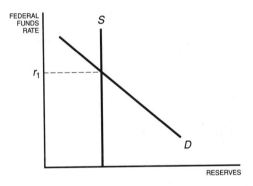

Step two: Observe the exogenous change and determine which curve shifts. The purchase of bonds increases reserves, shifting supply to the right.

Step three: Shift the curve.

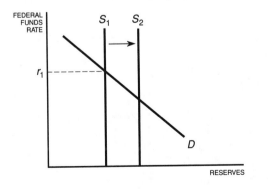

Step four: Find the new equilibrium. We see that the federal funds rate rises.

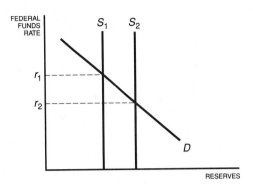

8 For each of the following, analyze the impact on the federal funds market.
a The Fed increases the discount rate.
b The Fed reduces the reserve requirement.
c The Fed sells bonds.
d Deposits increase.
e Deposits decrease.
f The Fed increases the reserve requirement.
g The Fed decreases the discount rate.

Answers to Problems

2

First Bank's Balance Sheet

Assets	Liabilities and net worth
Loans outstanding = $220 million	Deposits = $240 million
Government bonds = $10 million	
Reserves = $25 million	Net worth = $15 million
Total assets = $255 million	Total liabilities plus net worth = $255 million

3

Second Bank's Balance Sheet

Assets	Liabilities and net worth
Loans outstanding = $400 million	Deposits = $450 million
Government bonds = $25 million	
Reserves = $50 million	Net worth = $25 million
Total assets = $475 million	Total liabilities plus net worth = $475 million

5   *a*

El Dorado's Combined Balance Sheet

Assets	Liabilities and net worth
Loans outstanding = $200 million	Deposits = $210 million
Government bonds = $10 million	
Reserves = $30 million	Net worth = $30 million
Total assets = $240 million	Total liabilities plus net worth = $240 million

b

El Dorado's Combined Balance Sheet (round one)

Assets	Liabilities and net worth
Loans outstanding = $242 million	Deposits = $259 million
Government bonds = $10 million	
Reserves = $37 million	Net worth = $30 million
Total assets = $289 million	Total liabilities plus net worth = $289 million

El Dorado's Combined Balance Sheet (round two)

Assets	Liabilities and net worth
Loans outstanding = $278 million	Deposits = $301 million
Government bonds = $10 million	
Reserves = $43 million	Net worth = $30 million
Total assets = $331 million	Total liabilities plus net worth = $331 million

Final deposit expansion = 49/(1/7) = $343 million.

6   *a*

Erehwemos's Combined Balance Sheet (round one)

Assets	Liabilities and net worth
Loans outstanding = $45 billion	Deposits = $50 billion
Government bonds = $2 billion	
Reserves = $5 billion	Net worth = $2 billion
Total assets = $52 billion	Total liabilities plus net worth = $52 billion

b

Erehwemos's Combined Balance Sheet (round two)

Assets	Liabilities and net worth
Loans outstanding = $49.5 billion	Deposits = $55 billion
Government bonds = $2 billion	
Reserves = $5.5 billion	Net worth = $2 billion
Total assets = $57 billion	Total liabilities plus net worth = $57 billion

Erehwemos's Combined Balance Sheet (round three)

Assets	Liabilities and net worth
Loans outstanding = $53.55 billion	Deposits = $59.5 billion
Government bonds = $2 billion	
Reserves = $5.95 billion	Net worth = $2 billion
Total assets = $61.5 billion	Total liabilities plus net worth = $61.5 billion

Final deposit expansion = 5/(0.1) = $50 billion.

8   *a* Supply shifts to the left, increasing the federal funds rate.

b Supply shifts to the right, decreasing the federal funds rate.

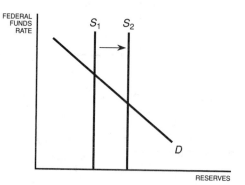

c Supply shifts to the left, increasing the federal funds rate.

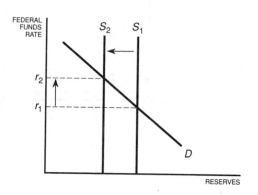

d Demand shifts to the right, increasing the federal funds rate.

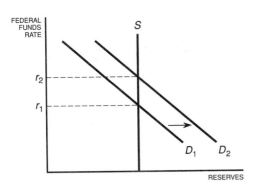

e Demand shifts to the left, decreasing the federal funds rate.

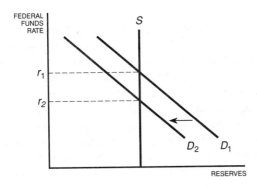

f Supply shifts to the left, increasing the federal funds rate.

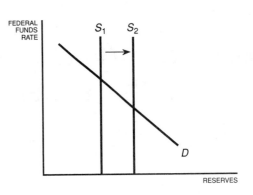

g Supply shifts to the right, decreasing the federal funds rate.

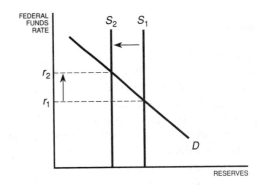

CHAPTER 26 | Government Finance and the Open Economy at Full-Employment

Chapter Review

The full-employment model, developed in Chapter 6, is put to use analyzing the fiscal deficit, or surplus, and the trade deficit. The center of attention is the capital market. Fiscal deficits and surpluses affect national savings, and through the capital market changes in national savings affect interest rates and investment. The openness of the economy to trade and investment means that some investment may be financed by foreign borrowing. This relationship becomes clear in two key ideas: the basic trade identity and the equality of savings and investment. Funds for foreign trade and investment flow through the market for foreign exchange, which is the final topic.

ESSENTIAL CONCEPTS

1 **National savings** is the sum of private savings and government savings. When the government runs a **fiscal deficit,** government savings is a negative number. Thus, an increase in the fiscal deficit reduces national savings and shifts the supply of funds in the capital market to the left. This raises interest rates and reduces investment. The same scenario follows a balanced budget increase in government spending, where again private investment is **crowded out**. Of course, a **surplus** has the opposite effect.

2 In an **open economy**, national savings plus foreign borrowing (also called net capital flows, NCFs) must equal investment. For a small open economy, interest rates are set on international capital markets. When government deficits reduce national savings, interest rates do not change and therefore neither does investment. The United States is a large open economy. Reductions in national savings do increase international interest rates and lead to lower levels of investment.

3 The difference between imports and exports in a given year is the **trade deficit** which, according to the basic trade identity, must equal the inflows of foreign capital. The exchange of currencies for imports, exports, and capital flows is governed by the exchange rate, which is the relative price of two currencies. The **exchange rate** adjusts to bring into balance the demands and supplies of all currencies.

4 International trade and investment require markets to exchange currencies. The market for dollars determines the **exchange rate,** which is the amount of foreign currency that trades for 1 dollar. Demand and supply in this market determine this exchange rate. It operates in a similar manner to other markets. For example, an increase in foreign borrowing causes the price of a dollar to rise (or **appreciate**).

BEHIND THE ESSENTIAL CONCEPTS

1 The connection between budget and trade deficits can be seen by examining the **basic trade identity** for an open economy. The basic trade identity is

trade deficit = imports − exports = **capital inflows.**

This means that if foreign capital flows into the United States (in greater amounts than U.S. capital flows abroad), then the U.S. must run a trade deficit.

2 **Federal budget deficits** rose dramatically during the 1980s, increasing the nation's debt to record levels even though the 1980s were a time of peace and relative prosperity. The high deficits can be linked to four causes. Taxes were reduced, defense spending increased, Social Security and Medicare payments grew, and the accumulated debt required higher interest payments. At the same time, the U.S. **trade deficit** reached record levels, causing the United States to slip from creditor to debtor nation status.

3 It is important to distinguish flows and stocks. The deficit is a flow variable. For example, if spending outpaces taxes by $100 billion, then there is an outflow from the government of $100 billion. This adds to the stock of debt, which is the accumulated amount that government owes. The large fiscal deficits of the 1980s added to the United States's stock of debt. Recent surpluses have reduced the debt both in absolute terms and as a percent of GDP.

4. There are three models of the capital market: closed economy, small open economy, and large open economy. In a **closed economy** national savings must equal investment. Any change in savings brings about an equal change in investment. In a small open economy, on the other hand, the interest rate is fixed. Changes in savings are exactly offset by net inflows of foreign funds, leaving investment unchanged. For a large open economy, changes in savings affect interest rates and change investment, but the change is less than the change in savings.

5 There is another view about how fiscal deficits affect capital markets. When the government increases spending without a tax increase, it finances its deficit by selling bonds. Today's bonds must be repaid, however. This means that future taxpayers are liable for the debts incurred to finance current spending. Households will save now in order to be able to pay the future tax liability, and these savings will completely offset the effects of the deficit. Thus deficits are equivalent to taxes. This idea is called Ricardian equivalence, but most economists reject it.

SELF-TEST

True or False

1 During the 1980s, the United States ran a fiscal surplus.
2 In a closed economy, investment equals private savings
3 An increase in the fiscal deficit raises the real interest rate.
4 Increased fiscal deficits reduce national savings.
5 A balanced budget increase in government spending has no effect on national savings or interest rates.
6 The federal debt is the difference between what the government receives in taxes and what it spends.

7 Both the budget deficit and the federal debt are much larger for the United States than for most European countries.
8 Ricardian equivalence implies that fiscal deficits have no effect on interest rates.
9 In a small open economy, increasing the budget deficit shifts supply to the left, increasing the interest rate and reducing investment.
10 In an open economy, national savings need not equal investment.
11 The United States is a large open economy.
12 The trade deficit always equals capital inflows from abroad.
13 The exchange rate is the relative price of two currencies.
14 When the price of a country's currency rises, the currency is said to appreciate.
15 Increased foreign borrowing causes the dollar to appreciate.

Multiple Choice

1 In a closed economy, investment equals
  a private savings.
  b private savings plus government savings.
  c government savings.
  d private savings minus government savings minus the budget deficit.
  e the trade deficit.
2 In a closed economy, an increase in the budget deficit
  a reduces the interest rate and investment.
  b does not change the interest rate or investment.
  c increases the interest rate and investment.
  d increases the interest rate but reduces investment.
  e decreases the interest rate but increases investment.
3 A balanced budget increase in government spending
  a reduces national savings.
  b shifts supply to the left in the capital market.
  c raises interest rates.
  d all of the above.
  e none of the above.
4 Which of the following is *not* caused by a balanced budget change in government spending?
  a A change in the composition of output
  b A change in interest rates
  c A change in national savings
  d A change in investment
  e A change in the deficit or surplus
5 During much of the 1980s, the United States ran
  a federal budget deficits and trade surpluses.
  b federal budget surpluses and trade deficits.
  c federal budget and trade surpluses.
  d federal budget and trade deficits.
  e balanced federal budgets and trade accounts.

6 Which of the following is true of the relative size of U.S. budget deficits and the federal debt?

  a Neither the deficits nor the debt are as large as those of many European countries and Canada.

  b The deficits are larger than those of European countries and Canada, but the debt has not yet grown as large.

  c The deficits are smaller than those of European countries and Canada, but the debt is greater.

  d Both the deficits and debt are larger than those of European countries and Canada.

  e Neither the deficits nor the debt are as large as those of Japan.

7 According to Ricardian equivalence, which of the following are equivalent?

  a Savings and investment

  b Real and nominal interest rates

  c Fiscal deficits and taxation

  d Trade deficits and net inflows of foreign funds

  e Private savings and government savings

8 In an open economy,

  a private savings must equal private investment.

  b private savings plus capital flows from abroad must equal investment.

  c private savings plus capital flows from abroad must equal investment plus the government deficit.

  d private savings plus capital flows from abroad must equal the government deficits plus the trade deficit.

  e private savings plus capital flows from abroad must equal the government deficit plus the trade deficit plus investment.

9 In an open economy, investment may be financed from

  a private savings.

  b government savings.

  c capital flows from abroad.

  d all of the above.

  e a and c.

10 In a small open economy, which of the following does/do *not* change when national savings changes?

  a The real interest rate

  b Investment

  c The trade of deficit

  d Inflows of foreign capital

  e a and b

11 In a small open economy, an increase in the budget deficit

  a reduces the interest rate and investment.

  b does not change the interest rate or investment.

  c increases the interest rate and investment.

  d increases the interest rate but reduces investment.

  e decreases the interest rate but increases investment.

12 In the U.S. economy, an increase in the budget deficit

  a reduces the interest rate and investment.

  b does not change the interest rate or investment.

  c increases the interest rate and investment.

  d increases the interest rate but reduces investment.

  e decreases the interest rate but increases investment.

13 To reduce the trade deficit, a country can

  a shift the investment function to the left or the savings curve to the right.

  b shift the investment function to the right or the savings curve to the left.

  c shift either the investment function or the savings curve to the right.

  d shift either the investment function or the savings curve to the left.

  e restrict the importation of foreign goods.

14 To increase investment in a closed economy,

  a shift the investment function to the left or the savings curve to the right.

  b shift the investment function to the right or the savings curve to the left.

  c shift either the investment function or the savings curve to the right.

  d shift either the investment function or the savings curve to the left.

  e negotiate with foreign countries to reduce world interest rates.

15 The basic trade identify says that

  a imports must equal exports.

  b imports must equal capital flows from abroad.

  c exports must equal capital flows from abroad.

  d the trade deficit must equal capital flows from abroad.

  e capital flows from abroad must equal capital flows to overseas economies.

16 Japan currently

  a exports more than it imports.

  b runs a trade surplus.

  c has net capital outflow.

  d all of the above.

  e a and b.

17 If a country invests more overseas than foreign countries invest in it, then

  a its trade account must be in balance.

  b it must run a trade surplus.

  c it must run a trade deficit.

  d it must balance its government budget.

  e its government deficit must equal the net flow of capital to other countries.

18 The exchange rate is

  a the trade deficit between two nations.

  b a country's net inflow of capital.

  c the relative price of two currencies.

  d the rate of appreciation of a country's currency.

  e the rate of depreciation of a country's currency.

19 When a German buys a U.S. government bond, the transaction is an example of

  a imports.

  b exports.

  c capital inflows.

d capital outflows.

e currency exchange.

20 An increase in foreign borrowing causes the U.S. dollar to

a remain fixed because it is set on world markets.

b depreciate.

c appreciate.

d move closer to the world interest rate.

e remain fixed because of Ricardian equivalence.

Completion

1 The _____ is the cumulative amount that the government owes.

2 The difference between government expenditures and revenues is the _____.

3 The basic trade identity says that the trade deficit must equal _____.

4 In an open economy, private savings plus capital flows from abroad must equal investment plus _____.

5 The relative price of two currencies is called the _____.

6 When the price of a country's currency rises, it is said to _____.

7 National savings equals investment for a(n) _____ economy.

8 The interest rate is set on world markets for a(n) _____ economy.

9 The United States is a(n) _____ economy.

10 When a balanced budget increase in government spending leads to a reduction in private consumption and investment, there is said to be _____.

Answers to Self-Test

True or False

1	f	6	f	11	t
2	f	7	f	12	t
3	t	8	t	13	t
4	t	9	f	14	t
5	f	10	t	15	t

Multiple Choice

1	*b*	6	*a*	11	*b*	16	*d*
2	*d*	7	*c*	12	*d*	17	*b*
3	*d*	8	*c*	13	*a*	18	*c*
4	*e*	9	*d*	14	*c*	19	*c*
5	*d*	10	*e*	15	*d*	20	*c*

Completion

1 federal debt

2 fiscal deficit

3 capital inflows from abroad

4 government savings

5 exchange rate

6 appreciate

7 closed

8 small open

9 large open

10 crowding out

Doing Economics: Tools and Practice Problems

The discussion of the three major topics of this chapter—budget deficits, trade deficits, and exchange rates—centers on the capital market. Government finances budget deficits by borrowing funds on the capital market. Trade deficits, through the basic trade identity, result in flows of foreign capital to the capital market. An essential aspect of the capital market is its openness to international borrowing and savings. We look at the model of the small open economy and then study the model most appropriate to the United States, the large open economy. Finally we consider exchange rates.

THE GOVERNMENT AND THE CAPITAL MARKET

We study the impact of government fiscal policy on the capital market. The starting point is the observation that national savings equals private plus government savings (tax collections − expenditures). Changes in tax or expenditure policy, then, affect national savings, interest rates, and, ultimately, investment. We show these effects through the usual approach of starting with the equilibrium, shifting the curve, and finding the new equilibrium.

Tool Kit 26.1 Government and the Capital Market

When taxes, spending, or both change, national savings is affected. Follow these steps to find the impact on the capital market.

Step one: Start with an equilibrium.

Step two: Determine which curve shifts. Government fiscal policy always shifts the supply (savings) curve. Refer to the following table.

Exogenous change	Effect on deficit or surplus	Shift
Taxes increase	Increases in surplus (deficit falls)	Supply to right
Government spending increases	Decreases in surplus (deficit rises)	Supply to left
Balanced budget increase in spending	No change in surplus	Supply to left

Step three: Shift the curve.

Step four: Find the new equilibrium and compare.

1 (Worked problem: government and capital market) The Bush administration pushes through a major tax cut. Find the impact on the government fiscal surplus, national savings, interest rates, and investment.

Step-by-step solution

Step one: Start with an equilibrium.

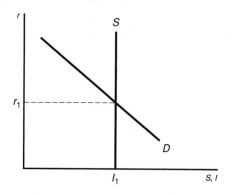

Step two: Determine which curve shifts. The tax cut decreases the surplus. National savings falls and supply shifts to left.

Step three: Shift the curve.

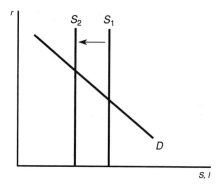

Step four: Find the new equilibrium and compare. The interest rate rises and investment falls.

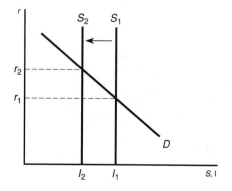

2 Show the effect on the fiscal surplus or deficit, national savings, interest rates, and investment of each of the following.

 a A major defense buildup increases government spending. There is a fiscal surplus.

 b The estate tax is eliminated. There is a fiscal surplus.

 c Both expenditures and taxes fall by 10 percent. There is a fiscal surplus.

 d Social Security payroll taxes are increased. There is a fiscal deficit.

 e Medicare benefits are reduced substantially. There is a fiscal surplus.

THE SMALL OPEN ECONOMY

The international capital market is so huge that a small country's borrowing and lending have no effect on interest rates. Thus, a small open economy can borrow and lend on international markets at a fixed interest rate. Because its investment equals its quantity demanded at that fixed interest rate, domestic savings have no effect on investment. This separation of savings and investment implies that the most important effects of budget deficits concern flows of foreign capital. Another implication identifies trade deficits as a result of domestic savings and investment decisions. Tool Kit 26.2 shows how the small open economy model works.

Tool Kit 26.2 Using the Small Open Economy Model

For a small open economy the interest rate is fixed, determined on international capital markets that are large relative to the size of the economy. If the interest rate clears the domestic market, the trade account is balanced. Higher interest rates imply a trade surplus; lower interest rates imply a trade deficit. Follow these steps to analyze the working of the capital market for a small open economy.

Step one: Identify the world interest rate, the demand, and the supply of funds.

Step two: Find the level of investment. This is quantity demanded, and it is read off the demand curve at the world interest rate.

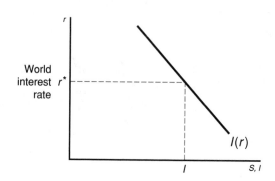

Step three: Find the level of savings. This is the quantity supplied, and it is read off the supply curve at the world interest rate.

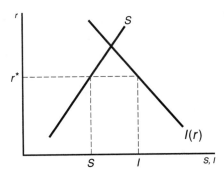

Step four: Find the level of capital inflows or outflows. If the quantity demanded exceeds the quantity supplied, then the country imports capital. Otherwise capital is exported.

Capital inflows from abroad
= quantity demanded − quantity supplied (if positive).

Capital outflows to abroad
= quantity supplied − quantity demanded (if positive).

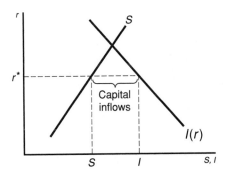

Step five: Find the trade deficit or surplus. If there are capital inflows, the country runs a trade deficit. If there are capital outflows, the country runs a trade surplus.

Trade deficit = inflows of foreign capital.

Trade surplus = outflows of foreign capital.

3 (Worked problem: small open economy) Costa Guano is a small open economy facing a world interest rate equal to 10 percent. Its domestic demand and supply of funds are given in Table 26.1.

a Find the level of investment.
b Find the level of savings.
c Find the level of capital inflows or outflows.
d Does the country run a trade deficit or surplus? How much is it?

Table 26.1

Interest rate percent)	Demand for funds (millions of guanos)	Supply of funds (millions of guanos)
15	100	100
14	110	90
13	120	80
12	130	70
11	140	60
10	150	50
9	160	40
8	170	30

Step-by-step solution

Step one: Identify the world interest rate, the demand, and the supply of funds. The world interest rate is 10 percent and the demand and supply of funds are given in Table 26.1.

Step two: Find the level of investment. When the interest rate is 10 percent, the demand for funds (investment) equals 150 million.

Step three: Find the level of savings. At an interest rate equal to 10 percent, savings (supply of funds) equals 50 million.

Step four: Find the level of capital inflows or outflows. The quantity demanded exceeds the quantity supplied, so the country imports capital.

Capital inflows from abroad
= quantity demanded − quantity supplied
= 150 − 50 = 100 million.

Step five: Find the trade deficit or surplus. If there are capital inflows, the country runs a trade deficit.

Trade deficit = inflows of foreign capital = 100 million.

4 (Practice problem: small open economy) El Dorado is a small open economy facing a world interest rate equal to 9 percent. Its domestic demand and supply of funds are given in Table 26.2.
a Find the level of investment.
b Find the level of savings.
c Find the level of capital inflows or outflows.
d Does the country run a trade deficit or surplus? How much is it?

Table 26.2

Interest rate (percent)	Demand for funds (millions of dorals)	Supply of funds (millions of dorals)
11	200	400
10	225	350
9	250	300
8	275	250
7	300	200
6	325	150
5	350	100

Table 26.3

Interest rate (percent)	Demand for funds (millions of wemos)	Supply of funds (millions of wemos)
20	50	50
19	60	45
18	70	40
17	80	35
16	90	30
15	100	25
14	110	20

5 (Practice problem: small open economy) Erehwemos is a small open economy facing a world interest rate equal to 15 percent. Its domestic demand and supply of funds are given in Table 26.3.
  a Find the level of investment.
  b Find the level of savings.
  c Find the level of capital inflows or outflows.
  d Does the country run a trade deficit or surplus? How much is it?

LARGE OPEN ECONOMY

The United States is a large open economy. This means that domestic savings affects interest rates and the level of investment. Approximately 80 percent of additional savings is invested in the United States. The remaining savings flows abroad. We can analyze large open economies by distinguishing between the domestic and total supply of funds. Tool Kit 26.3 shows how this is done.

Tool Kit 26.3 Using the Large Open Economy Model

Unlike the small open economy model, where foreign savings is perfectly elastic, for the large open economy foreign savings is upward sloping. The interest rate is determined where the total savings supply intersects the domestic demand for funds. Follow these steps.

Step one: Identify the foreign supply of savings, the domestic supply of savings, and the domestic demand for funds (investment function).

Step two: Calculate the total savings supply curve. For each interest rate add the quantity of foreign and domestic savings.

Total savings = foreign savings + domestic savings.

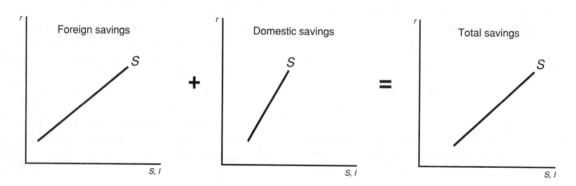

Step three: Find the interest rate that clears the market.

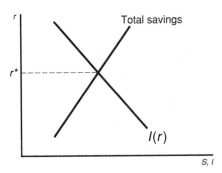

Step four: Find the level of investment. This is the quantity demanded at the equilibrium interest rate.

Step five: Find the level of domestic savings. This is read off the domestic supply of funds at the equilibrium interest rate.

Step six: Calculate the level of capital flows. Recall that this is also the level of the trade deficit.

Capital inflows from abroad = trade deficit = quantity demanded − quantity supplied (if positive).

Capital outflows to abroad = trade surplus = quantity supplied − quantity demanded (if positive).

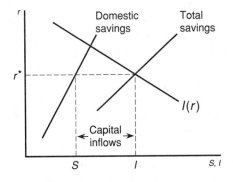

6 (Worked problem: large open economy) Table 26.4 gives the foreign supply of funds, the domestic supply of funds, and the demand for funds (investment function) for a large open economy.
   a Calculate the total supply of funds.
   b Find the equilibrium interest rate.
   c Does this country import or export capital? How much?
   d What is the size of the trade deficit or surplus?

Step-by-step solution

Step one: Identify the foreign supply of savings, the domestic supply of savings, and the domestic demand for funds. They are given in Table 26.4.

Step two: Calculate the total savings supply curve. For each interest rate add the quantity of foreign and domestic savings.

Total savings = foreign savings + domestic savings.

Table 26.4

Interest rate (percent)	Foreign supply (billions of dollars)	Domestic supply (billions of dollars)	Domestic demand (billions of dollars)
12	10,000	15,000	13,000
11	9,000	13,000	16,000
10	8,000	11,000	19,000
9	7,000	9,000	22,000
8	6,000	7,000	25,000
7	5,000	5,000	30,000

At 12 percent total savings = 10,000 + 15,000 = 25,000. At 11 percent total savings = 9,000 + 13,000 = 22,000. Continuing, we get the total supply.

Interest rate (percent)	Total supply (billions of dollars)
12	10,000 + 15,000 = 25,000
11	9,000 + 13,000 = 22,000
10	8,000 + 11,000 = 19,000
9	7,000 + 9,000 = 16,000
8	6,000 + 7,000 = 13,000
7	5,000 + 5,000 = 10,000

Step three: Find the interest rate that clears the market. Supply and demand are equal at $19,000 million when the interest rate is 10 percent.

Step four: Find the level of investment. This is the quantity demanded at the equilibrium interest rate, and it equals $19,000 million.

Step five: Find the level of domestic savings. This is read off the domestic supply of funds at the equilibrium interest rate. At 10 percent the domestic supply is $11,000 million.

Step six: Calculate the level of capital flows. Recall that this is also the level of the trade deficit. Since demand exceeds supply, there will be inflows of capital.

Capital inflows from abroad = trade deficit
= quantity demanded − quantity supplied
= 19,000 − 11,000 = $8,000 million.

7 (Practice problem: large open economy) Table 26.5 gives the foreign supply of funds, the domestic supply of funds, and the demand for funds (investment function) for a large open economy.
   a Calculate the total supply of funds.
   b Find the equilibrium interest rate.
   c Does this country import or export capital? How much?
   d What is the size of the trade deficit or surplus?

Table 26.5

Interest rate (percent)	Foreign supply	Domestic supply	Domestic demand
	(billions of dollars)		
15	1,000	500	900
14	800	400	1,200
13	600	300	1,500
12	400	200	1,800
11	200	100	2,100
10	100	50	2,500

8 (Practice problem: large open economy) Table 26.6 gives the foreign supply of funds, the domestic supply of funds, and the demand for funds (investment function) for a large open economy.

a Calculate the total supply of funds.
b Find the equilibrium interest rate.
c Does this country import or export capital? How much?
d What is the size of the trade deficit or surplus?

Table 26.6

Interest rate (percent)	Foreign supply	Domestic supply	Domestic demand
	(billions of dollars)		
8	200	50	100
7	180	45	110
6	160	40	130
5	140	35	140
4	120	30	150
3	100	25	160
2	80	20	170

EXCHANGE RATES

Supply and demand in international currency markets is the topic of this section. This is an application of basic supply and demand, so we follow the usual four-step procedure. All of the applications in this section deal with the market for U.S. dollars and the determination of the dollar exchange rate.

We will study three reasons for shifts in the supply and demand curves for foreign currencies. First, the demand for traded goods may change, shifting either the demand or supply curve for dollars. Second, interest rates may change, and because investors seek the highest relative return, both the supply and demand curves shift. One thing to keep in mind when both curves shift is that the shift reinforce each other. In other words, if the shift in the demand curve would cause the dollar to depreciate, then the supply curve will shift to cause further depreciation. Table 26.7 summarizes the possible causes of shifts.

Table 26.7

Shifts in demand and supply curves for foreign currencies

1 Traded goods and services: When the foreign demand for U.S. exports increases, demand for U.S. dollars shifts to the right; when it decreases, demand for U.S. dollars shifts to the left. When U.S. demand for imported goods increases, supply of U.S. dollars shifts to the right; when it decreases, supply of U.S. dollars shifts to the left.
2 Borrowing and lending: When U.S. interest rates increase, demand for U.S. dollars shifts to the right and supply shifts to the left. When they decrease, demand for U.S. dollars shifts to the left and supply shifts to the right. When foreign interest rates increase, demand for U.S. dollars shifts to the left and supply shifts to the right. When they decrease, demand for U.S. dollars shifts to the right and supply shifts to the left.

Tool Kit 26.4 Supply and Demand for Currencies

Step one: Start with an equilibrium.

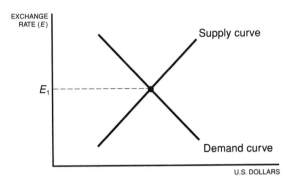

Step two: Observe the exogenous change, and determine which curve or curves shift.

Step three: Shift the supply curve, demand curve, or both.

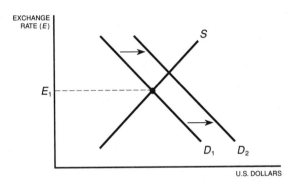

Step four: Find the new equilibrium exchange rate, and compare it with the original one.

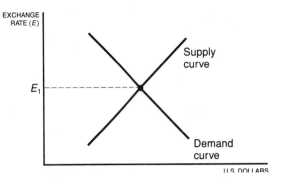

Step two: Observe the exogenous change, and determine which curve shifts. The increase in German interest rates shifts the demand for dollars to the left (because German investors keep their marks in Germany to earn high German interest rates), and the supply of dollars shifts to the right (because U.S. investors seek to trade dollars for marks and invest in Germany).

Step three: Shift the curves.

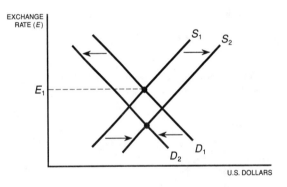

Step four: Find the new equilibrium, and compare. The U.S. dollar depreciates.

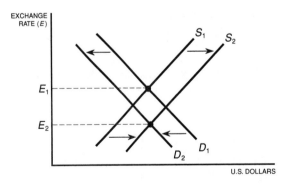

9 (Worked problem: supply and demand for currencies) What is the effect of an increase in German interest rates on the U.S. dollar exchange rate?

Step-by-step solution

Step one: Start with an equilibrium.

10 (Practice problem: supply and demand for currencies) U.S. energy conservation reduces the demand for imported oil. How does the exchange rate change?

11 (Practice problem: supply and demand for currencies) For each of the following, use supply and demand

analysis to show the effect on the exchange rate for U.S. dollars.

a Foreign demand for U.S. movies skyrockets.
b U.S. demand for African music takes off.
c Japanese interest rates rise.
d European interest rates fall.
e U.S. interest rates increase.
f U.S. interest rates decrease.

Answers to Problems

2 a The surplus shrinks, national savings falls, interest rates increases, and investment falls.

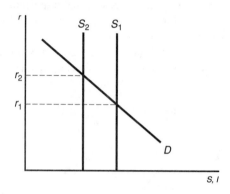

b The surplus stays constant, national savings falls, interest rates increases, and investment falls.

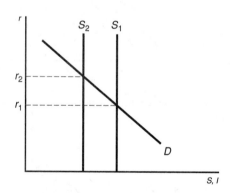

c The surplus shrinks, national savings falls, interest rates increase, and investment falls.

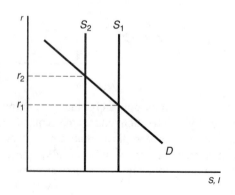

d The deficit shrinks, national savings rises, interest rates decrease, and investment rises.

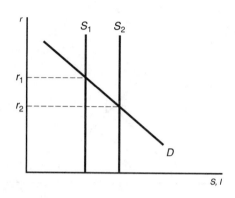

e The surplus increases, national savings rises, interest rates decrease, and investment rises.

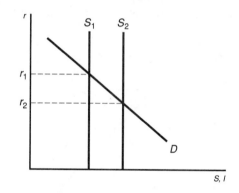

4 a Investment = 250 million dorals.
   b Savings = 300 million dorals.
   c Capital outflows = 50 million dorals.
   d Trade surplus = 50 milllion dorals.
5 a Investment = 100 million wemos.
   b Savings = 25 million wemos.
   c Capital inflows = 75 million wemos.
   d Trade surplus = 75 million wemos.
7 a

Interest rate (percent)	Total supply (billions of dollars)
15	1,000 + 500 = 1,500
14	800 + 400 = 1,200
13	600 + 300 = 900
12	400 + 200 = 600
11	200 + 100 = 300
10	100 + 50 = 150

b Interest rate = 14 percent.
c Capital inflows = 1,200 − 400 = $800 billion.
d Trade deficit = $800 billion.

8 *a*

Interest rate (percent)	Total supply (billions of dollars)
8	200 + 50 = 250
7	180 + 45 = 225
6	160 + 40 = 200
5	140 + 35 = 175
4	120 + 30 = 150
3	100 + 25 = 125
2	80 + 20 = 100

b Interest rate = 4 percent.
c Capital inflows = 150 − $120 billion.
d Trade deficit = $120 billion.

10 The supply curve of dollars shifts to the left, and the U.S. dollar appreciates.

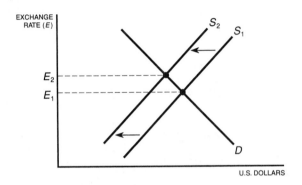

11 *a* The demand curve for dollars shifts to the right, and the U.S. dollar appreciates.

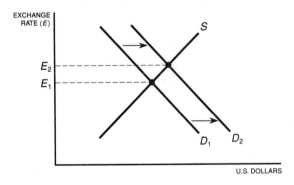

b The supply curve of dollars shifts to the right, and the U.S. dollar depreciates.

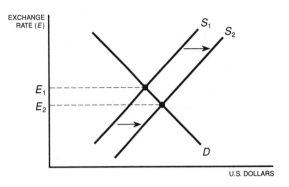

c The demand curve shifts to the left, the supply curve shifts to the right, and the U.S. dollar depreciates.

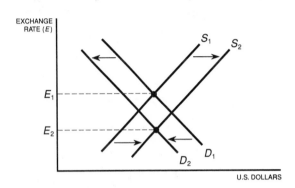

d The demand curve shifts to the right, the supply curve shifts to the left, and the U.S. dollar appreciates.

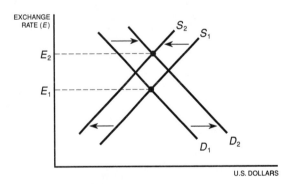

e The demand curve shifts to the right, the supply curve shifts to the left, and the U.S. dollar appreciates.

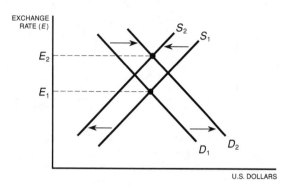

f The demand curve shifts to the left, the supply curve shifts to the right, and the U.S. dollar depreciates.

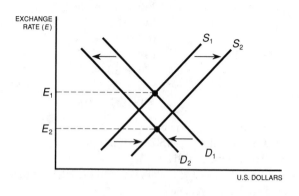

CHAPTER 27 | Growth and Productivity

Chapter Review

The previous three chapters spelled out the equilibrium in the full-employment model. This chapter turns to the issue of how the economy's equilibrium changes over time. The main focus is on improvements in productivity through capital investment and through improvements in technology. Key engines of growth include savings, human capital, research and development, and the ability of the economy to allocate capital to its most productive uses.

ESSENTIAL CONCEPTS

1   The U.S. economy has grown enormously in the twentieth century. This growth can be seen as the sum of the growth in hours worked and the rate of growth in productivity (output per hour worked). Although it has improved recently, productivity growth slowed in the past three decades. Economists watch productivity carefully because it ultimately determines the standard of living and because small changes in its growth rate lead to quite large changes in living standards.

2   The four causes of growth in productivity are the accumulation of capital goods, an improvement in the quality of the labor force, an increase in the efficiency of resource allocation, and technological advance. Concerns about productivity slowdown have led economists to propose policies designed to restore rapid growth.

3   Figure 27.1 represents the production function, which shows the relationship between inputs and outputs. It illustrates that the accumulation of capital goods per worker brings about an increase in output per worker; however, the increase is subject to the **law of**

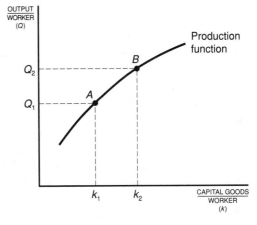

Figure 27.1

diminishing returns. Economists call the increase in capital per worker **capital deepening.**

4   Although today's world capital market allows international borrowing, **capital accumulation** clearly requires more domestic savings and investment. Savings rates in the United States have fallen because of a booming stock market in the late 1990s and more generous Social Security benefits have reduced incentives to save for retirement, while improved capital markets have made borrowing easier. Promoting savings through tax policy is likely to be ineffective because savings are relatively unresponsive to changes in after-tax returns, and investment is subject to diminishing returns.

5   Investment in skills and education improves the quality of the labor force. Economists call this **human capital.** Although the U.S. educational system has considerable

strengths, especially in higher education, there is concern about the level of funding, quality of teachers, and other problems.

6 The economy expanded during this century as resources moved from traditional agriculture to higher productivity employment in manufacturing. Presently, the movement is toward the service sector, where some economists think the potential for productivity gains is more limited.

7 **Technological change** shifts the production function up and can outstrip diminishing returns. Although not everyone benefits from every innovation, technological change increases productivity, employment, and living standards overall. **Research and development** is the source of technological progress. Sound macroeconomic policies that encourage full employment, R & D funding and tax subsidies, more science and technology education, and better government regulation all promote technological advance.

8 **Total factor productivity** analysis helps quantify the role of different factors in increasing productivity. After accounting for the increase due to more physical and human capital, economists attribute the residual increase to improvements in technology. This analysis shows that much productivity increase is due to technological change.

9 Other developed countries have experienced more rapid growth than the United States. One likely is that capital deepening is subject to diminishing returns. Thus the highest-productivity country will experience smaller gains from capital deepening than its somewhat less productive rivals will. Among developing nations, however, there seems to be no clear relationships between the level of productivity and the growth rate.

BEHIND THE ESSENTIAL CONCEPTS

1 You should be clear about the distinction between factors that lead to movements along the production function and those that cause shifts. Capital accumulation moves the economy along its production function, as shown in Figure 27.1. An improvement in technology, on the other hand, shifts the production function. In Figure 27.2, the technological advance increases output without increasing the capital stock.

2 Productivity equals output per worker. As population grows, capital goods must be accumulated for the new workers to use. Because output per worker depends on how much capital each has to work with, this extra capital only keeps productivity constant. Additional capital goods must be accumulated to increase the amount of capital per worker, so that productivity can grow.

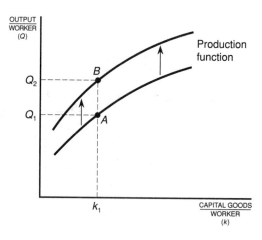

Figure 27.2

3 To see why U.S. savings rates are low, you need to understand the **life-cycle theory of savings.** According to this view, you save in order to consume in the future. Thus, the trade-off is current vs. future consumption. As Social Security and Medicare became more generous and individuals accumulated unexpected wealth through the increase in housing prices, the need to save for retirement declined. As private and public insurance improved, there has been less need to save for future emergencies. Many of these developments are good, but an unfortunate side effect is the accompanying disincentive to save.

4 Giving workers more capital to work with—capital deepening—accounts for only one-eighth of the growth in productivity. How do economists know this? One reason is that until recently productivity grew at a steady rate, a fact that cannot be explained by capital accumulation. If it were capital deepening, then the movement along the production function would run into diminishing returns. Therefore it must be a shift in the production function, probably brought about by human capital accumulation or technological advance.

5 Some have argued that the available natural resources set up limits to growth. Certain natural resources, such as petroleum and agricultural land, are privately owned and traded in well-organized markets. These markets provide good incentives for conservation and preservation. If oil becomes scarce, for example, its price will rise, and world oil stocks will be conserved. This type of natural resource will probably not limit the world's growth. The ozone, oceans, and the genetic diversity in threatened natural habitats, on the other hand, are natural resources that are commonly owned and not traded in markets. The world's economy provides no incentive to conserve or preserve these resources. Their destruction is an external cost, not captured by prices. These global environmental problems may pose threats to increased living

standards. Their solution requires cooperation among the world's governments.

SELF-TEST

True or False

1 The growth rate in output equals the growth rate in productivity.
2 Productivity measures output per unit of capital goods.
3 All of the industrialized countries have experienced slower productivity growth since 1973.
4 The low productivity growth continued through the late 1990s.
5 If productivity grows at 4 percent per year, it will double in 25 years.
6 Capital deepening refers to increases in the number of workers per unit capital.
7 Savings rates in the United States are lower than those in other developed countries.
8 Improved Social Security benefits reduce the incentive to save.
9 Rising stock prices increase the incentive to save.
10 The law of diminishing returns says that technological advance must bring about slower growth in the future.
11 A great strength of the U.S. educational system is its junior colleges and state universities.
12 Increased international trade raises U.S. productivity by shifting workers to export sectors where productivity is higher.
13 Low rates of return on research and development expenditures imply that there is too much investment in research.
14 Total factor productivity analysis is used to distinguish between growth due to increases in labor and capital from that due to technological advance.
15 Market incentives ensure that such natural resources as rain forests and the global environment will be preserved.

Multiple Choice

1 Productivity is
   a the extra output from the marginal worker.
   b hours worked divided by output.
   c output per hour worked.
   d the number of workers required to produce the next unit of output.
   e output divided by the total number of inputs.
2 The U.S. rate of growth in productivity
   a sped up in the late 1960s and 1970s.
   b has been nearly constant throughout the twentieth century.
   c slowed significantly since 1973.
   d increased steadily through the twentieth century.
   e rose dramatically in the 1980s.
3 If the growth rate of output is 5 percent and the growth rate of hours worked is 2 percent then the growth rate of productivity equals
   a 10 percent.
   b 3 percent.
   c 2.5 percent.
   d 7 percent.
   e −3 percent.
4 The causes of growth include
   a the accumulation of capital goods.
   b improvement in the quality of the labor force.
   c more efficient allocation of resources.
   d technological advance.
   e all of the above.
5 Capital deepening refers to
   a increased numbers of workers per unit of capital.
   b increases in capital per worker.
   c decreases in capital per worker.
   d reallocation of capital from less productive to more productive sectors.
   e government investment in infrastructure.
6 According to the law of diminishing returns, as the economy accumulates more capital, output increases
   a at the same rate as capital grows.
   b at a slower rate than capital grows.
   c at a faster rate than capital grows.
   d only if new workers enter the labor force.
   e only if the new capital equipment takes advantage of new and better technologies.
7 Savings accumulated for retirement are called
   a life-cycle savings.
   b target savings.
   c precautionary savings.
   d bequest savings.
   e permanent income savings.
8 If productivity grows at 7 percent per year, it will double in
   a 10 years.
   b $14\,^2/_7$ years.
   c $28\,^4/_7$ years.
   d 7 years.
   e 93 years.
9 During the 1980s, taxes on the return to capital
   a fell, leading to an increase in savings.
   b fell but savings also fell.
   c rose, leading to a decrease in savings.
   d rose but savings also rose.
   e did not change appreciably.
10 During the 1980s, Social Security benefits
   a fell, leading to an increase in savings.
   b fell but savings also fell.
   c rose, leading to a decrease in savings.

d rose but savings also rose.

e did not change appreciably.

11 When the economy is at full employment, which of the following will *not* increase investment?

a Reducing the fiscal deficit

b Shifting government spending toward infrastructure investment

c Subsidizing investment

d Using tax policies such as IRAs

e All of the above increase investment

12 The production function shows the relationship between

a the levels of inputs and the level of output.

b technology and growth.

c productivity and real wages.

d learning and experience.

e productivity and output.

13 In the long run, capital deepening results in

a higher level of productivity.

b higher growth rate of productivity.

c higher growth rate of output.

d all of the above.

e none of the above.

14 Human capital refers to

a the capital goods that individuals own.

b education and skills that increase the productivity of individuals.

c fertility.

d output per hour worked.

e the capital goods that workers use on the job.

15 Which of the following is *not* a strength of the U.S. educational system?

a The absence of early tracking of students in lower grades

b The relatively open system of junior colleges and state universities

c The research universities

d The high percentage of students choosing majors in science and technology

e All of the above are strengths.

16 Telecommunications deregulation and expanded international trade will

a raise overall productivity because productivity is higher than average in these sectors.

b raise overall productivity because productivity is lower than average in these sectors.

c reduce overall productivity because productivity is higher than average in these sectors.

d reduce overall productivity because productivity is lower than average in these sectors.

e leave overall productivity unchanged.

17 Technological change

a shifts the production function so that the same number of inputs produce more output.

b shifts the production function so that more output is produced but only if additional capital goods are used.

c shifts the production function so that more output is produced but only if additional workers are hired.

d increases productivity for capital but not for workers.

e increases productivity but does not shift the production function.

18 The method that attributes that part of the growth in productivity that cannot be explained by increases in labor and capital to technological advance is called

a total factor productivity analysis.

b partial productivity analysis.

c capital deepening.

d capital widening.

e sustainable development.

19 The economy's growth in output is equal to

a its growth in productivity.

b the sum of its growth in the labor force and its capital accumulation.

c the sum of its growth in hours worked and its growth in productivity.

d the marginal product of labor times the number of hours worked plus the marginal product of capital times the capital stock.

e the sum of private savings, government savings, and net inflows of capital from abroad.

20 Sustainable development refers to growth without

a excessive technological advance.

b excessive population increase.

c excessive capital investment.

d excessive natural resource exploitation.

e all of the above.

Completion

1 _____ is defined as output per hour worked.

2 The _____ relates the levels of inputs to the level of output.

3 A country's roads, airports, bridges, sewer lines, and railroads make up its _____.

4 Economists refer to education and skills as _____.

5 Increases in capital per worker are called _____.

6 Savings for a specific purpose, such as college tuition, are called _____.

7 According to the _____, successive increments in capital lead to smaller increases in output per worker.

8 The savings that a household sets aside in case of emergency or illness are called _____.

9 Economists use _____ to discover the magnitude of technological advance.

10 Advocates of _____ seek policies to preserve the environment and natural resources while increasing living standards.

Answers to Self-Test

True or False

1	f	6	f	11	t
2	f	7	t	12	t
3	t	8	t	13	f
4	f	9	f	14	t
5	f	10	f	15	f

Multiple Choice

1	c	6	b	11	c	16	a
2	c	7	a	12	a	17	a
3	b	8	a	13	a	18	a
4	e	9	b	14	b	19	c
5	b	10	c	15	d	20	d

Completion

1 Productivity
2 production function
3 infrastructure
4 human capital
5 capital deepening
6 target savings
7 law of diminishing returns
8 precautionary savings
9 total factor productivity analysis
10 sustainable growth

Doing Economics: Tools and Practice Problems

Two important factors in the U.S. productivity slowdown are low savings and misallocated investment. In this section, we study some reasons for low savings rates: improved opportunities for consumer borrowing and more generous Social Security benefits. Also, we see how favorable tax treatment of certain types of projects misallocates investment.

REASONS FOR LOW SAVINGS RATES: LOWER INTEREST RATES FOR BORROWING

One of the great strengths of the U.S. economy is its efficient capital market. Recently a combination of factors, for example credit cards, home equity loans, and bank deregulation, have increased access for borrowers. Lower interest rates for borrowers rotate part of the budget constraint out, giving the household more opportunities to consume more today. This is an application of the opportunity set with multiple constraints introduced in Chapter 2.

1 (Worked problem: low savings rates) Harold and Myla take home $60,000 each year. They can earn 4 percent

on any savings, but they must borrow at 14 percent.

a Plot their two-period budget constraint.

b A preapproved application for a new credit card arrives. The interest rate on the unpaid balance will be 8 percent. Plot their new two-period budget constraint, and compare it with the answer to part *a*.

Step-by-step solution

Step one (*a*): Plot the budget constraint with the 4 percent interest rate. The slope is 1.04, and it passes through the point $60,000 now and $60,000 next year.

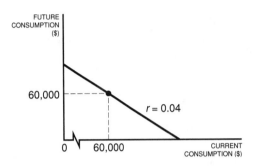

Step two: Plot the budget constraint with the 14 percent interest rate. The slope is 1.14, and it passes through the point $60,000 now and $60,000 next year.

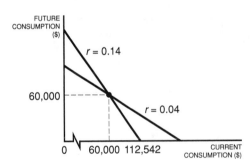

Step three: Darken the portion of each budget constraint that lies under the other constraint. This is the answer to part a.

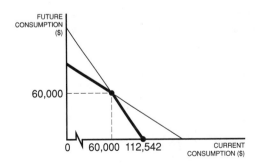

Step four (*b*): Again, plot the budget constraint with the 4 percent interest rate as in step one.

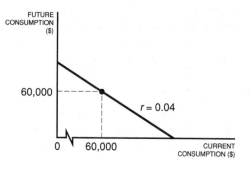

Step five: Plot the budget constraint with the 8 percent interest rate. The slope is 1.08, and it passes through the point $60,000 now and $60,000 next year.

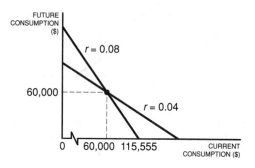

Step six: Darken the portion of each budget constraint that lies under the other constraint. This is the answer to part b.

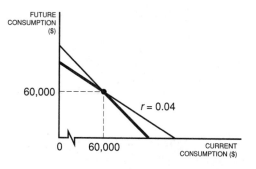

Step seven: Compare the two budget constraints. The lower interest rate gives Harold and Myla more opportunities, but the extra opportunities all involve borrowing.

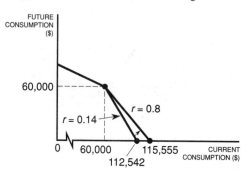

2   (Practice problem: low savings rates) Bill takes home $10,000 this year, but he anticipates taking home $30,000 next year. He can earn 8 percent on savings, but he has a poor credit rating and must pay 19 percent to borrow.
   a   Plot his *two*-period budget constraint.
   b   Through his credit union at his new job, Bill can obtain loans for 10 percent. Plot his new two-period budget constraint, and compare.

REASONS FOR LOW SAVINGS RATES: INCREASED SOCIAL SECURITY BENEFITS

Social Security certainly reduce people's incentives to save for retirement, and because it is financed on a pay-as-you-go basis, it reduces national savings. Increases in Social Security benefits during the 1970s further reduced savings incentives. The next two problems use the two-period budget constraint to illustrate this idea.

3   (Worked problem: low savings rates) Juwan has 10 years until retirement. He earns $40,000 after taxes and expects to receive $20,000 in Social Security benefits when he retires. He expects that over the 10-year interval until retirement he can earn a 100 percent rate of return, and he currently saves $5,000 per year.
   a   Calculate the present discounted value of his Social Security benefits.
   b   Draw his two-period budget constraint, and plot his chosen point.
   c   Suppose that his Social Security benefits are increased to $30,000. His Social Security taxes are also increased by $5,000, which reduces his current net income to $35,000. Draw his two-period budget constraint.
   d   How much does Juwan now save?

Step-by-step solution

Step one (*a*): The present discounted value of his benefit payment is $20,000/(1 + r) = $20,000/(1 + 1) = $10,000.

Step two (*b*): Draw his two-period budget constraint. Label the axes "Current consumption" and "Retirement consumption." The slope is $1 + r$, and the interest rate for the 10-year period is 100 percent. The horizontal intercept is the present discounted value of all income, which is $40,000 + $10,000 = $50,000.

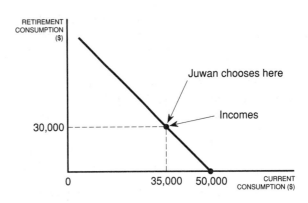

Step three: Plot his chosen point. Juwan chooses to save $5,000; thus, he consumes $40,000 − $5,000 = $35,000 now. The $5,000 grows to $10,000 in 10 years, which enables consumption of $20,000 + $10,000 = $30,000.

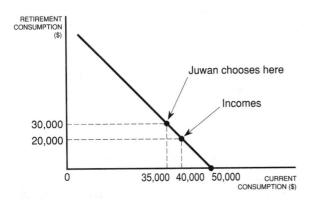

Step four (c): Plot his new budget constraint. The present discounted value of his benefits is now $30,000/2 = $15,000. The horizontal intercept is $15,000 + $35,000 = $50,000, which is unchanged. Because neither the present discounted value of his two-period income nor the interest rate changes, the budget constraint remains the same.

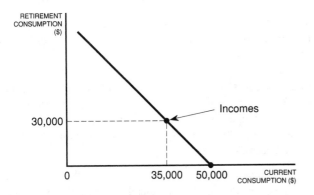

Step five (d): Because he has the same budget constraint, he chooses the same point. But he achieves this combination of current and retirement consumption by reducing his savings to zero. The increase in Social Security benefits has reduced Juwan's savings by exactly $5,000.

4 (Practice problem: low savings rates) Mai Lin is only 10 years from retirement. She can expect to receive $2 in interest for every $1 saved for retirement. She takes home $60,000 annually, saves $10,000 each year, and expects Social Security benefits of $30,000 when she retires.
   a Plot her two-period budget constraint.
   b Suppose the American Association of Retired Persons has a banner year lobbying Congress and wins a 50 percent increase in benefits. Taxes also rise so that the budget constraint does not change. How will Mai Lin's consumption now and during retirement change? How will her savings change?

Subsidies and the Allocation of Investment

Preferential tax treatment of certain types of investment can reallocate an economy's capital stock. A subsidy to a particular type of investment will raise its return, and since investors always seek the highest rate of return, they will reallocate their portfolio to take advantage of the subsidy. Tool Kit 27.1 shows the link between subsidies and reallocation.

Tool Kit 27.1 Showing How Subsidies Can Reallocate Investment

Subsidies shift up the demand for investment in the subsidized sector. This reallocates investment. These steps outline the procedure for analyzing the impact of a subsidy in one sector.

Step one: Add up the demands of each sector for capital.

Step two: Find the market-clearing rate of interest.

Step three: Substitute the market-clearing rate of interest into each demand to determine the allocation of investment that occurs without subsidy.

Step four: Add the subsidy to the demand for capital in the subsidized sector.

Step five: Repeat steps one through three.

Step six: compare the allocation found in step five with that found in step three.

---

5 (Worked problem: allocation of investment) The 1986 Tax Reform Act eliminated certain provisions that gave preferential tax treatment to real estate. To see the effect that these tax subsidies have, consider Table 27.1, which gives the demands for capital by the real estate and manufacturing sectors in billions of U.S. dollars. The supply of financial capital for the two sectors is $3,900 billion.

Table 27.1

Interest rate	Demand in the real estate sector (billions)	Demand in the manufacturing sector (billions)
10%	$1,000	$2,000
9%	$1,100	$2,200
8%	$1,200	$2,400
7%	$1,300	$2,600
6%	$1,400	$2,800
5%	$1,500	$3,000
4%	$1,600	$3,200

a Find the market allocation.
b Suppose the tax subsidy amounts to an extra 3 percent annual earnings for a real estate investment. Find the allocation.
c How does the tax subsidy alter the equilibrium allocation of capital?

Step-by-step solution

Step one (a): Add the demands of each sector for capital. We choose an interest rate, and sum the quantity demanded in each sector. When the interest rate is 10 percent, the total quantity demanded is $1,000 + $2,000 = $3,000 billion. Continuing, we derive Table 27.2.

Table 27.2

Interest rate	Real estate	Manufacturing	Total
10%	$1,000	$2,000	$3,000
9%	$1,100	$2,200	$3,300
8%	$1,200	$2,400	$3,600
7%	$1,300	$2,600	$3,900
6%	$1,400	$2,800	$4,200
5%	$1,500	$3,000	$4,500
4%	$1,600	$3,200	$4,800

Step two: Find the market-clearing rate of interest. Quantity supplied, which is $3,900 billion, equals quantity demanded when the interest rate is 7 percent.

Step three: Substitute the market-clearing rate of interest into each demand to determine the allocation of investment. The 7 percent rate of interest brings about an allocation of $1,300 billion in real estate and $2,600 billion in manufacturing.

Step four (b): Add the subsidy to the demand for capital in the subsidized sector. Simply add 3 percent to the interest rate column for the real estate sector. Table 27.3 gives the result.

Table 27.3

Interest rate	Real estate
13%	$1,000
12%	$1,100
11%	$1,200
10%	$1,300
9%	$1,400
8%	$1,500
7%	$1,600

Step five: Repeat steps one through three. Table 27.4 gives the new total demand.

Table 27.4

Interest rate	Real estate	Manufacturing	Total
13%	$1,000	$2,000	$3,000
12%	$1,100	$2,000	$3,100
11%	$1,200	$2,000	$3,200
10%	$1,300	$2,000	$3,300
9%	$1,400	$2,200	$3,600
8%	$1,500	$2,400	$3,900
7%	$1,600	$2,600	$4,200
6%	$1,600	$2,800	$4,400
5%	$1,700	$3,000	$4,700
4%	$1,800	$3,200	$5,000

The market clears at an 8 percent interest rate with an allocation of $1,500 billion to real estate and $2,400 billion to manufacturing.

Step six (c): Compare the allocation found in step five with that found in step three. The tax subsidy increases the real estate sector's allocation from $1,300 to $1,500 billion, reducing the manufacturing sector's allocation from $2,600 billion to $2,400 billion. In effect, $200 billion is reallocated from manufacturing to real estate.

6 (Practice problem: allocation of investment) Table 27.5 gives the demands for financial capital in the sector that produces goods for export and the sector that produces goods that compete with imports. The available supply of capital is $200 billion.

Table 27.5

Interest rate	Demand in the import-competing sector (billions)	Demand in the export sector (billions)
12%	$ 30	$ 40
11%	$ 50	$ 50
10%	$ 60	$ 60
9%	$ 70	$ 80
8%	$ 80	$ 90
7%	$100	$100
6%	$120	$110
5%	$140	$120

a Find the market allocation.

b Worried about lost market share to imports, a protectionist Congress passes a series of tax subsidies and trade barriers. Suppose that the tax subsidies and import controls amount to an extra 5 percent annual earnings for import-competing investment. Find the new allocation.

c How does the tax policy alter the equilibrium allocation of capital?

7 (Practice problem: allocation of investment) Preferential tax treatment can reallocate investment capital across regions. The enterprise zone idea offers tax breaks to firms that locate in specified areas such as impoverished inner cities. To see how this policy might work, consider Table 27.6, which gives demands for capital in enterprise zones and elsewhere. Assume that the tax breaks are worth 6 percent and the total quantity supplied equals $10 billion.

Table 27.6

Interest rate	Demand in the enterprise zones (billions)	Demand elsewhere (billions)
9%	$0.6	$ 8.2
8%	$0.8	$ 8.6
7%	$1.0	$ 9.0
6%	$1.2	$ 9.8
5%	$1.4	$10.8
4%	$1.6	$12.0
3%	$1.8	$15.0
2%	$2.0	$20.0

a Find the market allocation without the tax breaks and the corresponding interest rate.

b Find the demand curves with the tax breaks.

c Find the new allocation brought about by the tax breaks. How does the tax policy alter the equilibrium allocation of capital?

Answers to Problems

2 *a*

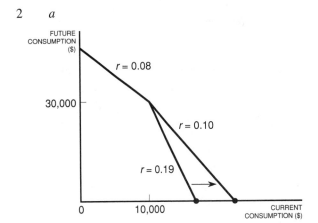

b With the lower interest rate for borrowing, Bill's budget constraint rotates out, giving him new opportunities, all of which involve borrowing more.

4 *a*

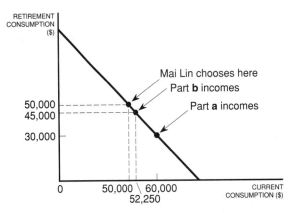

b The budget constraint does not change, so neither do her current and retirement consumptions. The increase in Social Security benefits reduces her savings by $7,500.

6 *a* The equilibrium interest rate is 7 percent, and the allocation is $100 billion to each sector.

b Table 27.8 gives the demands with the tax subsidy and trade protection policies.

Table 27.8

Interest rate	Imports	Exports	Total
17%	$ 30	$40	$ 70
16%	$ 50	$40	$ 90
15%	$ 60	$40	$100
14%	$ 70	$40	$110
13%	$ 80	$40	$120
12%	$100	$40	$140
11%	$120	$50	$170
10%	$140	$60	$200
9%	$140	$80	$220
8%	$140	$90	$220

c The market clears at an interest rate of 10 percent with an allocation of $140 billion to the import-competing sector and $60 billion to the export sector. The policies shift $40 billion from the export to the import-competing sector.

7 a The market allocation without the enterprise zone tax breaks is $1 billion in the zones and $9 billion elsewhere and the interest rate is 7 percent.

b Table 27.9 gives the demands with the tax breaks.

Table 27.9

Interest rate	Demand in the enterprise zones	Demand elsewhere	Total
15%	$0.6	$ 8.2	$ 8.8
14%	$0.8	$ 8.2	$ 9.0
13%	$1.0	$ 8.2	$ 9.2
12%	$1.2	$ 8.2	$ 9.4
11%	$1.4	$ 8.2	$ 9.6
10%	$1.6	$ 8.2	$ 9.8
9%	$1.8	$ 8.2	$10.0
8%	$2.0	$ 8.6	$10.6
7%	$2.0	$ 9.0	$11.0
6%	$2.0	$ 9.8	$11.8
5%	$2.0	$10.8	$12.8

c The new equilibrium allocation is $1.8 billion to the enterprise zones and $8.2 billion elsewhere at an equilibrium interest rate of 9 percent. The tax breaks shift $.8 billion to the zones from elsewhere in the economy.

PART SEVEN

Macroeconomic Fluctuations

Chapter Review

This chapter begins the study of the economy's ups and downs, sometimes called the business cycle. It presents the data on how output, unemployment, and other macroeconomic variables move and then explains why the full-employment model of Part Two cannot explain these facts. Finally, it outlines the nature of the explanation and gives an overview of how things will develop throughout Part Three.

ESSENTIAL CONCEPTS

1   Over time, the economy's output fluctuates around an upward trend. Periods of output growth are called **expansions.** Periods below the trend indicate **recessions,** and the deviation of actual GDP below its potential is called the **output gap.** During these periods, unemployment is above its trend and **capacity utilization** below its trend. The jobless workers and idle plant and equipment add up to lost output.

2   According to the full-employment model, during recessions the **demand for labor** shifts to the left and **real wages** fall (especially because labor supply is inelastic). In reality, however, real wages change very little even in times of high unemployment. This contradicts the full-employment model. Most economists reject explanations that claim labor supply is elastic, or likely to shift along with demand, during recessions.

3   **Real wages** may adjust slowly to shifts in demand and supply for three reasons.

   a   Explicit contracts may call for infrequent wage adjustment. Also, firms may have informal agreements, or **implicit contracts**, with their risk-averse workers to provide fixed wages as a kind of insurance against economic downturns.

   b   Firms may make higher profits by paying **efficiency wages** that are above the market clearing level, because this gives incentives for workers to work harder and be more productive. A higher-wage job is worth working hard to keep. Also, higher wages attract more productive workers and reduce labor turnover.

   c   Cutting wages may be risky. Depending on what its rivals do, a firm may lose too many, too few, or its best workers. It may be safer to simply lay off those unneeded workers.

4   The **model of macroeconomic fluctuations** rests on four fundamental ideas.

   a   **Sticky wages** fail to adjust to market-clearing levels, leaving a surplus of unemployed workers.

   b   **Sticky prices** adjust slowly and cause firms to respond to shifts in demand curves by cutting output and employment.

   c   The **short-run inflation-unemployment trade-off** results from nominal wages' rising faster than productivity in times of low unemployment, which leads to inflation. When there is high unemployment, wage increases moderate, reducing inflation.

   d   Inflation, monetary policy, and spending move so as to bring about reduced aggregate spending when inflation increases. How the central bank reacts to inflation is the key here.

BEHIND THE ESSENTIAL CONCEPTS

1   Some economists have tried to reconcile the full-employment model with the fact that real wages do not

fall in times of high unemployment. One idea is that labor supply is elastic. If this were true, when demand shifted to the left in downturns, the labor market would clear at a lower level of employment with little change in real wages. There is little empirical support for this idea.

2 Another attempt hypothesizes that when demand shifts to the left, supply also shifts to the left. The simultaneous shift in labor supply might keep the real wage from falling. This outcome would occur if during recession, people demanded more leisure. Again, there is little evidence that labor supply fluctuates in this way.

3 Keep in mind that the model in Part Three explains **short-run** fluctuations around the economy's trend. The model in Part Two on the other hand, explains the long-run trend. It is important to realize that these models do no contradict each other. Rather they explain different elements of the economy's short- and long-run performance.

4 The appendix to this chapter goes into greater detail about why wages and prices might be sticky. This topic is part of the microeconomic foundations of macroeconomics, a topic to which economists have devoted great effort over the last two decades.

SELF-TEST

True or False

1 Periods during which output declines substantially are called recessions.
2 The output gap measures the percentage deviation between actual and potential GDP.
3 During recessions both output and the unemployment rate decline.
4 The utilization of plant and equipment also falls during recessions.
5 As the name suggests, business cycles show regular patterns in the movement of macroeconomic variables.
6 Real wages fall significantly during recessions.
7 During times of inflation, the nominal wage rises faster than the real wage.
8 Rational, profit-seeking firms never pay more than the market-clearing wage.
9 The efficiency wage lies above the market-clearing wage and it brings about higher productivity.
10 Although sticky in the short run, real wages eventually adjust to the market-clearing level.
11 If prices are sticky, firms adjust output and employment when demand shifts.
12 Inflation means that prices are high.
13 In tight labor markets, wages rise more quickly.
14 In the short run, increases in inflation cause a reduction in aggregate spending.

15 If inflation rises, the Fed brings about an increase in the real interest rate.

Multiple Choice

1 Periods of significant output declines are called
  a peaks.
  b troughs.
  c expansions.
  d recessions.
  e the business cycle.
2 Periods of output growth are called
  a peaks.
  b troughs.
  c expansions.
  d recessions.
  e the business cycle.
3 High points in output are called
  a peaks.
  b troughs.
  c expansions.
  d recessions.
  e the business cycle.
4 Which of the following does *not* occur during a recession?
  a Output falls significantly.
  b Unemployment rises.
  c Capacity utilization decreases.
  d Real wages fall substantially.
  e All of the above occur.
5 Since 1960, the unemployment rate has averaged just above
  a 4 percent.
  b 5 percent.
  c 6 percent.
  d 7 percent.
  e 8 percent.
6 The longest post–World War II expansion happened during the
  a 1950s.
  b 1960s.
  c 1970s.
  d 1980s.
  e 1990s.
7 The Humphrey-Hawkins Act of 1978 mandates the federal government to promote
  a full employment.
  b higher real incomes.
  c price stability.
  d productivity growth.
  e all of the above.
8 According to Okun's Law, when the output gap declines by 2 percent (i.e., actual GDP falls below potential GDP by an additional 2 percent), the unemployment rate

   a rises above the full-employment level by 1 percent.

   b rises above the full-employment level by 2 percent.

   c rises above the full-employment level by 3 percent.

   d falls below the full-employment level by 1 percent.

   e falls below the full-employment level by 2 percent.

9 Which of the following countries did *not* experience a recession following the 1973 oil price shocks?

   a United States

   b Japan

   c Canada

   d United Kingdom

   e All experienced recessions.

10 Which of the following countries did *not* experience a recession in 1990–91?

   a United States

   b Japan

   c Canada

   d United Kingdom

   e All experienced recessions.

11 Unemployment results if

   a the demand for labor shifts to the left and wages fail to adjust.

   b the supply of labor shifts to the left and wages fail to adjust.

   c the demand for labor shifts to the right and wages fail to adjust.

   d the supply of labor shifts to the right and wages fail to adjust.

   e *a* and *d*.

12 Which of the following is *not* an explanation for why real wages do not fall when the demand for labor decreases?

   a Labor supply is elastic.

   b Labor demand is inelastic.

   c Real wages are sticky.

   d Labor supply simultaneously shifts to the left.

   e All are explanations.

13 What is the best description of the relationship between real wages and the unemployment rate?

   a Real wages are higher when unemployment is higher.

   b Real wages increase faster when unemployment is higher.

   c Real wages are lower when unemployment is higher.

   d Real wages fall faster when unemployment is higher.

   e There is no relationship.

14 If real wages are sticky and the demand for labor shifts to the left, then

   a employment falls.

   b there is a surplus of workers.

   c the supply of labor falls.

   d real wages fall.

   e *a* and *b*.

15 If nominal wages increase by 4 percent and prices increase by 3 percent, then real wages

   a increase by 1 percent.

   b decrease by 1 percent.

   c increase by 7 percent.

   d decrease by 7 percent.

   e increase by 12 percent.

16 Informal agreements to keep nominal wages fixed during recessions are called

   a implicit contracts.

   b efficiency wages.

   c cyclical wages.

   d implicit wages.

   e contract wages.

17 When demand shifts to the left in the labor market,

   a wages are sticky in the short run.

   b wages adjust to the market clearing level in the long run.

   c there is unemployment in the short run.

   d there is full employment in the long run.

   e all of the above.

18 When there are sticky prices and the demand for a firm's product falls, the firm

   a lowers its price.

   b reduces output.

   c increases employment.

   d reduces employment.

   e *b* and *d*.

19 In the short run, low unemployment causes

   a nominal wages and prices to rise faster.

   b nominal wages and prices to rise more slowly.

   c nominal wages to rise faster, but prices to rise more slowly.

   d nominal wages to rise more slowly, but prices to rise faster.

   e no change in the rate of increase of nominal wages and prices.

20 In the short run, increases in inflation lead to

   a reduced aggregate spending and higher real interest rates.

   b reduced aggregate spending and lower real interest rates.

   c increased aggregate spending and higher real interest rates.

   d increased aggregate spending and lower real interest rates.

   e no change in either aggregate spending or real interest rates.

Completion

1 The extra unemployment due to the fluctuation of output below its trend is called _____.

2 The percentage deviation of actual and potential GDP is called the _____.

3 _____ are periods of significantly falling output.

4 _____ are periods of rising output.

5 The high point of the business cycle is called its _____.

6 The low point of the business cycle is called its _____.

7 An informal agreement to keep wages fixed during recession is an example of a(n) _____.

8 The _____ lies above the market clearing wage and motivates workers to be more productive.

9 _____ cause unemployment when labor demand shifts to the left in recessions.

10 The _____ describes how inflation is higher in times of low unemployment.

Answers to Self-test

True or False

1	t	6	f	11	t
2	t	7	t	12	f
3	f	8	f	13	t
4	t	9	t	14	t
5	f	10	t	15	t

Multiple Choice

1	d	6	e	11	e	16	a
2	c	7	e	12	b	17	e
3	a	8	a	13	e	18	e
4	d	9	e	14	e	19	a
5	c	10	b	15	a	20	a

Completion

1 cyclical unemployment
2 output gap
3 Recessions
4 Expansions
5 peak
6 trough
7 implicit labor contract
8 efficiency wage
9 Sticky wages
10 short-run inflation-unemployment trade-off

Doing Economics: Tools and Practice Problems

In the aggregate labor market, the economy's levels of employment, unemployment, and real wages are determined. Unemployment results from the failure of wages to adjust to the market-clearing level, and several problems explore this relationship between sticky wages and unemployment. We also figure the cost of a recession.

Unemployment and Rigid Wages

When real wages remain stuck above market-clearing levels, the number of workers willing to work at the going wage exceeds the number of jobs available. This excess supply of labor is involuntary unemployment and is part of the overall unemployment rate. In this section we calculate the real wage by adjusting the nominal wage for inflation and then determine the level of unemployment. Tool Kit 28.1 shows how to proceed.

Tool Kit 28.1 Determining the Unemployment Level

Above market-clearing real wages lead to unemployment. The level of unemployment is the amount of excess supply in the labor market. Follow these steps to see this relationship.

Step one: Identify the demand curve, the supply curve, and the nominal wage and price level.

Step two: Find the real wage by adjusting the nominal wage for inflation:

real wage = (nominal wage/price index) $\times$ 100.

Step three: Substitute the real wage into the demand curve and find the quantity demanded. This is the number of jobs available.

Step four: Substitute the real wage into the supply curve and find the quantity supplied. This is the number of workers willing to work at the going wage.

Step five: Find the quantity of unemployment by subtracting the quantity demanded from the quantity supplied:

unemployment = quantity supplied − quantity demanded.

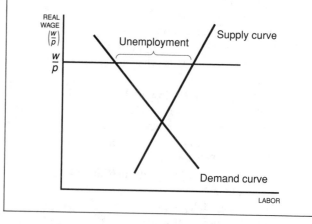

---

1 (Worked problem: unemployment level) The nominal wage level equals $2,400 per month, and the price

index equals 120. Table 28.1 gives the demand and supply of labor. Find the level of unemployment.

Table 28.1

Real wage	Demand	Supply
$2,400	6,000	18,000
$2,200	7,000	16,000
$2,000	8,000	14,000
$1,800	9,000	12,000
$1,600	10,000	10,000
$1,400	11,000	8,000
$1,200	12,000	6,000

Step-by-step solution

Step one: Identify the demand curve, the supply curve, and the nominal wage and price level. The demand and supply are given in Table 28.1, the nominal wage is $2,400, and the price index equals 120.

Step two: Find the real wage by adjusting the nominal wage for inflation:

real wage = ($2,400/120) × 100 = $2,000.

Step three: Substitute the real wage into the demand curve, and find the quantity demanded. It is 8,000.

Step four: Substitute the real wage into the supply curve, and find the quantity supplied. It is 14,000.

Step five: Find the quantity of unemployment by subtracting the quantity demanded from the quantity supplied:

unemployment = 14,000 − 8,000 = 6,000.

2 (Practice problem: unemployment level) Suppose that the nominal wage level remains at $2,400, as in problem 1, and the demand and supply curves remain as in Table 8.1 but the price level increases to 150. Find the new level of unemployment.

3 (Practice problem: unemployment level) Suppose that the nominal wage is $3,300, the price index is 150, and the demand and supply curves are as given in Table 28.1. Find the level of unemployment.

4 (Practice problem: unemployment level) For each of the following, find the level of unemployment given the demand and supply of labor shown in Table 28.2.
a Nominal wage = $50,000; price level = 100.
b Nominal wage = $50,000; price level = 125.
c Nominal wage = $50,000; price level = 167.
d Nominal wage = $60,000; price level = 120.

The Labor Market with Rigid Wages

When either the demand or supply of labor shifts and wages fail to adjust to the market-clearing level, there is unemployment. In modern economies, wages exhibit downward rigid-

Table 28.2

Real wage	Demand	Supply
$60,000	8,000	26,000
$55,000	10,000	25,000
$50,000	12,000	24,000
$45,000	14,000	23,000
$40,000	16,000	22,000
$35,000	18,000	21,000
$30,000	20,000	20,000
$25,000	22,000	19,000

ity, although they do adjust upward when conditions warrant. In the following problems real wages are assumed to be inflexible downward, but flexible upward. Tool Kit 28.2 shows how to analyze labor markets under these conditions.

Tool Kit 28.2 Analyzing the Labor Market with Rigid Real Wages and Unemployment

If the labor market is at its market-clearing equilibrium and demand or supply shifts, it may not move to the new market-clearing equilibrium if the real wage does not adjust. Follow these steps to analyze a labor market in which the real wage is rigid when market conditions call for it to fall.

Step one: Start with a market-clearing equilibrium in the labor market.

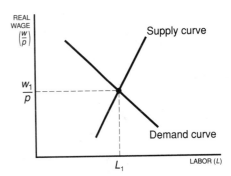

Step two: Identify a cause, and determine which curve shifts.

Step three: Shift the supply or demand curve.

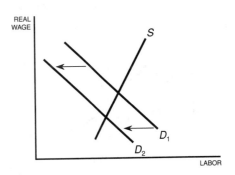

Step four: Find the new equilibrium. If there is excess demand, increase the real wage to the market-clearing level. If there is excess supply, keep the real wage constant.

Step five: Show the level of unemployment as the difference between quantity demanded and quantity supplied.

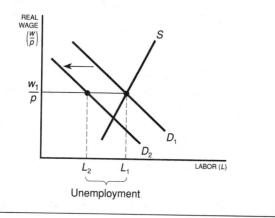

5 (Worked problem: rigid wages) Suppose a deep recession strikes the economy. Show the effect on real wages, unemployment, and the labor market.

Step-by-step solution

Step one: Start with an equilibrium.

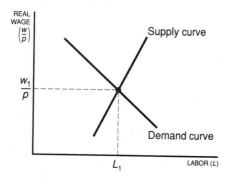

Step two: Identify a cause, and determine which curve shifts. The economy's output falls in a recession, and this reduces the demand for labor.

Step three: Shift the demand curve. It shifts left.

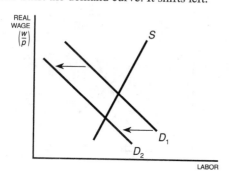

Step four: Find the new equilibrium. Although there is an excess supply of labor, wages do not adjust downward, because they are assumed rigid.

Step five: Show the level of unemployment.

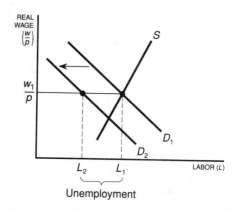

6 (Practice problem: rigid wages) Strife abroad leads to a wave of new immigration. Show the effect on real wages, unemployment, and the labor market.

7 (Practice problem: rigid wages) For each of the following, show the effect on real wages, unemployment, and the labor market.

 a The economy booms, and its output increases.
 b As barriers fall, millions of women enter the labor market.
 c The demand for U.S. exports soars, and the economy's output expands to meet the demand.
 d The baby bust generation reaches working age, and the number of new entrants declines.
 e Recession overseas reduces the demand for U.S. exports, and the economy falls into a recession.

THE COSTS OF RECESSION

When the economy has cyclical unemployment, idle workers do not produce output. This lost output is the opportunity cost of the recession, and it underscores the importance of reducing output fluctuations. Tool Kit 28.3 shows how to make the computation.

8 (Worked problem: costs of recession) In Costa Guano the unemployment rate is now 8 percent although the natural rate is only 5 percent. Current GDP is 2,000 million guanos (the local currency).
 a Compute the cyclical unemployment rate.
 b Compute the value of lost output.

Step-by-step solution

Step one: Identify the actual unemployment rate, the natural rate, and GDP. They are, respectively, 8 percent, 5 percent, and 2,000 million.

Tool Kit 28.3 Estimating the Cost of a Recession

Recessions bring with them lost output and high unemployment. Okun's Law tells us how to compute the lost output. Follow these steps.

Step one: Identify the actual unemployment rate, the natural rate, and GDP.

Step two: Compute the rate of cyclical unemployment.

Cyclical unemployment rate = natural rate of unemployment − unemployment rate.

Step three: Use Okun's Law to compute the lost output as a fraction of GDP.

Percent of GDP lost = 2 × cyclical unemployment rate.

Step four: Compute the value of lost output.
Lost output = percent of GDP lost × GDP.

Step two: Compute the rate of cyclical unemployment.

Cyclical unemployment rate = natural rate of unemployment − unemployment rate
= 8 percent − 5 percent = 3 percent.

Step three: Use Okun's Law to compute the lost output as a fraction of GDP.

Percent of GDP lost = 2 × cyclical unemployment rate = 2 × 3 percent = 6 percent.

Step four: Compute the value of lost output.

Lost output = percent of GDP lost × GDP = 6 percent × 2,000 million = 12 million dorals.

9 (Practice problem: costs of recession) El Dorado is suffering a recession with 9 percent unemployment, well above its natural rate of 6 percent. The GDP is 60 billion dorals (the local currency).
   a Compute the cyclical unemployment rate.
   b Compute the value of lost output.

10 (Practice problem: costs of recession) Erewemos is suffering a recession with 10 percent unemployment, well above its natural rate of 4 percent. The GDP is 16 billion wemos (the local currency).
   a Compute the cyclical unemployment rate.
   b Compute the value of lost output.

Answers to Problems

2 Real wage = ($2,400/150) × 100 = $1,600; unemployment = 10,000 − 10,000 = 0.

3 Real wage = ($3,300/150) × 100 = $2,200; unemployment = 16,000 − 7,000 = 9,000.
4 a Real wage = ($50,000/100) × 100 = $50,000; unemployment = 24,000 − 12,000 = 12,000.
   b Real wage = ($50,000/125) × 100 = $40,000; unemployment = 22,000 − 16,000 = 6,000.
   c Real wage = ($50,000/167) × 100 = $30,000; unemployment = 20,000 − 20,000 = 0.
   d Real wage = ($60,000/120) × 100 = $50,000; unemployment = 24,000 − 12,000 = 12,000.
6 The supply curve shifts to the right, and the wage fails to adjust downward; this results in unemployment equal to $L_s - L_1$.

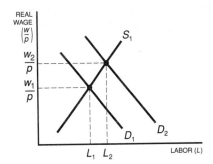

7 a The demand curve shifts to the right, and wages adjust upward to clear the market.

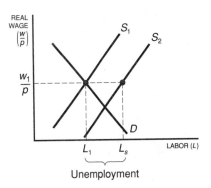

   b The supply curve shifts to the right, and the wage fails to adjust downward; this results in unemployment equal to $L_s - L_1$.

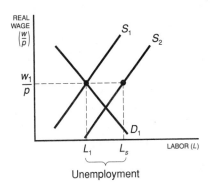

c The demand curve shifts to the right, and wage adjusts upward to clear the market.

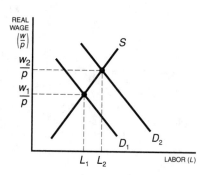

d The supply curve shifts to the left, and the wage adjusts upward to clear the market.

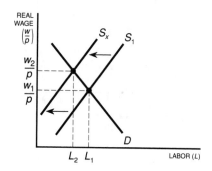

e The demand curve shifts to the left, and the wage fails to adjust downward; this results in unemployment equal to $L_1 - L_s$.

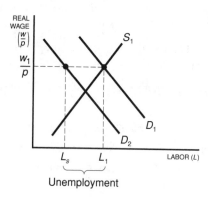

9 *a* 9 percent − 6 percent = 3 percent cyclical unemployment.

b 3 percent × 2 × 60 billion = 3.6 billion dorals in lost output.

10 *a* 10 percent − 4 percent = 6 percent cyclical unemployment.

b 6 percent × 2 × 16 = 1.92 billion wemos in lost output.

CHAPTER 29 | Aggregate Expenditures and Income

Chapter Review

Following the overview given in Chapter 28, the discussion now turns to the short-run performance of the economy in detail. One of the driving forces is aggregate demand: what household, firms, government, and the foreign sector spend on the goods and services that the economy produces. This chapter shows how aggregate expenditures are determined in the short run and, in particular, how it is influenced by changes in the real interest rate. The model is called income-expenditure analysis, and it is a key component of the study of macroeconomic fluctuations.

ESSENTIAL CONCEPTS

1 **Income-expenditure analysis** has three components.
   a The **aggregate expenditures schedule** shows the relationship between national income and aggregate expenditures. As shown in Figure 29.1 its curve slopes positively but is flatter than the 45-degree line. Also, at the left it lies above the 45-degree line, indicating that spending exceeds income for low levels of income.
   b The **national income-output identity** states that income must equal output. This allows the horizontal axis in Figure 29.1 to measure both national income and GDP.
   c **Equilibrium** occurs when aggregate expenditures equal output. This is shown as the intersection of the two lines in Figure 29.1. At this point, all of the economy's output is willingly purchased by consumers, firms, government, or the foreign sector.
2 Shifts in the aggregate expenditures schedule bring about changes in equilibrium output, as shown in

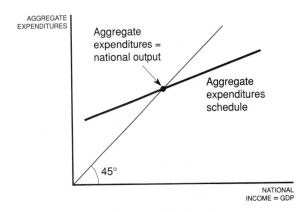

Figure 29.1

Figure 29.2, where *AE* shift up and output increases. The key idea is that output increases by more than the shift in aggregate expenditures. The factor that gives the change in output resulting from a $1 change in

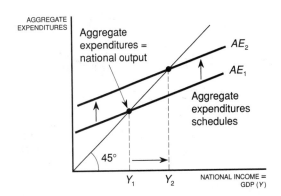

Figure 29.2

335

aggregate expenditures is called the **multiplier.** Mathematically, it is calculated as $1/(1 - b)$, where b is the slope of the *AE* curve.

3 The first component of aggregate expenditures is **consumption.** The **consumption function** describes the relationship between income and consumption. The additional consumption resulting from a 1 dollar increase in income is the **marginal propensity to consume** (*MPC*), which is the slope of the consumption function curve shown in Figure 29.3. In a simple model with only consumption's depending on income, then, the multiplier equals $1/(1 - MPC)$. The **marginal propensity to save** (*MPS*) is the additional amount saved out of a 1-dollar increase in income.

4 Two future-oriented theories imply that consumption will depend more on expectations of future income or wealth and less on current income; that is, the consumption function curve will be flatter. Of course, a flatter slope implies a smaller multiplier.

a The life-cycle hypothesis asserts that individuals plan their consumption over their entire lifetime. Thus, people save during their working years when income is high in order to provide for consumption during retirement. Because savings plays such an important role, current and expected future interest rates as well as expected future income have significant effects on the level of consumption. The life-cycle hypothesis is a future-oriented explanation. It implies that the relationship between consumption and current income would be quite flat, as shown in Figure 29.4.

b The permanent income hypothesis also argues that people rationally plan their present and future consumption, saving in good years to provide extra consumption in bad years. Again, the focus is on both current and future income, interest rates, and prices. The permanent income hypothesis reconciles the discrepancy between the aggregate and the individual: over time, aggregate consumption

increases in the same proportion as income, while for individuals consumption increases by a smaller proportion than income.

5 In reality, the relationship between current income and consumption is not as flat as the future-oriented theories suggest. Two explanations of why consumption seems to be more dependent on current income involve **durable goods consumption and credit rationing.** When incomes fall during recessions, individuals postpone purchases of durable goods. Because they are uncertain when and if good times will return, they take the safer alternative of making do with old durable goods. Further, when incomes fall, individuals find borrowing more difficult than the permanent income hypothesis asserts. Banks also are unsure of the future incomes of borrowers and are reluctant to lend money to the unemployed. It is safer for banks to lend money to those who do not need it!

6 The government enters with its spending and its taxation. Increases in government purchases shift the aggregate expenditures curve up. Income taxation makes the consumption function curve flatter because some of the extra income is taken in taxes, rather than spent. A proportional income tax rate equal to *t* reduces the multiplier formula to $1/[1 - MPC(1 - t)]$.

7 **Investment** includes firms' purchases of new plant and equipment and inventories, and households' purchases of new houses, which are durable goods. Business **investment in plant and equipment** is based on the expectation that future profits from the investment will more than outweigh the current investment expenditure. Of course, the firm must discount future revenues and costs; therefore, the interest rate is important. The investment schedule gives the total value of investment at each rate of interest. Lower interest rates increase the present value of profits and lead to more investment.

8 Firms face technological risks and market risks and they demand compensation, the size of which depends upon the size of the risks, their ability to share the risks, and

Figure 29.3

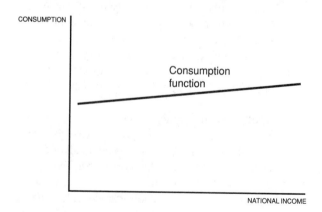

Figure 29.4

their willingness to bear the risks themselves. The other important factor is the availability of funds. During recessions the investment schedule shifts to the left because expectations of profits decrease, risks appear larger, risk-sharing opportunities diminish, firms grow less willing to bear risks, and available funds dry up.

9 **International trade** brings in the last component of aggregate expenditures. **Exports,** which are foreign purchases of domestic goods, shift *AE* up. **Imports** depend on income, as shown by the import function in Figure 29.4. Imports also depend on the relative price of domestic and foreign goods and on the exchange rate. Since some of additional income is spent abroad for imports, the *AE* curve is made flatter and the multiplier reduced further to $1/[1 - (1 - t)(MPC - MPI)]$.

10 A rise in the interest rate reduces investment, net exports, and durable goods consumption, shifting *AE* down and reducing output. This negative relationship between output and real interest rates is summarized in the *IS* curve shown in Figure 29.5.

BEHIND THE ESSENTIAL CONCEPTS

1 You might wonder what role prices play in income-expenditure analysis. Prices are determined by supply and demand, but here we are concerned only with the demand side. At this level of analysis, prices are fixed; one way of thinking about this is that the economy is operating on the flat portion of the aggregate supply curve.

2 How does the economy reach equilibrium without price adjustment? Inventories play the key role.

 a If GDP is below equilibrium, then households and firms want to buy more than the economy produces. Firms notice this when they sell the goods they have on inventory. Firms produce more to restore inventories, and GDP increases.

 b If GDP is above equilibrium, the story is reversed.

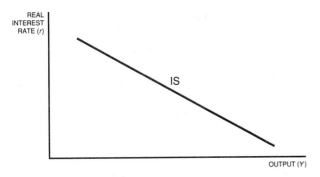

Figure 29.5

Households and firms buy less than the economy produces, inventories of unsold goods accumulate, and firms cut back on production. GDP falls.

3 A helpful way to understand the multiplier process and why the multiplier is smaller when there are taxes and trade is to think in terms of injections and leakages. Suppose that the economy gets an injection of new spending, say an increase in exports. Some people will receive this money, and they will save some and spend some. We say that the money that is saved "leaks" out of the system. The money that is spent becomes other people's income; they in turn save some and spend some, and the process continues. The total amount of spending generated is a multiple of the initial injection. But any leakage reduces the total amount of spending. Clearly, taxes go to the government. That is a leakage. Money spent on imports goes abroad—another leakage. More leakages means less spending and a smaller multiplier.

4 The marginal propensity to consume out of current income is quite high, and thus the consumption function slopes up rather steeply. Why, then, do we study the future-oriented theories of consumption, which stress the future and predict a flat consumption function? The answer is that the life-cycle and permanent income hypotheses provide a deeper understanding of consumption, especially of what factors might cause the Keynesian consumption function to shift and the stability of the relationship. For example, in recessions, people become pessimistic about future incomes and postpone durable goods purchases, shifting the consumption function and aggregate expenditures down. Remember that the central questions in macroeconomics involve the fluctuations in the economy; therefore, it is vital to understand the causes of the changes.

5 The life-cycle and permanent income hypotheses involve borrowing and savings; thus, they teach us the importance of capital markets. If you were always able to obtain credit, your consumption would not vary much. You could borrow in low-income years (such as during college), live well, and repay during high-income years. But capital markets are not perfect; credit rationing suggests that banks are reluctant to let you borrow against future earnings. When your income is less during recessions and you need money, the best available option is to postpone major purchases. Imperfect capital markets make consumption more variable, and thus they are at the center of the discussion about economic ups and downs.

6 To see why business investment is volatile and why it fluctuates over the business cycle, put yourself in the shoes of a business owner. The economy is in recession, and customers are not buying your products. Profits are

down, and you have little retained earnings to spend on investment. The bank will not lend to you because it perceives your precarious financial position. Even if you could obtain funds, a recession is not the time to take risks. During good times, a failed investment may only mean lower profits; during bad times, it may mean bankruptcy. The safest option is to postpone purchases of new plant and equipment, cut production, and sell off inventories.

SELF-TEST

True or False

1 The four components of aggregate expenditures are consumption, investment, government purchases, and net exports.
2 Aggregate expenditures include what households, firms, and government spend on goods and services produced in the United States.
3 The aggregate expenditures schedule gives the total desired spending at each price level.
4 A change in aggregate expenditures causes a greater change in output.
5 The relationship between a household's income and its consumption is called its consumption function.
6 Disposable income equals national income plus taxes.
7 The marginal propensity to consume equals the marginal propensity to save.
8 A higher tax rate on income means that the multiplier is larger.
9 According to the life-cycle hypothesis, people save during working years to provide for consumption retirement.
10 The future-oriented theories of consumption imply that the consumption function curve is relatively flat.
11 Spending on durable goods is less variable than spending on nondurable goods.
12 A borrower is credit rationed if she cannot afford the interest rate at which banks are willing to lend.
13 In the United States economy, inventories fluctuate less than output because firms try to smooth production and produce at a steady rate.
14 The slope of the *AE* curve is flatter in an open economy.
15 A recession in Europe will reduce exports and shift the U.S. *AE* curve down.

Multiple Choice

1 As income increases, aggregate expenditures
  a increase.
  b decrease.
  c remain the same.
  d increase or decrease depending on how product prices change.
  e increase or decrease of depending on events in the capital market.
2 The aggregate expenditures curve is
  a horizontal.
  b horizontal for low levels of output, upward sloping for intermediate levels of output, and steep at high levels of output.
  c upward sloping.
  d downward sloping.
  e a 45-degree line.
3 In equilibrium, it is true that
  a the output of the economy must be purchased.
  b aggregate expenditures equal national output.
  c aggregate expenditures equal what households, firms, and government want to spend at the equilibrium level of national income.
  d unplanned inventories equal zero.
  e all of the above.
4 An upward shift in the aggregate expenditures schedule occurs when
  a households, firms, and government decide to spend more at each level of income.
  b households, firms, and government decide to spend less at each level of income.
  c households, firms, and government decide to spend less at each price level.
  d households, firms, and government decide to spend more at each price level.
  e the economy is in recession.
5 Which of the following is *not* a component of aggregate expenditures?
  a Consumption
  b Investment
  c Government purchases
  d Net exports
  e Taxes
6 The household's consumption function traces out the relationship between its consumption and its
  a investment.
  b income.
  c taxes.
  d inflation rate.
  e total expenditure.
7 The marginal propensity to consume gives the
  a fraction of extra income that will be consumed.
  b ratio of consumption to income.
  c fraction of extra consumption that comes from wage income.
  d fraction of extra consumption that comes from interest and dividends.
  e ratio of consumption out of wage income to consumption out of interest and dividend income.
8 The marginal propensity to save equals
  a the marginal propensity to consume.
  b 1 plus the marginal propensity to consume.

c 1 minus the marginal propensity to consume.

d the reciprocal of the marginal propensity to consume.

e none of the above.

9 The view that current disposable income determines current consumption is consistent with the

a Keynesian consumption function.

b life-cycle hypothesis.

c permanent income hypothesis.

d all of the above.

e *b* and *c*.

10 The idea that individuals save during working years in order to provide for consumption during retirement is called the

a Keynesian consumption function.

b life-cycle hypothesis.

c permanent income hypothesis.

d all of the above.

e *b* and *c*.

11 The theory that people save in good years to provide for extra consumption in bad years is called the

a Keynesian consumption function.

b life-cycle hypothesis.

c permanent income hypothesis.

d all of the above.

e *b* and *c*.

12 Which of the following emphasize(s) that expected future income affects current consumption?

a Keynesian consumption function

b Life-cycle hypothesis

c Permanent income hypothesis

d All of the above

e *b* and *c*.

13 According to the future-oriented consumption theories, the multiplier is

a quite small.

b zero.

c large.

d small in recessions but large in booms.

e large in recessions but small in booms.

14 Adding taxes to the income-expenditure model causes

a disposable income to be less than national income.

b the aggregate expenditures curve to be flatter.

c the multiplier to be smaller.

d the aggregate consumption function curve to be flatter.

e all of the above.

15 The component of aggregate expenditures that is most variable is probably

a investment.

b consumption.

c government expenditures.

d net exports.

e They are equally variable.

16 For aggregate expenditure calculation, which of the following is *not* included in investment spending?

a Purchases of new capital goods

b Inventories accumulated in anticipation of sales

c Purchases of used capital goods

d Purchases of new homes

e None of the above

17 The investment function describes the total value of investment at each

a price level.

b level of disposable income.

c level of national income.

d level of GDP.

e rate of interest.

18 The amount of each extra dollar of disposable income spent on imports is the marginal propensity to

a import.

b consume.

c save.

d export.

e invest.

19 Adding international trade to the income-expenditure model causes

a the multiplier to be larger.

b the aggregate expenditures schedule to be flatter.

c the aggregate expenditures schedule to be steeper.

d the equilibrium level of output to be lower.

e *a* and *c*.

20 The balance of trade is

a exports minus imports.

b exports plus imports.

c imports minus exports

d imports divided by exports.

e exports divided by imports.

Completion

1 The relationship between the economy's total expenditures and national income is summarized by the _____.

2 The _____ traces the relationship between consumption and disposable income.

3 The fraction of additional income that is consumed is called the _____.

4 National output increases by more than the amount of a given increase in investment by a factor called the _____.

5 According to the _____ hypothesis, people save during their working years in order to increase consumption after retirement.

6 When firms cannot sell all that they produce, they experience an increase in _____.

7 Inventories generally _____ during recessions.

8 The relationship between national income and imports is summarized by the _____.

9 The additional imports purchased as a result of a one-dollar increase in income is called the _____.

10 An economy actively engaged in international trade and investment is called an _____.

Answers to Self-test

True or False

1	t	6	f	11	f
2	t	7	f	12	f
3	f	8	f	13	f
4	t	9	t	14	t
5	t	10	t	15	t

Multiple Choice

1	*a*	6	*b*	11	*c*	16	*c*
2	*c*	7	*a*	12	*e*	17	*e*
3	*e*	8	*c*	13	*a*	18	*a*
4	*a*	9	*a*	14	*e*	19	*b*
5	*e*	10	*b*	15	*a*	20	*a*

Completion

1 aggregate expenditures schedule
2 consumption function
3 marginal propensity to consume
4 multiplier
5 life-cycle
6 unplanned inventories
7 increase
8 import function
9 marginal propensity to import
10 open economy

Doing Economics: Tools and Practice Problems

The topic of this section is income-expenditure analysis. We begin with an explanation of the tools needed and follow with problems involving economies with no taxes or imports. For each, we find the consumption function, calculate the aggregate expenditures schedule, and solve for the economy's equilibrium output. We then study the multiplier process, which shows how a change in spending brings about a larger change in equilibrium output. Finally, we consider progressively more complicated problems with income taxes and imports, where the net export function must be calculated. An important lesson of these latter problems concerns how taxes and imports affect the multiplier and the stability of the economy.

1 (Worked problem: income-expenditure analysis) For years, Costa Guano has remained closed to foreign trade and investment. The government of the isolated nation spends no money and collects none in taxes. Autonomous consumption is 300 million guanos (the currency of Costa Guano), and the marginal propensity

---

> **Tool Kit 29.1** Finding the Aggregate Consumption Function
>
> Aggregate expenditures equal the sum of consumption, investment, government spending, and net exports. The first step is to find the aggregate consumption function, which shows the level of consumption that corresponds to each level of national income.
>
> *Step one:* Identify the marginal propensity to consume (*MPC*), autonomous consumption, and the income tax rate.
>
> *Step two:* Calculate the aggregate consumption function by substituting various values of national income into the following formula:
>
> aggregate consumption = autonomous consumption + national income (1 − tax rate) × *MPC*.
>
> (Note that the term in brackets is disposable income, which equals national income when the tax rate is zero.)

> **Tool Kit 29.2** Finding the Net Export Function
>
> In an open economy, net exports must be included in aggregate expenditures. The **net export function** shows the level of net exports that corresponds to each level of national income.
>
> *Step one:* Identify the marginal propensity to import (*MPI*), the tax rate, and the level of exports.
>
> *Step two:* Calculate the import function by substituting various levels of national income into the following formula:
>
> imports = national income (1 − tax rate) × *MPI*.
>
> *Step three:* Find the net export function by subtracting imports from exports for every level of national income:
>
> net exports = exports − imports.

---

to consume equals 0.8. Finally, domestic private investment equals 100 million guanos.

a Find the aggregate consumption function.
b Find the aggregate expenditures schedule.
c Calculate equilibrium output and national income.
d Brimming with confidence, Costa Guano's firms increase their investment spending by 100 million (for a total of 200 million). Calculate the multiplier and the ultimate change in output brought about by this increase in investment.

Tool Kit 29.3 Finding the Aggregate Expenditures Schedule

With the aggregate consumption and net export functions in place, the aggregate expenditures schedule can be calculated. The aggregate expenditures schedule shows the level of aggregate spending corresponding to each level of national income.

Step one: Identify the aggregate consumption function, the level of investment spending, the level of government spending, and the net export function.

Step two: Calculate the aggregate expenditures schedule by summing consumption, investment, government spending, and net exports for each level of national income:

$AE = C + I + G + X.$

Tool Kit 29.4 Using Income-Expenditure Analysis to Determine the Equilibrium

We find the equilibrium level of output and national income (which are always equal), where the aggregate expenditures schedule crosses the 45-degree line. At this point, consumers, firms, government, and foreigners spend just enough to purchase the economy's output.

Step one: Identity the aggregate expenditures schedule.

Step two: Choose a level of national income, and find the corresponding level of aggregate expenditures. If they are equal, stop. This is the equilibrium level of output.

Step three: If aggregate expenditures exceed national income, then inventories will fall, firms will increase production, and output will expand. Choose a greater level of national income, and repeat step one. If aggregate expenditures are less than national income, then inventories will rise, firms will cut back production, and output will decrease. Choose a lower level of national income, and repeat step one.

Step four: Continue until the equilibrium is found.

Step-by-step solution

Step one (a): Find the aggregate consumption function. Identify the *MPC,* autonomous consumption, and the tax rate. The *MPC* is 0.8, autonomous consumption is 300 million guanos, but the tax rate is zero.

Tool Kit 29.5 Using Multiplier Analysis to Find the Ultimate Change in Output Caused by an Initial Change in Spending

The great lesson of income-expenditure analysis is that an initial change in spending ripples through the economy and ultimately results in a larger change in output. The process by which this happens is the multiplier process, and the multiplier itself shows how much larger than the initial change in spending is the ultimate change in output.

Step one: Identify the marginal propensity to consume, the tax rate, the marginal propensity to import, and the initial change in spending.

Step two: Calculate the multiplier. Use the appropriate formula:

No taxes or imports	$1/(1 - MPC)$
Income taxes	$1/[1 - MPC(1 - \text{tax rate})]$
Open economy/no taxes	$1/[1 - (MPC + MPI)]$
Open economy with taxes	$1/[1 - (MPC - MPI)(1 - \text{tax rate})]$

Step three: Calculate the ultimate change in output by multiplying the initial change in spending by the multiplier:

change in output = change in spending × multiplier.

Step four: Verify the result in step three by adding the change in spending to the original aggregate expenditures schedule and solving for the new equilibrium level of output.

Step two: Calculate the aggregate consumption function. When national income equals zero, aggregate consumption equals autonomous consumption (300 million guanos). At 500 million guanos in national income, consumption equals $300 + 0.8(500) = 700$ million guanos. Continuing, we derive Table 29.1.

Table 29.1

National income	Aggregate consumption
(millions of guanos)	
0	300
500	700
1,000	1,100
1,500	1,500
2,000	1,900
2,500	2,300
3,000	2,700

Step one (b): Find the aggregate expenditures schedule. Identify the aggregate consumption function, investment, government spending, and the net export function. The aggregate consumption function is given in Table 29.1, and investment equals 100 million. Government spending and net exports equal zero.

Step two: Calculate the aggregate expenditures schedule adding investment and consumption, as shown in Table 29.2.

Table 29.2

National income	Aggregate consumption	Investment	Aggregate expenditures
	(millions of guanos)		
0	300	100	400
500	700	100	800
1,000	1,100	100	1,200
1,500	1,500	100	1,600
2,000	1,900	100	2,000
2,500	2,300	100	2,400
3,000	2,700	100	2,800

Step one (c): Calculate equilibrium output and national income. Identify the aggregate expenditures schedule. It appears in Table 29.2.

Step two: Choose a level of national income. When national income is 2,000 million guanos, aggregate expenditures equal 2,000 million guanos. Consumers and firms purchase exactly the economy's output of 2,000 million guanos.

Step one (d): Calculate the multiplier and the ultimate change in output brought about by this increase in investment of 100 million guanos (from 100 to 200). Identify the marginal propensity to consume, the tax rate, the marginal propensity to import, and the initial change in spending. The *MPC* is 0.8, the initial change in spending is 100 million guanos. There are no taxes or imports.

Step two: Calculate the multiplier. Because there are no taxes or imports, the multiplier equals

$1/(1 - MPC) = 1/(1 - 0.8) = 1/0.2 = 5.$

Step three: Calculate the ultimate change in output:

change in output $= 100 \times 5 = 500$ million guanos.

Step four: Verify the result in step three by adding the change in spending to the original aggregate expenditures schedule and solving for the new equilibrium level of output. The new aggregate expenditures schedule is given in Table 29.3.

Table 29.3

National income	Aggregate consumption	Investment	Aggregate expenditures
	(millions of guanos)		
0	300	200	500
500	700	200	900
1,000	1,100	200	1,300
1,500	1,500	200	1,700
2,000	1,900	200	2,100
2,500	2,300	200	2,500
3,000	2,700	200	2,900

The new equilibrium level of output is 2,500 million guanos which is 500 million guanos more than originally. It checks!

2 (Practice problem: income-expenditure analysis) El Dorado, an insular economy closed to foreign trade and investment, has no income-based taxes, and its government spends nothing. The marginal propensity to consume is 0.9, autonomous consumption is 5 billion dorals (the currency of El Dorado), and private investment totals 1 billion dorals. (Hint: Choose national income in intervals of 10 billion; that is, 0, 10, 20, etc.)
a Find the aggregate consumption function.
b Find the aggregate expenditures schedule.
c Calculate equilibrium output and national income.
d After a period of stability, investment in El Dorado jumps to 2 billion dorals. Calculate the multiplier and the ultimate change in output brought about by this increase in investment.

3 (Practice problem: income-expenditure analysis) In Erehwemos, there is no taxation and also no government spending. The economy is closed to the outside world. All investment is undertaken by private domestic firms, and the total is 2 billion wemos (the Erehwemosian currency). The marginal propensity to consume is 0.75, and autonomous consumption is 2 billion wemos. (Hint: Choose national income levels in intervals of 4 billion; that is, 0, 4, 8, 12, etc.)
a Find the aggregate consumption function.
b Find the aggregate expenditures schedule.
c Calculate equilibrium output and national income.
d Investment climbs to 4 billion wemos. Calculate the multiplier and the ultimate change in output brought about by this increase in investment.

4 (Worked problem: income-expenditure analysis) This problem builds on problem 1. Recognizing the need for infrastructure investment, the government of Costa Guano institutes an income tax with a flat rate of 25 percent and spends 300 million guanos. Private

investment continues at 200 million guanos, the marginal propensity to consume is 0.8, and autonomous consumption equals 300 million guanos. The economy remains closed to foreign trade.

a Find the consumption function.

b Find the aggregate expenditures schedule.

c Find the equilibrium level of output.

d Suppose that the government raises its spending by 200 million guanos (for a total of 500 million guanos). Calculate the multiplier, and solve for the ultimate change in output brought about by the increase in government spending.

Step-by-step solution

Step one (*a*): Identify the marginal propensity to consume, autonomous consumption, and the income tax rate. The *MPC* is 0.8, autonomous consumption equals 300 million, and the income tax rate is 25 percent.

Step two: Calculate the aggregate consumption function. When national income equals zero, aggregate consumption equals autonomous consumption (300 million guanos). At 500 million guanos in national income, aggregate consumption = 300 + [500 (1 − 0.25)] × 0.8 = 600 (million guanos). Continuing, we derive Table 29.4.

Table 29.4

National income	Aggregate consumption
(millions of guanos)	
0	300
500	600
1,000	900
1,500	1,200
2,000	1,500
2,500	1,800
3,000	2,100

Step one (*b*): Identify the aggregate consumption function, investment, government spending, and the net export function. The aggregate consumption function is given in Table 29.4, investment equals 200 million guanos, and government spending equals 300 million guanos. Net exports remain zero.

Step two: Calculate the aggregate expenditures schedule by adding consumption, investment, and government spending, as shown in Table 29.5.

Step one (*c*): Identify the aggregate expenditures schedule. It appears in Table 29.5.

Step two: Choose a level of national income. When national income is 2,000 million guanos, aggregate expenditures equal 2,000 million guanos. Consumers and firms purchase exactly the economy's output of 2,000 million guanos.

Table 29.5

National income	Aggregate consumption	Investment	Government spending	Aggregate expenditures
		(millions of guanos)		
0	300	200	300	800
500	600	200	300	1,100
1,000	900	200	300	1,400
1,500	1,200	200	300	1,700
2,000	1,500	200	300	2,000
2,500	1,800	200	300	2,300
3,000	2,100	200	300	2,600

Step one (*d*): Identify the marginal propensity to consume, the tax rate, the marginal propensity to import, and the initial change in spending. The *MPC* is 0.8, and the initial change in spending is 200 million. The tax rate is 25 percent, but there are no imports.

Step two: Calculate the multiplier. Because there is an income tax but no imports, the multiplier equals

$$1/[1 - MPC\,(1 - \text{tax rate})] = 1/[1 - 0.8\,(1 - 0.25)]$$
$$= 1/(1 - 0.6) = 1/0.4 = 2.5.$$

(In problem 1, there was no income tax and the multiplier equalled 5. Here, the income tax reduces the multiplier to 2.5.)

Step three: Calculate the ultimate change in output:

change in output = 200 × 2.5 = 500 million.

Step four: Verify the result in step three by adding the change in spending to the original aggregate expenditures schedule and solving for the new equilibrium level of output. The new aggregate expenditures schedule is given in Table 29.6.

Table 29.6

National income	Aggregate consumption	Investment	Government spending	Aggregate expenditures
		(millions of guanos)		
0	300	200	500	1,000
500	600	200	500	1,300
1,000	900	200	500	1,600
1,500	1,200	200	500	1,900
2,000	1,500	200	500	2,200
2,500	1,800	200	500	2,500
3,000	2,100	200	500	2,800

The new equilibrium level of output is 2,500 million guanos, which is 500 million more than originally. It checks. The economy is more stable with the income tax, for it took a 200 million change in spending to change output by 500 million guanos in problem 1, where there was no tax.

5 (Practice problem: income-expenditure analysis) This problem builds on problem 2. An income tax system is passed by El Dorado's Council of Ministers. The flat tax rate is 1/9 on all income, and the government plans to spend 3 billion dorals. The marginal propensity to consume remains at 0.9, autonomous consumption is 5 billion dorals, and private investment continues at 2 billion dorals.

a Find the consumption function.

b Find the aggregate expenditures schedule.

c Find the equilibrium level of output.

d Suppose that the government raises its spending by 4 billion dorals (for a total of 7 billion dorals). Calculate the multiplier, and solve for the ultimate change in output brought about by the increase in government spending.

6 (Practice problem: income-expenditure analysis) This problem builds on problem 3. Erehwemos institutes an income tax with a flat rate of 1/3. The government spends 2 billion wemos. The marginal propensity to consume remains at 0.75, autonomous consumption equals 2 billion wemos, and private investment equals 4 billion wemos.

a Find the aggregate consumption function.

b Find the aggregate expenditures schedule.

c Calculate equilibrium output and national income.

d Responding to the war threat from neighboring Erehwon, the government doubles spending. The increase in government spending is 2 billion wemos (for a total of 4 billion wemos). Calculate the multiplier and the ultimate change in output brought about by this increase in government spending.

7 (Worked problem: income-expenditure analysis) This problem builds on problems 1 and 4. Costa Guano has opened its economy to foreign trade. It exports 500 million guanos worth of goods in world markets. Its citizens have developed tastes for foreign goods, however, and their marginal propensity to import is 1/3. Autonomous consumption remains at 300 million guanos, investment equals 200 million guanos, government spending has returned to 300 million guanos, the marginal propensity to consume is 0.8, and the tax rate is 25 percent.

a Find the aggregate consumption function.

b Find the net export function.

c Find the aggregate expenditures schedule.

d Find the equilibrium level of output.

e Suppose that exports increase by 325 million guanos (for a total of 825 million guanos). Calculate the multiplier, and solve for the ultimate change in output brought about by the increase in exports.

Step-by-step solution

Step one (*a* and *b*): The aggregate consumption function is the same as in problem 4 and is given in Table 29.4. Identify the marginal propensity to import, the tax rate, and the level of exports. The *MPI* equals 1/3, the tax rate is 25 percent, and the level of exports equals 500 million guanos.

Step two: Calculate the import function. When national income is zero, so are imports. When national income is 500 million guanos, imports = $500 \times (1 - 0.25) \times 1/3 = 125$ million. Continuing, we derive the import function in Table 29.7.

Table 29.7

National income	Imports
0	0
500	125
1,000	250
1,500	375
2,000	500
2,500	625
3,000	750

Step three: Find the net export function. When national income is zero, net exports are $500 - 0 = 500$ million guanos. When national income is 500, net exports are $500 - 125 = 375$ million guanos. Continuing, we derive the net export function in Table 29.8.

Table 29.8

National income	Exports	Imports	Net exports
	(millions of guanos)		
0	500	0	500
500	500	125	375
1,000	500	250	250
1,500	500	375	125
2,000	500	500	0
2,500	500	625	−125
3,000	500	750	−250

Step one (*c*): Identify the aggregate consumption function, investment, government spending, and the net export function. The aggregate consumption function is given in Table 29.4, investment equals 200 million guanos, government spending is 300 million guanos, and the net export function appears in Table 29.8.

Step two: Calculate the aggregate expenditures schedule by adding consumption, investment, government spending, and net exports. Table 29.9 gives the results.

Step one (*d*): Identify the aggregate expenditures schedule. It is given in Table 29.9.

Step two: Choose a level of national income. When national income equals 2,000 million guanos, aggregate expenditures equal 2,000 million guanos, and this is the equilibrium level of output.

Table 29.9

National income	Aggregate consumption	Invest-ment	Govern-ment spending	Net exports	Aggregate expenditures
			(millions of guanos)		
0	300	200	300	500	1,300
500	600	200	300	375	1,475
1,000	900	200	300	250	1,650
1,500	1,200	200	300	125	1,825
2,000	1,500	200	300	0	2,000
2,500	1,800	200	300	−125	2,175
3,000	2,100	200	300	−250	2,350

Step one (e): Identify the marginal propensity to consume, the tax rate, the marginal propensity to import, and the initial change in spending. The *MPC* is 0.8, the tax rate is 25 percent, the *MPI* equals 1/3, and exports increase by 325 million guanos.

Step two: Calculate the multiplier:

multiplier $= 1/[1 − (MPC − MPI)(1 − \text{tax rate})]$
$= 1/[1 − (0.8 − 1/3)(1 − 0.25)] = 20/13 = 1.54.$

Note that in the open economy, the multiplier is smaller than in the closed economy of problem 4.

Step three: Calculate the ultimate change in output:

change in output $= 325 × 20/13 = 500$ million guanos.

Step four: Verify the result in step three by adding the change in exports to the original aggregate expenditures schedule (Table 29.9) and solving for the new equilibrium level of output. The new aggregate expenditures schedule is given in Table 29.10. (Note that the increase in exports increases net exports by 325 million guanos.)

Table 29.10

National income	Aggregate consumption	Invest-ment	Govern-ment spending	Net exports	Aggregate expenditures
			(millions of guanos)		
0	300	200	300	825	1,625
500	600	200	300	700	1,800
1,000	900	200	300	575	1,975
1,500	1,200	200	300	450	2,150
2,000	1,500	200	300	325	2,325
2,500	1,800	200	300	200	2,500
3,000	2,100	200	300	75	2,825

The new equilibrium level of output is 2,500 million guanos, which is 500 million more than originally. It checks. The open economy is yet more stable because it took a 325 million change in spending to change output by 500 million guanos.

8 (Practice problem: income-expenditure analysis) This problem builds on problems 2 and 5. The new economics minister wins the day with a brilliant argument against protectionism, and El Dorado opens its economy. Its exports surge to 14 billion dorals. The marginal propensity to import is 9/40, the marginal propensity to consume remains at 0.9, autonomous consumption is 5 billion, private investment is 2 billion, and the government spends 3 billion dorals.
 a Find the consumption function.
 b Find the net export function.
 c Find the aggregate expenditures schedule.
 d Find the equilibrium level of output.
 e Suppose that exports increase by 4 billion dorals (for a total of 18 billion dorals). Calculate the multiplier, and solve for the ultimate change in output brought about by the increase in exports.

9 (Practice problem: income-expenditure analysis) This problem builds on problems 3 and 6. With peace at hand, the Erehwemos economy is opened to foreign trade and investment. Exports equal 8/3 (2.67) billion wemos, and the marginal propensity to import is 0.25. Government spending has returned to 2 billion wemos, but private investment remains at 4 billion wemos. Autonomous consumption is also 2 billion wemos, and the marginal propensity to consume remains at 0.75. Finally, the tax rate is 1/3.
 a Find the aggregate consumption function.
 b Find the net export function.
 c Find the aggregate expenditures schedule.
 d Calculate the equilibrium output and national income.
 e Exports increase to 16/3 (5.33) billion wemos. Calculate the multiplier and the ultimate change in output brought about by this increase in exports.

Answers to Problems

Table 29.11

National income	Aggregate consumption	Investment	Aggregate expenditures
	(billions of dorals)		
0	5	1	6
10	14	1	15
20	23	1	24
30	32	1	33
40	41	1	42
50	50	1	51
60	59	1	60
70	68	1	69
80	77	1	78
90	86	1	87
100	95	1	96

2 Table 29.11 gives:
  a The aggregate consumption function
  b The aggregate expenditures schedule
  c Equilibrium output is 60 billion dorals.
  d The multiplier is $1/(1 - 0.9) = 10$. The change in output is $1 \times 10 = 10$ million dorals. Table 29.12 shows that when investment increases to 2 billion dorals, equilibrium output grows to 70 billion dorals. It verifies that equilibrium output increases by 10 billion dorals (from 60 to 70 billion), as indicated above.

Table 29.12

National income	Aggregate consumption	Investment	Aggregate expenditures
(millions of dorals)			
0	5	2	7
10	14	2	16
20	23	2	25
30	32	2	34
40	41	2	43
50	50	2	52
60	59	2	61
70	68	2	70
80	77	2	79
90	86	2	88
100	95	2	97

Table 29.13

National income	Aggregate consumption	Investment	Aggregate expenditures
(billions of wemos)			
0	2	2	4
4	5	2	7
8	8	2	10
12	11	2	13
16	14	2	16
20	17	2	19
24	20	2	22
28	23	2	25

3 Table 29.13 gives:
  a The aggregate consumption function
  b The aggregate expenditures schedule
  c Equilibrium output is 16 billion wemos.
  d The multiplier is $1/(1 - MPC) = 1/(1 - 0.75) = 4$. The change in output is $2 \times 4 = 8$ billion wemos. This is verified by Table 29.14, which shows that the new equilibrium output is 24 billion wemos.

Table 29.14

National income	Aggregate consumption	Investment	Aggregate expenditures
(billion of wemos)			
0	2	4	6
4	5	4	9
8	8	4	12
12	11	4	15
16	14	4	18
20	17	4	21
24	20	4	24
28	23	4	27

5 Table 29.15 shows:
  a The aggregate consumption function
  b The aggregate expenditures schedule

Table 29.15

National income	Aggregate consumption	Investment	Government spending	Aggregate expenditures
(billions of dorals)				
0	5	2	3	10
10	13	2	3	18
20	21	2	3	26
30	29	2	3	34
40	37	2	3	42
50	45	2	3	50
60	53	2	3	58
70	61	2	3	66
80	69	2	3	74
90	77	2	3	82
100	85	2	3	90

  c The equilibrium level of output is 50 billion dorals.
  d The multiplier is $1/[1 - MPC(1 - t)] = 1/[1 - 0.9$ dorals $(1 - 1/9)] = 5$. The change in output is $4 \times 5 = 20$ billion dorals. Table 29.16 shows that when

Table 29.16

National income	Aggregate consumption	Investment	Government spending	Aggregate expenditures
(billions of dorals)				
0	5	2	7	14
10	13	2	7	22
20	21	2	7	30
30	29	2	7	38
40	37	2	7	46
50	45	2	7	54
60	53	2	7	62
70	61	2	7	70
80	69	2	7	78
90	77	2	7	86
100	85	2	7	94

government spending is 7 billion dorals, the new equilibrium output is 70 billion dorals, which represents an increase of 20 billion dorals.

6 Table 29.17 gives:
   a The aggregate consumption function
   b The aggregate expenditures schedule

Table 29.17

National income	Aggregate consumption	Investment	Government spending	Aggregate expenditures
		(billions of wemos)		
0	2	4	2	8
4	4	4	2	10
8	6	4	2	12
12	8	4	2	14
16	10	4	2	16
20	12	4	2	18
24	14	4	2	20
28	16	4	2	22

   c Equilibrium output is 16 billion wemos.
   d The multiplier is $1/[1 - MPC(1 - t)] = 1/[1 - 0.75(1 - 1/3)] = 2$. The change in equilibrium output is $2 \times 2 = 4$ billion wemos, as is verified by Table 29.18, which shows that the new equilibrium output is 20 billion wemos.

Table 29.18

National income	Aggregate consumption	Investment	Government spending	Aggregate expenditures
		(billions of wemos)		
0	2	4	4	10
4	4	4	4	12
8	6	4	4	14
12	8	4	4	16
16	10	4	4	18
20	12	4	4	20
24	14	4	4	22
28	16	4	4	24

8 Table 29.19 shows:
   a the aggregate consumption function
   b the net export function
   c the aggregate expenditures schedule

Table 29.19

National income	Aggregate consumption	Investment	Government spending	Net exports	Aggregate expenditures
		(billions of dorals)			
0	5	2	3	14	24
10	13	2	3	12	30
20	21	2	3	10	26
30	29	2	3	8	42
40	37	2	3	6	48
50	45	2	3	4	54
60	53	2	3	2	60
70	61	2	3	0	66
80	69	2	3	-2	72
90	77	2	3	-4	78
100	85	2	3	-6	84

   d Equilibrium output is 60 billion dorals.
   e The multiplier is $1/[1 - (MPC - MPI)(1 - t)] = 1/[1 - (0.9 - 9/40)(1 - 1/9)] = 2.5$. The change in output is $4 \times 2.5 = 10$ billion dorals. Table 29.20 shows that the new equilibrium output is 70 billion dorals, which indicates an increase of 10 billion dorals.

Table 29.20

National income	Aggregate consumption	Investment	Government spending	Net exports	Aggregate expenditures
		(billions of dorals)			
0	5	2	3	18	28
10	13	2	3	16	34
20	21	2	3	14	40
30	29	2	3	12	46
40	37	2	3	10	52
50	45	2	3	8	58
60	53	2	3	6	64
70	61	2	3	4	70
80	69	2	3	2	76
90	77	2	3	0	82
100	85	2	3	-6	84

9   Table 29.21 shows:
   a   The aggregate consumption function
   b   The net export function
   c   The aggregate expenditures schedule
   d   Equilibrium output equals 16 billion dorals.

Table 29.21

National income	Aggregate consumption	Invest- ment	Govern- ment spending	Net exports	Aggregate expenditures
(billions of dorals)					
0	2	4	2	2 2/3	10 2/3
4	4	4	2	2	12
8	6	4	2	1 1/3	13 1/3
12	8	4	2	2/3	14 2/3
16	10	4	2	0	16
20	12	4	2	−2/3	17 1/3
24	14	4	2	−1 1/3	18 2/3
28	16	4	2	−2	20

e   The multiplier is $1/[1 − (MPC − MPI)(1 − t)] = 1/[1 − (0.75 − 0.25)(1 − 1/3)] = 1.5$ billion dorals. The change in output is $(8/3) \times 1.5 = 4$ billion dorals. Table 29.22 shows that the new equilibrium output equals 20 billion dorals, which is an increase of 4 billion dorals.

Table 29.22

National income	Aggregate consumption	Invest- ment	Govern- ment spending	Net exports	Aggregate expenditures
(billions of dorals)					
0	2	4	2	5 1/3	13 1/3
4	4	4	2	4 2/3	14 2/3
8	6	4	2	4	16
12	8	4	2	3 1/3	17 1/3
16	10	4	2	2 2/3	18 2/3
20	12	4	2	2	20
24	14	4	2	1 1/3	21 1/3
28	16	4	2	2/3	22 2/3

CHAPTER 30 | Aggregate Demand and Inflation

Chapter Review

This chapter continues the study of macroeconomic fluctuations, but for now it restricts attention to the closed economy. Building on the insights of last chapter's income-expenditure analysis, the discussion brings inflation into the analysis. The central idea is the aggregate demand-inflation curve. It shows how outbreaks of inflation lead the central bank to raise interest rates and how those higher interest rates cause output to fall and unemployment to rise Of course, these are short-run phenomena. Eventually, the economy returns to its long-run trend as explained by the full-employment model of Part Six.

ESSENTIAL CONCEPTS

1 When the economy slips into a downturn, output and income fall. In the capital market, this leads to a leftward shift in both the savings curve and the investment schedule, and it brings about lower levels of savings and investment. The new real interest rate may rise or fall from its full-employment level.

2 The Fed's **monetary policy rule** describes how it moves interest rates in response to economic conditions. Although it has other goals, the main one involves inflation. When inflation rises, the Fed increases nominal interest rates. The higher nominal rates lead to higher real rates of interest and this causes output to fall below its potential. Unemployment rises and inflation slows.

3 The **aggregate demand-inflation** (*ADI*) **curve** summarizes how spending falls when inflation rises. The slope of the *ADI* curve depends on two factors: how much the central bank adjusts interest rates when inflation changes and how sensitive spending and output are to changes in the real rate of interest. If the central bank changes interest rates by a great deal or if spending and output are very sensitive to the interest rate, then the *ADI* curve is quite flat. On the other hand, weak central bank responses and a tendency for spending to change little when interest rates change imply a steeper *ADI* curve.

4 The *ADI* curve shifts when there are changes in fiscal policy. For example, lower taxes or increased government purchases shift the *ADI* curve to the right. Monetary policy shifts the *ADI* curve if the Fed changes its monetary policy rule. If, for a given rate of inflation, the Fed lowers interest rates, the *ADI* curve shifts to the right. Other factors that shift the *ADI* curve to the right are increases in wealth (such as booms in stock markets) and more optimistic expectations. These factors lead households and firms to increase spending.

5 Figure 12 shows how the *ADI* curve is used to explain output fluctuations. The economy begins at point *A*, where the inflation rate is π_0 and output equals its full-employment level Y_f. The horizontal line drawn at π_0 is called the inflation adjustment (IA) curve. The *ADI* curve shifts to the left and output falls to Y_1. The higher unemployment causes inflation to adjust downward from π_0 to π_1. As this adjustment proceeds, the output level returns to full employment.

6 Output fluctuations can be caused by shifts in the *ADI* curve brought on by the government or by changes in household or business spending or by **supply shocks** that shift the *IA* curve. These fluctuations can also be offset by suitable fiscal or monetary policy. Another application involves an increase in potential GDP, which is a rightward shift in **long-run aggregate supply** Y_f.

BEHIND THE ESSENTIAL CONCEPTS

1   When inflation increases, the Fed wants to increase the real interest rate. We saw in Chapter 25 that the Fed can control the supply of reserves and thereby determine the federal funds rate, but this is a short-term nominal rate of interest. It is the real rate (the nominal rate adjusted for inflation), however, that influences output. Recall the formula

nominal rate of interest = real rate of interest + inflation rate.

If inflation increases and the Fed keeps the nominal rate constant, then the real rate would tend to fall. The Fed can raise the real interest rate, but it must increase the nominal rate by more than the change in inflation.

2   A movement along the *ADI* curve summarizes a great deal of economic activity. When the inflation rate rises, the economy works through these steps.

Step one: The Fed decreases reserves.

Step two: The Federal funds rate increases by more than the increase in inflation.

Step three: The real interest rate rises.

Step four: Aggregate spending shifts down.

Step five: Output falls by more than the change in spending due to the multiplier.

3   You can see what makes the *ADI* curve steeper or flatter by looking at the steps listed above. If the Fed changes interest rates by a large amount, if interest rate changes greatly affect spending, or if the multiplier is large, the *ADI* curve will tend to be flat. If the Fed changes interest rates by small amounts, if these interest rates have little impact on spending, and if the multiplier is small, then the *ADI* curve will tend to be steep.

4   How does the model of this chapter fit with the income-expenditure analysis of the last chapter? Income-expenditure analysis explains two of the steps. First, it explains the shifts in the *ADI* curve. For example, if business investment declines, output falls and the *ADI* curve shifts to the left. When output is below potential, inflation slows. The Fed is concerned about inflation, and when inflation is lower, it lowers interest rates. Here income-expenditure analysis does its second job, showing that changes in interest rates lead to changes in output (steps-four and five listed above).

SELF-TEST

True or False

1   This chapter focuses on the closed economy.
2   When interest rates rise, households and businesses increase their spending.

3   In the capital market, a fall in output shifts both the savings curve and the investment function curve to the left.
4   When output falls, interest rates must rise.
5   When inflation rises, the Fed reduces interest rates.
6   In order to change the real rate of interest, the Fed must change the nominal interest rate by more than the change in inflation.
7   The chapter assumes that the Fed's monetary policy rule targets the real interest rate.
8   If investment spending were less sensitive to the interest rate, then *ADI* curve would be steeper.
9   If the central bank reacts strongly to inflation with large changes in interest rates, the *ADI* curve has a steep slope.
10   A cut in taxes shifts the *ADI* curve to the right.
11   A decrease in wealth shifts the *ADI* curve to the left.
12   The Volcker disinflation is an example of a change in the monetary policy rule.
13   The Kennedy tax cut of 1963 shifted the *ADI* curve to the right.
14   Supply shocks, such as changes in oil prices, shift the *ADI* curve.
15   An increase in potential GDP shifts the *ADI* curve to the right.

Multiple Choice

1   The policymaking committee of the Federal Reserve is called the
   a   Senate Finance Committee.
   b   U.S. Department of Treasury.
   c   American Bankers Association.
   d   Federal Open Market Committee.
   e   International Monetary Fund.
2   Which of the following components of aggregate expenditures is *ignored* in this chapter?
   a   Consumption
   b   Investment
   c   Government purchases
   d   Net exports
   e   None is ignored.
3   Higher interest rates lower aggregate expenditures by
   a   reducing the profitability of investment.
   b   leading businesses to cut back on investment projects.
   c   leading households to reduce purchases of new homes.
   d   leading households to reduce purchases of new cars.
   e   all of the above.
4   When output falls, in the capital market,
   a   supply and demand both shift to the right.
   b   supply and demand both shift to the left.
   c   supply shifts to the right, but demand shifts to the left.
   d   supply shifts to the left, but demand shifts to the right.
   e   only supply shifts.

5　A fall in output leads to
   a　higher real interest rates.
   b　lower real interest rates.
   c　either higher or lower interest rates depending on the size of the shifts in the investment function and the savings curve.
   d　higher nominal interest rates.
   e　lower nominal interest rates.

6　This chapter assumes that the Fed's monetary policy rule targets
   a　inflation.
   b　unemployment.
   c　the exchange rate.
   d　the real interest rate.
   e　the nominal interest rate.

7　An increase in the inflation rate leads the Fed to
   a　decrease reserves, causing an increase in the federal funds rate.
   b　increase reserves, causing an increase in the federal funds rate.
   c　increase reserves, causing a decrease in the federal funds rate.
   d　decrease reserves, causing a decrease in the federal funds rate.
   e　none of the above

8　When inflation rises, the Fed will
   a　increase the nominal interest rate by more than the change in inflation.
   b　increase the nominal interest rate by less than the change in inflation.
   c　decrease the nominal interest rate by less than the change in inflation.
   d　decrease the nominal interest rate by more than the change in inflation.
   e　leave the nominal interest rate unchanged.

9　The *ADI* curve is steeper if
   a　spending is more sensitive to the real interest rate.
   b　spending is less sensitive to the real interest rate.
   c　the Fed responds weakly to inflation.
   d　*a* and *c*.
   e　*b* and *c*.

10　The *ADI* curve shifts to the right with
   a　an increase in government purchases and a decrease in taxes.
   b　an increase in government purchases and a increase in taxes.
   c　a decrease in government purchases and a decrease in taxes.
   d　a decrease in government purchases and a increase in taxes.
   e　The *ADI* curve is not affected by government fiscal policy.

11　The *ADI* curve shifts to the left if the Fed
   a　responds more strongly to increases in inflation.
   b　responds more weakly to increases in inflation.
   c　changes its monetary policy rule to lower the real interest rate at each level of inflation.
   d　changes its monetary policy rule to raise the real interest rate at each level of inflation.
   e　The *ADI* curve is not affected by monetary policy.

12　The *ADI* curve shifts to the right if household and business become
   a　more optimistic or if wealth increases.
   b　more optimistic or if wealth decreases.
   c　less optimistic or if wealth increases.
   d　less optimistic or if wealth decreases.
   e　The *ADI* curve does not shift with changes in optimism or wealth.

13　Which of the following is *not* associated with recession?
   a　The *ADI* curve shifts to the left.
   b　Unemployment rises.
   c　Inflation slowly adjusts downward.
   d　The Fed lowers interest rates as inflationary pressure abates.
   e　All of the above are associated with recession.

14　The Volcker disinflation began with a
   a　shift to the left of the *ADI* curve.
   b　shift to the right of the *ADI* curve.
   c　upward shift in *IA*.
   d　downward shift in *IA*.
   e　rightward shift in Y_f

15　The Kennedy tax cut caused an initial
   a　shift to the left of the *ADI* curve.
   b　shift to the right of the *ADI* curve.
   c　upward shift in *IA*.
   d　downward shift in *IA*.
   e　rightward shift in Y_f.

16　The oil price shocks of the 1970s caused an initial
   a　shift to the left of the *ADI* curve.
   b　shift to the right of the *ADI* curve.
   c　upward shift in *IA*.
   d　downward shift in *IA*.
   e　rightward shift in Y_f

17　The boom at the end of the 1990s caused an initial
   a　shift to the left of the *ADI* curve.
   b　shift to the right of the *ADI* curve.
   c　upward shift in *IA*.
   d　downward shift in *IA*.
   e　rightward shift in Y_f

18　Recessions may begin with
   a　a leftward shift in *ADI*.
   b　a rightward shift in *ADI*.
   c　an upward shift in *IA*.
   d　a downward shift in *IA*.
   e　*a* and *c*.

19　After the economy has recovered from a recession caused by a supply shock,
   a　output is at the full-employment level.
   b　inflation returns to its prerecession level.

c inflation remains above its prerecession level.
d *a* and *b*.
e *a* and *c*.

20 After the economy has recovered from a recession caused by a demand shock,
  a output is at the full-employment level.
  b inflation returns to its prerecession level.
  c inflation is lower its prerecession level.
  d *a* and *b*.
  e *a* and *c*.

Completion

1 The policy committee of the Federal Reserve is called the _____.
2 How the Fed moves the interest rate as economic conditions change is its _____.
3 This chapter assume that the Fed targets the _____.
4 The relationship between spending and inflation is summarized by the _____.
5 The *ADI* curve has a _____ slope.
6 With an increase in government purchases the *ADI* curve shifts to the _____.
7 The curve that gives the full-employment level of output at each inflation rates is called the _____.
8 The horizontal line at the inflation rate is called the _____.
9 When the Fed raises interest rates in response to increased inflation, there is a _____ the *ADI* curve.
10 When the Fed changes its monetary policy rule, there is a _____ the *ADI* curve.

Answers to Self-test

True or False

1	t	6	t	11	t
2	f	7	f	12	t
3	t	8	t	13	t
4	f	9	f	14	f
5	f	10	t	15	f

Multiple Choice

1	d	6	a	11	d	16	c
2	d	7	a	12	a	17	e
3	e	8	a	13	e	18	e
4	b	9	e	14	a	19	d
5	c	10	a	15	b	20	e

Completion

1 Federal Open Market Committee
2 monetary policy rule
3 inflation rate
4 aggregate demand–inflation (*ADI*) curve
5 negative

6 right
7 long-run aggregate supply curve
8 inflation adjustment (*IA*) curve
9 movement along
10 shift in

Doing Economics: Tools and Practice Problems

Because prices and wages adjust slowly, the economy does not respond to shocks with an instantaneous jump to the long-run equilibrium. Rather, it first moves to a short-run equilibrium that is determined by aggregate demand. Here output can exceed or fall short of potential GDP. Eventually, prices and wages do adjust, and the economy returns to produce the full-employment level of output. Tool Kit 30.1 shows how to use the aggregate demand–inflation curve to analyze the economy's fluctuations.

Tool Kit 30.1 Using the *ADI* Curve

In long-run equilibrium, inflation has adjusted to bring aggregate demand equal to potential GDP. We start here and analyze the impacts of shock in the usual way. Follow these steps.

Step one: Start with a long-run equilibrium.

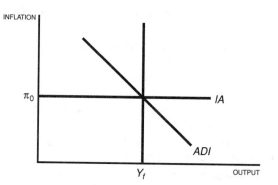

Step two: Determine the shift caused by the exogenous shock. The following table lists the main types of shocks.

Exogenous shock	Shift
Fiscal policy	
Increase in government spending	*ADI* curve to right
Decrease in taxes	*ADI* curve to right
Monetary policy rule changes	
Lower *r* for every inflation rate	*ADI* curve to right
Higher *r* for every inflation rate	*ADI* curve to left
More optimistic expectations	*ADI* curve to right
Increase in wealth	*ADI* curve to right

Supply shock (inflation shock) *IA* curve up
Higher productivity Y_f to right

Step three: Shift the curve.

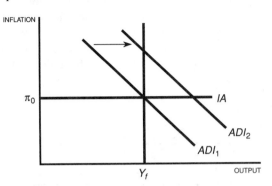

Step four: Find the short-run equilibrium.

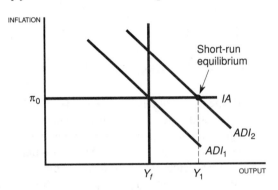

Step five: Show the inflation adjustment.

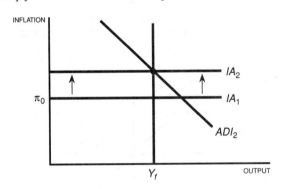

Step six: Find the long-run equilibrium.

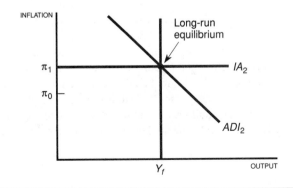

1 (Worked problem: using the *ADI* curve) A major stock market crash wipes output 20 percent of the value of stock market wealth. Use the aggregate demand-inflation curve to analyze the effects.

 a Find the short-run equilibrium.
 b Describe the inflation adjustment process.
 c Find the long-run equilibrium.

Step-by-step solution

Step one: Start with a long-run equilibrium.

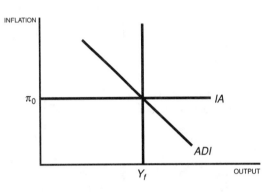

Step two: Determine the shift caused by the exogenous shock. The decline in wealth causes consumers to cut back on spending, and aggregate demand shifts to the left.

Step three: Shift the curve.

Step four: Find the short-run equilibrium. Output has fallen to Y_1.

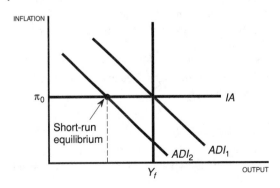

Step five: Show the inflation adjustment. With output below potential GDP, inflation slows. This shifts the *IA* curve down and the economy moves along the *ADI* curve. During this time the Fed responds to the lower inflation with a cut in interest rates, stimulating increased investment.

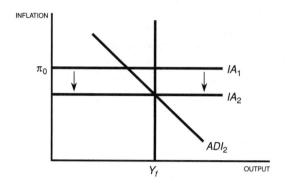

Step six: Find the long-run equilibrium. The economy returns to full employment at a lower rate of inflation.

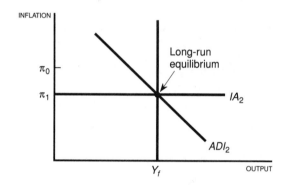

2 (Practice problem: using the *ADI* curve) For each of the following use the aggregate demand-inflation curve to analyze the short- and long-run effects on output and inflation.

   a The Federal Reserve adopts a looser monetary policy, targeting a lower real interest rate for every level of inflation.

   b A major tax cut is passed by Congress.

   c Business investors grow pessimistic about future economic conditions.

   d Following the end of the war, there is a significant decline in defense spending.

   e New technological breakthroughs lead to increased investment.

   f Oil prices fall.

   g Improved K-through-12 education increases productivity.

Answers to Problem

2 *a* From the initial long-run equilibrium at *E* with output equal to potential GDP, the *ADI* curve shifts

right as investment responds to the lower interest rates. The short-run equilibrium is at *A* and output increases to Y_1. Inflation begins to increase, shifting the *IA* curve up. The Fed responds with higher interest rates. This reduces investment and consumption, moving the economy back along the *ADI* curve to its long-run equilibrium at *C,* where output is again at potential GDP but inflation is at a higher level.

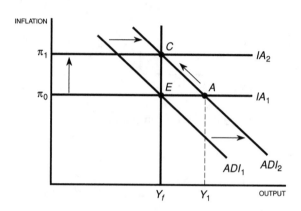

b From the initial long-run equilibrium at *E,* where output equals potential GDP, the *ADI* curve shifts right as households spend some of their increased disposable income. The short-run equilibrium is at *A* and output increases to Y_1. Inflation begins to increase, shifting the *IA* curve up. The Fed responds with higher interest rates. This reduces investment and consumption, moving the economy back along the *ADI* curve to its long-run equilibrium at *C,* where output is again at potential GDP but inflation is at a higher level.

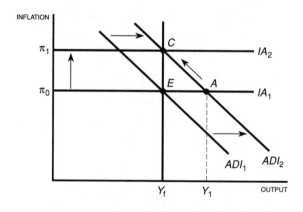

c From the initial long-run equilibrium at *E,* where output equals potential GDP, the *ADI* curve shifts left as the pessimism leads to lower investment. The short-run equilibrium is at *A* and output decreases to Y_1. Inflation begins to decrease, shifting the *IA* curve down. The Fed responds with lower interest rates. This increases investment and consumption, moving the economy back along the *ADI* curve to its long-run equilibrium at *C,* where output is again at potential GDP but inflation is at a lower level.

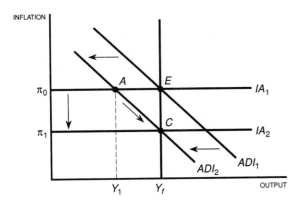

d   From the initial long-run equilibrium at *E,* where output equals potential GDP, the *ADI* curve shifts left as government spending declines. The short-run equilibrium is at *A* and output decreases to Y_1. Inflation begins to decrease, shifting the *IA* curve down. The Fed responds with lower interest rates. This increases investment and consumption, moving the economy back along the *ADI* curve to its long-run equilibrium at *C,* where output is again at potential GDP but inflation is at a lower level.

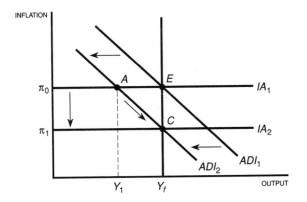

e   From the initial long-run equilibrium at *E,* where output equals potential GDP, the *ADI* shifts right, reflecting the increased investment. The short-run equilibrium is at *A* and output increases to Y_1. Inflation begins to increase, shifting the *IA* curve up. The Fed responds with higher interest rates. This reduces investment and consumption, moving the economy back along the *ADI* curve to its long-run equilibrium at *C,* where output is again at potential GDP but inflation is at a higher level.

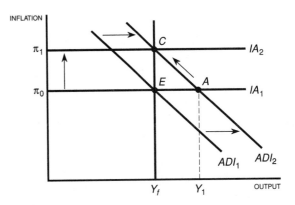

f   From the initial long-run equilibrium at *E,* where output equals potential GDP, the *IA* curve shifts down, reflecting the lower oil prices. The short-run equilibrium is at *A* and output increases to Y_1. Inflation begins to increase, shifting the *IA* curve back up. The Fed responds with higher interest rates. This reduces investment and consumption, moving the economy back along the *ADI* curve to its long-run equilibrium at *E,* where output is again at potential GDP and inflation returns to its original level.

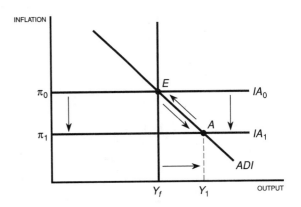

g From the initial long-run equilibrium at *E*, where output equals potential GDP, Y_f shifts right, reflecting the increased potential GDP. Inflation begins to decrease, shifting the *IA* curve down. The Fed responds with lower interest rates. This increases investment and consumption, moving the economy along the *ADI* curve to its long-run equilibrium at *C*, where output is at the higher level of potential GDP but inflation is at a lower level.

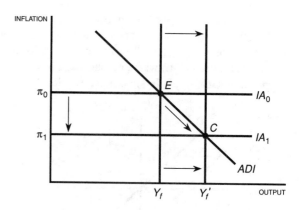

CHAPTER 31 | Inflation and Unemployment

Chapter Review

The foundation of inflation adjustment and its relation to unemployment are the main topics. The main tool is the short-run inflation adjustment curve, which shows the trade-off of inflation and output. This fits with last chapter's aggregate demand-inflation curve to provide a complete picture of the short-run determination of output and inflation. This sets the stage for next chapter's examination of macroeconomic policy.

ESSENTIAL CONCEPTS

1   The **Phillips curve** shows a negative relationship between the rate of growth in nominal wages and the unemployment rate. When unemployment is low, it is hard for firms to retain their current workers or hire new ones, and they tend to increase wage offers. Also, unions and other employees are in a better bargaining position and can demand larger wage increases. Increases in unemployment lead to more moderate wage increases.

2   The **short-run inflation adjustment** (*SRIA*) curve shows the relationship between inflation and output. It is upward sloping, indicating that when inflation is higher, so is output.

3   The **natural rate of unemployment** is the measured unemployment rate when the economy is at full employment, producing its potential GDP. It is also called the **nonaccelerating inflation rate of unemployment** (NAIRU). This measure includes frictional and structural unemployment. Cyclical unemployment refers to any additional unemployment above the natural rate.

4   The position of the *SRIA* curve depends on the expected rate of inflation. To underscore this dependence, it is termed the **expectations-augmented SRIA.** Higher rates of expected inflation shift the curve up, and lower expected inflation shifts it down.

5   The trade-off of output and inflation shown by the *SRIA* applies only to the short run. If output is kept above its full employment, people will simply expect more inflation. The *SRIA* curve will shift up, and output will decrease. In the long run, there is no trade-off between output and inflation. The **long-run inflation adjustment** (*LRIA*) curve is a vertical line at full employment.

6   The sacrifice ratio is the amount by which unemployment must be kept below the NAIRU for a year to reduce the inflation rate by 1 percent. For the United States, it is between 1 and 2.

7   Increases in potential GDP shift the *LRIA* curve to the right. Inflation expectations adjust it down and the economy moves to a higher level of output.

8   Combining the *SRIA* with the *ADI* gives a complete model of macroeconomic fluctuations and shows the determinants of inflation: expected inflation, output relative to potential GDP, and **inflation shocks**.

   a   Expectations of higher inflation shift the *SRIA* curve up, leading to a short-run equilibrium with higher inflation and lower output.

   b   An inflation shock, such as an oil price increase, also shifts the *SRIA* curve up, with the same consequences.

   c   When output exceeds potential GDP, inflation increases, bringing output back to the full-employment level.

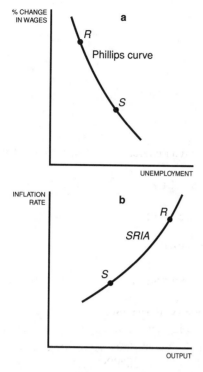

Figure 31.1

BEHIND THE ESSENTIAL CONCEPTS

1　You should see that the short-run inflation adjustment curve represents the basic idea of the Phillips curve in another way. Look at Figure 31.1, which shows a Phillips curve in panel A and an *SRIA* curve in panel B. At point *R* on the Phillips curve wages are growing fast and unemployment is low. In this situation, prices will also rise quickly as employers pass along their higher costs to consumers. And output will be high because so many workers are employed. Plotting the corresponding inflation rate and output level gives us point *R* in panel B. Similarly, at point *S* on the Phillips curve, wages grow slowly and unemployment is high. This implies that prices will also grow slowly but output will be lower because jobless workers produce nothing. Again, plotting the corresponding inflation rate and output level gives us point *S* on the *SRIA* curve.

2　In order to plan, workers and firms must form expectations about the future. As conditions change, of course, they will revise their expectations. One simple approach is to expect that current trends will continue. For example, if last year's inflation was 4 percent, then you expect this year's to be 4 percent. This is called **adaptive expectations.** There is other information, however. For example, in 1979 Paul Volcker announced that he intended to lower inflation. A rational person would also use this information. Using all available

information, including what you learn in this course, means acting on **rational expectations.**

3　We have seen that the economy eventually adjusts the its long-term trend, for which we have three synonyms: potential GDP, long-run aggregate supply, or full employment. Of course, it is not really full employment because some workers remain jobless for structural or frictional reasons. This level of employment is called the natural rate. At this rate of unemployment there is no pressure on inflation; so it is also called the nonaccelerating inflation rate of unemployment (NAIRU). Again, these are two terms for the same thing. Finally, the NAIRU itself may change over time with demographic shifts, such as the baby boom and the entry of women into the labor force.

SELF-TEST

True or False

1　Inflation may vary, but it is always positive.
2　The Phillips curve shows the relationship between unemployment and inflation.
3　Inflation and the rate of wage increase usually move together quite closely.
4　The natural rate of unemployment is zero.
5　The short-run inflation adjustment curve is upward sloping.
6　If inflation expectations increase, the short-run inflation adjustment curve shifts to the right.
7　Stagflation refers to a period of high unemployment and high inflation.
8　The NAIRU is larger than the natural rate of unemployment.
9　The long-run inflation adjustment curve is vertical.
10　The sacrifice ratio is the amount by which the inflation rate must be kept above zero to bring the unemployment rate down 1 percentage point.
11　Rational expectations are based on all available information.
12　The entry of women into the labor force increased the NAIRU.
13　An increase in potential GDP shifts both the *SRIA* and the *LRIA* curves to the right.
14　Inflation shocks produce permanent shifts in the *SRIA* curve.
15　The upward slope of the *SRIA* curve shows that unemployment and inflation cannot fall at the same time.

Multiple Choice

1　If inflation turns out to be lower than expected,
　a　both borrowers and lenders lose.
　b　both borrowers and lenders gain.

   c borrowers lose but lenders gain.

   d lenders lose but borrowers gain.

   e Inflation has no effect on borrowers or lenders.

2 Which is true of wages and prices?

   a Wages and prices are flexible in the short run but rigid in the long run.

   b Wages and prices are flexible in both the short and long runs.

   c Wages and prices are rigid in both the short and long runs.

   d Wages and prices are rigid in the short run but flexible in the long run.

   e Wages are always rigid, but prices are always flexible.

3 The trade-off between inflation and unemployment is illustrated by the

   a aggregate demand curve.

   b aggregate supply curve.

   c Phillips curve.

   d aggregate expenditures schedule.

   e money demand curve.

4 Which correctly describes the relationship between the rate of wage increase and inflation?

   a They move together.

   b There is no relationship.

   c The rate of wage increase is constant while inflation fluctuates.

   d The rate of wage increase fluctuates while inflation remains constant.

   e Wages rise when inflation falls and vice versa.

5 When the economy is producing its potential GDP, its unemployment rate

   a is zero.

   b equals the natural rate.

   c depends on the inflation rate.

   d equals the rate of cyclical unemployment.

   e none of the above.

6 The short-run inflation adjustment curve

   a shows the relationship between unemployment and inflation in the short run.

   b is upward sloping.

   c shows the relationship between output and inflation in the short run.

   d *a* and *b*.

   e *b* and *c*.

7 Stagflation refers to a period of

   a high unemployment and inflation.

   b high unemployment and low inflation.

   c low unemployment and inflation.

   d low unemployment and high inflation.

   e *a* or *c*.

8 An increase in the expected rate of inflation

   a rotates the *SRIA* curve clockwise.

   b rotates the *SRIA* curve counterclockwise.

   c shifts the *SRIA* curve up.

   d shifts the *SRIA* curve down.

   e has no effect on the *SRIA* curve.

9 The long-run inflation adjustment curve is

   a vertical.

   b horizontal.

   c upward sloping.

   d downward sloping.

   e none of the above.

10 The long-run inflation adjustment curve is a vertical line at

   a potential GDP.

   b the level of GDP where frictional and structural unemployment equal zero.

   c the natural rate of unemployment.

   d the NAIRU.

   e the natural rate of inflation.

11 If the government tries to keep unemployment below the NAIRU,

   a inflation will decrease.

   b there will be no effect on inflation.

   c inflation will increase.

   d there will be stagflation.

   e the Phillips curve will shift to the left.

12 The amount by which the unemployment rate must be kept above the NAIRU for one year to bring inflation down by 1 percentage point is called the

   a natural rate of unemployment.

   b NAIRU.

   c sacrifice ratio.

   d *LRIA*.

   e *SRIA*.

13 In the United States, the sacrifice ratio is between

   a 0 and 1.

   b 1 and 2.

   c 2 and 3.

   d 3 and 4.

   e 4 and 5.

14 When people form expectations based on the structure of the economy, their expectations are said to be

   a irrational.

   b rational.

   c adaptive.

   d unrealistic.

   e myopic.

15 The idea that there is no stable long-run trade-off between inflation and unemployment is due to

   a A. W. Phillips.

   b Milton Friedman.

   c Robert Lucas.

   d Paul Volcker.

   e Larry Martin.

16 In the United States, the baby boom generation has caused the NAIRU to

a increase from 1960 to 1980 and decrease since then.

b decrease from 1960 to 1980 and increase since then.

c increase from 1960 to the present.

d decrease from 1960 to the present.

e not change.

17 An increase in potential GDP shifts the

    a *SRIA* and *LRIA* curves to the left.

    b *SRIA* and *LRIA* curves to the right.

    c *SRIA* curve to the left and the *LRIA* curve to the right.

    d *SRIA* curve to the right and the *LRIA* curve to the left.

    e *SRIA* curve only.

18 The inflation shocks due to the 1970s oil price increases caused a

    a temporary shift in the *SRIA* curve to the left.

    b permanent shift in the *SRIA* curve to the left.

    c permanent shift in the *SRIA* curve to the right.

    d temporary shift in the *SRIA* curve to the right.

    e no shift in the *SRIA* curve.

19 During the 1990s, in the United States

    a unemployment fell as inflation increased.

    b unemployment rose as inflation decreased.

    c both unemployment and inflation rose.

    d both unemployment and inflation fell.

    e unemployment and inflation remained constant.

20 Unemployment rates

    a are approximately equal for different demographic groups.

    b are higher for African Americans than for whites.

    c are higher for teenagers than for adults.

    d are higher for whites than for African Americans.

    e *b* and *c*.

Completion

1 Higher than expected inflation injures _____.

2 The trade-off between unemployment and the rate of increase in wages is called the _____.

3 The short-run relationship between _____ and inflation is given by the short-run inflation adjustment curve.

4 The long-run inflation adjustment curve is a vertical line at _____.

5 If the government tries to maintain the unemployment rate below the _____, inflation will increase.

6 When both the unemployment rate and inflation rate are high, there is _____.

7 The oil price increases of the 1970s were an example of _____.

8 An increase in inflation expectations shifts the *SRIA* curve to the _____.

9 When people use all available information including the structure of the economy, they act on _____.

10 The _____ is the amount by which the unemployment rate must be kept above the natural rate to bring the inflation rate down 1 percentage point.

Answers to Self-test

True or False

1	f	6	f	11	t
2	f	7	t	12	t
3	t	8	f	13	t
4	f	9	t	14	f
5	t	10	f	15	f

Multiple Choice

1	*c*	6	*e*	11	*c*	16	*a*
2	*d*	7	*a*	12	*c*	17	*b*
3	*c*	8	*c*	13	*b*	18	*a*
4	*a*	9	*a*	14	*b*	19	*d*
5	*b*	10	*a*	15	*b*	20	*e*

Completion

1 lenders

2 Phillips curve

3 output

4 potential GDP

5 NAIRU

6 stagflation

7 inflation shocks

8 left

9 rational expectations

10 sacrifice ratio

Doing Economics: Tools and Practice Problems

In the last chapter we saw that when the economy diverges from its potential GDP in the short run, inflation adjusts to bring aggregate demand back to long-run equilibrium. In this chapter we study the short-run inflation adjustment. The key idea is the expectations-augmented short-run inflation-adjusted (*SRIA*) curve. There are two differences between the *SRIA* and the *IA* used in Chapter 30. First, the *SRIA* curve slopes upward, showing the short-run trade-off of inflation and output. Second the *SRIA* curve shifts when inflationary expectations change. Tool Kit 31.1 shows how, combined with the *ADI* curve, it helps explain fluctuations caused by changes in expectations, supply shocks, and aggregate demand.

Tool Kit 31.1 Analyzing Short- and Long-Run Inflation Adjustment

In the short run, changes in aggregate demand cause changes in output and inflation. These demand shocks cause a movement along the *SRIA* curve. In the long run, the *SRIA* curve shifts to restore long-run equilibrium. Other fluctuations are caused by shifts in the *SRIA* curve. Follow these steps.

Step one: Start with a long-run equilibrium.

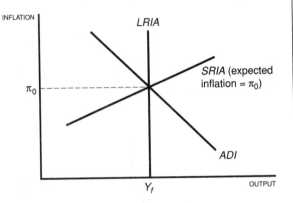

Step two: Determine the shift caused by the exogenous shock. The *ADI* curve shifts as explained in Tool Kit 30.1. The *SRIA* and *LRIA* curves shift as follows:

Exogenous shock	Shift
Rise in inflationary expectations	*SRIA* curve to the left
Fall in inflationary expectations	*SRIA* curve to the right
Inflation shocks	
Higher prices	*SRIA* curve to the left
Lower prices	*SRIA* curve to the right
Productivity improvements	*LRIA* and *SRIA* curves both to the right

Step three: Shift the curve(s).

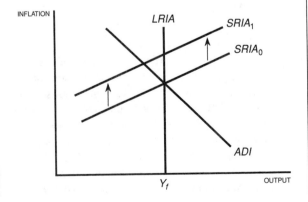

Step four: Find the short-run equilibrium.

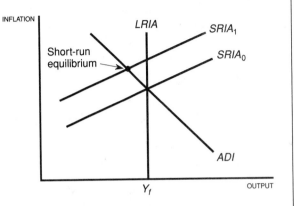

Step five: Show the inflation adjustment.

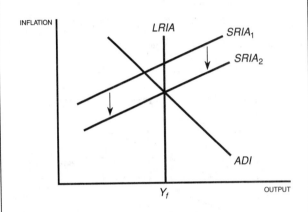

Step six: Find the long-run equilibrium

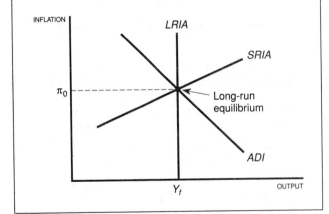

1 (Worked problem: short-run inflation adjustment) Spooked by the sudden death of the chairperson of the Federal Reserve and nervous about his or her successor, market participants expect inflation to rise from its current level of 3 percent per year.

Step-by-step solution

Step one: Start with an equilibrium. Notice that the curves intersect at the expected rate of 3 percent inflation.

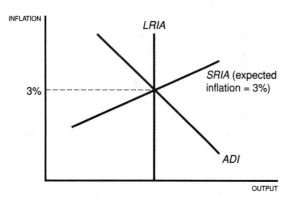

Step two: Determine the shift. Higher inflationary expectations shift the *SRIA* curve to the left.

Step three: Shift the curve.

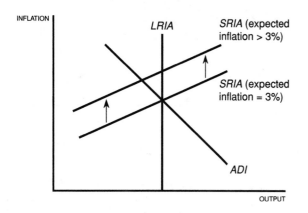

Step four: Find the short-run equilibrium. Inflation has increased, while output has fallen below potential GDP.

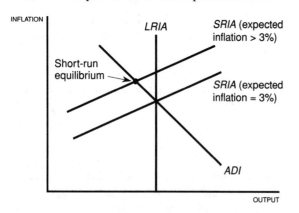

Step five: Show the inflation adjustment.

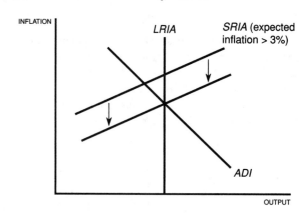

Step six: Find the long-run equilibrium. Note that both output and inflation have returned to their original levels.

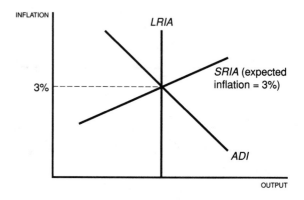

2 Analyze the impact of each of the following. Show the short-run equilibrium, the inflation adjustment, and the long-run equilibrium.

a The Federal Reserve adopts a tighter monetary policy, targeting a higher real interest rate for every level of inflation.

b Market participants expect lower rates of inflation.

c Oil prices increase.

d Widespread access to Internet Two enhances productivity.

Answers to Problem

2 a From the initial long-run equilibrium at *E* with output equal to potential GDP and inflation equal to its expected level of π_0, the *ADI* curve shifts to the left. Output falls to its short-run equilibrium (point *A*) level of Y_1, but inflation has fallen below expectations to π_1. With output below potential GDP, expectations of inflation fall and the *SRIA* curve shifts to the right until full employment is restored at a lower level of inflation at point *C*.

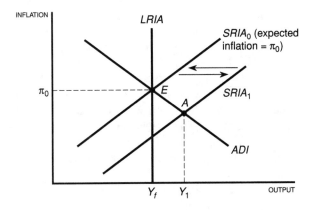

b From the initial long-run equilibrium at *E* where output equals potential GDP and inflation equals its expected level of π_0, the *SRIA* curve shifts to the right. Output rises to its short-run equilibrium (point *A*) level of Y_1, and inflation falls below expectations to π_1. With output above potential GDP, expectations of inflation rise and the *SRIA* curve shifts to the left until full employment is restored at the original level of inflation.

c From the initial long-run equilibrium at *E* where output equals potential GDP and inflation equals its expected level of π_0, the *SRIA* curve shifts to the left. Output falls to its short-run equilibrium (point

A) level of Y_1, and inflation rises above expectations to π_1. With output below potential GDP, expectations of inflation fall and the *SRIA* curve shifts to the right until full employment is restored at the original level of inflation.

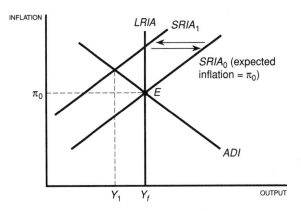

d From the intial long-run equilibrium at *E* where output equals potential GDP and inflation equals its expected level of π_0, both the *SRIA* and *LRIA* curves shift to the right. Output rises to its new long-run equilibrium (point *C*) level of Y_1, which is the new higher potential GDP, and inflation remains at its original level.

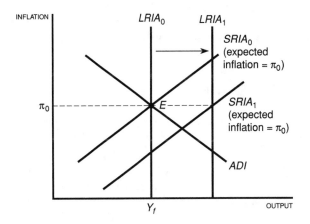

CHAPTER 32

The Role of Macroeconomic Policy

Chapter Review

With the basic model of macroeconomic fluctuations completed in the last chapter, the discussion turns to policy. The government has two types of policies at its disposal: fiscal and monetary. Fiscal policy is the use of government tax and expenditure policies; monetary policy involves the Federal Reserve and its instruments. How these policies affect the economy is the main topic. This discussion stays with the assumption of the closed economy, the next chapter moves forward to open economy issues.

ESSENTIAL CONCEPTS

1   **Automatic stabilizers** decrease taxes and increase spending during times of low output, thereby automatically limiting the decline in spending. The opposite occurs during times of high output. Examples of these stabilizers include income taxes and transfer programs, such as unemployment insurance. Strong automatic stabilizers make the *ADI* curve steeper and reduce its shifts.

2   **Discretionary fiscal policy** actions are deliberate changes in tax and expenditure policies, such as public works projects or tax rate changes. Although these policies shift the *ADI* curve and can in principle be used to counteract fluctuations, their inflexibility limits their use and effectiveness.

3   The actual budget deficit computes the difference between government expenditures and tax revenues. When the economy falls into recession, however, tax collections diminish. Households earn less income and pay less income tax. Business profits fall and so do corporate tax collections. Spending increases on unemployment insurance and welfare programs. All of these combine to bring about a deficit without any change in policy. The **full-employment deficit** measures what the deficit would be at full employment. Tax and expenditure policies that result in no full-employment deficit will nevertheless lead to actual budget deficits when the economy is operating below capacity.

4   The Federal Reserve implements **monetary policy** by setting a target for the federal funds rate, and it is almost always able to hit its target. Other nominal rates, such as the prime lending rate move in tandem with the federal funds rate. The real interest rate, however, is the nominal rate minus the inflation rate. The Fed can influence this rate but nominal and real rates do diverge unpredictably.

5   The **monetary policy rule** describes what the central bank targets and how it reacts. If the Fed targets inflation, then the monetary policy rule shows what nominal interest rate the Fed will achieve for every inflation rate. To lower real rates when inflation rises, the Fed must increase nominal rates by more than inflation. In the real world, however, it tries to anticipate future inflation and also to promote low unemployment, overall stability, and growth and even keeps an eye on stock markets.

6   Monetary policy cannot influence the real interest rate that occurs at full employment. This is another implication of the principle of the neutrality of money studied in Part Six. It can target an inflation rate by setting the nominal interest rate equal to the real interest rate plus the desired rate of inflation. If the full-employment real rate of interest changes, however, the Fed must alter its policy rule. For example, an increase in the full-employment real interest rate requires a higher nominal interest rate.

7 While the main channel through which monetary policy affects spending is interest rates, two other possibilities exist. Tighter monetary policy reduces credit and the supply of loans. Alternatively, changes in interest rates cause investors to switch from bonds to stocks, and the resulting higher stock prices make households wealthier, leading to additional consumption.

BEHIND THE ESSENTIAL CONCEPTS

1 When the economy experiences a downturn, a fiscal stimulus is called for. Government can tax less or spend more. Discretionary actions involve changes in laws and take time to implement. By the time the stimulus arrives, it may not be needed. After all, the economy does tend to recover on its own. Automatic stabilizers, on the other hand, work quickly. As output falls and unemployment increases, profits and incomes fall and so do tax collections. Laid-off workers draw unemployment compensation. Automatically, the economy is provided with the needed fiscal stimulus.

2 Monetary policy is not inhibited by the political and administrative lags of discretionary fiscal policy. The Fed can act on its own quite quickly in response to changes in economic conditions. This greater flexibility is the main reason that most developed economies rely on monetary policy to promote macroeconomic stability.

3 Although the discussion in this chapter assumes that the Fed targets inflation, targeting the money supply would achieve similar results. As inflation rises, households would withdraw money to use for transactions at the higher prices. Banks would demand more reserves to offset these withdrawals, and this increased demand would drive up interest rates. The policy works indirectly, but it still results in higher interest rates in response to higher inflation.

SELF-TEST

True or False

1 Automatic stabilizers reduce tax collections and increase government spending during times of low output.

2 Unemployment insurance helps stabilize the economy by increasing government expenditures during recessions.

3 Automatic stabilizers make the *ADI* curve flatter.

4 The effectiveness of discretionary fiscal policy is limited by the time it takes to recognize and react to changes in economic conditions.

5 When the economy is in recession, the appropriate discretionary fiscal policy is a tax increase.

6 When the economy's output falls, the actual budget surplus tends to decrease.

7 The full-employment deficit is what the actual budget deficit would be if the economy were operating at full employment.

8 A tax cut shifts the *ADI* curve to the left.

9 The Federal Reserve has difficulty hitting its target for the federal funds rate.

10 The prime interest rate moves together with the federal funds rate.

11 The nominal interest rate equals the real interest rate minus the rate of inflation.

12 To ensure that the real interest rate increases when inflation rises, the Fed must raise the nominal interest rate more than one for one with an increase in inflation.

13 The Fed targets only the inflation rate.

14 Through the use of its policy instruments, the Fed can change the real interest rate at full employment.

15 When interest rates fall, investors reallocate their portfolios from stocks to bonds.

Multiple Choice

1 Fiscal policy includes
 a maintaining a stable money supply.
 b using consumer product safety regulation to promote consumer confidence.
 c regulating the banking and securities industries to encourage sound investment.
 d using government expenditures and taxation to improve macroeconomic performance.
 e funding oversight agencies, such as the General Accounting Office, to ensure that government carries out its fiduciary responsibilities.

2 Mechanisms that increase the government deficit during recessions and decrease it during economic booms are called
 a balanced budget multipliers.
 b full-employment deficits.
 c automatic stabilizers.
 d political business cycles.
 e none of the above.

3 Which of the following is/are an example(s) of automatic stabilizers?
 a Federal government financing of roads and bridges
 b National defense expenditures
 c Unemployment insurance
 d Subsidies for research and development
 e Health and safety regulations

4 The tax system acts as an automatic stabilizer because tax
 a collections increase when output falls.
 b collections decrease when output falls.
 c rates are cut when output falls.
 d rates are increased when output falls.
 e *b* and *c*.

5 Automatic stabilizers
   a make the *ADI* steeper.
   b make the *ADI* flatter.
   c reduce the magnitudes of shifts in the *ADI* curve.
   d increase the magnitudes of shifts in the *ADI* curve.
   e *a* and *c*.

6 Which of the following is/are example(s) of discretionary fiscal policies during a recession?
   a The government embarks on a large public works program.
   b Tax collections fall.
   c Unemployment insurance claims rise.
   d The actual budget surplus declines.
   e All are discretionary fiscal policies.

7 Lags in implementation limit the effectiveness of
   a automatic stabilizers.
   b discretionary fiscal policy.
   c discretionary monetary policy.
   d the monetary policy rule.
   e accommodative monetary policy.

8 The appropriate discretionary fiscal policy during a recession is
   a the sale of bonds by the Fed.
   b a cut in the reserve requirement.
   c a cut in the discount rate.
   d a cut in tax rates.
   e wage and price controls.

9 The deficit that would occur if the economy were at full employment under current spending and tax policies is called the
   a balanced budget multiplier.
   b full-employment deficit.
   c trade deficit.
   d total accumulated government debt.
   e real budget deficit.

10 When the economy falls into recession, the
   a actual budget surplus falls.
   b the full-employment budget surplus falls.
   c the monetary policy rule shifts.
   d the equilibrium full-employment real interest rate falls.
   e All of the above.

11 Which of the following best describes the relationship between the actual and full-employment budget surplus?
   a The actual budget surplus is always less than the full-employment surplus.
   b The actual budget surplus is always more than the full-employment surplus.
   c The actual budget surplus may be more or less than the full-employment surplus.
   d The actual budget surplus equals the full-employment surplus.
   e None of the above.

12 Which of the following will change the full-employment surplus?
   a Unemployment insurance claims increase during a recession.
   b Tax collections fall during a recession.
   c Tax collections increase during an economic boom.
   d Tax rates are cut.
   e All of the above.

13 When inflation increases, the Fed increases interest rates. This represents a
   a shift to the left in the *ADI* curve.
   b shift to the right in the *ADI* curve.
   c movement up the *ADI* curve.
   d movement down the *ADI* curve.
   e none of the above.

14 The Fed changes its monetary policy rule to lower interest rates for each level of inflation. This represents a
   a shift to the left in the *ADI* curve.
   b shift to the right in the *ADI* curve.
   c movement up the *ADI* curve.
   d movement down the *ADI* curve.
   e none of the above.

15 Which of the following move very closely with the Fed target for the federal funds rate?
   a Federal fund rate
   b Prime rate
   c Real interest rate
   d all of the above
   e *a* and *b*

16 The nominal interest rate equals the sum of the
   a federal funds rate and the prime rate.
   b real interest rate and the inflation rate.
   c unemployment rate and the inflation rate.
   d unemployment rate and the real interest rate.
   e exchange rate and the inflation rate.

17 To ensure that the real interest rate rises when inflation increases, the Fed must
   a change its monetary policy rule.
   b use discretionary fiscal policy.
   c raise the nominal interest rate by more than the change in the inflation rate.
   d raise the nominal interest rate by more than the change in the real interest rate.
   e raise the nominal interest rate by less than the change in the inflation rate.

18 Which of the following are possible targets for the monetary policy rule?
   a Inflation
   b Unemployment
   c Macroeconomic stability
   d Growth
   e All of the above

19 Monetary policy works through the credit channel when interest rate changes affect

a investment.

b consumer durable purchases.

c credit availability.

d the relative demands for stocks and bonds.

e all of the above.

20 Monetary policy works through the portfolio when interest rate changes affect

a investment.

b consumer durable purchases.

c credit availability.

d the relative demands for stocks and bonds.

e all of the above.

Completion

1 _____ involves the use of taxation and government spending to improve macroeconomic performance.

2 Mechanisms that reduce government spending or raise taxes in recessions are called _____.

3 Automatic stabilizer make the ADI curve _____.

4 _____ fiscal policy involves deliberate changes in tax and expenditure policies.

5 The _____ equals the deficit that would have occurred if government revenues and spending were at their full-employment levels.

6 The nominal interest rate equals the real interest rate plus the _____.

7 To increase the real interest rate when inflation rises, the Fed must increase the nominal interest rate by _____ than the change in inflation.

8 The relationship between inflation and the interest rate set by the central bank is an example of a _____.

9 Monetary policy influences the economy through the _____ by affecting the availability of loans.

10 Monetary policy influences the economy through the _____ by affecting investors' relative demands for stocks and bonds.

Answers to Self-Test

True or False

1	t	6	f	11	f
2	t	7	t	12	t
3	f	8	f	13	f
4	t	9	f	14	f
5	f	10	t	15	f

Multiple Choice

1	d	6	a	11	c	16	b
2	c	7	b	12	d	17	c
3	c	8	d	13	c	18	e
4	b	9	b	14	b	19	c
5	e	10	a	15	e	20	d

Completion

1 Fiscal policy

2 automatic stabilizers

3 steeper

4 Discretionary

5 full-employment deficit

6 inflation rate

7 more

8 monetary policy rule

9 credit channel

10 portfolio channel

Doing Economics: Tools and Practice Problems

The topic for this section is the full-employment surplus or deficit. When output fluctuates, automatic stabilizers change government expenditures and tax revenues. The actual deficit or surplus will then differ from what it would be at full employment. The full-employment surplus or deficit is a useful tool in macroeconomic policy, telling us the fiscal position of the government when the effects of automatic stabilizers are removed. Tool Kit 32.1 shows how to calculate the full-employment surplus.

Tool Kit 32.1 Calculating the Full-Employment Surplus

If output is below full-employment, the actual fiscal surplus will be less than the full-employment surplus. The opposite is true when output exceeds potential GDP. Follow these steps to compute the full-employment surplus.

Step one: Identify the actual surplus or deficit, the unemployment rate, the natural rate of unemployment, the actual output, and the marginal expenditure and tax rates.

Step two: Calculate cyclical unemployment.

Cyclical unemployment = actual unemployment − natural rate of unemployment.

Step three: Calculate the output gap. Use Okun's law.

Output gap = cyclical unemployment rate × 2.

Step four: Calculate the change in tax revenue if the output gap were eliminated.

Change in revenue = tax rate × change in output.

Step five: Calculate the change in government expenditures if the output gap were eliminated.

Change in expenditures = expenditure rate × change in output.

Step six: Calculate the full-employment surplus.

Full-employment surplus = actual surplus + change in revenue + change in expenditures.

1 (Worked problem: full-employment surplus) Suppose that there is 4 percent unemployment, which is below the natural rate of 5 percent. The marginal tax rate is 20 percent, the marginal expenditure rate (the extra government spending that results from a $1 change in output) is 10 percent, and output is $6 trillion. Finally, the actual fiscal surplus is $100 billion. Compute the full-employment surplus.

Step one: Identify the actual surplus or deficit, the unemployment rate, the natural rate of unemployment, the actual output, and the marginal expenditure and tax rates.

Step two: Calculate cyclical unemployment.

Cyclical unemployment = actual unemployment − natural rate of unemployment = 4 percent − 5 percent = −1 percent.

Step three: Calculate the output gap. Use Okun's Law.

Output gap = cyclical unemployment rate × 2 × output = −1 percent × 2 × $6 trillion = −$120 billion.

That the gap is negative indicates that output is above potential GDP by $120 billion.

Step four: Calculate the change in tax revenue if the output gap were eliminated.

Change in revenue = tax rate × change in output = 0.20 × (−$120 billion) = −$24 billion.

Step five: Calculate the change in government expenditures if the output gap were eliminated.

Change in expenditures = expenditure rate × change in output = 0.10 × (−$120 billion) = −$12 billion.

Step six: Calculate the full-employment surplus.

Full employment surplus = actual surplus + change in revenue + change in expenditures = $100 − $24 − $12 = $64 billion.

2 For each of the following, compute the full-employment surplus.

	Actual unemployment rate	Natural rate	output	Tax rate	Expenditure rate	Fiscal surplus (or deficit)
a	4%	6%	$10 trillion	0.2	0.1	$80 billion surplus
b	8%	6%	$8 trillion	0.2	0.1	$100 billion deficit
c	6%	6%	$9 trillion	0.2	0.05	$50 billion surplus
d	6%	5%	$9 trillion	0.2	0.05	$0

Answers to Problem

2 a $40 billion surplus
   b $28 billion surplus
   c $50 billion surplus (The economy is at full employment.)
   d $27 billion surplus

CHAPTER 33 | Policy in the Open Economy

Chapter Review

This chapter returns to the open economy and integrates international trade and investment into the short-run macroeconomic model developed in Chapters 28 through 32. The expanded model is then used to explain how foreign events affect the U.S. economy in the short run and how U.S. fiscal and monetary policy work in the open economy. This chapter brings to a close Part Seven and its study of macroeconomic fluctuations. The next topics are the domestic and international financial systems.

ESSENTIAL CONCEPTS

1   In the open economy, net exports affect the *ADI* curve, which, to review, shows the level of aggregate demand for every value of the inflation rate. When inflation increases, the Fed acts to bring about an increase in the real interest rate. But higher real interest rates, as we saw in Chapter 26, cause the currency to appreciate. So in the open economy, movements along the *ADI* curve are accompanied not only by changes in the real interest rate but also by changes in the exchange rate.

2   The exchange rate affects net exports by changing the net relative price of domestic and foreign goods. An **appreciation** of the dollar makes foreign goods relatively less expensive than U.S. goods. Households both in the United States and abroad substitute away from U.S. goods toward the relatively cheaper foreign goods. Imports rise, exports fall, and net exports decline. The greater the decline, the flatter is the *ADI* curve.

3   Other factors may affect net exports and cause the *ADI* curve to shift. For example, recession in foreign countries reduces the demand for U.S. exports. Also, changes in foreign interest rates affect the exchange rate and net exports. Both foreign income and interest rates cause the *ADI* curve to shift.

4   The open economy can also cause the short-run inflation adjustment (*SRIA*) curve to shift. The most important examples are the oil shocks, but any change in the exchange rate makes imported inputs more expensive and acts as an inflation shock. Recall that inflation shocks shift the *SRIA* curve up temporarily.

5   The short-run impact of discretionary monetary policy actions is reinforced by the exchange rate. If the Fed raises interest rates, not only does U.S. investment decline, but the exchange rate appreciates and net exports fall. Similarly, Fed-induced lower interest rates have the additional effect of increasing net exports.

6   The impact of fiscal policy, on the other hand, is lessened in the open economy. Fiscal expansions drive up interest rates and, as we have seen, appreciate the dollar and reduce net exports. These lower net exports partially offset the stimulus of the fiscal policy itself.

BEHIND THE ESSENTIAL CONCEPTS

1   You should pay careful attention to the distinction between a movement along the *ADI* curve and a shift of the curve. Remember that the *ADI* curve shows the relationship between inflation and aggregate demand. Any change resulting from a rise or fall in U.S. inflation leads to a movement along the *ADI* curve. All other changes (foreign income, foreign interest rates) cause shifts. In each case, net exports change, but some changes are movements along the curve and some are shifts of the curve.

2 Remember that the exchange rate used in this chapter is the real exchange rate, which is, of course, the nominal exchange rate adjusted for differences in prices. If European inflation is 2 percent higher than U.S. inflation and the dollar appreciates 2 percent there is no change in the real exchange rate. This is because there is no change in the relative price of U.S. and European goods. It is true that your stronger dollar buys 2 percent more euros than before the appreciation, but you also need 2 percent more euros to buy the European goods. The price that matters to you and other U.S. consumers is the price in dollars, and that price is governed by the real exchange rate.

3 Is the open economy more or less stable than the closed economy? The open economy is subject to shocks emanating from abroad. For example, a recession in Europe may lead to a fall in exports and U.S. layoffs. On the other hand, some of the impact of domestic shocks leaks out of the United States. For example, lower U.S. investment may be offset by increased foreign investment in the United States. In the long run, the theory of comparative advantage tells us that foreign trade and investment make our standard of living higher, but there may be some instability that comes along with the benefits.

SELF-TEST

True or False

1 In 1990 exports accounted for about 25 percent of U.S. GDP.
2 Net exports equal exports minus imports.
3 An appreciation of the dollar increases net exports.
4 As we move up the *ADI* curve, the dollar appreciates.
5 As increase in European interest rates shifts the *ADI* curve to the left.
6 A boom in Asia will shift the *ADI* curve to the right.
7 In the late 1990s the dollar appreciated.
8 Real and nominal exchange rates have moved together in the United States over the past couple of decades.
9 The real exchange rate is the nominal exchange rate adjusted for inflation.
10 An increase in oil prices shifts the *ADI* curve to the left.
11 Monetary policy is more effective in the open economy because exchange rate changes reinforce interest rate changes.
12 In the long run, monetary policy cannot change real interest rates.
13 Fiscal policy is more effective in the open economy because exchange rate changes reinforce interest rate changes.
14 Since its introduction, the euro has depreciated relative to the dollar.

15 During the late 1990s, rapid U.S. growth shifted foreign *ADI* curves to the right.

Multiple Choice

1 Purchases in the United States of foreign produced goods are called
  a exports.
  b imports.
  c net exports.
  d direct foreign investment.
  e foreign aid.
2 Net exports equal
  a imports minus exports.
  b imports plus exports.
  c exports minus imports.
  d exports divided by imports.
  e imports divided by exports.
3 An increase in the U.S. real interest rate leads to a
  a depreciation of the dollar and a fall in net exports.
  b depreciation of the dollar and a rise in net exports.
  c appreciation of the dollar and a rise in net exports.
  d appreciation of the dollar and a fall in net exports.
  e none of the above.
4 A rise in U.S. inflation leads to
  a a fall in net exports and a leftward shift in the *ADI* curve.
  b a rise in net exports and a rightward shift in the *ADI* curve.
  c a fall in net exports and a movement up the *ADI* curve.
  d a rise in net exports and a movement down the *ADI* curve.
  e a rise in net exports and a movement up the ADI curve.
5 Recession in Europe leads to a
  a fall in net exports and a leftward shift in the *ADI* curve.
  b rise in net exports and a rightward shift in the *ADI* curve.
  c fall in net exports and a movement up the *ADI* curve.
  d rise in net exports and a movement down the *ADI* curve.
  e rise in net exports and a movement up the *ADI* curve.
6 An increase in Japanese interest rates leads to a
  a fall in net exports and a rightward shift in the *ADI* curve.
  b rise in the net exports and a rightward shift in the *ADI* curve.
  c fall in net exports and a movement up the *ADI* curve.
  d rise in net exports and a movement down the *ADI* curve.

e rise in net exports and a movement up the *ADI* curve.

7 For the United States, an increase in oil prices leads to
   a a leftward shift in the *ADI* curve.
   b a rightward shift in the *ADI* curve.
   c a leftward shift in the *SRIA* curve.
   d a rightward shift in the *SRIA* curve.
   e none of the above.

8 In the short run, a shift to the left in the *SRIA* curve brings about
   a higher real interest rates.
   b higher inflation.
   c lower output.
   d an appreciaton in the dollar.
   e all of the above.

9 Through its effect on the prices of imported inputs, an appreciation of the dollar can lead to
   a a leftward shift in the *SRIA* curve and higher U.S. inflation.
   b a rightward shift in the *SRIA* curve and higher U.S. inflation.
   c a leftward shift in the *SRIA* curve and lower U.S. inflation.
   d a rightward shift in the *SRIA* curve and lower U.S. inflation.
   e Any of the above is possible.

10 In the short run, which of the following is *not* brought about by an increase in U.S. inflation?
   a Higher real interest rates
   b Lower net exports
   c An appreciation in the dollar
   d Greater investment
   e Lower output

11 The real exchange rate is the nominal exchange rate adjusted for differences in
   a real interest rates.
   b nominal interest rates.
   c price levels.
   d unemployment rates.
   e trade deficits.

12 Over the past several decades the U.S. real exchange rate has
   a moved in tandem with the nominal exchange rate.
   b diverged greatly from the nominal exchange rate.
   c risen while the nominal rate fell.
   d fell while the nominal rate rose.
   e remained very nearly unchanged.

13 If the exchange rate has larger effects on net exports, the *ADI* curve will be
   a flatter.
   b steeper.
   c vertical.
   d horizontal.
   e none of the above.

14 Which of the following is true about monetary policy in the open economy as compared with its effectiveness in the closed economy?
   a It is less effective because higher interest rate crowd out direct foreign investment.
   b It is less effective because exchange rate changes offset the effects of changes in interest rates.
   c It is more effective because changes in foreign interest rates reinforce changes in domestic interest rates.
   d It is more effective because changes in exchange rates reinforce changes in domestic interest rates.
   e It is neither more nor less effective.

15 When monetary policy expands the economy be lowering interest rates,
   a the dollar depreciates.
   b imports decrease.
   c exports increase.
   d all of the above.
   e none of the above.

16 In the long run, in the open economy monetary policy can affect
   a real interest rates.
   b output.
   c real exchange rates.
   d all of the above.
   e none of the above.

17 When discretionary fiscal policy expands the economy, it
   a increases the real interest rate and crowds out private investment.
   b decreases the real interest rate and stimulates private investment.
   c increases the real interest rate and stimulates private investment.
   d decrease the real interest rate and crowds our private investment.
   e has no impact on private investment.

18 When monetary fiscal policy expands the economy, it
   a increases the real exchange rate and reduces net exports.
   b decreases the real exchange rate and increases net exports.
   c increases the real exchange rate and increases net exports.
   d decrease the real exchange rate and reduces net exports.
   e has no impact on net exports.

19 Suppose that the United States engages in expansionary fiscal policy. Its effects will be greatest if Europe
   a does the same.
   b engages in contractionary fiscal policy.
   c uses expansionary monetary policy.
   d uses contractionary monetary policy.
   e does nothing.

20 Which of the following is *not* true about the open economy?
   a It makes monetary policy less effective.
   b It makes fiscal policy less effective.
   c It causes shifts in the *ADI* curve.
   d It causes shifts in the *SRIA* curve.
   e All of the above are true.

Completion

1 Net exports equal exports _____ imports.
2 The relative price of currencies is called the _____.
3 When the dollar falls in value, it is said to _____.
4 An increase in the U.S. real interest rate cause the dollar to _____.
5 The real exchange rate is the _____ adjusted for changes in domestic and foreign price levels.
6 An increase in U.S. inflation leads to a _____ the *ADI* curve.
7 An increase in foreign income leads to a _____ the *ADI* curve.
8 An oil price shock shifts the _____ curve.
9 In the open economy _____ is more effective, and _____ is less effective.
10 When countries agree to simultaneously engage in expansionary fiscal policy, there is _____.

Answers to Self-test

True or False

1	f	6	t	11	t
2	t	7	t	12	t
3	f	8	t	13	f
4	t	9	f	14	t
5	f	10	f	15	t

Multiple Choice

1	b	6	b	11	c	16	e
2	c	7	c	12	a	17	a
3	d	8	e	13	a	18	b
4	c	9	a	14	d	19	a
5	a	10	d	15	d	20	a

Completion

1 minus
2 exchange rate
3 depreciate
4 appreciate
5 nominal exchange rate
6 movement along
7 shift in
8 short-run inflation adjustment (*SRIA*)
9 monetary policy; fiscal policy
10 policy coordination

Doing Economics: Tools and Practice Problems

In this chapter we fully incorporate the international sector into the basic framework of aggregate demand and inflation adjustment. There are two important new ideas. The first idea is that as we move along the *ADI* curve, not only do interest rates adjust but also exchange rates move. Thus, for example, movement up the *ADI* curve brings with it two types of changes. First, there are higher interest rates and lower investment and consumer durable spending. Second, the dollar appreciates, and this decreases net exports. The changes reinforce each other, causing aggregate demand to decline. The second idea is that changes abroad can cause shifts in the domestic *ADI* and *SRIA* curves. Tool Kit 33.1 shows how to analyze these changes.

Tool Kit 33.1 Analyzing International Shocks

Changes in foreign economies and in the exchange rate can lead to fluctuations at home. The *ADI-SRIA* framework makes the impact clear. Follow these steps.

Step one: Start with a long-run equilibrium

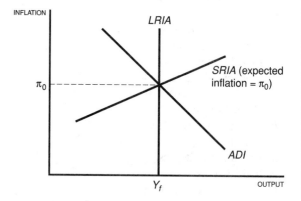

Step two: Determine the shift caused by the exogenous shock. The table gives the most important of the internationally driven disturbances.

Exogenous shock	Shift
Recession abroad	*ADI* curve to left
Boom abroad	*ADI* curve to right
Higher foreign interest rates	*ADI* curve to right
Lower foreign interest rates	*ADI* curve to left
Rise in exchange rate	*SRIA* curve to left
Fall in exchange rate	*SRIA* curve to right

Step three: Shift the curve.

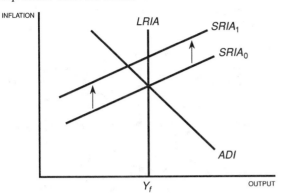

Step four: Find the short-run equilibrium.

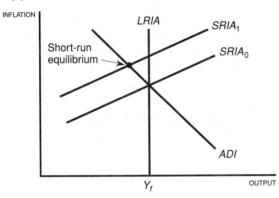

Step five: Show the inflation adjustment.

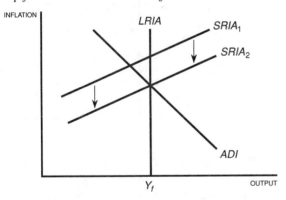

Step six: Find the long-run equilibrium

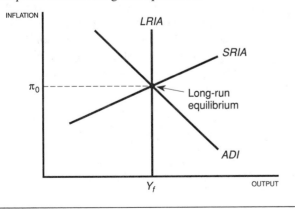

1 (Worked problem: international shocks) A worldwide loss of confidence in the U.S. dollar causes a major depreciation. Analyze the impact in the short and long run.

Step-by-step solution

Step one: Start with a long-run equilibrium. The economy is producing its potential GDP and inflation equals inflation expectations.

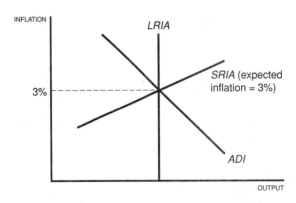

Step two: Determine the shift. The sudden depreciation makes imported inputs more expensive, creating an inflation shock. This shifts the *SRIA* curve to the left.

Step three: Shift the curve.

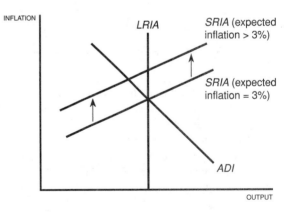

Step four: Find the short-run equilibrium. Inflation has increased, while output has fallen below potential GDP.

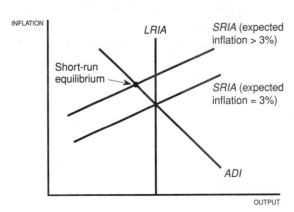

Step five: Show the inflation adjustment. With output below potential market participants expect lower inflation. This shifts the *SRIA* curve to the right.

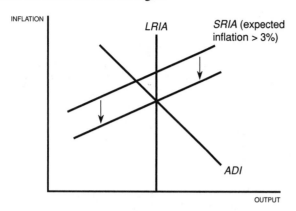

Step six: Find the long-run equilibrium. Output and inflation return to their original levels.

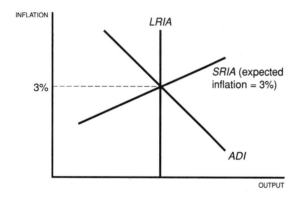

2 Analyze the impact of each of the following. Show the short-run equilibrium, the inflation adjustment, and the long-run equilibrium.

a A deep recession in Europe
b A rise in Japanese interest rates
c An appreciation of the U.S. dollar
d A boom in Latin America

Answers to Problem

2 *a* The deep recession in Europe reduces exports and thus net exports. This shifts the *ADI* curve to the left. Output and inflation fall to the short-run equilibrium at *A*. With output below potential GDP, expectations

of inflation fall and the *SRIA* curve shifts to the right until full employment is restored at point *C*.

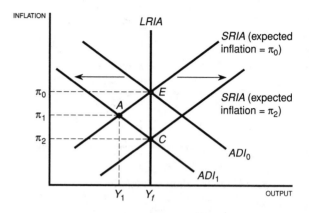

b The rise in Japanese interest rates causes the dollar to appreciate. This reduces net exports and shifts the *ADI* curve to the left. Output and inflation fall to the short-run equilibrium at *A*. With output below potential GDP, expectations of inflation fall and the *SRIA* curve shifts to the right until full employment is restored at point *C*.

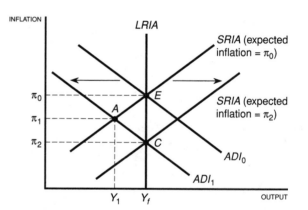

c The appreciation of the U.S. dollar lowers the prices of imported inputs, creating a positive inflation shock. This shifts the *SRIA* curve to the right. Output rises to its short-run equilibrium (point *A*) level of Y_1, and inflation falls below expectations to π_1. With output above potential GDP, expectations of inflation rise and the *SRIA* curve shifts to the left until full employment is restored at the original level of inflation.

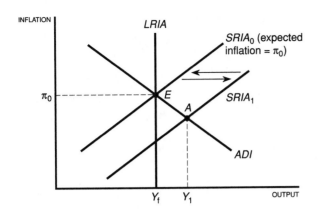

equilibrium at *A*. With output below above GDP, expectations of inflation rise and the *SRIA* curve shifts to the left until full employment is restored at point *C*.

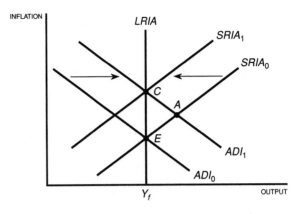

d The boom in Latin America increases exports and thus net exports. This shifts the *ADI* curve to the right. Output and inflation rise to the short-run

PART EIGHT | Topics in Macroeconomics

CHAPTER 34 | The International Financial System

Chapter Review

In this chapter, the discussion moves from the domestic arena to the international dimensions of the financial system. First, there is a discussion on what determines the exchange rate in the flexible exchange rate system. The chapter continues with a look at the fixed exchange rate policies employed by many smaller economies and government attempts to influence exchange rates.

ESSENTIAL CONCEPTS

1 International trade and investment require the exchange of currencies. One country's currency can be traded for another's on the **foreign exchange market.** Under the current **flexible exchange rate system,** the prices of currencies (**exchange rates**) are determined by supply and demand. Foreign households and firms demand U.S. dollars in order to purchase U.S. exports, to invest in U.S. assets, and to speculate. Households and firms in the United States supply dollars in order to import foreign goods, to invest in foreign assets, and also to speculate. Equilibrium in the foreign exchange market is shown in Figure 34.1

2 If there were no international borrowing or lending, then the demand for U.S. dollars would equal the value of U.S. exports, and the supply of dollars would equal the value of U.S. imports. When the foreign exchange market reached equilibrium, trade would be in balance. But because international capital is mobile (although not perfectly), trade deficits and surpluses are possible. A country can import more than it exports (run a trade deficit) and make up the difference by borrowing from abroad.

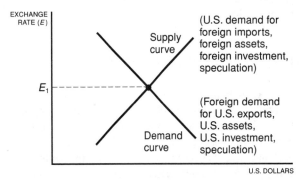

Figure 34.1

3 The supply of and demand for a country's currency will shift when there are changes in the world demand for its exports, its citizens' demand for imported goods, the attractiveness of investing in its assets relative to foreign investments, or expectations about changes in the exchange rate. Shifts in supply or demand will cause changes in the equilibrium exchange rate.

4 Speculators buy and sell foreign currency in order to gain from movements in exchange rates. Of course, in equilibrium there will be no further opportunities to profit from arbitrage. This fact implies the interest parity condition:

rate of return on foreign assets
= rate of return on dollar assets − expected rate of depreciation in the dollar.

5 Inflation expectations also shift demands and supplies for currencies. The nominal exchange rate moves when one country's inflation rate is expected to exceed that in another country. The real exchange rate refers to the nominal rate adjusted for inflation.

6 Many countries fix their exchange rate. If the equilibrium level diverges from the pegged level, there will be shortage or surplus unless the country intervenes with monetary policy or with buying and selling currencies. The **interest rate parity condition** implies that with fixed exchange rates, the interest rate at home must equal the foreign interest rate. This mandates that the central bank target interest rates in order to maintain the currency at its fixed level.

7 When the U.S. dollar appreciates, U.S. exports become more expensive to foreigners, while imported goods grow cheaper in the United States. Trade thus depends upon exchange rates. The volatility of exchange rates adds to the risks of importing, exporting, and also international borrowing and lending. Thus governments try to influence and stabilize the level of exchange rates. Stabilizing exchange rates is difficult for two reasons: no one can be sure of the equilibrium exchange rate, and international cooperation in this area is problematic.

BEHIND THE ESSENTIAL CONCEPTS

1 International currency markets closely resemble other markets governed by supply and demand, but they use a lingo all their own. The price of one currency in terms of another is not called the price, it's called the exchange rate. When this price rises, it **appreciates.** When it falls, it **depreciates.** A currency priced above equilibrium is **overvalued.** Under the abandoned fixed exchange rate system, when the government reduced the fixed price, it **devalued** its currency.

2 Do not confuse the supply of U.S. dollars in the international currency market with the supply of money you learned about in Chapter 25. The supply of *dollars* in currency markets shows for every exchange rate how much U.S. households and firms desire to spend in order to buy imported goods or invest abroad. The supply of *money,* on the other hand, is determined by the Federal Reserve. Although changes in the supply of money may bring about changes in the economy that affect the supply of dollars in international currency markets, the two supply curves are different animals. It's important to keep them straight.

3 The effects of changes in the demand for imports and exports in international currency markets are straight-forward. If foreign nationals want to purchase more U.S. export goods, then they need U.S. dollars, and the demand for dollars shifts to the right. If American citizens desire more imported goods, dollars must be traded for foreign currencies, and the supply of dollars shifts to the right. Notice that in each case, only one curve shifts.

4 When you analyze changes that affect international borrowing and lending, both curves will shift. The reason is that the capital flows toward the country that offers the highest *relative* return. If U.S. interest rates increase, for example, foreign investors will want to buy American assets (lend in the United States) and will therefore demand more dollars. At the same time, U.S. investors will keep their dollars at home to take advantage of the high interest rates. They will supply fewer dollars. Thus, the demand shifts to the right, and the supply shifts to the left. Later in the chapter, you will get lots of practice working with demand and supply in international currency markets.

5 Why are exchange rates so volatile? Exchange rates go up and down because borrowing and lending involve expectations about the future, and our expectations change as we get new information. To see this, imagine that you are a German investor thinking about buying a U.S. bond. You will earn the U.S. rate of interest, but to determine the rate of return in terms of your own currency, you must anticipate how the exchange rate will change. The following formula summarizes the issue:

rate of return in foreign currency
= dollar interest rate − expected rate of depreciation in the dollar.

Thus, the rate of return and therefore your demand for dollars depend upon the future happenings in the currency market. Whenever expectations are involved, things are volatile.

SELF-TEST

True or False

1 If the U.S. dollar depreciates relative to the French franc, then a dollar will buy more francs.

2 If the U.S. dollar appreciates relative to the Japanese yen, then the yen must depreciate relative to the U.S. dollar.

3 An appreciation of the U.S. dollar makes U.S. exports more expensive for foreign households to purchase.

4 If there were no international borrowing or lending, then the money value of exports would equal the money value of imports.

5 If interest rates are lower in one country, the investors must expect that country's currency to depreciate.

6 International capital markets are highly but not perfectly mobile.

7 An increase in European interest rates makes investing in Europe more attractive, shifting the supply of dollars to the right.

8 The supply of dollars in world currency markets is determined by the Federal Reserve.

9 The real exchange rate is the exchange rate adjusted for inflation.

10 The rate of return that a Brazilian investor earns on her U.S. T-bill is the dollar interest rate minus the rate of change in the exchange rate.

11 The European Monetary Union fixed exchange rates among the currencies of its eleven members.

12 Under the fixed exchange rate system, speculation always destabilized currency markets.

13 Under a currency board, the exchange rate between two currencies is fixed by law.

14 Dollarization, or abandoning the domestic currency and using the U.S. dollar, removes monetary policy from the control of the country.

15 Stabilizing the exchange rate is difficult because it is hard to know what the equilibrium exchange rate is.

Multiple Choice

1 If the U.S. dollar becomes more valuable relative to the Italian lira, then
   a the dollar appreciates.
   b the lira appreciates.
   c the dollar depreciates.
   d *b* and *c*.
   e none of the above.

2 The price of one currency in terms of another is called
   a the discount rate.
   b the inflation rate.
   c the exchange rate.
   d purchasing power parity.
   e the required reserve ratio.

3 Foreigners demand U.S. dollars in order to
   a buy U.S. goods.
   b invest in U.S. assets.
   c speculate, hoping that the dollar will appreciate.
   d all of the above.
   e none of the above.

4 If the U.S. dollar appreciates, U.S. goods become
   a more expensive in foreign currency.
   b less expensive in foreign currency.
   c more expensive in U.S. dollars.
   d less expensive in U.S. dollars.
   e *a* and *d.*

5 If there is no foreign borrowing or lending, then a surplus of U.S. dollars means
   a U.S. imports exceed U.S. exports.
   b U.S. exports exceed U.S. imports.
   c the U.S. trade account is in balance.
   d the U.S. dollar will appreciate.
   e foreign firms are competing unfairly in U.S. markets.

6 If U.S. consumers increase their demand for foreign goods, then
   a the U.S. dollar will depreciate.
   b foreign currencies will appreciate.
   c the U.S. dollar will appreciate.
   d the demand for dollars will shift to the left.
   e *a* and *b*.

7 An increase in foreign investment in the United States will shift the
   a demand for dollars to the left.
   b supply of dollars to the left.
   c demand for dollars to the right.
   d supply of dollars to the right.
   e *a* and *d*.

8 A German investor holding U.S. dollars for speculative purposes hopes that
   a the German mark appreciates.
   b the U.S. dollar appreciates.
   c the U.S. dollar depreciates.
   d the U.S. trade account is in balance.
   e purchasing power parity is restored.

9 An Italian investor who is holding a U.S. corporate bond earns, in italian lira, the rate of
   a interest on the corporate bond.
   b interest on an equivalent Italian corporate bond.
   c change in the exchange rate.
   d interest on the corporate bond plus the rate of change in the exchange rate.
   e interest on the corporate bond minus the rate of change in the exchange rate.

10 If capital is perfectly mobile between Germany and the United States and if the inflation rate is 10 percent in the United States and 5 percent in Germany, the nominal interest rate in Germany will
   a equal the interest rate in the United States.
   b exceed the interest rate in the United States by 5 percent.
   c be less than the interest rate in the United States by 5 percent.
   d equal 15 percent.
   e be twice as high as the interest rate in the United States.

11 If the U.S. interest rate increases, then
   a foreign capital will flow into the United States.
   b U.S. capital will flow abroad.
   c the demand for U.S. dollars will decrease.
   d the U.S. dollar will depreciate.
   e the supply of dollars will shift to the right.

12 Suppose that the equilibrium exchange rate has fallen below the pegged rate. If investors believe that the government is unable or unwilling to support the fixed exchange rate,
   a speculation will tend to restore confidence in the currency and bring the equilibrium rate back to equality with the pegged rate.
   b speculation will make the problem worse as

speculators try to unload currency before the currency is devalued.

   c the country will abandon the fixed exchange rate system.

   d the country will accept dollarization.

   e the interest rate parity condition assures that the equilibrium exchange rate will rise back to the level of the peg.

13 Higher U.S. interest rates

   a cause the U.S. dollar to appreciate.

   b discourage U.S. exports through the change in the exchange rate.

   c encourage U.S. imports through the change in the exchange rate.

   d reduce U.S. investment.

   e all of the above.

14 If speculators expect that the U.S. dollar will depreciate 5 percent over the next year, then

   a they will want to buy dollars now to realize a capital gain.

   b they will want to sell dollars now.

   c the dollar will depreciate now.

   d the dollar will first appreciate and then depreciate after the speculators have sold their dollars.

   e *b* and *c*.

15 Under the fixed exchange rate system.

   a the equilibrium exchange rate (which would prevail under the flexible exchange rate system) is irrelevant.

   b the equilibrium exchange rate (which would prevail under the flexible exchange rate system) is always lower than the fixed rate.

   c the equilibrium exchange rate (which would prevail under the flexible exchange rate system) is always higher than the fixed rate.

   d the equilibrium exchange rate (which would prevail under the flexible exchange rate system) always equals the fixed rate.

   e none of the above.

16 The system in which governments intervene in order to reduce the day-to-day variability of exchange rates is called the

   a flexible exchange rate system.

   b fixed exchange rate system.

   c gold standard.

   d dirty float system.

   e purchasing power parity system.

17 Under fixed exchange rate systems,

   a monetary policy is more effective because exchange rate movements do not offset the impact of interest rate changes.

   b monetary policy is less effective because exchange rate movements do not offset the impact of interest rate changes.

   c countries lose control of monetary policy.

   d countries lose control of fiscal policy.

   e *c* and *d*.

18 Volatile exchange rates make international trade

   a more profitable.

   b riskier.

   c safer than domestic trade.

   d impossible.

   e none of the above.

19 Volatile exchange rates add to the risks of

   a doing business in the world market.

   b doing business in the home market.

   c borrowing and lending on world markets.

   d all of the above.

   e *a* and *c*.

20 Under a currency board, the

   a country abandons its currency and uses a foreign currency.

   b country appoints a board to manage the dirty float of its currency.

   c country appoints a board to monitor the movements of its currency on world markets.

   d country appoints a board to run its monetary policy and target the exchange rate.

   e exchange rate between a country's currency and that of another country is fixed by law.

<u>Completion</u>

1 If the U.S. dollar becomes less valuable relative to the German mark, then we say that the dollar has _____ and the mark has _____.

2 The _____ allows exchange rates to be determined by the law of supply and demand.

3 If foreigners increase their demand for U.S. goods, the demand for dollars will shift to the _____.

4 Holding currency in anticipation of capital gains when it appreciates is called _____.

5 The rate of return that a French investor earns on a U.S. bond is the bond's interest rate minus the _____.

6 High inflation in the United States causes the dollar to _____.

7 The system under which exchange rates are pegged to particular levels is called the _____.

8 If governments take actions that cause the exchange rate to be higher than it would be in a free market, the currency is _____.

9 Under a _____, the exchange rate between the local currency and a foreign currency is fixed by law.

10 A country abandons its currency and simply uses the U.S. currency under _____.

Answers to Self-Test

True or False

1	f	6	t	11	t
2	t	7	t	12	f
3	t	8	f	13	t
4	t	9	t	14	t
5	f	10	f	15	t

Multiple Choice

1	a	6	e	11	a	16	d
2	c	7	c	12	b	17	c
3	d	8	b	13	e	18	b
4	a	9	e	14	e	19	d
5	a	10	c	15	e	20	e

Completion

1 depreciated, appreciated
2 flexible exchange rate system
3 right
4 speculating
5 change in the exchange rate
6 depreciate
7 fixed exchange rate system
8 overvalued
9 currency board
10 dollarization

Doing Economics: Tools and Practice Problems

Supply and demand in international currency markets is the topic of this section. This is an application of basic supply and demand, so we follow the usual four-step procedure. All of the applications in this section deal with the market for U.S. dollars and the determination of the dollar exchange rate.

We will study three reasons for shifts in the supply and demand curves for foreign currencies. First, the demand for traded goods may change, shifting either the demand or supply curve for dollars. Second, interest rates may change, and because investors seek the highest relative return, both the supply and demand curves shift. Finally, when inflation changes, investors expect that the exchange rate will change to offset the inflation, and again both curves shift. One thing to keep in mind when both curves shift is that the shifts reinforce each other. In other words, if the shift in the demand curve would cause the dollar to depreciate, then the supply curve will shift to cause further depreciation. Table 34.1 summarizes the possible causes of shifts.

Tool Kit 34.1 Supply and Demand for Currencies

Step one: Start with an equilibrium.

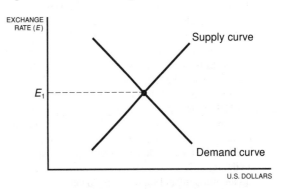

Step two: Observe the exogenous change, and determine which curve or curves shift.

Step three: Shift the supply curve, demand curve, or both.

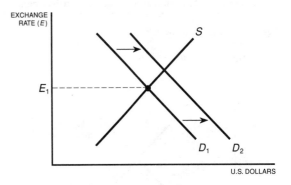

Step four: Find the new equilibrium exchange rate, and compare it with the original one.

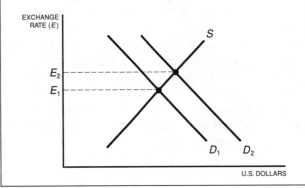

1 (Worked problem: supply and demand for currencies) What is the effect of an increase in German interest rates on the U.S. dollar exchange rate?

Table 34.1

Shifts in demand and supply curves for foreign currencies

1 Traded goods and services: When the foreign demand for U.S. exports increases, demand for U.S. dollars shifts to the right; when it decreases, demand for U.S. dollars shifts to the left. When U.S. demand for imported goods increases, supply of U.S. dollars shifts to the right; when it decreases, supply of U.S. dollars shifts to the left.

2 Borrowing and lending: When U.S. interest rates increase, demand for U.S. dollars shifts to the right and supply shifts to the left. When they decrease, demand for U.S. dollars shifts to the left and supply shifts to the right. When foreign interest rates increase, demand for U.S. dollars shifts to the left and supply shifts to the right. When they decrease, demand for U.S. dollars shifts to the right and supply shifts to the left.

3 Expected change in exchange rates: When the U.S. inflation rate increases, demand for U.S. dollars shifts to the left and supply shifts to the right. When it decreases, demand for U.S. dollars shifts to the right and supply shifts to the left. When the foreign inflation rate increases, demand for U.S. dollars shifts to the right and supply shifts to the left. When it decreases, demand for U.S. dollars shifts to the left and supply shifts to the right.

Step-by-step solution

Step one: Start with an equilibrium.

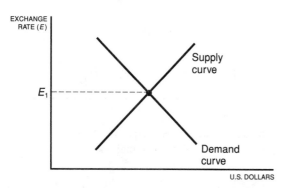

Step two: Observe the exogenous change, and determine which curve shifts. The increase in German interest rates shifts the demand for dollars to the left (because German investors keep their marks in Germany to earn high German interest rates), and the supply of dollars shifts to the right (because U.S. investors seek to trade dollars for marks and invest in Germany).

Step three: Shift the curves.

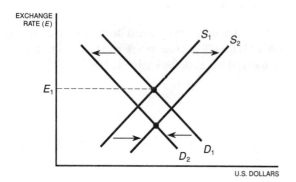

Step four: Find the new equilibrium, and compare. The U.S. dollar depreciates.

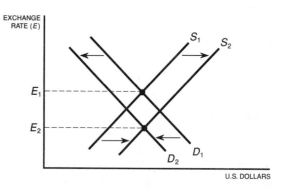

2 (Practice problem: supply and demand for currencies) U.S. energy conservation reduces the demand for imported oil. How does the exchange rate change?

3 (Practice problem: supply and demand for currencies) For each of the following, use supply and demand analysis to show the effect on the exchange rate for U.S. dollars:

a Foreign demand for U.S. movies skyrockets.
b U.S. demand for African music takes off.
c Japanese interest rates rise.
d European interest rates fall.
e U.S. interest rates increase.
f U.S. interest rates decrease.
g Inflation takes off in East Asia.
h South American inflation rates fall.
i U.S. inflation increases.
j U.S. inflation decreases.

Answers to Problems

2 The supply curve of dollars shifts to the left, and the U.S. dollar appreciates.

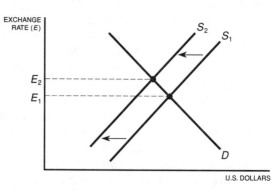

3 *a* The demand curve for dollars shifts to the right, and
the U.S. dollar appreciates.

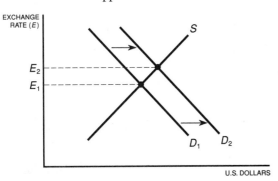

b The supply curve of dollars shifts to the right, and
the U.S. dollar depreciates.

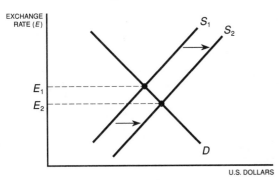

c The demand curve shifts to the left, the supply curve
shifts to the right, and the dollar depreciates.

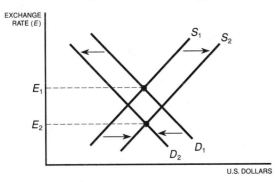

d The demand curve shifts to the right, the supply
curve shifts to the left, and the dollar appreciates.

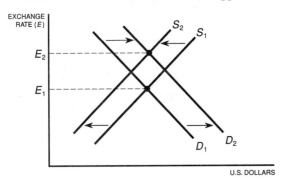

e The demand curve shifts to the right, the supply
curve shifts to the left, and the dollar appreciates.

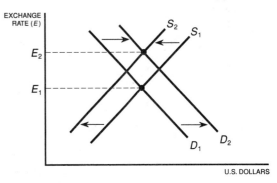

f The demand curve shifts to the left, the supply curve
shifts to the right, and the dollar depreciates.

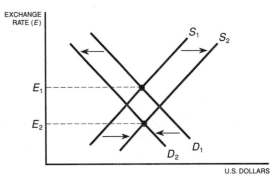

g The demand curve shifts to the right, the supply
curve shifts to the left, and the dollar appreciates.

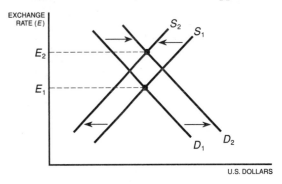

h The demand curve shifts to the left, the supply curve
shifts to the right, and the dollar depreciates.

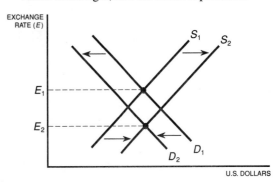

i The demand curve shifts to the left, the supply curve shifts to the right, and the dollar depreciates.

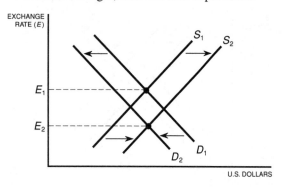

j The demand curve shifts to the right, the supply curve shifts to the left, and the dollar appreciates.

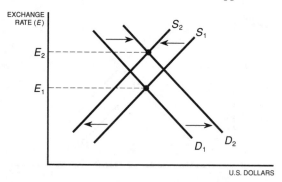

CHAPTER 35 | Controversies in Macroeconomic Policy

This chapter forms the capstone for Parts Seven and Eight, where the basic approach to macroeconomic fluctuations was studied. Here attention is paid to the deep questions of macroeconomics: the nature and causes of economic fluctuations and the role for policy. The key issues in economic policy are whether and to what extent the government should intervene to stabilize the economy, reduce unemployment, and control inflation.

ESSENTIAL CONCEPTS

1   The goals of economic policy are low unemployment, low inflation, and rapid growth. The debate about economic policy revolves around how aggressive the government should be and which goals deserve more emphasis. Economists disagree to some extent about the effectiveness of policy intervention. Also, because the costs of unemployment and unanticipated inflation are borne by different groups, economists advocate different policies even when they share the same view of the economy's workings.

2   Some economists take the noninterventionist perspective, denying that the government can successfully act to stabilize the economy.

   a   **Real business-cycle theory** attributes variations in economic activity to random, unpredictable shocks originating outside the economy (exogenous). This view stresses the importance of **shocks to productivity** but insists that markets clear throughout the ups and downs. The economy thus responds rapidly and efficiently to these exogenous shocks, and economic fluctuations are not an important matter for government policy.

   b   New classical economists do not claim that the economy is always efficient, but they emphasize the likely ineffectiveness of policy interventions. Rational households and firms anticipate the impacts of systematic macroeconomic policies and nullify their effects.

   c   Other noninterventionists go further and argue that intervention makes matters worse. Lags in implementation and the difficulty in forecasting make timely policy unlikely. Also, political pressures tempt policymakers to manipulate economic performance to win elections.

   d   Noninterventionists advocate fixed policy **rules**, such as a constant rate of increase in the money supply. This would reduce uncertainty. Also, they emphasize the problem of **dynamic inconsistency**, the government's inability to commit to a promised course of action.

3   Interventionists, on the other hand, believe that the economy's fluctuations are not efficient, that wages and prices adjust slowly, and that recessions may last for a considerable time with large opportunity costs in terms of forgone output.

   a   The **new Keynesian view** says that a variety of exogenous shocks, both supply and demand sided, may move the economy from its long-term trend, but various mechanisms in the economic system *amplify* these shocks and cause the variations in output to *persist*. Government can play an important role in offsetting these ups and downs.

   b   Interventionist believe that discretionary macroeconomic policy can be effective and also that automatic stabilizers can reduce the economy's volatility.

4   Almost all economists and policymakers agree that the long-run Phillips curve is vertical, that there is no long-

run trade-off between unemployment and inflation. There is disagreement on the magnitude of the short-run trade-off, the costs of disinflation, and the NAIRU. The relevant policy trade-off is whether to pursue more output stability or more inflation stability.

5 Although there has been little use of discretionary fiscal policy in recent decades, one should be clear on how its effects differ from those of monetary policy.

   a Monetary and fiscal policy differ in how they affect the composition of output. Monetary policy's lower interest rates bring about more investment. The impact of fiscal policy depends upon the mix of additional expenditures and tax cuts and also upon how government expenditures are divided between consumption and investment.

   b Monetary policy's impact is delayed by the time it takes lower interest rates to stimulate investment. Government spending in principle can work immediately. It does take time for government to pass laws and administer the spending.

6 The Fed can engage in **countercyclical policies** and focus on keeping average inflation rates low, but there are difficulties. Using **inflation targeting** exclusively risks exacerbating output variations. Using price level targeting requires deflation when prices rise, but the amount of deflation is limited because the nominal interest rate cannot fall below zero. The credibility of its commitment to low inflation helps keeps inflationary expectations low.

BEHIND THE ESSENTIAL CONCEPTS

1 When the economy is hit with a shock, such as an increase in oil prices, households and firms take actions. Some of these actions offset the impact of the shock and dampen its effects. For example, while you would reduce your demand for gasoline, you and others might buy high-mileage cars. Similarly, firms invest in energy-saving equipment, leading to increased production and employment in that sector. All of these responses to changes in relative prices keep aggregate demand, output, and employment high. On the other hand, there are mechanisms in the economy that amplify the shock. High energy use industries contract, firms go out of business, and their workers are laid off. Income and consumption fall and the multiplier process worsens the decline. Sometimes the dampening activities dominate; for example, when the stock market crashed in 1987, the economy continued its expansion. Other times the shock is amplified and the economy is thrown into recession.

2 The Fed's reputation as an inflation fighter is one of its most important assets. If people doubt the Fed's commitment, then the short-run inflation adjustment curve shifts to the left—a shift that brings both higher unemployment and more inflation. To combat the unemployment, the Fed must stimulate the economy, but that increases inflation. To combat the inflation, the Fed must raise interest rates, but that increases unemployment. Avoiding this dilemma requires that the Fed remain credible.

3 Supply shocks face the Fed with the same dilemma: to fight the inflation and increase unemployment or to fight the unemployment and increase inflation. Demand shocks, on the other hand, pose no such difficulty. When the *ADI* curve shifts left, this reduces inflation and increases unemployment. Countercyclical interest rate cuts offset both problems.

4 Most of the chapter's discussion focuses on stabilization policies, but there are also microeconomic policies that can improve the macroeconomic performance of the economy. For example, policies that increase worker mobility and skills can lower the NAIRU with no impact on inflation.

SELF-TEST

True or False

1 The costs of unemployment inflation are spread evenly throughout the economy.

2 If the government attempts to keep the inflation rate below the NAIRU, unemployment will accelerate.

3 Real business-cycle theorists attribute the economy's fluctuations to exogenous changes in factors such as oil price and productivity.

4 According to real business-cycle theory, fluctuations in output are efficient.

5 New classical economists stress that systematic government policies are dangerous because they have large and lasting effects.

6 One problem with fiscal policy is the time it takes for government to take action.

7 The impact of monetary policy is delayed while firms take time to respond to lower interest rates with new investments.

8 Interventionists favor fixed policy rules such as balanced budgets and steady money growth.

9 The dynamic consistency problem refers to the difficulty of maintaining full employment when wages and prices change.

10 New Keynesians differ from old Keynesian economists in their emphasis on microeconomics.

11 An exclusive focus on inflation may increase the variability of output.

12 With deflation, the nominal interest rate may be driven below zero.

13 When the aggregate demand-inflation curve shifts, policymakers face a fundamental trade-off: whether to fight inflation or unemployment.

14 An example of hysteresis occurs if an increase in the actual unemployment rate causes the natural unemployment rate to rise.

15 Under the direct control of Congress, the Fed has little independence.

Multiple Choice

1 The costs of unanticipated inflation are borne more by
  a low-wage workers.
  b holders of long-term bonds.
  c holders of short-term bonds.
  d issuers of long-term bonds.
  e b and d.

2 Real business-cycle theory holds that economic fluctuations are
  a due to endogenous forces and predictable.
  b due to random, exogenous shocks and unpredictable.
  c chiefly due to misguided monetary and fiscal policy.
  d due to exogenous shocks but are amplified and made persistent by the economic system.
  e none of the above.

3 The idea variations in output are due to exogenous shocks to which the market reacts quickly to restore full employment is a tenet of
  a real business-cycle theory.
  b new classical macroeconomics.
  c monetarism.
  d New Keynesianism.
  e supply-side economics.

4 The idea that actions of rational individuals offset the impact of government actions is associated with
  a real business-cycle theory.
  b new classical macroeconomics.
  c monetarism.
  d New Keynesianism.
  e supply-side economics.

5 Doubts about the government's ability to carry out discretionary fiscal and monetary policy are stressed by believers in
  a real business-cycle theory.
  b new classical macroeconomics.
  c Monetarism.
  d New Keynesianism.
  e supply-side economics.

6 The belief that government can be effective with discretionary fiscal and monetary policy is part of
  a real business-cycle theory.
  b new classical macroeconomics.
  c monetarism.
  d New Keynesianism.
  e supply-side economics.

7 According to new classical macroeconomists,
  a inflation is not a problem because markets are always efficient.
  b inflation occurs because automatic wage increases are built into union contracts.
  c inflation is due to deficit spending by government.
  d lower inflation requires increased unemployment in order to convince market participants that the inflation target has been lowered.
  e inflation may be reduced without additional unemployment if market participants are convinced that the inflation target has been lowered.

8 Noninterventionist economists view government as a source of instability and advocate
  a binding fiscal and monetary policy with fixed policy rules.
  b using fiscal and monetary policies with discretion.
  c returning oversight of the money supply to the private sector.
  d dynamic inconsistency.
  e repealing the accelerator.

9 Which of the following is *not* an example of a policy rule advocated by noninterventionists?
  a The money supply should increase at a fixed rate each year.
  b The moneysupply should be adjusted to stimulate aggregate demand in recessions and constrain aggregate demand in inflationary times.
  c The budget deficit should be zero.
  d Government expenditures should be a fixed percentage of GDP.
  e The money supply should increase with the rate of output.

10 Dynamic consistency refers to the
  a fact that most business cycles follow the same pattern.
  b recommendation that government policy follow certain fixed rules.
  c issue of whether the government will carry out its promises.
  d political business-cycle explanation for economic fluctuations.
  e need to harmonize fiscal and monetary policy.

11 New Keynesians advocate
  a policies to lower the NAIRU, such as reducing business regulation.
  b discretionary monetary policy.
  c discretionary fiscal point.
  d automatic stabilizers.
  e all of the above.

12 Most economists agree that in the long run, the Phillips curve is
   a vertical.
   b horizontal
   c upward sloping.
   d downward sloping.
   e inelastic.

13 Economists, such as John Taylor, emphasize the new trade-off of
   a unemployment versus inflation.
   b monetary policy versus fiscal policy.
   c output stability versus inflation stability.
   d the long run versus the short run.
   e the NAIRU versus the Phillips curve.

14 Mechanisms that increase the government deficit during recessions and decrease it during economic booms are called
   a balanced budget multipliers.
   b full-employment deficits.
   c automatic stabilizers.
   d political business cycles.
   e none of the above.

15 Which of the following relates to the issue of lags in monetary and fiscal policy?
   a Monetary policy's effectiveness is delayed while businesses wait to undertake new investments.
   b Governments take time to make decisions about tax and expenditure changes.
   c Exchange rates adjust slowly.
   d All of the above.
   e a and b.

16 Which of the following illustrates a concern with the effect of a policy instrument on the composition of output?
   a Even though the Federal Reserve undertakes policies that increase bank reserves, it may not be able to motivate banks to make new loans.
   b Looser monetary policy might cause the dollar to depreciate and increase net exports.
   c Monetary policy often concentrates its effect on particular sectors, such as export-competing industries or consumer durables.
   d There are lags in the government's ability to recognize and implement fiscal programs.
   e Individuals may treat tax cuts as temporary and increase consumption.

17 Which of the following relates to the issue of the flexibility of a policy instrument?
   a Even though the Federal Reserve undertakes policies that increase bank reserves, it may not be able to motivate banks to make new loans.
   b Looser monetary policy, even though it was designed to increase investment, might instead cause the dollar to depreciate and increase net exports.

   c Monetary policy often concentrates its effects on particular sectors, such as export-competing industries or consumer durables.
   d There are lags in the government's ability to recognize and implement fiscal programs.
   e Individuals may treat tax cuts as temporary and increase consumption.

18 Monetary authorities are faced with an unemployment-inflation trade-off
   a when the *ADI* curve shifts to the left.
   b when the *ADI* curve shifts to the right.
   c when the *SRIA* curve shifts to the left.
   d when the *SRIA* curve shifts to the right.
   e at all times.

19 If the real rate of interest is 3 percent and there is deflation at the rate of −4 percent, then the nominal interest rate is
   a −3 percent.
   b −7 percent.
   c −1 percent.
   d −12 percent.
   e The nominal interest rate cannot fall below zero.

20 If when unemployment increases, workers lose skills and the natural rate of unemployment also increases, there is/are said to be
   a dynamic inconsistency.
   b dynamic consistency.
   c hysteresis.
   d recession.
   e rational expectations.

Completion

1 Holders of long-term bonds bear the costs of _____ inflation

2 The _____ view of the economy places the blame for economic fluctuations on supply shocks but believes that the economy adjusts quickly and efficiently.

3 _____ economists emphasize the likely ineffectiveness of systematic government policies.

4 New Keynesians stress that although externally generated shocks may hit the economy, the system can _____ them and cause the effects to _____.

5 The issue of whether government will actually carry out its promised economic policy is called _____.

6 New classical economists distrust discretionary policies by government and would restrict any intervention to _____.

7 Private investment will be lower if the government uses discretionary _____ policy to increase aggregate demand.

8 When the government uses _____, a temporary inflation shock requires deflation to hit the target.

9 If the natural rate of unemployment depends on the actual rate, there is said to be _____.

Answers to Self-Test

True or False

1	f	6	t	11	t
2	f	7	t	12	f
3	t	8	f	13	f
4	t	9	f	14	t
5	f	10	t	15	f

Multiple Choice

1	b	6	d	11	e	16	b
2	b	7	e	12	a	17	d
3	a	8	a	13	c	18	c
4	b	9	b	14	c	19	e
5	b	10	c	15	e	20	c

Completion

1 unanticipated
2 real business-cycle
3 New classical
4 amplify; persist
5 dynamic consistency
6 fixed rules
7 fiscal
8 price level targeting
9 hysteresis

Doing Economics: Tools and Practice Problems

The economy is continually buffeted by shocks. Consumer tastes change, new technologies are discovered, bad weather appears, or import prices surge. There are mechanisms within the economy that dampen the impact of shocks. These include flexible prices, rational expectations, labor mobility, and government policies, such as automatic stabilizers. On the other hand, there are factors such as the multiplier and accelerator that amplify shocks. Tool Kit 35.1 illustrates how these mechanisms can exacerbate instability.

Tool Kit 35.1 The Multiplier-Accelerator Process

The accelerator is the capital-output ratio. Firms in many industries try to keep this constant. The multiplier determines how much aggregate demand shifts when there is a change in spending, such as an increase in investment. These mechanisms can combine to amplify shocks. Follow these steps.

Step one: Identify the accelerator, the multiplier, and the change in spending.

Step two: Multiply the change in spending by the accelerator. This gives the extra investment needed to keep the capital-output ratio constant.

Required investment = change in spending × accelerator.

Step three: Multiply the product in step two by the multiplier. This gives the change in output resulting from the extra investment.

Change in output = new investment × multiplier.

Step four: Multiply the product in step three by the accelerator. This gives the second round of additional investment needed to keep the capital-output ratio constant.

Required investment = change in output × accelerator.

---

1 (Worked problem: multiplier-accelerator) Output is $5 trillion and the capital stock equals $15 trillion. The multiplier is 2. Suppose that a new investment project of $10 billion is undertaken.
 a Trace through the impact of this using the multiplier-accelerator
 b Do you think the process can continue unabated? Why or why not?

Step-by-step solution

Step one: Identify the accelerator, the multiplier, and the change in spending. The accelerator is 15/5 = 3 and the multiplier is 2. The initial change in spending is $10 billion.

Step two: Multiply the change in spending by the accelerator. This gives the extra investment needed to keep the capital-output ratio constant.

Required investment = change in spending × accelerator
= $10 billion × 3 = $30 billion.

Step three: Multiply the product in step two by the multiplier. This gives the change in output resulting from the extra investment.

Change in output = new investment × multiplier
= $30 billion × 2 = $60 billion.

Step four: Multiply the product in step three by the accelerator. This gives the second round of additional investment needed to keep the capital-output ratio constant.

Required investment = change in output × accelerator
= $60 billion × 3 = $180 billion.

Of course, the process cannot continue too long, because the economy has capacity constraints.

2 (Practice problem: multiplier-accelerator) Output is $2 trillion and the capital stock equals $4 trillion. The multiplier is 2.5. Suppose that a new investment project of $30 billion is undertaken.

a Trace through the impact of this using the multiplier-accelerator.

b Do you think the process can continue unabated? Why or why not?

3 (Practice problem: multiplier-accelerator) Output is $7 trillion and the capital stock equals $14 trillion. The multiplier is 1.5. Suppose that a new investment project of $15 billion is undertaken.

a Trace through the impact of this using the multiplier-accelerator.

b Do you think the process can continue unabated? Why or why not?

Answers to Problems

2 *a* Required investment = $30 billion × 4/2 = $60 billion; change in output = $60 billion × 2.5 = $150 billion; additional investment = $150 billion × 2 = $300 billion.

b No. The economy will eventually run into capacity constraints.

3 *a* Required investment = $15 billion × 14/7 = $30 billion; change in output = $30 billion × 1.5 = $45 billion; additional investment = $45 billion × 2 = $90 billion.

b No. The economy will eventually run into capacity constraints.

CHAPTER 36

Government Fiscal Policy, Deficits, and Surpluses

Chapter Review

The U.S. fiscal deficit, the difference between government spending and taxes, exploded in the 1980s, greatly adding to the public debt. During the last decade, the deficit was reduced, and the U.S. government is currently running a surplus. How does the federal government raise and spend its money? What caused these drastic shifts in the fiscal situation and how did they affect the economy? And what budgetary problems lie on the horizon? This chapter addresses these and other issues related to the fiscal policy of the United States.

ESSENTIAL CONCEPTS

1 Spending by the U.S. federal government includes **discretionary** items, such as defense, education, and government operations, which are decided on an annual basis, and **nondiscretionary** items, which comprise **entitlements** and interest. Changes in certain revenue and spending programs help explain the movement to high deficits and then to surplus.

   a Tax cuts in 1981 reduced the federal tax share of GDP back to its historic level of 17 or 18 percent. Taxes were increased during the 1990s.

   b In 1991 and again in 1997 caps on discretionary spending reduced growth in this category.

   c Spending on the elderly through Social Security and Medicare has risen steadily both absolutely and relative to the elderly population.

   d Health care expenses have increased dramatically.

   e Strong economic growth in the late 1990s increased tax collections.

2 The deficits of the 1980s reduced national savings and shifted the savings curve to the left in the capital market. This raised real interest rates and reduced investment. In the 1990s, the fiscal surplus had the opposite effect. In an open economy, deficits lead to inflows of capital from abroad.

3 Government borrowing can affect future generations in three ways. First, the burden can be shifted directly to the future generation by increasing taxes after the current generation has retired. Second, borrowing drives up interest rates and crowds out private investment. Finally, since much of the borrowing comes from abroad and foreign investors are attracted by higher U.S. interest rates, current borrowing increases foreign indebtedness. Repayment of foreign debt then requires reduced future living standards. The Ricardian equivalence argument that private savings will offset the future effects of current deficits has not proven true.

4 The long-term budgetary problem in the United States is entitlement spending for Social Security and Medicare, because of anticipated increases in both the size of the elderly population and health care costs. Proposed reforms in Social Security include reducing benefits by increasing the retirement age, means testing for benefits, and investing **Social Security Trust Fund** assets in equities. On the Medicare issue one set of reforms, including Medical Savings Accounts, focuses on patient incentives. **Managed care** moves in another direction, seeking to give doctors incentives to reduce the use and expense of medical care. Ultimately, the problem rests on the question of how much of society's resources should be allocated to health care for the elderly, especially for expensive technological innovations. Another option would partially privatize the system, allowing some of one's tax payment to be invested in an individual account.

BEHIND THE ESSENTIAL CONCEPTS

1 If you are the age of the typical college student, say 19 or 20, you will pay for some of the federal budget deficit of the past decades. Government borrowing is sopping up private savings and crowding out private investment. Currently capital goods are not purchased, research and development is not undertaken, and businesses are not started. Furthermore, the trade deficit caused by the budget deficits is financed by selling off U.S. assets. Reduced investment and the sale of assets will result in lower living standards in the future.

2 The distinction between stocks and flows is important in this chapter. The annual federal buget deficit is a flow, and the corresponding stock is the federal debt, which is the sum of past accumulated deficits. The trade deficit is also a flow variable. It is the difference between what U.S. households and firms import and export. The basic trade identity makes it clear that the trade deficit is financed by capital flows. Now capital flows into the United States when foreign nationals buy U.S. assets and when U.S. firms borrow from abroad. Both of these activities affect the credit position of the United States. The relationship between these trade deficits and the U.S. status as a debtor nation is that the accumulated trade deficits have led to a stock of foreign indebtedness.

3 The Ricardian equivalence argument claims that current budget deficits have no impact. Specifically, whether government expenditures are financed by taxes or borrowing makes no difference in either the present or the future. If the spending is paid for with taxes, then current disposable income and consumption fall. If the government borrows, then rational individuals anticipate future taxes and put aside the money now. This increase in savings is just enough to pay for the future tax liability. In either case, the impact on the economy is the same.

SELF-TEST

True or False

1 During the 1980s the U.S. budget deficit was high, but there have been other episodes of equally high peacetime deficits.

2 Early in the Reagan administration, taxes were cut well below their 1970s levels.

3 Interest payments have accounted for an increased share of federal outlays since 1980.

4 Government borrowing does not matter because the bonds sold to finance the deficit are purchased by Americans.

5 Government borrowing drives up the interest rate and crowds out private investment.

6 The largest single component of government spending is national defense.

7 Welfare and foreign aid accounted for a substantial portion of the high deficits of the 1980s.

8 The Ricardian equivalence argument claims that when the government runs a deficit, private savings increase to offset the government dissaving.

9 Defense spending is an example of a nondiscretionary expenditure.

10 In a small open economy, fiscal surpluses and deficits do not affect the level of investment.

11 One reason for the emergence of fiscal surpluses in the late 1990s was that strong economic growth increased tax collections.

12 Over the next few decades the proportion of the population that is elderly will remain about what it is today.

13 While health care costs have been rising, the rate of increase is no faster than the rate of inflation.

14 The Social Security Trust Fund currently is not invested in equities.

15 Managed care refers to reforms designed to give health care providers incentives to economize on health care.

Multiple Choice

1 During the 1980s, the United States ran
   a very high federal budget deficits.
   b very high federal budget surpluses.
   c typical peacetime federal budget surpluses.
   d typical peacetime federal budget deficits.
   e balanced federal budgets.

2 The tax cuts enacted early in the Reagan presidency reduced the percentage of GDP taken in taxes
   a to historically low levels.
   b well below the levels taken in the 1970s.
   c to about the level of the 1970s.
   d to levels somewhat higher than in the 1970s.
   e none of the above.

3 Which federal expenditures increased during the 1980s?
   a Defense
   b Social Security
   c Medicare
   d Interest on the debt
   e All of the above

4 Federal budget deficits
   a increase private investment by reducing the interest rate.
   b crowd out private investment by increasing the interest rate.
   c may not reduce future output if the borrowing finances government investments such as roads or research and development.

d always reduce future consumption because future generations must pay taxes to repay the debt.

e *b* and *c*.

5 In a small open economy, government fiscal deficits

a raise the real interest rate.

b reduce investment.

c increase the inflow of capital from abroad.

d all of the above.

e *a* and *b*.

6 Which of the following is *not* true?

a The burden of current government deficits necessarily falls on the current generation.

b The burden of current government deficits may be shifted to future generations if taxes are increased after the current generation retires.

c The burden of current government deficits may be shifted to future generations if current borrowing replaces private investment.

d The burden of current government deficits may be shifted to future generations if current borrowing increases foreign indebtedness.

e All of the above are true.

7 The largest single component of government expenditure is

a defense.

b interest on the debt.

c social Security.

d education.

e welfare.

8 The Ricardian equivalence argument states that

a government deficits crowd out private investment and consumption.

b the burden of government deficits falls on future generations.

c private savings increase to offset government deficits.

d increases in interest rates crowd out private investment.

e the deficit does not matter because we owe it to ourselves.

9 Which of the following is an example of discretionary spending?

a Medicare

b Medicaid

c Social Security

d Interest on the national debt

e None of the above

10 Which of the following is an example of nondiscretionary spending?

a Defense expenditures

b Most education and training expenditures

c Money for roads and bridges

d Medicare

e Money to run the government

11 Which of the following is an example of an entitlement?

a Medicare

b Medicaid

c Social Security

d Aid to Families with Dependent Children (welfare)

e All of the above

12 Which of the following did *not* substantially affect the fiscal deficits and surpluses in the 1980s and 1990s?

a Higher social spending on the elderly

b Caps on discretionary spending in the 1990s

c Increasing health care expenditures

d Increased welfare expenditures

e Strong economic growth following the 1990–91 recession

13 The debt does not matter because the "we owe it to ourselves" argument is

a wrong since borrowing to finance the debt raises interest rates and reduces investment.

b wrong since some debt is financed by borrowing from abroad.

c wrong since the interest payments require higher taxes.

d all of the above.

e right.

14 Subtracting the change in the real value of the outstanding debt from the fiscal deficit gives the

a primary deficit.

b inflation-adjusted deficit.

c structural deficit.

d deficit to GDP ratio.

e none of the above.

15 Subtracting interest payments from the fiscal deficit gives the

a primary deficit.

b inflation-adjusted deficit.

c structural deficit.

d deficit to GDP ratio.

e none of the above.

16 Measuring what the deficit would be if the economy were at full employment gives

a the primary deficit.

b the inflation-adjusted deficit.

c the structural deficit.

d the deficit to GDP ratio.

e none of the above.

17 Because of the increase in life expectancy,

a the proportion of elderly in the population will increase.

b the number of workers per retired person will decrease.

c Medicare payments will increase.

d Social Security payments will increase.

e all of the above.

18 The fraction of the Social Security Trust Fund currently invested in equities is about
  a 0.
  b one-fourth.
  c one-half.
  d three-fourths.
  e 1.

19 During the 1980s and 1990s, health care costs have
  a increased on a pace with inflation.
  b increased less rapidly than inflation.
  c increased more rapidly than inflation.
  d fallen.
  e remained constant.

20 Programs that give health care providers greater incentive to economize on costs are called
  a means testing.
  b entitlements.
  c managed care.
  d capital budgeting.
  e fee for service.

Completion

1 The difference between government expenditures and revenues is the _____.
2 The total accumulated sum of past deficits is the _____.
3 The _____ equals what the budget deficit would be if the economy were at full employment.
4 The _____ subtracts interest payments from the budget deficit.
5 The program that pays health costs for the elderly is called _____.
6 The _____ says that private savings rise to offset government deficits.
7 Interest on the government debt is an example of _____.
8 _____ gives incentives to health care providers to economize on health care.
9 _____ allow households to put aside money in tax-free accounts to pay for medical expenses.
10 Excess tax collections put aside to pay for future Social Security benefits are deposited in the _____.

Answers to Self-Test

True or False

1	f	6	f	11	t
2	f	7	f	12	f
3	t	8	t	13	f
4	f	9	f	14	t
5	t	10	t	15	t

Multiple Choice

1	a	6	a	11	e	16	c
2	c	7	c	12	d	17	e
3	e	8	c	13	d	18	a
4	e	9	e	14	b	19	c
5	b	10	d	15	a	20	c

Completion

1 fiscal deficit
2 government debt
3 structural deficit
4 primary deficit
5 Medicare
6 Ricardian equivalence
7 nondiscretionary spending
8 Managed care
9 Medical Savings Accounts
10 Social Security Trust Fund

Doing Economics: Tools and Practice Problems

The fiscal surplus or deficit may seem like a simple calculation: government spending minus government revenues. For different purposes, however, economists argue for different measures. We know that automatic stabilizers, such as unemployment insurance, bring about an increase in the budget deficit during recessions, even though there is no change in law. The structural deficit or surplus corrects for the effects of economic downturns by calculating what the budget deficit would be if the economy were at full employment. Another measure, the inflation-adjusted deficit, looks at the change in the real value of the outstanding government debt. Finally, the primary deficit ignores interest on the current debt. Tool Kit 36.1 shows how to keep all of this straight.

Tool Kit 36.1 Calculating the Deficits (or Surpluses)

The various deficit measures are explained. Follow the steps.

Step one: Identify the average tax rate, national income, full-employment national income, government expenditures, the outstanding debt, the nominal interest rate, and the inflation rate.

Step two: Calculate the budget deficit. This is just government revenues less its expenditures.

Fiscal deficit = government expenditures − average tax rate × national income.

Step three: Calculate the structural deficit. Here we use what revenues would be if the economy were at full employment.

Structural deficit = government expenditures
 − average tax rate × full
 employment income.

Step four: Calculate the inflation-adjusted deficit. This measures takes into account the change in the real value of the outstanding debt.

Inflation-adjusted deficit = government expenditures
 − average tax rate ×
 national income
 − inflation rate ×
 outstanding debt.

Step five: Calculate the primary deficit. This measure ignores interest on the debt.

Primary deficit = government expenditures
 − average tax rate × national
 income
 − nominal interest rate × outstanding debt.

1 (Worked problem: deficits) The Costa Guanoan Economic Report of the Dictator gives the following information:

Table 36.1

National income	$60 million
Average tax rate	20 percent
Full-employment national income	$80 million
Government expenditures	$25 million
Outstanding debt	$80 million
Inflation rate	10 percent
Nominal interest rate	15 percent

a Calculate the fiscal deficit.
b Calculate the structural deficit.
c Calculate the inflation-adjusted deficit.
d Calculate the primary deficit.

Step-by-step solution

Step one: Identify the average tax rate, national income, full-employment national income, government expenditures, the outstanding debt, the nominal interest rate, and the inflation rate. All are given in Table 36.1.

Step two: Calculate the budget deficit.

Budget deficit = government expenditures
 − average tax rate × national income
 = 25 − 0.20 × 60 = $13 million.

Step three: Calculate the structural deficit.

Structural deficit = government expenditures
 − average tax rate × full employment
 income
 = 25 − 0.20 × 80 = $9 million.

Step four: Calculate the inflation-adjusted deficit.

Inflation-adjusted deficit = government expenditures
 − average tax rate × national
 income
 − inflation rate × outstanding
 debt
 = 25 − 0.20 × 60 − 0.10 × 80
 = $5 million.

Step five: Calculate the primary deficit.

Primary deficit = government expenditures
 − average tax rate × national income
 − nominal interest rate × outstanding
 debt
 = 25 − 0.20 × 60 − 0.15 × 80 = $1
 million.

2 (Practice problem: deficits) The El Dorado Economic Report of the Government gives the following information:

Table 36.2

National income	$8 billion
Average tax rate	25 percent
Full-employment national income	$8 billion
Government expenditures	$4 billion
Outstanding debt	$6 billion
Inflation rate	20 percent
Nominal interest rate	30 percent

a Calculate the fiscal deficit.
b Calculate the structural deficit.
c Calculate the inflation-adjusted deficit.
d Calculate the primary deficit.

3 (Practice problem: deficits) The Erehwemos Economic Report of the Oligarchy gives the following information:

Table 36.3

National income	$ 80 billion
Average tax rate	40 percent
Full-employment national income	$100 billion
Government expenditures	$ 50 billion
Outstanding debt	$500 billion
Inflation rate	5 percent
Nominal interest rate	10 percent

a Calculate the fiscal deficit.
b Calculate the structural deficit.

c Calculate the inflation-adjusted deficit.
d Calculate the primary deficit.

Answers to Problems

2 *a* Fiscal deficit = 4 − 0.25 × 8 = $2 billion.
 b Structural deficit = 4 ≈ 0.25 × 8 = $2 billion.
 c Inflation-adjusted deficit = 4 − 0.25 × 8 − 0.20 × 6 = $0.8 billion.

d Primary deficit = 4 − 0.25 × 8 − 0.30 × 6 = $0.2 billion.

3 *a* Fiscal deficit = 50 − 0.40 × 80 = $18 billion.
 b Structural deficit = 50 − 0.40 × 100 = $10 billion.
 c Inflation-adjusted deficit = 50 − 0.40 × 80 − 0.05 × 500 = $7 billion surplus.
 d Primary deficit = 50 − 0.40 × 80 − 0.10 × 500 = $32 billion surplus.

CHAPTER 37 | Development and Transition

Chapter Review

This chapter takes up the topic of developing countries, the problems of their development, and the prospects for bringing their living standards up to those of the developed countries. Particular focus is placed on the largely successful strategies of East Asia. It then considers the topic of the failure of communism and the difficulties involved in the transition to capitalism.

ESSENTIAL CONCEPTS

1 In **developing countries** GDP per capita was less than $725 in 1999. The per capita income gap among developed countries has narrowed over the past century, while it has widened between the developed and less developed world. Although a few countries have successfully raised their living standards, most of the LDCs remain in grinding poverty. Agricultural gains from the **green revolution,** improvements in health and life expectancy, and the emergence of the **newly industrialized countries** of East Asia are some examples of successful economic development.

2 Although there is considerable variation among developing countries, agriculture dominates the economy in most. In the rural sector, farming takes place on small, labor-intensive farms with poorer techniques and less fertilizer than in the developed world. **Sharecropping** remains a widespread arrangement. Redistribution of land ownership through **land reform** has at times been successful, but dramatic inequality remains. In the urban sector, wages are far higher, and many individuals have migrated to the cities. Such migration has caused massive

unemployment and squalor. The term *dual economy* describes the vast difference between the rural and urban sectors.

3 The success of the East Asian economies points to several policy successes. These countries practiced the sound macroeconomic policies of low budget deficits and low inflation. Other policies encouraged high savings rates, literacy, college education, and the explicit promotion of certain export-oriented industries, especially technology. One final benefit is the high level of economic equality, suggesting that there is not necessarily a trade-off between growth and equality.

4 Government planning approaches and protectionist policies, such as import substitution, dominated the early postindependence development strategies. The Washington Consensus developed in the 1980s, stressing the need to reduce government involvement and liberalize the economy. This approach underestimated the important government roles of providing or facilitating the legal, financial, and educational systems. There remains debate about the effectiveness of foreign aid.

5 Remaining trade barriers in **developed countries** and the aftereffects of the financial crisis in 1997 has led to some distrust of **globalization** among the developing countries. The central economic question of the financial crisis in the desirability of capital market liberalization. The basic story of the crisis as it appeared in Indonesia, Thailand, South Korea, and Brazil involved huge inflows of foreign capital during the boom and rapid outflows as the crisis emerged. International Monetary Fund recommendations to raise interest rates may have exacerbated the downturn.

6 In communist countries, the state owns the means of production and coordinates economic activity through a

system known as **central planning**. Low production levels of consumer goods require rationing and lead to underground markets. Although the emphasis on industrialization and development brought some early success, eventually the communist economies stagnated. As living standards fell behind those in the capitalist countries, communism was abandoned.

7 The transition to capitalism required privatization of state-owned resources and a liberalization of the economy. Advocates of shock therapy recommended quick transitions. Others proposed more gradual approaches that stressed the need to establish legal and financial infrastructures. The relative success of China and Poland, as compared with Russia, argues for a more gradual approach.

BEHIND THE ESSENTIAL CONCEPTS

1 Observing varying levels of success and failure around the world, we can compile a list of good development policies. First, there must be sound macroeconomics, that is, fiscal responsibility and a stable monetary system. Second, the economies must direct themselves toward the rest of the world by reducing trade barriers, encouraging foreign investment, and promoting exports. This approach helps to transfer more advanced technology from abroad and provides a natural test for success. Government can allocate more of its budget to investment and less to consumption, such as food subsidies. Finally, policies such as land reform and universal education (including women) not only contribute to development, but also promote equality.

2 The term *vicious circle* is often used with respect to developing countries. Poor households cannot afford education and must scratch out a living in labor-intensive activities, such as subsistence farming. They not only lack the education to practice birth control, but also have incentives to raise more children, who are economically useful. The population growth reduces capital per worker, keeping the economy in underdevelopment.

3 The education of women plays an especially important role in development. You can see this in terms of the costs and benefits of children. More-educated women understand and practice birth control. Also, as education allows their earnings to increase, they realize that the opportunity cost of having children is high and limit family size. Lower population growth means more capital per worker and higher output.

4 The main disadvantages of central government control are gathering the information needed to determine the optimal decisions, and giving incentives to managers and workers. Every organization, whether it operates within a market or a socialist economy, faces these problems. The difficulty with the socialist system is that the economy is simply too large an organization to control from the center.

5 Real world markets are complicated, and the institutions that help them work have taken time to evolve. Reputations, repeated business arrangements, implicit contracts, and other institutions help ease the information problems that trouble imperfectly competitive markets. In the developing countries, these institutions are not present, and in their absence, resource allocation is worse.

SELF-TEST

True or False

1 Over the past century, the income gap between the industrialized and less developed economies has narrowed.
2 One success story in the less developed world has been the emergence of the newly industrialized countries, such as Singapore and Taiwan.
3 Increases in life expectancy and improvements in infant mortality have allowed rapid population growth in many developing countries.
4 In poor countries, agriculture plays a more prominent role, often accounting for 80 percent in GNP.
5 The developing countries have much less capital per person than the United States because her savings rates are very low.
6 Inequality can inhibit development by leading to political instability and a poor climate for foreign investment.
7 Central planning enables developing countries to coordinate all the related activities in a single coherent development strategy.
8 An important element of a country's infrastructure is its legal system.
9 The successful East Asian economies have achieved high growth rates, but this has occurred at the cost of extreme inequality.
10 Educating women leads to lower birth rates because as their education brings higher wages, the opportunity cost of devoting time to raise children rises.
11 Under socialism, the state owns the means of production.
12 Under central planning, important decisions are made at the plant level.
13 Most economists believe that the experiment in Soviet-style socialism was a failure.
14 The movement from socialism to a more market-oriented economy has caused prices to increase.

15 Privatization refers to the process of eliminating price controls and returning the function of setting prices to private firms.

Multiple Choice

1 What fraction of the world's population lives in developing countries?
   a One-fourth
   b One-half
   c Three-fourths
   d One-third
   e One-sixth

2 Over the past century, the income gap has
   a widened among high-income countries.
   b narrowed among high-income countries.
   c grown wider between high- and low-income countries.
   d narrowed between high- and low-income countries.
   e *b* anc *c.*

3 The green revolution refers to
   a the spread of concern for the environment in the developing countries.
   b the World Bank's largely successful efforts to aid development by lending money for infrastructure investment.
   c the development and spread to developing countries of new agricultural technologies, which brought about huge increases in output.
   d improvements in life expectancy and infant mortality statistics in the developing countries.
   e none of the above.

4 Agriculture in developed countries
   a uses larger farms than in the developing countries.
   b uses fewer workers per acre than in developing countries.
   c uses more fertilizer per acre than in developing countries.
   d is more mechanized than in developing countries.
   e all of the above.

5 Sharecropping refers to the
   a fact that much of the agricultural output in the developing countries is taken in taxes.
   b World Bank's policy of matching agricultural gains in developing countries with food shipments.
   c sharing of technological know-how between agricultural research centers in the developed world and the developing countries.
   d system in which the landlord takes a share of the output of a farm.
   e system in which farmers set aside a fraction of their output to support religious institutions.

6 The term **dual economies** refers to the disparity between

   a the developed and developing economies.
   b men's and women's earnings in the developing countries.
   c upper and lower incomes in the developing countries.
   d rural and urban life in the developing countries.
   e the efficiency of the market sector and the inefficiency of governments in developing countries.

7 In developing countries, it is generally true that
   a savings rates are low.
   b because it is in short supply, capital is used very intensively.
   c because the capital stock is so low, the marginal return to capital is much higher than in developed countries.
   d the lack of effective capital markets keeps capital from its most productive uses.
   e the stable political environments attract foreign investment.

8 In developing countries, the population is
   a large and well educated.
   b falling because of the poor medical care and meager diets.
   c growing too rapidly, causing an excess supply of trained workers.
   d growing too rapidly, but includes too few vocationally trained, skilled workers.
   e none of the above.

9 Export-led growth strategies have promoted
   a agriculture, where developing countries have had a comparative advantage.
   b substitution of domestic production for imported goods.
   c land reform.
   d export industries aligned with the principle of dynamic comparative advantage, which is based on acquired skills, education, and technology.
   e government control of production in order to maximize exports.

10 What best describes the relationship between inequality and economic growth?
   a The countries that have developed most rapidly have lower levels of inequality.
   b The countries that have developed most rapidly have higher levels of inequality.
   c There is no consistent relationship between inequality and the pace of development.
   d Planned economies have developed rapidly with low inequality, but unplanned ones have only developed when inequality is high.
   e Planned economies have developed rapidly with high inequality, but unplanned ones have only developed when inequality is low.

11 Encouraging the production and export of goods in which the country has a comparative advantage is the strategy called
   a export-led growth.
   b central planning.
   c dynamic comparative advantage.
   d import substitution.
   e laissez-faire.

12 Encouraging the development of a domestic market by substituting domestically produced goods for imports is called
   a export-led growth.
   b central planning.
   c dynamic comparative advantage.
   d import substitution.
   e laissez-faire.

13 The financial crises of the late 1990s hit which country(s)?
   a Brazil
   b Indonesia
   c South Korea
   d Russia
   e All of the above

14 Under communism,
   a the state owns the means of production.
   b there is a heavy reliance on firms and households interacting in markets.
   c there is a heavy reliance on markets and a considerable role for government.
   d workers own and manage the firms.
   e none of the above.

15 Under central planning,
   a the government makes all significant economic decisions.
   b government-owned property is sold or given to individuals.
   c workers own and manage their firms.
   d prices are set by the interplay of supply and demand.
   e land is redistributed to those who have worked it.

16 The Soviet Union pursued a policy of
   a high investment and low consumption.
   b high consumption and low investment.
   c high investment and high consumption.
   d low investment and low consumption.
   e none of the above.

17 Amomg the problems of central planning are
   a the lack of incentives that managers have to operate firms efficiently.
   b the lack of information needed to make efficient decisions.
   c the fact that prices, not determined by markets, could not provide informative signals.
   d the difficulty in monitoring the performance of managers and workers.
   e all of the above.

18 Privatization refers to
   a the transfer to individuals of property formerly owned by the state in the Soviet Union.
   b the fact that managers in the Soviet Union kept information private.
   c the consolidation of agriculture into large firms.
   d the policy that allowed private farmers in China to sell much of what they produced.
   e the attempt to combine the best features of socialism and private enterprise.

19 Which of the following are problems involved in the transition from socialism to market economies?
   a Inflation
   b Unemployment
   c The lack of a safety net
   d Falling living standards
   e All of the above

20 Shock therapy refers to
   a rapid privatization and liberalization of the economy.
   b establishment of legal and financial systems.
   c distributing the state's assets to their most productive users.
   d setting in place durable democratic reforms.
   e all of the above.

Completion

1 Economists refer to the poorest nations of the world as _____.

2 Nations that have recently moved from being quite poor to being middle-income countries, including South Korea and Hong Kong, are called _____.

3 The development of new seeds, fertilizers, and agricultural practices that brought about increases in agricultural output in the developing countries during the 1960s and 1970s was called the _____.

4 In many developing countries, there is a _____, which includes a poor rural sector alongside a relatively more advanced urban sector.

5 A country's roads, ports, bridges, and legal system compose its _____.

6 _____ is a strategy according to which governments encourage exports to stimulate growth.

7 _____ is a strategy whereby the focus is on substituting domestic goods for imports to develop self-sufficiency.

8 Countries that have large numbers of unemployed or underemployed workers are said to have _____.

9 The _____ is the most important of the international agencies that lend funds to developing countries to aid in development.

10 The government owns and operates the means of production under _____.

Answers to Self-Test

True or False

1	f	6	t	11	t
2	t	7	f	12	f
3	t	8	t	13	t
4	t	9	f	14	t
5	f	10	t	15	f

Multiple Choice

1	c	6	d	11	a	16	a
2	e	7	d	12	d	17	e
3	c	8	d	13	e	18	a
4	e	9	d	14	a	19	e
5	d	10	a	15	a	20	a

Completion

1 developing countries
2 newly industrialized countries
3 green revolution
4 dual economy
5 infrastructure
6 Export-led growth
7 Import substitution
8 labor surplus
9 World Bank
10 Communism

Doing Economics: Tools and Practice Problems

Two important problems that impede growth in underdeveloped countries are the absence of markets to allocate resources efficiently, and the prevalence of institutions, such as sharecropping, that provide weak incentives. We study both of these problems in this section. Underdeveloped economies not only have limited supplies of capital and skilled labor, they also lack good markets to allocate what supplies they have. In this section, we consider the efficient allocation of resources, how markets achieve this allocation, and the losses that result from misallocation.

1 (Worked problem: absence of markets) The World Bank has made $10 million available for development projects in Costa Guano. Two possible uses for the money are building roads and building irrigation systems. The present discounted value of investments in each sector is given in Table 37.1.
   a Find the efficient allocation of the $10 million.
   b How would competitive markets allocate the money?
   c The party in power in Costa Guano draws much of its support from agriculture. If it used all of the money for irrigation, how much less would the benefits be?

Table 37.1

Investment	Irrigation projects	Roads
	(millions)	
$ 1	$10	$ 25
$ 2	$18	$ 45
$ 3	$25	$ 60
$ 4	$31	$ 72
$ 5	$36	$ 83
$ 6	$40	$ 93
$ 7	$43	$102
$ 8	$45	$110
$ 9	$46	$116
$10	$46	$120

Step-by-step solution

Step one (*a*): To find the efficient allocation, we adapt the procedure outlined in Tool Kit 36.1. Identify the production functions for each possible use. Here we are given the relationship between investment and the benefits of investment in Table 37.1.

Step two: Compute the marginal benefit for each quantity of the resource. We compute marginal benefit in the usual way. For example, the marginal benefit of the first $1 million in investment in irrigation is $10 million. Continuing, we derive Table 37.2.

Table 37.2

Investment	Irrigation projects	Marginal benefit	Roads	Marginal benefit
		(millions)		
$ 1	$10	$10	$ 25	$25
$ 2	$18	$ 8	$ 45	$20
$ 3	$25	$ 7	$ 60	$15
$ 4	$31	$ 6	$ 72	$12
$ 5	$36	$ 5	$ 83	$11
$ 6	$40	$ 4	$ 93	$10
$ 7	$43	$ 3	$102	$ 9
$ 8	$45	$ 2	$110	$ 8
$ 9	$46	$ 1	$116	$ 6
$10	$46	$ 0	$120	$ 4

Step three: Allocate the first unit of the resource to the activity with the highest marginal benefit. The first $1 million is allocated to road building, where it has a marginal benefit of $25 million.

Step four: Allocate the second unit of the resource to the activity with the next highest marginal benefit. The second $1 million is allocated to road building, where it has a marginal benefit of $20 million.

Step five: Continue until the available supply of the resource is exhausted. We allocate $8 million to roads and $2 million to irrigation.

Step one (*b*): To find the competitive market allocation, simply interpret the marginal benefits as the demand for the investment money. Add each sector's demand for capital. When the price is $25 million, the total quantity demanded is $1 million by the road-building industry. When the price falls to $20 million, the quantity demanded is $2 million. Continuing, we derive the demand in Table 37.3.

Table 37.3

Price (million/million)	Quantity (millions of investment)
$25	$ 1
$20	$ 2
$15	$ 3
$12	$ 4
$11	$ 5
$10	$ 7 ($1 each for roads and irrigation)
$ 9	$ 8
$ 8	$10
$ 7	$11 etc.

Step two: Find the market-clearing price. The market clears at a price of $8 million.

Step three: Substitute the market-clearing price into each demand to determine the allocation of investment. At a price of $8 million, road builders will purchase $8 million, and irrigation firms will purchase $2 million. This is exactly the efficient allocation.

Step four (*c*): If all the investment money is used in irrigation projects, then the total benefit will be $46 million. The efficient allocation gives benefits equal to $18 million (irrigation) + $110 million (roads) = $128 million. Thus the waste that is due to misallocation is $128 − $46 = $82 million.

2 (Practice problem: absence of markets) Eight engineers return to Zaire with their diplomas from MIT. They can work for the government building bridges or in the mining sector. The (U.S. dollar equivalent) value of output produced in each sector is given in Table 37.4.
   a Find the efficient allocation of the 8 engineers.
   b How would competitive markets allocate the engineers?
   c The president for life likes roads. How much is wasted if all 8 engineers are sent to build roads?
3 (Practice problem: absence of markets) The Zambizi River can provide up to 100 million gallons annually for irrigation. Both the cotton and millet crops would benefit from irrigation, and the benefits are given in Table 37.5.

Table 37.4

Engineers	Roads	Mining
1	$200,000	$100,000
2	$280,000	$190,000
3	$350,000	$270,000
4	$410,000	$330,000
5	$450,000	$360,000
6	$480,000	$380,000
7	$500,000	$400,000
8	$500,000	$400,000

Table 37.5

Water (millions of gallons)	Cotton (millions)	Millet (millions)
1	$ 50	$ 25
2	$ 95	$ 50
3	$135	$ 75
4	$170	$100
5	$200	$125
6	$225	$150
7	$245	$175
8	$260	$190
9	$270	$200
10	$275	$200

a Find the efficient allocation of the water.
b How would competitive markets allocate the water?
c The president for life allocates 80 million to millet and the rest to cotton. How much value is wasted?

SHARECROPPING

In underdeveloped economies, much farming takes place under conditions of sharecropping, where the landlord receives a fixed percentage of the output of the farm. The landlord's share of output is an externality from the point of view of the tenant, and as in all similar situations, there are incentive problems. Tool Kit 37.1 shows how to analyze sharecropping.

Tool Kit 37.1 Analyzing Sharecropping

Under sharecropping the farmer pays a fraction of the output to the landlord. This creates poor incentives to work hard and maintain the land and equipment. Follow these steps.

Step one: Find the full marginal benefits and costs of the tenant's effort.

Step two: Find the efficient level of effort, which is the level at which marginal benefits equal marginal cost.

Step three: Calculate the tenant's marginal private benefits, multiplying the full marginal benefits by the tenant's share.

Step four: Find the equilibrium level of effort, which is the level at which marginal private benefits equal marginal cost.

Step five: Compare the equilibrium and efficient levels of the activity.

4 (Worked problem: analyzing sharecropping) Mahragh grows sorghum on 20 acres in Chad. He gives one-half of his output in rent to the landlord. The current price is $1 per bushel, and Table 37.6 gives the production function. Finally, Mahragh could devote time each day to his wife's bicycle manufacture business, where he could earn $30 for each daily hour.
a Find the efficient level of effort.
b Find the equilibrium level of effort.

Table 37.6

Effort (hours per day)	Sorghum (bushels)
1	120
2	210
3	270
4	300
5	315
6	321
7	324

Step-by-step solution

Step one (*a*): Find the full marginal benefits and costs of the tenant's effort. We first compute the marginal product in bushels of sorghum and then multiply by the price of sorghum to find the dollar value. The first 2 hours of daily effort increase output to 120 bushels, which sell for $120. Continuing, we derive Table 37.7.

Table 37.7

Effort (hours per day)	Sorghum (bushels)	Marginal product (bushels per daily hour)	Marginal benefits (per daily hour)
1	120	120	$120
2	210	90	$ 90
3	270	60	$ 60
4	300	30	$ 30
5	315	15	$ 15
6	321	6	$ 6
7	324	3	$ 3

Step two: Find the efficient level of effort, which is the level at which marginal benefits equal marginal cost. The marginal cost, which is $30, equals marginal benefits at 4 hours per day.

Step three (*b*): Calculate the marginal private benefits by multiplying the full marginal benefits by the tenant's share. Mahragh's share is one-half; so if he works 1 hour each day, his marginal private benefits equal $120 × 1/2 = $60. Continuing, we derive Table 37.8.

Table 37.8

Effort	Marginal private benefits (per daily hour)
1	$60.00
2	$45.00
3	$30.00
4	$15.00
5	$ 7.50
6	$ 3.00
7	$ 1.50

Step four: Find the equilibrium level of effort, which is the level at which marginal private benefits equal marginal cost. The marginal private benefits equal marginal cost at 3 hours per day.

Step five: Compare the equilibrium and efficient levels of the activity. Mahragh works 3 hours each day, which is 1 less than the efficient number of hours.

5 (Practice problem: analyzing sharecropping) Mr. Droulig is a sharecropper on a farm owned by the bank. He gives one-third of his revenues from farming 20 acres in rural Mali to the bank. Table 37.9 gives the relationship between his effort and the revenues from the farm.

Table 37.9

Time (hours)	Total revenues
1	$18
2	$33
3	$45
4	$54
5	$60
6	$63

Mr. Droulig, when not sharecropping, can work in town and make $6 per hour.
a If he owned the farm himself and did not share revenues with the bank, how much would he work on the farm?
b How much does Mr. Droulig choose to work on the farm?

6 (Practice problem: analyzing sharecropping) Protecting farms against soil erosion is vital in the Sahel region of sub-Saharan Africa. The benefits of effort (in U.S. dollar equivalent) for a typical farm are given in Table 37.10. Assume that the marginal cost of effort is $100 and that sharecroppers pay one-half their yield in rent.
a Find the level of effort for owners.
b Find the level of effort for sharecroppers.

Table 37.10

Effort (days)	Benefits
1	$ 500
2	$ 900
3	$1,200
4	$1,400
5	$1,500
6	$1,500

Answers to Problems

2 The marginal benefits of the engineers in each sector are given in Table 37.11.

Table 37.11

Engineers	Roads	Marginal benefits	Mining	Marginal benefits
1	$200,000	$200,000	$100,000	$100,000
2	$280,000	$ 90,000	$190,000	$ 90,000
3	$350,000	$ 80,000	$270,000	$ 80,000
4	$410,000	$ 60,000	$330,000	$ 60,000
5	$450,000	$ 40,000	$360,000	$ 30,000
6	$480,000	$ 30,000	$380,000	$ 20,000
7	$500,000	$ 20,000	$400,000	$ 20,000
8	$500,000	$ 0	$400,000	$ 0

a The efficient allocation is 4 engineers to each sector.
b The market would allocate 4 to each sector with a wage of $60,000.
c The total benefits if all are allocated to roads equal $500,000. At the efficient allocation, the total benefits equal $410,000 + $330,000 = $740,000. The waste is $740,000 − $500,000 = $240,000.

3 Table 37.12 gives the marginal benefits of irrigation water for each crop.
a The efficient allocation is 6 million gallons to cotton and 4 million to millet.
b The market would allocate 6 million to cotton and 4 million to millet with a price equal to $25 million.
c Using 8 million for cotton and 2 million for millet gives benefits equal to $260 + $50 = $310 million.

The efficient allocation gives benefits equal to $225 + $100 = $325 million. The waste is $325 − $310 = $15 million.

Table 37.12

Water	Cotton	Marginal benefit	Millet	Marginal benefit
1	$ 50	$50	$ 25	$25
2	$ 95	$45	$ 50	$25
3	$135	$40	$ 75	$25
4	$170	$35	$100	$25
5	$200	$30	$125	$25
6	$225	$25	$150	$25
7	$245	$20	$175	$25
8	$260	$15	$190	$15
9	$270	$10	$200	$10
10	$275	$ 5	$200	$ 0

5 Table 37.13 gives the full marginal benefits and the private marginal benefits of time.

Table 37.13

Time	Total revenues	Full marginal benefits	Private marginal benefits
1	$18	$18	$12
2	$33	$15	$10
3	$45	$12	$ 8
4	$54	$ 9	$ 6
5	$60	$ 6	$ 4
6	$63	$ 3	$ 2

a The efficient amount of time is 5 hours.
b Mr. Droulig works 4 hours each day.
6 Table 37.14 gives the owner's and sharecropper's marginal benefits of efforts to reduce soil erosion.
a The owner would devote 5 days.
b The sharecropper would devote 4 days.

Table 37.14

Effort	Benefits	Owner's marginal benefits	Sharecropper's marginal benefits
1	$ 500	$500	$250
2	$ 900	$400	$200
3	$1,200	$300	$150
4	$1,400	$200	$100
5	$1,500	$100	$ 50
6	$1,500	$ 0	$ 0